Cecil Beaton

Cecil Beaton

A BIOGRAPHY

Hugo Vickers

DONALD I. FINE, INC.
New York

Library of Congress Catalogue Card Number: 86-46384

ISBN: 1-55611-021-9

Manufactured in the United States of America

10 9 8 7 6 5 4 3 2 1

For my Mother,
whose copy of
The Glass of Fashion
I stole in 1965

Contents

Illustrations   *ix*
Acknowledgements   *xiii*
The Diaries   *xvii*
Beaton Family Tree   *xix*
Sisson Family Tree   *xx*
Introduction   *xxi*

   Part One: The Formative Years 1904–25
1   The Blacksmith and the Chemist   *3*
2   A Harsher Reality   *12*
3   Adolescent Emotions   *20*
4   Cambridge and the Pursuit of Publicity   *27*

   Part Two: The Struggling Years 1925–7
5   Anything for the Uprise   *51*
6   The Office   *62*
7   The Breakthrough   *77*

   Part Three: The Wild Years 1927–30
8   Cecil Masked and Unmasked   *95*
9   The Americans   *109*
10   The Funniest Place in the World   *122*
11   Cecil in Arcadia   *137*

   Part Four: The Lovelorn Years 1930–39
12   I Love You, Mr Watson   *147*
13   Roses and Tuberoses and Chalk White Flowers   *157*
14   The Girls of Radcliff Hall   *171*
15   Malice in Wonderland   *180*
16   The Means to an Achievement   *193*
17   All the Damned Kikes in Town   *201*
18   Rest and Recuperation   *214*

Part Five: The War Years 1939–45

19 Winged Squadrons   235
20 Near East   255
21 Far East   274

Part Six: The Garbo Years 1945–52

22 The Passing of a House   297
23 My Greatest Triumph   312
24 The Return of the Prodigal   334
25 Man Proposes, God Disposes   350

Part Seven: The Victorious Years 1953–65

26 Tunnelling Towards Something New   363
27 Magpies Against a White Drop   381
28 The Crest of a Wave   396
29 Noses to the Grind   413
30 June   426
31 Royal Photographer   435
32 The Severing of Links   443
33 Cecil Goes to Hollywood   461
34 Kin   477

Part Eight: The Swinging Years 1965–70

35 Rip-Van-With-It   497
36 Growing Old, Staying Young   510
37 Forty Years On   524
38 Little Black Dresses   538

Part Nine: The Declining Years 1971–80

39 Garbo Reviewed   557
40 The Stroke   574
41 No Fear of Oblivion   584

Bibliography   590
Source References   594
Index   627

Illustrations

Unless otherwise indicated all the photographs listed below are reproduced by courtesy of Sotheby's, London.

Between pages 98 and 99
Etty Beaton with Cecil and Reggie, Langland Gardens (*Eileen Hose's collection*)
Cecil photographing his sister Baba
Lily Elsie, 1910 (*Eileen Hose's collection*)
Cecil at Cambridge, 1922
Cecil in *All the Vogue*, Cambridge, 1925 (*photo: Dorothy Wilding, © Tom Hustler*)
Nancy and Baba, June 1927
Daphne du Maurier, 1926
Nancy with her father at her wedding, 1933
The Sitwells, 1927
Cecil with Stephen Tennant, 1927 (*photo: Maurice Beck and Helen MacGregor, Eileen Hose's collection*)
Cecil dressed as George IV (*Eileen Hose s collection*)
Marjorie Oelrichs
Adèle Astaire
Doris Castlerosse
Lilia Ralli
Marlene Dietrich in Hollywood
Cecil and Peter Watson on their travels (*Eileen Hose's collection*)
Peter Watson
Ashcombe (*Eileen Hose's collection*)
Ashcombe table setting (*Eileen Hose's collection*)

Between pages 226 and 227
Lady Diana Cooper
Princess Natasha Paley
Cecil sketching Mona Harrison Williams (*Eileen Hose*)
Three stages of retouching
Bébé Bérard (*Hugo Vickers*)
Princess Louise, Duchess of Argyll
Tableau from *My Royal Past*, 1939 (*Eileen Hose*)
Wallis Simpson sketched by Cecil, November 1936 (*Hugo Vickers's collection, © Eileen Hose*)
Cecil photographing Mrs Simpson, Château de Candé 1937 (*Hugo Vickers*)
Princess Paul of Yugoslavia, 1939 (*Eileen Hose*)

Queen Elizabeth at Buckingham Palace, 1939 (*Eileen Hose*)
The bombed-out child, 1940
London bomb damage, 1940
Patterns of broken tanks, 1940 (*Crown copyright, Imperial War Museum*)
Cecil in improvised luxury, the 'Ritz', 1942 (*Crown copyright, Imperial War Museum*)
Lieutenant-General Adrian Carton de Wiart, vc, 1944 (*Crown copyright, Imperial War Museum*)
Cecil watching a troop exercise, Pihu, China, 1944 (*Crown copyright, Imperial War Museum*)

Between pages 386 and 387
Diana Wynyard in *Kipps*, 1941
Isabel Jeans in *Lady Windermere's Fan*, 1945
Vivien Leigh in *Anna Karenina*, 1947
Clarissa Churchill (*by courtesy of Vogue © The Condé Nast Publications*)
Cecil in *Lady Windermere's Fan*, 1946
Edith Olivier
Cecil by George Platt-Lynes (*Eileen Hose's collection*)
Valentina and Georges Schlee with friends at El Morocco (© *Jerome Zerbe*)
Garbo in New York, 1946
Cecil's sketch of Garbo as *Queen Christina* (*Hugo Vickers's collection*, © *Eileen Hose*)
Garbo in her garden, California, March 1948
Cecil and Garbo in London, October 1951 (*Fox Photos*)
The Queen in Garter Robes, 1955 (*Eileen Hose*)
The Queen and Prince Charles, 1950 (*Eileen Hose*)
The Ascot scene, *My Fair Lady*
Marilyn Monroe, New York, February 1956
Cecil with Leslie Caron, *Gigi*, Hollywood 1957
June Osborn
The dying Isak Dinesen, 1962
Cecil photographing Nureyev and Margot Fonteyn

Between pages 514 and 515
Cecil photographing the Duchess of Gloucester, 1961 (*Eileen Hose*)
Victoria Heber-Percy
Audrey Hepburn in one of her *My Fair Lady* costumes, 1963
Cecil with Audrey Hepburn on the set of *My Fair Lady* (*Eileen Hose's collection*)
George Cukor and Audrey Hepburn before the ball scene
Princess Marina at Vaynol, 1964
Kin and Cecil, 1964
Garbo on the yacht, Greece 1965
Cecil greeting the Queen Mother at the National Portrait Gallery, 1968 (*photo: Desmond O'Neill*)
Truman Capote

Sir Francis Rose
Mick Jagger and Anita Pallenberg in *Performance*, 1968
Barbra Streisand in *On a Clear Day*, 1969
Jane Birkin at the Rothschild Ball, 1971 (*by courtesy of Vogue © The Condé Nast Publications*)
Cecil after the announcement of his knighthood, 1972 (*photo: Kevin Brodie, Sunday Times*)
Diana Vreeland (*Hugo Vickers's collection, © Eileen Hose*)
Katharine Hepburn with Cecil, New York 1969
Eileen Hose in the winter garden at Reddish House
The drawing-room at Reddish House
Lady Diana Cooper at Reddish House, 1972
Sir Ralph Richardson and Cecil at the National Theatre, 1979 (*photo: Richard Young, Rex Features*)

LINE ILLUSTRATIONS

Unless otherwise indicated, all the line illustrations are reproduced by courtesy of Eileen Hose.

Extract from Cecil's diary, December 1933   xvi
Cecil's famous glass dome   80
A drawing in a letter from Stephen Tennant   95
Gladys, Duchess of Marlborough (*by courtesy of Vogue © The Condé Nast Publications*)   100
Virginia Woolf   142
Cecil's offensive *Vogue* drawing, February 1938 (*by courtesy of Vogue © The Condé Nast Publications*)   209
Two drawings from *My Royal Past*   229
General Li Mo-an, Pihu, 1944   285
Greta Garbo   302
Garbo as *La Dame aux Camellias*   333
Christian Bérard   336
Noël Coward   357
The Queen's Coronation sketched in the Abbey   366
Drawing of Gaby Deslys from *The Glass of Fashion*, 1954   373
Cecil's first Ascot drawings in *Vogue*, July 1930 (*by courtesy of Vogue © The Condé Nast Publications*)   388
Design for an opera-goer in *My Fair Lady*, 1956   389
Julie Andrews as Eliza   390
A lady from Cecil's book *Japanese*   402
The *Gigi* logo   408
Flower drawing from *First Garden*   455
Princess Marina from *The Glass of Fashion*   523
The *Coco* logo   538
Cathleen Nesbitt, Cecil's first Mrs Higgins   547
A white hyacinth drawn after Cecil's stroke   575
Finis from *The Book of Beauty*   583

PHOTOGRAPH SOURCES

There are five main sources of Beaton photographs.

Sotheby's of Bond Street: The Beaton archive is lodged at Sotheby's, who retain all the original negatives (except the royal ones), a number of original prints which are auctioned from time to time, and all Cecil's other photographs whether taken by him or not. The archive is available to those who wish to reproduce photographs in books, but copies are not sold privately, and prints must be returned after use. It is a rich source and well indexed. The copyright in these pictures belongs to Sotheby's.

Miss Eileen Hose: Eileen Hose retains the negatives and prints of Cecil's royal photographs, as well as a few photographs that he took after the sale of his other work to Sotheby's. Some of these pictures are available at Camera Press.

Imperial War Museum: The Imperial War Museum hold the work that Cecil undertook in the war for the Ministry of Information. There are about 7,000 negatives in their archives.

National Portrait Gallery: Certain Beaton photographs are available at the National Portrait Gallery.

Condé Nast: The Condé Nast archive in London and New York house the work that Cecil undertook for *Vogue* and their other publications. By commissioning him they also acquired the copyright of these pictures.

Acknowledgements

My first debt of gratitude is to the late Sir Cecil Beaton for selecting me to write this biography. After his death his promise of help was more than fulfilled by Eileen Hose, who answered endless questions, provided vital clues and helped me to see many of the other sources. For several weeks after Sir Cecil's death I worked at Reddish House and was allowed total access to his papers. I would like to express particular gratitude to the Countess of Avon for her guidance on many points and for letting me work at Alvediston for part of two summers, and to Lady Diana Cooper, to whom I read a considerable part of this book as it progressed. In New York my research was guided by Diana Vreeland, who, amongst other kindnesses, ensured that I knew exactly where to find the vital American sources.

I am most grateful to Her Majesty Queen Elizabeth The Queen Mother, HRH The Prince of Wales, HRH Princess Alice, Duchess of Gloucester, and HRH Princess Alexandra, the Hon. Mrs Angus Ogilvy, for permission to quote from their letters to Sir Cecil; to HRH The Duke of Kent for permission to quote from a letter written by the late Princess Marina, Duchess of Kent, and to Maître Suzanne Blum for allowing me to quote extracts from the Duchess of Windsor's letters. I would also like to thank HRH Princess Paul of Yugoslavia for recalling her first photographic encounter with Cecil in 1939, and the late HSH Princess Grace of Monaco for an interview in Paris.

For interviews, the loan of letters, permission to quote from copyright material and for help and advice, I would like to thank the following:

Jane Lady Abdy; Sir Harold Acton; Mr Derek Adkins; Hon. Charles Allsopp; Mrs Susan Mary Alsop; HH Princess Joan Aly Khan; Mr Mark Amory; Miss Julie Andrews; Margaret Duchess of Argyll; Mr Dennis Arundell; Dame Peggy Ashcroft; Lady Ashton; Sir Frederick Ashton; Hon. Mrs Chiquita Astor; Miss Maxine Audley; the Countess of Avon;

Mr John Badcock; the late Enid Bagnold; Mr David Bailey; Lord Balfour of Inchrye; Mr Andrew Barrow; Sir Brian Batsford; Mr Alan Bell; Mr James Berry; Mrs Lesley Blanch; Mrs Alfred Bloomingdale; Lady Bonham Carter; Mr John Bowes-Lyon; Mr Mark Boxer; Count Brando Brandolini; the late Frederick Brisson; Dr and Mrs Christopher Brown; Miss Coral Browne; Mr Buck (Librarian, St John's College, Cambridge); Mrs Gail Buckland; Mr Richard Buckle; Mr Hal Burton; Mr W.G. Butler;

the late Truman Capote; Miss Jane Carmichael; Miss Barbara Cartland; The Lord Charteris of Amisfield; the late June Churchill; Countess Anna Maria Cicogna; the late Ina Claire; Mr Gerald C. Clarke; Mr Peter Coats; Mrs

Anne Cockerell; Hon. Artemis Cooper; Lady Diana Cooper; Miss Louise Corrigan; the Noël Coward estate; Miss Lydia Cresswell-Jones; Mrs Teresa Cuthbertson;

Mrs Louise Dahl-Wolfe; Mr Allan Davis; Mr Jonathan Dawson; Miss Angeline de Core; Mrs Constance de Hamel; Madame Dilé; the late Sir Anton Dolin; Dr Christopher Dowling; Maureen Marchioness of Dufferin and Ava; Dame Daphne du Maurier;

Mr and Mrs John Ellert; Air Vice-Marshal John Elton; Mrs Meredith Etherington-Smith;

Mrs Frank Fearnley-Whittingstall; Miss Sheila Fermoy (H.M. Tennent Ltd); Hon. Mrs Daphne Fielding; Miss Ann Firbank; Mr Alastair Forbes; Miss Ruth Ford; Mr Edward Fox; Dr Noble Frankland; Lady Freyberg;

Mr Philippe Garner; Paula Gellibrand (Mrs Long); Mr Christopher Gibbs; Sir John Gielgud; Miss Lillian Gish; Lady Gladwyn; Lady Glendevon; Mr Peter Glenville; Mr Jack Gold; Mr Francis Goodman; Mr William Grant; Mrs Austen T. Gray; the late Colonel T.H.H. Grayson; Mr Samuel Adams Green; the late Sir John Grotrian; Mrs Winston Guest;

Mr Brodrick Haldane; The Dowager Viscountess Hambleden; Mr Leo Handley-Derry; Mr Waldemar Hansen; the late Felix Harbord; the late Lady Hartwell; Madame Allanah Harper Statlender; Mr Derek Hart; Lady Harvey; Mr Nicholas Haslam; Lady Selina Hastings; the late Viscount Head; Mr Robert Heber-Percy; Mrs H.J. Heinz; Mr Christopher Hemphill; Mr William Henderson; Miss Audrey Hepburn; Hon. David Herbert; Mr Derek Hill; Mr John Hill; Miss Marianne Hinton; Mr and Mrs Anthony Hobson; Mr Eliot Hodgkin; Mr Horst P. Horst; Miss Eileen Hose; Miss Nicola Howard; the Lady Hutchinson of Lullington;

Mr Christopher Isherwood; Mrs Arthur James; Miss Isabel Jeans; Sir Charles Johnston; Mr Timothy Jones;

Miss Mary Kerridge; Mr Lincoln Kirstein; Mr Eardley Knollys; M. Boris Kochno;

Mrs Eleanor Lambert; Lord Lambton; Mr Kenneth J. Lane; Mr Valentine Lawford; Miss Katell le Bourhis; Graf Friedrich Ledebur; Mr James Lees-Milne; Mr Patrick Leigh Fermor; Mr Leo Lerman; Mr Alan Jay Lerner; Mrs Anita Leslie-King; Mr Herman Levin; Mr Alexander Liberman; M. Serge Lifar; Hon. Lady Lindsay (formerly Loelia Duchess of Westminster); the late Anita Loos; Mr Adam Low; Lady Caroline Lowell;

Mrs Nesta Macdonald; Mr Frank Magro; Mr Leo Maguire; Miss Joanna Malley; Laura Duchess of Marlborough; Mr I.L. May; Mr David Mellor; Mr Ivan Moffat; Hon. Lady Mosley; Mr Paul Motter; Mrs Tertius Murray-Threipland; Mr Lawrence Mynott;

Dame Anna Neagle; the late Cathleen Nesbitt; Miss Louise Nevelson; Major Donald Neville-Willing; Miss Christine Norden; the Viscount Norwich; Lady Nutting;

Miss Rosemary Olivier;

Mr Michael Parkin; Mr Burnet Pavitt; Mr Graham Payn; Mary Countess of Pembroke; the Earl of Pembroke; Mr Irving Penn; Mr Stewart Perowne; Mrs Edward Phillips; Sir John Pope-Hennessy; Lady Violet Powell; Mr Harry Porter; Mr Stuart Preston;

Mr and Mrs Peter Quennell;

Mr Wayne Radziminski; Mr and Mrs Robin Raybould; Mr Peter Reid; Mr John Richardson; Frederica Lady Rose; Anne Countess of Rosse; Hon. Sir Steven Runciman; Mr George Rylands;

the late Frank Scarlett; Mrs Valentina Schlee; Mr Dudley Scholte; Mr Alan V. Schwartz; Mrs Anne Sebba; Mrs Irene Selznick; the late Marie Seton; Lady Seymour; Mr Nicholas Shakespeare; Dr Michael Shelden; Mr Francis Sitwell; Sir Sacheverell Sitwell; Sir Hugh and Lady Smiley; Mrs A.J. Smith; Mr Oliver Smith; Mr Philip Smith; Madame Ginette Spanier; Sir Stephen Spender; Mrs Charmian Stirling; Sir Roy Strong; the late Raymond Sturge; the Duke of Sutherland; Mr and Mrs John Sutro; Dr Wayne Swift;

Dr Frank Tait; Mr Paul Tanqueray; Hon. Stephen Tennant; Mrs C.E.M. Thornton; Mr Michael Thornton; Mr Geoffrey Toone; Group-Captain Peter Townsend; Mr George Traill; Mr Michael and Lady Anne Tree;

Mr and Mrs Gérald Van de Kemp; Mrs Diana Vreeland;

Miss Mona Washbourne; the late Major Erik Watts; Lord Weidenfeld; Mr Roger Williams; Mr Reece Winstone; Mr Michael Wishart; Miss Annette Worsley-Taylor; Miss Irene Worth; Mr James Wright;

Mr Richard Young; HRH Princess Paul of Yugoslavia.

It would be a long list if I enumerated all those who offered me hospitality while I worked, but I would like to mention the kindness of David Herbert who had me to stay in Tangiers for a week, and Mrs Joan Lazar and Miss Dorothy Safian for putting me up and putting up with me in New York.

I thank my agent Gillon Aitken for his protection, my editors John Curtis and Linda Osband for their patience and help, and Hugh Montgomery-Massingberd for his close scrutiny of my text. I am grateful to Susan Duffus (now Devitt), Sigi Stansbury and Louise Corrigan for gallant help with typing. Above all I am grateful to Alexandra Clayton, who rescued me in 1983 when I was floundering amongst the papers, helped to sort them, annotate them and date them, typed the majority of the manuscript more than once and offered valuable editorial advice and support at all times.

Hugo Vickers
Easter 1985

December
1933

A Trip to Tunisia
(with George Hoare)

Extract from Cecil's diary, Tunis trip, December 1933

The Diaries

There remain 145 volumes of Cecil's manuscript diaries, written in large exercise books or beautiful marbled books from Venice, dating from 1922 to 1974 (when he suffered his stroke). He began keeping a diary at Harrow, but he destroyed it when he was about twenty because he was frightened that it might be found. Today only a minute fragment of this school record survives. He began a day-to-day diary when he went up to Cambridge in October 1922 and filled fifty-six volumes with closely scrawled material, most of which was written on or soon after the day. This he continued until February 1927, by which time life was being led so fully that he could hardly keep up: 'I felt somewhat guilty at the sight of my journal lying apart like a discarded lover,' wrote Cecil, 'but life had become too busy for regrets.'[1] Entries were written in a snatched moment sometimes several months later. Therefore they lose the appeal of immediacy.

Cecil resumed a day-to-day diary on his first trip to America from 1928 to 1929 and he wrote a great deal during times when he was lonely and bored, for example during the war (twenty-two diaries) and his year in Hollywood working on *My Fair Lady* (nine diaries). At all other times, he wrote retrospectively, summing up a particular summer or weekend. After an occasion such as the Duke of Windsor's wedding, he would turn to the diary at once so that the most important events were covered in his attempt at all times 'to preserve the fleeting moment like a fly in amber'.[2] Interestingly Cecil wrote his diary in the morning rather than before going to bed.

During his lifetime Cecil edited and published six volumes of his diaries in what James Pope-Hennessy called a 'thirst for self revelation'.[3] Shortly before Cecil's death, a composite volume appeared, *Self Portrait with Friends*, edited by Richard Buckle in 1979. An historian should always mistrust a diary edited by the diarist himself. In *The Wandering Years*, the first volume, entries were rewritten with hindsight, some extracts were added that do not exist in the original manuscript diaries, events were kaleidoscoped and dates tampered with. For instance in *The Years Between* there is a fictional account of a day spent with his Delhi secretary, Jean MacFarlane, in 1944. This was in fact spent with his Cairo secretary, Pamela Burns, in 1942. In this biography only the original manuscript diaries are quoted, especially when a published version also exists. Readers should not be surprised therefore if the entries in this biography differ from those previously published. Dates have also been corrected on numerous occasions.

The purpose of Cecil's diary almost certainly changed over the years. Yet in its unpublished (and at times unpublishable) form it remains a candid and thorough portrait of its writer and a valuable mirror to the many worlds in which he moved.

In the early years it was clearly not written with publication in mind. On 9 October 1923, Cecil wrote: 'If I knew anyone had read this I'd almost go mad and yet I feel I have to write it. It's so much myself – the real self that not a single person alive knows.'[4] On the same day he added: 'I don't want people to know me as I really am but as I'm trying and pretending to be.'[5]

Cecil told me that only one tenth of his diary was published. This proved an accurate estimate. When he suffered his stroke in 1974, the diary was necessarily laid aside, but such was his recovery that unbeknown to anyone (though suspected by his secretary Eileen Hose), he resumed it in 1978. He filled three-quarters of a volume, writing with his left hand. The last entry is dated exactly one week before his death.

Beaton Family Tree

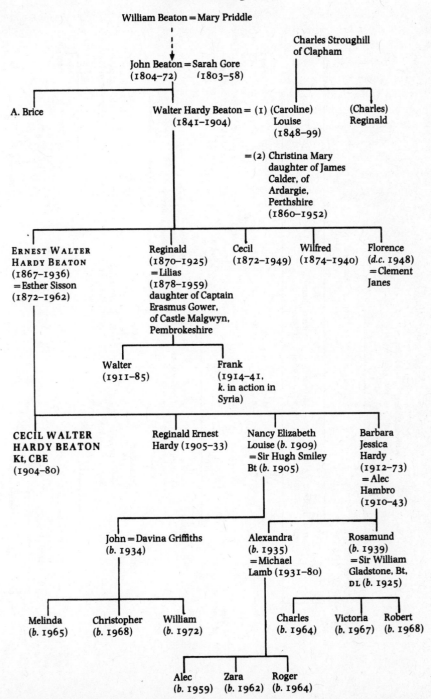

William Beaton = Mary Priddle

John Beaton = Sarah Gore
(1804–72)   (1803–58)

Charles Stroughill
of Clapham

A. Brice

Walter Hardy Beaton = (1) (Caroline)
(1841–1904)   Louise
                        (1848–99)

(Charles)
Reginald

= (2) Christina Mary
daughter of James
Calder, of
Ardargie,
Perthshire
(1860–1952)

ERNEST WALTER
HARDY BEATON
(1867–1936)
= Esther Sisson
(1872–1962)

Reginald
(1870–1925)
= Lilias
(1878–1959)
daughter of Captain
Erasmus Gower,
of Castle Malgwyn,
Pembrokeshire

Cecil
(1872–1949)

Wilfred
(1874–1940)

Florence
(d.c. 1948)
= Clement
Janes

Walter
(1911–85)

Frank
(1914–41,
k. in action in
Syria)

CECIL WALTER
HARDY BEATON
Kt, CBE
(1904–80)

Reginald Ernest
Hardy (1905–33)

Nancy Elizabeth
Louise (b. 1909)
= Sir Hugh Smiley
Bt (b. 1905)

Barbara
Jessica
Hardy
(1912–73)
= Alec
Hambro
(1910–43)

John = Davina Griffiths
(b. 1934)

Alexandra
(b. 1935)
= Michael
Lamb (1931–80)

Rosamund
(b. 1939)
= Sir William
Gladstone, Bt,
DL (b. 1925)

Melinda
(b. 1965)

Christopher
(b. 1968)

William
(b. 1972)

Charles
(b. 1964)

Victoria
(b. 1967)

Robert
(b. 1968)

Alec
(b. 1959)

Zara
(b. 1962)

Roger
(b. 1964)

Sisson Family Tree

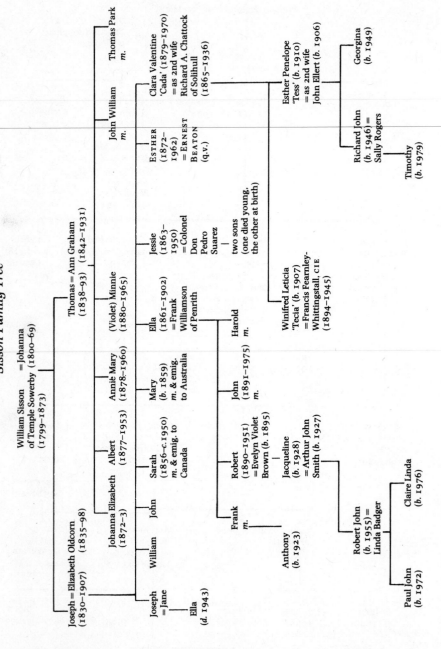

Introduction

Cecil Beaton asked me to write his biography in December 1979 and died two days after I started work in January 1980. He invited me to write about him after reading my biography of Gladys, Duchess of Marlborough. whom he had met in the 1920s but who had been beyond his grasp. Before meeting me he wrote about Gladys: 'I should have enjoyed her so much and could have learnt a lot from the way she behaved.... I now find her very accessible and to someone like myself she must have been remarkably sensible ... she must have been very much at home with artists and writers.'[1] When we met, we talked about Gladys and, although he sometimes struggled for the right word due to his incapacitating stroke, I found his questions sharp and on the mark. I never had the chance to tell him how strong his influence was on someone of my generation. I was just old enough to see the Drury Lane production of *My Fair Lady* and remember it vividly. Later as a family we twice saw the film in London. At home in the country the music of *Gigi* was often playing on the gramophone. (In fact, it was through Alan Jay Lerner's song 'The night they invented champagne' that I became aware of that delicious drink before ever tasting it.) I was familiar with a great number of Cecil's photographs. By no means a regular attender of exhibitions I had nevertheless queued to see his National Portrait Gallery exhibition in 1968 and visited his fashion exhibition at the Victoria and Albert Museum in 1971. I had once been to his Pelham Place house in 1972 to collect some royal photographs for the first book I worked on. In the same year I recall seeing Cecil Beaton and Lady Diana Cooper sitting together at the Duke of Windsor's funeral in St George's Chapel, and on 26 October happened to sit behind him at a performance of *Crown Matrimonial* at the Haymarket. My next sight of him was at a wedding reception at Fonthill in the last summer of his life. I saw a very distinguished old man being helped across the lawn to sit with Lady Margadale to listen to the band. At first I did not recognize him. He bore the aged venerability of Chagall or the late Paul-Henri Spaak. Then suddenly I realized who it was.

My two meetings with Cecil at Broadchalke were enjoyable and stimulating. As Eileen Hose wrote after he died: 'I cannot bear to think of Cecil not being here to work with you as planned. There was promise of much enjoyment for him, and, I feel, for you too.'[2] His sudden death was more than disappointing and it changed the nature of the book I was to write. There is always something unsatisfactory about a biography published in the lifetime of the subject. However much authors protest that they have written as though the subject were dead, I cannot believe that they were not inhibited. I am sure that Cecil Beaton would have helped me enormously. It would have been fascinating to see him at work, photographing fashions for French *Vogue*, or to observe him with his friends and to ask him about the many adventures of his extraordinary life. But equally he might have influenced me. Because he was tired one day he might have brushed aside something I might have explored with interest. He might even have tried to hoodwink me. After all, he wrote in his diary in December 1964 about his reactions to the possible posthumous sale of his papers:

> The thought came to me that those left in charge of clearing up the debris would have a sticky time of it.... The idea of a Texas undergraduate looking into my private life filled me with strange reactions. I kept thinking of ways to taunt the student, of intriguing him, of showing him how bad my work could be, as well as how good.[3]

However, that was not to be. On our second meeting on 15 January he and Eileen took me over to the studio to show me the diaries, the press cutting volumes, the folders of stage designs and other paintings. I was to have total access to these and to the letters in their leather boxes in the library. Cecil gave me a number of his books, signing each in turn with a black felt-tip pen held confidently in his left hand. I departed for London, not a little daunted by the amount of work ahead, but looking forward to visits planned later in the month. But then Cecil died. It was as though he had outlined the scope of the work and then left me to continue my labours on my own. Though at first I regretted his loss deeply, I soon discovered that his diaries and letters contained the key to all mysteries and that by persevering with them I could find the answers I needed. This was my work for the next five and a half years.

One of the best tributes one can pay to Cecil is that his friends (and indeed the occasional foe) enjoy talking about him. No author can have been given so much help and constructive advice in the years that followed. Because Cecil had given his blessing, his friends were happy to talk and, because there was no fear of my returning to him and telling him what they had said, they spoke freely. Eileen gave me Cecil's handsome black overcoat and it travelled to many of the same houses with me inside it instead of him. Such is the role of the biographer that it even went to certain apartments where its previous owner would have refused to go or where indeed he would have been unwelcome. During the course of the work it was a rare privilege to be able to meet people from the many worlds in which Cecil operated. I was able to talk to school friends from Heath Mount and Harrow, to other photographers, directors, stars of stage and screen, collaborators, his elegant sitters and members of royal families. Here and there I encountered those who loved him and those who loathed him, ranging in age from ninety-three to eleven. It was helpful to know that a Cambridge contemporary, Stewart Perowne, could answer his telephone and cast his mind back to university life sixty years ago. Dennis Arundell played and sang 'I'm just a little piece of seaweed', which he had composed for Cecil in 1923. Cecil's surviving sister, Lady Smiley, talked to me about early family life and the parties and pageants they attended in the late 1920s. Lady Diana Cooper answered numerous enquiries about an age of which she was the only front-line survivor. Eileen Hose, Cecil's secretary and the mainstay of his life for a quarter of a century, could recall or find the answer to nearly every question I asked. Nor was I ever able to ask a question which in any way disconcerted her. One of the most perceptive sources was Stephen Tennant, still living at Wilsford Manor near Amesbury, to which an excited Cecil was first summoned in January 1927. For many years a recluse, Stephen Tennant is a poet, artist and writer. In 1929 he was the author and artist of an entertaining (now rare) book called *Leaves from a Missionary's Notebook*. He was notorious for inviting friends to Wilsford and then losing his nerve at the last moment. The guest would find the doors of Wilsford closed against him. But I was admitted several times to that haunted domain with its profusion of shells, polar bear rugs, paintings, and strewn jewels and fabrics. I sat for several afternoons on the landing of Wilsford's first floor and it was soon hard to believe in the existence of cars and televisions in the world outside. Stephen Tennant warned me: 'You have tackled a big fish in Cecil.' Then, in conversation and in a series of letters (seven arrived in one day), he explored the character of his old friend:

I think Cecil was a 'self-created' genius. In some senses he is very impressive. I never thought he had 'imagination'. But at times his talk was very bright, witty and succinct. He hated the very big businessman behind himself, the artist. How great an artist he was is questionable. He made himself read great fiction, and at times he could be very dry and bleak (rather *mauvaise langue*) because he was so terrifically critical and how! I think he was many men and the enigmatic social sparkler made him take hurdles that no one else would have tackled.

Without being an idealist he wished to be one. He was not vain, insincere or pretentious. He was very unique in his approach to high fashion. He was a worldly Peter Pan. He never aged. Personally I think his genius for exotic photographs is his greatest contribution to modern life and art. One must pay him this sincere compliment. Many have copied his vast output of ideas and beauty dedication. Some very discerning people adore his prose but to me it's rather a smart jumble of cute cunning (in the USA sense), stuff of very questionable merit or charm, trivial, trifling, very silly at times.... How good his books are is a moot point. They are like good writing and rattle along like a smart buggy, a tiny bit metallic and chill for my taste.

Cecil had a deep love for fame. Success was his fairy wand! When I told him that in New York I'd met Felia Doubrovska,* he said: 'Failure, did you say? How *awful*!'

He was always shy of showing affection, deeply soul-shy, and that is why his eyes became sad. Of course Cecil, more than most bachelors, valued his social freedom. His Birthday morning joy was very strong in him. I think behind a rather cool manner (distinguished poise he had), there was a curious intensity.... One sensed also a curious hard quality, difficult to put into words, not heartless, but an analyst of others. Cecil is the best 'grown-up child' in painting, I feel. He can't draw at all and his vibrant, vivid works evoke a smile (is he a Dufy?) – a joy that is pure and unrestrained.

If he had a lack, perhaps it was because he was surprised if you were depressed. Like Willa Cather he said: 'Snap out of it.' All his thrilling life he scorned 'when life showed a dark wing'. He was a realist, an aesthete, a man both certain and uncertain of his aims, much too clever to feel absolute, total, crude self-confidence. He was a very delightful, eager man to be with.... He was only lonely because the perfect response was unattainable. Like A.E. Housman and Lawrence of Arabia, he feared to give full expression to his feelings unless they could be returned in equal ratio. He longed for perfect love.

Had he much sense of humour? Not really. Hectic fun at parties, yes. He did say very witty things. He was a real friend, bless him, and had very good qualities and a lot of fashion-plate talent in him. I never feel that he quite achieved all he wished for. His diaries? It's like chewing sawdust, so monotonous, yet witty at times. The man behind all this – what was he like? A problem. A Jekyll and Hyde. Lord Byron and the Sun King. Like these two men he worshipped beauty and he, like them, was a luxury man. A Roman Emperor. Yes, now we have 'netted' him.[4]

As I travelled amongst the friends, I found that Cecil emerged as a much more interesting character than his public image might suggest. Foremost amongst his qualities were energy and determination. Oliver Smith, who did the sets for the play of *My Fair Lady*, said:

Cecil had more energy than anyone I've ever known – drive, ambition and·the talent to follow it through. He would come and go like a marvellous old comet. He held very strong moral points of view. I was always impressed by how organized Cecil was. Incredibly busy.[5]

Alan Jay Lerner, who wrote the lyrics for *Gigi* and *My Fair Lady*, described

*Felia Doubrovska (1896–1981), Russian–American dancer

Cecil as a star in a world where stars are a dying breed. He too was impressed by Cecil's dynamism:

> We used to say that inside Cecil Beaton there was another Cecil Beaton sending out lots of little Cecils into the world. One did the sets, another did the costumes. A third took the photographs. Another put the sketches in an exhibition, then into magazines, then in a book. Another Cecil photographed the sketches and sold these.... He was the only designer whose sketches were stunningly beautiful and outrageously funny at the same time.[6]

Beautiful women appreciated his skill as a photographer. The late Ina Claire, who starred as *The Girl from Utah* in London in 1913 and was the Grand Duchess in the film *Ninotchka* in 1939, refused to be photographed by anyone but Cecil. In San Francisco she declared that she would say: 'Only Cecil Beaton. He knows my faults and how to get round them.'[7]

Julie Andrews, Cecil's first Eliza Doolittle, had a daunting experience the first time she submitted to his lens. From Switzerland she said:

> I was quite nervous of him, this eminent gentleman who always looked so very stylish, and I felt in those days particularly, terribly gauche and green and absolutely not sure of who I was at all and he kept saying as he was photographing me: 'Lovely, oh beautiful, wonderful, yes, yes, more.' Then eventually he ended up by saying: 'Of course you do have the most unphotogenic face I've ever seen.' I suddenly went down like a pricked balloon.[8]

Audrey Hepburn, the film's Eliza, spoke of Cecil from Rome:

> Owning a really fine Cecil Beaton photograph is like owning a beautiful painting.... I really adored him because he was always very tender with me, very sweet to me.... There's nothing terribly unusual about me, but perhaps there was a sensitivity about him and I think he understood me. ... Like every woman and every young child I said I always would have loved to be beautiful and for a moment I was. If somebody loves you very much then they make you feel beautiful and he did it with his tenderness, but also with his art. Between the clothes and the photographs I looked smashing![9]

Interestingly neither of the Eliza Doolittles fully appreciated Cecil's contribution at the time. Audrey Hepburn said:

> I couldn't at the time quite evaluate who I was with. Today I can say I knew the great Cecil Beaton. When I was this kid on Broadway I didn't quite know who Cecil Beaton was.[10]

Similarly Julie Andrews said:

Now I appreciate it far more than I did at the time. You're so busy doing
your thing, getting on with your job, and it's only over the last ten or
fifteen years that I've come to appreciate his contribution and how amaz-
ingly talented he was.... He was, no doubt, as you probably realized, a
very imposing figure in spite of a look of certain fragility. There was an
undeniable strength in the man.[11]

Lillian Gish, star of the silent screen, said in New York:

Every memory I have of him is pleasant. He was interested in everything
and everybody. And, like all photographers, he had that blessing, which
is curiosity.[12]

Dame Anna Neagle cited one of the great figures she had portrayed –
Florence Nightingale: 'So much to do, so little time to do it.'[13] Peter Quennell
said: 'The publicity was just the froth on top. He worked very hard';[14] and
Diana Vreeland, high priestess of fashion, declared: 'He was a Capricorn.
Oh, yes, that old goat keeps climbing up the hill and always gets there in
the end.'[15] Lady Diana Cooper judged: 'Well, he was not a genius, but he
was immensely unusual.'[16]

Kenneth Tynan wrote perceptively of Cecil, stressing the importance of
the theatre in Cecil's life. Cecil told him that his other careers were 'all alibis
for the basic fact that he should have gone on the stage and stayed there'.[17]
Tynan left a sharp visual picture of Cecil:

He enters a room for all the world like an actor who has just made a
superb exit: You would think he had come straight from some garish and
exhausting rout on the floor above. He strides lightly towards you, smiling intimately, soaplessly washing his hands. His 'hello' is a commisera-
tion, a condolence exchanged; like much of his talk, it emerges as a
quizzical, heartfelt sigh. He drops naturally into his favourite posture, the
left foot turned out like a dancing master's, the right hand carefully
poised on the right hip, and the head, greying and benign, tilted to catch
the light.[18]

Cecil himself liked to quote the comments made to him by John Irwin, a
depressed ADC, in Calcutta. In his diary for 13 February 1944, Cecil wrote:

About myself he said I had rare powers of application for a person with
my temperament, that I had made my mark by allying my feminine
talents, by utilizing them in an unfeminine way and by doggedly applying
myself. I was no genius. My talents in another would have amounted to
little, that my powers of adaptation and feminine instinct were at the
same time a weakness but my great strength. I was in no way an intellectual.[19]

Other friends judged other aspects. The artist Michael Wishart said: 'His courage was an immense quality.'[20] Doyen of King's, George Rylands thought: 'He was as clever as a monkey',[21] while Truman Capote judged him: 'one of the three or four best photographers in this century'.[22] Irene Selznick, the distinguished theatre producer and daughter of Hollywood mogul L.B. Mayer, said: 'Photography was a means to an end to people.' She continued:

He attached the least value to the things he did best. He despised his photography because it came easily to him. He wanted to be a designer and a playwright. He was very good at photographing the sets. A lot of photographers are very *chi-chi* about it, but in a few minutes he got wonderful results. And he wouldn't accept extra payment. It would have lowered him.... He had great flair, great eye, but he was not that inventive. He had no end of rows. He was not the white knight![23]

Cecil was aware of his capacity for rows. The photographer David Bailey once asked him: 'Why don't you go into films, Cecil?', and he replied: 'I can't afford a whole new set of enemies.'[24]

While some people coined expressions about Cecil, such as that of Hank Brennan of the *Vogue* studio in New York: 'His baroque is worse than his bite',[25] so too did Cecil have a particular way of expressing himself. Some found this funny, others thought it bitchy or cruel according to taste. Once, when delayed fitting an opera star of giant proportions, Oliver Messel telephoned to ask how he was getting on. Cecil replied despairingly: 'Well, I've *found* the waist.'[26] Sometimes he was more arch: 'You can tell a woman's beauty by reading between the lines.' And Paddy Leigh Fermor recalled Cecil's description of Professor Tancred Borenius, while staying with the Sacheverell Sitwells during the war: 'Oh! that halitosis. It's so thick – a greyhound couldn't jump it. It would kill a mosquito at a yard.'[27]

The novelist Caroline Blackwood recalled the disconcerting effect that Cecil had on people, making them behave completely out of character:

His worship of his own perfect life-style made one rebel. It created some kind of unconscious longing to dynamite it by introducing outrageous imperfections of manners and behaviour. He gave everyone the feeling that he alone had been exquisitely brought up. This produced a perverse desire to confirm Cecil's worst fears and beliefs, and commit social suicide under his pale and appalled blue eye.

Dining at Pelham Crescent, Lucian [Freud], for no obvious reason, suddenly pushed back his chair and placed both his feet on Cecil's flawless gleaming dining-table. Cecil watched in silent and shuddering torment as Lucian's hefty shoes sent his beautiful plates and his Waterford glass scratching across it's flawless surface.

Every time that Cecil came to dinner in the country, I found that I burnt the food; I seemed to be unable to offer him any dish that had not been reduced to a catastrophically blackened crisp. And somehow whenever he came to the house he was served cream for his disgusting charcoal-coloured *tarte de fraise*, not from the jug that he would have liked, but from the plastic container. He was often a martyr to the backlash that he created by his astringent demand for ideal decorum.[28]

In America Betsy Bloomingdale, close friend of Mrs Reagan, observed: 'Cecil made you feel *you* were special by entertaining him.'[29]

The playwright and novelist, Enid Bagnold, who suffered a long row with Cecil, enquired: 'I wonder if he had heart. He seemed to, but I wonder if he did.'[30] David Herbert maintained: 'His head ruled his heart.'[31] Yet he was passionately involved in everything he did. The image of Cecil is of a cold, rather remote man, yet several have testified that he was a pouncer. Ina Claire, for one, recalled a Christmas in America when he pounced after a party. 'Come off it, Cecil,'[32] she said and they remained friends. The actress Coral Browne recalled that upon reading Cecil's diaries, *The Happy Years*, with their revelations about Greta Garbo, she had thought: 'It was a trip down memory lane so far as I was concerned.'[33]

I asked a number of Cecil's friends whether or not they thought he was a happy man. His San Francisco friend, Kin, replied:

> I never knew anyone who had nearly as much joy in being a member of the cast of the play we all act out, and it is only in terms of that joy that one can really know him.[34]

Cathleen Nesbitt, sitting in her New York dressing-room about to play Mrs Higgins in *My Fair Lady* at the age of ninety-three, said: 'He was not an effusive man. But he achieved a lot of what he wanted and that makes for happiness.'[35] Oliver Smith thought:

> Yes and no. He was happy when he was working. But he had to do a lot of work he had disdain for. He had a strong protective shell – mistrust, cynicism.[36]

I said to Irving Penn: 'He could have been much happier if he had relaxed a bit.' To this he replied: 'Yes, but he wouldn't have been Cecil then.'[37]

Cecil gave his own opinions on the merits of happiness to the *Palm Beach Post*:

> I suppose I would want for a child most of all to be happy. But it's not necessarily the most interesting life, to be always happy.... The more intelligent people are, the more likely they are to be unhappy.[38]

Cecil was driven by a strong ambition. When in 1955 Sir Roderick Jones said to him: 'I hear of you everywhere, Cecil, you are getting so famous', he replied: 'I hope to God I am. I've worked hard enough for the damn thing.'[39]

The way that Cecil achieved his fame is one of the themes of this biography. It interested me to know how a boy born in a middle-class Hampstead family had turned himself into Cecil Beaton. He was that very rare creature – a total self-creation. A journalist commented that he had not been born with a silver spoon in his mouth and with pride Cecil added: 'But I managed to put it there.'[40] Thanks to his very detailed diary it is possible to trace his rise to fame step by step. To Greta Garbo Cecil wrote:

I have been reading a lot of my early diaries and am quite amazed at their contents. It seems that I must have spent most of my youth putting my most private actions and thoughts onto paper. I am rather glad now that I did. They will make amusing reading and I shall trust one evening I may inflict some of the juicier passages onto you. I am also quite appalled to discover what a ghastly little tick I used to be, and sympathize so much with my father who must have been very upset to find his son turning out to be so very different from the sportsman he hoped I'd be.[41]

In a later diary Cecil recorded Garbo's vindication of the way he had emerged:

Some people when you were very young and effeminate may have found you most obnoxious to begin with, but then you worked and proved yourself useful.[42]

Fearing an oncoming war, Cecil wrote in his diary of September 1938:

I suddenly see myself as a person a few future young men may be curious to ask questions about. Had he charm? What was he like? Just in the same way I have asked similar questions about Rupert Brooke and so many others who were figures before the last annihilation.[43]

More than a few people, young and old, ask questions about Cecil today and the other purpose of this book is to answer them.

Author's Note
The episodes relating to Miss Greta Garbo are derived from Cecil Beaton's unpublished diaries. The author did not interview Miss Garbo.

Part One

The Formative Years 1904–25

The Blacksmith and the Chemist

*Somehow I had always felt I came from nothing, but if I
do go back any distance there is nowhere I'd rather be
than Tintinhull.*

Cecil's diary, August 1973

In ancient times at Acornbank there stood a solid stone table around which,
it was said, the Knights Templar used to gather. The village of Temple
Sowerby is supposedly named after this stone and lies between Penrith in
Cumberland and Appleby in Westmorland. There have been Sissons (or
Syssons) in that vicinity for over 450 years. Some were mercers and lawyers, but the family from which Cecil descends were millers or poultry
farmers. In the latter part of the nineteenth century, Joseph Sisson was the
village blacksmith at Temple Sowerby. He was also Cecil's maternal grandfather. Known as 'Auld Jossie' to the villagers, his smithy was a popular
spot for young children. One of its attractions was a red and green Amazon
parrot chained to a pump in the cobbled yard. Alice Lowthian spent many
hours there as a child: 'He was so jolly and handsome and always a kindly
word for the tots watching the great bellows and the patient fine horses.'[1]
Alice thought Cecil bore a striking resemblance to his bewhiskered old
grandfather. Auld Jossie was married to Elizabeth Oldcorn, a handsome if
rather austere woman who had probably married beneath her. They had a
family of nine and were often so poor that the children went barefoot to the
doors of the better houses begging for waste for their pigs. Of the children
of the marriage, the three sons led unremembered lives, and the two elder
daughters married and disappeared to Canada and Australia respectively.
Ella, the third daughter, married the well-to-do Frank Williamson of Penrith
who, alas, proved a gambler. It was the three youngest daughters, Jessie,
Etty and Cada, who were to prove exceptional.

These three girls were outstandingly beautiful and caused such a sensation in the village that the memory of them lingers there to this day. Some
say that the girls owed their particular beauty to the fact that their fathers
were young bloods who came to Temple Sowerby to fish and that they were

not Auld Jossie's girls, but this can be no more than a matter for speculation. The girls attended the village school and for a while entered private service. But they were destined for more glittering futures and none lacked the self-confidence to take their chance when it came.

The King's Arms, which still dominates the village today, was the place where visiting young gentlemen would stay. Elizabeth Sisson was ambitious for her daughters and realized that here, if anywhere, they might meet suitable husbands. She was once seen with binoculars trained on the pub awaiting the arrival of fashionable prey from London. She would then send her pretty daughters to walk past the pub and hope that hearts would be stirred.

Two young boys, Romulo Suarez and Claud Chattock, used to come to Temple Sowerby at this time. Romulo's uncle, Don Pedro Suarez, was attached to the Bolivian Legation. Cecil described him as having 'large velvety eyes, thickly lashed, black hair centre-parted and a Ghengis Khan moustache'.[2] He was considered devastatingly attractive and he certainly proved so to Cecil's Aunt Jessie. After a whirlwind romance she and Pedro married in 1890 and set off on a life of adventure in the exotic if feudal world of Bolivia. After many bizarre adventures, Jessie contracted malaria and she and her husband were forced to return to England. She remained in bed for two years, and became little more than a wraith. Later she gave birth to a son, which she took to Temple Sowerby to show her father. Here it was injected against smallpox, but the doctor used a dirty needle: the child contracted septicaemia and died.

Following Jessie's marriage to Suarez, Auld Jossie gave up his smithy and moved from his thatched cottage to 'The Cedars', a fine old house opposite the maypole on the village green. Alice Lowthian recalled: 'I seem to see him now in an impeccable grey suit and panama hat and with a beautiful flower in his buttonhole, and his smiling face and curly hair.'[3] Auld Jossie's wife died on 23 September 1898, shortly before Jessie returned from her Bolivian adventures. Jessie and Pedro set up home at 74 Compayne Gardens in West Hampstead, where they entertained a motley crew of fellow South American diplomats. Pedro, now known as Lieutenant-Colonel Don Pedro Suarez, served as Military Attaché in London from 1900 and later as Consul General. In 1913 he was promoted Envoy Extraordinary and Minister Plenipotentiary. He also represented Bolivia in Paris, and this account by Eduardo Aramayo represents the way Cecil liked to think of his aunt: 'At the end of the *Belle Epoque* the elegant coach, drawn by a team of white horses in which Don Pedro and his beautiful English wife drove along the Champs Elysées and the Avenue du Bois, attracted much attention.'[4]

Esther, Cecil's mother, always known as Etty, was born on 14 November 1872. As a young girl she liked to take bicycle rides with her father and sometimes she accompanied her sister Ella to watch the football at Penrith. She was good-looking and when she grew up she acquired an admirer called Ted Tandy, a keen shot, who used to send her salmon and wild duck. In time they became engaged, but Ted caught a bad cold as a result of shooting until four in the morning. This developed into tuberculosis and he died in Switzerland. There was another man who was on the point of proposing, but Jessie summoned Etty to London to join the fun there, part of which was to see the local amateur company in *A Bunch of Violets*. The male lead was Cecil's father, Ernest Beaton. On Christmas Day 1902, in Jessie's drawing-room, Ernest Beaton proposed to Etty and was accepted. The wedding took place on 7 March 1903. The invitations were sent in the name of Lieutenant-Colonel and Madame Suarez and there is no evidence that Auld Jossie (who did not die until 8 December 1907) took any part in it. In 1928 Cecil wrote: 'It is extraordinary how unintimate we all are with our parents and never hear anything about things past. I've no idea what sort of people Mummie's parents were, what their house was like, where Mummie met Daddy or any other such sentimentally interesting thing.'[5] Nor did Mrs Beaton ever discuss her past with her children. Cecil only learned of his maternal origins after his mother's death, when he began to piece together the details of his aunt's life for his book, *My Bolivian Aunt*. Even so he did not mention the blacksmith, either in print or to his friends. Of Auld Jossie he wrote: 'He loved all country trades, including farrier work, and was pleased when his cart and horses needed shoeing.... But if Joe Sisson was in a mood to explore the woods, or make his way down the River Eden, the world and all in it could go hang.'*[6] Cecil's case is proof of the fluidity of the English class system. It might be thought impossible that a blacksmith's grandson could turn into a Cecil Beaton, but then the exotic novelist, Ronald Firbank, was the grandson of a coal-miner.

Cecil was hardly better informed about his Beaton ancestors. His great-uncle Brice tried his hand at some amateur genealogy and came up with the story that the Beatons descended from an ancient family who had come over with William the Conqueror and that they belonged to the same family that produced Cardinal David Beaton, Archbishop James Beaton (the faithful Ambassador to Mary, Queen of Scots), and Mary Beaton, one of her four maids-of-honour attendants. This unreliable information caused Cecil some trouble in society later on.

---

*Cecil's youngest aunt, Cada, also forged a marriage within the world of Temple Sowerby and yet, like Etty, she was married in Hampstead. She married Richard Chattock, the widowed father of young Claud. Claud was about fifteen when he used to come to Temple Sowerby and had just started at Rugby. He was killed in the Great War. Richard Chattock, who became Chief Electrical Engineer to Birmingham Corporation, lived at Silhill Hall, a beautiful timbered Elizabethan house at Solihull. They had two daughters, Tecia and Tess.

The earliest known ancestor of the Beatons is John Beaton, who was born in Somerset on 31 March 1804. He descended illegitimately from William Beaton, of Tintinhull, near Yeovil, and Mary Priddle, who married in 1770. One day when Cecil was on holiday with his parents, his father shattered any illusions he may have had concerning grand origins. Mr Beaton said his father began life dispensing medicines in a chemist's shop in Kilburn, and that his grandfather (the aforementioned John) owned the shop. Mrs Beaton then interjected, 'And a very good business too, I expect', but Mr Beaton snapped, 'No, it wasn't. He was just an ordinary chemist in Kilburn.' Cecil was upset about this: 'I just was dumb and numb. I had hoped we were better than that. Daddy's father got terribly prosperous and had an enormous house and wonderful gardens, stone balustrades etc. So he sprang from a Kilburn chemist. ...' [7]

Not long after this Cecil was with his father when they looked him up in the Sherborne School register: 'There he was, the nice E.W.H. Beaton, son of [Walter] Hardy Beaton of Nightingales, Clapham Common! Rather a nasty hit for me, the snob, but I comforted myself that Nightingales may have been the most wonderful place.' [8]

Cecil's grandfather lived at different times in Calne (Wiltshire), Newington (Kent), Oxford Street (London), Shoreditch High Street and Grange Road, Dalston (Hackney). He married Louise Stroughill, who was engaged at fifteen, married at seventeen, and a mother at twenty. The Stroughills were said to be 'men of Kent who were never beaten'. [9] Some of them had been knights. Walter Hardy Beaton was one of the original founders in 1858 of the firm of Beaton Brothers, which specialized in importing sleepers. Cecil's youngest uncle Wilfred inherited that business. The grandfather prospered and ended his days at Hazelwood in Abbots Langley (Hertfordshire).

In this house Ernest Beaton presented his bride to his family. After their wedding they travelled to Monte Carlo for their honeymoon. Visiting Monaco in September 1965, Cecil noted:

There is every reason to believe that I was conceived here. My parents spent their honeymoon at the Hotel Hermitage and nine months later I was born. One of my earliest memories is of a photograph of my proud and smiling parents standing in an exotic garden with the spikes of the black feathers on my mother's hat complementing the cacti and palms of the background. My mother's dress was rose velvet. [10]

Cecil was born at 21 Langland Gardens in Hampstead, a house he described as 'a small, tall, red brick house of ornate, but indiscriminate taste'. [11] He came into the world at 11.30 in the morning of 14 January 1904. By 18 January he weighed 7¼ pounds and on 5 March he was baptized with the names Cecil Walter Hardy by the Reverend William Stone, Vicar of St Mary, Kilburn. His godfather was his uncle, Cecil Beaton. By a curious coincidence

Uncle Cecil was also chosen to be godfather of Dame Peggy Ashcroft's brother, the first of Cecil's many links with the theatre. Cecil was the eldest of four children. His brother Reginald was born at Langland Gardens on 3 April 1905. So was his sister Nancy on 30 September 1909. In 1911 the family moved to Temple Court, Templewood Avenue, a 'vaguely neo-Georgian mansion',[12] close to Hampstead Heath and generally more spacious. Here Barbara (known as 'Baba') was born on 21 January 1912.

Cecil, or Toto Binnun (his first name for himself), remembered his earliest childhood days as 'a mixture of wonder and surprise', but was soon aware that not far away 'danger lurked, and the grown-ups laughed sympathetically about it, and tried to protect one against the worst'.[13] His first memory was of a spring holiday at Shanklin on the Isle of the Wight. He remembered bluebells, a ride in a carriage and a Pomeranian dog.

At the end of their plot at Langland Gardens was a gate which led on to a communal public garden. Here Cecil encountered 'the strangeness of vegetation'. He recalled 'frighteningly large, dark bushes of flowering privet and also weigelia which has pink blossom of a waxy trumpet variety: even as an infant I did not like the colour of this pink'.[14]

On a particularly magical summer evening, when he was about three, Cecil was picking daisies in the long grass. Suddenly he was interrupted:

> The atmosphere became less calm, and more electric; someone was smiling at me in a rather alarming, excited way. It was my father returned from America. This was my first reunion with him. He wanted me to remember him, but I did not know he had been away. I did not know whether to be frightened and to start to cry, but instead tried to regain the pleasure of the calm evening and invited him to 'pick daisies, pick daisies'.[15]

The face that looked down on him was a kind one. Cecil liked to describe the Beatons as coarse, or like walruses. He described his great-uncle Brice, in September 1923, as: 'a typical fat Beaton that had fallen in the dustbin'.[16] Uncle Wilfred fared little better. He looked like 'a bloated bladder'. Ernest Beaton had simple tastes from which he derived much enjoyment. His favourite work, *Vanity Fair*, he read thirty times. Cecil often bemoaned the fact that he was not more like his father, as life would perhaps have been easier. Ernest Beaton and his brothers and sister were keen amateur actors in the 1890s: he was the popular Honorary Secretary of the Thespis Dramatic Society in the days when the family lived at 8 Netherhall Gardens, Hampstead. He gained quite a reputation as an amateur actor, whose performances were described as spirited, lively and energetic and 'decidedly in advance of the average amateur in style and finish'.[17]

After his marriage Mr Beaton gave up acting, but never lost his love for the theatre. He greatly enjoyed mimicking the great actors of his day for the benefit of his family. 'His Herbert Tree as Svengali sent shivers down our spines,' wrote Cecil, 'and he made terrible faces, dilating his eyes, widening his nostrils, and stretching his mouth to reveal his black teeth.' Sometimes the family nurse complained that Nancy and Baba had been disturbed in the nursery by 'bloodcurdling noises accompanied by raucous outbursts of laughter'.[18] Nancy always maintained that her father missed a good career as a barrister.

His other great passion was cricket. He played some forty-six seasons for Hampstead, very often as wicket-keeper. He was a member of MCC, and the editor of *Timber and Plywood* noted: 'We have heard tales, not from him, of mighty smites associated with his name on that famous ground.'[19] He was born in 1867 and, after Sherborne, was educated first in Germany, then in Sweden. In 1887 he started work in one of his father's timber agency businesses, which specialized in all types of European and Baltic softwoods. Later he spent eleven years on the Council of the Timber Trade Federation and became its President in 1933. He had one other curious appointment. He was listed as Vice-Consul of Bolivia in London. During Cecil's early years the family business prospered, and the Beatons bettered their standard of living. Only later did matters take a downward turn.

Cecil was born in the Edwardian era, and was considerably influenced by this period and particularly by the two women closest to him, his mother and his Aunt Jessie. He admitted that his child's eye, like his later adult's vision, 'always sought out the detail rather than the conception as a whole'.[20] He would take in and never forget the 'miraculously soft' materials his mother wore as she bade him good night, or some imitation lilies pinned to her pale green chiffon scarf. He loved to watch his mother disguise herself in the fashion of the day and to witness the transformation of their house into a stage setting for a party. Spellbound, he observed his mother completing her efforts while her bedroom became more chaotic, with powder spilled on the dressing-table and floor, and discarded garments, trimmings and feathers littering the bed. One night a governess told Cecil that in Heaven people's shapes were different. As he wrote in 1923, 'I was so upset at the idea that I wouldn't see Mummie that I cried until I was quite exhausted.'[21] Cecil loved his mother better than anyone in the world, and when he was little he held the illusion that she was an important society figure. He was bitterly disappointed to discover that she was not, but resolved to improve her.

Aunt Jessie was altogether more flamboyant. Cecil loved her personality ('built on heroic proportions')[22] and her beautiful, small, straight nose. He was prepared to overlook her lack of stature and plumpness. In his childhood he would hear her infectious laugh. He thought her 'grand and gaudy and gay'.²³ In her days as wife of the Bolivian Minister she could offer Cecil a glimpse of herself on the way to court. Sometimes he was allowed to powder her back before a ball. Jessie herself acquired a somewhat exaggerated foreign accent, mixed in with a touch of north-country. Her husband, Pedro, she referred to as 'Peth-er-orh'; tomato was 'tomm-art-tohh'; she emitted curious exclamations such as 'Orch-ta-taie' and 'Tutte, tutte, tutte'. Less exotically she would complain, 'Orh, rotten cotton', and the family often heard aunt and mother in close discussion: 'Eh! Etty, but do you know!' ... 'Eh! Jessie, but have you ever?'

Aunt Jessie was considered a comic character in the Beaton household with her strange and often unbelieved stories of Bolivian life. But to Cecil she was the spoiler and rule-breaker. At Compayne Gardens he encountered spiced food, magically scented soaps and a Yorkshire terrier with gold medallions around its neck. She dressed extravagantly and wore huge, elaborate hats that proved an inspiration for many a stage production (most notably *My Fair Lady*), and in 1943 Edith Evans, starring in Shaw's *Heartbreak House*, would complain: 'I *won't* wear a train just because Cecil's Aunt Jessie did.'²⁴

Aunt Jessie paid a second visit to Bolivia, but when Pedro ran off with the young housekeeper she sold her wedding ring and came home, impoverished and sad, with only an assortment of old clothes in trunks and her jumbled memories. Thereafter she was a less romantic figure. She would walk about with a small cigarette staining her upper lip yellow, the ash inches long and precariously balanced, perhaps carrying a vegetable dish in either hand. Once a part of the diplomatic world, she was now neglected. She lived on £500 a year. Cecil sometimes amused himself by drawing caricatures of her, and a friend who saw her in later years described her as looking 'like a down-at-heel fortune-teller'.²⁵

There was a third, important influence on the young Cecil in the form of his first theatrical heroine. It was his habit to climb into his mother's bed and nestle close to her while she opened letters and sipped her tea in the mornings. One day when he was about three, his eye was caught by a tinselled, hand-coloured picture postcard of Lily Elsie, with her hair piled high in a billowing cluster of curls. Cecil wrote: 'the beauty of it caused my heart to leap'.²⁶ The picture showed the famous musical comedy star as a swan-like profile 'yearning towards some unknown romantic horizon'.²⁷ This gentle creature exuded a sweet sadness, compassion and dignity. Cecil thought her the kind of woman that other women emulate and men want to protect. Not only did he fall for Lily Elsie, but he also fell for the idea of the picture postcard and thus acquired an early interest in the photographic image. Presently he obtained a picture of Lily Elsie in her black hat, a short brim at the front, a large one at the back, adorned with wisps of paradise. This 'Merry Widow hat' created a craze for huge hats, and part of Lily Elsie's charm was that she never quite knew why she was so popular. Nor did she understand the dazzling effect that she had on London. Cecil never saw her in Franz Lehár's musical because she was ill on the matinée to which his father took him. However, at a children's party at the Carlton Hotel in Haymarket, Aunt Jessie introduced them. Gallantly he rose to the occasion, obliging his uncle to buy him some Parma violets, which he presented to the smiling lady in furs. Another meeting occurred when Lily Elsie and Gertrude Glyn took tea with Aunt Jessie at Compayne Gardens. Cecil and his brother, Reggie, attempted to re-enact the Merry Widow waltz, Cecil taking the part of the widow in too long a pale green nightgown with Reggie following meekly as Prince Danilo. Although Cecil's performance was appalling, the adults loved it and Miss Elsie rewarded him with a kiss. In such ways was a love of theatre born in him, and he never forgot the lovely creature whose beauty he so often tried to capture in crayon. 'Lily Elsie wrapped the whole of my childhood in a haze of roses,' he wrote, 'and since then has never failed to cast her spell.'[28]

Cecil's early life was enriched by further visual wonders. His interest in picture postcards widened to include other leading ladies of the day. On afternoon walks he would make a beeline for the local stationer's shop and spend half an hour turning the revolving stands of postcards. He cut out magazine pictures of Gertie Millar, Florence Smithson and the extraordinary Gaby Deslys. He was delighted if the editors had granted her a full-page spread. At the age of four his mother took him to be photographed by Miss Lallie Charles, the lady responsible for the pictures of many of his stage goddesses. Cecil began the session very shyly until he recognized the bouquet of false roses that Lily Elsie used to hold. Miss Charles had some difficulty persuading him that it would not be suitable for him to clutch them during his sitting.

Mr Beaton welcomed the daily enthusiasm with which Cecil awaited his return from the office, but presently he became aware that Cecil was really wanting the *Evening Standard*, which contained a daily fashion plate by Bessie Ascough. If he were lucky there would be a lady in court dress with feathers, bouquet and train. Cecil particularly admired the skill with which she drew roses (an art that he himself developed to a high degree). One day his father forgot the paper and Cecil flew into a rage. His father then told him that Bessie Ascough was on holiday for a while. This was not true, but the Beatons had decided that this obsession with fashion was unhealthy. As Cecil put it: 'The child was becoming peculiar.'[29]

Once a passion is within a child there is little chance of controlling it. Cecil found photographs of stage sets and designs and studied them through a magnifying glass with professional dedication. He loved the 'tricks and artifices of the stage' and sought to discover how the sets were constructed, where the joins came in the canvas. His father was also stagestruck and, whenever he came back from New York, he brought with him a bundle of playbills and theatrical magazines. Cecil bombarded his father with questions which poor Mr Beaton was rarely expert enough to answer. For years this situation would continue, the youthful Cecil squirrelling away a vast collection of images of lovely ladies, gathering ideas and plans, but being too young to find a satisfactory outlet for them. His taste would change, of course, over the years. By 1925 he 'loathed' Gertie Millar and 'detested' Florence Smithson, while remaining loyal to Lily Elsie and declaring himself proudly to be 'of the Gaby Deslys period'. He was forever grateful to have been a child of the Edwardian era and able to enjoy youthful glimpses of that world before the Great War swept it away. He believed it gave him 'a sense of solidity and discipline and helped to crystallize a number of homely virtues and tastes, by which, consciously or unconsciously, I have been influenced in my life'.[30]

2

A Harsher Reality

I found school appalling – such a waste of time.

Cecil to John Freeman, *Face to Face*, 1962

For ten years from 1911 the Beaton family lived at Temple Court on the corner of Templewood Avenue in Hampstead. They were happy there; Mr Beaton's business was flourishing, he had plenty to occupy him with four growing children, riding on the Heath and his love for billiards and cricket. There were servants in the house, though one butler, Paget, left voluntarily, confessing, 'I'll have to leave, Sir, I'm in love with the Missus.'[1] The only curious thing about this house was the library, which, because Mr Beaton only read the cricketing almanacs and the *Economist*, never contained a book. There was a garden where Reggie practised his cricket, following keenly in his father's footsteps, while Cecil experimented with his first snapshots. When Nancy and Baba were old enough they wheeled their dolls' prams beside the rock plants and there were energetic games of catch-as-catch-can. An oak tree dominated the scene. Beyond was Mrs Beaton's rose garden where pink, red and salmony-yellow blooms flourished before being taken indoors in huge bunches.

This house held the happy memories of childhood – Cecil poring over his Buster Brown books; the day when two young neighbours, Gwen and Molly Le Bas, were offered a bar of chocolate if they would run round the billiard table 300 times; the rocking horse in the nursery which Cecil didn't like because it made his hands smelly and sticky; and the time when Cecil painted his first picture, on the inside of a white cardboard dress-box lid. He had been to the Crystal Palace and was under the influence of Japanese hanging blossoms:

I'd never been more delighted, because it was theatrical and beautiful. If the mauve wisteria hanging from the tresses had been real I shouldn't have adored it so much but the fact that it was artificial and that the blue sky one could see above was of blue paper made the whole thing so intensely wonderful for me that I used to dream of it for weeks.[2]

He acquired at an early age a fondness for mimicry and imitation. When he was about five he saw an old man limping along the street, one leg shorter than the other. Immediately he began to walk like that, greatly enjoying the affectation. The nurse became worried and the family doctor was summoned. Cecil was stripped naked and told to walk round the room. He limped round and round while the doctor laughed till tears rolled out of his eyes. Likewise he adopted the poses of the actress Isobel Elsom, stretching his neck and sticking out his chin in the way that she did.

Cecil began school at Miss Dale's in Hampstead, where he enjoyed the painting class. He was also taught the polka and hornpipe at Madame Sherwood's Dancing School. Then, at the age of eight, in 1912, he entered Heath Mount as a day boy.

Heath Mount Preparatory School was founded in 1790 and remained in Hampstead opposite the Admiral's house. Evelyn Waugh described it as 'the best school in the neighbourhood',[3] to which two brothers came from as far afield as the Channel Islands. No boys took scholarships, but most passed their school certificate without undue problems. Cricket coaching was just adequate. As Waugh put it: 'Nothing was attempted that was not being done better in fifty other schools. But it prospered.'[4] Among its pupils besides Evelyn Waugh were Dudley Scholte (son of the famous tailor and Cecil's earliest surviving friend), Burnet Pavitt (a few years younger), and Robert Nesbitt (the producer who created The Talk of the Town).

As he crossed the Heath on his first day, together with Reggie, both carrying their satchels and wearing their emerald green caps, Cecil dreaded that the masters would be cruel. However, morning break at eleven arrived without disaster and the boys were let out 'to rampage over the asphalt playground'.[5] The new boys looked lost, but none more lost than Cecil. A terrible fate awaited him and, as so often when he was the victim, he described with an exaggerated sense of drama how the bullies arrived, at once 'recognized their quarry' and advanced upon him. While the larger boys encircled him, their leader, 'a boy half the size of the others, wearing Barrie-esque green tweed knickerbockers', darted towards him and then halted very close to him, fixing him with 'a menacing wild stare'.

> He then stood on his toes and slowly thrust his face with a diabolical stare, closer and closer to mine, ever closer until the eyes converged into one enormous Cyclops nightmare. It was a clever inauguration to the terrors that followed, and my introduction to Evelyn Waugh.[6]

Cecil wanted to publish that Waugh 'bared his black pitted teeth in a further effort to frighten me',[7] but was restrained by the laws of libel. It was not an isolated incident. They often bent Cecil's arms back to front. Waugh recalled with pleasure the tortures they inflicted:

The tears on his long eyelashes used to provoke the sadism of youth and my cronies and I tormented him on the excuse that he was reputed to enjoy his music lessons and to hold in sentimental regard the lady who taught him. I am sure he was innocent of these charges. Our persecution went no further than sticking pins into him and we were soundly beaten for doing so.[8]

Only then did the tortures cease, but a lifelong enmity grew from these incidents. In 1962, Cecil told John Freeman: 'Evelyn Waugh is my enemy. We dislike one another intensely. He thinks I'm a nasty piece of goods and, oh brother! do I feel the same way about him.'[9]

A normal day at Heath Mount began with a gathering of the sixty pupils in the gymnasium. The headmaster, Mr Granville Grenfell, was an elegant man and a senior Freemason. Burnet Pavitt recalled that he often wore a smart black silk cravat and pearl pin. Each morning he bounded up three steps and greeted the school: 'Good morning, Gentlemen' – 'Good morning, Sir'. On Saturdays Mr Grenfell appeared with a ledger and went through the elaborate charade of praising the commended pupils and shouting at the idle ones in sudden and startling changes of mood and tone. Few boys were beaten, though lying and cheating were considered heinous crimes. The assistant masters varied considerably in calibre and were treated either with awe or mockery. George Traill,* a contemporary of Cecil's, recalled that Hynchcliffe used to make miscreants bend over a footstool. He would then jump over them delivering a kick on the backside. (In time, Hynchcliffe was dismissed for pinching little boys' bottoms.) Stebbing, on the other hand, was more scientific. He covered his ruler with chalk so as to be sure to hit the same spot. At the end of the day Cecil and some of the other boys would be met by a man who worked for the Beatons and escorted home over the Heath which, as light faded, became the pitch of prostitutes.

All Cecil's schoolmates, whether from Heath Mount or Harrow, recall that he was a very beautiful child. In a portrait of the school group he is the only one with a thick fringe. He gazes bright-eyed and cheerfully from amongst his schoolmates, though, in view of his later reputation for sartorial elegance, his tie is far from well knotted. His beauty tended to make him a favourite of the masters and to some extent eased his progress through school. Some of the pupils thought him too beautiful to be a boy. They used to take surreptitious glances in the school lavatory to reassure themselves.

His schoolmates also remember that while they subscribed to *The Captain*, a schoolboy's weekly, Cecil would spend his time cutting out silhouette portraits of actors and actresses from the theatrical page of the *Tatler* or the *Sketch*. These he pasted into a scrap-book. Cecil also made models of stage personalities by cutting out photographs, painting the faces in stage make-

---

* Father of Sir Alan Traill, Lord Mayor of London 1984–5.

up and colouring the evening dresses with pastel colours dotted in gold and silver liquid paint. He constructed a toy theatre from a hat box and faithfully reproduced the scenery. The tableau was lit with an electric torch and the characters pushed on stage with tin clips attached to long handles. Cecil himself mouthed all the parts and sang the songs. His first production was the musical comedy, *Oh, Oh, Delphine*. The masters at Heath Mount tended to be fond of amateur theatricals so they condoned this unusual hobby. One of them, Aubrey Ensor, had a collection of 36,000 postcards of actresses. He contributed to revues at the Everyman Theatre, and Dudley Scholte remembered that when they were at work Mr Ensor often danced round the classroom, singing to himself the popular songs of the day. Cecil was so involved in his own exploits that he often spent his lessons sketching in an album so small he could hide it in the palm of his hand. Eventually he was caught by the history master, during a lecture on the early Saxons. His album was confiscated. Neither he nor Reggie were good readers. When faced with *Middlemarch* as a holiday task, Cecil skipped so much that he made no sense of it, while nothing would induce his brother to do anything but play cricket in the garden.

One thing that Cecil had to face at Heath Mount was his first confusing attempt to understand sex. A boy called Geoghegan minor sometimes waited for Cecil to finish his school tea and then took him part of the way home on his bicycle. Cecil recalled:

There was quite an electric current running from me to him as I mounted the metal step and clung on to his shoulders. I had to dig deeper into his shoulders whenever the bicycle shook and I was more likely to lose my balance. Geoghegan had already been initiated into the rites of sex, but he did not explain the facts to me and would occasionally produce for my delectation a naughty word. It was he who taught me the word 'fuck' but I still had no idea of its meaning when he recited the lines:
When apples and pears are ripe for plucking,
Sweet girls of sixteen are ready for fucking.
However, I would feel beholden to him to produce on my own accord some smutty word for him at our next meeting. But the dictionary did not produce any word that could compare with his. The best I could do would be to say 'entrails' to him.[10]

It fell to another friend, Dudley Brown (who was destined to take a sinister path and throw himself to an early death from his window in the rue Jacob in Paris at the age of twenty-two), to enlighten Cecil further about the facts of life. He whispered that children were produced by the man 'mixing his "stuff" with the woman's'.[11]

Boys could remain at Heath Mount until they went to public school, but after three years the Beatons sent Cecil and Reggie away to board. Thus

Cecil prepared to say farewell to 'an idyllically happy childhood'[12] and face a harsher reality. He realized that he was exchanging his nice warm bed at Temple Court for the cold of school. He would lie there 'lumpy in the throat' and his throat would become sore with swallowing lumps. In 1915 the two brothers set off by train for the grim St Cyprian's School at Eastbourne, later made notorious by the writings of two contemporaries, Eric Blair (George Orwell) and Tim Connolly (Cyril Connolly). St Cyprian's was an ugly building with a square of asphalt in front of it. The schoolrooms smelt inky and dusty, the swimming-pool was stagnant, the lavatories cold and damp. A flat playing-field stretched out to a steep bank with a low brick wall marking the road. It was wartime and things were naturally bleak. In winter the pupils suffered intensely from the cold.

George Orwell wrote a memorable account of the school entitled 'Such, Such were the Joys', and Cyril Connolly devoted a chapter to it in *Enemies of Promise*. Orwell believed that 'the public schools aren't so bad, but the people are wrecked by those filthy private schools long before they get to public school age'.[13] In his bitter essay he painted a terrifying picture of the tortures he underwent. Desolately lonely and helpless, he was beaten for wetting his bed and flogged like a foundered horse towards his Eton scholarship. He suffered from insufficient food, draughty dormitories and dusty, splintery passages. The pewter porridge bowls had overhanging rims in which lurked accumulations of sour porridge. Lumps, hairs and unidentified black objects turned up in the soup, the plunge baths were filled with slimy water and pupils dried themselves with damp towels, smelling of cheese. In the public baths a human turd floated towards him. Orwell wrote:

> Almost as in the days of Thackeray, it seemed natural that a little boy of eight or ten should be a miserable, snotty-nosed creature, his face almost permanently dirty, his hands chapped, his nails bitten, his handkerchief a sodden horror, his bottom frequently blue with bruises.[14]

Cecil himself recalled the miserable first days of homesickness, how the tears almost froze on his face in the cruel wind and how he and Reggie developed papillomas on the soles of their feet due to undernourishment. Nor did the icy swimming-bath into which they jumped each morning help the chilblains from which he suffered on and off all his life. The gymnasium was 'medieval torture' and he lived in terror of Mr and Mrs Vaughan Wilkes ('Sambo' and 'Flip'), the headmaster and his ferocious wife.

Cecil greatly admired George Orwell's piece on St Cyprian's and wrote:

> It is uncanny how a boy of that age could have seen through all the layers of snobbery and pretence of the Vaughan Wilkes. It is hilariously funny – but it is exaggerated: God knows I *loathed* the Wilkes and loathed every minute of the school regime, and was just as appalled as he by the

stink and squalor of the loos, the swimming-pool, just as appalled by the cold and the filthiness of the food. Even so I never saw a turd floating in the bath. I do not remember the rind of old porridge under the rim of the pewter bowl, and I have the feeling that Orwell made a fetish of the sordid and enjoyed playing up the horror of life among the miners, or the down-and-outs in any city of the world. He is looking everywhere for class hatred and I did not find the boys at St Cyprian's were themselves snobbish and heard no word until I went to Harrow of their parents' grandeur, the grouse moors and butlers and chauffeurs. But his description of 'Flip' and 'Sambo' bring back with an extraordinary vividness these two major characters in the earliest scenes of one's life.... [Flip] was a non-stop study. I was fascinated by her, terrified, had absolutely no affection for her, in fact hated her almost as much as Orwell did.

The escape from Flip when at last we left St Cyprian's was one of the great milestones in my early existence.[15]

Cecil was never a friend of Orwell's ('there could hardly be two people further apart than Orwell and myself'),[16] though for a while they worked together on an allotment – 'but even at an age when politics had no bearing on either of us, there was so little rapport'.[17] In retrospect he was 'intrigued and fascinated' by Cyril Connolly, though he thought him 'always rather preciously clever'.[18] Not long after leaving school he wrote:

He is extraordinarily intellectual, but I think he has no real sense of beauty. One feels he has no fundamental basis and he always falters when talking about pictures. In a way he is charming but he can be dreadfully nasty and deceitful. Sometimes I detested him like poison at St Cyprian's when, the greedy, dirty little beast, he used to continue eating bread and honey, surreptitiously, during scripture, after breakfast....* He likes me but one feels one cannot trust him whole-heartedly for any moment.[19]

Connolly did indeed like Cecil: 'He had a charming, dreamy face, enormous blue eyes with long lashes and wore his hair in a fringe. His voice was slow, affected and creamy. He was not good at games or work but he escaped persecution through good manners, and a baffling independence.'[20] All the pupils aspired to remain in the favour of Flip, and there were ways of achieving this – being born rich or titled, heading for a scholarship which would bring acclaim to the school, or by having read the most worthy books. This assured Connolly a secure place, while Cecil merely made lists of the books without reading them. When in favour Cecil would be allowed to practise the piano in Flip's private sitting-room. Music held no allure for

* Later Cyril Connolly justified this by claiming he was underfed. To obtain extra food was a great school victory.

him but the sitting-room held other treasures. While one hand ran up and down the scales in a somewhat cursory manner the other turned the pages of the weekly magazines and Cecil's heart beat faster as he examined the ladies of fashion, their extraordinary clothes and hats and the stage pictures. Here he encountered Mrs Vernon Castle, 'with a waist like a scimitar',[21] and the actress Ina Claire, 'like a sugared almond'.*[22]

Cecil took part in the end-of-term plays and loved to dress up and put on make-up. For a production of *The Mikado* he spent many hours painting designs on fans. Sometimes he stepped forward on stage and sang the great hit of the day, 'If you were the only girl in the world and I was the only boy'. His small voice had quite an effect on the audience, as Cyril Connolly recalled:

> The eighty-odd [pupils] felt there could be no other boy in the world for them, the beetling chaplain forgot hell-fire and masturbation, the Irish drill-sergeant his bayonet practice, the staff refrained from disapproving and for a moment the whole structure of character and duty tottered and even the principles of hanging on, muddling through, and building empires were called into question.[23]

Cecil quite liked riding but he hated football and went to some lengths to avoid it. One bad moment occurred when he was discovered hiding under the stage, his coat covered with shavings and cobwebs. There was a blind boy at the school. He was a terrifying character because he had 'an uncanny way of using his long supple fingers like pincers and really torturing one in the most relentless way'.[24] The pupils were told that if they interfered with his bulgy eyes, his eyeballs would burst. This boy discovered that Cecil kept an old-fashioned nail-polish buffer in a pocket of his corduroy trousers and made full use of this 'ammunition' against him. There was also a boy of great charm, character and good manners, a Scottish boy in a kilt, called Nigel Kirkpatrick. Cecil wrote:

> One felt he knew all about life already and in his gentle way could cope with everything. I was in love with him and the greatest disappointment came when having imagined I could share a bath with him at Temple Court, a letter arrived at the eleventh hour saying that Nigel could not after all come to spend a week staying with us in the holidays.[25]

The majority of the boys of St Cyprian's were destined for Harrow and Cecil duly sat his exam. He knew he could never pass the school certificate honestly and therefore cheated, by cribbing at his exams, but so successfully that he passed into Harrow with honours. Looking back on St Cyprian's (which was eventually burnt down), he concluded:

*Hearing this in 1931, Ina Claire commented: 'Huh, hope when he says I'm an almond he doesn't mean I'm a nut.'

I learnt how to suck up, to curry favour, to be a sycophant – in order to survive, to get 'into favour' – to get a coconut cake. But many of the things I learnt were those I could have well remained ignorant of for some time to come. Altogether it was a bad school – but not as black as painted by Orwell with his beady eyes for the sinister, and the unfair.[26]

Years later, at Cambridge, another former pupil, Lord Charles Cavendish, the black sheep of the Devonshire family, decided in a drunken moment to write an abusive letter to Flip. Cecil regretted later adding his name to this unworthy missive.

3

Adolescent Emotions

*By the fireside I looked through early negatives of myself
at Harrow and Cambridge (what a horror I was!).*

Cecil's diary, 14 May 1968

Cecil entered Harrow in January 1918, not long before the end of the Great War, having passed into a higher class than his academic prowess merited. From this upgrading he was never able to escape. He struggled with incomprehensible reading-matter, was baffled by long division and algebra; he found it hard to concentrate. Outside the classroom he loathed cricket and football, dreaded the gymnasium and feared the prospect of army drill so much that he went to the trouble of ordering a pair of boots with irons from a Harley Street specialist in order to masquerade as a cripple. These were not worn when his parents came to see him.

In those days Harrow had a sense of isolation, perched on its hill ten miles from London in leafy Middlesex. English painters such as Turner had come there through the ages to paint its views. Cecil rather liked its formidably Victorian architecture of hearty and confident gloom, especially the beautiful rose-coloured fifth form which seemed an appropriate setting for the Elizabethan plays acted within. He liked the uneven steps trodden by generations of boys, assembling there for roll-call. He even liked 'an eyesore-brick-red-building'[1] known as the Stink School, where they worked with sulphuric acid and iron filings, because it overlooked terraced gardens with balustrades and flaming azaleas. The scent of these flowers in springtime was so strong that throughout his life azaleas stirred in Cecil 'abstract adolescent emotions ... dreads and happiness'.[2]

He enjoyed the smartness of the clothes, the top hats worn on Sundays, the fezes with tassels of the boys who excelled at 'footer'. He was amused by the petty distinctions in the way clothes were worn: the blue blazers of the new boys had to be entirely buttoned; after one year, a single button could be left undone and, after three, the coat could be open entirely.

Above all, Cecil loved the art school. Here he painted happily, his style dominated by that of the art master, W. Egerton Hine, affectionately known as 'Eggie'. He won prizes and good mentions during his years at the school. In 1919 he won a term prize, his work being dubbed 'both prolific and clever'.[3] In 1920 he won first prize in the Lower School and in 1921 was equal second with his friend Boy Le Bas, losing to D.W. Strachan. He was often to be seen setting off with the sketching class (still wearing the awful boots), to record churchyard scenes, bluebell woods and other rural landmarks, often inserting a Bacchante into the picture.

Eggie Hine had a lifelong influence on Cecil's art but, frankly, he was no artist. His skill lay in the tremendous enthusiasm which he instilled into his pupils. He remains an important pioneer in the teaching of art in public schools because it was he who persuaded the headmaster and governors to build an art school soon after he arrived at Harrow in 1892. He took the boys up to the National Gallery where they ragged him mercilessly because he resented the inclusion of the El Grecos.

Cecil was Eggie's favourite pupil. Through Vallance, Eggie Hine's junior, Cecil sold his first picture. He obtained 10s. 6d. for a little sketch of Pavlova. It was following a visit they made to the Royal Academy that Cecil believed he had found his vocation. He would be a Royal Academy portrait painter, with 'a high-ceilinged dingy studio with dusty suits of armour standing about, lengths of old brocade, and Carmen's Spanish shawl idly draped over the minstrel's gallery'.[4]

During his time at Harrow, Cecil boarded at Bradby's (called High Street until May 1919), the house of Major E.W. Freeborn, always known as 'Juggins'. Tris Grayson, Cecil's fagmaster, recalled the Major as a 'colourless man', while his wife was 'the life and soul of the pair'.[5] 'Mrs Juggins' was a competent painter in oils and theatrically minded. The house had a dramatic society which used to put on a play each winter term in which Cecil invariably took a female lead. These were performed at the Harrow Mission for the poor in Latimer Road. One song, called 'Goblin Golliwog Trees', that he performed with a friend in 'The Follies' in 1919, was deemed 'excellent' by the school magazine.

Cecil won the Lady Bourchier Reading Prize in 1918 and 1920. It was reported in *The Harrovian* that 'Beaton then read Arthur's dying speech, and he read it well; but the King seemed to die in such sprightly fashion, hardly decorously as it were, with a twinkle in his eye'.[6] Nevertheless the 'bloods' sitting in the front row cried out, 'Oh, jolly good!'[7] and Cecil relished the applause.

He was not bullied at Harrow. By and large he was left to his own devices. He is remembered mainly for the elegant if slightly flashy way he dressed at the school. He longed for a pair of gauntlet gloves and took real pride in being encountered in his house in a new pair of silk pyjamas. It was considered effeminate to have a smart room and most boys lived rather spartanly. The more aesthetically minded would discuss their fantasies of emerald green walls, black carpets and four-poster beds, dreams that were invariably dashed by the door being kicked open and the summons: 'You're wanted for slacking at corps.'[8]

Cecil shared his first room with Bobbie Horton (another of his friends destined to die young, during a Cambridge vacation). Horton wanted the room decorated pink, but Cecil declared that any pink would clash with Bobbie's head. It should be mauve. Once he painted everything in his room blue to the horror of Major Freeborn. He and Bobbie were great raggers. Cecil loved to come up behind Bobbie's chair and push him over with a scream of laughter. Bobbie retaliated by ramming a huge sponge down Cecil's throat, which Cecil duly bit in half. Once they nearly set the room on fire, then swamped it with water. On another occasion Cecil spilt a jug of water into Bobbie's bed.

His best friend at Harrow and later at Cambridge was Edward Le Bas, a rich boy who was a neighbour in Hampstead. 'Boy' became a serious painter who exhibited at the Royal Academy. Cecil also made friends with Jack Gold and they giggled a lot together before Jack took stock of his character and, in Cecil's words, 'became the county squire'.[9] They collaborated enjoyably on a burlesque of Elinor Glyn's *Three Weeks* and used to go to theatre matinées together. Jack also encouraged Cecil to read. One day, returning from a sketching expedition, Cecil saw an advertisement for *Punch*, marked 'copiously illustrated'. He asked Jack what 'copiously' meant and Jack reprimanded him: 'Really Cecil, you should read a bit!'[10] Cecil tried to read a Compton Mackenzie novel when Jack was in the room, but was distracted. In later life he read with difficulty if people were in the room and not at all if they were talking. Jack Gold recalled that Cecil found it hard to keep up with school work and had to cheat a lot, but he got away with it because the masters liked him. He never thought Cecil would do well in life. He was surprised when his uncle, Major Arthur Dillon, remarked of Cecil: 'He'll never beg for his bread.'[11] Another of Cecil's contemporaries was Charles James, later famous as a dress designer, but he was removed from Harrow after a while, allegedly because he did no work and because his father disliked his artistic 'sloppy' friends, though more likely because of a sexual escapade. There were also two boys that Cecil and Boy Le Bas used to tease, who were nicknamed 'Hodgepot' and 'Jeffpot'. The former, Eliot Hodgkin, became an artist and writer, while the latter, Arthur Jeffress,* an exotic figure in Venice, was the subject of a memorable portrait by Graham Sutherland.

There were also less innocent friendships at Harrow. One boy found him-

---

* Arthur Jeffress (1904–61). He was obliged to leave Venice, tried to settle in Japan but was unhappy there. He returned to England, and later committed suicide in Paris.

self in another's bed on his first night at the school, while another crossed the hill from West Acre to The Grove for the same purpose. The situation varied from house to house. In some there was 'open naughtiness', in others very little. Cecil acquired a bad reputation at the school unfairly and without justification, due to his good looks. For example, his fagmaster, Tris Grayson, recalled that he had been in love with Cecil, but this only meant that he protected him, and another boy wrote awful poems about Cecil's 'lovely eyes'. Bradby's was full of petty intrigue and plot, passed notes and misinterpreted glances, but not much more. Cecil was 'cold-blooded' by his own definition and acutely sensitive about how people thought of him. Two years after leaving the school he analysed his predicament:

> I was quiet and weak and rather effeminate at Harrow. I never played football or did anything like that. I dressed nicely and wanted to look nice because it pleased me, and wretched people thought just because I was frightfully pretty and luscious that I must be a little tart and just dressed nicely to get off with people. It just makes me sick and everything I did was taken in the wrong way.... Most people were frightfully naughty and used to go to bed with tons of people but I didn't. I only went to bed with G. [Gordon Fell-Clark] ...
>
> It's only the people who know me well now that think, or know, I'm unphysical.[12]

His contemporaries cannot be blamed entirely for jumping to these conclusions because Cecil also confessed in secret:

> I wondered why I had painted my face [at Harrow]. I always used to powder and often put red stuff on my lips. It's so idiotic to think people don't notice it.... Now I squirm to see a man powdered. I must have been rather awful at Harrow and I used to think I was so marvellous, so witty and bright and subtle and interesting.[13]

The main outcome of the tryst that Cecil shared with Gordon Fell-Clark, whom he had known since Heath Mount days, was a series of 'housemaidish' letters and soliloquies exchanged between the two. Gordon's letters expressed 'blatant adoration'. But there was some happening remembered by Cecil as 'a stupid field day years ago'.

A more important sentimental friendship kept Cecil in a 'pent-up' state for two years at Harrow: 'that really was a lump in my life. It meant much more to me than Gordon.'[14] Cecil's admirer was Tris Bennett, two years his senior and 'the youngest flannel ever'. Tris played in the Harrow Cricket xi from 1917 to 1921 and was its captain in his last year. He went on to play for Cambridge and Middlesex. He was one of those perennial public-school boys who reached his zenith at Harrow and thereafter began a decline towards a lonely old age. He also wrote Cecil letters, which were much treasured though they were dull and ordinary and full of commonplace remarks. Cecil thought Tris 'the most sophisticated, rich and outwardly grown-up man imaginable'.[15] Unwisely Cecil sang his praises to Boy Le Bas. Boy stepped in and won Tris's affection. When Cecil discovered this he fell into a state of 'abject misery' and smashed his photograph of the white-flannelled Tris with a clenched fist, shattering his illusions along with the glass.

When Cecil went up to Cambridge he ended any Harrow romances most decisively, but rather than lose his friendship with Boy, he was forced to condone the Tris situation. In the 1960s, when Tris became redundant, he asked for some 'temporary assistance' and Cecil sent £15. At that time Tris wrote to Cecil:

> You could not know then I acted with unhappy restraint. I was more than fond of you – a most lovable person, but would not jeopardize your obvious brilliant future. There were many heartaches but the consolations have been great following your triumphs. Memories are also sweet.[16]

It was during his Harrow days that Cecil became an enthusiastic amateur photographer. He had been making attempts for some years with a Box-Brownie, but with rather poor results. His first subjects were cows and horses and the children he played with. He was never skilled on the technical side and large lumps of cotton wool tended to float in front of his subjects. But help was at hand in the shape of Alice Louise Collard, always known as 'Ninnie', who came to the Beaton family as nanny in June 1913.

Ninnie had been trained as a hospital nurse, but was slightly deaf owing to a severe attack of scarlet fever and so became a children's nurse. She was only five foot tall and plump like a robin with beady eyes and steel-rimmed spectacles. She wore grey alpaca dresses with tight bodices buttoned to the neck and edged with lace. Her influence was felt throughout the house, protecting Nancy and Baba from the teasings of their elder brothers, and complaining about the food with the result that cooks came and went often. She was a passionate gardener, rallying the family to replant the herbaceous border or dig a small plot. She was also a keen photographer, as Baba Beaton, the younger sister, recalled:

> One often wonders whether her artistic efforts of 'the children in the flower border' were taken not for the artistic effect, but as a lasting memento of her prowess as a gardener. Her enthusiasm for photography was equalled and surpassed by Cecil's. Though his photographs were always, from the earliest days, taken with a view for effect, Ninnie was never happier than when she was photographing an unposed episode: the results of which were innumerable snapshots of us all back-view![17]

Ninnie developed and printed her own films. She laid her printing-frames on the nursery window-sill to develop in the sun. As Cecil progressed, she allowed him to watch her developing and, when he began to take studio portraits, she often held the lights or manipulated the looking-glass to catch certain effects (though she did not approve of these unnatural endeavours). Cecil was sometimes rather jealous of her success and irritated by the sharpness of her focus.

Harrovians passing Cecil's window in the High Street would invariably find a couple of printing-frames on his window-sill. Yet he was isolated from other camera enthusiasts in his house as he found their labours too technical and their subject-matter too boring. He preferred theatrical poses. The theatre was after all his first love and he was drawn to photography as an extension of his love of anything theatrical. That photography later proved the medium in which he made his name famous was as much by chance as by design. Throughout life he deeply resented being described solely as a photographer. Nevertheless he was certainly 'bitten by the bug' of photography and even at Harrow would use his mother and sisters as models, and have them pose on the school terrace looking as much like actresses as possible.

Thus Cecil's Harrow days passed. He painted and drew, photographed and acted. He struggled through his work and avoided sport and army drill. Harrow was unable to teach him how to spell. He wrote 'here' when he meant 'hear', he wrote 'eat' for 'ate', and at university he wrote of 'Mordlyn' College, Oxford. But he did learn how to acquire a temperature in order to get out of unpleasant activities (he drank hot water and sometimes it worked). He continued to gaze at the outer world in awe and wonder, acquiring at this time a passion for Rupert Brooke and Hazel Lavery.

As the time came for Cecil to leave the school, the question arose as to his future. He went for private coaching with a rather dubious figure called Billie Bullivant, who took perhaps too close an interest in the private lives of his pupils. At one point Cecil wanted to go to Cambridge, then he changed his mind. It was decided that he would enter his father's business as an apprentice. Finally, however, after some muddles, he was persuaded to go to Cambridge by Gordon Fell-Clark and Bullivant.

Thus his father went to see Mr B.W.F. Armitage of St John's College, Cambridge, who took a shine to Mr Beaton and Cecil believed he was admitted because his tutor liked his father's whisky. Armitage told Cecil later that he liked his father because he was so kind and such a sportsman which, he said, was a rare combination. He added that he saw hundreds of parents, many of whom were famous, but seldom one he had liked as much as Mr Beaton. This was backed up by a 'thoroughly good' character reference from Major Freeborn, which would scarcely get him into Cambridge these days:

As an artist he is quite exceptional and he is also good at English. During his time here, he won the Senior Reading Prize.

With the ordinary school subjects such as Mathematics and Latin, he is very weak indeed, in fact, bad.

He left Harrow at Easter to be coached for the 'Little Go' but I regret to say he has failed to get through. But he is a very nice boy and I feel sure you would not regret admitting him to the College for a degree. I believe he would read English and French, perhaps, if one is able to take such a degree.

During his last term, he was a House Monitor, and was able to enforce his authority. At games he is quite useless and they do not appeal to him.[18]

Though Cecil's Harrow career was hardly likely to earn him many laurels at the time, when he died *The Harrovian* recorded the death of 'one of Harrow's most distinguished and celebrated sons'.[19]

4

Cambridge and the Pursuit of Publicity

Roy Plomley to Cecil: *So you went up to Cambridge.*
What did you read there?
Cecil: *I've really forgotten. I don't think it was very*
important.

Desert Island Discs (broadcast posthumously),
26 January 1980

Cecil liked to make light of his years at Cambridge in the manner of his remark on *Desert Island Discs*. In one of his lectures in the United States he would dismiss these years as follows:

> During the three years I spent at Cambridge, I put myself down to do a vague mixture of studies, but I never went to lectures. Instead I became a whole-hearted aesthete, joined the Theatre Club, designed costumes and scenery, and performed in the stage productions. I hired an attic for fifty cents a week, in which I took romantically agonized photographs of the dons' wives. I came to the end of my Cambridge years without a degree, having failed, as usual, in all my examinations. Now, I was more than ever in a state of indecision about the future.[1]

This is a fair assessment, although Cecil attended many lectures and often worried about his lack of academic progress. He entered Cambridge at a very interesting period. Due to the war there was a wider range of ages than usual. People as diverse as Rab Butler, Norman Hartnell and Michael Ramsey (later Archbishop of Canterbury) were to be found wandering the university's narrow streets. George ('Dadie') Rylands, the distinguished Fellow of King's, recalled that Cambridge went through a particularly fruitful period between 1921 and 1928, while Oxford flourished a little later. 'Oxford would have been very bad for Cecil,' he said. 'He would have gone straight down the Evelyn Waugh drain. They drank champagne at eleven in the morning, while we drank beer at night – or occasionally Burgundy.

We lived in a rather poverty-stricken, priggish way.'[2] There was nothing as exciting as the incident in Oxford when hearties burst into an aesthete's room and the aesthete severed an invader's thumb with a sword.

Oxford's acting life was confined to outdoor productions by the Oxford University Dramatic Society (OUDS), while Cambridge had the Amateur Dramatic Company (ADC, in those days exclusive to men) and the Marlowe Society (which by tradition never named its actors), where ambitious plays were attempted by brilliant interpreters such as Frank Birch, a Don at King's, and Dennis Arundell, a Fellow of St John's. For lighter entertainment Cambridge had the Footlights. By nature an aesthete, Cecil might have found life more comfortable if he had followed Cyril Connolly to Eton instead of going to boorish Harrow. Oxford too would have held an allure for him. Yet by going to Harrow and Cambridge there was less competition and he had more scope to emerge as a prominent personality in his own right.

Cecil went up to Cambridge on 4 October 1922, travelling with two huge trunks and the first of the thirty-eight diaries that he would fill during his university days. He prayed that Cambridge would be a success and, as the train bore him away, he wrote: 'I did want courage.'[3]

He did not live in St John's College, because it was already full, but lodged at 47 Bridge Street, just next door, above the fruiterer and florist, Biggs and Sons. The rooms proved charming, with sloping floors and ceilings, white walls and black beams, and plenty of possibility for adaptation to Cecil's particular taste. He was soon hanging decorative Pamela Bianco illustrations in black frames and generally creating a 'cottagey' effect. When he looked out of his window over the little roofs around him, he imagined it all rather like a pretty back street in Venice.

Presently Cecil went to meet his tutor 'Bif' Armitage, whom he found 'delightfully vague'. Armitage at first suggested that Cecil should attempt the English Tripos, but after the surprise of Cecil passing the maths exam he had failed in the summer, Armitage changed his mind and put him down for art, history and architecture. Cecil would try for an 'ordinary' – a 'special' – degree. He was given a programme of lectures on Shakespeare and the seventeenth-century dramatists and poets. The initial sympathy that Armitage felt for his father extended to Cecil himself, to the extent that Cecil wondered if Armitage harboured impure thoughts on his account. Once he even suggested that they might visit Oxford together and stay a night in Bedford. Cecil seemed only to visit his tutor when he wanted to be signed off Hall or given leave to attend a party. After keeping him waiting for at least three quarters of an hour, Armitage always gave his permission. Over the years Armitage became scruffier and more dishevelled, sporting a beard and wearing extremely baggy trousers. When, on 28 February 1924, he made a precipitate departure from Cambridge in his Hispano-Suiza, leaving debts and rumours of homosexuality behind him, Cecil was sorry to see him go: 'What a sensation!! My tutor and the only decent cultured man in Johns.'⁴

The first excitement of Cecil's term was a visit to Oxford on 22 October in the car of a Harrow friend, Robert Blundell. Cecil went there to see Kyrle Leng, whom he had met at Harlech in the summer holidays with Jack Gold and Jack's cousin, Peggy Broadbent.* Cecil and Kyrle had climbed mountains and taken motorbicycle rides. There had been a pageant at which Cecil had worn mock armour. At other times he wore a red tie given to him by Kyrle. They had slept under the stars and talked late into the cold nights. Cecil had confided that he contemplated calling himself Cecil Hardy-Beaton. Kyrle said it sounded like a plant. While Kyrle slept deeply, Cecil gazed lovingly at him, longing, but not daring, to touch his hand.

Cecil had high hopes of this friendship, but it was doomed from the start because the anaemic Kyrle was destined for Oxford where he shared rooms with Robert Gathorne-Hardy, who became his lifelong friend. Even his visit to Oxford began badly. Cecil felt as nervous as when waiting in the wings of a theatre, uncertain of his words. Hardly was he alone with Kyrle and beginning to relax than Bob Gathorne-Hardy joined them and the three ended up lunching in his High Street rooms to Cecil's deep confusion. In due course Kyrle and Cecil were again alone and settling down to listen to a Schumann Quartet when the door flew open and nine energetic Oxford undergraduates burst in – Eddy Sackville-West, Billy Smith (of the W. H. Smith family), Lord David Cecil ('who talked even quicker than Bob. He seized a hairbrush and puffed his hair out like the Barber in Happy Families. He was about the most affected youth I've seen but quite amusing'),⁵ Teddy Hogg, Eardley Knollys ('quite handsome'),⁶ Lord Morven Cavendish-Bentinck, Lord Sudley and two young peers. Everyone talked at once, showing off madly and staring at Cecil, but they amused him. At length Kyrle announced that he was taking Cecil out for a walk:

> There was a great silence as we left, but soon more gabbling and Kyrle said none of them minded what he said or did to them: Kyrle and I walked arm in arm to see Mordlyn [sic] which was very beautiful, but I didn't pay much attention to the surroundings because I was so busy trying to get the old way of being with Kyrle.... Oh! it was all so marvellous! Kyrle looked very wonderful. His face was very thin – but he has been ill poor dear. His eyes are gorgeous and I love the shape of his head....⁷

Occasionally Kyrle came to Cambridge to visit Cecil. On one such occasion they sat alone on cushions in Cecil's rooms in the soft candlelight: 'both our

---

*Peggy Broadbent (d. 1978), married Sir Austin Hudson, Bt, in 1930. In 1978 Walter Scott-Elliot, the former Labour MP, was murdered by his butler. One of the five corpses in the case was found in a shallow grave on her Dumfriesshire estate.

eyes were sparkling ... I don't think I shall ever be happier in my life. I was just nicely sad too.'[8] Likewise a letter from Kyrle that reached Cecil in his holidays could send him into a state of ecstasy: 'My tummy quivered and I was so weak and cold streams ran up and down my neck.'[9]

It was Cecil's prime ambition at Cambridge to join the ADC and Marlowe Society and work really hard on a play, acting, designing and even conducting rehearsals. In this respect Blundell was his benefactor by introducing him to the acting crowd. The night of the Oxford visit he found he had been elected to the ADC. 'Cambridge wouldn't be so bad after all,' he thought, 'with some nice people, the ADC and the Marlowe.'[10] He had been at the university less than three weeks.

Boy Le Bas was his closest friend at this time. Another Cambridge friend, John Hill, recalled that they were 'very similar in appearance, very elegant and with very high standards of behaviour and taste'.[11] They spent part of most days together. Presently they called on Dennis Arundell to see if they could join the Marlowe Society:

> Mr A. was quite good-looking – a trifle affected with the baggiest trousers I've ever seen. He took our names and asked us what parts we'd acted in and I screamed with laughter when Boy said he'd played Celia! Anyone less suited to the part is impossible to imagine!![12]

Cecil was soon reading the part of Princess Angelica for the ADC's forthcoming production of *The Rose and the Ring*, though he did not think it fitted his personality: 'A stupid little Victorian girl doing silly things and being so innocent with lovers galore and always simpering – a Fay Compton part!'[13] However he dared not risk turning it down for fear of upsetting his new friends. On 6 November he was introduced to his fellow actors by Dennis Robertson,* the producer. One of them was 'that absurd-looking youth with the fringe',[14] he had spotted in a lecture. Cecil continued: 'He really is rather marvellous. I should adore to model him. He's so huge and ugly and strong with the most fruity voice.'[15]

The youth turned out to be the historian Steven Runciman of Trinity, on whom in due course Cecil did indeed model his appearance, by wearing Fair Isle sweaters. Runciman had magnificent but sparsely furnished rooms on the first floor of Nevile Court and when visitors arrived they would be confronted with one little round table on which rested one little book. Even the incurious could not fail to be impressed by the royal inscription which read 'To dear Victoria from her aunt Adelaide'.[16] Runciman first noticed Cecil when he threw a cigarette from his Bridge Street window. It landed on a lady's straw hat and an altercation ensued. Cecil also met the President

---

*Later Sir Dennis Robertson (1890–1963), Fellow of Trinity College, Cambridge, one-time President of the Cambridge ADC, described as 'the only really good performer in *The Son of Heaven*'.

of the ADC, 'Dadie' Rylands: 'He's quite nice-looking . . . and spoke exactly like Bobbie Andrews [the actor boyfriend of Ivor Novello]. I think it's rather a pose here to talk very quietly and softly and slowly.'[17] All the actors sat round a huge fire discussing the play. Cecil did not have the courage to say it was 'piffle'. They then read it through, while Cecil admired the balding Robertson's many books and Botticelli prints. The next day they held a rehearsal in the theatre during which 'lots of rather affected and dull people rushed about'.[18]

Cecil was very pleased with himself:

> Billie [Bullivant, Cecil's former tutor] says I'm very perfect just now and Kyrle likes me. I want to be like this for a long time – not to be absurd – but just before I came here I was getting rather nice I think. I do hope Cambridge won't spoil me.[19]

He then proceeded to spend far too much money decorating his rooms in a style unlike that of any other undergraduate. He blamed Boy Le Bas for encouraging his extravagance and for not making him adapt to his more hearty friends. Preoccupied with rehearsals, Cecil often neglected his lectures but congratulated himself in one on Caesar when he was 'very clever in talking at great length about things I had not read'.[20]

Both he and Boy Le Bas (also elected to the ADC) became more closely involved in theatre work. Cecil was depressed by the lack of originality in the sets designed by Roger Hinks and Charles Lambe. He began to make his influence felt, which meant insisting on everything being done his way. He wanted very elaborate and vivid dresses as a contrast to Hinks's plain scenery. He was disappointed to learn that some of the costumes would come from Nathan's: 'One knows what that will mean! Olive green instead of emerald, dingy red velvet instead of scarlet, plum colour instead of magenta. . . .'[21]

Presently Dennis Arundell played the incidental music he had written for the play. Cecil gained confidence and got into trouble for improvising too much: he had very specific ideas about his appearance and gave precise instructions to the make-up man:

> The man did what I told him very well and I finished it off – a dead-white face – huge blue and black eyes – cerise lips – and when I'd got the wig in the correct shape it all looked wonderful. Everyone got a terrific shock when they first saw me, especially the Producer. He was speechless – and then I said I thought it was remarkably effective. I looked like a Rossetti picture. I most certainly did look, as [Graham] Ogden said, terrific.[22]

Hinks disapproved of the changes to the wig and Arundell eyed him with disgust. Cecil could not wait for the first night.

For the first time ever he felt ill at ease before a performance, but it went better than expected. The next day he was surprised to see a long column in *The Times*, in which he was criticized for not having enough 'go'.

> Princess Angelica and Betsinda her maid need 'go' to give them their chance, and though Mr Beaton and Mr Herbage play them with an oddity which is good to laugh at, when first one encounters it, the touch of the grotesque loses its effect after a scene or two.[23]

Saturday's matinée had the writers Maurice Baring and St John Ervine in the audience. The latter singled Cecil out as one of those who was particularly good. So imbued by the general atmosphere was he that on the last night Cecil let his enjoyment get the better of him, broke six eggs, kicked over the footlights and became convulsed with laughter. Crowds in the wings hooted at him and in the interval he was 'severely scolded and quite right too for the breakfast scene was spoiled'.[24] Cecil's participation in *The Rose and the Ring* had a number of important consequences. He was invited to read the part of Lady Would-be for the Marlowe Society's *Volpone*. He was summoned by Frank Birch in order that he should submit some scenery designs for the play. He earned the admiration of Stewart Perowne, of Pembroke College, who showed him a good criticism in *Isis*. Perowne, the orientalist and historian, admired Cecil's determination and flair from the start, particularly since 'he had none of the advantages of his contemporaries. We knew nothing about him except that he had been at Harrow.'[25]

Looking back, Dennis Arundell commented: 'He was amateur, but in a thoroughly professional way.... I always thought he was more interested in getting his sisters into the *Tatler* than in the University.'[26] 'Dadie' Rylands recalled: 'We welcomed him into our set. He liked being with people who were fairly intellectual.'[27] Steven Runciman agreed to lunch with Cecil in his rooms.

Thus Cecil's first term at Cambridge ended on a high note.

Cecil sent his *Volpone* designs to Frank Birch during the Christmas holidays. He forgot the commission until the last moment when, he confessed: 'I scribbled off a lot of bad things.'[28] One of his designs derived from 'two lovely red candlesticks against long vivid curtains'[29] seen by Cecil at Barton, the Oxfordshire home of Peggy Broadbent's mother, Mrs Arthur Dillon. Returning to Cambridge in January 1923, Cecil found he would be working on the *Volpone* sets under young Vulliamy, the principal scene director. The work was to be based on designs executed by Alec Penrose* before he went down. Cecil soon found Vulliamy's ideas at some variance from his own: he was full of new ideas but Vulliamy always said: 'It's all very difficult.' It was not long before Cecil resolved: 'I'd like to do it all myself or not at all.'[30] Vulliamy liked dirty salmon-pink silver polish colours, while Cecil favoured

---

* Alec Penrose (1896–1950), brother of Sir Roland Penrose.

a vivid orange. Cecil wanted scarlet curtains with gold lions. Vulliamy wanted them Cambridge blue with brown ones. Cecil proved strong and Vulliamy weak and retiring. Feeling 'a horrible traitor',[31] Cecil complained to Dennis Arundell and Frank Birch. He argued with Vulliamy, who adhered resolutely to Alec Penrose's designs, saying: 'We are only slaves.'[32] Cecil took no notice. Finally a dreadful argument ensued: 'I lost my temper and Vulliamy lost his. I was backed up by everyone and then Vulliamy climbed a ladder and forbade anyone to touch the canvas.'[33]

But Vulliamy had lost. He was gated, and no sooner had he left the theatre than Cecil repainted everything he had done: 'The curtains really began now to look exceedingly nice.'[34] It was Friday and Cecil only had until Tuesday to complete the dresses, wigs, properties and scenery, not to mention learning his part in the play. But he never shirked hard work, when it interested him. After a nightmarish week he rejoiced that the scenery was of a kind that had never before been seen at Cambridge. Frank Birch congratulated him on his sense of colour and Stewart Perowne on his sense of proportion. He said: 'The highest praise I can give you is that you are a worthy successor to Alec Penrose.'[35] Penrose himself added his congratulations. On the first night the *Daily Mail* critic told him he thought the scenery better than that in the productions at the Everyman. By and large the notices were good, though Cecil was put out by a malicious review in *Granta* and by W.A. Darlington of the *Daily Telegraph*, who accused him of acting as though he were impersonating Athene Seyler. Francis Birrell, Alec Penrose's Bloomsbury friend, wrote that he did not like the curtains but that Cecil was young and would improve. The play was also seen by Cecil's parents, Kyrle Leng (who, to Cecil's sorrow, was soon to go to Biarritz for a long recuperation), 'Topsy' Lucas (the novelist), Clive Bell, Roger Fry, Lydia Lopokova and Sebastian Sprott. Cecil was also congratulated by Armitage, who told him he had thoroughly fulfilled his reputation as an artist. On the other hand his lavish sets and designs succeeded in temporarily bankrupting the ADC – to him but a minor consideration.

From time to time Cecil received a visit from his sinister former tutor Billie Bullivant, who would stay at the University Arms and invite him to dine in order to assess his progress and give him some sharp advice. For example, the previous November Bullivant had written warning him not to make contrived remarks:

> Remember at Cambridge to be clever and witty is Victorian and to be aesthetic is to be even more archaic – for Oscar Wilde plagiarized the late Georgians. But what is always unique is to find anyone who can survive a Public School and one year at Cambridge and still be natural. . . . There is little fear that your affections will get the better of your judgement but there is always the fear that your vanity may.[36]

Just before *Volpone* a meeting with Bullivant took place. Cecil summed up the advice he was offered. He was becoming unpopular because he had sprung up all of a sudden and was now going round 'saying that people, whose opinion has generally been regarded as right before, are absurd fools and not the least artistic'.[37] He was not backed by the Bishop–Schofield* crowd, who did not like people to have success without their help. Having behaved at rehearsals in a generally conceited manner, Cecil would then disappear to the sanctity of his Bridge Street room. Billie said people were wondering if this behaviour was natural or a pose. Cecil admitted to himself that it was 'a good deal affected'.[38] Billie warned him that he must try his hardest to make a success of his designs. He must succeed this year or never. On a lower note, Billie suddenly said, 'You must find some good cold cream and put it on your hands, which are almost your best feature.'[39] He added that Steven Runciman liked him very much and wanted him 'to get on and not be squashed by the Schofield–Bishop crowd',[40] while Sheppard† was professionally jealous. Later, when *Volpone* was a success, Billie congratulated Cecil. He said that although the ADC crowd disliked him, they could not now do without him.

Cecil's theatrical success helped his social progress. Frank Birch introduced him to his wife Vera,‡ whom Cecil (a great admirer of the play *Dear Brutus*) found 'young and Barrie-ish'.[41]

> She is exquisitely thin with a long face and a lovely shaped head, and nice bobbed hair and the most marvellous eyebrows that ever were – very black and even and perfectly straight.[42]

Vera Birch and he were destined to share many adventures, not least dining with a rich Dutchman called Englebrecht, who served a pudding of his own invention flavoured with Chanel No. 5. Vera Birch wrote: 'I always liked Cecil in the far-off days when I knew him. We laughed a lot together.... He might have become a famous dress designer, like Molyneux or Norman Hartnell, but whatever it was his road upwards would have been very slightly overdone.'[43]

Cecil took tea with Steven Runciman. They smoked Russian cigarettes and ate 'roseleaf' jam, while Benedict, the parakeet, continually interrupted their conversation. Here he met 'Topsy' Lucas, whose influence he later described as 'the beginning of the opening of a door onto the intellectual world'.[44] When Cecil lingered on after the party, Steven Runciman said: 'What extraordinary people I have round me – crowds of parasites and

---

* Adrian Bishop and A.F. Schofield (1884–1969, a keen member of the ADC and the Marlowe who had acted in *Faustus*). Schofield became librarian to the University of Cambridge.

† Sir John Sheppard (1881–1968), who had produced all the Greek plays for over twenty years.

‡ Hon. Vera Birch (1899–1983), sister of 6th Viscount Gage.

dowdies.'[45] Cecil was an eager listener when 'Topsy' told his fortune or Runciman teased him by predicting he had only two years to live:

> That really did make me quiver. I was going to die full of promise. I was in a panic. Oh I should loathe to die insignificantly and be forgotten. Oh I was in a panic. I would have to be so energetic![46]

During the summer term of 1923 Cecil acquired a Gyp,* because his landlord had complained about the amount of extra work Cecil caused by his tea-parties. So on 3 May Bill Butler arrived, sent by Armitage: 'He looks very nice and clean,' wrote Cecil, 'and is very willing. I am pleased with him and he is going to be my Gyp for 3 pounds a term. He took some clothes to press and will wait on Wednesday.'[47] Butler was to stay with St John's College for forty-five years. At the age of eighty-six he remembered the young man:

> He was a very nice gentleman, a refined man. He didn't wear a hat in those days. He was very fond of beautiful flowers. He didn't go to Hall often or mix much with other undergraduates. He just had one or two special friends who came for lunch or dinner. I used to clean his shoes, see what clothes he needed. He came to depend on me. He only played tennis under pressure from friends such as Mr Le Bas.[48]

Butler did not recall ever seeing any academic work being done in Cecil's rooms, but he was 'always drawing women's dresses and hats'.[49] The room was full of sketchbooks. He remembered a smart man who came to see Cecil from time to time. Butler wondered who he was. Later he discovered: 'It was his tailor from London.'[50]

The most pressing problem of the summer term was to pass an exam. On 16 May Cecil went to see his supervisor, Mr Bennett, a man who lived in a shabby house and whose sham leg hung on the wall. The meeting gave him a shock: 'I never realized until just now what an enormous amount of work I have to get through between now and my exam which is in a fortnight's time.'[51] Back in his room, he attempted an essay on the humour of Chaucer and Shakespeare, but found it took ages as he was out of practice. Then he began to read about Chaucer's life, but as so often when faced with tedious academic work, he soon felt sleepy and went to bed. On the other hand he never fell asleep when conjuring up stage sets, perusing the *Tatler* or writing his giant diary, never fewer than two pages a day and sometimes considerably more.

He was easily diverted from his revision. He accepted an invitation to design the cover of *Granta*, but, lest Steven Runciman should disapprove of his doing it, he submitted the design unsigned. As a guide he was shown the cover of the Christmas *Granta* 'done by that horrid N.B. Hartnell [later

* Gyp – the Cambridge name for a gentleman's gentleman, the precursor of the Cambridge bedder.

Sir Norman Hartnell, dress designer to the Queen]. It's the worst thing I've ever seen.'[52]

At the beginning of June, he sat his exams, writing 'pages and pages of rot'[53] until he felt exhausted. He obtained a third and went down for the holiday more or less satisfied with his results: 'I had passed my exam and I had been busy doing other things, designing dresses, acting and painting and then those dances at the beginning of May.'[54] Only one thing bothered him: 'I shall be in my second year next term. I shall be livid if there are some successful freshers to act or paint or talk.'[55]

Cecil came down for the summer holidays to the Beaton family home. They had recently moved from Hampstead to a house at 3 Hyde Park Street, just off the Bayswater Road. Philip Guedalla, the historian, lived next door and Cecil soon discovered that a number of fashionable figures lived nearby, including the Spender-Clays and the Prince of Wales's mistress, Freda Dudley Ward. The move from Hampstead delighted the entire family except Mr Beaton, who preferred a simple life. Cecil despised his father's reluctance to ask a 'title' to dinner, in favour of being kind to 'some penniless relation, or some old fool who wants a square meal'.[56] Mr Beaton maintained the old-fashioned standards of Victorian morality. He did not permit his wife or daughters (let alone Cecil) to wear make-up. A woman in make-up was to him 'that woman with the painted face',[57] and seeing an old lady in a wig he would ask: 'What's that old geyser got on her head?'[58]

Cecil loved Hyde Park Street and on Sundays he greatly enjoyed church parade in the park, where he could spot well-known faces. He was an expert at recognizing people, and at the 1922 Bicester Hunt Ball made the astonishing, but no doubt accurate, claim: 'I knew most of the 500 people by sight. Most figure in the *Tatler*.'[59] Thus it was no problem for him to identify Allanah Harper, leading a motley collection of boys and girls through the park, one of whom was Lord Birkenhead's eccentric daughter, Lady Eleanor Smith.

He was not particularly popular at home, and his mother often accused him of being conceited and artificial. She was cross that he got up late and seldom went out until after dark. But when a party loomed he came into his own and manipulated the event from behind the scenes.

In June 1923 the Beatons gave a dance at Hyde Park Street. A form arrived from the *Daily Telegraph* asking for details. Mrs Beaton put this aside, but Cecil rescued it and retired to his room with a secret plan.

His pursuit of publicity derived from an idea planted in his head by Aunt Jessie. In April 1923 he was staying with his aunt and some of her friends at Turner's Hill. 'Modom', as he called her, told him that when she was in the diplomatic world notices of her parties appeared on the court page of *The Times*. Sometimes the social editor rang up asking for more details. Every time a good list of names was published Uncle Pedro had to send *The Times* man a box of cigars or a pound note. Thus the Suarezes remained in the social swim.

Cecil therefore filled in the form and sent it to the *Daily Telegraph*. 'Mummie would be very annoyed,' he wrote. 'I was later naughtier still cos I paid a guinea to have an announcement of the dance put in *The Times*.'[60] Two days later he went downstairs early:

> I peeped at *The Times*. Yes, it was in! I was terribly pleased, I rushed upstairs and said, 'I see Mama, from *The Times* that you are to be a dance hostess.' Mama wouldn't believe it until *The Times* was brought and then Mummie went all pink and burst into a pouting lash and was very sweet. Reggie was pleased and Mummie kept saying, 'Well I never' and 'What cheek' and 'How can they have got hold of it'. I tried to look innocent and said, 'Mrs Le Bas must have done it.' When Mummie got over the shock I think she was very pleased. (It looked tremendously grand – with a line to oneself and most people having dances all on the same day! We were lucky not to have dances on our day!) Mummie said what an eye-opener all the Hampstead people would get and also Aunt Lilias.* I think it was a guinea well spent indeed![61]

Later in the day a letter arrived from the social editor of *The Times* asking Mrs Beaton for more details: 'What amazing luck being asked!' noted Cecil. 'I posted the thing off with details of everything. I was so excited.'[62] Then on the day of the dance, 19 June, Mrs Beaton went to rest while Cecil manned the telephone. *The Times* man rang for yet more details. Not every son would be able to describe his mother's dress with accuracy, but this was no problem for Cecil.

There was nothing exceptional about the dance itself. Cecil forced his Aunt Cada to wear her train and he revelled in his mother's beauty in a pale green dress, embroidered with crystals and a diamond head-dress of leaves: 'Mummie looked much more beautiful than a hundred Lady Lattas.'†[63] He was also amused by his father's distaste for 'Bubbles' Beauchamp,‡ an exquisite flapper with 'a pale green face, purple lips, brilliant hair scraped back, red eyes and eyebrows'.[64] Seeing her Mr Beaton exclaimed: 'Someone must have left the cage door open.'[65] That night Cecil noted: 'Mummie never thought she'd give a dance like this and right at the height of the season. It was splendid. I couldn't sleep for thinking about it all and longing to see the papers.'[66] The next day he rushed to his mother's room:

* Wife of Cecil's Uncle Reggie.

† Ada May Short, wife of the shipowner Sir John Latta, Bt (1867–1946).

‡ Irene (1899–1951), daughter of Sir Frank Beauchamp, Bt. Married Ashley Hall of Bristol in 1923.

How different Mummie looked now from last night, hair screwed back and face all creamed: we talked about the dance. All day we talked about the dance. An unexhaustable [*sic*] subject. I got dressed quickly and hurried to Jackson's. I bought all the likely papers. I peeped at *The Times*! Yes it was in! I rushed back here so excited. I didn't know what to do. I was pleased. It meant such a lot! There were descriptions in *The Times*, *Telegraph* and *Graphic* – 'Last night's dance' with a description of Mummie's dress – the decorations and a list of famous guests. Everyone will see it and become so livid and jealous and we'll be marvellously sought after.[67]

Some days later Cecil sent the social editor of *The Times* a box of cigars.

The appearance of Mrs Beaton's name in the social columns had the effect that the photographers, Swaines, sent a card offering her a complimentary sitting. Cecil took her along, they were both photographed, but Cecil was disappointed with the results. He preferred his own, especially some of his mother at Ranelagh which he touched up and sent secretly to the *Tatler*, hoping they might be published.

At the end of July he wandered along to the studio of Hugh Cecil, the society photographer, to inspect the portraits: 'They are absolutely marvellous! Lewis is awful compared to him. The soft sharpness of them is gorgeous.'[68] Cecil conceived a new plot – to get his mother photographed at this studio. That very day he rang up and asked if they had any portraits of Lady Alexander, Mrs Post Wheeler and Mrs E.W.H. Beaton for publication. The receptionist asked him: '*Vogue*, did you say?' and Cecil replied, 'Yes.' 'I'll look it up and ring you up in a few minutes.'[69]

Cecil was amused at the idea of her ringing *Vogue*: '*Vogue* would be astonished. Anyhow I also sent the names and addresses of these three people to them so that if they like to write to the three people they can and I shall be delighted: I went out to post this anonymous missile and then I came back here to play with the kitten.'[70]

The very next day Mrs Beaton called Cecil to her: 'Come here. How have you managed this?'[71] she asked, smiling. Cecil's heart leapt as he saw a letter from Hugh Cecil, enclosing a portfolio, in which he said he was anxious to take her portrait because the editor of the *Tatler* had written for a photograph! Cecil was so excited that he could not sleep: 'I nearly leapt out of bed.'[72] The next day he gave his father his own photograph of Nancy dressed to look like Mrs Vernon Castle. Mr Beaton framed it and put it on his desk. Mr Beaton also had to make the decision as to whether or not his wife should go to Hugh Cecil's studio, the results appearing perhaps in the *Tatler*. Surprisingly he was pleased and thought it might be good for business. He pointed out that thousands of people saw his cricket scores in the papers. Therefore Mrs Beaton made an appointment and allowed Cecil to experiment with her hair to find an appropriate new style for the picture. The day of the session was set for 2 August. Cecil himself dressed carefully because he too had hopes of being photographed. Mrs Beaton had her hair waved while Madame Rudolph Valentino [Natcha Rambova] was photographed in a black taffeta crinoline. Cecil was thrilled to be allowed to see the studio with its windows curtained over with magenta silk. There was an altar and several large screens on wheels and only one light, which surprised him. Layers and layers of muslin were used to diffuse the light. Hugh Cecil himself was a tiny little man, chinless with prominent teeth, wearing spectacles, dancing pumps and a knitted bow tie. He jumped about the room displeased with everything. He threw shawls over Mrs Beaton's shoulders and then a cloth of silver. Then he took only four poses. Cecil came away rather dissatisfied, but having learned a lot from his first-hand glimpse of the society photographer at work.

Cecil's summer included a family holiday in Devon, which put him into a long-lasting sulk. At Instow he wrote:

> I've never never never been so near screaming with rage in all my life. I can hardly write of the filthy meal, the filthy place, everything filthy, filthy. . . . My soul revolts against anything like this.[73]

He returned to London in August and drew caricatures of Margaret Bannerman, Sybil Thorndike, Constance Collier and Leon Quartermaine. Egged on by his father (who wanted him to earn some money) he sent these to various papers. Two were accepted by the *Sketch* and, although they were never published, Cecil was greatly encouraged.

Just before Cecil returned to Cambridge, Billie Bullivant rang to invite him to lunch at the Carlton to meet Noël Coward.

> I said yes but couldn't speak when I got into the dining-room. Mummie seems to hate Billie and I've heard so much about Noël Coward – rather nasty things about his mother being a charwoman and he being very naughty. But he's clever and well known since *London Calling*.[74]

Cecil went along, sick with nerves, and found Billie alone. He wanted to see Cecil to discuss his future, he said, so he had put Noël off. It is more than likely that Noël Coward had never been invited. Billie asked if Cecil would go into his father's business. He thought not. He would like to design scenery. Billie said Noël was the 'coming youth' and Cecil should do his ballets and lighting. Ivor Novello and Bobbie Andrews would help. If he failed he would have to go into business. Cecil noted: 'I just half wondered later if I wanted to get into the Ivor, Noël naughty set. They're rather cheap and horrid and yet sometimes very nice. If I got my start through them I should soon give them up and get on myself.'[75] He continued:

Billie understands me so well and I do so adore being talked about – to myself – and Billie knows and says that I'm the most self-centred person in the world! It's so terribly true! I just don't care what other people think. I know I'm right. I don't care if anyone says my scenery is putrid. It's always been my pose to say, 'It's perfectly wonderful scenery and you're mad if you can't understand it.'[76]

Billie believed that plays in the Russian manner would be the next vogue. This was the theatrical decade of Basil Dean – why not Cecil Beaton's decade next? Billie thought Cecil could squeeze £500 a year from his father and earn the same again himself. He asked if Cecil thought he would ever marry. Cecil said he would only marry someone very exotic. Billie said the bride must be rich:

Billie asked me what my attitude was towards women. (What I am now writing is tremendously private and I should be horrified and I'd quiver inside ever afterwards if some friend or relation read it!) My attitude to women is this – I adore to dance with them and take them to theatres and private views and talk about dresses and plays and women, but I'm really much more fond of men. My friendships with men are much more wonderful than with women. I've never been in love with women and I don't think I ever shall in the way that I have been in love with men. I'm really a terrible, terrible homosexualist and try so hard not to be. I try so terribly hard to be good and not cheap and horrid ... it's so much nicer just to be affectionate and ordinary and sleep in the same bed but that's all. Everything else is repulsive to me and yet it's awfully difficult![77]

The same day Cecil returned to Cambridge, restless and depressed. He missed Kyrle Leng and he envied Boy Le Bas his sumptuous new rooms. A few days later he found himself discussing domesticity, marriage and children with Boy. Cecil was against all three. They fell to discussing Tris Bennett, who had been Boy's friend and companion since their last week at Harrow. Boy wanted to drop him but it was not easy. 'It's terribly difficult,' said Boy, 'because you don't know how naughty I've been with Tris.'[78]

I only slowly realized. It's just been like marriage. All the time at Miss Harris's [Boy's landlady], nagging away and hating one another all day and then just being horrid, revolting. Ugh, I was genuinely disgusted.[79]

Boy had hated it, but could not stop himself. Cecil thanked his stars that his own friendship with Tris had not ended that way.

From a shy and innocent standpoint Cecil had revealed the second of his two problems. The first was that he had been born into an inartistic, unpretentious middle-class family and he sensed that he did not belong there. By the harnessing of publicity to his cause he was beginning to change that. As Diana Vreeland, the dramatic editor of *Vogue*, put it years later: 'Now Cecil may have been born from the middle classes but he didn't have a middle-class bone in his body.'[80] His second problem was the insecurity he felt about his homosexuality. As late as December 1966 he returned to the subject, greeting the acceptance of the Wolfenden Report as 'one of the most important milestones in English Law'. Cecil wrote in his 1966 diary:

Of recent years the tolerance towards the subject has made a nonsense of many of the prejudices from which I myself suffered acutely as a young man. Even now I can only vaguely realize that it was only comparatively late in life that I would go into a room full of people without a feeling of guilt. To go into a room full of men, or to a lavatory in the Savoy, needed quite an effort. With success in my work this situation became easier. But when one realizes what damage, what tragedy has been brought on by this lack of sympathy to a very delicate and difficult subject, this should be a great time of celebration.... For myself I am grateful. Selfishly I wish that this marvellous step forward could have been taken at an earlier age. It is not that I would have wished to avail myself of further licence, but to feel that one was not a felon and an outcast could have helped enormously during the difficult young years.[81]

Cecil did no work in the winter term of 1923 because no exams threatened. Some of the lectures he found so dull that he thought he could do better by reading *Apollo*. When he was ordered to attend supervision one day and preferred to play tennis, he wrote a note to say he had damaged his ankle. He bandaged the ankle and hobbled off on a stick to deliver the note. He was forgiven.

At this time he and Boy acquired a studio with electric light in Ram Yard for six shillings a week. The walls were whitewashed, the ceiling a mass of huge beams, and there was a finely shaped fireplace. The only access was via a ladder. Cecil was soon using it for paintings and photographs. His first sitter was Steven Runciman: 'He sat still and firm and looked quite gorgeous. I was very professional and smooth and took such a lot of photos in a very little time.'[82] Later Cecil painted him, though Steven made his work difficult by pursing up his mouth and staring as though mad. Cecil was now perfectly accepted in the Rylands–Runciman set, christened by Frank Birch the 'Tea Party Cats'.[83]

On 21 October 1923 Cecil was elected to the Committee of the ADC and put in charge of all dresses and scenery. Their next production was the musical comedy, *The Gyp's Princess*, and he laughed enormously when Dennis Arundell played him the song he had composed for him: 'Just a little piece of seaweed'. Cecil had considerable problems getting his clothes fitted in time and the expense was exorbitant: 'The ADC will be ruined!! This production is costing the most enormous amount. It does make me feel awkward. Money always makes me have the sinking feeling. It goes so quickly!'[84] Nor was it easy to find all that was needed – swords, guns, tables, chairs, cloaks, etc. *The Gyp's Princess* received good notices and Cecil was thrilled to find his picture in a number of papers. Lytton Strachey and Maynard Keynes saw him act: 'They hardly smiled altho' they loved the show.'[85] The cast learned later that the older members of the ADC were annoyed that the chorus girls winked and that the play had attracted a number of dirty old men, who came up from London.

During this production Cecil acquired an admirer. Following the unfair rumours that used to spread about him at Harrow, he had sworn a private oath that he would not get involved with anyone at Cambridge or allow his name to be tarnished by smutty gossip. Throughout his Cambridge years he kept his oath, but partly in the spirit in which the leading lady must have her admirers, Cecil, in the coveted role of Princess Tecla, did not discourage 'the tall Thomas', who 'hugged and kissed'[86] him behind the scenes during the dress rehearsal. Ben Thomas,* two years Cecil's senior, was studying law at Trinity. Steven Runciman remembered him as 'a very tall bespectacled rowing man who looked a pillar of respectability but proved to have acting and other more exotic tastes (including a taste for Cecil)'.[87] The liaison soon became a matter of as much interest to the members of the ADC as to Cecil, who wrote: 'It's such fun being mauled slightly by some quite strange person with whom one has nothing in common.' But when Cecil missed one of his cues, Frank Birch was livid. Cecil confessed: 'I was carrying on a flirtation in the wings.'[88]

Cecil enjoyed the aloof role he played at Cambridge. When a friend called Hazlitt said he did not dare invite him to his rooms for fear that he would hate them, Cecil was very amused. He thought that a number of people were in love with him, but he rebuffed them all so successfully that they never dared come near him again. The six-foot-six Thomas was not so easily deterred.

When the show was over, Cecil was deluged with gifts of chocolates, fruit and flowers from his admirers. Ben Thomas sent 'an avalanche of white chrysanthemums'. There was a drunken celebration during which Cecil remained 'cool and calculating'. On his way home a policeman saw him staggering under the weight of his trophies and spluttered, 'There's a bloody flower show.'[89]

One evening before the end of term Cecil invited Ben Thomas to a candlelit dinner in his rooms. As the evening progressed Thomas told him he had never been in love before. Ever conscious of his reputation, Cecil was pleased they were alone. Then for an hour they kissed: 'the most sensual thing

* Benjamin Crewdson Thomas CBE (1902–75), Barrister Inner Temple 1926, Controller Central Office of Information 1952–68.

imaginable.'⁹⁰ When at length Thomas departed into the night, Cecil wrote: 'I came to bed very happy and tired and unphysical. What a giddy rush these last weeks have been.'⁹¹ Ben Thomas continued to press his suit the following term but Cecil came to consider him a nuisance and their friendship cooled.

At the beginning of the spring term of 1924 Cecil asked Boy Le Bas about his holidays. Boy had been to the opera with Miradia Unwin, a beautiful half-caste Japanese pianist, who wore tight-bodiced dresses with high waists, and her hair piled high on the back of her head. 'Ma Unpot', as Cecil called her, was a gentle creature. She made Cecil feel loud, crude and artificial. Boy was so much taken with her that he first dropped Tris Bennett and later Cecil himself.

The Marlowe Society staged *The Duchess of Malfi* in the spring term. The producer, Tom Marshall of Trinity (Frances Partridge's brother), hoped Cecil might act in it, but he failed the audition. The star part went to 'Dadie' Rylands and Cecil took his revenge by publishing a mean caricature of him in *Granta*.

Cecil continued his pursuit of publicity. In Oxford he talked to Valentine Whitaker,* who told him that the OUDS got their publicity through having two publicity managers continually sending things to the papers. Besides the wish for self-advertisement, which was strong, there was logic to Cecil's wish for publicity:

If one advertises in papers, people (like myself) get excited. Rush to see the show. The theatre is crowded. They get money enough to pay for an elaborate production. With Frank B's pettiness no one out of Cambridge should go. Theatre half empty – rotten meagre production.⁹²

Cecil also arranged for photographs to be taken of himself in his rooms and began to send them to newspapers. He loved it when his photograph appeared: 'Few things thrill me more.'⁹³ Presently one appeared in the *Sketch*. Boy spotted it and screamed. Cecil feigned ignorance, went white and exclaimed, 'Oh I say! Billie must have sent it. He took it.'⁹⁴ Boy was livid because the caption read that Cecil was designing scenery for the Marlowe Society – currently the occupation of Boy. Normally Cecil's photographs were returned to him unused, but from time to time one went in.

When peace was restored between Cecil and Boy, they gave a performance as 'Beattie and Bass (straight from their phenomenal success at the Kilburn Empire) In Selections from their Repertoire including Wagner and Rubinstein'. The members of the ADC were livid, accusing the concert of being like a Footlights revue, but 'Dadie' Rylands thought them hilariously

---

* Valentine Whitaker (1904–30) acted as Valentine Ware.

funny. Trouble brewed again when the *Daily Mirror* printed Cecil's picture stating that he had done the sets and costumes for *The Duchess of Malfi*, again a falsehood. There was a blazing row between him and Boy. Cecil became cautious, thinking he was about to lose his only real friend at Cambridge: 'All the others use me as I use them.'[95] He wrote to the president of the Marlowe Society denying that he had put the notices in. Meanwhile Boy, who had got the designer's job through Cecil, was fêted among the Duncan Grants and Maynard Keyneses, while Cecil was left in the cold.

In March 1924 he was cajoled into taking part in a concert for his college, a skit on *The Merchant of Venice*. He was very put out to have to do it, because St John's was thought of as a hearty establishment and rather 'dank and remote'.[96] Cecil claimed, 'I don't know a soul in it and I don't want to either.'[97] When he appeared in a gold crinoline, the drunken St John's men called out, 'Keep her away from me',[98] but the performance itself was greeted with more than usual hilarity. Nevertheless *The Eagle*, the magazine of St John's, recorded:

> Had the words been written more than two days beforehand and the play rehearsed more than two hours previously, and lastly the parts learnt, the performance might have been excellent, for the Opera contained much humour, and the audience was appreciative.[99]

This term Cecil had still done no work (except one essay, his first for two years) and no acting. He resolved to be 'frightfully energetic' the following term, designing scenery, acting and working. In the Easter holidays he was in a disagreeable mood. He accompanied his father and Reggie to Bournemouth. But when an 'entertainer woman' at the hotel tried to get him onto the stage, saying with a nudge: 'You haven't got a face like yours for nothing',[100] Cecil remained silent, resolutely refusing to move. His father then embarrassed him further by announcing that he took all the leading parts at Cambridge.

Back at Cambridge for the summer term Cecil realized that 'Summer is here and one thinks of silky hair, white hands, a river and shady trees and laziness – one ought to think of the exam in six weeks time!'[101] His dilemma was to master the difficult part of the Marchioness Matilda Spina in the ADC's production of Pirandello's *Henry IV* (the first time it had ever been performed in English),* to do the scenery, and to pass his architecture exam. *Henry IV* ran into considerable difficulties because it was such an ambitious undertaking, and the rehearsals were a strain because of a violent conflict between Cecil and Frank Birch. Cecil was told by Frank that he had excellent elocution but no voice projection. Like his father, he could not express emotion. Worse, he was told that no photographs were to be published.

---

*It was first performed professionally in English at the Everyman Theatre, London, on 15 July 1925. Godfrey Winn took the walk-on part of Ordulph.

This was the most bitter blow: 'If I'd known there were to be no photographs in the press I wouldn't have acted. It's all I care about – well no – but still it's one of the things I like the best. Everyone sees them!'[102] However, Cecil decided to take no notice and to send a piece in to *The Times*. When it was printed Frank Birch came up to him and enquired, 'Do you know anything about this, Beaton? It's obviously something to do with you or your name wouldn't be down here twice and in such important positions. There is someone who evidently does you a lot of good up here in getting you thrust forward. Is it Le Bas?'[103] Cecil went very red and pretended that it was someone to whom he had been talking casually at Lady Ferguson's dance in London. Frank made him write to *The Times* correcting various errors; Cecil dreaded being found out more than anything. He was terrified he would be fired and his reputation ruined. He lay in bed praying that he would escape. Nevertheless within a week he was conjuring up new publicity schemes. He longed for a suitable picture of himself to send the press despite Frank's wrath:

> I do so want to make my name – and a full-page thing of me as the Marchioness looking like a Madonna would make the most terrific sensation and I should hold my head high all the season.[104]

Whenever Cecil disobeyed one of Frank's edicts, he felt sick with worry but he could not stop himself from doing it. Frank had identified the problem correctly: Cecil was using the ADC for personal advancement, an unforgivable crime. For this reason Frank complained about the flamboyance of Cecil's green and silver dress. Meanwhile Cecil tried his costume on and was delighted: 'I looked so like the most sumptuous society woman.'[105]

The dreaded exams just preceded the first night of *Henry IV*. Cecil found he could answer none of the questions: 'What a waste of days sitting doing nothing and too terrified to go. I might just as well have shown up a blank paper. There is not the thousandth chance that I've passed my exam.'[106] The play did not go brilliantly for Cecil either. He missed his cue on the first night and then caught a bad cold, but his sets got good mentions, especially in the *Spectator* whose critic, Humbert Wolfe, wrote: 'In Mr Beaton who designed the scenery and dresses, [Frank Birch] has (unless I am much mistaken) chanced upon one who may well prove a legitimate successor to Lovat Fraser.'*[107]

The play was seen by Lytton Strachey and by Harold Acton from Oxford, who liked the 'decorative little groups'.[108] Of Cecil he wrote: 'Mr Beaton, as the Marchesa Matilda, exuded a Coty-perfumed atmosphere of Roman–Venetian society as we read of it in the novels of Ouida and Marion Crawford.'[109] When Cecil failed his exam, Armitage said that probably his

---

* Claud Lovat Fraser (1890–1921), the artist and designer, best known for his colourful sets and costumes for *The Beggar's Opera*.

other achievements justified it. Cecil then returned to the 'squabbles and pettiness of family life'.[110]

There was talk about Cecil having private coaching when he returned to Cambridge for his last year in October 1924. For a long time he aspired to become a member of the exclusive Pitt Club but did not succeed because, he believed, his female roles had made him too flashy. He continued to worry about his reputation. He did not enjoy a surprise visit from a very affected young actor who turned out to be Godfrey Winn: 'He talked terribly vivaciously and intimately and kept saying, "Oh my dear, you really should have ..." etc. It was amazing.'[111] And he was sickened that his Heath Mount friend, Dudley Brown, now well advanced on the louche path that would lead to an early death, went around saying: 'Oh I've got someone you'd like. He plays all the female parts at Cambridge.' As Cecil said, 'Ugh!'[112]

The winter term was taken up with more study than generally appealed to Cecil and a new diversion, writing 'The Letters of Pamela' secretly for a Cambridge paper. He attended a talk by T.S. Eliot and longed to stand up and contradict him just to see his reaction. He re-took the exam and was pleased to find that some of the papers were the same as in the summer.

In January 1925 Cecil celebrated his twenty-first birthday with a dance. Despite the death of his black-bearded Uncle Reggie, and his mother's command that he should not send out notices, the event was well publicized. He made his brother Reggie post the notices, thus technically not breaking the rules.

Cecil was determined to end his Cambridge career on a high note. Thus in the summer term of 1925 he hovered between two options. Either he could take a man's part in the ADC or do something frivolous in the Footlights. Despite his worries about his reputation, there was some appeal in going down 'in a flash of diamanté'.[113]

The Footlights performed in a professional theatre for seven nights to an audience of 1,400 people, while the ADC performed for only three nights to 200 in a room like a cigar box. Cecil had not forgotten the sensation Norman Hartnell had created there in the summer of 1922. He thought Hartnell was no actor but conceded that his dresses were superb and clearly the whole house had adored the show. 'Dadie' Rylands and 'Topsy' Lucas advised him to go ahead. Cecil also asked the advice of Billie Bullivant, telling him that he was in trouble with the ADC. 'Well, what does it matter,' said Billie. 'You'll think the whole thing so petty soon!'*[114]

After further wavering, Cecil took the plunge and, on 29 April, he went to see Harry Warrender,† the Footlights President. Having put in his applica-

---

* Not long after coming down from Cambridge, Cecil took offence because Bullivant accused him of looking like a tart. He never spoke to him again.

† Harry Warrender (1903–53), son of Lady Maud Warrender; minor actor in such films as *Scott of the Antarctic* (1949).

tion, he dreaded being blackballed, but all went well and he was duly elected. They even revealed that there was a plan to take the production to the Coliseum: 'My God that would be a flash! I feel almost ashamed. One would be branded for ever more as a female impersonator. What a riot of photographs one could have outside the theatre. My Gosh! That really would be cheap fame. No ADC surreptitious smirking. I chuckled to myself....'[115] He began to rehearse with the Footlights, but found them unprofessional and in rather a muddle. He found it embarrassing to perform in front of these strangers. He began to practise high kicks for his show and found himself incapable of preparing for his exam: 'I've done absolutely no work!'[116] Then he went to London to buy bright peppermint pink chiffon for his dress.

His last days at Cambridge were a mixture of exams and Footlights preparations. Not having the requisite number of essays to show up, Cecil prevailed upon another Footlights actor, Mark Griffith-Jones, to lend him two of his, which he copied out at the back of the lecture room. On 26 May he went to see his supervisor, who was distinctly pessimistic. But Cecil was beyond caring.

The exam week overtook him after a whole week in which he did no academic work. He was resigned to failure. Reading the questions in his first paper he realized he had never heard of either Edward II or Edward III. In fact, in history he never got further than William the Conqueror. 'I made an attempt to answer one question. Then I wrote two letters and off I went.'[117] The subsequent three papers were no more successful. Not surprisingly Cecil failed.

The Footlights production, *All the Vogue*, interested him very much more. When he should have been revising, he had his hair waved by a Cambridge hairdresser and rushed to London to be photographed in his costume by Dorothy Wilding. He was frightened of what Miss Wilding would think of him, but the session proved a great success. 'She is a funny, fat, vulgar little woman,' wrote Cecil, 'very motherly, smart and amusing.'[118] He adopted poses favoured by Gladys Cooper and Mary Curzon (later Countess Howe) and was far from disappointed with the results: 'They really are simply marvellous just as I had expected them to be.'[119]

Cecil felt 'grey and oysterish' about the prospect of the first night, after a bad rehearsal watched by the young actor John Gielgud.* Cecil took no account of the fact that he was a newcomer to the Footlights and deeply resented not being allowed to dance, so much so that he had a fierce row with the producer, Gordon Sherry, while Frank Corbett, formerly of Princeton University, was obliged to stand at the door of the dressing-room

---

* Sir John recalled that Harry Warrender had to kiss a girl. Cecil stood at the top of the stairs and said, 'We are *not* amused.'

barring others from coming in. 'I was simply desperate,' noted Cecil, 'and so much more desperate because in the end I didn't get my own way.'[120]

The next day Cecil was ticked off for his lack of team spirit but he continued to be hostile to Sherry until the latter relented about the dance on the third night. Alas, however, Philip Shaw, who would have been his partner, was now teamed up with another Footlights man, Gordon Alcock. Finally Frank Corbett brought Cecil to heel by telling him that he had the best opportunities in the show and was being greedy. Furthermore he was making himself unpopular, a bad fate in the Footlights. Corbett wondered why he was trying to 'hog the whole show'.[121] He pointed out that while Harry Warrender, the president, had only one photo outside the New Theatre, Cecil's were 'plastered' all over the place. Cecil admitted; 'I suddenly did realize that I had been rather too much of a good thing and too grabbing.'[122] He wrote apologizing to Sherry for his selfishness and resolved to call on Harry Warrender to explain that he 'wasn't clear-headed at the time and only intent on the one thing – in fact rather temperamentally insane'.[123]

The chastened Cecil then relaxed to enjoy the last two shows, whose audiences included members of his family, H.G. Wells and Philip Guedalla. There was hilarious laughter and great admiration for his stunning costumes, particularly when he wore a ballet skirt and black stockings. On the last night he received an 'embarrassing' number of bouquets of lilies and roses, while Alcock, his rival as 'leading lady', left the stage with but one. He was sad when it all ended: 'I so liked the excitement, the theatrical thrills, the publicity. It was marvellous to see one's name up all over the town.'[124] After a rush of packing and amidst much nostalgia, Cecil went down on 19 June.

Part Two

The Struggling Years 1925–7

5

Anything for the Uprise

*It's so easy to be overwhelming in Cambridge but London
is such a large thing to grapple with.*

Cecil's diary, 24 October 1925

'Oh dear, oh dear the last day of the play, the Trinity Ball, the end of
Cambridge and after this the squalor of being shut up with one's family like
cabbages – boxed away in one's bedroom and impossible to see one's friends.
Oh! dear, oh dear! The best of one's days then really are finished.'[1] Cecil had
been worried for some time about life after university. He had come down
unqualified and badly educated, which, as his sisters often reminded him,
was his own fault. Later he made some attempt to rectify the situation by
pinning cards all over his bedroom with the key dates of kings and artists.
Having seen these cards in the 1930s, his publisher, Brian Cook (later Sir
Brian Batsford), observed that this enabled him to appear more knowledgeable than he was. He could comment: 'Yes, and of course that was two
years after Michelangelo was born.'[2]

The life Cecil led in London had already assumed a certain pattern. During
his university holidays he had had the chance to go to the theatre on many
occasions. He saw Cathleen Nesbitt as Yasmin in *Hassan* and wrote: 'I
nearly went mad. With wonderful costumes and scenery it would be too
gorgeously perfect.'[3] He worshipped Cathleen Nesbitt from afar: 'I should
like to know her. She is too splendid.'[4] He took a standing-room ticket at
the Coliseum to see Beatrice Lillie do her sketch 'Tea Shop Prattle'. Worried
that richer Cambridge colleagues would spot him there, he hid in a corridor
behind a curtain in the interval. In April 1925 he saw Tallulah Bankhead
in Noël Coward's *Fallen Angels*. All his life he had a blind spot concerning
Noël Coward: 'I do think the play will help to ruin old Coward. It is quite
definite that he won't live long. People will get so tired of him.'[5]

Cecil also enjoyed his walks down Bond Street and elsewhere, inspecting
the photographers' windows and the photos of actresses outside theatres.
He was delighted if Hazel Lavery or Gladys Cooper was on display. Sometimes he spotted a heroine in the flesh. The Modigliani beauty Paula Gelli-

brand swept past in a Rolls-Royce with her husband, the Marquis de Casa Maury. In July 1923 Lady Diana Cooper pulled up outside the Times Bookshop in her little car. Cecil followed her into the shop to take a closer look at this legendary beauty: 'She did look perfect and caused a great sensation. . . . I adore her side face. Her chin almost slides away.'[6] Once Cecil was himself recognized by two youths in Bond Street. He enjoyed the experience so much that the next day he returned there to walk up and down several times, but in vain.

During a visit to his friend Peggy Broadbent, in December 1922, the Duke of Marlborough came to dinner. Cecil was mortified to see that the Duke had three pearl studs the size of his one. In July 1924 when the Beatons were on holiday at Sheringham, they went to Sandringham and Cecil saw Queen Alexandra, now aged seventy-nine, attend the flower show. For him she represented the glamour of the Edwardian era with its laced corsets, sequins and diamonds. Cecil thought the Queen, now very old, 'still beautiful, thinner and haggard'. He studied her face, 'painted scarlets and whites and black and magenta'.[7] In December he met Lady Ottoline Morrell and declared, 'I have hardly ever enjoyed myself so much before.'[8] These were among the visual images that he retained throughout his life. Later they found an outlet in his work.

Cecil devoted much of his time to drawing or photographing his two sisters. He copied the lens effects of Hugh Cecil and paid visits to photographers such as Maurice Beck. Baba was his favourite sitter. He was almost in love with her and he enjoyed doing her hair in different styles and dressing her in gold. He developed and printed late into the night and his parents complained that he took no exercise. One night he had a dream in which he saw Nancy and Baba playing with titled children. In his dream he sent their photograph to the *Tatler*: 'Little snob! Even in my dreams I long to make Mummie a society lady and not a housewife.'[9] The *Tatler* was very important to him. Even when he had a headache and streaming eyes he could not resist reading it, though once this caused him to be sick. At this time he charged his family 4d. for every print he made.

Cecil was depressed by his parents' life. In 1923 he wrote:

There's nothing that excites Mummie now. She doesn't care about going out, reading, anything except a mild interest in golf, but Mummie hasn't played for nearly a year! . . . Daddy is fairly nice. He's really sweet. He's very good natured but he really is getting an infirm and an annoying old fool! and rather a common fool at that![10]

Whenever he showed enthusiasm for any plan, it was usually squashed by one or other parent saying: 'We're not millionaires you know.'[11] He was relieved when Nancy passed her fourteenth birthday and joined the family at dinner, easing the tension with her youthful chatter.

Cecil exerted considerable influence on his two sisters, so much so that his mother complained that he taught them to speak of people as being common. Cecil got on less well with his brother Reggie, who failed his 'Little Go' and went straight into Mr Beaton's timber business. Cecil observed: 'Reggie returned very quietly from the office. His first day. Poor wretch. I do feel sorry for him, but he doesn't seem to have much feeling about it either way.'[12]

Just as he had sent photographs of himself to newspapers from Cambridge, Cecil now sent in photographs of his sisters. In October 1924 he had two successes. The *Queen* published his photograph of Madame Gutiérrez, the wife of the Bolivian Minister in London, a friend of Aunt Jessie who looked like an ageing Spanish Infanta. 'At last a success. I hope I shall get paid. I sat looking at the *Queen* for ages after breakfast.'[13] The same day Aunt Jessie arrived with a letter from the *Tatler* addressed to her house in one of the pseudonyms Cecil sometimes used. His tummy 'quivered and jerked' with delight at the news that they would publish two photographs of Nancy: 'I had been depressed but this was a triumph.'[14]

At Easter 1925 Cecil had some more 'triumphs'. His mother's photograph appeared in the *Bystander* with the caption 'A London Hostess'. Cecil chuckled all the way home. Then he was asked to exhibit some of his designs at Wembley. Later he attended the Max Beerbohm exhibition and the editor of *Vogue* came up to him. Dorothy Todd was (in the words of Rebecca West) 'a fat little woman, full of energy, full of genius',[15] and a great editor. The fashion editor of *Vogue*, Madge Garland, described her as 'a brilliantly perceptive editor whose aim was to make *Vogue* into a magazine of such literary and social importance that it would be acceptable everywhere'.[16] Dame Rebecca believed that these two editors 'changed *Vogue* from just another fashion paper to being the best of fashion papers and a guide to the modern movement in the arts'.[17] They helped Roger Fry bring Post-Impressionism to England; they promoted Picasso, Matisse, Derain, Bonnard, Proust and Cocteau. Dorothy Todd commissioned Virginia Woolf and other Bloomsberries to write for them. Photographers such as Maurice Beck and Helen MacGregor were set to work. Thus it was an important step for Cecil when Dorothy Todd told him that he was the only person who sent in good photographs but that they always arrived too late. She went to press ten days before the magazine appeared. She urged him: 'Do try and get them out sooner.'[18] This was Cecil's first introduction to the world of Condé Nast.

Helpful though this was, Cecil's immediate problems were not solved. He had no job and no ideas for a job. He was allowed a holiday after coming down from Cambridge in July 1925 before parental pressure was applied. He began by attending some parties and concluding that something had to be done to go to better ones. After Lady Clementine Waring's party, he thought: 'how small we are'.[19]

At this period Mrs Beaton and Cecil were prepared to put up with any boring charity committee in order to meet new people, surely the dreariest path ever trod by the social climber. Cecil tolerated anything: 'That old Baroness Goldsmid was with us and looked awful in red but we must cultivate her as she gives good parties.'[20] And he was angry if he was left out: 'Lady Walpole was there and I cut her. I was livid at not being asked to her party tomorrow.'[21]

By his own confession he would do anything for the 'uprise'. Of one charity lady he wrote, 'she doesn't know I'm a scheming snob. She thinks I'm just charming.'[22] He was forever jealous of the Le Bas family because they were very rich whereas his own family was rather poor. His diaries are full of the complaint, 'How they've got on!'[23] He manipulated charity ladies like Mrs Frank Braham shamelessly. He danced with her and she was thrilled: 'but little did she know that I was doing it because I knew she was a very influential woman who had got the Le Bas on so splendidly and could do the same with Mummie if only Mummie worked with her!'[24] Of course as he progressed he readjusted his values. He went to tea with Lady Wyndham,* who produced an old gramophone for dancing. Cecil danced with his former heroine, Isobel Elsom, 'who is charming, unconceited and very fresh and healthy and natural', but he noted, 'I wouldn't admire her at all if I hadn't been so mad about her in my youth.... I have lately met so many people without a thrill that I should have gone mad about ten years ago.'[25]

Amongst the older ladies in the Beaton set, Cecil was very struck with Madame Gutiérrez and Lady Alexander,† the widow of the well-known actor-manager Sir George Alexander. She looked like a female impersonator, invariably dressed in a confection of silver and garter blue, bedecked with ostrich feathers. Lady Diana Cooper recalled that 'she was totally grotesque'.[26] Cecil loved the stories that surrounded Lady Alexander and rather overrated her place in the social hierarchy. It was said that when her Pekinese died and was buried near Sir George at Chorley Wood, the London florists had sent miniature wreaths. Soon afterwards Lady Alexander met a lady friend in deep mourning, whose husband and son had been killed in a terrible accident. She shed a tear, saying: 'I too have a great sorrow ... my little Pekinese.'[27] Cecil attended charity functions with Lady Alexander and danced with her to the amusement of other guests. He was delighted when he engineered a photograph to be taken of them both at the theatre. It was published on the front page of the *Daily Mirror*: 'Yes, I'd been clever about that. The Le Bas would be livid!'[28]

---

* Lady Wyndham, the actress Mary Moore, produced early Noël Coward plays.

† Lady Alexander, *née* Florence Théleur, married Sir George in 1882.

It was through Lady Alexander that Cecil met his first member of the royal family in November 1925. She gave him the job of escorting Princess Arthur of Connaught to her car after a charity *thé dansant*: 'She was thoroughly nervous and like a little servant, but I felt very proud.'[29]

Cecil always enjoyed the annual Theatrical Garden Party and this year a chance encounter was to help him. He wandered among the stars:

Lady Diana Cooper was being a terrific success and enjoying herself so much – Tallulah Bankhead was too wonderful with her gorgeous face, gruff voice and pale marcello waved hair.... Binnie Hale was [having] a triumph. Sybil Thorndike looked like a haggard governess.[30]

But Cecil was out of it: 'I did feel insignificant here and at Cambridge one is so famous.'[31] So lonely did he look that Gerald Hoare and a friend of his came over to talk to him. The friend was Paul Tanqueray, the photographer, who had worked as an assistant to Hugh Cecil. The meeting was well timed because Cecil was about to have a blazing row with his mother about his latest plan to become a photographer. Driving in the car one day,

Mama and I did nothing but quarrel and get simply livid about my being a photographer. Mama blamed Cambridge for that. She wished I'd never gone – that if I hadn't I would have done better than that. Mama said all my friends would be snobby about me if I was a photographer and I said well what can I do – and a dead silence – surely everyone can do anything nowadays – altho' I don't expect Suffield-Jones [the gossip columnist] would mention me in his paper again. I wonder.[32]

Paul Tanqueray had felt sorry for Cecil ('He looked so sad'[33]) and meeting him at the ballet on the night of this row, he reintroduced himself. Cecil had heard of him. He bombarded him with questions and Tanqueray explained some of the tricks and dodges of the trade. He had paid Hugh Cecil £250 a year to be in his studio. Cecil thought: 'If I have got to get some training I might as well do it in his business without having to pay £250 at Hugh Cecil's!! I was pleased with my evening's work.'[34]

Five days later, on 29 July, Cecil rang up Paul Tanqueray and went to see him at his studio in Kensington High Street. He was shown photographs of Tom Douglas* in various stages of retouching. Paul Tanqueray recalled: 'In those days [Hugh] Cecil used a folding camera. The process was called orthochromatic. Blue eyes came out better, hair darker and pink as very black. Both Cecil and I had to re-touch heavily. We were both exponents of glamour.'[35] Cecil thought Paul Tanqueray's photos 'quite excellent just like Hugh Cecil in technique',[36] but thought he would do better to set up more

* Tom Douglas, an outrageous American actor, who became famous in London in the play *Fata Morgana*. Later he ran an antique shop in Hollywood.

cheaply in a smarter area. Cecil asked 'a thousand questions without being too inquisitive and positive'.[37]

The time had now come for Mr Beaton to ask some pertinent questions about the future. For this ritual his wife took Nancy and Baba out and Mr Beaton came to see Cecil in his bedroom. Mr Beaton's business had been declining since the middle of the war. Timber was having to give place to the new materials of steel and concrete. The firm had lost the American business, which represented half the family income, to a man in Manchester. Then at Christmas 1923 a cargo from Ireland had gone astray, causing an immediate loss of £6,000. The house in Hyde Park Street was too expensive and a move was threatened. Cecil had long worried over how this would affect him. 'If we did lose our money I'd not know how to look at people.'[38] He was determined not to follow Reggie into the family business. 'I certainly won't slave away in that business all my life. It wouldn't matter if it were a marvellous one like the Le Bas where one really would make money. It's so unclever to hack on at this rotten business and then always be feeling the pinch.'[39] Mr Beaton asked Cecil if perhaps he wanted to do dress design-ing, and was told that he had thought of photography. Mr Beaton seemed interested, his only reservation being the initial outlay of capital and the risks involved. 'He was rather nice about it,' recorded Cecil, 'and we got on quite well together.'[40] Fortunately any further discussion on the subject was prevented by a row at lunch. Mrs Beaton said it was vulgar of her husband to eat cheese off his knife; he said it was merely old-fashioned. The next day Cecil sent off a batch of photographs to the *Tatler* – of 'Mrs Beaton, the beautiful wife of Mr E.W.H. Beaton'. 'It takes a great deal of time doing these things up carefully and remembering under what various names they are being sent.'[41] One name that Cecil used was 'Carlo Crivelli' (after the fifteenth-century Venetian painter). This particular batch was sent back unused.

Over the ensuing weeks, Cecil's father got into more of a state about his son's prolonged holiday. Cecil invited Paul Tanqueray to tea in order to learn more secrets: where to get good cheap photographic paper, the diffi-culty of getting perfect results, how for this most photographs had to be enlarged. He was discouraged by the technical problems and the amount of gadgets required, and asked if he could come and work just for fun:

> He said yes to begin with but later said there'd be nothing for me to do as I couldn't enlarge or print, that that was frightfully skilled labour. I was disappointed. He seemed utterly amazed that I should want to work!! That I, Cecil Beaton, should want to work. He is very impressed with me and I suppose I have got rather a glamorous name among young men of a certain brand. And I suppose that's through my hacking away at publicity and also being so cold and formal and conceited when I meet young men.[42]

Cecil prevailed upon Tanqueray to photograph Nancy and Baba. This was done the next day amidst great excitement. Cecil went to see the results and ordered some prints, which he could ill afford, and on 20 October (1925) he was delighted when Tanqueray told him there was a full page of Nancy and Baba reproduced in the *Bystander*. 'I was in such a state of excitement that I almost gave a terrible scream down the telephone.' Baba rushed off in the rain to get a copy. It said they came 'from an old Scotch family'.[43] It was a 'double triumph' because Cecil's picture of Vera Birch was on the next page.

His photograph of Vera was taken at the house in Buckingham Street which her brother Lord Gage shared with Chips Channon, 'a terribly popular young American, who is very rich and very popular and a snob [and who] spends his time running after Lady Curzon of Kedleston'.[44] Vera Birch wrote of Cecil:

> I often sat for him at Cambridge. One of these ventures included a full-length portrait of me in an oriental dressing-gown with disordered hair and a sponge which appeared, neither with my knowledge or consent, covering an entire page of that week's *Bystander* to my moderate embarrassment.... By the time we all left Cambridge, Cecil had developed his chief talent considerably. He went to my horror 'society' (I by then being inclined to socialism).... It probably shocked me then that he had become what I considered in my priggish way to be 'climbing' as we snootily called it. Later in my more advanced years I realized he had to reach these heights to further his career as a photographer. Also he was a bright young man tempted by rich and alluring invitations. But one was young and intolerant and from my awful political angle believed him to be lost for ever.[45]

At this time Vera advised Cecil that he would achieve nothing until he got away from his family.

During this uncertain time in Cecil's life advice poured in from all quarters. An eccentric old friend called Mrs Ruffer advised him not to be a photographer, but either to paint or do interior decoration. Boy Le Bas (now increasingly under the influence of Mrs Miradia Unwin) urged him to get a studio and start work. Boy believed he should concentrate on one thing, but Cecil did not dare ask his impoverished father for the £1,000 needed for a studio. The charity lady, Mrs Braham, thought he should follow his parents' wishes for a year, so that they would not be disappointed in him. Meanwhile Cecil remained confused. At one moment he veered to photography:

> Photos are the only thing – just to make money. It is so difficult to get a permanent job with scenery and dresses. Oh! I'm very desperate. When-

ever Daddy sees me reading in a chair he feels I ought to be working and I feel that he is feeling that. Also I'm feeling horribly poor. I've paid off such a lot of Cambridge bills out of my own pocket money and there are still more lagging on. I'm really getting very desperate. That Lenare photo bill has just been paid after great delay and difficulty.[46]

Then soon afterwards he contemplated the stage:

I must get a start. I should frightfully like to act, I believe, but what terrible parts one would get if one got one at all! I am feeling very discontented and grudging everyone else their triumphs and publicity.[47]

The best he could do was keep meeting people and see what came of it.

At this time many important new people came into his orbit. A family friend called Mrs Brennan, who lived in Chapel Street, always had faith in Cecil's talents. At her house he met Charles Fry, who worked at Batsfords, the publishers. Cecil thought him 'frightfully nice looking, all very fine and smooth and pale – a gorgeous complexion and very pale yellow hair brushed right back. He did look nice and he was too. So very unflashy.'[48] By contrast Cecil felt rather cold:

All the people I meet now seem to have an intimate personality which just shoots out and makes one a friend from the start, but I've suddenly realized I'm not a very attractive personality or else I should have a lot more intimate friends.[49]

A very important new friend to him was Allanah Harper, whom he had met a number of times. She was a rich young lady, whose father was one of the British consultants working on the first Aswan dam. She was widely travelled and had been at Miss Wolfe's school in London with Baba d'Erlanger and Iris Tree and Miss Douglas's at Queen's Gate with Lady Eleanor Smith and Zita Jungman. Although showing no particular artistic or literary bent at that time, she had developed into an intellectual who subsequently edited a literary magazine in Paris. She turned against the conventional side of her upbringing and became a close friend of Edith Sitwell, Brian Howard and others. One day she saw Cecil's photographs of his mother and sisters and became an important catalyst in his career (as in so many others, most notably Sybille Bedford's) by making the simple suggestion that he must photograph other girls too. This she arranged. She invited him to tea, which delighted Cecil:

I was looking forward to that as the Harpers were terrifically rich and I've lately found that Allanah Harper has an artistic appreciation and is thoroughly well read and amusing without being brilliant. The house is simply lovely and we had tea in Allanah's room which has an excellent collection of books. A. looked much younger and fresher than when she

first came out six years ago. She has a gleam in her eye now – I suppose
since she broke out from her silly friends and parents and gained an
artistic appreciation! ... We talked about Jean Cocteau, André Gide,
Picasso, the Bloomsberries and the amusing people there are – I enjoyed
myself and stayed there a very long time.[50]

In this atmosphere of general uncertainty it is not surprising to find
relations within the Beaton family taking a turn for the worse. Aunt Jessie
came to dinner two nights running and got on Mr Beaton's nerves. Normally the family ignored him when he was in this state, but on this particular evening he flared up and raged about a forthcoming society wedding
to which the family were eagerly looking forward. He said it incited Bolshevism. He complained that nobody allowed him to get a word in. His rage
was so fierce that Mrs Beaton and her sister left the dining-room. Aunt
Jessie complained that Mr Beaton would allow nobody to have their own
personality, and Cecil quickly agreed with her.

The next day Mrs Beaton was haggard and weeping. She told Cecil how
difficult his father was, and he incited her to be more domineering: 'I felt
annoyed that she wasn't stronger and firmer in her dealings with Daddy –
other husbands are quietly and gently squashed – Mr Noad, Mr Le Bas, Mr
Agar!'[51] Fortunately Mrs Braham came to the rescue by inviting Mrs Beaton
to work on a new charity appeal. Cecil envisaged the fulfilment of his 'life
work since we left Hampstead',[52] which was to make his mother important
and have photographs of her in the popular press.

One can't get on at all if one doesn't have a little glamour about one's
home. I have done wonders considering how poor we are – photos in lots
of papers and a continual fight for more![53]

In view of this development, Cecil retired to his room to cut his fingernails
to a respectable length. (Once in Bond Street a man had spotted them newly
enamelled and muttered, 'Ought not to be allowed on the streets.'[54] His
thumbnail on the left hand had been $1\frac{3}{4}$ inches long.)

On the last day of October 1925, Cecil escaped from his dreary domesticity
to attend a wild fancy-dress party in Cambridge, given by his Harrow friend,
Jack Gold. Jack had got into what Cecil thought a 'select set', including
people such as Sir Richard Sykes, Maurice Bridgeman, John Ramsden, Philip
Dunn and Lord Charles Cavendish. His other friends at Cambridge were
very envious that he was going to this party. Cecil thought: 'I suppose they
take me up because I'm the Gladys Cooper of my world – I think they think
of me as an intellectual Joy Boy.'[55]

For the party Cecil put on pink chiffon and a bustle. The theme was to
have been a middle-class party, but it ended up as 'a banquet of fish-wives'.
Cecil drank cocktails and champagne. As glass followed glass, his natural

reserve wore down and he become increasingly carefree. He laughed and waved his arms about. The room 'rather deliciously whirled along' with Cecil in it. Champagne was now poured into tumblers and the assembled young gentlemen began to dance with each other.

It was marvellous!! So abandoned! I was flying round the room and falling over people and shouting and twirling and I suddenly realized that John Ramsden and Philip Dunn were after me and I in my tightness and un-soundedness [sic] of mind gave way to the little Dunn. If I had been sober I should have paid more attention to the silly Ramsden. He is so smart and dances with the Duchess of York. I was so tight and so pleased with myself.... I was in a state, rushing with Philip Dunn and John Ramsden after me from one couch to another and then falling over a sofa and being smothered with kisses from Philip Dunn, and John Ramsden saying, 'Oh Philip I shall never speak to you again. Oh Cecil. Oh Cecil. I thought your shingle was too marvellous.... I would look at something and gradually it would become focused and I could see what it was – and I could see Charles Cavendish staring with a smile on his face and I heard him say 'Cecil's tight'.... My hair was being stroked and my face kissed and my lips and mouth licked. It was the most abandoned thing and I so enjoyed it and my heart beat with pure un-lustful love! I tried to dance and fell over everybody and I tried to get away from the pursuers and shouted to Jack to look after me. There was a terrible fight and I rushed out and was sick all over Anthony Jenkinson's couch. God I was so full of remorse.*[56]

The next day Cecil was in a dreadful state: 'I've come to Cambridge and lost my reputation in a night that I've built up for three years.'[57]

Cecil's Cambridge escapade caused him to turn a cold eye on his parents when he went home:

I was so struck ... with the childlike simplicity of Daddy and Mummie. They were so silly getting in and out of buses, so fussy and ridiculous and never knowing the way and their talking about whether our seats were worth the money. I said to Nancy when we came here that I thought it was pitiful that Papa at his state of impotence should be so meagre and poor – not selfish and miserly – no – just can't afford it – poor.[58]

---

* All these men later married and most of them undertook respectable occupations. Sir Richard Sykes, Bt (1905–78) was Chairman of the Driffield Magistrates and President of the Bridlington Conservative Association. Hon. Sir Maurice Bridgeman (1904–80) was Chairman of British Petroleum. John Ramsden married Lady Catherine Heathcote-Drummond-Willoughby, divorced in 1947 and was assassinated in Malaya in June 1948; and Sir Philip Dunn Bt (1905–76) was married to Lady Mary St Clair-Erskine, divorced but remarried to her later. Lord Charles Cavendish did not work. He married Adèle Astaire.

Due to their increasing poverty, the Beatons dismissed their servants for a while and Mrs Beaton had to do the housework. No. 3 Hyde Park Street was put on the market and Cecil was terrified that they might move back to the 'dreadful suburban desert'[59] of Hampstead, which his father so dearly loved. This coincided with Mr Beaton's announcement that he would like Cecil 'to get a little idea of business by going to his office and keeping accounts'.[60] Cecil agreed to this 'but gosh how I'll loathe it'.[61] Boy Le Bas was horrified to hear the news, but the Le Bas parents were delighted: 'So he's had to knuckle down and throw to the winds all his fanciful ideas.'[62]

Before the axe fell on his freedom Cecil went to stay with Peggy Broadbent:

> How remote I was now from the striving middle-class family or arty Boy and his thoroughness – I was far from everything else – just having a good rest in a select way – that appealed to my snobbery – so nice being so select – and Peggy was taking me to the Leicester Races and I'd got all the most suitable clothes and I would thoroughly enjoy it and we'd very likely be photographed and appear selectly in the *Tatler* and all the unselect people would see it and be rather annoyed.[63]

They duly attended the Leicester Races and his photograph subsequently appeared in the *Tatler*. Although in the picture he looks a reassuringly sporting figure, he admitted privately that he 'didn't know one horse from another'.[64]

On 18 November Cecil became restless: 'Daddy would be getting impatient for me to start at that bloody office so I was quite resigned to my fate.'[65] Peggy drove him to Oxford and there was a small accident when their Essex motor hit a lorry. But Cecil returned safely in time to be 'hemmed in at that filthy office'.[66]

6

The Office

*[Cecil's] father could only puff ineffectual flames from his
dragon's lair in the city and reach out a great paw to put
him on an office stool.*

Cyril Connolly, *Sunday Times*, 16 July 1961

The night before Cecil began work on 23 November the four Beaton children
tried to joke about the awe in which their father's office had always been
held. They said it was 'a mere toy for taking up Daddy's time'.[1] The following morning the jokes had worn very thin as Cecil was marched to the tube
station to take his place alongside 'Daddy and a thousand other men smoking pipes, the morning paper under their arms'.[2] Pointedly he did not buy
a paper. He sat there glaring at his travelling companions, haunted by the
ever recurring taunt in his mind: 'He's had to knuckle under.'[3]

They arrived at the 'small and unimportant'[4] office, which Cecil thought
smelt 'like an underground lavatory'.[5] A series of grim-faced men brought
letters into his father's room, their expressions 'as sordid as their collars'.[6]
The heating gave him a throbbing headache. He could hear his younger
brother talking rather professionally on the telephone and he soon felt
thoroughly inadequate. His father's instructions were a mass of unintelli-
gible phrases: 'The first rule in business is ... or put it another way ... the
simple plan is ...'.[7] Cecil's job was to list and add up a lot of 'fee-guires'[8]
(as Mr Beaton pronounced them). If a mistake was made it was to be erased
sharply with an India rubber. Cecil thought it 'petty and ridiculous'.[9] He
lunched with Reggie, before returning to the office, where his head spun
with figures all afternoon. He dreaded what his friends would say if they
could see him: 'Fancy Cecil Beaton in his father's office in the city – doing
a clerk's work.'[10] Eventually his first day was over and, as it was Friday, a
weekend of freedom loomed. Queen Alexandra, 'the Rose Queen', had died
and he spent much of his time poring over photographs of her 'in all her
periods of beauty'.[11]

On Monday he went back to 'that bloody city'[12] again, to earn his weekly
£2, and his headache returned. That night in bed he cried with exhaustion

and depression. By Thursday he was reading *The Man of Destiny* in the underground as a protest to the newspaper-readers. On Friday his father went to Paris, so he slipped out of the office early. He worked there the following Monday and Tuesday, and then it was all over.

Cecil's career in his father's firm had lasted no more than eight working days. He was saved by a timely, if worrying, letter from Cambridge informing him that he must retake his history exam on Monday 7 December. His father realized for the first time how slack Cecil had been. However, he gave him permission to stay at home to swot. Cecil set to work on William the Conqueror, but soon became discouraged: 'I thought I knew all about him but there were masses of damned Kings I'd never heard of.'[13] To cram three months' work into four days was an impossible task; nor could Cecil resist Lady Latta's tea party: 'She is so superb and so is her house.'[14]

Further troubles lay in store for him when his father had a chance to review his office work:

Daddy came back from the office in a most foul mood. He was livid and turned Reggie out of the room while he ticked me off about the books at the office. He said I couldn't do work that a child of twelve could do. There were mistakes, scratchings out, blanks and altogether I'd made the books in the most terrible state and he would be afraid to let me do them. I couldn't do a simple addition of 'feeguires'. I made mistakes. Why, the business would soon be bankrupt if I continued. Daddy even went so far as to say he didn't want me at the office again, but he wasn't going to let me do nothing. He was furious and I was very little touched by his fury.[15]

At the end of the day Cecil fell into a morbid state: 'I was thoroughly depressed. I shouldn't have minded dying not for any particular reason or that I was unhappy but just because there was nothing immediate to live for.'[16]

Cecil made preparations for his four history papers:

I did a thing which I feel ashamed at having to write and that was – I wrote out a crib – on a very small piece of paper, the dates of various kings and a word about each, so that I could glance and have a reminder of who was what when I was in the Exam Hall. It was terribly inferior and dishonest of me but I wanted to get through the Exam and I thought with luck and with the aid of these scraps of paper I'd be able to.[17]

He covered sheets and sheets with scribblings, relevant or irrelevant, and was delighted when the exam was over ('no matter the result'[18]). It is not altogether surprising that he failed 'by quite a few marks',[19] something he did not dare tell his father.

While in Cambridge, Cecil was soon 'screaming with laughter'[20] at another riotous gathering. He paired off with Lord Charles Cavendish, who hugged him tight round the waist and kissed him: 'I decided I liked Charles Cavendish. Also Charles was a Lord and there was some glamour in that.'[21] Further revelry followed over the next few days and one night Charles got very drunk tossing back bumpers of champagne. Richard Sykes shouted out: 'Cecil, you'll lose your virginity tonight for certain.'[22] Charles and Cecil walked home arm in arm, and Cecil thought he loved Charles 'most terribly'. At Charles's digs, Cecil lay on the sofa while Charles went away, returning presently in his pyjamas, 'nice ordinary unflashy ones, dull pink and bluey grey and all buttoned up with a handkerchief in his breast pocket'.[23] After a while Charles leapt to his feet saying, 'Good night, I'm so sorry I can't show you to your bedroom.'[24] He fled from the room.

Cecil groped his way to his own room with enormous difficulty, tortured with unhappiness at this sudden, unexplained parting. The next morning he apologized nervously. 'Oh poor Cecil,' said Charles. 'No, no, no, that wasn't it.'[25] Charles had merely rushed out to vomit.

Later in the day Cecil called on his old friend 'Topsy' Lucas to relate his adventures. He found Lytton Strachey staying there with her:

> He is tall and anaemic! with lovely hands, pale yellow long and thin but useful.... Topsy told him about my triumphs with the hunting people and Lytton was amazed and interested and asked me even more difficult psychological questions than Lucas. He was thoroughly interested in me and his eyes twinkled. He said he would like to be liked by the cultured hearty hunting men more than by anyone else. Lucas gave a horsey scream 'Oh no' and Lytton in his genteel dairy maid voice said 'Yes, I would'.[26]

These Cambridge parties were about the only highlight in these difficult days. Cecil was thrilled when, a little later on, Charles Cavendish offered him a lift to Cambridge. He announced to his mother and Loins, the butler: 'Lord Charles Cavendish is coming for me in ten minutes. Prepare.'[27] When Charles appeared, Cecil's mother made a theatrical entrance that impressed Cecil but left the unobservant Charles quite unmoved. Once again Cecil revelled in young men falling off canoes, and alcohol being consumed in excessive measure. On the last night his trousers got stuck on the revolving spikes of the Trinity railings as he tried to climb in. The ensuing rush for safety caused Cecil to forget six steps and leap into space. Then he hared off, ducking the flashing torches of the porters. Fun though it all was, Cecil realized that he did not belong in this milieu and in due course he tired of the general 'slackness'.

Returning from his history exam, Cecil asked his angry father if he was expected at the office. At first Mr Beaton could not decide, but when Cecil said he had enough photographic work to occupy him for a week, he let him stay at home. Then another axe fell.

On 17 December 1925 Mr Beaton sold their Hyde Park Street home to Captain Alan (Tommy) Lascelles, the Prince of Wales's Assistant Private Secretary. He obtained only £200 more than he had paid in 1922. Cecil was furious and prevailed upon his mother and sisters to be as nasty as possible to Mr Beaton.

It was now imperative that Cecil should come up with some work before his father found him something else to do. One straw came from Mrs Brennan, who offered to show his stage designs to Nigel Playfair. Cecil then deserted his family to spend Christmas in Gloucestershire with some friends and to drink 1880 champagne. One of the guests, Norma Mitchell-Innes, predicted his future with uncanny accuracy. On 28 December Cecil recorded:

> I was going to have a dreadful time for a year falling between stools and my friends' advice, but after that I was going abroad and coming back with my mind made up and setting hard at work, most enthusiastically. I would be an enormous success, my work my recompense. I was going to have a lot of friends around me.[28]

The New Year of 1926 began with Nancy and Baba taking part in the annual Peter Pan party. Cecil saw this as an ideal opportunity for publicity. He designed their dresses and was especially pleased with Baba as the Duchess of Malfi in a long white and gold dress with trailing magenta and gold sleeves. In the afternoon a *Daily Mail* photographer came to take their pictures. At the ball itself at Claridge's, Mrs Braham stirred up the press. Mrs Whish of the *Daily Express* and Mrs Settle of *Eve* were very enthusiastic. Cecil posed Nancy and Baba before a panelled wall and thirty photographers snapped away eagerly. Each girl on her own was appealing, but together they made the effect all the more stunning. Baba and Nancy won second and third prizes, while Peggy Gordon-Moore, whose mother was a key member of the committee, was the winner. The competition over, the three Beatons rushed around excitedly, receiving ecstatic praise:

> Everyone was running after us. And who would think how poor we are! We spend our last penny on advertisement.... Everyone at the Peter Pan must have thought us terribly sumptuous. The reporters are such snobs that they wouldn't have taken any notice of us unless they'd thought N and B were two promising debutantes! ... a little batch of children thought Baba was a Princess and kept following her and touching her dress and hand.[29]

The scene was an extraordinary forerunner to the musical *My Fair Lady*, which was to prove Cecil's most famous stage and film work. He dressed his sisters up, took them to the ball and passed them off as princesses. Queen Victoria's daughter, Princess Beatrice, the patron of the evening, was heard to say: 'Oh look at those lovely girls',[30] a scene very similar to the arrival of the Queen of Transylvania. Then the actress Zena Dare sent a messenger to Cecil asking him to design for her. Nothing came of that in 1926, but he dressed her as Mrs Higgins at Drury Lane thirty-two years later. No wonder he understood the Lerner and Loewe production so well.

Mrs Braham had arranged for Cecil to submit designs to C.B. Cochran for a Cochran revue. With the photographs of his sisters in many of the newspapers the next day, it seemed an auspicious moment for Cecil to beard Cochran in his office. He was disappointed to find 'a very ordinary little man ... just like the provincial manager with cigar, whisky and soda and talking about pretty girls'.[31] He asked if Cecil knew anything about the West Indies, the Bermudas, the vivid colours, the blues, the yellows. Cecil merely said: 'Oh, lovely.' He asked Cecil to submit some designs for bathing dresses in a week's time, but warned him: 'They must be suitable for modern dancing, high kicks, cartwheels and splits!'[32] Cecil was disappointed – 'a bathing suit of tinsel and nothing more! How vulgar and commonplace.'[33]

Cecil tackled his Cochran work without inspiration, but was pleased to meet him and his wife a few days later at the party Seymour Hicks* and Ellaline Terriss† gave for their daughter Betty's coming-of-age. Seymour Hicks gave him quite a boost by rushing up to him when he was dancing with Angela du Maurier to enquire: 'Are you Cecil Beaton? Well I must shake hands with you. I've heard such a lot about you, the brilliant things you've said. Why you are the wittiest young man in London. Whenever I'm feeling dull, Betty suggests sending for Cecil Beaton. Be amusing, my young man. I wonder what you've said about us all tonight.'[34]

Cochran told him to bring his designs in the next day, so in a last-minute panic Cecil polished off several sketches. Cochran liked some but not all. A fish curtain appealed a lot, but overall he remained non-committal. Months of delay, raised hopes and suspense followed until Cochran wrote to say he would not be using any of the designs. However, when Cecil next went to the Pavilion he spotted that several of his designs had been pirated. There was nothing he could do as he had never had a firm contract (something he would never let happen again). This was a serious blow because, since his spell in the office, his small allowance from his father had been stopped. His only source of income was the small sums he got from photographs published here and there. Meanwhile he was haunted by debts, including a £25 Cambridge tailor's bill and another £7 owed for frames for the Wembley exhibition.

*   *   *

* Sir Seymour Hicks (1871–1949), actor-manager.

† Ellaline Terriss (1871–1971), Gaiety actress, daughter of William Terriss, the actor, who was stabbed to death in the Adelphi Theatre by a poverty-stricken mad actor in 1893. William Terriss was also a sheep farmer in the Falkland Isles. Ellaline was born at the Ship Hotel, Port Stanley.

In February 1926 the Beatons left Hyde Park Street, to Cecil's deep chagrin because the house marked: 'our development into the sun, the coming forth from Hampstead'.[35] At a farewell party he forbade Nancy to dance with any of Reggie's friends. Meanwhile he concentrated on Allanah Harper, because 'she has got beyond social parties of this sort',[36] and Madge Garland, *Vogue's* fashion editor, 'who looked perfect in a most lovely costume by Nicole Groult, very influenced by Marie Laurençin, in pale blue and pink'.[37]

The family moved to 61 Sussex Gardens, W2. 'It's not a nice house,' thought Cecil, 'and a horrible neighbourhood of Paddington.'[38] Cecil succeeded in avoiding taking a new job by supervising the decoration of the new house. He longed to have it all his own way, but his mother was over-economical and his father soon complained that the heavily gilded rooms made the house look like a gin palace. If he did not always have a free hand downstairs, Cecil made up for it in his own room. He painted lilies on the peppermint walls. He acquired a four-poster bed, which he draped with curtains of scarlet and gold stencilled silk and covered with a bedspread of puce-pink silk, edged with gold. The bedroom curtains were oilcloth, the colour of red sealing-wax. A journalist, who saw the room later, wrote: 'One could not call it a restful room, but it certainly was as original as its occupant and designer.'[39] To his surprise Cecil found the family had acquired a dog. 'It's such a sterile waste of time and when we are trying to reduce the staff it is an absurdity to add a dog to the establishment.'[40]

Simultaneously Cecil expanded his list of contacts. Mrs Whish of the *Daily Express* invited him to take photographs for her social column at 10/6d a picture. Cecil called on the critic, Raymond Mortimer, and admired the colours and modern pictures in his flat. They walked over to see Clive Bell in Gordon Square and shared a taxi to Victoria: 'Clive Bell is podgy and arty and one imagines an awful old rake, fond of a good laugh, a good glass of wine and a good ——! [*sic*]'[41] Arriving at Mrs Brennan's, Cecil reached for his share of the fare. Clive Bell said: 'No. Don't bother to fumble for money',[42] while the less generous Mortimer reached out for a florin from the pile in Cecil's hand.

At Allanah Harper's party at the Gargoyle Club he met Zita Jungman and 'there was really a good feeling of mutual understanding'. Allanah invited him to lunch at Boulestin's where he had never dared to go ('It's so expensive! Still Allanah's terribly rich so that's all right').[43] He met Lady Eleanor Smith, 'terribly alert and sharp like a bird'.[44] While delighted to enter this world, Cecil still admired his friend Boy Le Bas who had left home for a flat in Golden Square, in Soho, and seemed to relish every moment of the day. Meanwhile Cecil found himself surrounded by dull fools, who craved only comfort! 'I'm doped with society,' he wrote, 'a silly liking for fame which I know is ridiculous as I so loathe the mob.'[45] He contemplated the uncertain future:

I didn't want to be stamped an actor, out of snobbery. I didn't want to be stamped this or that. Least I should like to be stamped a photographer. Oh! I didn't know what to do. I felt so thoroughly weak and unenergetic to decide anything in case it wouldn't be a success. I wondered how long it would be before I was plonked somewhere else.[46]

He was right to worry. Time was running out. Cochran having failed to produce anything or even pay him for his work, the future looked empty. At breakfast on Saturday 10 April his father asked him if he had found a job. Cecil had hardly begun to say, 'I'm afraid not', when his father interrupted with the news, 'Well, if you haven't I have. Mr Schmiegelow will take you in his office. You start on Monday morning at half-past nine and get £1 a week and I'll leave you to work your way up from the bottom.'[47]

Cecil was furious, but beaten. He resented not only the choice of office but the fact that his fate was due to the chance that his father had read Arnold Bennett's essay 'Father's Sons' in a Sunday paper, which related how Swiss hotel proprietors sent their sons to neighbouring hotels for experience. He was miserably depressed. He resolved to escape as soon as possible. If he could get work he would plonk £1 down on Schmiegelow's desk and walk out. He was spurred on to new energies, praying that a miracle would happen and he would be spared his fate. On the Sunday he met Paul Cohen-Portheim, a 'little frog of a Jew',[48] who offered to help him get some work published, but it was too late. Cecil tried a last-minute argument with his father that night but to no avail. He was handed a slip of paper with the address of his new office and that was that.

All very unfortunate. A misunderstanding that will never be understood. I didn't say anything at breakfast, just munched and felt rather uneasy with that nasty empty throbbing feeling in one's stomach. I had to go to this office evidently.[49]

Cecil presented himself at Schmiegelow's office, full of deep resentment. His father was content that he should start at the bottom of the business world, but Cecil could not understand why he was not allowed to start at the bottom of his own world. On Cecil's first day Mr Schmiegelow took him out to lunch at the Holborn Restaurant. He won Cecil's respect by letting him know that he understood what the young man was going through – his distaste for business and business methods – how there was no real friendship when money was at stake – how he loved art – but how, sadly, life was ultimately governed by hard cash. Cecil thought him 'thoroughly decent'.[50] But he soon discovered that Schmiegelow was not a worker. He often disappeared for a game of tennis, returning to the office pretending he had seen a number of firms. Cecil could never bring himself to enjoy working in this office, but he had a soft spot for Schmiegelow's staff and this was reciprocated. They helped him learn to type and do invoices, and they instilled into him a rudimentary idea of how a small business is run. When he made mistakes they let him off lightly. They knew he did not belong in their world and they told him so. They urged him to achieve other goals. Nor did they seem to mind when he wrote his diary in the office or (later) retouched photographs in office time. Miss Robertson was 'rather a nice old bird, very motherly and very feminine and giggly'.[51] In cases of emergency she panicked dreadfully, screamed and lost her head. Mr Skinner talked a lot about art and asked Cecil about prices. Cecil found him 'sensible and so business minded'.[52] When Cecil told them he sent photographs to news-papers, Mr Skinner was thrilled. He instantly rang up the *Sporting and Dramatic News* on Cecil's behalf and negotiated a fee of two guineas for a photo of Peggy Broadbent. Cecil sent off a most professional invoice.

Cecil's arrival at this office had the good effect of spurring him to greater efforts on his own account. He took to visiting the British Museum in his lunch hour to snatch a look at costume books. He went to see the American photographer, Helen MacGregor, in her studio – 'she is rather like an apple that has been kept rather a long time in a loft'[53] – it was she who gave him the idea of taking photographs of sitters reflected in piano tops. In the evenings, although he was tired, he worked on scale drawings of designs of eighteenth-century opera costumes. He tried out new photographic ideas on his sisters, whom he often found sullen and unwilling models. They got bored having to wait patiently in uncomfortable positions, with heads upside-down or looking in different directions. Cecil found a Victorian dome in the Caledonian Market. He forced Baba to pose under it though she almost wept with aggravation. He refused to bribe her with a sixpence as had been his early habit because photography was expensive enough with-out that. Finally he achieved from his little sister a 'marvellous, subtle and amusing'[54] expression. He worked hard and discovered that, despite the 'damned office',[55] he felt alive and aware. Even so he took out his resent-ment on his parents, and this was a period of bitter family rows. At its worst moment Mr Beaton shouted at Cecil 'like a cross crabbed old woman. His voice was pitch pent full of absolute hate and fury.'[56] For a time Cecil and his father did not speak.

On 27 April Allanah Harper took Cecil to an early performance of Edith Sitwell's *Façade* after a 'crude little dinner' at the Blue Cockatoo in Oakley Street, which cost him three shillings. Cecil had first seen Edith in Cambridge in May 1925 when she had come up to talk on modern poetry and to harangue the critics. He had been impressed by how natural and sincere she was, and he longed to meet her. His unpublished account of this occa-sion differs somewhat from his frequently quoted description:

The Chenil Galleries were crowded with arty people and not a seat to be had in the place. There were masses of people standing and we had to stand. Everyone seemed very thrilled and expectant: the artiness of the place was terrific. The poems started. They were recited through a mega-phone put through a hole in a painted scene representing a face, and they were accompanied by modern music by Walton.* I rather liked the music. I rather liked the poems but I felt too restless to settle down properly to understand them. There were too many distractions – arty people moving about and arty people in the outer room talking loud.[57]

He spotted Augustus John, Harold Acton, Alison Settle, Dorothy Todd, Madge Garland and the Jungman sisters, Zita and 'Baby', and Georgia Sitwell, whom he thought smug and flashy. He concluded:

I found the programme much too long and monotonous and didn't bother or couldn't concentrate to listen to the poems towards the end. The reception was extremely friendly and enthusiastic and the Sitwells were only too delighted to give repeated encores.[58]

Allanah took him and a group of friends to the Eiffel Tower for supper, where Cecil observed Lady Milford Haven getting very drunk and the arrival of Tallulah Bankhead with a Sapphist: 'I loathe actors and actresses. They are acting their entire life on and off the stage and it is so unfresh and so aggravating.'[59]

Cecil took to visiting publishers in his lunch hour. Through his Cambridge friend Billy Williams (the author, Robert Herring), he had met J.C. Squire, the poet and man of letters. Squire sent him to see Robert Longman, the chairman of Longmans, and told him that Cecil had been in an office for six weeks now and still did not know what was being sold. Cecil was commis-sioned to do the cover for Robert Herring's book, *The President's Hat* (in which he found a number of remarks that he had made at Cambridge quoted directly). The fee was four guineas, thanks to Squire's recommen-dation. Cecil then resolved to write a *Book of Letters*, but the idea came to nothing. He thought of becoming a writer: 'I'm sure once I got the habit I should be successful and enjoy it.'[60] He also conceived the beginning of a life-long obsession to write a play. He visited more and more publishers and was pleased that whenever he got an appointment he was allowed by his office to keep it. 'I was quite accustomed to wandering about London with a portfolio and I didn't care a bloody damn if people did look at me – I was myself, Cecil Beaton, not a silly unsuccessful persevering artist.'[61] In the office he typed a draft article called 'The Triumph of the Charleston'.

Cecil had no money at this time and yet he felt he did well on nothing

---

* Sir William Walton (1902–83).

but personality, looks and reputation. He realized that not only did he waste his time at the office but that the people he used to think of as select party-givers were really very dreary and out of the main stream. He had funny dreams. One was that he saw a full-page photograph of his mother in the *Tatler*, but always he awoke disappointed for in reality few of the photographs he sent were ever used. He wished his mother would get on in society but felt his father was a drawback. Cecil thought his mother looked slimmer and younger than in Hampstead days, but 'has never thought about anything and is on completely the wrong end of the street about pictures, art, religion and anything really serious'.[62] Cecil knew he had to make a break, but as yet he could not find the way.

Cecil's lifeline was his fascination with his two sisters. Baba he thought 'the more genuine of the two ... completely definite and decided, sensitive and intelligent, observant',[63] while Nancy sometimes preferred opinions that she thought smart without really having felt them – 'very like me in fact',[64] he noted. He loved weddings, even 'dowdy' ones, and longed for the day when his sisters went up the aisle: 'I couldn't help picturing vividly the lurid scene when Nancy and Baba got married to some titled person and they appear looking marvellous in silver.'[65] Meanwhile he felt a bit guilty about influencing his sisters to think as he did.

Advice continued to reach Cecil from extraordinary sources. The Prince of Wales was guest of honour at a charity dinner at the Mansion House and, to Cecil's great excitement, he found himself seated next to the Prince's mistress, Freda Dudley Ward. She smoked twenty-five cigarettes during dinner and wore a scent specially made for her called 'white butterfly orchid'. They got on famously but, as she hated photographers, she told him to avoid that profession. She thought he should concentrate on acting, producing, designing and writing plays.

At the end of July 1926 Cecil went to see Schmiegelow to broach the matter of leaving the office. Schmiegelow said it was quite clear that he was not a bit interested in the work but thanked him for showing willing. He realized that Cecil's talents lay elsewhere. He offered to help in any way he could, particularly by talking to Cecil's father. Amidst much shaking of hands, Cecil bade farewell to Mr Skinner and Miss Robertson. Years later Cecil discovered that his father had paid Schmiegelow the pound a week he gave Cecil as salary.

Boy Le Bas urged Cecil to make a clean break once and for all:

If you *really* feel fed up why not do something about it: go away *quite* by yourself & decide what you want to do and then do it entirely without reserve – widening into the subject instead of eating up one's own substance – anyway I'm finding that works.[66]

As it happened, Cecil had conceived the plan to accept the invitation of the journalist Alison Settle to go to Venice. He therefore wrote to Boy asking if he could borrow the necessary money if his father refused to pay:

> I want to go to Venice for a soul's uplift, to rid myself of London and the family for a bit and think, also to get in with other people through this woman, a very nice woman, middle class but pure, good and definitely aware and alive.... It is my last week at the office and I'm feeling alert and as observant as any poor relation up to London for a short trip.[67]

Returning from holiday with Peggy Broadbent and her family at Etretat, Cecil found a scribbled note from Boy: 'Sorry, can't lend you the money as I haven't got it.'[68] He was livid and a death-knell sounded for their friendship.*

He then tried to borrow from Peggy, but without success. When he joined his mother in Sandwich, she was livid when she heard that he had tried to borrow from a young girl: 'I went to bed really awfully unhappy, realizing for the first time that I was not after all going to Venice this year, that I would not be meeting my saviour.'[69] Nancy and Baba sweetly offered their savings. In the end, the only solution was to write to his father.

The letter written, Cecil sat nervously by the telephone, feeling sick with nerves each time it rang. At last it was his father who, after giving him a brief lecture, said that if it was a pleasure trip he would have to decline but 'if you do think there is a chance of something coming out of it, I'll let you have the money'.[70] Cecil was thrilled but apprehensive:

> I so hoped Venice would bring something big to me, I'd be able to repay all the money I owed and help in many other ways. How silly of me to have said, and said not only once but often to Nancy, 'What fun it will be when I get lots of money and am rich to show off in front of Daddy and be thoroughly extravagant and overtip taxi-drivers.[71]

Two days later Cecil was on the train in the company of Alison Settle of *Eve* and Mrs Whish of the *Daily Express*. Mrs Whish brought along her fourteen-year-old daughter, Mary Diana ('a fresh little dumpling'). Cecil wore a pink

---

*Boy Le Bas later dropped Cecil completely because he represented a worldliness that no longer appealed to him. There was an unfriendly chance encounter in 1930 which caused Cecil to conclude: 'Now he may be a great painter but it seemed that he was no longer a person at all. His mouth was horrid, feminine and precious, his voice dull, his phraseology humdrum to a degree' [Diary, 30 May 1930]. Boy dedicated his life to painting. Due to his friendship with Mrs Unwin he became estranged from his family, but after her death he became close to his one surviving sister. In later years Cecil heard rumours of his high blood-pressure, drunkenness and failing memory. He made no effort to get in touch. After Boy's death on 18 November 1966, Cecil concluded: 'Boy was not in fact a very nice character' [Diary, 27 November 1966].

flannel scarf proudly round his neck and, as the train rattled on and the journalists gossiped, he succumbed to a bad headache: 'It throbbed and piercing pains went right through my head. It was agony!'[72]

He was disappointed that the sun had already set when the train rolled into Venice on the evening of 23 August 1926. The weary group was met by Mrs Whish's friend, Ivy Van Someren,* a lady who many years earlier had given a home to Frederick Rolfe (Baron Corvo) and was now eking out a living in the *Daily Express* office in Venice. She yapped at porters in Italian and steered the travellers past many hazards to the Casa Petrarca, a moderate but iron-gated hotel on the edge of the Grand Canal. Cecil crawled under his mosquito net and attempted sleep while a horde of English trippers tried to make conversation with a parrot under his window.

The mission of Mrs Settle and Mrs Whish was to report the forthcoming costume ball which the Baroness d'Erlanger was giving in the Fenice Theatre. Cecil had been allowed to come along for the trip and his mission, declared or otherwise, was to 'get in' with the d'Erlanger set. He also had photographs and designs with him in case these could be used to get him some work.

On the first day the little group set off to explore. They made a funny team: the eager Cecil running on ahead with Mary Diana, the two lady journalists struggling to keep up and the inevitable flock of starving cats following in their wake. Their sightseeing included a trip to the Lido. The steamer passed the island of San Sérvolo where the lunatics were kept. 'It's almost worth being a lunatic to be sent to such a lovely place.'[73] The Lido, on the contrary, he thought 'horrid, bare and ugly like Ramsgate',[74] but he cheered up when they reached the Excelsior Hotel. Settling down in the terrific heat to admire the passing spectacle, Cecil's only regret was that his red-and-white bathing costume had a top to it. The other men wore 'small little trousers, the smaller the better. I would buy a pair immediately.'[75]

On the following day the group visited the Palazzo on the Grand Canal occupied by Baroness d'Erlanger's daughter, Baba, the Princesse de Faucigny-Lucinge. They found themselves in a magnificent room over 150 feet long, hung with red brocade. The journalists went into her bedroom, but Cecil had to wait outside, inspecting the books and records and the brand of cigarette they smoked. Then they went off to see 'the scarlet-haired Baroness',[76] who was in the garden gilding stone pumpkins with her lover, Bertie Landsberg. Mrs Whish asked to borrow some clothes, but Lady Diana Cooper had just walked off with the few remaining ones. 'I had no look in whatsoever,' wrote Cecil. 'I was disappointed. I wouldn't get a look in with the d'Erlangers. That was certain. They were too busy with their business and they were surrounded with their

*Ivy Van Someren, wife of Dr Ernest Van Someren. Daughter of the American Horace Fletcher, a famous food faddist who believed people should only eat when hungry.

own friends.'[77] This realization was followed by another afternoon on the Lido beach after which Cecil suffered bad sunburn. That night he lay in bed under the mosquito netting, doused in cream which mingled with the sand on his body. The Italians made a frantic din outside – 'such excitement that one might have thought a murder had been discovered. It was only very likely two men saying "what a nice day it has been. I hope it will be as nice tomorrow".'[78] After hours of 'absolute Hell', Cecil finally got to sleep.

The next day there was a chaotic rehearsal for the ball, at the end of which Cecil got saddled with a huge box containing Mrs Robin d'Erlanger's dress (which somehow got mislaid to her rage). He began to wish he had not come. He hated Mrs Settle and Mrs Whish and the young d'Erlanger flappers. Only the sight of Lady Diana Cooper at Florian's caused him any joy: 'When one sees her after a long time she almost takes one's breath away with her complete loveliness and she knows how to make the very best of herself.' Lady Diana was with the eccentric composer Lord Berners, 'a ridiculous-looking man – like a particularly silly tailor's dummy'.[79] At the next table sat two Bright Young Things, Loelia Ponsonby ('who is very amusing')[80] and Zita Jungman (who 'would be so beautiful if her mother would allow her to make herself up').[81] Meanwhile Cecil sat on the outside with the two journalists. Zita remembered him and asked him to dance with her 'on the scrumptious floating raft',[82] but Cecil could not escape.

Worse was to follow. At the dress rehearsal Cecil appeared with his camera to find an official photographer at work. He was treated like dirt and pointedly not offered any sherry. He asked Baba Faucigny-Lucinge if he might photograph her, explaining that he was an amateur. Reluctantly she agreed but was far from co-operative thereafter. He ended up with three photos. He smarted 'with fury' at the way he had been dealt with and the way the d'Erlangers assumed the ill-treated journalists would turn their 'failure into a triumph' in the newspapers. For these reasons, Cecil decided to judge the pageant ball harshly.

Cecil thought the ball itself looked very beautiful and that the costumes were original and well made. He wore a white and silver page's uniform run up by Ninnie and made up his cheeks to be scarlet. 'It was beautifully cut and very tight and short and it showed to full advantage my willowy figure',[83] he wrote. But apart from that the arrangements were something of a fiasco. Crown Prince Umberto was expected and there could be no dancing until he arrived. Then, because he did not feel inclined to dance, no one else was allowed to. Because of the presence of royalty, no masks could be worn and Lady Diana was forced to go home in a fury and swap her white dress for a crinoline and turban that she had already worn at Count Volpi's ball. There was a dreadful crush at the buffet. Loelia Ponsonby and Zita Jungman were far from pleased with the hideous costumes the Baroness had allotted them. The two lady journalists were fêted by some rich Americans and Mrs Whish became distressingly noisy.

Mrs Whish filed a report to the effect that the ball was the most beautiful function for centuries, while Cecil wrote a treacherous letter to a friend on the *Daily Graphic* telling the true story of the Pageant. 'I felt dreadfully unsuccessful and venomous and hated being a nobody or back number while all these brainless fools were having such a triumph.'[84]

During the next few days Cecil remained an observer on the outside. He crossed to the Lido in the same steamer as Lady Diana Cooper and Lord Berners and listened in to their conversation. They all talked at the top of their voices while Lady Diana told them that the food was so bad at the Excelsior that she now did her own cooking. Her chief successes were eggs and spaghetti. They spoke of a riotous party the night before and Cecil thought enviously that they behaved 'like silly children. Lady Diana was delighted with her performance in the boat.'[85] Cecil also spotted Baron de Meyer, whose work had influenced him considerably:

> I adore his photographs but he is revolting himself, so like a silly affected woman, swaying at the hips, displaying his hands and puckling up his nose and mouth and talking incessantly of lady's fashions.[86]

Time passed and, though Cecil continued to lie on the Lido, his conscience weighed heavily upon him. How could he justify his visit to his father? Who would save him?

> I was getting desperate. Cooped up with journalists, I saw no chance of meeting the saviour. The journalists are sucked up to in private but not really received. I got hold of Miss Gibson [an American journalist] to try and get me an interview with Diaghilev – but she's such a vague casual sloppy person that I didn't think it would come to anything. I gave her no peace at all.[87]

However, this plan showed some signs of working, so Cecil rushed back to Venice to get his portfolio of drawings and photographs. He made the mistake of attempting a short-cut back to the hotel with the result familiar to many visitors to Venice: he got totally lost and had to start again. At the hotel he hurriedly made himself 'as pretty' as he could, before racing back to St Mark's Square.

Miss Gibson and a nervous Cecil waited in vain for Diaghilev to appear: 'It was a dreadful scene – two wretches waiting unsuccessfully for someone to turn up.'[88] As seven o'clock passed Miss Gibson went off to send him a note. Cecil waited 'just on chance':

> Oh! God there he was. I rushed up and spoke in English, a marvellous fat pale man, such a funny face and so smartly dressed, and with him was Lifar, so young and smartly dressed too – both in superb white

flannel trousers and blue double-breasted coats with tuberoses in their buttonhole. Diaghilev was as quiet and meek as a lamb – He was rather nice – so furry. I can't think what animal it is he reminds me of – perhaps a mole – perhaps a very nice monkey. He is like a baby – very fat and dignified.[89]

Diaghilev examined the entire portfolio without saying a word, but insisting on seeing every design. Finally Cecil asked his advice on some. Diaghilev knew at once where each design went wrong. Sometimes he said 'nice', sometimes 'original'. Then he asked, 'You take photos too? Yes, I like this. It is very curious.'[90]

At the end of the interview Cecil thanked Diaghilev for his time and Diaghilev in turn thanked Cecil profusely. 'We all shook hands and he walked away. That's that! That's useless!'[91] He was in despair. Alison Settle reassured him later that the meeting had not been a failure, that Diaghilev would now know who he was in the future. But he never saw Diaghilev again, though on later visits he used to see Serge Lifar, who recalled the young unknown Cecil as 'très chic, très snob'.[92] Cecil spent his last day in Venice carrying a huge portfolio in the hope of running into Lord Berners and proposing himself for the scenery of one of his ballets. In the end he was too afraid to go directly to Lord Berners' cabana, where he feared he would also find the Duff Cooper crowd and 'would be treated like dirt and no good would come of it'.[93]

Cecil left Venice in a depressed and miserable frame of mind. In the train he asked his neighbour if he might glance at the papers, which were full of nothing but a picture of Lady Diana Cooper feeding the pigeons in St Mark's Square. He felt guilty that his expedition had cost his father £30 and had come to nothing.

7

The Breakthrough

I like publicity and it's necessary to me and no one has taken any notice of me in Venice – treated me as dirt. Wait till I have success with my play! Then I'll ignore Lady Vyvyan.* It all went to show I must be thoroughly energetic, work hard and have a success and then I'll turn the tables on these damned journalists and have Lady Vyvyan grovelling on her knees to me.

Cecil's diary, 7 September 1926

Thus wrote Cecil on his return to London. His only success was the promise that his picture of the Princesse de Faucigny-Lucinge would appear in the *Tatler*. His father, however, welcomed him back and thought he looked well. Then Jack Gold reminded him that they had a plan to write a play together. Cecil told Jack of his adventures and they decided it should be based on Mrs Whish and all the society secrets that she knew. 'Let the *Times* social column go to hell for ten days. ... Please be thoroughly engrossed ...', wrote Cecil. 'We will be able to rush about in Hispano Sweezers [*sic*] wearing green hats and covered in scent if the play is a success.'[1] Again Cecil confronted his father with the idea. 'My next mad plan is to write a play,' he said. Mr Beaton listened quietly and when Cecil assured him he could afford to go to the West Country thanks to some money from photographs, he said, 'Good. Well then, all right. Go ahead then.'[2]

Jack Gold and Cecil set off for Mrs Childs's boarding-house in Charmouth, Devon, on 13 September 1926 with grandiose schemes about having Lady Curzon and Laura Corrigan in boxes for the first night of their play. But soon, as with many a collaboration, they found working together a trial. Each morning Jack had his breakfast and then an hour later he had his bath, while Cecil yearned to make an early start. Jack wanted the play to be a melodrama; Cecil wanted only the three characters already invented. Jack did not like Cecil to smoke; Cecil hated Jack's suggestions but did not wish to be

* A lady connected with the *Tatler*.

discouraging. By Friday Jack had had enough of Mrs Childs's establishment and said he was leaving. Cecil was secretly delighted.

As soon as Jack had gone, Cecil went off on his own to read and to swim: 'I bathed naked and the idea of my lean body kicking energetically in the cold water pleased me.'[3] Mrs Childs gave him good lunches but talked to him excessively, thinking he must be lonely. He then began to draft a tragedy based on Beaton family life. He worked on this late into the night but, being alone, his imagination played tricks on him and he was quite scared going up to bed. Cecil stayed on until the following Friday when his money ran out. He worked extremely hard, which was never a problem if he enjoyed what he was doing. For all the work done, Cecil's first attempt at a play – *A Charmed Circle* by 'Ada Mallowes' – never got past the first act. After Charmouth Cecil went to stay with his Cambridge friend, John Hill, returning to London 'penniless' on 28 September. Cecil's debts were considerable:[4]

His father	£20 }	Venice trip
His mother	10 }	
Webster & Gerling	8	theatre tickets
Peers	9	decoration of bedroom
Burnet	5	bed materials
Kyrle Leng	4	photographic materials
Boy Le Bas	3	a cupid
Hills & Saunders	10/–	Cambridge photos
Reggie	5	the journey back from Charmouth
His mother	4.10/–	photographic materials
	£69	

One or two people owed Cecil money for photographs that he had taken. He resolved to take a lot more pictures in order to clear his debts. This was the only lucrative source of income. He wrote later: 'At no stage of my photographic career could I ever have believed that photography could be my life's work. It was a fascinating hobby, made much more fascinating by the cheques I received for my efforts; but I felt I had become a professional photographer by accident.'[5]

Cecil was disappointed when one prospective sitter, John Fraser, let him down: 'Hell. I could have got a good deal of money for his photos. He's so thoroughly extravagant and would have been carried away with the photos because I would have made him look so young and beautiful.'[6] He decided to take Nancy instead. Together they created an elaborate background. Nancy wore her crinoline and Cecil arranged a bower of blossoms with a distance of tulle, tinsel and silver mackintosh. The screen was raised on three chairs. Stepladders were brought in, billiard cues rested on them, with bunches of Michaelmas daisies hanging from the cues; then a towel rack was turned upside-down on the top of one of the steps and a billiard cue fastened to another screen with string. Nancy sat on an upturned waste-paper basket. Cecil thought the whole arrangement 'just like one of those absurd Heath Robinson drawings "how to boil an egg" or something idiotic. Really this erection was a marvel of balancing!'⁷ Cecil's work was dogged by two problems. First the camera burst open and he had to retreat into darkness to fix the film. His sister Nancy confirmed that many of these sessions would be delayed as Cecil fumbled about with the camera in a bag or cursed the implement for its bad behaviour. He also hated the fiddly work of retouching and making duplicate prints. Second, Cecil's mother came in to say that she had a message from Aunt Cada in Birmingham. Violet Vanbrugh, the actress, might want him to design scenes for her new French play. 'Now then, Cecil,' said his mother. 'Do take your work seriously this time. Do for goodness' sake work hard and don't waste your time doing photographs.'⁸ Alas, when Cecil went to Selfridges to collect the results, he found the negatives badly underdeveloped.

Three days later Angela du Maurier came to pose. The Beatons were friends of Sir Gerald du Maurier, the distinguished actor-manager, who was born in Hampstead and lived at Cannon Hall. Sir Gerald was amused by Cecil's in-talk. He was particularly struck by the expression 'un-funny'. Cecil used to make Angela giggle a lot at dances: 'I tell her there's nothing so luscious as a candelabra or a piece of diamanté. She gasps and laughs.'⁹ He also noted with some prescience that her sister Daphne 'writes stories very cleverly'.¹⁰ Angela was then making a name as an actress. Cecil posed this bright and perky girl under his glass dome. On another occasion he photographed the two sisters together, a scene recalled by Angela du Maurier:

> I distinctly remember we went to be photographed by him in the nursery, and I rather think his helper was his old nanny. There was a lot of shilly-shallying with small cameras on tripods, and we thought it a heap of fun. The result was Daph's and my heads appearing magically under wine glasses. Certainly neither of us have ever had lovelier (or I'm afraid, more flattering!) photographs than these in the old days taken by Cecil in his advent.¹¹

Despite disappointments Cecil continued to work hard at his photography. Nancy and Baba were his most regular sitters, while his mother remained disapproving and reluctant to sit. He began to give ambitious lunch-parties, obliging Ninnie to disguise herself as the parlourmaid. He invited Madge Garland, lately of *Vogue*, 'Dadie' Rylands, Steven Runciman, Billie Williams and others. His mother helped him behind the scenes but was hurt when

Cecil's famous glass dome

he did not want her there. 'It is so silly,' wrote Cecil. 'One doesn't want to waste time making the silly conversation that Mummie makes.'[12]

Through Allanah Harper, Cecil was swept into the dizzy worlds of Brenda Dean Paul and Lady Eleanor Smith. The former danced 'energetic and hilarious' Charlestons, while the latter talked at a rattling pace and used 'extraordinary obsolete and long words'. At one of Allanah's tea-parties he met Inez Holden, who yearned to be photographed. Cecil duly photographed the girls. Already he had developed a certain style of behaviour. When Marie Novello put off their photographic session before a concert she was giving, Cecil wrote her a rude note saying it was a pity that she had missed her chance.

Cecil and Allanah went to tea with Madge Garland and Dorothy Todd,* who had been sacked from *Vogue* because, by making it too intellecual, the London office was losing £25,000 a year. Here he met such people as the artist William Rothenstein, the composers Constant Lambert and William Walton, and the Sacheverell Sitwells.

His first breakthrough came at an enormous tea-party at Allanah's on 10 November 1926. Everyone talked at the top of their voices and Cecil began by feeling rather out of it. He brought with him a picture of fawns that he had painted and sold to Allanah for two guineas:

---

*Dorothy Todd was in a weak position because she was a lesbian. Mercedes de Acosta jokingly described her as 'the bucket in the well of loneliness'.

My picture was discovered on the stairs and dragged up for universal applause, which rather embarrassed me. Also the photos of Allanah were shown and these were raved over. Wouldn't I take the others? Baby, Zita and Eleanor. I pretended at first not to jump at it, but I was really highly delighted. What fun. They certainly would get into the papers![13]

Not only was Cecil paid for the occasional photograph that was published, but Mrs Whish paid him for any society news he passed on.

On 18 November Zita Jungman and Eleanor Smith were due for lunch and Cecil was excited as Eleanor was 'so very saleable to papers – Lord Birkenhead's elder daughter!' He was put out that his guests were so 'casual and rude' in not arriving on time. Then he was even more put out when Eleanor forgot to appear at all. Nevertheless, with the aid of Nancy, a lot of photographs were taken of Zita.

Zita loved it and I did too. She loved doing her hair in various exotic ways and looked quite beautiful and quite extraordinarily funny. She is a perfect young lady. She has a completely different personality to anyone I know, thoroughly unflashy, quiet, but very original.[14]

Eleanor Smith came four days later with Zita's younger sister, Teresa, then always known as 'Baby'. They arrived when Blunt, the new butler, was dressing. Ever anxious to keep up appearances, Cecil had to devise a quick and elaborate plan to save the day:

I with terrific courage took my hat, rushed to the door as though going out, pretended to be thoroughly surprised and then explained I was just rushing out to send a telegram.[15]

Lunch was a great success with the two Bright Young Things shrieking and yelling with laughter. Upstairs in the nursery Baby began to taunt Eleanor: 'That's right, put on the well-known Lady Eleanor Smith wistful expression.'[16] The two girls teased one another like schoolchildren. Somehow a lot of photographs were taken, the girls ending up 'almost naked – just bits of gold tinsel round their middle ... one a dashing brunette, the other a dazzling blonde'.[17] Cecil was worn out at the end of it and his sisters' bedroom was a mass of lights, leaves and tinsel strewn everywhere. Sadly Cecil found that when he collected the negatives, he had often set the distances wrong and many were out of focus: 'Life is very hard for a climber,'[18] he noted.

Another sitter was his old friend Kyrle Leng: 'Poor Kyrle has gone off in looks. He used to be so beautiful and now he's got a mouth full of false teeth and the shape is quite wrong. It is pitiful.... I used to love him, but it's a terrible pity to see him now so ill, so unfresh and grey and looking really rather middle-aged trying to be young.'[19]

He took Baba and Nancy to a fancy-dress ball, where they won first and third prize respectively. Peggy Gordon-Moore, who was accustomed to winning, was as angry as Cecil was delighted. He observed his charges with pride, as they stood as still as waxworks, Baba in medieval dress, Nancy as a Winterhalter lady. He rushed off to the telephone booth to tell Mrs Whish the news and to inform her of other social details such as that Lady Dorothy Ashley-Cooper was wearing a sequin toque. 'I was like an old mother or nurse and kept rushing up to N and B making them do this and that ... planning how to stalk more reporters.'[20]

Cecil was invited to a party given by Mrs Richard Guinness, the mother of Zita and Baby Jungman. Cecil had never seen such a spectacle:

As soon as I got there I decided I would be one of the last to leave. Oh what fun it was, really quite marvellous, such a crowd.... What food! Too marvellous for words – oysters, caviar, pâté – pots and pots – great turkeys, hot kidneys and bacon, hot lobsters, the best meringues I've ever tasted, champagne flowing like water and a steady flow of marvellously amusing people.... I was busy tucking into food and busy making the best of every opportunity. Zita and Baby were rushing round having a very good time and not looking at all excited at having such a glorious party.[21]

He gazed in wonder at the guests – Gladys Cooper, Ivor Novello, Olga Lynn, Maureen Guinness and Tallulah Bankhead. Oliver Messel was doing his impersonations in one room, Richard Sykes playing the piano in another. The next morning Cecil passed on the news to Mrs Whish, which ensured that his taxi fares were paid. Now and then he would be given press tickets to attend a ball. He always rubbed the word 'PRESS' off the ticket.

Over the weekend Cecil and a very tired Baba (working for 5d an hour) settled down to enlarge the better portraits of Zita and Baby. Baba went to bed at ten and Cecil pressed on. Eventually he fell wearily into bed, leaving the prints dripping from a screen on the landing. In the morning they were brittle and curled up on the floor.

When Zita saw the results, she 'lay back in a chair looking at them for ages never speaking, just occasionally grunting a grunt of satisfaction'.[22] Cecil knew that Zita's and Baby's aunt was giving a dance that night. 'I happened to remark on purpose that I'd been badly let down tonight by Lady Alexander and wasn't after all going to Mrs Benjamin Guinness's dance. That was so maddening. The Jungmans were going and I hoped they would later ring me up to ask me to join them.'[23] Baby Jungman duly swallowed the bait and Cecil was presently on his way to the Embassy Club. Here he met and made friends with their formidable mother, 'Gloomy Beatrice'. She asked him to bring his photographs round and described them as 'like a handful of rose petals thrown in the sunlight'.[24] She said that one must be sent at once to the *Sketch*. It was clear to Cecil that Mrs Guinness was going to take him up: 'I feel that she will very likely be a great help to me and I'm delighted to have got in with her.'[25]

For a while now Cecil had lived with the realization that his mother's friends were 'the worst sort of people, dowdy, common and brainless'.[26] Even Lady Alexander fell from favour. He was embarrassed when he accompanied her to a charity evening: 'Tonight the old harridan rather repulsed me; I thought perhaps, like the people on the cinema, people would think I was being kept by her. It made me shy and I hated the party.'[27] Cecil was in many ways like a jack-in-the-box, continually jumping up, but failing to burst out. The lid had remained firmly shut in Venice, for example. However, in December 1926 there occurred two events which finally released the latch enabling Cecil to jump into the world he had so long admired from afar.

The first of these two events was a professional one, the first flowering of his career as a photographer. On 7 December Allanah brought Edith Sitwell and Madge Garland to lunch. Edith Sitwell arrived, 'a tall graceful scarecrow, really quite beautiful with a lovely, bell clear voice and wonderful long white hands'.[28] She had been lured to Sussex Gardens to see Cecil's photographs, to lunch and then to pose in her brocade dress and little jet hat. Cecil found Edith a natural sitter. He loved the fresh pink of her cheeks, her beautiful hands and her enormous ring. The more exaggerated the pose the more Edith loved it. Maurice Beck and Helen MacGregor had already photographed Edith lying down with hands clasped and eyes closed. Cecil tried similar poses. Edith went under the dome. She knelt on the floor, her knees and joints cracking, and said it was a Chinese torture. Cecil wrote:

> What fun but I had agony with the camera going wrong, the film getting stuck and it being impossible to wind further.... I prayed to God – a thing I never do now, that the film might be all right. I had to keep rushing to my room pulling down the blind and unrolling the films.[29]

When Cecil got the photographs he was disappointed to find Edith looking 'haggish', but noted that her hands were like 'ivory'. Taking tea with her a few days later Cecil spotted that she had a twinkle in her eye when talking to him: 'We get on well together. We have the same intimate flame within us. We are going to be friends.'[30]

Cecil now found his life taken up in a rush of photographic assignments. Inez Holden brought her friends in streams and hinted that she should get commission on each girl. These girls relished their photographic sessions. For them it was the latest 'in thing'. Meanwhile he tried to keep his mind on his new stunts: 'The cubistic background suited the hefty Miss [Sybil] Vincent very well indeed,'[31] he found. He experimented with new ideas of lighting, posing and backgrounds. Often the mindless chatter of the girls got on his nerves, but he tolerated them as they were the means to several ends. Once when entertaining a group of them to cocktails, he confessed secretly that he longed to turn them all out and get on with his work. As Christmas approached they all wanted more and more prints for presents.

One morning he was on the point of leaving for Peggy Broadbent's for a hunt ball (the prospect of which now bored him), when 'a lovely fat painted tulip' appeared on his doorstep. Cecil was in a panic but could not tell her to go away: 'Besides I wanted to take her. I'd get photos in the papers – Miss Tanis Guinness, daughter of London's most celebrated hostess, Mrs Benjamin Guinness. ... I enjoyed taking the girl. She is fat and lovely. She is rather like a stolid Greuze and that is rather fun I think. She has simply gigantic eyes with shiny long lids. She talks in a nice slow voice. . . .'[32]

The days before Christmas were intensely hectic. Besides a stream of lucrative developing and printing work, there was a string of parties at which Cecil met many people who were to be important friends for the rest of his life. At Madge Garland's party he met the actor Tom Douglas, Charles Fry of Batsford (again), Elizabeth Ponsonby and Cynthia Noble (later Lady Gladwyn), and a young man called Freddie Ashton who 'did rather shy-making imitations of various ballet dancers and Queen Alexandra, the sort of thing one is ashamed of and only does in one's bedroom in front of large mirrors, when one is rather excited and worked up ...'.[33] He was cautious of these new people. At Lady Wyndham's he talked to John Gielgud 'whose manner repulses me. It's so very stagey and unfresh, so suave, such a well-gradated voice.'[34]

Cecil had promised to deliver some photographs of Zita and Baby to the younger sister who was sitting for her portrait to Oliver Messel in a studio he had borrowed in St John's Wood. After an expensive taxi ride Cecil found himself in 'a forced atmosphere'. Oliver Messel, 'really rather nasty and trashy, though a good deal of brilliant superficiality', was busy painting an awful portrait of Baby's head:

Baby raved in an empty way about my photographs and I felt altogether not at all comfortable or at home. I was also a bit afraid of meeting a lot of snobby young men, who all knew one another very well and who were coming in to tea a little later. They are the sort of people who think more of one if one is a bit distant and so far I'd never met them – Brian Howard, the Queen of the troupe – with his floppy eyes and fish face. His voice so terribly cultured and affected. Oh God give me the open spaces and ploughed fields! The superficial smartness nearly made me sick – the slow sensual drawl of his speech – the awful things he said about Selfridges jewellery being so much more amusing than Cartier's! Oh gosh I was cold and quiet. . . . I rang up Allanah as I was expected there to tea. It was difficult to get away from here but I would go if I could. Troupes of smart people came to the telephone to say a word of love to Allanah.

It was disgraceful, insincere, disgustingly smart and was so dreadfully like the party in a Noël Coward play! Then someone said that Stephen Tennant was in London – screams and more telephonic rot.[35]

On the same day Cecil was delighted to find a long-awaited two-page spread about the Beaton home in Sussex Gardens, published in *Eve*. He thought it 'the most terrific triumph we've yet had in the press'.[36]

That evening, 21 December 1926, was the coldest night of the year. However, for Cecil it marked the second crucial step in his uprise. Everything he had aspired to for so long was suddenly his. The setting was a dance given by Tanis's mother, Mrs Benjamin Guinness:

> I enjoyed the party as here I met Stephen Tennant for the first time and I liked him enormously and I felt puffed with pride that he so gushed at me. I was already a name with him and he'd noticed masses of things I'd done and seen things about me in the paper and for years had wanted to know me just as I'd wanted to know him. We sat in a corner with Tanis and Meraud [Guinness] and talked wildly and made elaborate plans for photographs of us all to be taken doing ballets – matelots or something like that. We became thrilled and excited.[37]

Then Brian Howard came up and said that he too had always wanted to know Cecil:

> And when this afternoon he had, he was enchanted (a favourite word and he puts a horrid nasal accent-stress on the *chant*) but I had looked upon him with evident 'suspicion'! I felt very elated with praise and was so happy to think that after all I had built up for myself a reputation otherwise these smart young men wouldn't want to know me. It is right that I should have a certain opinion of myself, which I was gradually losing in that awful Holborn office, and being bullied at home.[38]

Stephen Tennant was to prove an important influence on Cecil, who now modelled his life on that of his fashionable friend. There was much for Cecil to envy in Stephen and his way of life. Born in 1906, he was the youngest son of Pamela, Lady Glenconner, one of the Wyndham sisters in Sargent's 'Three Graces'. His mother, a legendary beauty, had been widowed when Stephen was fourteen and had then married Viscount Grey of Falloden, the former Foreign Secretary. They shared a passion for wild birds, while she also fostered a love of poetry and literature, of her children and her home, Wilsford, near Amesbury. Of this Elizabethan-style manor house (built by Detmar Blow) Lady Grey's niece, Lady Cynthia Asquith, wrote: 'Wilsford, with its chalk streams, enchanted water-meadows bordered by the Avon, and the downs rising behind it in a natural amphitheatre, is one of the loveliest places I know.'[39] Here she brought up her children and welcomed to the house a wide circle of talented and cultured friends. For Osbert Sitwell and for Rex Whistler it became a second home. One of Pamela's literary works was entitled *The Sayings of the Children*, in which she recorded things her children said. Stephen is 'Four' in this little book, which proves that from an early age he was destined for his strange life as a poet and artist. His mother wrote of his telling stories in a voice 'filled with intonations of melting emotion'. While she cosseted and spoiled Stephen, his mother did nothing to toughen him up. Nor did she squash a cruel streak in him. As a child he stamped on one of his two goldfishes, explaining: 'I only wanted one.'[40] Stephen did some dramatic illustrations for her book, *The Vein in the Marble*, at a very young age and from then on, as Cecil wrote, 'he was brought up by his mother to be a genius'.[41] He was also allowed to live a semi-invalid life which, as Cecil again pointed out, 'encouraged him to evade the more unpleasant aspects of reality'.[42] Edith Olivier described him as 'the most sparkling talker' who ever came to her house 'and perhaps the most amusing', adding: 'He can be by turns poetic, malicious and nonsensical.'[43] He was also extremely funny, well read and possessed of a love of the exotic.

Cecil envied him his connections with the world of Bright Young People, artists, writers and poets. Stephen was very rich, while Cecil was very poor. Stephen was also very beautiful, like a youthful Shelley. A peppery admiral who once saw him in a restaurant in Soho declared: 'I don't know if that's a man or a woman but it's the most beautiful creature I've ever seen.'[44] He possessed a fantastic imagination which was to guide Cecil in many ways. He loved outrageous poses, photographs taken through splintered mirrors and drapes of rich fabric. While Stephen was far from short of ideas, he lacked the stamina to carry them out himself. Thus he was often the inspiration of an idea and Cecil its executor.

Nancy Mitford used Stephen's looks when describing Cedric in *Love in a Cold Climate*. Cedric's conversation was based on a mixture of Brian Howard and others. No sooner had he met them than Cecil was impressed at the complete self-confidence of both Stephen and Brian. They were oblivious to what people thought of them, while he minded the smallest slight. Similarly Stephen Tennant recalled: 'When I first met him, he was bursting with élan, éclat. Sparkle was life to him. He was only truly joyous when he had taken on much too much.'[45] Cecil went home elated with the thought of accompanying the Guinness girls and Stephen to the circus the next day. 'This is a great opportunity and the photograph orders of Miss Franks and that Jew can go to Hell.'[46]

On the following day Cecil made his way to the Gargoyle Club by bus as he only had a few shillings in the world. Presently they drove to Olympia in a large car belonging to Stephen's mother:

We talked so hard and had such great bonds of sympathy in common with one another. We were in an ecstasy of happiness. The only thing that slightly marred my pleasure was in wondering how far my ten shillings would go without my running short and being embarrassed. At the Gargoyle I made up an elaborate story about 'life' today having given me a nasty knock. I'd been brought down to worldly squalors as I'd had my pocket picked in the Christmas shopping crowd. This I thought a good excuse for not having come with money and for that reason I told it, but when I received heartfelt sympathies, I felt guilty and embarrassed that these people should be sorry and sympathetic for nothing.[47]

Cecil adored the circus itself, as they rushed about in an abandoned manner. He was so happy on the Great Switchback Railway that he thought: 'I wouldn't mind if I met my death on it. In fact I should very much like to die in such company.'[48] He was still aware of the difference in class between him and his new friends:

I admit I felt a little less un-selfconscious than the others. They were so earnest themselves about enjoying themselves and thinking about nothing else, but I, rather middle-class-ly, was noticing that people stared and glared and even laughed at us.[49]

When eventually Cecil went home, worn out with the thrills of the day, he noted, 'It was wretched to come back to a cold banal atmosphere.'[50]

Over the next two days Cecil worked hard at photography. He estimated that he would be quite rich after the Christmas rush. He had Nancy and Baba photograph him as a 1904 beauty draped in old-fashioned furs and sent these out as Christmas cards. And he worked away retouching his subjects, putting in eyelashes and making the lips curl until he was bored to distraction by the process.

The year 1926, therefore, ended considerably better than it had begun. At Tanis's and Meraud's New Year's Eve party he achieved the ambition of meeting Cathleen Nesbitt: 'a disappointment as I'd always held great opinions or illusions about her – she was one of my passions when I was fourteen. She was the lover of Rupert Brooke and tonight she was ogling me and being dull and silly.'[51]

The Peter Pan party came round again on 3 January 1927. This time Cecil dressed his sisters in outré mackintosh material. Baba was billed as Lady Mary Beaton:

Every year we have managed to get a bit of publicity out of it and this year we hoped to top even last year's successes. Everything was planned for tripping up reporters and for making news – the mackintosh material itself would make a very good story besides all the nonsense that could be made about children posing as their ancestresses and Baba as the Lady in Waiting to Mary, Queen of Scots, Lady Mary Beaton.[52]

– the sauce of terror, I mean. But the Mad Hatter's tea party simply won't be in it.'[58] The person destined for this grim experience proved to be none other than Baba Brougham, whom Cecil had met with his new friends and who would be at Wilsford for the long-awaited weekend. After the tea Edith wrote, 'Wasn't tea on Saturday one of the most appalling experiences of your life? It was of mine.'[59] These excitements had the effect that Cecil found his own home 'so unamusing' and pitied his parents' lives, 'so very uninteresting, sparkless and dim'.[60] One reason that Cecil enjoyed being a photographer was that it nourished the actor in him: 'Not only do I take photographs but I am an entertainer as well and this afternoon my performance was much appreciated and the audience laughed at all they should.'[61]

Life became 'a mad whirl'.[62] Cecil was commissioned to do two more book covers for Longmans, Ninnie finished making him a leopard-skin dressing-gown and his plus-four suit was ready: 'it is very hearty; a bit too so'.[63]

When his sisters were away at school, Cecil wrote to describe a successful lunch party on 12 January:

> Edith Sitwell came in a black toque from which fell masses of black lace, and a tweed dress. She dropped a little potato or spud off her plate onto the floor and grovelled for it becoming quite hysterical with laughter and saying that it was quite pardonable to drop a little potato as it looked so amusing and like a marble rolling along the floor. Baba Brougham came and nearly went potty with delight at my bedroom, she said she'd never seen anything so Jezebelesque, and I thought that such a good adjective. Others present were Todd and Garland, Billie Williams, whom Ninnie says is growing a moustache, Paddy Brodie and Brian Howard. The last two named smart young men had their photographs taken for hours before and after the meal. Really their vanity surpasses that of Ladies! I could hardly keep them away from the mirror, and after each photo they dabbed on a little more liquid powder, or rouge, or eyelash muck.[64]

Cecil felt it was a mistake to see too much of Brian Howard and Paddy Brodie,* nevertheless he agreed to join them for dinner at the Gargoyle. Here he found Charles Fry and Eddie Gathorne-Hardy as the other guests. They went on to a party and Cecil was surprised that all four declared their intention 'to find a man' and brought out powderpuffs. In the end, when Cecil found himself amongst a crowd that included Raymond Mortimer (looking like 'a poodle') and Nancy Cunard with wooden bracelets up her arm, he too donned make-up. Eddie Gathorne-Hardy was being made up by Brian Howard and in Cecil's opinion being ruined. So he had an altercation with Brian, scraped Eddie's make-up off and began again:

*Brian Howard and Paddy Brodie are generally thought to have been Evelyn Waugh's models for 'Anthony Blanche' and 'Miles Malpractice' respectively.

Brian, drunk and disorderly, shouted all sorts of very unpleasant names at me – such as harlot, shit etc. – and I, not drunk, was mortally offended and quivered with impotent rage. I was really upset and, although told by Eddie and others that I was the Queen of the Party, I felt my evening was not a success and I was miserable. Damn Brian. I hated him now.[65]

Cecil told Brian he would not attend his lunch-party and Brian went home in a huff. This evening's party was altogether something of a shock for Cecil. It was an extension of the kind of party he had relished at Cambridge, but it soon got somewhat out of hand:

I was falling for Eddie – so quiet and cold and unreal; his body looking as though it were made from pieces of a Meccano and his suit made of pale brown tweed that smelt nicely tweedy, his eyes like large hard boiled eggs, or doves or at any rate like the eyes in the Epstein portrait of Lady Drogheda, his voice like the cracking of coke and his neck pale and anaemic.... Ribaldry was rife and Eddie and I were thrown into a cupboard where most exciting thrilling things happened. My heart beat until it nearly burst. Eddie's face was sliding all over mine. His face was soft and like a peach, his skin felt, and he was doing thoroughly perverted things new to me, so thrilling and perverted that they were complete and quite unnecessary to go to bed or become conventionally lustful was it after the complete satisfaction of having one's ear licked – that is as far as we got mercifully – any farther and I should have been embarrassed. ... My heart strings had been racked for the first time after a very long interval and I was in the throes and agonies of being in love again.[66]

Cecil and Eddie shared a taxi home, but when Eddie wanted to come in, Cecil panicked. He paid his share of the fare and swiftly said good-bye. He crept nervously upstairs to bed.

Cecil went to Wilsford the day after his twenty-third birthday. He prepared for this by submitting himself to a strenuous massage, 'almost like a rape'.[67] The masseur had problems because his client was exceedingly ticklish. Finally he was in the stiff clay, hoping to emerge with a 'Paula Gellibrand mask'.[68] In due course he set off in the train with Dorothy Wilde, Oscar's niece, Steven Runciman, 'looking extremely foreign and intellectual',[69] and Baba Brougham, who told him that Stephen Tennant's mother was very beautiful and could recite the whole of Shakespeare and the Bible by heart. They arrived at Wilsford amid screams and yells of joy, and Cecil was reunited with Stephen, Zita and Baby. Cecil thought his whole visit 'like being at the most perfect play'.[70] He was overawed by Lady Grey, who told funny stories with a rare eloquence. One involved a woman who wanted to have diamonds put in her teeth in order to say good morning 'brilliantly'.

Stephen showed Cecil to his room: 'My dressing-gown caught his eye and he nearly went mad with joy of it and I was glad he liked it so.... I managed to let Dorothy Wilde see me in it and she too was amazed and enraptured.'[71]

Downstairs they played games and Stephen was 'quite brilliant – as brilliant as one is when one is tight – talking as fast as a rocket goes off and brilliant things slipping off his tongue ... no facile flashy superficial epigrams or Noël Coward rot, thank God'.[72]

Cecil made a good impression on the household. Lady Grey liked him for his good manners and allowed him to photograph her. She scrutinized the result with close attention: a heavy pearl earring looked like part of the ear; this must be rectified. Lady Grey was also concerned about her eye: 'A slight enlargement of the iris of the eye would diminish the white and improve the likeness and really be more like me,'[73] she wrote.

At eleven o'clock, on account of Stephen's ill-health, they all retired to bed and Cecil wandered around his room in a trance of happiness:

> I undressed and wore a flimsy pair of speckled pyjamas which completely went with the room. I wanted to eat all the books, and all the flowers and Stephen as well. I am sure I went to bed with a beam of happiness on my face.[74]

He could not but contrast all this with life at 61 Sussex Gardens: 'At home one is completely misunderstood – considered an idiot and a nuisance. Here one was treated like some divine and exquisite genius.' He went on:

> How glorious this was and if I hadn't made a move away from that rotten Holborn office I should still have continued in that rotten, miserable, unsuccessful, unhappy, undeveloped state. This weekend I considered a great moment in my life. I was at last among really lovely people, the sort of people I want to be among – not middle-class brainless idiots. These delightful people were perfection to me. I was gloriously happy and thankful.[75]

Cecil's only general worry was that his life still lacked a definite plan. He knew he had to press on with photography while he was 'all the rage'. He was sure he 'could really make masses of money once I started in a business way'.[76]

Stephen knew that Cecil had suffered from coming from such an uninspiring and unimaginative background. Cecil's mother had told Stephen: 'We don't want him to be a photographer.' Stephen observed:

> She could not surmise the dazzling career this was to give him. She was sweet but, frankly, not clever. His father was even less sympathetic. Cecil was a very keen organizer of his career to be. Sensible, matter-of-fact, his

love of beauty and the arts was, at first, not very noticeable. He adored parties and he liked many kinds of gaiety. His knowledge of the stage was amazing. ... One did sense in him rather ambiguous elements. He was not an open book, believe me."

Part Three

The Wild Years 1927–30

8

Cecil Masked and Unmasked

I think you had much better have a little house of your own somewhere or a studio and have intimate relations with T.S. Eliot and Virginia Woolf, Helen MacGregor, the Sitwells etc. etc. You would probably evolve a style of painting, or writing which would make you famous and rich.

Kyrle Leng to Cecil, *c.* 1927

Stephen Tennant became Cecil's keenest sitter: 'I want to be photographed drowned in picturesque rags, like this

or would it be too funny? A sham moon would be such fun. Your lighting always looks like moonlight any way and it is the loveliest I've ever seen in any photographs.'[1] Stephen invited Cecil to stay with him and his mother at their villa at St-Jean-Cap-Ferrat in March 1927: 'I can't tell you what it's like now! a sea like gentian glass – a sky of crystal clear Madonna blue, and flowers that make one shriek.'[2] He arrived bearing a portfolio filled with photographs of his sisters. He loved the 'theatrical' display of primulas, Bougainvillaeas, pansies, roses and tulips, and Lady Grey putting sprigs of peach blossom in the bird cages and talking about Emily Dickinson. In the daytime they drew and in the evening; they re-enacted biblical and historical scenes. One night they danced 'Les Biches', and Stephen gave such a star performance that the party was hysterical with laughter. Later Cecil described his stay as 'the first time life started to be nice to me after the sordid greyness of the years in that office'.[3] He made new friends at the villa, notably Rex Whistler and Edith Olivier, who would presently lure him to live in Wiltshire.

Edith Olivier appeared to Cecil 'a rather swarthy and formidable middle-aged woman wearing a tall purple pixie hat'.[4] Lady Grey explained: 'Miss Olivier comes of an old Huguenot family, and is a figure in the archaeological and ecclesiastical life of Wiltshire.'[5] Edith Olivier was one of the ten children of the Rector of Wilton and a first cousin of Laurence Olivier's father. She lived amongst a strange collection of objects in the Daye House, the former dairy house of the Wilton estate. Here she received all kinds of visitors, many of them the young and talented of the day, such as Rex Whistler, Lord David Cecil and the slightly older Siegfried Sassoon. She had a mystical side and claimed to possess second sight. She loved to read aloud and might take a group of friends to Stonehenge and read them the last chapter of *Tess of the D'Urbervilles*. She wrote stories herself, one of them, *The Love Child*, a delightful tale about a 'pretend' friend. She gave good advice. When A.G. Street came rushing in to show her his first novel – about the high life of Monte Carlo – she urged him to write instead about the countryside he knew and loved, and he set off on a much better tack. The author of *Farmer's Glory* even found himself lecturing on rustic matters in Canada and the United States.

Stephen Tennant recalled:

> Edith Olivier stimulated Cecil as no one else has done. Cecil loved her most appalling vitality, her writing a diary at 3.30 in the night.... She was utterly adorable.... She galvanized a man already galvanized by his own rare gifts. Her talk was a blitz of fireworks. Her interests were legion. ... She was Cecil's Egeria, Erda. She was all the muses to him.... She lived ten lives glowing with joyous, subtle appreciation.[6]

Cecil paid the first of many visits to the Daye House in May 1927. For some years he regarded it as his 'spiritual home'.[7]

The summer of 1927 reflected the world that Noël Coward parodied in his song: 'I've been to a marvellous party', two lines of which read:

> Dear Cecil arrived wearing armour
> Some shells and a black feather boa ...[8]

Costume balls and pageants filled every moment and Cecil took his full share of dressing up and designing. On 6 May the Great London Pageant of Lovers through the Ages took place at the New Theatre in the presence of Princess Mary and Princess Arthur of Connaught. Cecil designed Baba's Heloïse dress and several others. He went as Lucien Bonaparte in a pink satin coat with very long tails. Stephen Tennant was Prince Charming in a pink wig and had difficulty with Cinderella's slipper. Tallulah Bankhead was Cleopatra, but her dress got caught on one of the slave girls' wigs and nearly came off.

Oliver Messel attended as Bacchus and his sister, Anne Armstrong-Jones, as Ariadne. Gladys Cooper was Helen of Troy. The rehearsal was chaotic with champagne and sandwiches being served at 2 a.m. and Captain Evelyn Fitzgerald telling his wife, 'You'll be lucky if you get out of this by five o'clock.'[9] The actual performance was of course a wild success with unhappy lovers making their exits on opposite sides and Henry VIII's executed wives clasping their necks as they departed.

A little later in the summer Mrs Benjamin Guinness gave a costume party. Stephen tried to impersonate a beggar but was 'as elegant as a fairy', making a dramatic entrance in a billowing silver cloak which hid the rags beneath. Cecil came as a seventeenth-century dandy in pink satin and Oliver Messel in a similar costume. On 18 July there was a nautical party with Lytton Strachey as an admiral and Cecil in 'pale pink trousers and a white shirt with his rather long hair thickly powdered with gold dust'.[10] Such was the competition that Rex Whistler observed to Stephen Tennant:

Have you noticed that when a very smart fancy dress ball is impending and goading all of us to be deeply original and outstanding, Cecil says in a bored tone: 'Oh yes I love a fancy ball but I'm not taking much interest in this one – just a very dull outfit for me', while really he is designing a dazzling costume to emerge and eclipse us all dressed as a peacock?

In turn Stephen observed: 'You may think Cecil is listening intently to what you say. He isn't. He's counting the hairs in your nostrils as you speak.'[11]

Cecil was capable of making unkind remarks that were not forgotten. To Nancy Mitford he said: 'My mother thinks you are a beauty, but I'm afraid nowadays we only admire Clara Uriburu.'[12] Stephen Tennant recalled:

He made a lot of enemies soon after his 'sunburst' had electrified London. He said very sharp things, often witty and cogent but people hate being mocked. His extreme elegance of clothes stirred up much bad feeling ... and the society women (his prey) were not easy to net, because he saw too deeply into them, into all their exotic tricks and affectations. Very soon they deeply dreaded his 'lorgnette' fixed on their carelessness. ... Nothing impressed him very much. A great deal jarred on him. Soon they said 'Can I stand any more of this pungent suave watching me?'[13]

Cecil used to tell Stephen that he was always recreating himself in a better image. Lincoln Kirstein, who founded the New York City Ballet in 1934, remembered that Cecil spoke in an unnatural affected manner like Brian Howard. Beverley Nichols enjoyed describing Cecil's voice:

It was, and still is, one of the most astonishing sounds in the contemporary symphony. When he is serious it resembles the sounds made by an extremely fatigued corncrake, when he is amused it recalls an obscene laughing jackass. Nor are those the only birds whose cries his voice evokes. In moments of depression he has a seagull wail and when excited he can chatter like a spiteful starling. Oddly enough, though the voice is totally unmusical, it is not displeasing, but it is definitely an acquired taste.[14]

Cecil was soon included in Oliver Messel's repertoire of impersonations.

While Cecil's image amused the aesthetes, it aggravated the young bloods who watched his antics. They resolved to teach him a lesson. He had become friends with the Herberts: 'Sid', the heir to Lord Pembroke, and his younger brother, David, who described Cecil at this time:

Tall, thin and willowy, he had the most remarkable eyes; violet and piercing, set flat against his face and as far apart as a goat's. Each profile boasted a full-face eye. His hair was long for those days, light brown in colour and grew beautifully. Like Agag in the Bible, he 'walked delicately', unlike most Englishmen he used his hands expressively when talking.[15]

Cecil was duly invited to attend the coming of age of Lord Herbert at Wilton on Friday 5 August. 'Sid' Herbert had celebrated his actual birthday in January with a small party including Lord David Cecil, Freda Dudley Ward and Maureen Guinness. For this grander occasion in the late summer he had a house party of thirty-seven, including Robert Laycock, a young officer in the Royal Horse Guards, and Roger Chetwode. Friends gathered in the vicinity, Cecil staying with Edith Olivier at the Daye House. In *The Wandering Years* (though not in his diary at the time), Cecil gave an exaggerated account of how his evening became a nightmare.* The story goes that he was hijacked by three of the guests and 'catapulted into the darkness',[16] that he ended up 'hip deep in the Nadder',[17] and that, with characteristic courage, he returned to the ball, water running down his legs and oozing out of his shoes. David Herbert points out: 'It was summer and the river very low. He only got wet up to just below the calf.'[18] Both David and his sister Patricia (Lady Hambleden) remember seeing Cecil return to the dance and that their mother, Lady Pembroke, was rightly furious with the assailants. Robert Laycock (later a Major-General and Governor of Malta),† Roger Chetwode (son of the Field-Marshal) and 'Sim' Feversham‡ (the 3rd Earl who married Lord Halifax's daughter) were ordered to leave. Lord Herbert's son Henry (the present Earl) recalled that his father was very upset about the incident, particularly because Roger Chetwode was his closest friend. Next day Cecil went over to Wilsford with Edith Olivier and

---

* See *Self Portrait with Friends*, pp. 6–8.

† Laycock was, by chance, the friend and sometime commanding officer of Evelyn Waugh, another of Cecil's tormentors.

‡ It is a nice irony that 'Sim' Feversham's call to the Sinnington hounds was the cry, 'Greta Garbo, Greta Garbo'.

Etty Beaton with Cecil and Reggie, Langland Gardens

Cecil photographing his sister Baba

Lily Elsie, 1910

all my kindest thoughts
to you Lily Elsie

Cecil at Cambridge, 1922

Nancy (as Lady Mary
Carmichael) and Baba (as Lady
Mary Beaton), June 1927

The Sitwells, 1927

Daphne du Maurier, 1926

Nancy with her father at her wedding, 1933

Above, Cecil with
Stephen Tennant, 1927

Cecil dressed
as George IV

Marjorie Oelrichs

Adèle Astaire

Doris Castlerosse

Lilia Ralli

Marlene Dietrich in Hollywood

Peter Watson

Cecil and Peter Watson on their travels

Ashcombe table setting

Ashcombe: Cecil by the studio

Brian Howard to see some cinema films with Stephen and his party. He resolved never to mention the incident again.

Cecil's most important and most eager sitters were Edith Sitwell and her brothers, Osbert and Sacheverell. Edith posed as Botticelli's Primavera. On a sofa she sat in a Longhi tricorne resembling a Modigliani painting; on the floor she lay on a square of chequered linoleum disguised as a figure on a medieval tomb. Cecil went to Renishaw, the Sitwell seat in Derbyshire, to photograph her in the style of Zoffany, against tapestried backgrounds and taking morning coffee from a coloured attendant, as she sat in a four-poster bed wearing a turban plucking harp strings. Osbert and Sacheverell joined their sister in a series of ring-a-ring-a-roses heads amid much jollification.

Edith loved her photographs: 'I realize now that it was well worth while nearly dying of a rush of blood to the head,'[19] she wrote to Cecil. Later she grew even more enthusiastic: 'I simply can't tell you what excitement there is at Renishaw about the marvellous photographs – or what joy and gratitude. We are all, including mother, half off our heads with excitement. ... But Oh how well worth it was to turn green with terror at the top of that chest, to have such photographs as these. ...'[20]

Stephen Tennant also adored the photographs Cecil took of him: 'I am *nearly crazy* at their beauty,' he wrote on 30 August from Falloden. 'I can't believe that even for *one moment* I've looked as beautiful as this but I suppose you touch [retouch] them up brilliantly ... how flattering are they?? I cast desperate glances at the mirror while looking at them without very reassuring results. But I LOVE them!'[21] As early as July 1927, Stephen was describing Cecil as 'the King of *Vogue*'.[22]

Edna Woolman Chase, the formidable Quaker editress, who had created *Vogue* with Condé Nast out of Lucien Lelong's *Gazette du Bon Temps*, made a trip to London and Cecil came to see her recommended by Alison Settle, now editor of London *Vogue*. In her memoirs Mrs Chase recalled that his first contributions were caricatures of well-known London actresses or celebrated partygoers. Cecil might, for example, draw Gladys Marlborough with the caption 'How the Duchess of Marlborough wears her diamond and pearl tiara'.[23]

From now on and for the next eleven years a feature of *Vogue* was to be these 'fragile and spidery' caricatures, accompanying an article, later sometimes written by Cecil too. Mrs Chase recalled her first encounter with him:

> I remember the day Cecil first came into my London office – tall, slender, swaying like a reed, blond and very young. The aura emanating from him was an odd combination of airiness and assurance.
>
> He used a small amateur kind of camera and had no studio. When he had been working for a few months I one day asked him who did his

Gladys, Duchess of Marlborough, in her Russian tiara

developing for him. 'Oh, Mrs Chase,' he said. 'Nannie does it for me at home, in the bath tub.'[24]

As he became more successful, Cecil found it harder to keep up with the business of doing drawings for *Vogue*, writing letters, sending out bills (at £2 a photograph) and preparing enormous prints for the annual Photographic Salon exhibition.

In November 1927 he held his first exhibition at the Cooling Galleries in Bond Street, a mixture of photographs, drawings and stage designs. This required an intense period of hard work. Many glamorous sitters came to Sussex Gardens and Manley,* the butler, helped Cecil by holding heavy lights and then sliding down the bannisters to open the front door. Tallulah Bankhead was pictured against a background of balloons, Sheila Milbanke under the glass dome, Tilly Losch in a tree-trunk. Paula Gellibrand, an early heroine who had become the Marquise de Casa Maury, remembered Cecil posing her in front of a mauve-green curtain and complaining in the excitement: 'But you're *just not* taking it seriously.'[25] Fortunately Paula proved a good natural sitter. Her beautiful profile and exquisite hands lent themselves well to any pose, though Cecil forbade her to smile. In the foreword to the catalogue, Osbert Sitwell described Cecil as 'the stern Nemesis who transmutes his various sitters into so many flowers, simple or orchidaceous'.[26] He recalled an incident in which Cecil was poised on a ladder and fell,

* Stephen Tennant recalled that Cecil was very amused that the family had employed butlers called Loins and Manley.

entangling the three Sitwells, the ladder and the camera in an inextricable confusion'.[27] One who refused to sit for Cecil was Virginia Woolf. On 5 October she declined rather formally: 'Unfortunately I am afraid that I cannot accept your offer as I am staying down here in Sussex.'[28] To Vita Sackville-West she was more explicit. She refused because judging from Cecil's 'style and manner' she thought him 'a mere Catamite'.[29] Cecil always claimed when he was famous that only Queen Mary and Virginia Woolf refused to submit to his lens.

The exhibition received welcome publicity. The *Sunday News* thought it a 'most interesting exhibition, not to say remarkable'. They concluded: 'With all his eccentricities Mr Beaton has extraordinary skill in the arrangement of light and shade in such a way as to bring out the characters of his sitters. Many of the photographs are beautiful pictures of beautiful women.'[30] They noted his love of vivid colours, his sense of pose and movement, but noted 'the painting of the human face is not his strong point'.[31] The *British Journal of Photography* found at the Cooling Galleries 'great examples of photographic portraiture, works to be ranked with the best which is done by perhaps the best half-dozen portrait photographers in London'.[32] They cited the portraits of Baba Beaton, Lady Alexander, Nancy, Paula Gellibrand and one of the Edith Sitwells: 'In these portraits Mr Beaton exhibits a sense of line and pose, which is translated into exceedingly fine work by his evident mastery of photographic technique. They are remarkable achievements. One can only smile at most of the others.'[33] Meanwhile the *Sunday Express* declared: 'I cannot see how a young Society man has contributed anything of importance to modern photography by including in his exhibition portraits of people seen upside-down, or showing both profiles at once.'[34]

There were curious scenes at the private view. Some of the beauties tried to pose looking as much like their photographs as possible. A large lady observed the portrait of Maud Nelson 'as seen by a dog' and frightened her companion by saying: 'I feel I must lie down and see what view my Peke gets of you.'[35] The relentless society hostess, Lady Colefax, was so intrigued by what she saw that, after battling with the crowd in the morning, she returned in the afternoon for a second look. Edith Olivier wrote: 'I knew your photographs. The drawings were a revelation.'[36]

His old friend, Kyrle Leng, who had been advising Cecil assiduously about photographic paper and accounts as well as obtaining film for him at a discount, now gave his views on the work he saw: 'I was very struck by the *finish* of all your photographs. Not long ago you didn't bother with it much and bits of retouching were occasionally rather clumsy, but now it seemed to me quite perfect.'[37] Kyrle Leng was less keen on the drawings, not being a great enthusiast of what he called the Marie Laurencin period.*

---

* Kyrle Leng drifted out of Cecil's life. He shared a dwelling with Robert Gathorne-Hardy and they were never apart for more than a few weeks for thirty-seven years. He died in 1958.

Cecil followed this success by advancing on all fronts. He designed a production by Osbert and Sacheverell Sitwell at the Arts Theatre Club entitled *First Class Passengers Only*. He covered stools with oilcloth from which some of the cast had difficulty in rising. He wrote about dressing up in *Vogue*, attacking the tendency of dressing in tawdry crushed-strawberry velveteen. He urged an extravagant approach to make-up: 'Make the cheeks look like strawberry ices and weighten the eyelids with pomatum.'[38] Young women wishing to display curvaceous legs should don doublet and hose and go as Romeo. Following the exhibition he was inundated with requests to take portraits, and immediately became more exclusive: 'But I'm not interested in making portraits of strangers,' he told Charles Vivian of *Pearson's Magazine*, 'unless I'm intrigued by their personality or achievements.'[39] He was determined to be considered an artist as well as a photographer. The camera should be looked upon more as 'an instrument of art than one of record'.[40] He saw himself as a pioneer of photography, believing that the photographer should give full vent to his imagination and his intuition 'to find the character'[41] of the sitter. Writing on *Photography of the Future*, he declared:

> To my mind, in many ways, a photograph is a far more satisfying medium to work in than paint; for example only the camera can differentiate the subtle differences in the texture of various materials.
>
> It is also not only more accurate in every sense of the word, but it can be depended upon to reveal the sitter as he actually is, not as he appears to the imagination of the observer.[42]

Cecil also established himself as an arbiter of beauty, examining its current trends and speculating on how it would change over the years. Here again he employed a vivid imagination. Just after the Dream of Fair Women Ball, he wrote: 'Women are at last growing tired of appearing like a troupe of consumptive messenger boys.'[43] He hoped science would improve beauty:

> The secret of eyelash growth will have been mastered, and every woman will have lashes like a peacock's spreading tail. ... She will be able to grow fatter or thinner at will, by the miraculous methods of electrical massage; the whole world of beauty will be within her reach, for her to choose out those particular graces that she would make her own. ... It will be a race of Robot-looking women, uncaring and unreal looking but perfectly lovely, for money will be able to buy beauty mechanically.[44]

Cecil began to live more expensively. In 1927 he made a gross profit of £549 12s, which dwindled to £31 4s 6d after payments and expenses had been taken into account. By 11 May 1928 he had spent £331 12s 6d, and by 22 June this had risen to £1,016 5s 3d. Cecil enjoyed the way he spent his money as much as the way he earned it. He served mauve cocktails with cream on top before a lunch at which Syrie Maugham and Tallulah

Bankhead were present and he attended the Eton and Harrow match at Lord's in an elegant cigar-brown suit and Homburg with a sister on each arm, when the more traditional were in top hats and tails. Cecil and Stephen Tennant often used to stay at Savehay Farm with Sir Oswald and Lady Cynthia Mosley. In May 1928 they dressed up in old clothes belonging to the first Lady Curzon (Mary Leiter) and did what Lady Ravensdale described as 'the most fantastic dances as passed description for effeteness tho' brilliance was in every line'.[45] The Mosleys made an amateur cine-film in which Cecil played the Madam in a brothel, made up like Margot Asquith. Cimmie Mosley was one of the girls in his charge. Cecil had one scene in which he was to drown himself, but his wig fell off. Stephen Tennant gave a convincing performance as a blind boy.

After consulting a teenage psychic friend called Valerie Domville, Cecil took a flight to Holland with his eccentric Cambridge host, Englebrecht. He felt rather courageous, although there had been a daily air service to Holland for more than five years:

> On the other hand never have I wanted to die less than I do at this moment for my family would be absolutely lost without me and very likely Nancy and Baba, divine and exquisite creatures that they are, without me would not have the strength or opportunity to fight against the middle-class squalor that the family might so easily sink into.[46]

Nancy came out in the summer of 1928 and, suitably adorned by Cecil, she was taken to curtsey to King George V at one of his Courts. Under Cecil's guidance she seemed set for a good season. She was readily accepted by his friends, indeed welcomed into their world. On the night of 9 July 1928, however, a hideous incident occurred which echoed in the press for weeks afterwards in a way which now sounds incredible. Known in society as 'The Ellesmere Ball Row', it occupied so many columns of newsprint that it fills almost an entire album in Cecil's collection.

The Countess of Ellesmere was holding a ball in honour of her daughters, the Ladies Anne and Jane Egerton, at Bridgewater House, the family's London home. Lady Ellesmere, resplendent in gold and green lace, received the guests, who included Princess Andrew of Greece (the Duke of Edinburgh's mother), her daughter, Princess Cecilie, Princess Aspasia of Greece (the widow of King Alexander, who had died from a monkey bite), Lady Maud Carnegie and her husband. In the ballroom the 'Yellow' Earl of Lonsdale was waltzing with Lady George Cholmondeley while the Duchess of Roxburghe was to be seen wearing a narrow tubular skirt of pink satin, beaded with a quantity of diamonds and pearls. But as Violet Ellesmere stood in the receiving line, she had the subject of gatecrashers in the forefront of her mind, because the previous year an American debutante, Charlotte Brown of New York (later Mrs Coudert Nast), had been brought uninvited by Lady

Muriel Paget, who, as everybody agreed, should have known better. Lady Ellesmere had complained bitterly. She even hoped Queen Mary might intervene and duly wrote to her Lady of the Bedchamber, the Countess of Minto. On 13 July 1927, Lady Minto had replied from Holyroodhouse:

> I told the Queen about Lady Muriel Paget's behaviour in bringing an uninvited guest, but both the Queen and I are so behind the times that neither of us has ever heard of Miss Brown. Anyway it is unpardonable anyone inviting people to houses that don't belong to them and you are quite right to make a fuss.[47]

Lady Ellesmere had given up receiving when Stephen Tennant and David Plunket Greene* arrived from the Russian Ballet bringing with them Nancy Beaton and Elizabeth Lowndes (later the Countess of Iddesleigh). The two girls had been invited by Stephen and Plunket Greene and had naturally not considered that any trouble could possibly arise from it. But Prince George of Russia spotted the girls and quickly said to his hostess: 'I didn't know you knew Miss Beaton', upon which the irate Lady Ellesmere swept up to the girls and asked them:

'Why have you come?'

'Oh! We came with Mr Tennant.'

'Would you kindly leave the house.'[48]

The affair might have rested there but Miss Horner, a journalist, happened to witness the scene and the story broke in the newspapers. The next evening at seven o'clock Nancy found a reporter awaiting her outside 61 Sussex Gardens. Cecil rose at once to his sister's defence and wrote to Lady Ellesmere:

> I am horrified to find that a newspaper reporter has been given the name of my sister as having been the uninvited guest at your Ball last night and that she was asked to leave the house instantly, but I must hasten to explain that this was not the case and I beg of you to allow me to give your permission that her name should not appear in the newspapers. My sister had been to a theatre with Mr Tennant who invited her as his partner, to accompany him to your dance, but by the time they arrived at your house you were no longer receiving the guests and thus she had not the opportunity of being introduced by Mr Tennant, who is also writing to explain, as, of course, he, alone, was responsible for her entire evening and it is most unfortunate that through him my sister should find herself in the dreadful predicament of being named 'an uninvited guest'.[49]

* Plunket Greene used to be a great friend of Cecil's at Harrow until, in the second year, they had a row. Later Cecil thought him 'milk soppy and Victorian' [Diary, 21 August 1923]. His nephew married Mary Quant, in whose honour Cecil addressed a Foyle's luncheon in April 1966.

The next morning the *Daily Express* printed the story in lurid detail with a comment from Lady Ellesmere:

> I wish the fullest publicity to be given to the name of my uninvited guests as I consider this the only way of dealing with a nuisance which I understand many hostesses have suffered from this season.

Cecil also spoke:

> I cannot see why Lady Ellesmere should have singled out my sister as an uninvited guest, as she had previously told a friend of mine that there were at least 300 people at her ball she did not even know by sight.[50]

Stephen and Plunket Greene wrote to Lady Ellesmere to apologize. Nancy wrote that she was 'extremely hurt'[51] and reserved the right to send a copy of her letter to the press (the *Daily Express* printed it on 13 July). Thereafter the matter became a subject for earnest letters of support for Lady Ellesmere from the aristocracy, humorous leaders written in national newspapers and music-hall jokes. Amongst the former, Lady Ellesmere's father, the Earl of Durham, wrote:

> I think in the next honours list you should receive the OM or VC and doubt if anyone who does not possess Lambton blood would have dared. ... At the balls here when looking about guests I have often hoped some of them were uninvited.
>
> Of course you did the right thing and I admire you for it.[52]

The Duke of Northumberland wrote: 'The principal culprit is a youth whose strange behaviour has caused considerable comment in Northumberland!'*[53] The Duchess of Roxburghe: 'What intolerable impertinence bringing guests unasked and uninvited through your portals – I should certainly punish them soundly.'[54] Lord Lambourne, a former Coldstream Guards colonel, referred to them as 'howling cads'.[55] While the *Daily Express* headlines continued to read 'The Great Mayfair War Develops',[56] Archie de Bear, the impresario, joked in the Duke of York's Theatre: 'Where are you going to, my pretty maid? ... Nobody asked me, Sir, she said', while at parties the joke was 'I did not send you an invitation as I *knew* you would come.' The *Morning Post* decried the idea of guests having to produce invitation cards at the door: 'the undignified situation may be reached when the guest will have to prove his claim to a welcome before receiving it'.[57] Finally Lord Castlerosse had his say on what he called 'the unwanted hostess' in his column in the *Sunday Express*:

> A week never passes but I receive several of those familiar envelopes containing an important card which announces to me that some lady with a resonant name will be at home to me.

* Stephen's step-father, Lord Grey of Falloden, lived at Falloden in Northumberland.

In nine cases out of ten I do not know her, and I do not want to know her, and yet she asks me; more, she demands an answer, without doing me the courtesy of enclosing the usual stamped and addressed envelope. At the height of the season the mere expense of postage becomes considerable.[58]

The incident was another that the Beatons had to overcome and it rankled with Cecil to the extent that, when some twenty years later Lord Lambton (Lady Ellesmere's nephew) declined a dinner invitation for a perfectly justifiable reason, Cecil seriously thought it was because of the Ellesmere Ball row. The whole episode remains important because, as Diana Mosley points out: 'In those days there were a few people who knew everything about everybody but the papers knew nothing. ... It was rather *ghastly* for Nancy to find herself on the front page of the *Daily Express*.'[59] The writer, Anita Leslie, stresses that this was the first time that a society hostess had spoken publicly, with the result that the squabble was vaunted in the press with the open collaboration of all concerned. As a result of this incident, more than any other, have the Nigel Dempsters of today gained their freedom. Lady Ellesmere never gave another ball.

At the end of the London season Cecil was exhausted:

We have all been very busy indeed – I with work as well as play and both quite strenuous with the dances, theatres, dinners, lunches, cocktail parties and my writing for *Vogue* and the *Oxford and Cambridge Magazine*, with my drawing and photography and keeping in touch with the hair-raising speed of gossip – news among the Sitwells, Stephen set, with the intense heat-wave and above all, with the horrors of the Ellesmere row. ... My mind was dulled with over-fatigue, my face was thin, lined, spotty and white, and with the cares and anxieties of the Bridgewater House Ball affair with its thousand nightmarish beastlinesses.[60]

There was more trouble to follow. Breaking his holiday in Sandwich, Cecil attended a boisterous American jazz show called *Good News*. He went along with Tom Driberg, a dissolute young journalist on the *Daily Express*. In the foyer Cecil was tapped on the shoulder by an old Harrovian called Toby Milbanke:*

Tonight he started abusing me in the most foul way and, as I had seen him drunk each time I'd lately set eyes upon him, I considered he was still in that condition and I was so amazed at what the little swine was saying that I put up a very bad show of back chat. However there was no fight, no spectacle and a friend of Milbanke's dragged him away, but

*Ralph Mark Milbanke (1907–49), later 12th Bt, younger son of Sir John Milbanke, 10th Bt, vc.

I was left quivering with fury and profound sorrow. It all seemed so unfair and filthy and as I walked home by myself I felt the only thing for me to do was to take up boxing. It seems unfair that that should be the final technique, that one's mind and work go for nothing in the most final yet primitive combat. ... For weeks I was miserable at this foul insult. I almost felt I might as well throw up the sponge and not go out. And I knew that would be the stupidest thing. It was all such unfair persecution.[61]

This unpleasant incident was followed by the publication in September 1928 of Evelyn Waugh's novel, *Decline and Fall*. Cecil found himself pilloried as David Lennox, the photographer, who took a picture of Mrs Beste-Chetwynde's head from the back. This was based on his photograph of Margot Asquith. Stephen Tennant thought he was also in the book as Miles Malpractice (though Paddy Brodie is the accepted model).

Finally, as if the Beatons had not suffered enough, one of Cecil's publicity schemes backfired rather dangerously. Cecil had often dressed his sister Baba as Lady Mary Beaton. In the summer of 1927, Princess Mary had presided over a *thé dansant* at which Georgiana Curzon had been Mary, Queen of Scots, with her four ladies-in-waiting, Baba as Mary Beaton, Jeanne Stourton as Mary Seton, Nancy as Mary Carmichael and Margaret Whigham as Mary Hamilton. Ironically the Beatons had a young friend called Marie Seton* (the daughter of Lady Walpole), who recalled how useful the fake Lady Mary Beaton connection was to them. She quoted Mary Hamilton's famous line: 'There was Mary Beaton, Mary Seton, Mary Carmichael and me.'[62] Cecil had not been slow to see the publicity possibilities of this.

In the late summer a letter arrived from an irate wing-commander complaining of the description of Nancy as a descendant of Lady Mary Beaton. Cecil wrote a letter of appeasement, but the wing-commander insisted that an apologia be published in the *Tatler*. In December it appeared:

In a recent issue we referred to Miss Nancy Beaton as a descendant of Mary Beaton, the famous lady-in-waiting to the ill-fated Mary, Queen of Scots. We are informed that this is incorrect and we desire to apologize for any annoyance which has been caused by this mis-statement. Mary Beaton married Alexander Ogilvy of Boyne in 1566, and W/Cmdr J.W. Ogilvy-Dalgleish† and his family are descended from them.[63]

This *Tatler* was hidden from Mr Beaton and Nancy's spirits remained low until one night King George of Greece asked her to dance at a ball.

By this time Cecil had departed for New York to try his luck over there.

---

* Marie Seton (1910–85), biographer and film scriptwriter.

† Wing-Commander James Ogilvy-Dalgleish, OBE (1888–1969).

When he heard of the *Tatler* piece, he noted: 'I was rather upset and hoped people wouldn't talk much about the correction. People can be so spiteful. In a way it was a good thing that I was so far away not to be worked up about it although I felt caddish about being so unmoved.'[64]

9

The Americans

How thrilling that you are going to America! How you will love it, to gaze with one's old-world intelligence upon that vast material 'rush-hour' of progress that is a sensation one must not miss, the feeling of another planet is so queer there.

Stephen Tennant to Cecil, autumn 1928

Cecil departed for New York on 3 November 1928, very early on a bleak Saturday morning. He was disappointed that no reporters noticed his departure: 'I am only half a celebrity which is such a maddening plight to be in. I'd seen many journalists lately and had been interviewed for gossip paragraphs and alas there was nothing about me but a lot about Oliver Messel.'[1] But his family were there and Cecil thought how dull life would be for them in his absence: 'They would miss my hair-raising flurries and pain-stricken flusters and the rushes that have become my life.'[2]

He had always wanted to go to New York. His father had made fourteen trips, returning with appetizing Broadway programmes. More recently Beverley Nichols had excited him with talk of his own success there and told him how he had been taken up by Otto Kahn and his family, how he had stayed for six weeks with Schuyler Parsons, a noted party-giver, and how he had met the aviator, Charles Lindbergh. Nichols also said he could guarantee Cecil at least £100 of photographic commissions and introductions to 'all sorts of millionaires'.[3]

Thus Cecil sailed on the *Aquitania*, dreading that it would sink, drowning him at this stimulating moment in his career and casting to the ocean a crate of his paintings, photographs and negatives, his faithful No. 3A folding Kodak and a miscellany of backdrops. All trace of him would disappear simultaneously. When the *Aquitania* docked at New York six days later, he again looked about for eager reporters, who might ask him for his first impressions. He went so far as to write his name in large letters on an envelope hoping that it would attract attention, but his arrival passed unnoticed.

Cecil loved New York: 'The beauty of Venice by night is nothing compared to this. This is essentially modern, utilitarian and stark, and yet it possesses all the glamour of eighteenth-century palaces.'[4] In later years he told the story that his first days in New York had been blank and empty, the telephone never rang, his only letters were ones from home or the dreaded weekly hotel bill. In fact on this trip he established important contacts almost immediately and many new and important friendships were forged. His first week was indicative of how events would go in the future. On 10 November, the day after his arrival, he went to see Edna Woolman Chase at *Vogue*. She was impressed with his work and a number of articles and drawings were planned. Mrs Dudley Brown, the mother of the same Charlotte who had upset Lady Ellesmere, lent him her car to deliver his letters of introduction and asked him to dine that evening. The next day Elizabeth Marbury, 'a colossal old woman',[5] responded to Cecil's introduction from Osbert Sitwell. Here he met the actors Irene Browne and Clifton Webb, and Lady Mendl,* who jumped about the room 'looking like a humanly dressed monkey'.[6] The same day Schuyler Parsons invited him to dine and on 13 November Condé Nast gave a luncheon for him. Here he met Frank Crowninshield, the editor of *Vanity Fair*, and thought him 'one of the most charming men I have ever met, wise, kind, witty and extremely knowledgeable'.[7] The following day he gave his first interview:

> A reporter sent by Beverley Nichols came to interview me and was rather frightening for just as he was about to leave, after I had been as garrulous and helpful to him as possible, after I had gone through piles of photographs, he asked me if when I had my exhibition in London the critics 'roasted' me pretty thoroughly. Sinister sluggish little man. Little swine. I wait in fear and trembling to read the review.[8]

Cecil thought this man came from *The World*, and had been told by Beverley Nichols that this would be important publicity for him. He was deceived on three counts. *The World* proved to be 'a common rag', the article never appeared, and much later Cecil discovered that Nichols was in fact employing this man for his own magazine. He was furious.

At dinner with the interior decorator Syrie Maugham, the estranged wife of Somerset Maugham, who proved a welcome link with home, he compared New York experiences. She told Cecil she had once spent three nights in Central Park, too miserable to go home. That Friday, a hostess called Mrs Fleitman invited him to tea, saying he would soon be the lion of New York and his life a hell. Meanwhile Cecil read that Mrs Vanderbilt was having a large dinner and felt his letters of introduction to her from Hazel Lavery and Myrtle d'Erlanger should have secured him an invitation. Then a lunch engagement with Beverley Nichols prevented him spending a day in the

---

*Lady Mendl is better known as Elsie de Wolfe, the Sapphic interior decorator.

country with the Harrison Williamses, whom Cecil was most anxious to meet. This, then, was Cecil's first week in New York City.

The most important link established was that with *Vogue*. Cecil's first job was to produce a batch of drawings. As so often, he left this commission until the last moment. However, he called on Mrs Munroe and then Elsie Mendl and drew them both quickly. The latter sat perfectly still for him while rattling instructions to her secretary. Cecil knew they would become great friends. 'She is the sort of wildly grotesque artificial creature I adore.' He then wrote an article about his New York experiences, in which he described the evening he came back to the Ambassador Hotel to find an enormous box, evidently of roses, awaiting him on a chair:

> Everyone in London had told me how I would be overwhelmed with people's hospitality and I was conjuring up to myself the various people who might have sent these roses – Schuyler Parsons, Elizabeth Marbury, Mrs Wellman [another hostess]. I ran through a string of possibles and imagine my chagrin when I discovered the box to contain my returned laundry.[9]

To his great relief Mrs Chase liked the article. Later she recalled that he wrote 'acceptably'.[10]

The photographic side of Cecil's life now took a leap forward. Condé Nast summoned him to photograph his daughter, Natica, in his apartment. He found Steichen there:

> Nast introduced me to Steichen, a good looking, goatishy-fawnish grey-haired man and both were so patronizing that I felt like a humiliated schoolboy and said quite honestly that my photography was so amateur that I felt it might cease to exist any moment. Steichen adores my sketches and complimented me upon them being slightly sinister, but he said I thought of photography too much in terms of paintings (and this I agree) and that some of the results therefore were rotten (this I will not agree to – especially since he is talking of my favourite photographs and mentioned, as a particular instance, the photograph group looking like a Winterhalter group of four debutantes). An agony followed in which I had to photograph with lamps I have never been used to. I had no idea of the negative potence and there was no unshaded bulb that I could put behind the sitter's head to give an effect of sentimental radiance and without this I am lost. The photographs I took I am sure were merely poor imitation Steichens.[11]

Quite early on Cecil found an old man who could print his work for him. The rate was extortionate but the results were just what he wanted. Both Edna Chase and Carmel Snow (the American editor of *Vogue*), whom Cecil immediately thought 'charming', were delighted with the Natica Nast portraits. Carmel Snow took him up at once. He was introduced to the society editor, Margaret Case, an important person in his New York life for the next forty-three years. He was commissioned to take more photographs and to write about New York night life. Theatre tickets were arranged and paid for by *Vogue*, and he was to work with the illustrator Carl Erickson whom he much admired.

His attitude to this work, however, was often surprisingly casual. On Saturday 15 December Edna Chase telephoned him to know how his photographs of her daughter had turned out. Cecil had not seen them yet, but dared not admit it. Instead he adopted a nondescript tone and told her they were very good.

'Are they what you wanted to get?'

'Oh. Yes.'

Following this exchange, Cecil sauntered into his sitting-room and found the negatives had arrived:

> When I saw the results I was so delighted that I skipped and jumped and danced naked kicking high and praising God, beaming, laughing, delighted and I got back into my bath.[12]

Frank Crowninshield too was attracted to Cecil's work: 'Gosh it was good to hear him enthuse so extravagantly: Myself, Steichen and de Meyer the *only* photographers!'[13] Crowninshield kept saying to him: 'But it's amazing you can do things like this with a toy camera.'[14]

Cecil gave a lunch-party and persuaded Carl Erickson, whom he had not yet met, to come at the last minute. Later the four English members of the party from London were left together, the Casa Maurys, Olive Snell (the portrait painter) and Cecil. They had a post-mortem on their experiences of America. Cecil declared:

> I have come here to rook the Americans, to make money and to have a good time. I have come here determined to enjoy myself and I can see the faults and snags, but enjoying myself I am.[15]

He had luckily received advice from 'Kaetchen' Kommer,* which would stand him in good stead throughout his long New York career. Kommer told him that Americans were impressed by people who stayed at smart hotels and urged Cecil to be sure to charge very high prices for his work. When a sitter was expected, Cecil knew he would earn enough to take care of two weeks in his hotel. He set his price at $300 for twelve prints. Back at home in the Beaton household in Paddington Nancy and Baba consulted old uncles Wilfred and Cecil as to how much they thought Cecil would get per dozen. Uncle Cecil volunteered about £20 and when they were told $300, Uncle Wilfred's only comment was 'By Jove!' When sitters did come

---

* Dr Rudolf 'Kaetchen' Kommer (d. 1943), Max Reinhardt's right-hand man.

Cecil was careful to leave press-cuttings and drawings lying around, along with smart addresses casually scribbled on the back of envelope. It often brought him further customers.

To give Cecil a boost, his faithful friend, Syrie Maugham, commissioned him to draw her young daughter Liza. 'Liza is a perfect darling. I adore her,' he wrote. 'She is unique, wise, sophisticated and yet very childish.'[16] The older she looked in Cecil's drawings, the more pleased she was. Some days later he photographed her as a Christmas present for her mother. Liza, the future Lady Glendevon, always remembered the great kindness of her mother's artistic friends, such as Cecil and Noël Coward.

Cecil's long-awaited meeting with Mona Harrison Williams took place at tea. At first he found her 'charming and delightful'.[17] Later he realized she was also 'alert and intelligent, and knowing exactly what was what'. He loved her 'lovely wide urchin's mouth' and 'enormous starry eyes'.[18] After a fortnight in New York, he thought that despite the expense involved he must have a sitting-room in the hotel, so that he could entertain and show his photographs and paintings. Mona Harrison Williams was one of a number of fashionable New Yorkers sufficiently interested to come along. In due course she invited Cecil for the weekend at Oak Point, Bayville, Long Island (and later he spent a luxurious Christmas there with them). He was staggered by their plutocratic way of life, especially as he had only £20 left of the £200 he had brought with him a month before. Even the footman's razor, which he was loaned, proved to be gold and much grander than his own. However, at the end of the weekend he was sickened by the talk of money and longed to go: 'It was all very well staying with the most sumptuous of people in America but what good if they bored me.'*[19]

When Cecil first arrived in New York he felt 'timid and unadventurous', a state he soon overcame. New York was expensive, particularly when no cheques were coming in, but even when they did, the weekly bills and the cost of getting from one appointment to another soon swallowed up his profits. Later he was obliged to cable for his £150 savings, which worried his father. His mother added: 'I think it's time now you were making some money and not spending so much. ... Do try and take lots of good photographs and bring some money home with you.'[20]

He was often annoyed to be asked if he was related to the Mrs Beeton of cookery book fame. He found he invariably misestimated the time of a .journey and was often late, though this never seemed to matter. There were many lunches and dinners. To his annoyance, Cecil found Noël Coward

---

*Back in England the following summer, Cecil gave an interview to the *Sketch*, which infuriated Mona. On 3 September 1929, Cecil wrote to her: 'It has been a worry to me the whole summer to think how ungrateful and treacherous you must have thought me to be.' The friendship survived.

enjoying 'the triumph of his New York career'.[21] Cecil even met Coward, who was the guest of honour at a lunch given by Mrs Schiff:

> He was very charming and gracious to me which was touching and I liked him for it, but although he talked hard and the entire time he didn't succeed in saying anything amusing or clever. He was extremely badly dressed in trousers too short and his face was sweating at every pore.[22]

He attended debutante parties and was shocked by the casual and sometimes rowdy behaviour of the guests (particularly when they threw bits of bread at one another), he had cheerful lunches and dinners with Paula and Bobby Casa Maury, and he made friends with Mercedes de Acosta. She took him to a party for Carl Van Vechten (author of *Nigger Heaven*) who proved

> completely unlike what I had imagined him to be for instead of a white, dessicated, powdery ghost I saw a fat, florid, unhealthy, plump and rosy business man with a kind, slow smile, white hair, a smart rich brown suit with fabulous suede shoes. He was very quiet and sheepish and I should imagine not a nice person, slimy – a vicious slug.[23]

In her memoirs, Mercedes de Acosta recalled her first impressions of Cecil:

> He was extremely slender and willowy. It was the vogue then for young men of artistic pursuits to appear to be falling apart. And this resemblance to a swaying reed or willow tree gave an impression of fragility, although actually many of them proved unusually durable.[24]

Cecil also attended Charlotte Brown's wedding and photographed the bridesmaids, but was depressed at the way the bride had clearly dressed hurriedly and persisted in smoking a cigarette in her bridal gown. Relating his disappointment to Mrs Henry Russell some days later, she looked at him quizzically and said, 'You're an idealist, I see.'[25]

While all seemed to be going well for Cecil, Elizabeth Marbury announced that one of his sitters had commented: 'That young man was heavily made up.'[26] Beverley Nichols was deputed to warn him that this had to stop. Cecil was enraged at the story, particularly because it was totally untrue.

> I adore *maquillage* and so wish that young men could paint their faces, but they definitely can't without being branded as social nuisances and if one renounces all things social one misses so much. This is my first set-back in New York and I am only slightly annoyed and I feel very high hatted so that if I find out who is the culprit she will be thoroughly abused by me.[27]

It seemed that the story had come from the other side of the Atlantic and was based on the make-up worn for pageants, though Beverley Nichols later revealed that the 'culprit' was Bessie Marbury herself.

Cecil went to the theatre as often as possible. He attended the first night of Somerset Maugham's short-lived play, *The Sacred Flame*, and saw for the first time some of his New York actress heroines in the flesh. Lillian Gish was exactly as he hoped, 'like a little old maid, spinsterish with a bundle of spidery, unkempt hair, a pale, sallow dumpling little face',[28] whereas Ina Claire was a shock: 'Oh surely no. I remembered the loveliest photographs of her like a tall thin almond with the most perfectional face and a heap of the loveliest, finest nut brown silk hair. It was such a blow to find her quite a solid young woman, very tall with the usual shrivelled hair, pale canary yellow.'[29] One night he saw Mae West on stage:

Mae West is terrific, a huge, blowsy, lustful blonde with a very painted face, high gold wig and curved figure of peachey pink. It made one feel that this thinness really was unsatisfactory sexually. This fat, pink, creamy, fleshy creature looked so lewd and naturally, healthily, amorously, lustful that in one scene where a Spanish lover mauled her, felt her breasts and buttocks, one had to cross one's legs and scream hysterically with laughter.[30]

Although Cecil appeared to be making a meteoric rise in New York society, something which Somerset Maugham believed was more difficult to do than in London, he was disappointed that he was not even more overwhelmed by New Yorkers.

He was fairly put out that none of Beverley Nichols's promises had come to much. It even transpired that the magazine he was editing would not have any photographs after all. Of course once *Vogue* entered Cecil's life, this no longer concerned him. One evening, early in his visit, Cecil and Nichols dined alone together. Cecil was still quite naïve in many ways. It fell to Nichols to tell him a few surprising stories about the ways of the world, for instance about his 'shatteringly unsuccessful love affairs',[31] and how he went 'to male brothels', or to various points of the town 'to pick up sailors, marines, guardsmen ...'. Cecil noted:

I heard more that staggered me this evening than I have during the past few years. I who have not been to bed with anyone but myself since I was at school had begun to think that the amount of people who actually went to bed together was very small. That one talked a bit, imagined a lot, but to get down to brass tacks – that few people did strip off boots, suspenders, socks, undo braces etc. and get into bed.[32]

As the twenty-four-year-old Cecil listened, wide-eyed, Nichols assured him of his first-hand knowledge of the homosexuality of Oliver Messel, Noël Coward, Somerset Maugham, Sydney Howard (the plump comedian known for fluttering gestures), Edward Knoblock (the playwright), and others. In the course of this rather disturbing evening, Nichols declared:

I'm not ashamed of it. I'm proud of it! Sex is everything in life. The trees, the flowers, everything exists through sex. Some people are born one way, others another. I adore my sexual experiences. They are the most thrilling moments in my life, and if I were castrated there would be no future interest ... to live for.[33]

Cecil wondered if one day he too would be as lonely as Beverley Nichols:

Now I have Nancy and Baba to take an interest in my press cuttings and my every action, but perhaps when they are married, I shall feel the want. I returned home very early, amazed at what I had heard from Beverley, shocked, excited and utterly amazed.[34]

In December, Cecil found another expert to discuss this with in the shape of Charles James, whom he had scarcely seen since their Harrow days, but he too was now in America, making his way in the fashion world. James had left England following a row with his family and arrived in New York with $60 to his name. After months of indescribable poverty, he succeeded in creating a millinery establishment, making the hats himself. Now he owned two cars and had an office in Chicago, but thought he had only three real friends in the city. The previous year, after an unhappy love affair, James had tried to commit suicide in a mirrored room by candlelight. He soused his handkerchief with ether and was sinking away when suddenly the ether burned the inside of his nose. He screamed in acute agony and, before he knew it, he was being stomach pumped in front of a group of students in the Chicago hospital his grandfather had founded. In time he became a famous dress designer, of whom Madge Garland said: 'He had more knowledge of fashion in his little finger than the whole world of couture put together.'[35]

James told Cecil some even more startling details about the facts of life. Cecil noted: 'Here at last was someone who would explain things and no one could do so better than little James. He is blushless and primed with information. ... It was all very interesting and I was grateful though staggered and disgusted by what I learnt.'[36] Cecil hoped he could help his old school friend to get on in New York. As so often with very talented people, this proved a thankless task on many occasions.

Conscious of the need to be remembered in London, Cecil occasionally passed news of his activities back to newspapers at home. In some articles for the *Sunday Dispatch*, he painted the New York scene as 'marvellous' and 'fabulous', with expensive parties every night of the week. Naturally he passed on the news of his forthcoming exhibition, saying he was painting his new friends 'to give it a local kick'.[37]

When Lady Mendl came to see his pictures, she at once offered him the use of the Elsie de Wolfe Gallery on 5th Avenue, without charging him commission. Mindful of Edna Chase's advice that he should hold his show somewhere where people did not expect too much, Cecil was as confused as he was delighted to accept. The exhibition opened there in January 1929 and, though it did not cause as great a stir as in London, it helped make Cecil's name known in New York.

Cecil used some of the same pictures as in the London exhibition, but committed a crime that Osbert Sitwell never forgave by altering his catalogue foreword without permission. Sitwell had written: 'And who has ever seen Lady Ottoline Morrell look more splendidly herself than in the portrait here displayed?' To fit his requirements Cecil changed Lady Ottoline to the very different figure of Mrs Walter Rosen, a Jewish American socialite. It was not until September 1941 that Osbert Sitwell delivered his stern rebuke.

The exhibition gave Cecil the chance to talk to reporters and he took the opportunity to address the Americans on the subject of beauty. This resulted in a prolonged exchange with Florenz Ziegfeld, the creator of the Ziegfeld Follies, and welcome publicity for all concerned. Cecil told David P. Sentener, of the *New York Times*:

> As an average, American women are more beautiful but individually, British women have it all over American women for pulchritude. From the neck down, American girls are gorgeous but from the neck up, literally speaking, give me English women. Where is there anyone over here to compare with Lady Diana Cooper, for instance?[38]

The appalled interviewer asked Cecil if he had been to any musicals and seen the glorified showgirls. 'Yes, I have been to your musical shows,' replied Cecil disdainfully. 'The girls are vulgarly pretty but hardly beautiful. I know Ziegfeld will be wild at me, but I must be honest, shouldn't I?'[39] Cecil's idea of a contemporary beauty was as follows:

> A ripping, ravishing Venus is a woman with a very long, thin, almost scrawny neck, no chin at all, an abbreviated nose, three cherries for a mouth and big pansy eyes.

Ziegfeld took the bait and entered the fray:

> When Cecil Beaton, the English artist, says our American girls are 'hideous', he makes himself ridiculous; and I have to laugh right in his face. I wonder where he has been since his arrival in America that he has seen so little beauty.[40]

The impresario then listed a number of beauties he was promoting, such as Claudia Dell, Billie Burke and Noel Francis. 'Our girls are simply superb,' he declared. 'No other nation can match them.'[41] He threw Cecil the gauntlet:

My shows are rosebud gardens of girls. I invite Beaton to look them over and then make an abject apology or else visit an oculist at my expense.[42]

On 6 February 1929 Cecil left for Palm Beach where he knew only two people. He arrived there feeling dirty and depressed, but he soon regained his spirits and rejoined battle:

Mr Ziegfeld need not conduct me to an oculist. There is nothing whatever the matter with my eyesight, and if any of his 'showgirls' possesses a wrinkle, pimple or blackhead my eagle eye will be the first to notice the dilemma. Mr Ziegfeld's eyesight, on the contrary, does seem to be in need of repair for he has obviously missed what I had to say about American beauties.

It was the debutantes of the winter season that I said were hideous and monstrous, and I still claim my privilege as an individual to stick to my opinion. I said I considered the average beauty in New York much higher than in London or Paris, but that in New York there were no absolute front-rank beauties, first-rate Venuses, comparable to the immortal loveliness of Lady Diana Duff Cooper, who would still be a vision of beauty if you scrubbed her hair and combed out the wave and hung her upside-down until the blood rushed to every vein in her head.

None of Mr Ziegfeld's beauties could come through this test.[43]

Ziegfeld again replied at length, concluding that Cecil 'went a long way for notoriety in making, to say the least, a very ungentlemanly statement'.[44] Now Cecil decided that Anita Loos was the 1929 Venus 'and a potent one at that'.

He made this statement at the time when he met Anita Loos, the diminutive author of *Gentlemen Prefer Blondes*. He was presently to be spotted relaxing on the beach with her, wearing a pair of beige satin beach pyjamas specially designed for him by Charles James. Cecil often produced lists of the best-dressed and most beautiful women. Invariably these turned out to be women who were in his immediate circle at the time and therefore of some use to him.

On 13 February Cecil's exhibition opened in Palm Beach at the Everglades Club Ballroom. He was hailed in the *Palm Beach News* as 'either a pioneer of a new beauty or back with the Italian primitives'.[45] The actress Gertrude Lawrence bought three pictures and commissioned two of herself.

Back in New York Cecil's sitters became more glamorous and famous. They included Alfred Lunt, Lynn Fontanne, Ina Claire, Fred and Adèle Astaire, Mrs Nelson Doubleday, Rosamond Pinchot and Edith Gray (who did not pay her bills, a fact which Cecil never forgot until the day he died). Accordingly his backdrops and props also became more glamorous. Once, under the aegis of *Vogue*, Cecil was bidden to use Condé Nast's drawing-room, with the Chinese wallpaper which came originally from the Duke of Rutland's seat, Belvoir Castle. The days when Cecil used to buy one lily to add glamour to his photographs were superseded by the expense account extravagance of the magazine. His sitters were often surprised at the new, exaggerated antics he adopted behind the camera. The Lunts, for example, had heard of his successes, yet they found a very young man, trembling with shyness, battling with his tripod as it slipped about on the marble floor. On the other hand they found Cecil surprisingly efficient. Lynn Fontanne recalled that he knew exactly what he wanted to photograph 'and set about it in a most direct and businesslike manner'.[46] Alfred Lunt, her husband, was amazed at the peculiar angles of the photographs. At one moment Cecil was on a ladder, photographing them from above as they sat at the piano. Once he had captured the tops of their heads, Cecil would shoot from under the music-rest, capturing nothing but their chins. The results appeared in *Vogue*.

After four months in America, Cecil felt he had achieved his goal and it was time to come home. He had earned money and he had secured an exclusive and generous contract with Condé Nast Publications to photograph for them for several years to come. 'I hate to leave,' said Cecil, more successful at getting press coverage for his departure than he had been on arrival. 'I feel like the Student Prince who is called away from Paradise, knowing that, even if he does return, everything may have become changed and wretched.'[47]

On the homeward journey Cecil received a dressing-down from Noël Coward about his affectations and mode of dressing. Then he found himself back at home with his parents in April 1929. Cecil showed his father his new contract with pride. Mr Beaton eyed it suspiciously and said: 'It sounds all right, but is it?'[48]

New York life had given Cecil a degree of new confidence. Stephen Tennant, who was in Bavaria recovering from his mother's death the previous November, wrote that he had heard of Cecil from Rex Whistler: 'Your life giving off sparkling *mondanité* like electric sparks. I feel I shall not recognize you so smartly equipped by New York *savoir faire*.'[49]

In comparison the Beatons' family life looked even more drab than hitherto. Mr Beaton's business suffered a further relapse and it seemed that he might have to close down his Liverpool office, then run by a Beaton called Theodore. As Mrs Beaton wrote on 4 March, 'it seems one set-back after the other and I'm so cross about it all as we have done so much for those Beatons'.[50] Mr Beaton found life confusing. He fought a strong rearguard action against Nancy and Baba wearing make-up and he insisted that they be present at breakfast at nine o'clock sharp, however late they had been out. He used to ride in the park each morning at seven and the girls were often hiding in the drawing-room until it was safe to creep up to bed.

Likewise, when they went out in the evenings, they applied the necessary lip-stick and powder in the taxi. Cecil thought his father's life desolate and empty:

> Daddy who like the man in the Sickert picture 'Erasmus' just sits blinking, blindly staring, never upping and doing, never doing anything on the spur of the moment. 'Why don't you go to the theatre tonight Daddy?' – 'Oh – er – well – er the theatres are so far away. How would you get there? There's nothing close by here', when in ten minutes a taxi can take one anywhere. ... One will never be able to alter Daddy's mentality now. All I can do is to try and save Nancy and Baba and Mummie from being victims of it.[51]

Reggie had given up working in his father's office since the so-called wood wool part of the business had closed down. Despite a 'sticky valve' in his heart, he had been accepted in the Flying Corps in February 1929. His life was also a contrast to Cecil's. He was fond of squash, skating, and the club dinners that followed. He revelled in night-clubs such as the Kit Kat, 'a great place', and occasionally he had a spree and 'spent a hell of a lot of money and Dad was not best pleased about it'.[52]

Cecil kept an eye on his two sisters. As early as March 1928 he had written: 'The only moment I am living for is when Nancy and Baba are married.'[53] Nancy was having an altogether better season, attending pageants, and writing articles when she needed extra pocket-money. In June 1929 she wrote one for the *Daily Chronicle* entitled: 'These Pageants are great fun'. In the late summer Cecil took her to the South of France. John Gilbert and his new wife Ina Claire were at Cannes and so was Noël Coward, fresh from his triumph with *Bitter Sweet*, the songs of which so aggravated Cecil and Anita Loos that they claimed they only went to America in 1930 to escape them.

Cecil now focused his attentions on projecting Baba, who was about to leave school and would come out in the summer of 1930. Asked in July 1929 to choose a favourite photograph he selected Baba in one of his own costumes:

> I like the idea of such a young and exquisite creature being weighed down by so many trappings. I like gilded lilies, and here, obviously, is one. ... I like this picture because it looks like an illustration to a fairy story – the romantic princess who was miserable at being imprisoned in her fabulous court.[54]

There were beauties to be photographed for *Vogue* and for Cecil's forthcoming *Book of Beauty*. Subjects included Tilly Losch as the Manchu Marchioness, Daisy Fellowes and Marie Laurençin. A particular excitement was the chance to photograph his childhood heroine, Lily Elsie, now almost a neighbour at Stanhope Court, W2. She arrived at Sussex Gardens and at once rekindled all Cecil's childhood dreams. In Paris Cecil photographed Colette, but not having read her books found it hard to understand her personality. His attempts to flatter her resulted in failed pictures. One hoped-for sitter was Lady Diana Cooper. But this was not a good moment. She wrote from Bognor:

> I admire your work more than anyone's and am longing to sit in spite of the agony. Alas! I am due to have a baby in August or September* and my appearance is so grotesque and generally absurd that I dare not be seen by the human eye far less by the cameras.
>
> If I survive it might be possible afterwards before you leave for America. Some people put on 2 stone for a year afterwards, some recapture a remnant of lost looks. Please ask me again after the ordeal.[55]

Eventually the sitting took place at Sussex Gardens and Lady Diana recalled Cecil beseeching the help of his butler: 'Oh! Manley, Manley, do come and help, Manley.'[56] She was portrayed in her famous role as the Madonna in *The Miracle*. She loved the results, but urged Cecil to lighten the eyes. 'I have a peculiarity shared with elephants and a certain sheep dog collie of having almost white eyes,'[57] she wrote.

On 9 November 1929 Cecil sailed for New York once more. Anita Loos was on the same boat, and this time the press were out in force to see them off.

*John Julius Norwich was born on 15 September 1929.

10

The Funniest Place in the World

*Greetings from Hollywood, the funniest place in the
world. Here with the Emersons and Irving Berlins seeing
all sights and meeting the stars. Weather tropical. Bought
weekly* Daily Sketch *on Hollywood Boulevard. Xmas
dotty – Cecil.*

Cecil to *Daily Sketch*, 27 December 1929

Cecil returned to New York in order to make more money and to gather
beauties for his forthcoming book. When asked about this he said that
Venus de Milo would not fulfil his requirements, but he was dead set to get
Greta Garbo: 'Oh, she's going in regardless of her measurements. She has
personality, and she has perfect lines, aside from academic beauty.'[1] This
time he underplayed his lecture on beauty or the lack of it in favour of
talking about enticing gimmicks such as climbing ladders to photograph
film stars.

Cecil arranged to go to Hollywood with Anita Loos and her old-fashioned
theatrical producer husband, John Emerson. He thought that under Anita's
tutelage he would 'see all the sights and we'd have some grand laughs'.[2]
They were due to set off on 10 December, but the trip was delayed a week
as Anita received the offer of a contract.

The extra week in New York proved nothing if not memorable for Cecil.
He had been thoroughly overworked with drawings to do for *Vogue* and
photographic print work. He hoped for a quiet week to get it all sorted out,
but gradually the telephone began to ring again and he took on more and
more work: 'My last-minute work panic was worse than ever, I felt ill with
pains in my head and a longing to sleep, but no time for that.'[3] *Vogue* and
Vanity Fair were calling up, appointments were being made for people to sit
for drawings and a half-witted secretary allocated to Cecil was coping badly.

In the midst of all this Cecil elected to lose his virginity:

This time my life was a nightmare. I had had a very momentous week.
I'd hardly slept at all and for the first time I had been to bed with a

woman. With one on Wednesday and another, a longer and more serious
affair, on Friday. We got up and dressed and went to Child's for some
hot coffee and eggs. I was deathly tired. She was alert and as pretty as
ever. I felt very sentimentally [sic] and slightly hysterical. I took her home
and then returned to retouch photographs – a dog's work but I can find
no one to do it. I slept for about three hours and then the storm started
again.[4]

With a certain modesty, Cecil did not at once confide the identities of his
benefactresses to his diary, but in time the names slipped out.

The first was Marjorie Oelrichs, a lively New York girl, with 'waxen skin
and eyebrows like butterflies' antennae',[5] who shocked her family by advertising Lucky Strike cigarettes. Of her Cecil wrote in *The Wandering Years*:
'More than any other woman I had met before, she was responsible for
giving me a modicum of self-confidence and the satisfaction of gaining some
worldly experience.'[6] In his book *Cecil Beaton's New York* he paid further
tribute to her:

Not only in character and appearance was she one hundred percent
American but she possessed all the best qualities of the young New York
woman – loyalty, courage and a wonderful sense of humour. Yet unlike
most women in her milieu, she was adaptable. Her friends, chosen from
every walk of life, had varied interests. She was equally sympathetic to
musicians, artists, sportsmen and businessmen, and fitted perfectly into
the national life of Austria, France, England, Scotland or Poland. ...
Though much of the time with her was spent in laughter, one took her
very seriously, minding very much what she felt, and her gentle reproof,
'Now really', was more effective than the most stringent criticisms or all
the threats of damnation.[7]

And Anita Loos, her friend, wrote of Marge: 'Soft, plump, and beautiful, she
was a high-society version of Mae West. Her voice was a sort of sexy wheeze
but, contrary to Mae, her brain was like a bag of popcorn.'[8] The affair came
about in a curious way. Cecil confided to her that he had never been to
bed with a woman. 'She volunteered her services as my first experiment,'
Cecil wrote in 1937, 'and if this sounds comic it was done from the best
motives.'[9]

The second girl was one of his early heroines, the dancer Adèle Astaire,
Fred's sister. Cecil had first seen the Astaires performing in *Stop Flirting* in
Birmingham in January 1924. He was 'delirious with happiness'[10] whenever they were on stage. 'She is so American and perfect and slim and
graceful and smart,' he wrote at the time. 'I adore her ugly face and the
pearls tight around her neck.'[11] He obtained Fred and Adèle's autographs at
the Theatrical Garden Party in 1924 and again saw them dance in London:

'I adored the Astaires so much that I nearly died in my stall.'[12] Adèle was very nearly eight years Cecil's senior. Like Marge he had met her in Palm Beach on his first visit. In *Vogue* he described her as 'rather too roguish but a delightfully brittle puppet'.[13] Cecil was still undergoing his grim week, when she reappeared on the scene. He stuttered, 'I'm so grateful to see you', and asked her up to help him wrap a vital parcel. Then he gave her a present: 'Did she like these? These were her photographs. Her Christmas present, hers and Fred's. She seemed rather quiet and sheepish and sour. Surely the little thing must realize I couldn't stop and devote my whole attention to her.'[14] His diary account continued:

Adèle and I went to the station in her car holding hands. 'I do think you're nice' and she would say 'Balls' – I was feeling very sentimentally [*sic*] and hysterical and when at the station Miss Platt my secretary and the luggage could not be found I was almost demented. Marge and Kitty [Miller] and Joe Schenck* were at the station to see us off [to Hollywood] and lovely presents were exchanged. Anita looking diminutive and screaming with laughter. Marge seemed quietly hysterical and sentimental. Kitty was just a kind and sympathetic stranger, Adèle was vague and quiet – 'Here's a little present I have for you but I'm furious with Cartier's for not having done what I wanted. I asked Liles Gleneazers to have Cecil stamped on it', and I producing the gold pencil realized that Adèle seeing the handsome and generous gift of photographs I was giving her felt she ought to give me something in return and dashed off there and then to Cartier's. I was rather annoyed and hurt. I hated her not being honest. I hated her getting me a present because she felt she had to.[15]

Thus Cecil departed for Hollywood leaving his two ladies behind. In later life Adèle, who adored Cecil, nevertheless related to friends how her shy young lover approached the bed, demurely holding a towel in front of himself.

'Gaga with exhaustion' Cecil settled down for his four-day train journey to Hollywood. He could not have been in better company. Anita Loos, whose exact age was never known (she was then about forty-two) and John Emerson (then aged sixty-four) were intelligent travelling companions with the added boon of a riotous sense of humour. Anita could laugh for four hours at a time without seemingly being exhausted by the process: 'There's no one who laughs more than she,'[16] Cecil wrote. He was impressed by her knowledge and statistics about goings-on in the cities they passed through and by her industry. She began work every morning in the train by 7.30 or 8.00 and continued until they met for a late lunch. Together they pored

---

*Joseph M. Schenck (1878–1961), Russian, chairman of United Artists 1924. Later founded Twentieth Century Fox. Then married to Norma Talmadge.

over ridiculous cinema magazines, one of which had a series entitled 'If Venus got her arms back'[17] and showed an actress in a variety of bizarre poses.

Cecil was relieved to be on his way: 'It was next morning when I was woken by the coon bringing a telegram from Marge: "The idea of you leaving is too frightful." I was glad to have left. Troubles were left behind. I wouldn't mind so much if I heard later that all my photographs had been lost or were received and considered unsatisfactory.'[18] He sent telegrams: 'To Adèle – I didn't quite know what to say to her but I like her. To Marge – I felt the same about her!'[19] A while later he wrote a letter to Adèle, noting, 'Adèle, about whom I had lustful thoughts, but with whom I am definitely not in love – and only hope our friendship will fizzle out happily as fizzle out it obviously must. We have nothing in common. She frankly doesn't like flowers.'[20]

At Chicago the songwriter Irving Berlin and his wife joined the train with

a lovely assortment of film people, Jew producers very flashily dressed, pale mauve collars, purple ties, custard blondes, with cream-coloured faces, scarlet lips and eyes swollen with make-up and curly headed young men all on their way to make good, to become stars. It was my first real glimpse of Hollywood and very exciting.[21]

At dinner Irving Berlin talked about his collection of wine, books and glass: 'Now what's the name of that blue glass I used to collect – er – not Wedgwood – something-staff – Lowestaff! Yes, that's it.' John Emerson chewed gum and muttered, 'Well, that's better than collecting stamps.'[22] There was talk of the cancellation of the romantic actor John Gilbert's contract after his failure in talkies, and of the aloofness of Garbo, for whom Cecil was already developing a powerful obsession: 'The loveliness of that exquisite lily in black velvet crinolines leaning on ornate mantelpieces fired me with inspiration and excitement.'[23]

The train rattled on towards Hollywood, a goal Cecil had longed for since childhood. They passed huge fruit markets, bakeries built like windmills, extraordinary ice-cream shops, and thousands of Christmas trees all vividly illuminated with scarlet, yellow and magenta lights. Christmas was big business in Hollywood. The boulevard was renamed Santa Claus Lane for the festive season, Santa Claus getting higher ratings here than Jesus Christ. Cecil concluded: 'It is as though rich children had been allowed to run amuck.'[24] Cecil had thought that Hollywood would be like a large village street with one big hotel, a few shops and an interminable procession of stars walking up and down it. Instead he found a city larger than Birmingham, ablaze with electric lights.

He was stunned by the beauty of everyone in Hollywood – even the typists, cashiers and waitresses, and the young men with plucked eyebrows: 'Some look like thugs and crooks, lots are fairies, all men and women look as though they feel the next moment is the one moment when they will be picked up to stardom. They have a rather desperate glint in their eyes.'[25] He observed at least a hundred people whom he felt worthy of his *Book of Beauty*. On the other hand, beauty and brains were not united. There was a plethora of 'vapidly blank faces'. In the back of his mind Cecil yearned to be spotted himself: 'How I would adore to be given a good part in a good film. There would be no excitement or satisfaction like it! But alas I am afraid I am not likely to realize that ambition.'[26]

At the Roosevelt Hotel a reporter called on Cecil, who was in the bath, but soon ready to receive him and his cameraman:

> I drying my hair and unpacking was saying the usual things about American women. The average good looks higher, no superlative beauties, from the neck up England wins but from the neck down America gets the prize.[27]

He wanted Anita to come and be photographed with him. John Emerson accompanied them to stop the picture looking compromising. Anita Loos realized that her husband was jealous of Cecil, though with no foundation. Later she recalled: 'When I met Cecil we clicked immediately. ... Yes, he met people through me, but he was popular. He soon didn't need that.'[28]

The following day Cecil had his first taste of a studio, when they lunched at United Artists with Irving Berlin. They passed deserted Belgian villages made of canvas and plaster, and decaying Russian palaces:

> Oh the glamour and romance of owning a mock Russian Palace. I would like to live in scenery; to have the doors painted to look like wood and to have the columns empty.* I was thrilled with all this and couldn't have been more excited than when we went into a huge building to see them making Dolores del Rio's talkie.[29]

He was disappointed with Dolores del Rio, but not with a glimpse of Lillian Gish walking to her dressing-room with a faded pink shawl around her shoulders. Overall he was depressed by the time spent on fundamentally bad films and how the photographic side was at present the least important.

Part of Cecil's Hollywood assignment was to photograph stars for *Vogue*. Condé Nast imposed one condition on the job. He had worried that the results Cecil obtained from his little folding Kodak were often technically deficient; they lacked contrast and definition and often became mottled in enlargement. He insisted that Cecil buy himself a camera that would take

---

* At Reddish House, Broadchalke, in Wiltshire (his last home) he was to achieve the goal of empty columns.

8 × 10 inch plates. Cecil had received this ultimatum with horror and complained that he would no longer be able to photograph from ladders. But
Condé Nast was insistent and so was *Vogue*'s new lay-out artist, Dr M.F.
Agha, a somewhat unsavoury Turk, who had worked for Nast in Berlin and
did not relish Cecil's welcome into the bosom of *Vogue*.

Cecil was greeted by Al Kaufman, of Paramount, at the start of his assignment. Here he observed a crowd of medieval beggars on their way to
lunch, smoking and chewing gum, a hooded old friar driving off in a little
car and a painted blonde stepping out into the sunlight in full evening dress,
tiara and tulle. Elsie Janis, a star of Cecil's childhood, was encountered. She
now wrote screenplays. So too was Ernst Lubitsch,* 'the god, the master
producer, the only producer, the man that produced *The Marriage Circle*, the
first good film I ever saw'.[30]

The new camera was tried out at Paramount on William Powell,† then
considered a ham actor who was acting in a detective drama. To begin
with, the new camera proved a menace: 'I hated the cumbersome thing,'
wrote Cecil. 'I felt rooted to the earth with it. I could not assert my domi-
nation over it.'[31] Gradually, though, Cecil came to see that it had the
advantage of picking up the tiniest detail with enormous clarity. He used
the set with ropes, lamps and property men all in evidence, as background
to the photographs. Powell was pleased and said, 'That's a very original
"thot" you have. Generally we spend our time trying to hide the implements
of our trade.'[32] Gary Cooper was next:

> He was absolutely charming, very good looking with black eyelashes as
> thick as the lower lid on the upper. Very tall, a good figure and such a
> good sort that he made one feel such a swine. He was on such good
> terms with everyone. The electrician offered him a cigar. 'Are they all
> right?' – 'Well they should be. The three cost 25 cents', and so Gary lit
> up and the cigar did not explode. He was extremely smartly dressed with
> a brown hat to match his suit and gloves, very elaborate gloves with
> green spots in the lining. He is just a very charming cowboy and it was
> amusing to see him so smartly turned out. His success is stupendous. He
> is about the most popular actor on the screen and is paid fabulous sums.
> It is an extraordinary phenomenon this suddenly leaping to fame. He has
> only been in the business three years and now it saps him entirely. He
> longs to get away, but can't – he can't spend his money even, he longs
> for the sun to stop shining but it never does. '*Terrible* weather this for the
> day before Christmas!' The sun was boiling hot. I took quite good pictures

*Ernst Lubitsch (1892–1947), German film director and former comic actor. Paramount's
leading producer. His many films included *The Marriage Circle* (1924) and *Ninotchka* (1939).
Won a special Oscar in 1946.

†William Powell (1892–1984). He and Myrna Loy became overnight stars in *The Thin Man*
in 1933. At one time married to Carole Lombard.

of him, that is unless they go wrong technically and the last person to be taken was little Mitzi Green,* the nine-year-old wonder-monster, who behaves like a tough old trouper who has been on the job for years.[33]

In addition to the photographs Cecil drew the set of the film *Young Eagles* for *Vogue*. The electricians and helpers took great interest in what was going on, asking questions of Cecil's work such as 'Do you think this looks anything like it's supposed to look?' and 'Well, what's it for anyway?'

'A magazine.'

'Oh, *publicity*.'[34]

Cecil was totally bemused by the characters that peopled Hollywood – Wilson Mizner, the brother of Palm Beach architect Addison Mizner, was a fund of odd stories. Talking to Al Cohen about a Greek Jew of their acquaintance, he burst into fury and cried, 'Jesus Christ. God damn the son of a bitch. Why he started his career as a waiter and invented rubber pockets so that he could steal soup.'[35] As the Christmas rush overtook Paramount Studio, a clerk proposed marriage to a secretary and was turned down, and a stenographer rushed in, seized a ringing telephone and addressed the caller: 'Hullo you silly sucker. Merry Christmas to you.'[36] Cecil went to a party at the Beverly Hills home of John Gilbert and Ina Claire; the actress was in jubilant mood, later to be seen 'in a corner cuddling and kissing a newly acquired dog that seemed to be resigned to its fate'.[37] At the end of the evening Cecil attracted the attention of a young starlet, who made a great play for him. John and Anita called this 'a big break' for Cecil, but he thought she just wanted him to photograph her for publicity purposes.

Other experiences included a visit to a religious rally drummed up by the evangelist Aimée Semple Macpherson and the exaggerated Hollywood-style wedding of Bessie Love ('the only person who was in the studio who had never had a beau').[38] The *Vogue* drawings pressed so heavily on Cecil that he felt exceptionally sorry for himself: 'I stamped with rage, kicked books sky high, talked and swore loud, tore pieces of paper to bits and wept. I recovered and went in to see John and Anita. The latest news was that Marion Davies arrived in Hollywood for one hour on Monday and wants us to go on with her up to her ranch for New Year's.'[39] Exhausted with overwork Cecil pressed on with an article for *Vogue*, ran into more stars such as Gloria Swanson 'looking at once terrible, old and hideous, like a pig, and also beautiful, soignée, flawless',[40] but failed to set eyes on the ever-elusive Garbo. Things reached a fever-pitch of panic, before they departed on Monday 30 December. High-spirited guests including a number of stupid but polished blondes mounted the special train which took them

* Mitzi Green (1920–69), American child performer. In 1930 she played in *Honey* and *Tom Sawyer*.

overnight to the Hearst stronghold at San Simeon. William Randolph
Hearst, the super-rich newspaper proprietor, arrived from New York with
the modest Marion Davies, his beautiful mistress, a 'sincere' film-star if such
a creature existed. Cecil dined with two blondes and retired to the compartment he was to share with Eddie Kane, 'a natty little counter skipper' who
bade him a cheery 'Good night, old man'.[41]

On New Year's Eve a 'coon's voice' gave the command: 'It's after nine
o'clock and Mr Hearst is up.'[42] It was an unshaven Cecil who joined John
and Anita. They passed signs declaring 'Danger. This road dangerous to
pedestrians on account of wild animals.' They saw buffalo and zebra, cypress
trees and statues and finally arrived at the castle:

> I was speechless at the place. Mr Hearst was standing smiling at the top
> of one of the many flights of garden steps. My room was enormous with
> carved gilt ceiling, huge carved Jacobean beds with gold brocade covers
> and on the walls hung old tinselled velvets and gosh the view from the
> window! One was in heaven looking down on pale green mountains, pale
> blue, misty hills, and a silver sea in the distance. Gosh the beauty. The
> pain of enduring the beauty.[43]

Anita Loos commented: 'To have this Palace and then ask these tough
blondes is what I call true aristocracy.'[44]

It was in such surroundings with delicious food awaiting him, bleached
blondes in breeches going riding, animals in the zoo being fed, Mr Hearst
terrifying all the guests, and the angelic Marion Davies attending to her
place à table, that Cecil bade farewell to the Twenties. It had been an extraordinary decade for him. He had transported himself from stifling domesticity in a suburban home to success in the cut-throat glamorous world of
Hollywood. There was no reason why this boy from Hampstead should
represent the decade, yet as early as 1930 Osbert Sitwell was writing: 'It is
to his photographic portraits that the people of the next century will turn
when they want to rediscover the character of this one.'[45] And in 1933,
Patrick Balfour cited Cecil as one of three typical products of the 'Twenties',
alongside Beverley Nichols and Oliver Messel. He continued:

> All three are talented, hard-working and successful. All three are bach-
> elors. All three are amusing and socially popular. Mr Nichols as some-
> thing more than a journalist, Mr Beaton as something more than a
> photographer, Mr Messel as something more than a stage-designer are
> entitled the respect due to all artists, and must be congratulated on the
> position which they have each achieved.[46]

The new decade began dramatically. Although Cecil had not ridden since
St Cyprian's, he and Anita set off together in borrowed riding clothes. The
sun set, the sky turned a blue-mauve colour, and the white palace at the
top of the mountain looked more beautiful than ever. But when Cecil tried

to open and close a gate from the saddle, his horse bolted and he was caught holding onto the saddle and to the rope of the gate. The skin on his fingers was burnt almost to the bone, upon which a 'scarlet blonde' commented: 'Oh that's too bad!'[47] Back at the ranch the hand was dressed, but the pain continued to soar and Cecil took refuge in whisky. He supervised his packing, calling out drunken instructions to the servant. He took a hot shower 'in a stupor'. Later he recovered sufficiently to dance wildly with Marion Davies (until her formidable overlord appeared) and later he tangoed with Eileen Percy. Cecil was fortunate not to be personally involved in the subsequent high jinks that resulted in the breaking of a priceless gold chest (at which point, of course, Hearst reappeared). It was the moment for the party to catch their train back to Hollywood. Cecil had enjoyed the luxury of the ranch but in conclusion he disliked the uninspiring house-party of toughs.

Cecil's last week in Hollywood proved frantic and exhausting. At the studios of Fox he photographed Lilyan Tashman and Marguerite Churchill. Due to a dreadful accident in which two aeroplanes had crashed during filming and ten people had been killed, he had to carry his own equipment which made his hand smart with pain once more. At Paramount his pictures of Mary Astor, Fay Wray, Jack Oakie and Kay Francis 'were so slickly taken and as I afterwards discovered were the best I'd taken'.[48] Dolores del Rio proved difficult because she had fixed ideas on how she should pose. She thought Cecil wanted to make her too exotic. Her ideas struck Cecil as being 'vulgar, garish and senseless'.[49] Cecil was sufficiently confident to call off the sitting when he had taken enough shots of her. Irving Berlin was another awkward sitter because of 'an enormous nose which catches the lights wherever they are placed'.[50] Ed Lowe in a sailor suit was submitted to what Cecil called 'brutal pictures which Beaton is getting good at'.[51] Sometimes the stars failed to inspire him at all – Joan Crawford was too inclined to pose, Anita Page 'easy and pliable',[52] Buster Keaton 'a disappointment too'.[53] But he loved his work on Pathé's *All Quiet on the Western Front*. He went up in a crane to view the scene below. A battalion of soldiers under fire were marching into the slush amidst tremendous explosions. A church was blown to the ground. 'Gosh this was thrilling,'[54] he noted. Meanwhile an ambulance was poised ready for calamities; indeed the director's nose and eye were cut by a piece of flying wood. Cecil was delighted to hear later from Carmel Snow that the photographs he had taken with his new camera were a great success.

Throughout this last week Cecil was obsessed with the idea of seeing Greta Garbo.

She is the only person with glamour. She is flattered and pleased that she is an amazing success but she does not want to meet her fans.

Women send orchids to her every day, men telephone on long distance calls to try and hear her voice. She is so casual and dreamy. She doesn't give a damn and the fact that she doesn't give a damn and will not come out of hiding only increases the frenzy and as with me they are almost driven insane with desire to see her and incidentally she gets more publicity in this way than if she were at everyone's beck and call.[55]

He persuaded the former child star, Elsie Janis, to ring Garbo's house. 'Mees Garboh away for weekend,'[56] came the reply. Howard Strickling, Metro-Goldwyn's head of publicity, also called her to ask if she would see Cecil. She replied: 'Oh I don't know about it. Oh well.'[57] Hopes faded and then hopes were raised again. On his last full day, Cecil began to think there was a chance:

I at last got through to Strickling and, after having my hopes raised so high yesterday in answer to my 'What about getting Garbo?' there was the deadly 'Not a chance'. Hell. Damn. Blast the bitch. I almost wept with fury, exhaustion, pique. Hell.... She'd got nothing else to do.*[58]

From this crushing blow Cecil returned to the business of photographing Norma Shearer. 'Where in Hell is Miss Shearer?' he cried. 'If she doesn't arrive in three minutes, I go.'[59] It is a tribute to Norma Shearer that, even in his unreceptive mood, her appearance completely won Cecil over. He was very impressed with her fastidiousness and perfectionism and thought her quite lovely. But Garbo's rejection continued to rankle with him:

Bloody Hell to Garbo – the independent and foolish bitch. Perhaps some day she may wish she *had* been photographed by me. If *only* I had gotten a load of her my visit would have been complete.[60]

After the usual panic of packing, the Emersons and Cecil left Hollywood on 8 January and travelled via New Orleans, Jacksonville and Florida to Palm Beach. On the train he wrote articles about Hollywood and worked out that these and his photographs would earn him 'quite a good deal of money'.[61] They arrived at Palm Beach on 13 January, where Cecil observed 'the coal-black coons peddling their white-fringed basket-chairs, the pseudo-Moorish buildings, the bushes of scarlet hibiscus down the sidewalks, the huge hotels, the whiteness and bright green-ness'.[62]

Cecil stayed at Anita Loos's house in Sea Spray Avenue for sixteen days. He tried to work but spent most of his time 'tomfooling about' with the gang. His twenty-sixth birthday was celebrated on 14 January with a dinner given by Anita, at which cigarettes sprang up when touched, matchboxes buzzed, *petits fours* squeaked and the sugar floated in the coffee. Cecil was surrounded by Palm Beach society: Addi Mizner, Mr and Mrs Gilbert Miller,

* Garbo's first 'talkie' film, *Anna Christie*, was due for release on 4 March 1930.

Jules Bache (Kitty Miller's father, dubbed 'Jew Bitch' by Cecil in an unattractive joke), and 'Laddie' and Jane Sandford. Cecil was not in a social frame of mind. On his first visit to Venice in 1926, he had asked permission to photograph Baba Lucinge. Now he was placed next to her at dinner and, far from being impressed, he was put out to find 'an intelligent person being ruined by being social'.[63] He cast a cool eye on society people:

> They are very good picking ground for business. They are rich, foolish and the easiest people in the world to fool if you approach them from their level and anyone with the patience to subjugate themselves can get on in society – but my God! What a game for intelligent brains to indulge in and yet it gets so many people.[64]

Years later Cecil's publisher, George Weidenfeld, recognized in Cecil an ambivalent attitude to the rich: 'He needed them and he liked being in their company, and their way of life. But if he was given a good enough pew, he would gladly have witnessed their execution.'[65]

This period in Palm Beach was also a time for personal reappraisal. One lady told Cecil that he was 'no longer an exotic lily but much better looking'.[66]

He thought his outlook had been widened by his travels with Anita and that he had toughened up in an American way. He believed he had escaped from his earlier superficiality. Along with his new image came a new laugh: 'My old laugh is so falsetto and absurd that I now laugh on an ingoing breath and the result is like a bad chauffeur changing gears.'[67] He felt more masculine. It was therefore with healthy anticipation that he learned that Marge Oelrichs was about to join them. When the press photographers became excited on the beach, he hoped this heralded the arrival of his girlfriend:

> Surely Marge. Yes there she was as casual as ever but extremely pretty. I have never seen her look so well and all day and all the evening I could not keep my eyes off her.[68]

That night the new Embassy Club opened:

> Marge looked ravishingly lovely and was in excellent form. She wore a lovely perfume and was excitingly attractive to me and I felt very amorously about her and kept pawing her and putting my hand under her cloak and down the back of her back.[69]

For the next few days life was filled with laughter and fun, while Cecil became more and more enthusiastic about his glamorous friend. He left a party early because he wanted 'to join up in every sense of the expression'[70] with Marge, but he was disappointed to find she had already gone home to her mother. The next night they danced with feverish abandon at a party given by Kitty Miller. They loved their dancing but deemed the party a failure. 'Poor old Kitty,' noted Cecil. 'She tries so hard to be one of the gang but she just doesn't belong.'[71]

On 28 January Cecil took Marge for dinner at the Patio Lameza. They talked about Anita and both said how fond they were of her, how they wanted to stroke her and bounce her up and down. 'I long to bite her head and it is all I can do to keep my hands off her,'[72] Cecil announced, possibly explaining the foundation for John Emerson's earlier jealousy. The evening progressed:

> I felt very sentimentally towards Marge and wanted very much to go to bed with her – was just in the mood for it. The scene seemed ripe but there was nowhere to go. Addi's [Mizner] Palace was shut. That would have been ideal. I didn't think it was playing fair to go to Anita's house. Marge's mother would be hanging around screaming in their apartment. We wandered round arm in arm making indecent jokes and pinching one another. No good. We were baulked. No good minding about it anymore so I said goodnight and walked home.[73]

The next day Cecil's friends bade him farewell. Addi Mizner expressed himself in his own idiom: 'Well you big bum, you old bastard, we shall miss you horribly.'[74] Later, at the station, the Emersons said they felt they were losing their child. It was a tearful farewell. Cecil hated the idea that their jaunt was over, although he was more restless than ever to go back to work. He hung sadly out of the train window as the car with John, Anita and Marge in it was driven off. Then his train lurched off on its two-day journey to New York.

Cecil stayed at the Barclay Hotel from 30 January until 14 March. His first adventure was to go and see Adèle Astaire, now living in a new apartment. Adèle was lying in bed 'looking like a bitter Felix the cat with her large amusing head on a minute and exquisite little body'.[75] Adèle was entertaining a boring and sluggish beau called Bill White and her conversation consisted of phrases like 'Oh it gives me pain where I should have pleasure.'[76] She was delighted to see Cecil and kissed him 'like a vicious little ape' and bit his chin 'unendurably hard'.[77] Sometimes he went for tap-dancing lessons with Adèle and they had several dates. 'She likes me more than anyone else at the moment,' he wrote on 8 February. 'Her feelings are maternal, sensual and full of admiration. So that's that. Good for Beaton.'[78] They went to a film and held hands:

> I liked the unusual feeling. It made me feel young and clean and I liked sucking Adèle's hand and biting her soft cheek – and I liked feeling her soft cheek on my, at present, soft face. Whenever a man looks at me amorously or even lecherously I feel old and haggard, a woman of fifty

trying to be young, but with Adèle I feel strapping and young and it is a very pleasant sensation. I longed for Adèle to come back to the Hotel with me.[79]

But Adèle was tired. She had been up until 5 a.m. the night before. A chastened Cecil had to console himself by reading Virginia Woolf wearing 'spectacles and the cream satin pyjamas'.[80] One evening he would indulge in 'a little petting party' in his rooms with Adèle, and the next day the 'exquisite' dancer, Tilly Losch, would come to lunch. Cecil entertained a desire for her too: 'I adore her and would love to go to bed with her.'[81] Of Lillian Gish, whom he met and photographed at this time, he wrote: 'She is just the sort of looking person I would like to marry.'[82] Cecil was also very taken with his lesbian friend, Mercedes de Acosta, who used to furnish him with curious stories about Garbo: 'I thought her delightful and would even have liked to have gone to bed with her. I told her I had had an affair with Adèle and I could have killed myself for doing so.'[83]

One evening Cecil showed Charles James some drawings he was submitting for Anita Loos's projected book on Hollywood. James was offended that a drawing of a 'fairy' bore a distinct likeness to himself. This led to a conversation in which Cecil summed up his attitude to men and women:

> We had a real 'set to' about fairies, Charles saying he thought I had become intolerant and mean about fairies suddenly, that last year I wasn't and that now I was pretending not to be a fairy to save myself humiliation and being sneered at. But I replied that if any pretence was necessary it needed as much and more to pretend one was a gay and coy young girl than to be a strapping and healthy young dog. I told Charles that I have always hated fairies collectively. ... I am sure I shall turn mean about fairies because they frighten and nauseate me and I see so vividly myself shadowed in so many of them and it only needs such a little grip and dash to get oneself out of that sad and ridiculous predicament.[84]

Cecil may have believed for a while that he had escaped from his homosexuality, but this hope was to prove optimistic. Through friends of Adèle, he met a virile black boxer, called Jimmy. Originally he came to see Cecil to be drawn as a character for Anita's book. He remained nine hours and thereafter became a regular visitor, regaling Cecil with fantastic and detailed stories of his sex life with women, and how 'pansies' beseeched him to go to bed with him, but he always replied: 'I happen to be a real man.'[85]

Cecil took some photographs of him in boxing poses. 'Gee, it's good to get into the old togs again,' said Jimmy. Cecil was impressed by his broad shoulders, his very thin hips and trunk-like waist:

I was thrilled and we returned for more pictures – complete nuders this time.... His body could not be more beautifully proportioned. I smeared him with cold cream and in the bright lights it shone like wet stone and he is, my gosh, what Grace Moore would describe as being 'well built' to the point of being almost a monstrosity.[86]

Later they talked and laughed together. Then Jimmy asked Cecil: 'And you then. You're bisexual?' 'Not except when you're around,' was Cecil's reply.[87]

After an afternoon photographing Gertie Lawrence and extracting $500 from her for a previously unpaid session, Cecil rushed to a party given by Hoytie Wiborg for Segovia, Misia Sert and Mrs Otto Kahn. Then he returned to his hotel for his last meeting with the well-endowed boxer:

It was hard to interrupt and get him to talking about what I wanted. He is an independent bastard and so am I and after a terrific struggle I won and it was not worth the bother and once I had won the delight had left. He was so very drunk but sobered up terrifically and said a thousand times: 'Gee I hate to have you go, Sees. Say, Baby, I'll miss you.' He told me that he was fonder of me than anyone else, that I was kind of different and he was so pleased and proud of the photograph I gave him of myself. ... I feel very triumphant at having been the first person to overcome him for he's a tough proposition and it's very difficult to sway him at all. I was very sleepy and he went and I went to sleep at once.[88]

These weeks in New York were frustrating as far as Cecil's work was concerned. Dr Agha of *Vogue* attacked his photographs at some length – Cecil understood composition and had some imagination, but technically he was hopeless. He knew nothing about lighting. As Cecil became more depressed, Dr Agha recommended that he should attend a night school of photography to learn about the technical side. When Margaret Case tried to sympathize after this onslaught, Cecil only felt sorrier for himself. He had a battle with the perfumier Elizabeth Arden who, having enthused over his very flattering photographs of her, had placed a considerable order. When Cecil went to see her, however, she looked 'terribly tired, swollen and bunged up ... a very bad advertisement for the shop'.[89] She now told Cecil his work was odious and, when he walked out in a languorous manner, she had a fit of hysterics and tore up the photographs 'in a blind rage'.*[90] Finally the drawings Cecil was doing for Anita Loos were rejected by Ray Long of *Cosmopolitan*. He thought them too amateur and too exaggerated, too much like caricatures. Cecil had been upset enough when Dr Agha told him to draw for *Vogue* in his 'normal technique'. He commented: 'Alas that I should be bound by my own technique so soon.'[91]

*This story is related at length in Cecil's *Photobiography* (Odhams, 1951, pp. 50–52, and Doubleday, 1951, pp. 66–8).

Cecil worried about money, but before he left New York Carmel Snow of Condé Nast presented him with new rates. She reassured him by telling him: 'Now you know, Beaton, you're very valuable to *Vogue* because you are a personality. We have so many clever and intelligent people working for us but few are personalities and it's very important to us that you're happy.'[92] When Cecil returned to London, his dollars bought him £80, a sum he had never had on his person before. This was a great thrill: 'Imagine £80 worth of orchids and roses,'[93] he wrote.

On 15 March, the day after he sailed, Anita Loos wrote and gave him some advice. She thought Cecil was 'on the crossways between being an artist and being a dilettante'. She continued:

It is great that you have had several years of frivolity – it will be a fund of satirical material for you always. *But* I think that now is the time to pull up.... I think a very great danger to you now is the fact that in London you are surrounded by young dilettantes who are so talented and full of charm and personal success that it would seem silly not to emulate them.

But I do not believe that, in your heart, you will ever be satisfied with the kind of drawing-room fame which satisfies them. You have so much more than any of them, believe me! ... Cecil, dear – do not feel that I could lecture you like this if I had not had exactly your problems. You have more solid talent than any one person I know – but I know that you can easily drift into a scrambled, footless life so far that you will never be able to pull up. And I know that the only real artistic satisfaction comes from a regime of honest work. To be 'professional', to win the respect of 'workers' in the arts and cut out the 'players' at art – is the only way to make a career that will last and get more and more important, as time goes on, to yourself and to others.[94]

11

Cecil in Arcadia

But while our eyes these distant landmarks greet
One curious object lies beneath our feet,
And ASHCOMBE'S *concave the attention draws,*
Like landscape pictured on a porcelain vase,
Strange it appears who'er could build a seat
In such an inaccessible retreat.

From 'The Invitation' (Anon., 1833)

Back in England Cecil joined Edith Olivier and Rex Whistler at the Daye House for the weekend of 5 to 7 April 1930. Edith launched into an elaborate monologue describing how the streams which carved the hills and valleys were the first architects of Wiltshire, a county that she felt was endowed with a mystical feeling as well as immense dynamic power, successfully igniting in Cecil a love for her county. In the light of his recent relative prosperity, he wondered if he might perhaps own a cottage in this beautiful stretch of southern England.

Edith happened to remember that the sculptor, Stephen Tomlin, had recently been walking on the downs and had discovered a deserted house with a grotto in the garden. The idea of a grotto conjured up Sitwellian visions of baroque fantasy. The house party set off at once. Stephen Tomlin was routed from his work to joint the quest for what he described as 'a sort of Grand Meaulnes place'.[1] It was hard to find but at length they came upon the brow of a steep hill below which lay the hidden house. Cecil described his first sight of his future home (on 6 April 1930):

With intense excitement we got out of the motor. Below, stretching to the distant sea, lay an extraordinary sylvan carpet. There were hills wooded with a variety of beautiful trees. Among a cluster of ilex trees a coil of smoke arose. We walked down the rough track of white chalk and flint stones which was bordered with nettles and yellow tansy. After we had descended for nearly half a mile we came to an arcade of low hanging beech trees, and an archway of pink brick faced with stone.

None of us uttered a word as we came under the vaulted ceiling and stood before a small compact house of lilac-coloured brick. We inhaled sensuously the strange, haunting and rather haunted atmosphere of the place.[2]

The discovery of these outhouses of the 'Palace of the Sleeping Beauty' had an extraordinary effect on Cecil:

It was as if I had been touched on the head by some magic wand. Some people may grow to love their homes: my reaction was instantaneous. It was love at first sight, and from the moment that I stood under the archway, I knew that this place was destined to be mine.[3]

Ashcombe had many visitors during Cecil's tenure and all bear testimony to the magic of its setting. Lost in the depths of the Wiltshire downs, the house is nevertheless perched at the top of a long, curving valley. Far from being exposed to fierce winds it is protected by a horseshoe of tree-covered hills around it. The drive leads first to the L-shaped building with the arch, which later became the studio, and acts as a barrier to the outside world. Beyond it is a gently sloping lawn at the end of which nestles the little jewel of a house, a sturdy, even a rather grand little house, well and compactly built. From its other side stretches the extensive view of the valley beneath.

'I would so love you to be there ...' wrote Edith on 11 April. 'I feel it would be the place to inspire real creative work, either writing or painting – and it might make a new epoch in your life, and show you the way for some great achievement. Also, *what fun for us all!*'[4] Edith entered most earnestly into the business of helping Cecil acquire the house, urging him to write to the owner, Mr R.W. Borley, of Barton Hill House, Shaftesbury, asking him if he would sell Ashcombe. 'Say you are a very quiet invalidish gentleman with no dogs or guns and you would not interfere with the game,'[5] she suggested.

On 23 April, Mr Borley wrote that he could not entertain the sale of the house as the property would be spoiled without it. He added that he had heard that Cecil was a friend of Miss Olivier, 'who is considered hot stuff in this part of the world'.[6] Edith was most amused by this, pointing out to Cecil that every reviewer described her as 'cool and restrained'.[7] On 31 May, Mr Borley took Cecil and Edith on an inspection of the house. Ashcombe was built in 1730. They found it well-proportioned and delightful, with dazzling views from every window. But they also found decay and disintegration, and there was neither plumbing nor electricity. But Cecil was bewitched and already planning elaborate improvements. Mr Borley said that he could have the house for seven years at an annual rent of £50 in view of the proposed work. At this point Cecil wavered, discouraged by his parents, but reassured always by Edith:

You won't find such another place and the rent, I should say, not high for what it is. But I don't know whether 'what it is' is the sort of thing to make you really happy if you possess it.... Are you too urbane and civilized to enjoy a bucolic existence when you begin to *live* it? And would the kind of work you do be at all possible there?[8]

In July Cecil made up his mind and took the house. He never regretted his decision: 'At this time life took on a sudden colour and warmth.'[9] He summoned the Austrian architect, Michael Rosenauer, a friend of Anita Loos, to advise him on how to alter it. In due course a passageway was tunnelled between the front and back of the house, bricked-in windows opened, flooring and rafters replaced. Plumbing was installed. Ornamental urns were placed on the parapet of the house and an ornate front doorway would be added to a design by Rex Whistler. Edith's tweed-clad builder friend, Mr Brazier, gave an estimate for the changes, and the great work began. Meanwhile Cecil remained impatiently at Sussex Gardens in London.

The results of Cecil's work in Hollywood, both written and photographic, appeared in magazines over the course of the summer. Greta Garbo's new career in 'talkies' was his favourite subject. 'Have you glamour?'[10] asked Cecil in the *Sunday Dispatch* of 11 May. He then compared Garbo to Edith Sitwell and Lady Diana Cooper. Meanwhile, ever pressing the case of photography as art, he asked to be described as 'a photographer of the fantastic'.[11] In *Vogue* he illustrated 'Ascots of the Past' (28 May 1930) – a prelude to his later work on *My Fair Lady*. He was invited to take over Lady Eleanor Smith's gossip page on the *Sunday Dispatch* at a salary of £1,000 a year but declined for fear of losing his independence.

Cecil wrote an article, 'Good Manners are in Fashion Again', for the *Daily Mail* (30 May 1930), which was subsequently attacked in the same column by Evelyn Waugh. He accused Cecil of trying to start a fashion of good manners by stating that this fashion already existed. Evelyn Waugh also attacked Charles Graves,* who had written a book on society and dug up the Ellesmere Ball row. Graves, of course, replied. Then Gilbert Frankau, an arrogant novelist from an older generation, saw this flurry of attacks and counterattacks as a splendid oppportunity to launch into a virulent on-slaught on four young writers – Waugh, Cecil, Godfrey Winn and Beverley Nichols. Writing in the *Sunday Chronicle* on 22 June, Frankau sneered:

Brilliant, these sucklings of the pen may be. And startling, as all infant prodigies are startling. But is there anything solid, anything of permanent value, underneath the brilliance? When they cease to startle will they continue even to entertain us?[12]

His theme was that young men who had never lived in the real world should not make exaggerated pronouncements on how others should

---

* Charles Graves (1899–1971), author and columnist, brother of the poet Robert Graves.

conduct their lives. Evelyn Waugh wrote that for £21 he would reply: 'You cannot obtain free copy from responsible authors simply by lining up an old hack like Frankau to insult them.'[13] Cecil, who had been described as 'the blue-eyed Cecil Beaton',[14] was rather more vicious:

Thank heavens blue eyes are my only fault! Alas an hereditary one, since I am of mingled English and Scottish origin, and these races are much given to eyes of that colour. Is it possible that the 'black-eyed Gilbert Frankau' (if he continues to write like this of his younger confrères it is possible that he may soon be black eyed in more than one sense) has some mingling of foreign blood to account for his swarthiness?[15]

The storm raged on, only ending when a blimpish letter arrived from one Charles Davis, of Oxford, who recalled Frankau's gallant efforts during the Great War:

Possibly our young friend does not know when throwing the challenge of blacking eyes that Mr Frankau was badly gassed. But here's one who was only wounded and who with Mr Frankau's permission is quite willing for our young Beaton to try and black his eyes instead of the eyes of such a man as Mr Frankau.[16]

Cecil's journalistic efforts were also attacked privately by Stephen Tennant, who for some years had been laid low with ill-health. Stephen wrote:

Now I'm going to scold you! those articles!!!!! *so* unworthy of you! so base to deny your true heritage of genius and rare brilliance – for you are an entrancingly brilliant creature – but I think you spend yourself too prodigally ... but don't you join all those poor washed-out drearies like Viola Tree and Alan Parsons with their thin vapid idle commentaries – you are so infinitely above them.[17]

Cecil's younger sister Baba was presented at Court on 15 May. Waiting in the long queue of cars, the Beatons listened to the exclamations of the watching crowd. One woman pointed at Baba and exclaimed, 'Oooh, ain't that lovely? All white and silver – just like Helen of Troy!'[18] Baba was adorned in a classical pseudo-Grecian costume and looked exquisite. Cecil was equally enchanted:

I have never seen her look more ethereal. Her breasts small and round, her arms like slender fronds and her skin milk white and hair in silky curls. I was quite touched by her loveliness as she sat with crossed feet and hands, so pansy-eyed and yet so delicately dignified.[19]

With Tallulah Bankhead, Osbert Sitwell, Stephen Tennant and others, Cecil sat for a head by Frank Dobson. He attended a celebratory lunch at the Savoy for the aviatrix, Amy Johnson; and he designed a parade of dresses for *Charlot's Masquerade* (a revue at the Cambridge Theatre, starring Beatrice Lillie).

There was a flurry of photography, drawing and writing for the *Book of Beauty*, Cecil's parody of a sentimental Victorian album. The idea for such a book had come to him in Canterbury in the summer of 1927. He found two volumes of Victorian society beauties on a market-stall. Osbert Sitwell mentioned the idea to Thomas Balston, of Duckworth, and Cecil's first book was commissioned. For the book Cecil photographed Lillie Langtry (who ordered two dozen prints). If ever he failed to get a sitting, he drew his subject and wrote about her, as in the case of Garbo.

Cecil found his work very stimulating. He made hurried research trips to the British Museum, and then he sat in Hyde Park going through the work with Dorothy Joseph,* an attractive, lively girl, who arrived to be his first secretary. Edith Olivier gave Cecil considerable help over the text of the *Book of Beauty*, with which he had struggled for many months. In describing the various beauties included he had tended to repeat adjectives. As Edith pointed out: 'Deliriously blonde is a heavenly expression, but if you use it, you ought to use deliriously in no other place.'[20] She also urged Cecil to write the absolute minimum about his sisters: 'You know how spiteful people are, quite ready to say the whole book is a boost for them.'[21] This advice Cecil did not heed. When the work was done Edith declared: 'Artistically it is a real achievement, and a lift for photography, proud and haughty as that art has already become.'[22]

The *Book of Beauty* was published by Duckworth in November 1930 and the first edition at once sold out. At the same time there was a second exhibition of photographs and drawings at the Cooling Galleries. By and large he got good reviews for both. T.W. Earp wrote in the *New Statesman*: 'The Goncourts of the future will be grateful to him for providing a useful document, and he is among the few worthy, if too modish, successors of Mrs Cameron.'†[23] Beverley Nichols quoted some of Cecil's descriptions of the lovely ladies – 'her subtle nose is knotty.... Her fingers are chicken bones' – and commented: 'If he had written in the days of the duel, he would already be lying in some dark corner of Hyde Park, slashed from tip to toe.'[24]

Though not slain, Cecil was subjected to other rapier thrusts. Lady Cunard threw the book on the fire and drove a poker through it, commenting, 'He calls me a hostess, that shows he's a low fellow.'[25]‡ Lord Berners settled down delightedly at Faringdon to deface his copy, blacking in faces, extending teeth and planting a bottle in the outstretched hand of Mrs Vernon

Castle. Lady Colefax warned Cecil: 'I wish you hadn't put in Virginia – she will never forgive it – and she's so worth having for friend.'[26] Sure enough Virginia Woolf entered the fray in a letter to *The Nation and the Athenaeum*:

> To my surprise, I find that two sketches of myself are included. My permission was not asked. I have never had the honour of meeting Mr Beaton. He has twice kindly asked me to sit to him, and I have twice, I hope politely, refused.[27]

The drawing to which Virginia Woolf took exception

She went on to protest against 'a method of book-making which seems to me as questionable as it is highly disagreeable to one at least of its victims'.[28]

Cecil, of course, welcomed the chance for a battle with such a distinguished literary figure. He wrote back with some justification:

> Which caricaturist ever asks his victim's permission to include him in a book of caricatures – all the less reason to protest against inclusion in a Book of Beauty? In fact Mrs Woolf's complaint should be addressed to her Creator, who made her, rather than me.[29]

Virginia Woolf complained further that her protest was made because everyone assumed she had consented to appear in the book. 'My protest was against the principle and not against the individual case, which, as I said before, is of no importance whatsoever.'[30] Christabel McLaren* came to Cecil's support in the same magazine. His troubles were not over. He believed (wrongly) that Lady Howe had taken offence and wrote to apologize. Finally there came a savage review from John Piper, the young artist and

*Later Lady Aberconway.

writer, who declared that the book would be out of date in six months and not back in fashion for at least a hundred years.* John Piper concluded:

> His drawings have a certain delicacy, though they are anything but sensitive. But as a whole this book is a monument of vulgar advertising, and apart from a little good photography, it is notable chiefly on the pictorial side for a few clichés manufactured from a superficial view of post-impressionism, and on the literary side for a deliberate submergence of taste.[31]

Cecil was a bit disappointed that the book had not caused more of a blaze and that the exhibition had not been more crowded. But now he had a more serious preoccupation: 'Nothing matters compared to my heart affair.'[32]

* In 1982 an adequate copy changed hands for nearly £40 in London.

Part Four

The Lovelorn Years 1930–39

12

I Love You, Mr Watson

Peter Watson was the only great love of his life, the only thing that absorbed him.... In Cecil's house there was a book on the desk – a nineteenth-century novel and a book mark in the place where one of the characters says 'I love you, Mr Watson.'

Truman Capote to the author, 28 June 1983

Sir George Watson, 1st Bt, Lord of the Manor of Sulhamstead Abbots, died on 12 July 1930. He was a self-made man from Warwickshire. The myth was that he started life in poverty pushing a wagon along the streets selling eggs and milk until one day he miraculously invented margarine. His business, the Maypole Dairy Company, brought in millions. In 1923 Sir George handed over £30,000 to the notorious honours broker, Maundy Gregory, to buy a peerage, but this never came and on his death his executors sued for the return of the money – the first step in Maundy Gregory's downfall.

Sir George had three children: the elder son, a conventional man and a Fellow of the Royal Geographical Society; the daughter a keen racehorse trainer; and his second son, Victor William, always known as Peter, over a decade younger than the other two, who was born on 14 September 1908. He was sent to Eton, but suffered the stigma of being considered *nouveau riche*. David Herbert recalled that the family Daimler contained two silver-embossed vases, attached to each side of the back seat, filled with bunches of sweat peas or carnations, and another vase attached to the glass dividing the family from the chauffeur.

Alan Pryce-Jones, who knew him for thirty-three years, remembered that 'he grew up in a spacious Thames-side house, Sulhamstead, where the bedroom furniture had been bought *en suite*, and the hall held a pipe organ'.[1] Pryce-Jones also recalled that aestheticism came to Peter 'through the medium of brilliantine'.

Peter went on to St John's College, Oxford, where his riches soon gathered him some very fashionable friends. He was duly sent down and resumed his studies in Munich, where he became interested in music. There he bought his first Picasso drawing. Sir Stephen Spender thought he developed his tastes and his sensibility in those years after university 'through love of beautiful works and through love of people in whom he saw beauty. He detested politics, officialdom, priggishness, pomposity and almost everything to do with public and bureaucratic life.'[2] With the exception of Truman Capote (who could not stand him), those who knew Peter look back on him as a charming and attractive man with exquisite manners. But there was another side to him. He suffered from a deeply cruel and masochistic streak which made him an unpredictable friend and led him into sinister and dangerous company. Spender considered the complications of his character:

> He was too perfectionist to be an easy person to live with and he seems to have driven those who were very close to him into a kind of sympathetic despair. He was, as it were, essentially made for honeymoons and not for marriages. I mean that the best possible relationship to have with Peter was to be taken up by him very intensely for a few weeks, and then simply to remain on his visiting list for the rest of one's time.[3]

Alan Pryce-Jones described him particularly well:

> I can see him very clearly: rather tall, rather languid, with the face of the frog just as he is turning into a prince: a face lit by inner amusement and a kind of reluctant practicality, the face of a born professional who preferred to be an amateur.[4]

At Sir George's death Peter Watson inherited a considerable fortune. He ordered new suits and a vast black and orange Rolls-Royce. His interests would change over the years and he would become a creative connoisseur of modern art, an intelligent and discreet patron to a new generation of painters, the financial backer of Cyril Connolly's *Horizon* and one of the founders of the Institute of Contemporary Arts. But at this time he was enjoying what Michael Wishart called 'the guilt-free extravagances of the *jeunesse dorée* of the period'.[5]

Cecil met Peter Watson in Vienna in the late summer of 1930, and on first acquaintance did not find him interesting. Cecil had joined Anita Loos and Michael Rosenauer, while Peter was travelling with Oliver Messel. Oliver was clearly intrigued by Peter and Cecil asked him incredulously: 'Do you like him?' Messel smiled. 'There was something louche and tarty about his way of conveying to me that he was interested,'[6] noted Cecil, whose first emotion, envy, soon turned to yearning.

Peter and Cecil went sightseeing together and Peter escorted Cecil on visits to antique shops, searching for furniture for Ashcombe. One day, coming down in the lift together, Cecil caught his eye. He recalled what then happened:

He shot me a glance of sympathy, of amusement – it may have been a wink – but it did its work – it went straight to my heart – and from that moment I was hypnotized by him; watching every gesture of his heavy hands, the casual languid way he walked.[7]

Cecil examined Peter more closely:

An ugly but charming face, sandy coloured and easily recognizable, although unstriking, subtle and I did not know of what features the face was composed, puffy eyes, pointed features, tall, stooping slightly, great male chic with hat perched forwards on one side, smiling, beaming, bustling with hurried small steps through the revolving doors. Shock at so sudden a use of my Christian name, but was grateful and pleased.[8]

Cecil was meant to accompany Anita to Berlin, but instead he went to Venice with the boys. They stayed in a dismal little house on the Grand Canal. There was some discussion as to who should share the double room with Peter. Cecil did not want to barge in, so entrusted this privilege to Oliver. Peter was travelling with an electric gramophone, on which over and over again they played a particular German record. This 'wonderful, haunting tune' became for Cecil 'the theme song for my increasing besottedness'.[9] Peter then succumbed to a fever which only served to strengthen Cecil's passion. He bought him tuberoses and nursed him. But then Cecil had to return to London to deal with the page proofs of *The Book of Beauty*. It was only after Cecil had gone and on their last night in Venice that Oliver and Peter became lovers. Though Cecil was dreadfully upset when he found out, he did not despair. He was encouraged by the sympathy Peter had shown him and resolved to win his love.

Thus Cecil entered a period of obsession which was to dominate his life for the next four years. He imitated Peter in every respect. They wore the same clothes, the same scent and even talked in the same manner, so much so that Cecil's sisters never knew which one it was on the telephone. Charles James commented: 'It's extraordinary. You used to have a rump like your mother's – rounded and curved. Now you've got a flat backside like Peter Watson.'[10] Peter had the power to throw him from moments of ecstatic happiness into long periods of deep misery. Cecil's work and social life became of secondary consideration to this great passion, from which he never wholly freed himself.

Back in England, Cecil was preoccupied with his book and with Ashcombe. The building work was progressing and lorryloads of strange acquisitions began to tackle the steep hill down to the house. Ashcombe had begun to take on its own personality, 'garish and gay, lots of silver trumpery, window-boxes and nice warm smells ... flowers in pots!'[11] The time had come to spend a first weekend in the house. Rex Whistler and Cecil went down in advance to set up the gramophone and ensure that the chickens on the stove were browned and crackling in readiness for the arrival that night of Oliver and Peter. Cecil had a plan. He took Peter for a walk in the valley and sat him down on a tree-trunk. He asked him to come with him to America, Mexico and Honolulu. Peter had never crossed the Atlantic and agreed readily. 'I felt that if I could get him away from everyone, from Oliver and all my friends, that then surely I must be able to have him as my own,' Cecil confessed later. 'But things weren't easy.'[12]

Cecil was due for the first of a series of extremely unpleasant shocks. Generously he had allotted the double bedroom to Oliver and Peter. On the last morning Cecil breezed up to their door to wish his guests good morning, but the door was locked and Cecil's heart 'turned to stone'. His mouth went dry and he could hardly speak for the rest of the day. The incident was particularly beastly as far as Cecil was concerned because he had gone to such trouble to make his first guests welcome. He could not believe they would do 'such a thing under my roof.'[13] Later in the day Oliver questioned him about his sadness. Cecil confessed that he was very much in love and very upset. Oliver seemed genuinely sorry that he was suffering so.

The American trip was planned and their departure set for early January 1931. Two nights before they sailed, Cecil left Sybil Colefax's party to drive Peter to the station. The next morning he rang the Watson house in Berkshire but there was no Peter. Cecil himself was giving a farewell cocktail-party that night but Peter never turned up because he was spending the last night with Oliver. Cecil therefore drank too much and got into a frenzy, worrying whether or not Peter would be on the boat. Cecil motored to Southampton and there was no sign of him. But just before the *Aquitania* sailed, he jogged up the gangplank laden with parcels and wreathed in smiles. Cecil was furious and they talked late into the night, as a result of which Cecil thought all would be well: 'I try to forget my mortification and bring myself up into thinking life is heaven. It kills me with shame now' (he wrote in October 1931) 'to think how hoodwinked I was being all the time, but then I was happy – in such good spirits, never dashed however cold the douche of disappointment.'[14] And later he described the voyage:

Titania was never so besotted of her Bottom than I with my travelling companion. My eyes were glued to him throughout the day and as he lay asleep. The sea air knocked him out most of the time and as he lay, big hands clasped on his chest with his head thrown to the side, I would get out a sketching book and make drawings of him. It was the most heavenly experience in the world to live here in this cabin with him, to dress together in the morning and evening, to play the gramophone (Dancing on the Ceiling) – to have baths together.... Once I made a bad

mistake in giving words to my wishes: 'One day when we are lovers ...
then ...' Peter was obviously annoyed. It rankled. The humiliation is not
what hurt me but the fact that I was no nearer to what I wanted most
in the world.[15]

In New York Cecil had arranged in advance that a huge box of lilies of
the valley and violets would arrive with the note 'To Peter whom I love so
much'. They discussed this message. Outwardly Peter was friendly, called
him 'Poppet' and 'My sweet', but back at the hotel he never relented. Their
privacy was invaded by an Italian homosexual and Cecil suffered agonies of
jealousy. Then Cecil presented him to his girlfriends. They went to see Adèle
dance and held hands in the theatre. Cecil introduced Peter to Marge, who
thought Peter 'the louse of the world'[16] because she saw how he tortured
Cecil. The old lesbian, Bessie Marbury,* on the other hand, welcomed the
fact that Cecil now had found his direction in life.

Cecil described his endeavours at this time as 'one long procession of
physical work, photographs and drawings rushed through in the hope that
they will scrape through the examination and pass muster'.†[17] He wore
himself out with Condé Nast work to make money for their forthcoming trip
and with plans for his new exhibition at the Delphic Studios on 57th Street.
He produced a list of the six most beautiful women in motion pictures,
earning himself the accolade 'the bravest man in Hollywood'. They were
Marlene Dietrich, Norma Shearer, Greto Garbo, Lilyan Tashman, Marion
Davies and Ina Claire. Some of them commented on his choice, but, as ever,
Garbo stayed silent.

Peter refused to be bound by definite plans, which made Cecil's work even
more difficult; however, eventually they set off for Washington, Palm Beach
and Miami and then sailed to the Bahamas. Nassau proved a disaster in
every way, 'a wretched petty social, second-rate little place', as Cecil wrote
to the writer Patrick Balfour (later Lord Kinross), 'everyone drinking so
much too much, gossiping and fighting and all the snobbery of the Isle of
Wight clubs!'[18] Peter distanced himself as much as possible, always saying
'I' instead of 'we'. He was annoyed when Cecil was recognized by some
debutante fans and he ruthlessly dropped out of dinner-parties at the last
moment, leaving Cecil to go alone and make apologies. Then another homosexual, a 'boring young American', arrived and travelled with them to
Havana, causing Cecil further agonies of wild jealousy, this time with rather
more justification. Cecil tried to persuade himself that he was no longer in
love:

* Bessie Marbury died on 22 January 1933.
† *Time* Magazine's file on Cecil includes a note dated 23 January 1931, part of which says
of him: 'Has designed a good many parties etc. Very much of a snob. Has never been really
accepted. Takes pictures with ordinary camera. No quick work.' This was cabled from London.

It only amazes me to realize how badly I have played my cards, how absolutely wrong I have been about Peter.... He likes ruthless people who make their own way over others. He is independent, selfish, rude, insolent, conceited, young and silly and completely unimportant. Oh that I should realize this now when he had such magic for me. His dirty handkerchiefs, his every belonging possessed a glamour. Now he seems a fickle, facetious cad, cruel beyond dreams with no forgiving or leniency at all. His retorts are so rude 'I, I, I', 'How right you are!' – every remark is a taunt to one to be on one's metal and I am so thankful that [the boring young American] has come with us from Nassau to Havana for the dreary situation of my doting forever would have gone on and now I am sure how I feel. How stupid I have been to be so nice. He is a strange character. He likes one to be his master.[19]

The 'boring young American' dropped Peter in Havana, and Cecil and he continued alone to Mexico. Cecil had become very sunburnt, his eyes were swollen and his face looked like a football. This extracted no sympathy from Peter. The battle was now for Cecil to survive the trip without conceding a triumphant victory to Oliver. Once his emotions overwhelmed him and he sobbed hysterically in his cabin through the night. It was not easy for Peter either. He had hoped for a civilized travelling companion. Instead he found he had an over-demonstrative wreck on his hands, offering him besotted love at every waking hour.

Mexico held some appeal for them with its baroque churches, gilt madonnas, bazaars, bullfights and huge wreaths of gardenias at fourpence a bunch. It was memorable too for an idiotic row about who should turn out the bedroom light. For once Cecil refused and they fell to serious wrestling. They rolled about for an hour, the bedroom was wrecked and the next day the management complained. When Cecil rose to turn the switch because he could not sleep, Peter jeered childishly, 'Who put out the light?' At other times they had more frolicsome pillow fights which Cecil enjoyed because 'they were the closest to sex that I was ever to get with Peter'.[20]

On the last night before flying to Hollywood Peter suddenly announced that he mistrusted Mexican pilots and would follow later by train. Cecil had no choice but to go because he could not afford to waste the expensive £25 air ticket. Thus 'sunk in despair' he made his cold dawn departure while Peter slept peacefully in bed, without stirring to say goodbye.

Hollywood provided a brief respite. Cecil was reunited with old friends, and Gary Cooper suggested they should go off and 'take some shots at some tin-cans'. But Cecil was determined to welcome Peter, who arrived four days later. Only afterwards did he realize that he could have made a strategic move by being nowhere to be found. But as he put it: 'the only thing that mattered was that I loved the wretch'.[21] The Hollywood visit was reasonably happy with a visit to San Simeon, masses of work and masses of parties. Mary Pickford gave a dinner at Pickfair.

Although Cecil was forever on the brink of emotional turmoil, this Hollywood visit represents an inspired period in the composition of his photographs. Sometimes he employed his former ruses, for example by perching precariously on a heavy chimneypiece to photograph Lilyan Tashman relaxing on a chaise-longue below. And he continued to behave in an extrovert manner to ensure that he was not forgotten. 'You've done the lady justice,' commented one Hollywood producer. 'I've done her more than justice,' shrieked Cecil. 'She should have kept that profile of hers a secret!'[22] But instead of using the realistically painted commercial film sets, he became fascinated by the possibilities of the structures of the studios themselves, the fire-escapes, the air-vents, the great ropes and chains and the piles of discarded props – the plaster statues, balustrades and staircases leading nowhere. Thus a surrealist effect was often created. Cecil captured the real-life star, waiting to enter the fantasy world. The presence of cameramen and microphones are suspected – sometimes they are seen. Thus the photographs show Gary Cooper framed by the set's scaffolding, Adrianne Allen (Mrs Raymond Massey) leaning on piles of film reels, Ruth Chatterton and Fay Wray (of *King Kong* fame) amongst the props. On the other hand he also enjoyed highly romantic settings: Loretta Young amidst bowers of blossom and Lilyan Tashman in a swirl of softly painted leaves. Mirrors, hailed as a new device in portrait studies, enabled Cecil to show Lillian Gish and Mrs Allan Ryan (Janet Rhinelander Stewart) full-face with both profiles and the backs of their heads. The results filled the *Vogues* of the following summer and many have survived to be thought of as 'the Best of Beaton'.

Cecil found he could confide his worries about Peter to Adrian, the talented costume designer who was a friend of Garbo. Adrian revealed that Peter was unhappy because Cecil thought so highly of him. Presently Peter became restless to go home, so they took the train back to New York. As the trip neared its end Cecil became 'terribly sentimental about it', while Peter 'couldn't be more cold-blooded'.[23] In New York they parted and Cecil bade him farewell as he sailed on the *Bremen*:

> The last day I felt very quivery and weak and little cool streaks ran down my spine, but the final wrench was an anti-climax, strangely undramatic. He with no word of thanks, he very materialistic and I who had imagined myself sobbing helplessly all the way home after the departure felt relieved and independent.[24]

Cecil's last fortnight in New York proved very much happier. Anita (still working hard), Adèle (still dancing with Fred),* and Marge (still drifting),

*The following year Adèle gave up the stage. On 9 May 1932 she married Cecil's Cambridge friend, Lord Charles Cavendish. They had a daughter, who died at birth in 1933, and still-born sons in 1935. Charlie Cavendish inherited Lismore Castle (the Duke of Devonshire's Irish seat)

came to his rescue, heaping friendship and praise onto the lovelorn traveller. Whereas Cecil had prayed his friends would like Peter when first he introduced him, he now welcomed their criticism of him.

At the same time Cecil's work looked up. Edna Woolman Chase wrote to him reminding him that he had earned over $7,000 in 1930 and had already amassed $4,035 in the first quarter of 1931. She hoped to increase his revenue from *Vogue*. She asked for six or eight London letters, illustrated with drawings, snapshots or photographs. She wanted a double-page spread of English beauties in tweed, for which she offered $200, and colour spreads at $350. Cecil could therefore earn $10–12,000 that year, but she warned: 'Of course, if you are flitting about too much, it may not be possible for you to do as much as we would like.'[25] Cecil, however, hoped for 'the glamour of a contract', and W.R. Hearst helped him beat Condé Nast up to a handsome new deal guaranteeing him £3,000 a year.

Peter was there with Nancy and Baba to greet Cecil at Southampton in April 1931. As soon as he asked 'How are ye?', Cecil realized he was still under his spell. It transpired that there had been a rift between Peter and Oliver, that the latter had written saying he never wanted to see him again. However, when Oliver realized that Cecil was still interested, his competitive spirit was awakened. Cecil aggravated the situation by begging Oliver to relinquish his hold on Peter. Weeks went by during which Cecil's sole occupation was keeping Oliver and Peter apart, without letting them accuse him of 'any real mischief'.[26]

Peter took Cecil to Paris and they lay in the same bed. Chastened by Oliver's behaviour, Peter admitted he had behaved 'swinishly' in America. But the torture was never over. Peter took Cecil to bars and there was always the threat he might pick somebody up. When Cecil said he was tired Peter decided to go elsewhere with Niki Gunzburg. When he came back to the hotel, giggling, three hours later, Cecil threw a lamp covered with red silk at him.

Cecil spent a lonely morbid summer, only longing for Peter's telephone calls and yet hardly ever seeing him:

> I felt very lonely and unhappy and the terrible weather did not improve matters. My great comfort was lovely Ashcombe. What a thrill to return there and to find so much done. The dining-room curtains were up and divine. Each weekend brought vast improvements. I would travel down with the car packed to the skies with cupids, chairs, provisions, flowers and there were some heavenly parties, writing games in front of the fire, hysterical laughter around Edith. I was always very busy and tired.[27]

overlooking the Blackwater in County Waterford. He took to the bottle and died on 23 March 1944. Adèle, who remained a life-long friend of Cecil's, married Kingman Douglass, sometime Assistant Director of the CIA. He died in 1971 and Adèle died in Phoenix, Arizona, on 25 January 1981, aged eighty-four.

Edith Olivier thought Cecil had preserved the romance of the exterior and even enhanced it with new urns and statues, while inside he had succeeded in bringing initially dismal rooms to life.

Peter never came alone to Ashcombe, but he was always the most eagerly awaited guest and he was always late. Cecil made elaborate preparations each time to ensure that Ashcombe looked at its most romantic. One weekend the guests were Nancy, Nada Ruffer (the Marquise de Casa Maury's sister), Lord Berners (who arrived bearing a tuberose from Stephen Tennant) and Christabel McLaren. After the guests had gone to bed, Peter and Cecil took a stroll in the moonlight on the downs. Then they climbed into Cecil's new circus bed, adorned with Baroque animals that looked more fantastic than ever in the moonlight:

> How we gossiped. We giggled and I felt particularly tense with Christabel likely to be awoken by any of our squeaks or the bathwater running away, in her room next door. We fought gaily in bed, completely upsetting the bedclothes. We tickled each other, lay in one another's arms and I was completely happy – as completely as I ever will be with this poppet because he is the most unperturbed bastard, uninfluencible and I shall never alas become his lover.[28]

The next night, without explanation, Peter went to sleep alone in the studio without saying good night. Such hysterical highs and desperate lows gradually took their toll on Cecil. He became overtired and tetchy, he demanded sympathy from friends, he drank too much, and he endured tortured sleepless nights. Before the summer holidays he wrote: 'For once I have thought of suicide and it is only the thought of leaving Nancy and Baba that stops me.'[29] Their summer holiday together was likewise fraught with intrigue, a mixture of bliss and purgatory, and in the South of France Oliver Messel made an unwelcome reappearance. Staying with Lady Mendl, Cecil went along the corridor to wake Peter, but found unruffled sheets and no Peter. Though Oliver was no longer interested in him, he could not resist luring him back. Cecil began by collapsing in a fit of sobbing, but a kind confidante fired him to be vengeful. Uneasy and spiteful days followed before Cecil at last succeeded in giving Oliver the slip and he and Peter then drove away to Switzerland. Peter was in a good mood and Cecil in consequence blissfully happy. In a small hotel in St Moritz they almost became lovers after a dinner capped by a number of cream and Cointreau cocktails.

They often shared a bed together on their travels: 'I would spend half the night looking lovingly and longingly at him in his poses of profound unconsciousness,' Cecil recalled in 1956. 'I loved his big fat veiny hands and would clasp them around me in his sleep. But no more. I couldn't somehow make the overture that might have made things more easy for us both. Or would it? At the end of a lifetime I still don't know what the answer might have been?'[30]

Peter took Cecil on to Germany, a country he knew well but which Cecil had never previously visited. They went to Munich, where they saw the sights and heard *The Marriage of Figaro*. In the night, alas, Peter could not resist delving into Munich's murky night-life. Cecil resolved to accompany him: 'I hate going to these sort of places with anyone I like and I was anxious in case I should be made agonizingly jealous and envious.'[31] Fortunately their guide never materialized, so instead they went to bed, but Peter threatened Cecil that if there was any 'horseplay' he would go straight out for diversion elsewhere. Another night, however, Peter was more adventurous and found a boyfriend in a club. This time Cecil succeeded in remaining calm. And so the persecution went on and on, Cecil's hopes raised and dashed, his work and peace of mind suffering equally. He was continually made to feel trivial, ignorant and inconsequential. He was a gaffed fish and could not escape.

13

Roses and Tuberoses and Chalk White Flowers

*My love life is not as disastrous as it has been for three
years for I feel a little more secure and my sex life is
eased by the fact that I have a mistress. That expression
pleases me so much.*

Cecil's diary, May 1933

Cecil's voyage to New York in October 1931 was both a solitary and working one, his diary and a batch of unfinished drawings demanding his full
attention. He found that New York had lost its glamour for him: 'It seems
to hold few thrills, to be monotonous and a poorer edition of what it was
four years ago. It is no place for a slump and depression.'[1] Because Condé
Nast had lost so much money, Cecil had to take a cut in salary. His earnings
dropped by $3,000 to $12,000 per annum. Condé Nast was very reasonable
about his work appearing in other publications such as Hollywood movie
magazines, but on no account was it to appear in a Hearst publication.
Condé Nast urged that at all times the quality of his work as a photographer
should be stressed. Meanwhile Cecil's father, whose Liverpool business was
now closed, continually admonished Cecil about his extravagance.

His trip was not an altogether unsatisfactory one. Distanced from Peter,
he escaped his yoke somewhat. He found his drawings had improved, that
he was a more relaxed and easy-going person. He fell in with the Winston
Churchills (who were staying on the floor below him)* and he photographed
Winston's wife Clementine and his daughter Diana. He attended relays of
tea-parties. Sometimes he indulged in 'hilarious drunkenness'[2] and he became close to 'divine'[3] Tilly Losch. He went to Chicago to witness a charity
performance of *tableaux vivants* based on his *Book of Beauty*, performed at
Orchestra Hall on 17 November. The cream of Chicago society impersonated

* Winston Churchill had come to the United States to make money by lecturing. On 13
December 1931 he was knocked down by a car in Fifth Avenue, a serious accident as a result
of which he developed pleurisy.

Cecil's sitters in identical costumes and poses, while the organizer, Mrs Howard Linn, recited Cecil's 'deathless prose'[4] through a megaphone. He observed: 'I felt that fame had at last come to me in a most unaccountable and disturbing way.'[5]

In January 1932 he went to Hollywood once more. He photographed stars such as Marlene Dietrich, the Marx Brothers, the eleven-year-old 'genius of the screen' Jackie Cooper, Dolores del Rio, adorned with shells and garlands, the muscular 'Tarzan', Johnny Weissmuller, and Gwili André (in the style of Marlene). Above all, Hollywood held one 'tremendous thrill',[6] which made the trip forever memorable.

Cecil had not relaxed his distant obsession for anything that concerned Garbo. He nurtured the hope that he might photograph her but the dream had never been realized. At the end of his visit in March 1932, Cecil was invited to stay with an English couple, Edmund Goulding* and his wife Marjorie Moss,† who lived in a Hollywood mansion built in the Spanish style. Eddie Goulding had just directed Greta Garbo in *Grand Hotel*, and Cecil knew that he was one of the few people she visited at weekends. He accepted the invitation with alacrity. Sunday was the day when she might come. She did telephone, but she did not want to meet Cecil. Having no doubt read some of the articles he had written about her, she told Eddie Goulding: 'No. He speaks to newspapers. I don't want to meet him.'[7] Cecil was angry and tried to ring a friend who also knew Garbo, so that if he could not talk to Garbo herself at least he could talk about her. There was no reply, so he took a long bath and dressed himself in his newly purchased white kid coat, snakeskin shorts, white shoes and socks.

Thus attired he looked out of the window and spotted his hosts with Garbo 'sitting cross-legged on a white garden seat, smoking a cigarette held high in two definite fingers'.[8] She too was in white, wearing a Debureau cap. With a thumping heart he crept downstairs to telephone again. Once more there was no reply. He 'catwalked' into the drawing-room and found the Gouldings and Garbo sitting there:

> Somewhat breathy with surprise, I gasped 'Oh! sorry', turned about on my heels and sharply left the room. Half-way up the stairs, I heard Marjorie's Cockney voice tinklingly bidding me to come down and join them. This time I walked across the drawing-room on air.[9]

---

*Edmund Goulding (1891–1959), British stage actor, who went to Hollywood in the 1920s as a writer and later director. He directed the film *Grand Hotel*, whose première was on 12 April 1932. The film's star-studded cast also included John and Lionel Barrymore and Joan Crawford (whom Goulding had discovered).

† Marjorie Moss was a ballroom dancer. In 1924 Diaghilev had been persuaded to watch her dance a number with George Fontana. Sir Anton Dolin believed their dance was in part the inspiration for the waltz in *Le Train Bleu*.

In his book *The Wandering Years* Cecil related how Garbo directed the full barrage of her magnetic charm at him; how she complimented him on his youth and beauty, his white Indian shoes; how the Gouldings 'hardly existed in the presence of their guests'; how he and Garbo 'crab-walked with arms round each other's waists, and much friendly hand-squeezing'. It was on this occasion that Garbo picked a yellow rose from a vase and declared: 'A rose that lives and dies and never again returns.'[10] Just as, in Proust, Swann pressed Odette's rose to his lips and then locked it away in a secret drawer of his desk, so Cecil concealed the rose in his diary, took it home, framed it and hung it above his bed. After his death it was sold to a New Zealand photographer for £750.

The party ate, played charades and drank Bellinis. Garbo then accepted Cecil's invitation to go to his room and see photographs of Ashcombe. Cecil claimed in his unpublished diaries to have kissed her. He wrote that she said to him: 'You are like a Grecian boy. If I were a young boy I would do such things to you. . . .'[11]

Downstairs the party continued until dawn: 'The lights were turned out and our bacchanalia became wilder in the firelight.'[12] At dawn Garbo left in her big motorcar. Cecil could not believe that he would not see her again. 'Then this is good-bye,' he cried plaintively. 'Yes, I'm afraid so. *C'est la vie!*'[13] she answered. As he wrote: 'The Gouldings were rather too baffled by the evening to talk about it. I could hardly believe what had happened. The only concrete proof was the yellow rose which she had kissed.'[14] Cecil did not see Garbo again until after the war.

To put this curious adventure in perspective it is worth bearing in mind that at this time Garbo was closely involved with Mercedes de Acosta. Soon afterwards Garbo and she had terrible battles, following which Garbo suddenly left for New York without saying good-bye. Mercedes tried to see her there, but in vain. She returned to Hollywood and lost her job with MGM. In the winter of 1933, Mercedes wrote to Cecil: 'Greta told me yesterday that she had met you when you were out here last. You didn't tell me about it.'[15] Eddie Goulding also left Hollywood at twelve hours' notice after giving a party for eight girls, as a result of which two girls ended up 'having to be sent to the hospital'.[16] Hearst was furious, but there was little fear of the story being printed 'as it was so filthy it couldn't be'.[17] Therefore, as with so much of Cecil's involvement with Garbo, the situation was considerably more complicated than he realized. Nor was Garbo's initial reservation about Cecil talking to newspapers to prove misplaced. He remained silent only until 25 July 1934, when he wrote an article about her in the *Sketch*: 'Since her distaste for publicity about her private existence is so great, for fear of offending her susceptibilities, I shall curb my pen. But surely she will not mind if I tell you what she looks like off the screen.'[18] The description that followed was similar to that in *The Wandering Years* and his private notes of the time. The *Sketch* article was largely reproduced in *Cecil Beaton's Scrapbook*, published in 1937.

Cecil returned to London and to Ashcombe. 'There is always excitement at returning to this darling spot each time I have been away,'[19] he noted. He found that the ground had been levelled for the tennis-court and the grass was cut, giving the impression of sweeping lawns. He was soon overseeing the arrival of plants, arranging flowers in urns and vases and watching the new doves settle into the dovecot. At night soft candles in faint gold candelabra winked against the pink walls, and hessian curtains, covered with hand-sewn pearl buttons like a costermonger's coat, rattled gently in the evening breeze.

Ashcombe was often filled to the brim with guests, who played charades, ate delicious but simple food in huge quantities, and played elaborate games. This summer they staged high-jumping over a silver tissue scarf hung between two easels. There was an egg and spoon race over hurdles with fat little Oggie Lynn given a start and Oliver Messel, dressed as Miss Smithkins, presenting the prize to Randolph Churchill. They staged Sibyl Colefax's production of *The Miracle* with Oliver as the nun, Cecil as the Madonna, and 'Coalbox' cooing with the excitement of it all. Before leaving, the new guests traced their hands on the bathroom wall or ceiling.

While Cecil was always a thoughtful and generous host, he also revelled in the peace of Ashcombe when he was alone. He was never lonely there, though he often felt pangs of stark loneliness in big cities. He went for long walks, sat in the sun, sketched in the studio, and sometimes hung his head between his legs to gaze at the view upside-down. He relished every moment of possessing the place. He felt like 'the master upon Olympia, looking down upon my heavenly world'.[20] Cecil had been sad that he had not seen Peter on his return from New York, but late in the summer they were reunited at the Ritz in London. Malicious gossips had speculated as to whether they could ever be happy, and Peter had delighted Cecil by saying: 'Well, I wouldn't be as miserable as I have been not seeing you and I really mean that.' Cecil concluded they were now 'affectionate companions'.[21] Peter invited Cecil to come on holiday with him and though Ashcombe was at its best, he could not resist accepting.

On the surface their travels were all that Cecil could hope for – a weekend at Syrie Maugham's in Le Touquet; a visit to the ballet to see Lifar dance *Le Spectre de la Rose*; the Manet Exhibition in Paris; a stay in Majorca, then on to Nîmes, Arles, Aix-en-Provence, Marseilles, Cassis, Toulon and Cannes; a visit to Maxine Elliott at L'Horizon; parties with Elsa Maxwell; watching Hindu dancers in Daisy Fellowes's colonnaded garden in Monte Carlo and then on to Parma and Venice. But under the surface there arose again the old pangs of jealousy, leading to an inability to work, read or write. Cecil was drawn close to Peter and then rejected. He had 'sunk so deep having to make the best of the predicament'. Venice at least was full of friends. The Duff Coopers and Chips Channon were at the Palazzo Brandolini with the American hostess, Laura Corrigan; Mona Harrison Williams was giving candlelit dinners at tables scattered with gardenias at the Vendramin; Emerald Cunard, Lady Juliet Duff, Lady Castlerosse, Lady Mendl, Oliver Messel and Randolph Churchill were daily to be seen on the Lido. There were the usual bouts of uncouth behaviour that perennially gave the English a bad name in Venice. Sir Richard Sykes was much taken by the lantern-jawed Lucky Strike heiress, Doris Duke, but when he had made a pass at her in a car her chauffeur had stopped, a detective had appeared from another car and he was deposited in the road. On the night of Lady Diana Cooper's fortieth birthday, on 29 August 1932, a party was given on one of the islands. Sykes, angered by Miss Duke's behaviour, purposely burned the back of her hand with a Lucky Strike and Randolph Churchill, who was also keen on the heiress, engineered a dreadful fight. Lady Diana recalled the incident, which gave Cecil the chance to get even with Oliver Messel:

> Everyone had been drinking like fishes for an hour before. Now all the wives were clinging to their men to stop them joining in. . . . Oliver Messel and Cecil Beaton were fighting like bears and, as I thought, doing *splendidly*! . . . The next day I was covered with tuberoses, which were sent when you'd behaved outrageously.[22]

By September Peter had became bored with Cecil, who nevertheless longed to stay on and was urged to do so by everyone except Peter himself.

'What are your plans?' asked Peter.

'I suppose to leave by the six o'clock today.' This was greeted by silence. Cecil dreaded leaving on such a dismal note. He asked, 'May I stay on?'[23] and, having thus humiliated himself, Peter relented. Cecil confessed to Princess Jane di San Faustino that they passed a charming last evening after somewhat unhappy days. Peter then accompanied Cecil to the station and watched as his train left. Alone in the carriage, Cecil howled 'because the situation was so helpless'.[24] It was aggravated by Princess Jane's loose tongue: she broadcast Cecil's words all over Venice. Peter, travelling in Austria and Germany, heard of them in Vienna and Munich. He rebuked Cecil: 'I do feel an idiot when someone comes up and says that Jane has announced that you and I had a very *happy last night together* which is what I did hear.'[25] Meanwhile Cecil wrote from Le Touquet: 'Please, please let's always be friends. I shall try not to make it difficult.'[26]

In Venice Peter had told Cecil: 'I'd be delighted if you had an affair.'[27] Cecil did precisely that – with Doris Castlerosse, three years his senior. She was an arrogant, temperamental and generous girl, said to be Noël Coward's inspiration for Amanda in *Private Lives*. Doris Delavigne was born in

Streatham in 1901, the daughter of a Belgian merchant. Her mother was English and Doris was brought up in Beckenham. She became a talented musician. Later she made money by selling second-hand clothes to chorus girls and eventually bought 'Louis', a coiffeur's establishment in the Champs-Elysées. As a young girl she shared rooms with a then unknown actress called Gertrude Lawrence. They had one evening dress between them and whichever of them had the more important date would wear the dress. Doris had lovely legs and wore very short shorts to show them off. She knew she had much to offer and was consequently surrounded by rich admirers, who financed different aspects of her life. In time, young girls flocked to her house in Deanery Street because they met boys there, and because Doris passed on her expensive silk stockings. She never wore the same pair twice.

Doris drove around London in a Phantom Rolls-Royce. Determined to be a peeress, she had married the corpulent gossip columnist, Lord Castlerosse, in 1928, to the chagrin and rage of his employer, Lord Beaverbrook. This tempestuous marriage had soon come adrift and on 26 October 1932 Castlerosse sued for divorce. For all her peccadilloes, Doris's friends remember her as a thoroughly nice girl. She was totally uninhibited, and believed that there was no such thing as an impotent man – only an incompetent woman. There is even a myth that Winston Churchill said to her: 'Doris, you could make a corpse come.'[28]

It was Doris who developed 'a decided penchant'[29] for Cecil. At the beginning he was disinterested but, partly to make Peter jealous, he gradually warmed to the idea of having an affair with her.

Daphne Fielding, then Viscountess Weymouth, recalled that Doris seduced Cecil in a room filled with tuberoses. The intoxication of their scent helped to overcome him. 'He wouldn't have to do a thing,'[30] recalled Mrs Fielding. There was a story of a weekend party at Faringdon. Doris and Cecil retired upstairs and, being Faringdon, a house noted for its eccentric activities, the house-guests tiptoed upstairs to listen outside the closed bedroom door. Suddenly Cecil's voice cried out: 'Oh! Goody, goody, goody!'[31] Doris instructed him in the arts of love-making. In bed, if he performed too precipitately, she would slow him down by saying: 'Think of your sister's wedding!'[32] This unlikely affair was to last for some time to the surprise of their friends and not least of Lord Castlerosse. One night he went into a restaurant and saw Doris dining with Cecil. 'I never knew Doris was a Lesbian!' he muttered.[33] Diana Vreeland, who remembered that Doris also had an affair with Sir Alfred Beit,* recalled the *bon mot* that circulated in London about Doris: 'Beaten by Beaton and bitten by Beit.'[34]

Cecil himself obtained little joy from the affair. Ill-treated by Peter, he was content to behave just as badly to Doris. In January 1933 he wrote:

* Sir Alfred was sent to South Africa to cool down.

Peter loves people that are not in love with him and I in my turn am now worshipped and adored by Doritzins for whom I hold no emotion whatsoever. It seems so terribly unfair that there cannot be a great straightening out and saving of waste. It really seems so terrible that I go to bed with Doritzins in desperation when it could be so celestial with the bedfellow I love and it is doubly hard for me that though Peter does not love me he is incensed by my relations with Doritzins whom he loathes and becomes bitter so that he doesn't want to see me.[35]

Presently things became more serious. In February 1933 a man arrived at Sussex Gardens to subpoena Cecil in the Castlerosse divorce case,* but, fortunately for him, he had by then sailed once more for America.

Before he sailed, Cecil oversaw the arrangements for Nancy's wedding. Both his sisters announced their engagements almost simultaneously in the winter of 1932. Baba was first to the post with an unofficial engagement to Alec Hambro, while Nancy followed on 4 November with her official engagement to Sir Hugh Smiley, 3rd Bt, a twenty-seven-year-old Grenadier Guards officer. 'I can see no point in making a marriage a dull, quiet, obscure thing,'[36] Cecil declared. He decried 'the same hymns, smilax, asparagus fern, wired roses, lumpy girlfriends looking like bad imitations of musical comedy bridesmaids in tulle skirts of pastel shades'.[37]

Tall silver Venetian posts were placed in St Margaret's, Westminster, by Constance Spry, who also arranged bouquets of chalk-white artificial flowers and palm leaves to add fantasy to the hazel branches sprayed with chalk. Nancy wore an ivory chiffon gown, lavishly embroidered with pearls and silver sequins, the hem trimmed with ermine. She looked, as Cecil intended, like the snow queen. The wedding day on 18 January 1933 was cold and the bridesmaids, who were harnessed to each other with garlands of white flowers, shivered in sleeveless, low-necked tulle dresses. They included Baba, Lady Violet Pakenham (a journalist on the *Evening Standard* who presently married the writer, Anthony Powell), Joan Buckmaster (Gladys Cooper's daughter, now Mrs Robert Morley), the Hon. Joan Monsell (now married to Patrick Leigh Fermor), and Margaret Whigham (who was about to marry Charles Sweeny and is now Margaret, Duchess of Argyll). In the church the whitewashed garlands flaked, leaving a chalky trail up to the chancel steps. 'It was quite a time before we were allowed in St Margaret's again after that,'[38] admitted George Foss, Mrs Spry's right-hand man.

The wedding was a glittering success† with thronging crowds and Cecil prominent in pale lavender-grey trousers, white satin stock and white Ascot top-hat. However, it marked for Cecil the end of the 'Beaton-circus-home

* In March 1933, the Castlerosses entered into a deed of separation.

† Sir Hugh and Lady Smiley had one son, John, born 24 February 1934. In 1983 they celebrated their golden wedding at the Guards' Club.

fun', a phase that Cecil knew could never be repeated: 'Oh the excitement of the dressing-up scenes at 61 Sussex Gardens! Oh the pretence and make believe!'[39]

Setting off for America a few days after the wedding, Cecil noted:

> I have realized my two ambitions of the winter. Nancy has been married in a blaze of happiness and success and on my way to the boat I get a charming letter from Prince George calling me by my first name. My life is sensibly planned and he is definitely in my plan of campaign.[40]

Cecil's important letter from Prince George (later Duke of Kent) congratulated him on some portraits Cecil had made of him. Prince George gave him permission to publish one, but only in an American Condé Nast magazine. The Prince was duly published in a light checked suit. Prince George was not Cecil's first royal sitter. He had previously photographed Queen Victoria's Bohemian sculptress daughter, Princess Louise, Duchess of Argyll, 'in a variety of conventional period poses in a grey tea-gown'.[41] The Princess came to Sussex Gardens to be photographed and then entered into lengthy correspondence about every minute detail of the touching up. Finally one picture was chosen.

The visit Cecil paid to America in 1933 marks his closer involvement with fashion photography. To begin with he photographed famous named sitters, such as the actress Helen Hayes, wearing products of the famous fashion houses. One of his models was Mary Taylor, a girl who was told by her doctor that she was dying and went into fashion as a last wish. But she got better* and Cecil was soon linking her with Princess Natasha Paley as among 'the most significant beauties of today ... completely natural' and 'pale with the rare quality of convolvulus'.[42] Cecil's compositions became accordingly more romantic again with painted backdrops of snow scenes and desolate trees, while sometimes the models were portrayed in looking-glass frames.

His efforts were greatly assisted by having professional lighting men and any number of women to help place his 'Baroque gadgets'. Cecil continued to describe himself as a camera artist. He explained:

> His lens will permit him to reproduce only exactly what is in front of it. The camera is a mirror of actual facts. Hence if the photographer is also to be an artist he must pose his sitters and prepare his decorations so as to place before the camera in physical reality those inward facts of life with which an artist is concerned.[43]

---

*Cecil visited Mary Taylor at Malibu Cliff in 1963 and found her leading a 'Brontë existence' there.

His *Vogue* contract was duly renewed until April 1935.

Cecil stayed at the Waldorf-Astoria, delighted to have escaped from both 'the poverty' of his parents' lives and 'the chaotic disturbances of [his] unrequited love'.[44] He converted his hotel rooms into a private apartment with borrowed Picassos and Matisses, odd junk, shells, artificial flowers and rubber plants.

In these carefree New York days Cecil enjoyed flirting with Tilly Losch until he became annoyed at her casualness. 'After that our relationship never recovered its former lovingness.'[45] David Herbert was in New York. Cecil and he became great friends: 'I have found him a most delightful, gay, alive and witty personality and companion – so generally sympathetic and kind and understanding.'[46] Sir Michael Duff then appeared. The immensely tall son of Lady Juliet Duff, he was a man of great charm, combined with an engaging stammer. Cecil had decided in advance that he would be a good person 'on whom to tag my affections,'[47] so he adopted a casual air with him. Michael Duff fell under the spell. 'We are not lovers,' wrote Cecil, 'but all the trappings are there.'[48] Their affectionate friendship resulted in midnight feasts and pillow fights, and endless gossiping either together or on the telephone. Eventually Cecil thought he might clinch the situation by 'rushing in' in the style of their friend Francesco Mendelssohn (formerly a leader of Berlin's intellectual life), but this plan was frustrated by Michael becoming close to Tilly. Cecil was at first disappointed and jealous. However, they remained good friends, drawn together by grim shared experiences such as witnessing a dance marathon: 'one of the most barbaric pieces of cruelty that continues in this so-called civilized age'.[49]

Cecil contemplated his return to London with some misgivings. He hoped he would not suffer further over Peter; he dreaded complications with Doris; and he hoped he could manage more serious work – 'but that's the way I feel every year and I never get down to it'. He arrived home to find 'Mummie rather tired, Baba not very chic and Daddy really very decrepid in a terrible old raincoat'.[50]

Marge, who had spent most of the winter in St Anton where she had seen a great deal of Peter, strongly advised Cecil not to see him again. Though they talked until dawn, Cecil was not convinced. A few nights later, Cecil met Peter at the Royal Opera House and noticed that he was wearing a ring, something he normally hated. He demanded to know with whom Peter had been in Rome and received a curt rebuff.

Cecil was only in England for a few crowded days in London and a quick visit to Ashcombe, where he ran round the garden exclaiming with joy. He attended the Circus Ball with Diana Cooper, Chips Channon, Daphne Weymouth and others. Doris Castlerosse was dressed as an equestrienne and Cecil, as a cowboy, pursued her with a whip.

Cecil persuaded Doris to cross to Paris with him before he set off on a sightseeing tour with William Odom,* a mysterious, very rich American with a smile like a snarl, whose only attraction was his willingness to pay for the entire trip. Cecil and Doris lunched at the Ritz with Elsie Mendl and her effeminate young escort Johnnie McMullin.† They gossiped madly and Elsie suddenly declared, 'I love whores', which brought a yell from Doris: 'What about homosexuality?'[51] This outburst was inspired by Doris's recent shock discovery (when perusing his diary at Madresfield, the Beauchamp seat) that Cecil was in love with Peter.

After lunch Doris bought a mass of clothes and then Cecil pretended he was going to a gallery, while in reality he paid a sneak visit to Daisy Fellowes at Neuilly. In the evening Doris and he saw Harlem dancers and an exceptional Hungarian band:

> Back to the Crillon which I enjoyed very much indeed. Situation the same. No truth is ever sought. The big day of explanation is still afar for with the questions asked I am so capable of tying the string a bit tighter and it flatters me a lot. It is an exciting game and I am always fond of anyone that is fond of me.[52]

The next morning Cecil and Odom set off on their European tour in the back of his open Duesenberg motorcar, visiting Aix-en-Provence, Genoa, La Spezia and Florence, by which time Cecil's face was thoroughly wind-burnt. They drove to Montegufoni to call on Lady Ida Sitwell, hobbling about with a broken ankle, and her six-year-old grandson, Reresby: 'What a charm the child has! ... with an extraordinary mind and with the fantasy of the rest of the family.'[53] In Rome, where Cecil observed: 'Michelangelo here draws bigger crowds than Rudy Vallee or Charlie Chaplin',[54] he heard of Cimmie Mosley's death (on 16 May): 'I am so upset I could cry.... I owe much of my happiness and success to her appreciation and friendliness.... She loved Peter and it made me rather jealous but I am glad she did like him.'[55] Doris wrote to tell him this news and urged him: 'Enjoy yourself, darling, and do come back the same sweet Cecil you were before you went to New York.'[56]

Odom's generosity to Cecil was ill-rewarded. He learned how to play on Odom's inferiority complex by asking difficult questions such as: 'What date is the villa we're going to see?' – 'What is incense made of?'[57]

Finally they reached Paris, where Cecil remained for three weeks of the

---

* William Odom came from Kentucky, where he began life as a gentleman jockey. He inherited the Parsons School of Design in Paris and New York. He liked Louis XVI art. For several summers he rented the Palazzo Barbaro in Venice, where he entertained any friends recommended by Sir Robert and Lady Diana Abdy.

† Johnnie McMullin (1889–1944), social columnist and fashion editor on *Vogue* for some years. He once wrote in *Vogue*: 'A complete jewelry kit is a most important part of a well-dressed man's wardrobe.' On another occasion he was overheard crying out: 'Cancel all my appointments; I have just heard of a white dress waistcoat with one button in Jermyn Street. I must fly!'

season. Marge was there and she spent further hours talking to Cecil about his predicament:

> Marge said that I used to be such a gay person, inspired and full of life; that since I met Peter I was a changed person, sadder and forcing my gaiety, being hysterical and crazy and drunken, that I'd lost my natural gaiety and had only been marking time with my existence – all *so* true alas. . . . [58]

Cecil hoped that Peter might be in Paris, but he had disappeared, presumably with a new friend of his, a young American. Meanwhile Cecil was happy in Paris, going to the ballet and enjoying the company of Daisy Fellowes (then enjoying a brief-lived career as Paris editor of *Harper's Bazaar*), the photographer Horst, who was to prove something of a rival, George Hoyningen-Huene, Pavel Tchelitchew and Edith Sitwell. Doris arrived and Cecil became the envy of the city. He described her stay as a 'great sex interlude. I become a peacock and feel so self-assured and even beautiful.'[59] Doris suffered, which made Cecil sad, but he thought 'being the loved one does me good morally'.[60] But soon he longed to be free and Doris went home taking her coroneted luggage and dozens of pairs of shoes and stockings with her. Then Peter arrived, causing the habitual mixture of elation and depression. Cecil found himself weeping in taxis or in the bright sunlight of the Ritz Bar, but pulled himself together and tried to enjoy his worldly success. He met Jean Cocteau and Christian Bérard, both of whom liked his work. Princess Natasha Paley* thought he was beautiful, and Daisy Fellowes thought him witty. And yet still nothing mattered but Peter: 'I have no best friend after all these years of dogged concentration. The one to whom I would go if I were dying finds I make him nervy.'[61]

Back in London Cecil composed a long letter to Peter, saying farewell. It began:

> My dearest Darling, This is so much the saddest thing that happened in my life. It is *so* serious for me to make the painful wrench but I *cannot* continue being made miserably unhappy constantly by your peculiar vagaries. . . . I cannot weep any more, my eyes are swollen and my face unrecognizable from so many tears and so much hysteria. [62]

Cecil never sent the letter, but one evening he read it to Peter, who said at once, 'No, that must never happen.'[63] Peter had been preoccupied with the American, the latest cause for Cecil's jealousy, and wrote that he had not wanted to make Cecil unhappy. Like Cecil he found the whole situation a nightmare and urged that they should be 'sane and friends again'.[64] In

---

*Princess Natasha Paley (1905–81) youngest daughter of Grand Duke Paul of Russia by a morganatic marriage. She married Lucien Lelong and later Jack Wilson.

July, after a particularly fraught week, Peter joined Cecil at Ashcombe for a few days to try and re-establish their friendship on a happier basis. This attempt proved successful, at any rate for a while, and they spent their time 'expounding, gossiping and giggling'; Cecil wrote 'I would have liked it never to end.'[65]

Peter showed no sign of wanting to share his summer holiday with Cecil this year, so in August Cecil joined Doris at Maxine Elliott's villa, near Cannes. Doris did everything possible to boost his morale, and he was happy there until a desolate letter arrived from Peter in Salzburg. Cecil made the obvious mistake of setting off to join him. Peter was not at the station to meet him and a note at the hotel announced that he had gone to the mountains for the day. Cecil spent a desperately lonely Sunday waiting about for Peter, who returned only when it suited him. Their first evening was rather cold. Fortunately Cecil soon became fed up with being made to grovel and departed for Venice. He joined Odom's party at the Palazzo Barbaro. Here he found the Abdys, the Channons and the Sacheverell Sitwells enjoying Odom's lavish hospitality. Cecil found that sightseeing with experts such as Bertie Abdy and Sachie Sitwell revealed his ignorance of Italian art and he was more comfortable relaxing on the Lido beach.

At the end of the season he settled down to paint and produced 'the least bad things I have yet done in oils'.[66] Later Odom drove him to Austria, where he stayed with the Channons and the Duff Coopers. In Munich he joined Gerald Berners and Robert Heber-Percy and there was a certain amount of rivalry. Peter almost succeeded in causing another upset by his 'sudden disconcerting arrival',[67] but Cecil was supported nobly by the Sitwells. He then spent some 'free and contented' days in Paris before returning to London to work.

On 7 October 1933 Cecil's cousin, Tecia, was married to Frank Fearnley-Whittingstall at St George's, Hanover Square. All the Beaton family were present and Reggie, who was in fine spirits, was an usher. Eleven days later, on 18 October, Reggie was killed by a tube train at Piccadilly Circus underground station. The train driver told the inquest that Reggie put his hands in front of him and dived under the train. He believed it was a deliberate action. Cecil was told the news by Baba when he returned from dropping Doris home after a dinner party given by Sybil Colefax for Mona Harrison Williams. At first he was strangely unmoved by the tragedy:

I couldn't believe it to be true that Reggie should not appear again – and uncannily enough I had been musing to myself only today or maybe yesterday what would happen if Reggie should die. How much difference would it make to me; and it would make so little difference really for I see him so seldom, and unlike Peter and his brother have so little in common with him, I hardly ever write to him and now the appalling news is given to me and it leaves me so cold that I am amazed.[68]

At first there seemed no particular reason why Reggie should have committed suicide. He was a reasonably happy person, he had many friends, he was adored by his cousins and was his father's favourite son. He loved his career with No. 101 Bomber Squadron at Andover. Occasionally he dated a pretty debutante called Jeanne Stourton, who later married Lord Camoys. But it transpired that he had eye trouble and continual blackouts. His best friend, Mrs Margery O'Brien, who lived in Dover, revealed that he had had a blackout in her drawing-room the previous weekend. He had another on the day he died as he got out of the bath and, though Mrs O'Brien did not say so at the inquest, he had telephoned a friend that evening to say 'he was feeling so rotten he thought he'd throw himself under a bus'.[69] Reggie's health threatened his career and the coroner concluded: 'I believe he was worrying and brooding about this, and gave way to a sudden impulse to get rid of anxiety and trouble by ending his life.'[70] Other friends have recalled a deeper unhappiness in Reggie and it is possible that the fear of losing his commission made him feel even more inadequate and inferior to Cecil, whose career appeared to grow daily more glamorous. His father never recovered from the tragedy.

Cecil found life at home particularly depressing in the days that followed. He escaped with Peter to the National Gallery, to Fortnum's, to the Ritz Grill and to a play which had run for a time and where he was unlikely to be spotted by friends. The funeral was grim, with Mrs Beaton sobbing dejectedly throughout. After the interment at Hampstead Cemetery the family gathered in the drawing-room, everyone in black, with sherry and brandy on the sideboard. Nobody spoke much. Cecil could bear it no longer:

> I felt helpless and selfishly though wisely decided to leave for Ashcombe right away and I was lucky to have Peter and Rex to go down there with me. There was rather a disturbing long before the two boys arrived. I drank several glasses of sherry, which perhaps weakened my resistance, with the result that I left utterly shattered and sank into the car weeping feebly.[71]

Sympathy poured in from friends: 'There is nothing that one can say in the face of anything so heartbreaking,'[72] wrote Edith Sitwell. 'I was so sad for you,'[73] wrote Mercedes de Acosta. And Ninnie, who was now in retirement, wrote: 'Poor dear Mr Reggie, he is probably saved from a lot of trouble.'[74] Cecil sent his mother a generous cheque when she went to Biarritz to recuperate.

The Ashcombe weekend immediately after the tragedy was at least a contrast to the recent horrors. Peter, Rex and Cecil listened to gramophone records, looked at albums and lay together on the circus bed, gossiping as they gazed up at the red, white and blue canopy. But Peter demanded his own room without explanation. One day Peter and Cecil found that a previous owner of Ashcombe, Sir Gerald Grove, still had a picture of the house, painted in about 1770, which showed the panorama as it used to be. Cecil bought it for £50 and it became his favourite possession.* Edith Olivier came over and Cecil painted Lady Juliet Duff. Cecil called on Stephen Tennant and found him almost well again after a protracted illness. He thought that 'to be with Stephen puts new life into one's veins'.[75] Cecil relished especially 'his joy of living' and ability to make ordinary things 'wildly exciting'.

Cecil returned to London but did not go to Doris's large dinner at Ciro's for the sole reason that 'it would offend people if I am to be seen out so soon after Reggie's death'.[76] Instead he dined quietly with Peter at the Savoy. At Ashcombe during a weekend party, the hat of Alison Settle, his journalist friend, was thrown into the fire. Then one day David Herbert came round to see him. They gossiped about Peter, whom David said he hated, and Cecil learnt some most disturbing news.

* This picture was sold to the Salisbury Museum for £7,500 in the Reddish House sale on 10 June 1980 (Lot 492).

14

The Girls of Radcliff Hall

*Daisy when about to perform some action that was parti-
cularly mischievous, invariably pretended that she was
acting with the highest ends in view. In this instance, she
went about the school saying: 'I do think it is perfectly
monstrous that Lizzie should give Millie a car. It is so
unfair on poor Cecily, who is simply longing for a new
car. Cecily is Lizzie's best friend and Lizzie has never even
thought of giving her a bicycle.'*

by Adela Quebec (alias Lord Berners),
The Girls of Radcliff Hall

Lord Berners wrote *The Girls of Radcliff Hall* in a rage in forty-eight hours in
1937. In his wicked spoof he related the romances and intrigues of Cecil
(Cecily Seymour), Peter Watson (Lizzie Johnson), Oliver Messel (Olive
Mason), Robin Thomas (May Peabody), David Herbert (Daisy Montgomery),
Jack Wilson (Helena de Troy), Doris Castlerosse (Mr Dorrick, the dancing
master), and Robert Heber-Percy (Millie Roberts). The story was set in a
girls' public school and Gerald Berners himself appeared as the headmistress,
Miss Carfax.

Written in pseudo-romantic vein, it is particularly naughty because,
within its code and disguise, all the stories were true. It is also a rare edition
because apparently Cecil succeeded in destroying most of the copies. He
believed himself the victim of the book because the plot revolves around his
love of Peter Watson and Peter's various infidelities.

The incident quoted above relates the scene when David Herbert prepared
to tell Cecil that Peter had given Robert Heber-Percy a car. Robert Heber-
Percy was a protégé of Gerald Berners, who inherited the Faringdon estate in
Berkshire after the mischievous peer's death, and was still living there in
the 1980s. Though he mellowed somewhat with age, Robert was a tempestuous youth, who earned the nickname 'The Mad Boy'. Michael Duff parodied him in a spoof of his own, *The Power of a Parasol*, under the name of
'Robert Oddman':

He was dressed in brown corduroys, a yellow polo shirt, and round his neck, arranged in an untidy mass, was a blue and white spotted scarf; his eyes were hazel and very gentle, and he resembled an attractive ape with his protruding lower lip.[1]

Gerald Berners had lately been travelling with him and, though given to exaggeration in his stories, had clearly enjoyed an eventful summer. He related to Cecil how the Mad Boy 'nearly killed a woman in the street at Salzburg by hurling down a glass tankard'[2] from a restaurant, how he had tried to commit suicide and had had to be removed, heavily drugged, to Florence. Lord Berners continued:

> Our arrival at the Hotel Excelsior in Florence was, to say the least of it, sensational, as the Mad Boy had to be carried into the hotel in a semi-conscious state still dressed in his Tyrolean costume and with his hair hanging all over his face to the amazement and stupefaction of Bobbie Casa Maury and the entire Dudley Ward family whom I found seated in the hall. (It required some explaining away I can assure you!)[3]

Later in Amalfi there was a further fracas:

> The Mad Boy woke up in a Neapolitan mood, put on a scarlet shirt, a blue jumper, green trousers and a yellow belt and then suggested that I should go down and have breakfast with him on the crowded terrace. I said no, certainly not. Whereupon the creature flew into a rage and hit me over the head with a button-hook; the same button-hook with which Pauly Sudley* was struck at Vaynol.[4]

Lord Berners and Robert Heber-Percy met Peter in Munich and, as is often the case in such matters, Peter fell for Robert and the car in question soon followed as a token of his affection. When Cecil heard this, he demanded that he too be given a car. 'Did I understand you when you say Peter is going to give you a new car,' wrote Cecil's mother from Biarritz. 'What has happened to him and what luck to have one given. I'm all excited to see it.'[5] Peter deposited a blank cheque with Cecil's father, which was later converted into an Alvis worth £1,000. Innocently, Mr Beaton enquired of Cecil why this gift had been vouchsafed: 'On account of your blue eyes?' As Cecil noted wryly: 'Oh dear, how much nearer the point he was than he believed.'[6]

Edna Woolman Chase advised Cecil not to come to New York this winter because *Vogue* had 'a flood of foreign talent' on their hands. Cecil would be competing with the Spanish artist, Eduardo Benito, the fashion illustrator, Jean Pagès, and others.

---

*Viscount Sudley, later 7th Earl of Arran (1903–58). Elder brother of 'Boofy', 8th Earl of Arran. He was at Oxford on the day Cecil visited Kyrle Leng in 1922.

It was essential that Cecil should escape because, following the car incident, there had been more Peter trouble – 'intrigues to fill a life'.[7] Gerald Berners had stirred up trouble and involved Cecil more than was necessary. Peter had announced he was leaving for America and Cecil had succeeded in stopping him. Meanwhile Cecil drank too much and became a nervous wreck. He managed to persuade Peter to come to Paris for two happy days, during which they saw Tchelitchew and Cecil bought Peter a Bérard watercolour.

Cecil visited North Africa with the Baltic Baron, George Hoyningen-Huene, who was *Vogue*'s chief photographer in Paris until 1934 when, like Christian Bérard, he defected to *Harper's Bazaar*. Huene convinced Cecil that he must work with a Rolleiflex (the negatives of which could enlarge to almost any size). Thus armed with his new toy, Cecil set off with Huene to explore the desert. The Rolleiflex proved a success and the possibility of high-quality travel photographs was added to Cecil's range. From that day on he always used a Rolleiflex:

> It is an all-weather camera which can be employed on almost every occasion, and is so simple to manipulate that the handling of it becomes automatic. It is a great advantage to be able to see the composition one is about to take in the ground glass; its sole disadvantage to me is that it has no adjustable back, so that if one tilts the camera up at high buildings there is a considerable distortion.[8]

Cecil was also on commission to write an article about his Tunis trip for *Vogue*. The article hung over him daily 'like a storm cloud',[9] but he revelled in the colours and sights and enjoyed learning about the native customs. His mind continued to dwell on Peter, the death of Reggie, Baba's hoped-for marriage with Alec Hambro and the future of his own career.

He spent Christmas at Ashcombe, and concluded that 1933 was a year in which he had been both 'rapturously happy and suicidally miserable'.[10] In January 1934 he reached the age of thirty: 'I still think of myself as being young and find myself judging myself as quite apart when I see my school contemporaries slightly bald and grey and settled down to the uneventful lives of dreary marital bliss and domesticity.'[11] Nevertheless Cecil looked tired and drawn himself; and his receding and greying hair was a threat to his vanity. He remained determined to win Peter 'for it means most of all my life to me'[12] and, despite all the odds, he was optimistic.

Arriving in New York much later in the year than usual, Cecil was soon swept up into the energetic gossiping and party-going world of David Herbert and Michael Duff. They gave a 'grand and glorious' party in a private suite at the Waldorf-Astoria in February at which Doris Castlerosse was present with the New York crowd. Everyone called everyone else 'darling' and spoke with exaggerated enthusiasm on any topic that came into their heads. One guest at the party was the lovely Lilyan Tashman, whose sudden death from a brain tumour a few weeks later upset Cecil enormously. He photographed Katharine Hepburn and undertook other photographic work for *Vogue*. Influenced by his meetings with Cocteau and Bérard, Cecil now took trouble to paint appropriate backdrops for his fashion photographs, occasionally drawing a caricature of Napoleon or a sailor to match some element in the character of his sitter. He draped fish-netting, paper decorations or lengths of chiffon round his subjects and he continued to frame them with flowers. Both his drawings and his photographs became considerably more stylish in their composition.

The pace of New York life overtook Cecil. Business was better, drink laws repealed, there were no more speakeasies, everyone was spending madly. Due to lack of sleep Cecil succumbed to headaches. His doctor gave him powerful injections, which made him apathetic. He wandered about feeling dazed and drugged. It was a 'jittering wreck' that greeted Peter at the dock for a few days in New York before they set off together to Charleston, Haiti and Jamaica. Later the Faringdon world delighted in a story that emanated from this trip. Cecil found a butterfly farm and thought it would be a vision of wonder if Peter awoke to find his room glowing with the myriad colours of these delightful creatures. One night he inserted some chrysalises under Peter's door. But in the morning, instead of fluttering butterflies, Peter awoke to find slimy undeveloped caterpillars crawling over his face. The boat journey to Jamaica was less successful than that to Haiti. Cecil became tense and Peter had to warn him to eschew the rum bottle. Nor did Peter care much for Jamaica. They returned to New York, where Cecil completed seventy-six costumes for a negro production of *Romeo and Juliet* within a week. Then they sailed for London.

Peter knew that Cecil would be restless unless he had the neighbouring cabin to Peter's, so, without telling him, he moved his cabin, which Cecil thought 'proof of his independence and selfishness'.[13] Cecil soon found an empty one next door to it. He was saddened that Peter had criticized him, accusing him of being 'spiky and governesslike'.

Ashcombe was one of Cecil's most constructive consolations. Removed from the torments and intrigues of arch-tormentors, he revelled in the simple joys of nature. The sun blazed strongly throughout the summer. Roses blossomed fatly, lasted a day, but then new buds burst. Juniper and tulip trees flowered for the first time in a generation. The evenings were warm and starlit. Visitors flocked in droves and Cecil and Peter fled there to escape the intrigues of Gerald Berners.

There were periods of happiness but, inevitably, Cecil had to conclude once more:

Now as I write at the end of the summer I am again conscious of my failure, that my beloved will never be in love with me and will always fall for strumpets, and that continuously I am going to be miserable through each intrigue.[14]

Cecil was always extravagant. He spent his more than reasonable earnings to obtain the maximum visible benefit from Ashcombe. All his life he spent gross earnings rather than net proceeds, and thus was always on the brink of financial worry. But at this time he felt unhampered and independent of financial cares. His contract with *Vogue* now guaranteed him $15,000 a year. In August 1934 Condé Nast increased this to $17,000, backdated to 1 April. At his best moments life was 'overcrowded with treats, delights and excitements'[15] – plays, pictures, music, books, people, parties, wine, food and flowers. His old Cambridge friend 'Dadie' Rylands thought he was one of those rare people who is improved by success. Having created for himself a lucrative and enjoyable way of earning a living, having made numerous glamorous friends, and having created a gem of a house in which to live and entertain, he veered towards more artistic and intelligent people. He was anxious to learn and to develop. Conscious of his inability to concentrate properly when reading he took to synopsizing and reviewing the books he read, a process that he found 'a great burden'.[16] He relished his travels and under new mentors his eyes were opened to more spiritual experiences.

Such a guide was Pavel Tchelitchew, with whom he visited Spain in the summer of 1934. Tchelitchew was a Russian expatriate painter, whose 'entire life was dedicated, with fanatic mysticism, to the cause of art'.[17] He was famed for his neo-romantic canvases of clowns, acrobats and unhappy girls and a number of revolutionary ballet designs. Cecil had met him with Edith Sitwell, who was not only his great supporter but a martyr to tormented love for the temperamental homosexual artist. Cecil is credited with having saved Edith's life on one occasion. Edith was sitting for her portrait when, for no understandable reason, Tchelitchew flew into a rage and, amidst many flying objects, declared his intention to kill her. Cecil arrived at the studio and called out, 'Oh, what is happening? Let me in at once. Pavlik, do you hear?'[18] But there is no evidence that anything was happening (other than a bad case of histrionics). Tchelitchew had recently fallen for Charles Henri Ford, a handsome young boy from Mississippi, the brother of Ruth Ford the actress. Ford had just written a novel, *The Young and Evil*, which Edith described as 'that foul and unspeakable book'.[19] Cecil was drawn to Tchelitchew for another reason – Peter, whose opinion on all matters was sacrosanct, became an admirer and supporter of the artist. Cecil wrote:

Tchelitchew at first intimidated me (he could be devastating in his disapproval) but soon cast an almost hypnotic influence over me, and under
his spell my photographs became 'neo-romantic'.[20]

Toledo was the home town of El Greco and Cecil revelled in finding thirty
El Grecos in two small rooms:

Here was something that one had only dreamt of, each a whirlwind, a
vision, muscular, sensitive, trembling with vitality and sensitiveness;
painted with skill beyond dreams, restrained, and with a colour so bold
and perfect, so metallic and vivid that all other paintings seemed to
quail.[21]

Tchelitchew was not only a guide to art. The next day he took Cecil and
Charles Henri Ford on a tour of Madrid's night-life: 'Our eyes big with expectation and I looked wistfully at my bed before leaving as much as to say I
wonder if I shall sleep on you tonight and if so with what strange company.'[22] They visited a number of highly indecent strip shows and Pavlik
became very excited and cried out: '*Oh la folle!!* Like Miss Sitwell in all her
states, *beaucoup de* taffetas, and such swishing skirts ... and oh my gosh,
and such tits and titties ... and such a picture to do all rose and yellows
and blues.'[23] Cecil observed that one of the women 'came out with a magnifying glass with which she showed us to the fullest advantage her extrem-
ities',[24] after which he became tired and short-tempered and returned gratefully to his bed. The next day was filled with those disasters peculiar to
foreign travel. Cecil rushed to the Royal Palace, but got locked in the Banqueting Hall by mistake. Pavlik, who had a sore throat, lost his cheque-
book. Therefore they bundled into a third-class compartment and spent
eleven hours in crowded and intense heat before arriving at Seville. When
they found a mediocre hotel, Cecil was upset by his image in a distorted
mirror in his bedroom, and the next morning he discovered a black cat
wedged miserably under his table. It was not long before he tired of the
squalor and discomfort and flew via Madrid and Barcelona to join Stephen
Tennant in Avignon. He came away with Tchelitchew's advice not to drop
Peter because, said the artist, it is 'a deep and serious background to an
otherwise superficial life'.[25]

The late summer produced the fulfilment of his long-awaited chance to
work for the theatrical impresario, C.B. Cochran. Cochran's new show,
Streamline, opened at the Opera House, Manchester, on 1 September with
designs by Cecil, Rex Whistler, Cathleen Mann (the Marchioness of Queens-
berry) and Doris Zinkeisen, all of whom, in the words of James Agate, served
Cochran 'wittily, wisely and well'.[26] Tilly Losch and Florence Desmond were
among the dancers. Cecil drew caricatures of famous society figures seated

in boxes either side of the stage. As with *The Book of Beauty*, Lady Cunard, one of those depicted, took offence and had to be replaced at the last moment by Lady Diana Cooper. The show went to London after three weeks.

Meanwhile Cecil, who had looked tired at the opening night in Manchester, set off for Venice, a holiday with Peter that proved more tortured than ever.

'Do you think we're getting along as well as usual this trip?' asked Cecil.

'Oh *really* Cecil. You are so extraordinary. You do say such odd things,'[27] replied Peter evasively.

Together they visited many Italian towns, including Bologna, Ravenna, Arezzo and Urbino. Much of the time was spent in long, brooding silences. By Milan all sparkle had gone and Cecil thought they were just 'a bored married couple'.[28] At last he had had enough:

> Yes I must free myself. I am very grateful for the electives of bliss lying by him when he is asleep – our good-night kiss and for all that he gives but it is hopeless and bad for me and at last I see how bad it is for me and I hope to be free to start off on something else and we will *I hope* remain as close as friends – and everything I plan may fail. I may not be able to fall out of love. Maybe nothing will alter though much as I do love him I do see it as high time I did.[29]

In London Cecil visited Dr Leahy, of 45 Clarges Street, a self-styled mind healer, who had lost his leg in the Great War and had learned how to transcend the pain by power of thought. On 5 October this tough and yet very understanding Irishman gave Cecil two cards. They read:

> There is nothing in the atmosphere to defeat you. You'll feel and be absolutely at ease, gay and happy, refreshed.
> Shut your eyes and your left hand will lift.

and

> You've achieved some ease. You'll go from ease to strength no matter what the conditions.
> Shut your eyes and your left hand will lift.[30]

Dr Leahy told Cecil that he could not alter the facts but that he could alter his reaction to them. As Cecil wrote:

> Each evening I would hold his card in my left hand, shut my eyes and make my mind a blank. Without any effort on my part my hand would rise, gently at first, jerkily, then very swiftly. By degrees I felt calmer. After a few months I could meet Peter with a certain self-confidence and everything became less difficult for both of us.[31]

Gradually Cecil learned how to be elusive and mysterious himself. Though there was still much pain to be endured, he coped better in public. 'I am now capable of being much less hurt,' he wrote in a melancholy moment in December 1934, 'but it is sad to know how hard I work on manufacturing a situation that does not exist – my life work.' Meanwhile Peter said: 'I'll give you a dinner when you fall in love with someone else.'[32]

Thereafter the situation became more relaxed. When Cecil suffered an appendicitis operation, Peter was considerate and took him to stay with Juliet Duff and later to the Abdys in Cornwall. When Sussex Gardens was sold and Cecil no longer had a home in London, Peter allowed him to stay at his Mayfair house, in Shepherd's Close. Their meetings became more superficial and Peter's role in Cecil's life became important only when he praised or criticized his work. Presently Peter became obsessed by 'the black angel', Denham Fouts (the model for Paul in Isherwood's *Down There on a Visit*), who behaved to him in an even worse manner than he had to Cecil.

Cecil's younger sister Baba was engaged officially to Alec Hambro on 19 September 1934. There had been a delay while the groom, son of Captain Angus Hambro, of Milton Abbey in Dorset, sometime High Sheriff of that county, was sent to farm in Zambesi and Rhodesia in order to earn enough to support a bride. Meanwhile Baba was forever a bridesmaid – to her sister Nancy, to her cousin Tecia, to Margaret Whigham when she married Charles Sweeny, and to Karen Harris when she married Osbert Lancaster. In June 1933 she advertised *The New Eastern Foam* and in August that year she had to dive to safety from a burning motor yacht off the Isle of Wight.

Baba's wedding at St Mark's, North Audley Street, on 6 November was considerably less dramatic than Nancy's. Happy at last, she wore a close-fitting gown of white satin, with a tulle head-dress, and carried a bouquet of dark red roses. Her one bridesmaid, Tess Chattock, wore crimson velvet with a wreath of red roses in her hair. Cecil's plan this time was for a red and white wedding. Though the event had a certain Elizabethan charm, the *Tatler* thought it bad taste to adorn the church with dyed lilies, red pampas grass and Flanders poppies – the latter being 'symbols of blood and death'.[33] Cecil wore a lavender tie. With his thinning hair (he could no longer hide a thin streak of baldness from the forehead to the crown) and drawn expression, he looked older than his thirty years.*

Cecil's parents joined him at Ashcombe for Christmas 1934, a depressing few days during which Cecil studied his poor old father's broken life. While he thought Mr Beaton a sport with a good sense of humour and pluck, he

---

* Baba and Alec had two daughters, Alexandra, born 5 August 1935 (now Mrs Michael Lamb), and Rosamund, born 27 September 1939 (now Lady Gladstone). Alec died of wounds in Tripoli, North Africa, on 8 August 1943, and Baba died on 18 March 1973 at the age of sixty-one.

found his life one of total boredom and lack of imagination. His father had his habits, his newspapers, his helpings of food. He checked his watch frequently throughout the day, he seldom picked up a magazine that Cecil might place by him to tempt him. Often he stared blankly into space. At night he coughed and groaned, while 'the noises when he is in the bathroom' sounded 'as though he was in the throes of a death agony'.[34] Cecil was determined never to become like him, and yet he noticed 'he has an honest look of benign magnanimity in his warm blue eyes'. Mrs Beaton was depressed and had even considered going to live alone in the country. Her husband raised his glass for his traditional toast – it was thirty-two years since they had become engaged – and asked, 'Now is this to be continued for another seven, fourteen or twenty-one years?' But Mrs Beaton just replied: 'Oh, I shan't be here for another seven years.' Mr Beaton tried gallantly to save the situation by adding: 'Oh! but you're too late. You should have given notice before.'[35] After Baba's wedding Cecil's parents moved from Sussex Gardens into two bed-sitting rooms at 31 Linden Gardens, Notting Hill Gate. Thus the Beaton family life ended for ever. At the end of March, in fact the day after the Timber Trade Federation annual dinner, Mr Beaton had a seizure at the office.

Mrs Beaton duly put him in a nursing home in Devonshire Terrace; he had suffered a slight stroke without knowing it. Within a fortnight Mrs Beaton broke an arm when she accidentally tripped over a council roadsweeper's broom, and joined her husband in the nursing home. The specialist suggested that Mr Beaton should give up his business. 'This is all very sad,' wrote Mrs Beaton on 7 April, 'as to me it seems the beginning of the end.'[36]

15

Malice in Wonderland

Cocteau says I am Malice in Wonderland.

Cecil's diary, 1935

Cecil's escape from his infatuation with Peter Watson freed him to work harder. He was also bequeathed an introduction to the intellectual world of Paris, which he found both stimulating and challenging. Yet he wondered how he would cope in that city in which Peter had been held in such esteem. Cecil arrived in Paris in the New Year of 1935, and hardly had he registered at the Hotel George v than Hoyningen-Huene telephoned and 'the fun of Paris' started.

Cecil was delighted to hear that Huene had left *Vogue* for *Harper's* (in a fit of temper following a misunderstanding with Dr Agha). So had Christian Bérard, removing a serious rival from his path: 'That would be too lovely for me. That gave me such stimulus to work well and not consider the magazine a rubbish heap.'[1] Cecil threw himself with enthusiasm into both work and play, with never enough time to sleep. He gathered an enormous portfolio of work to take to New York and only suffered three setbacks: Paris *Vogue* did not like one day's drawings (though Cecil did); there was an unfortunate accident at Mainbocher's when Cecil's ladder was upset, splashing paints, Indian inks, dirty water and broken glass all over the couturier's expensive new carpet, and the monocled British Ambassador, Sir George Clerk, complained that Cecil had breached etiquette by not asking to be presented to him at one of Kitty Rothschild's huge dinners. (Cecil thought this minor diplomatic *faux pas* probably brought him good publicity.)

While these adventures were occurring, poor Doris Castlerosse languished in her hotel, neglected by Cecil, who became the 'heavy beau' of Audrey James, Marshall Field's recently divorced wife (once the fiancée of Lord Louis Mountbatten and a girlfriend of the Prince of Wales).

Cecil relished the company of Bébé Bérard, who declared that he had 'real poetry, that I was the most sensitive of persons, with great depth of feeling, all the things I want to hear'.[2] Cecil spent many happy evenings with Bébé and his companion, Boris Kochno, the former secretary of Diaghilev (who had died in 1929). He was intrigued and fascinated when Cocteau began to take him seriously:

> Jean Cocteau said I was the best-dressed young man, of an elegance unforeseen. He would perhaps wear his hair flat too. And meanwhile I smiled so gratefully, so sadly, that there was a nice side to myself, still, in spite of having such rough wear and tear lately.[3]

Cocteau analysed Cecil's career for him:

> Cocteau says I am Malice in Wonderland and I have succeeded in spending my life in an unreality made up of fun, so much too much fun and my interests are limited to the joys of certain superficial forms of beauty, to sensual delights only to a certain blunt degree, and with too many people, too many light quick sketches, quickfire articles and photographs galore. The crowded weeks gave place to others and I am under the delusion that I am 'living' so much more vitally than I should have if I had 'gone my own way'. My quickfire effects have been successful but with the result that I am only sensitive to a millionth part of what is going on around me.[4]

In turn Cecil was fascinated by Cocteau's charm and childish exuberance, his tremendous brittle hands, his sparrow claw thin feet and fakir thin body. When silent, Cocteau's eyes looked anguished and helpless; when alert, he had an infectious chuckle. He could launch into 'annihilating descriptions of people with whom he is displeased'.[5] He lived in an atmosphere both claustrophobic and 'frenziedly alive'. Cecil noted the 'fishy smell of opium, the indecent postcards' and was impressed at how Cocteau had 'sufficient strength of personality to be outré yet accepted by the most conservative elements of society'.[6]

Cecil sailed once more for New York, longing for adventure: 'I crave a trip and, in spite of my great love, I crave romance.'[7] While staying with the Harrison Williamses in Palm Beach, Cecil found himself at a dinner-party organized by 'Nin' Ryan. One of the guests was the young Marchioness of Dufferin and Ava (the former Maureen Guinness), whom Mrs Ryan had put up as her guest at the Everglades Club. Her rooms included a sitting-room which Mrs Ryan described as 'a mixture between a Turkish harem and a brothel'. The rooms were about four minutes' walk from the dinner-party.
Maureen Dufferin recalled:

> It was a terribly shy-making evening. Mrs Ryan was unable to be there, so I found myself thrust into a group of young Americans all telling 'in' jokes, and not in the least interested in a completely unknown English lady in their midst. It was the sort of party one finds oneself in – in a

nightmare. The kind where at a dinner party one hears a voice next to one saying 'Would you care to dance?' and then discovers that the question is directed to the woman opposite. So it was a God-send to find Cecil dining.

Cecil told me that he longed to see my extraordinary sitting-room and that he would happily escort me home. I was delighted to escape, and we walked back through the palm trees. When Cecil had seen the sitting-room he said, 'I *must* see the bedroom.' Before I knew what was happening, Cecil had rushed me onto the bed. Utterly astonished and a little fearful, the chief thought which flashed through my mind was that no one, least of all my husband, would ever believe my plight. This resulted in my bursting out laughing, which wounded Cecil's pride. He left the bedroom immediately.

The next night Nin arranged that I should join a small dinner-party of about six people, given by some other friends. To my horror, I found that Cecil had been asked to balance me. As we sat down, he declared in his high nasal voice: 'Do you realize that you have here, in Maureen Dufferin, the biggest bitch in London!' There was a moment of horrified silence, and then everyone laughed, assuming this to be a new form of small talk.

These two amazing events caused me to make enquiries which revealed that Cecil was trying to become completely heterosexual, and that he had had a walk-out with Doris. This being over, he presumably wanted to keep his hand etc. in with me. Because of his unforgivable remark at dinner it was some years before we once again became friends.[8]

In New York Cecil enjoyed the company of Nicolas Nabokov, the composer, and Tchelitchew, who was savouring the enormous success of his ballet, *L'Errante*, which he had reproduced for George Balanchine. Michael Duff was not there, having recently married. Nor was David Herbert, which suited David's friend Jack Wilson, who was about to marry the ravishing Princess Natasha Paley ('her quality of beauty so rare and alluring').[9] Cecil worked hard, and his famous profile portrait of Marlene Dietrich in black feathered hat dates from this trip. Miss Dietrich was as specific about the pictures as his other beautiful sitters: 'Please take a look at the left hand of the profile-one in the black hat – the line that you put on there is *clear to see* – but it is done in pencil and the *rest* of the hand that we wanted *cut* is still *there*.'[10] One evening Mona, Tchelitchew and a Balinese dancer dined in Cecil's rooms and Hindu musicians played. The musicians were dressed up in fantastic costumes and photographed. Another night there was a cocktail-party for Kommer, at which Nicolas Nabokov played the piano and Marlene Dietrich sang. Tchelitchew told Cecil that he was 'like a glass that could never be drained' and that he 'had no idea of [his] depth and capabilities'.[11] Cecil felt generally more relaxed. He wondered how he would feel when he reached home:

> Would I carry on with the manufacturing of romance out of an old perfume, a wisp of fragrance from the past. Would I turn on the 'Pain' machine again? ... It is lovely to love but terrible to be never free, to walk into any room as a guilty murderer must feel, anxious that something may go wrong, one's peace of mind a thing of the past, chaos and destruction of the immediate future.[12]

There was no recurrence of trouble when Cecil returned for the Silver Jubilee of King George and Queen Mary. He enjoyed the carnival atmosphere of London and was awe-inspired by the sight of Queen Mary, riding at the King's side, 'for however tiresome and perverse we may be about our Queen's clothes in our more analytical moments there is no one who can give an effect such as she. Any beauty one could mention pales beside her, and to see her today was an unforgettable sight'.[13]

Cecil took part in the Pembrokes' Jubilee pageant, dressed as Charles I, holding his false beard on with difficulty while walking miles through Wilton streets, hazardous with horse dung. He went to the theatre with Stephen Tennant, who was as conspicuously dressed as ever. Cecil had forgotten what a stir his presence caused and he 'suffered from the barrage of rude remarks showered on him by total strangers'. In his maturity Cecil's appearance was relatively conventional: 'and so I have forgotten the torture of undergoing such bullying'.[14]

He went to Rome to stay with Gerald Berners in June, taking Tilly Losch with him, 'still sad and suffering from the results of her fiascotic marriage'.*[15] He found his host 'a very odd character with very little heart', who could not resist 'joking about one's softest spot and prodding one's Achilles heel'.[16] Tchelitchew and Charles Henri Ford arrived. Days went by in which they ate, slept or painted. Cecil noted: 'the light in Rome is of an unusual golden clear quality, rather like New York, and the nights were miraculous, certain parts of the town illuminated as for a play and the ruins appearing like ghosts in the moonlight'.[17] In the presence of Gerald Berners it was inevitable that they would soon be up to mischief. One evening they 'explored the bourgeoisie' by attending a soirée given by an English spinster, Miss Christine Radclyffe, who sang while playing the violin. This event inspired numerous jokes, drawings and imitations. Then they fell to designing a procession to mark 'the Jubilee celebration for David Horner's† reign with Osbert Sitwell in Carlyle Square'.[18] Pavlik designed the costumes while Cecil caricatured David Horner looking like Queen Alexandra or Queen Mary.

---

* Tilly Losch (1907–75) married the eccentric art collector, Edward James (1907–84), in 1931. They went through an untidy divorce in 1934. In 1939 she married Porchy, the Earl of Carnarvon. They were divorced in 1947. She died in New York on Christmas Eve 1975.

† David Horner (1901–84), novelist and life-long friend of Osbert Sitwell.

After Rome Cecil went on to Paris and designed an instant dress for Tilly Losch to wear at the Oriental Ball. Paris was in a fluster about the ball and also about René Crevel, the gifted young Surrealist poet, who had just committed suicide. Telephones buzzed all day long with a mixture of 'C'est effroyable – oh ma robe, c'est une merveille – pauvre petit garçon – oh ma robe!' Tony Gandarillas, the Chilean diplomat, arrived at the Ritz Hotel from the hospital panting for opium, complaining that this would have to happen just as he was in Paris for a few days' holiday. Dinner at Marie-Blanche de Polignac's surpassed Cecil's wildest dreams:

> The dinner was the best I have ever eaten in the world. There was lamb cooked in a casing of maize that was of such deliciousness that I could not believe such things exist. The sauces unbelievable. ...[19]

Cecil spent the rest of the evening with Bébé Bérard at Maxim's: 'We talked with charming interruptions from Figgi Ralli'[20] (Lilia Ralli), who presently became Cecil's girlfriend. Bébé flattered Cecil until 4 a.m., which he appreciated:

> I kept reminding myself that there was nothing in the world I would rather be doing than this. For Bébé has enormous magic and inspiration for me. He holds great glamour and for hours he talked about myself handing me all the bouquets I am greedy to have, for which I am starved at this moment, having been feeling rather down on my luck. Bébé smoked and talked with [the] eager avidness of a haunted creature desperate to rid himself of some devil: 'You do like me Cecil, don't you?' and my reply was such a relief to him that it went through him as an electric shock.[21]

They discussed Cocteau, whom Bébé loathed: 'an opium brilliance that does not linger, opium which gives calm takes from him the power to consider his work after it is done'.[22] Bébé 'despised' Cocteau's influence, but he said he loved Cecil 'for the intense love for *the things* I love'. And Cecil, so often untrusting, noted:

> I have complete faith in Bébé. He will never turn against me. He has more complete honesty than anyone I know and from the moment we became friends we became intimate and without having known each other long we know one another deeply and I really love him as a noble and great character very sincerely and deeply.[23]

Cecil spent the rest of the summer at Ashcombe, where rooms had been repainted, a new bedroom added and electric light installed, without detracting from the house's magic: 'It is impossible to describe how much I enjoy everyone's enjoyment, the beauty of the scene, the charm and strange romantic melancholy of the house that has become the gayest maddest house.'[24] House parties often swam nearby in the lake at Fonthill, Beckford's romantic ruins, in 'dark green and glacial'[25] water while 'proud swans'[26] swam majestically by.

John Sutro was a regular visitor to Ashcombe. He had wonderful powers of mimicry and could relate recent happenings in instantly composed perfectly rhyming couplets. Cecil thought he could have been a really great actor. In the evenings he became a company director, a pompous parliamentarian or a puffed-up schoolmaster. Oggie Lynn, the rotund and diminutive singer, was equally impressive in diverse female roles. Oliver Messel, once more a friend, went through his repertoire and David Herbert brought crowds of friends from Wilton.

That summer John Sutro decided they should attempt to make a private film of David Garnett's *The Sailor's Return*. John Sutro was a director of London Film Productions and soon the exercise became very elaborate. Arc-lights arrived with a camera director, a cameraman and a few technicians. The costumes were run up in a day, the cast of amateurs assembled. Cecil played the sailor who returned with his inky bride, Tulip (Lady Caroline Paget), to be innkeeper in his native village. The story relates how he falls victim to all the complications of village snobbery and religious difficulty and is eventually killed. Meanwhile Tulip has to escape home to avoid the village clergyman (John Betjeman, then a journalist on the *Architectural Review*), who wants to make her son as white as snow. John Sutro played Tom, the life and soul of the pub, and so convincing was he that while awaiting filming a genuine local leaned on a gate with him and passed the time of day.

The cameras began to roll early, but they soon ran into problems. The make-up was not good enough, the black baby was not on the 5.15 to Westbury from Paddington, and as Cecil wrote: 'it is very difficult a hundred miles from London to get hold of a black baby at a moment's notice, especially on Saturday afternoons when shops are shut'.[27]

The next day the cart collapsed under the weight of its load and Caroline Paget got slight sunstroke; Cecil nearly broke his toe and he pushed over a 'country boy' so forcefully that the lad claimed damages for an operation on a swollen knee and three weeks out of work. The film was never completed, but the experience deemed a wild success. Cecil learned at first hand the many problems of film-making and 'why it is that so many film stars appear to be living in a haze, unmindful of the postman, the books beside the bed and the generally considered important activities of the outside world'.[28]

Vogue was not making Cecil's life easy, nor he theirs. There were frequent disputes over relatively minor aspects of his contract. Edna Woolman Chase suggested that he should not come to New York this autumn, because his new rival, Horst, would be there. There was not room for both of them. At the same time Cecil's style of drawing and photography was now showing the French influence he had learned from Bérard, Cocteau and Tchelitchew. On 15 July Condé Nast noted that an edition with Cecil's colour sketch of a lady with her hair swept up against a background of leaves like snowflakes 'sold poorly. I gave this the "B" rating largely because it was different. This is always a poor seller.'[29] Dr Agha was also against Cecil's work appearing in *Vanity Fair*: '*Vanity Fair* should publish only the work of people who are excellent art-photographers,' he wrote to Condé Nast. These problems became more acute in the winter of 1936, when Cecil suffered many complications and disappointments. His work had changed and he feared that conventional people only wanted to see 'what they have seen a hundred times'. He concluded: 'It was altogether a bad winter for the artists.'[30]

In November Cecil worked again for Cochran, designing the scenery and costumes for Frederick Ashton's new ballet, *The First Shoot*, part of Cochran's revue, *Follow the Sun* (which opened in Manchester in December 1935, and at the Adelphi in London in February 1936). *The First Shoot* was a parody on Edwardian shooting-parties by Osbert Sitwell with music by William Walton. Cecil made his initial sketches on menus after lunch in a Soho restaurant with Freddie Ashton. His first efforts took twenty minutes to complete. Cecil sketched conventional ballet skirts, but Ashton declared, 'No tutus!' Cecil simply removed the skirts. In this very happy production, Sir Winston Churchill's daughter, Sarah, made her stage debut. Cecil launched her as a decorative pheasant.

Denied a New York winter, Cecil headed east for Russia. He began his trip in a luxurious train in the company of the couturier Elsa Schiaparelli and her blue-haired publicity agent, Mrs Macdonald. It soon became a nightmare, because, having no visa to cross Poland, he was decanted from the train to await the return journey to Berlin. Matters were arranged there and Cecil spent an unexpectedly enjoyable day with his rich art collector friends, Lalli and Freddy Horstmann (who later died of starvation in a Russian prison camp), before catching the next train, in which he slept for fifteen hours. He arrived in Moscow with a headache and two days' growth of beard.

Cecil was appalled by the drabness of the crowds he saw, the squalor of the shops and the general ugliness of Moscow. The Revolution Museum had caricatures of the former Tsar and his family and Lenin depicted as a God. He was 'shocked with so much horror and ugliness and could take in nothing more for the time being. So great a shock paralyses one.'[31] He filed past Lenin's body, the first time he had seen a corpse: 'He is lying in red, beautifully preserved, embalmed with the same process as the Egyptian mummies, in a glass case. He is extremely beautiful, pallid, delicate, with sensitive features and a wise and bold head.'[32] He saw the Russian jewels at the Kremlin. His life in Russia was a mixture either of energetic sightseeing in the four hours of daylight, during which he was confronted with the poverty of the people and the incompetence of officials, or of the contrasting richness of life in the British Embassy and even more so the French. He attended the theatre, but thought there were too many false noses on stage. Leaving the country he felt like a child let out of school. And yet there lurks in Cecil's diary a surprising remark written during his stay which is characteristic of that period when intelligent Englishmen still looked at the Soviet tyranny through rose-coloured spectacles: 'Mrs Macdonald ... became so sentimental about the new Soviet regime and I am fighting so hard against it although in my heart of hearts I am convinced that it is a great idea though the present hideousness is so cruel that there is no sop offered to life.'[33]

In February 1936 – the same month that saw the opening of *Follow the Sun* in London – Freddie Ashton's latest ballet, *Apparitions*, was staged at Sadler's Wells with costumes and sets by Cecil. The Australian dancer Robert Helpmann and the young ballerina Margot Fonteyn were the stars. As for *Follow the Sun*, the costumes were made by Madame Karinska, a wonderful Russian dressmaker, who understood how to create exactly what the designer wanted. She had set off to Monte Carlo in 1933 with 300 borrowed francs and announced her intention to create costumes for Derain's set for *La Concurrence*. Her reputation had grown steadily ever since.* Lilian Baylis, the proprietor of Sadler's Wells, paid Cecil a flat fee of £50 for his efforts. This Cecil passed on to Karinska so that the ballroom costumes could be more lavish. Karinska had the alarming knack of delivering her costumes at absolutely the last minute. Nevertheless Margot Fonteyn thought them 'ravishing', and Victor Stiebel based a collection of evening dresses on them.

Margot Fonteyn was somewhat in awe of Cecil. When she first met him, she intended to say what an honour it was. Instead she mumbled, 'Oh, I have heard of you.' Later, being photographed at his flat, she was amazed by the artificial grass he put on the floor and his apparent lack of knowledge about his camera settings. She was ready for anything when she emerged in stage make-up and Cecil said, 'Oh dear! Couldn't we have something a little more glamorous in the way of eye make-up?'[34]

In his early designs Cecil liked to assert himself, whereas later he learned to work closely with the director. In this ballet he wanted petals strewn all over the stage. Ninette de Valois said: 'But all the dancers will slip on them', to which Cecil replied: 'But you're so damned practical.'[35] His décor was hailed by the *Sunday Times* as of 'a mother-of-pearl delicacy'.[36] The *New Statesman and Nation* described him as 'an eclectic artist, very much aware

---

* Cecil later employed Karinska to dot felt flowers on the grass-green carpets at Ashcombe and to make birds for the bedroom curtains.

of what's afoot'[37] and detected the influence of Bérard and Tchelitchew. So did Peter Watson, who was not pleased:

> But Cecil, I was disappointed in your things. The Cochran Ballet is *infinitely* superior – you know I think highly of that. You have assimilated Bébé and Pavlik to no advantage to yourself. Perhaps it was the story that made me dislike it so much but I couldn't compete with the white beauties and the funeral procession and I defy Michelangelo to have made good costumes and scenery for such a wet mess. But you could have done better than that. Goodday.[38]

But a much more weighty figure, Constant Lambert, the composer, who arranged Liszt's music, wrote with enthusiasm: 'It was a real collaboration and everyone agrees that it knocks spots off any ballet since *Cotillon*.'[39]

Cecil was in New York when *Apparitions* opened (postponed due to the death of King George V on 20 January). He took many parties to see it on his return:

> The reality is of a great loveliness ... the music and choreography are superbly matched and the music is of an impossible romanticism and beauty. The dancing of Margot Fonteyn makes one weep a little for here is a combination of extreme youth, tenderness, elegance and virtuosity. ... I am delighted with my work and know it is the best and most serious I have yet done. Karinska has made in my absence the ballroom dresses very beautifully but the final additions that were made by me during these weeks helped the general effect enormously.[40]

Cecil's parents urged him to curtail his travelling, because he was overdrawn by £239. Nevertheless in the spring of 1936 he visited Havana and Mexico with Mona Harrison Williams and others. The party asked Cecil to tell them the story of his life. He was amused that they should think him 'a strange figure out of nowhere'.[41] In June Cecil was sent to cover the maiden voyage to New York of the *Queen Mary*. He suffered one of his occasional bouts of superstition, convinced that they would sink, but set off resigned to any eventuality.

The voyage began in an atmosphere of tense excitement with 'droves of ant humans'[42] overwhelming every deck, corridor, lounge, staircase and hall. There were too many people on board, Cecil had to share a cabin and there was nowhere to hide. It felt like being back at boarding school. But when the liner arrived in New York the welcome was so enthusiastic, with 'airplanes' buzzing overhead and every sort of vessel alongside, that it brought lumps to Cecil's throat.

Cecil had never been in New York in the summer. He found that the normal bustle and restlessness was subdued by the torpid heat. He also found that other photographers were aping his work in picture magazines. He in turn was influenced by Tchelitchew. When he photographed Pavlik's *Orphée*, the perfectly ordinary American boys and girls emerged as Tchelitchew paintings. Cecil tried to work as best he could, though he felt ill from the sudden change in temperature. Mary Taylor became his favourite sitter: 'She is so delicately exotic and mysteriously attractive. I believe I really quite love her.'[43] He saw old friends such as Marge Oelrichs and Mona Harrison Williams. He met and photographed Grand Duchess Marie of Russia, 'a pathetic but great émigré'.[44] In turn the Grand Duchess arranged for him to photograph Madame Valentina Schlee, the Russian dress-designer, by telling her: 'I command you as a Grand Duchess of your country to sit for Cecil.'[45] But the most surprising person to find in New York was Jean Cocteau.

Cocteau had decided to leave Paris on a whim to re-enact Phineas Fogg's voyage in Jules Verne's *Around the World in Eighty Days*. His Passepartout was Marcel Khill (shortly to be superseded in his affections by Jean Marais). Cocteau, on the last lap of his journey, was in a continual fever of activity to see everything and keep his deadline. Just as Tchelitchew influenced Cecil visually, so he found that Cocteau had the power to project his personality onto such unlikely places as an automat or a drugstore. Cecil described him:

His vitality is that of a monkey on a stick. His elegance is basic. His sweetness deeply tender. His eyes have wonderful compassion with pained eyebrows belied by the amusement of his upward laughter-closed eyes. He enjoys a joke more than anyone. ... He is one of the gayest people to be with and his macabre nature is as though an appendage that has no real bearing on his being. He looked from my windows to the roofs below where businessmen were having a banquet: 'Oh to get a gun and ping, ping, ping from left to right! Oh! the flutter, the commotion!' To us that is more sinister than to him. And yet he has a great heart. On arrival at the automat he made us stop still and watch carefully a boy eating his soup: 'You have seen Raymond Radiguet.'*[46]

Cecil, Cocteau and Marcel Khill motored round New York in an open car, seeing the docks, the Bowery, the Battery, the steamship piers. Cecil felt very free. By subway they went to Coney Island – 'If it had been a trip to the Far East it could not have been more exciting.'[47] They swung on hand-rails, went on a scenic railway, which shook every bone in their bodies, and saw the 'blood-curdling' wax shows 'which might have been designed by Jean himself'. They were photographed in booths. Then suddenly Cocteau lost his vitality completely. Cecil was relieved, 'for it showed him to be human'.[48]

---

*Raymond Radiguet (1903–23). Child poet and author of the sensational *Le Diable au Corps*. Cocteau was in love with him but said: 'He was hard. It took a diamond to scratch his heart.' He died of typhoid, weakened by his excesses.

After three days in New York Cocteau sailed home to France with two of his eighty days in hand. Cecil had one more day before he too sailed home yet again on the 'boring' *Aquitania*. That summer a rumour circulated in America that Cecil was going to marry Lady Ribblesdale,* the mother of Vincent Astor and Alice von Hofmannsthal. Even the gossip writer had to admit that it might be 'just a heat-wave brainstory'.[49]

On Cecil's return, Boris Kochno came to tea and asked him to design his ballet, *Le Pavillon*. This appealed to Cecil because it harked back to the world of Diaghilev. He began to design it all in blue – hydrangea blue for the sets, and all the skirts in varying shades of the same colour. Unfortunately Kochno saw the dresses half-finished and liked their effect so much that he forbade Cecil to add the gauze skirts, wings and flowers that he planned in the brightest colours imaginable. 'C'est un spectacle adorable,'[50] he wrote in August. The result was that all the audience saw was blue upon blue upon blue. In an exhausting summer Cecil noted:

> This more than anything else reduced me to a complete state of pulp. I have only a few times in my life felt as miserable as I did after the première, for my nerves were already distraught and all the faults I had to find with the work for which I was responsible were magnified.[51]

Le Pavillon opened at the Royal Opera House, Covent Garden, on 11 August. Cecil got bad reviews – 'excessively ordinary'[52] (*Evening News*) and 'disappointing'[53] (*Manchester Guardian*). The *New Statesman and Nation* declared: 'In *Apparitions* at Sadler's Wells, Mr Beaton showed delicate taste and vigorous imagination. But for some reason in *Le Pavillon* he has merely flopped.'[54]

Irina Baronova, one of Colonel de Basil's† three 'baby ballerinas', thought the illuminated kiosk that Cecil placed centre-stage for the lover's tryst resembled a *pissoir*. Immediately after the first night Cecil, who wore a blue moth in his lapel, impressed Godfrey Winn by telling him that he was going to sit up all night altering the costumes. Cecil asked permission to alter the costumes, but Colonel de Basil refused it. Cecil then took 'a most unethical step'. He paid Karinska out of his own pocket to add the overskirts, birdwings and flowers at the very last moment. Karinska's work was thorough and however hard the *corps de ballet* tried to remove the new adornments, they failed and had no choice but to go on stage looking the way Cecil wanted

---

* Ava, Lady Ribblesdale (d. 1958), born Ava Willing, of Philadelphia, married, first, John Jacob Astor IV and second, Lord Ribblesdale. She was noted for her many lovers and her outrageous remarks. Ironically, very much later, Cecil tried to marry her step-granddaughter, June Osborn.

† Colonel de Basil (1888–1951), successor to Diaghilev. He co-founded the Ballet Russe de Monte Carlo in 1932. From 1939 to 1948 he was its sole director.

them. Cecil was delighted with the result and even Colonel de Basil's fury and the stern dressing-down that followed did nothing to dampen his pleasure. 'I did not care,' wrote Cecil later. 'I had salvaged my own integrity as a designer. In the future I need not be ashamed at the appearance of my ballet, and when the company toured the United States, *Le Pavillon* met with an excellent reception.'[55]

Gratefully, Cecil departed on holiday with Nicolas Nabokov. After two idyllic days in Alsace, Cecil took the night train to Salzburg to stay at Schloss Kammer, a sinister, possibly haunted, castle, where Eleanor Mendelssohn and Alice von Hofmannsthal had large groups staying, including David Herbert, Rex Whistler and the Ladies Caroline and Elizabeth Paget. Cecil enjoyed sightseeing, riding, walking in the mountains and unravelling the intrigues of the various guests. By night he relished dining on a barge by torchlight, while music wafted across the lake from another barge, moored nearby. Nabokov read Cecil his lectures on music, and he seemed set for a stimulating holiday. All this came to a sudden end.

On 24 August a telegram announced: 'Daddy gravely ill. Come.' When Cecil telephoned, his mother told him in wails that his father had died at dawn. He was sixty-eight. Cecil drove at once to Munich but missed the last flight. To console himself, he ate at the Walterspiel, went to see Greek and Roman sculptures and attended a Mozart opera.

None of the family had been at home, because Mr Beaton had seemed a little better. It was a dreadful shock for Nancy to return unaware from holiday and see her father's coffin leaving Rutland Gate:

> It was a Websterian horror to see the lying-in in the Funeral Parlour, theatrically, garishly trapped out with sombre lighting, horrible lying prostitute flowers and the face arranged in death, dusted with a powder.[56]

Mr Beaton was cremated and buried in the family tomb at Hampstead. Cecil thought a lot about his father over those days. He concluded he had more 'admiration and respect'[57] for him than 'devotion and sympathy'.[58] He recalled the compassion that could be seen 'in the kind regard of his bright eyes',[59] his pride at paying out of all proportion for Nancy and Baba's weddings, how life had gone badly for him (in April he had closed his office to work from home), how his clothes had become shabby and how he prayed by his bed each night, but seldom went to church. Years later he concluded that in many ways he was like his father. Re-reading his letters, he found them full of sensible advice. He shuddered to think how irritating his father must have found his pretentious children with their snobbery and social climbing. 'I like him so much more now I look back on him,'[60] wrote Cecil in 1950. At the time of his father's demise, his thoughts turned to the possibility of his own death:

For myself I am not averse to the thought of dying except for the appalling suffering it would bring to my mother who has suffered so much more than enough already.[61]

Mrs Beaton had more to suffer, as Cecil discovered when he returned from a recuperative trip to Hungary and Dalmatia with David Herbert in September. He was now very precious to his mother: 'We are the only two left,' she wrote to him, 'and I always worry while you are away in case of accidents or illness.'[62] From now on he would have to support her because the family trustees revealed that all Mr Beaton's capital was eaten up by his business losses. She would receive only £15 a month from the Beaton trust. Cecil felt his life was in a groove, and that his work was trivial and devitalizing:

> At home there have been appalling disturbances with the trustees' news of Daddy's financial tragedy and the resultant effect on Mummie's shattered nerves. Minor trials have been legion. The car breaking down. An appalling chauffeur irrevocably ruining the Alvis which must now be sold. My hand has gone through a glass window playing hide and seek.[63]

Cecil thought that to acquire some serenity he should distance himself from the world:

> I have now realized how bad all the lunches are at the Ritz in between photograph sittings nearby at *Vogue*. They sap more of vitality than one knows. My argument has been that I must eat somewhere, somewhere near, but in spite of my outward poise that is remarked upon, inwardly I have very little self-assurance and it is only by becoming more of a mystic that this result can be achieved.[64]

Nor did he derive any joy from exhibiting his ballet designs at the Redfern Gallery. The *New Statesman and Nation*, always his sternest and most perceptive critic, noted:

> He is haunted by images of a world which he cannot remember, except perhaps from his perambulator, a world which is just beginning to acquire picturesqueness – where the ospreys, parasols, boas and Parma violets of bejewelled aunts are confused with the preposterous clothes of pantomime transformation-scenes and Mme Rasimi's Revues.[65]

However, this dull downward phase did not last long. Presently Cecil was catapulted into the middle of the most enduringly fascinating drama of the century.

16

The Means to an Achievement

Photographs are a good excuse to see people and luckily the day has not yet come when beckoned people do not come. Mrs Simpson was punctual and arrived rather nervously or maybe without great assurance.

Cecil's diary, November 1936

Wallis Simpson, a name breathed in whispers for some time, was a name on everybody's lips in the latter months of 1936. Cecil had first met her in the early 1930s 'in a box of American bums at the Three Arts Club Ball – Thelma Furness and her rawboned jaw sister and a lot of unmentionables were there'.[1] In those days he found her 'a brawny great cow or bullock in sapphic blue velvet'.[2]

> To hear her speak was enough. Her voice was raucous and appalling. I thought her awful, common, vulgar, strident, a second-rate American with no charm. Now she is all that is elegant. The whole of London flocks after her as the mistress and possible wife of the King.... I am certain she has more glamour and is of more interest than any public figure.[3]

Cecil first photographed her during the Jubilee summer of 1935: 'I found her bright and witty. She had become enormously improved in looks and chic.'[4] These now forgotten portraits show Wallis in a dress of black crêpe de chine lightly scattered with matchsticks with a black Circassian cap, and in an evening dress of white matt crêpe with bands of gleaming sequins massed on top. Mrs Simpson stood beside a masked statue which was draped in black crêpe veiling. When writing of the Jubilee for *Vogue* (21 August 1935), Cecil could not resist planting a clue that he knew the Royal Family was heading for trouble: 'Princess Marina's picture hats have put Mr Winston Churchill's in the shade and are seriously weighed in comparison with the Duchess of York's smile, and only a certain American hostess, whose head has been turned by "rankers", has not been impressed by the pomp and beauty of the court balls.'[5]

It was not easy for Cecil to resist forbidden topics when he photographed

Wallis in November 1936. His mock-prophetic idea of posing her against an ermine background was firmly squashed. When he asked her to lower her chin, 'as though bowing', he received a sharp look. At the same time he detected the haunted, sad look of one who had suffered. Cecil thought their long session a success: 'Her claim to looks is her dazzling brightness and freshness.'[6]

In the afternoon of 20 November Cecil went to Wallis's rented house in Regent's Park, 16 Cumberland Terrace, to draw her. He found his sketching difficult, but they talked freely:

> I really found my hostess quite alluring. Her skin today was incredibly bright and smooth like the inside of a shell, her hair as sleek as only the Chinese women know how to make it. The dress was incredibly simple and the aura of gossip and the expensive flowers did the rest. She amused me a lot with staccato sentences and explosive bursts of laughter. I like her surprised eyebrows when she laughs and her face has great gaiety. Whereas two days ago she had seemed slightly shopsoiled and middle-aged and her breath smelt a bit, today she was immaculate and as soignée yet fresh as no girl could be.[7]

Cecil gradually steered the talk round to the forthcoming Coronation and her plans. He asked if she knew what a sensation she was: 'Do you realize that as a topic I have banned you?'[8] She told him what 'absolute rot' any talk of marriage was. It was just something drummed up by the American papers. Cecil asked if he might photograph the King and at that moment Edward VIII walked in unexpectedly. Cecil had the chance to observe them together. He was impressed by the King:

> He knows an enormous amount of general knowledge, never forgets names, knows statistics and really has the mind of the average man *par excellence*. He will be a very popular King and one cannot help respecting him. His quips and sallies were trite and often vulgar ... but he has no pettiness, no interest in gossip and gossip of personalities, society consisting of Chips and Mrs Greville does not exist for him.[9]

They were joined by Mrs Simpson's 'fat aunt', Mrs Merryman. Eight different kinds of canapés were served (Oliver Messel used to imitate Elsie Mendl being impressed by these), and there was much laughter:

> The King talked very quickly and darted around the room and rang bells, his hands very red and slightly horny, busily unravelling parcels. He had a bad cold and wore a heavy silk jersey instead of a vest, with stiff collar attached. Wallis's eyes sparkled. Her mouth turned down at the corners as she laughed and her eyebrows mocked pained surprise. The aunt sat back wisecracking. The King like a child during his play hour before dinner was told that we all must go. Wallis had only a few minutes to dress for Emerald's dinner. Already she had unbuttoned her dress. I had

missed many trains to the country but what did it matter. There were so many secrets with which to regale the family and an armful of drawings, all bad, but perhaps the means to an achievement.[10]

Very soon after this, Mrs Simpson fled London for the sanctity of Fort Belvedere and Cecil went to New York for the winter.

He was in America when the King abdicated. It was perfect timing because Cecil was about to hold an exhibition at the Carroll Carstairs Gallery, and one of his sketches of Mrs Simpson was on show:

> The crowds that had come in their thousands arrived to see Mrs Simpson's pictures and stayed to admire the exhibition and be conscious of the fact that I painted as well as photographed. The publicity done through Miss Lambert,* a new friend, was excellent and after the first few days of hanging around the show I became too busy to go near the gallery.[11]

Meanwhile, in London, Cecil's secretary was invited to name her fee by the editor of a national newspaper to release one of the *Vogue* portraits of Mrs Simpson. Wisely she resisted the temptation. In New York, however, one photograph was released in a blaze of publicity. *Vogue* published Cecil's exclusive portraits of Mrs Simpson in their edition of 1 January 1937. She is shown heavily bedecked in jewels – in one a diamond and emerald necklace, in the other a heavy necklace of rubies. Mrs Simpson liked it as she wrote to Cecil from the Villa Lou Viei in Cannes: 'a relief after the one as a baby lying on the fur rug in the press!'[12] She also wanted to buy the sketches, 'the last link with my house'.[13]

Cecil's exhibition was attended by Mr and Mrs Salvador Dali, by Marge† (now married to the pianist, Eddy Duchin) and by Doris Castlerosse – who quietly bought nine pictures for a total of $760 (Cecil made about $1,800 in all from this exhibition). Cecil did not invite Peter Watson to the opening on 4 January and Peter was duly put out: 'It is all very strange and can help none of us,' wrote Peter from the St Regis Hotel. 'Please use a little more of your understanding. Life is difficult enough as it is.'[14]

Soon after this Cecil was influenced by a helpful clairvoyant called Bathsheba Askowith,‡ and by Nicolas Nabokov, who said: 'To grow one must prune.'[15] He wrote to Peter, making a final break and asking that there should be no reply.

---

* Eleanor Lambert, a famous New York publicist, still very much in action in the 1980s.

† Marge died in the summer of 1937, after giving birth to her son, Peter Duchin, also a jazz pianist. In her death Cecil lost one of his best friends: 'It is as if all trees had died,' he wrote, 'all skies, all fruit, all music' [diary, August 1937]. In 1956 Kim Novak played Marge in the film *The Eddy Duchin Story* opposite Tyrone Power.

‡ Bathsheba Askowith used to teach acting. She was devoted to Eleanore Duse (who called her 'La Russa') and gave up her job to accompany Duse on her American tour. She was with her when she died in a drab hotel in Pittsburgh in April 1924.

Returning to London in the spring of 1937, Cecil worked hard for the Coronation number of *Vogue*. He took 'particularly English' portraits in the 'grand old-fashioned manner' of stiff-looking peeresses with jewels that had been in the family for centuries. Sometimes he went to Garrards to search through leather boxes in tin trunks for the most photogenic tiaras or neck-laces. He photographed the Duchesses of Marlborough, Sutherland, West-minster, Northumberland and Buccleuch. Cecil also photographed the in-corrigible Margot Asquith (Countess of Oxford and Asquith) because she asked him and because *Vogue* wanted her. Unfortunately she did not pay for her pictures, explaining:

> I think you are the kindest of men and if I had a farthing in the world (or in my Bank!) I wd. pay you highly for yr. proficiency. But alas! I am up to my eyes in debt. I suppose I am frivolous, as I accept all *grand* invitations, Court banquets Court balls etc. wh. all cost me money wh. I can't afford.[16]

Amongst the peeresses photographed was Lady Nunburnholme in a Gre-cian tiara and a simple draped dress. She was one of the Queen's Ladies of the Bedchamber, and Cecil heard later that she was to show his portraits to Her Majesty. He did not photograph Queen Elizabeth at this time, but from a mass of press pictures and postcards, he painted a portrait of her in evening dress which he thought 'gave an effect of her lovely thrush-like eyes and delicious royal, pink and white skin'.[17] Cecil did, however, photo-graph the Hereditary Grand Duke and Grand Duchess of Hesse (who were killed in an aircrash with members of their family in November that year), and Princess Beatrice's daughter-in-law, the Marchioness of Carisbrooke.

He was thus getting nearer his goal of becoming a royal photographer. In November 1935 he had photographed Lady Alice Montagu-Douglas-Scott (now Princess Alice, Duchess of Gloucester) before her wedding. He also drew her for *Vogue*. In this respect his royal career was on a par with that of his old Cambridge Footlights rival, Norman Hartnell, for she was the first royal bride he dressed. Lady Alice was somewhat critical of the results: 'I thought two of the photographs very charming, though some people did not seem to think likewise and said I looked "somewhat hard" in them.'[18] Although she was the sort of person Cecil might well have liked, the Duchess of Gloucester was never his favourite royal sitter, perhaps because she criticized his work. Before her marriage the Duchess had won a Diploma of Honour for a photograph in a world contest arranged by Kodak in Geneva.

Cecil had longed to photograph Princess Marina ever since she arrived in Britain as the Duke of Kent's romantic bride in 1934. He admired her chic and beauty enormously and it was therefore a great excitement when she agreed to sit for him in Coronation summer:

The Duchess looked excessively beautiful in a huge brown tulle crinoline, ruched like a Queen Anne window blind, or a lampshade, with old-fashioned jewellery, a bow knot, large drop earrings. She looked like a Winterhalter painting and it was thus that she was photographed, slightly nervous at first and very Royal, with her deep, clipped accented voice, but soon she was as pliable as any sitter I have ever had and we made many jokes and got along splendidly.[19]

The Duke of Kent then arrived in a bad temper 'and there is no one bloodier than he in a bad mood'. Cecil took some of him in naval uniform and some of them together. A few days later he went to the Kents' house in Belgrave Square to present his work. The Duchess asked him, 'Well, and how are they?', and he went into raptures:

Oh Ma'am, I think they're incredibly romantic. There are some as nostalgic and summer scented as if Winterhalter had painted your great-aunt Queen Mary. Some are an idyll, the feathery trees and the summer lighting are really ...'[20]

The Duchess cut him short. Cecil and the Kents then selected the pictures for each magazine. 'Oh! I hate to be in the *Sketch* and *Tatler* and *Vogue*,' said the Duchess, adding, 'but *Vogue*'s a fashion magazine.' To this the Duke screwed up his nose with a laugh and said, 'Well, what about it? Aren't we fashionable?'[21]

Soon after this Cecil was summoned to the Château de Candé for the weekend to photograph Mrs Simpson, who was languishing there before her divorce became absolute.

He found his weekend 'extremely interesting, extremely enjoyable', but by Monday he had had enough 'because in Mrs Simpson's entourage there is no smattering of culture, no appreciation or interest in art of any form. As a diversion it is gay and successful. As a steady diet it would be impossible.'[22] He arrived at the château and was soon enjoying excellent cocktails and a delicious dinner prepared by a chef who had lately been with the Duke of Alba. The advent of a guest from the outside world was a significant event in the dull lives of Wallis, and her friends the Herman Rogerses and the Charles Bedauxes. After dinner the party talked in the games pavilion. Then, at midnight, Cecil and Wallis were left alone:

Wallis and I started talking in full earnest until late into the dawn. I was amazed at the clarity and vitality of her mind and went to bed, eventually, feeling that I had spent the evening with someone who not only has individuality and personality, but is a personality, a strong force. I find she is intelligent within her vast limitations. Politically she may be ignorant, aesthetically she is so, but about life she knows a great deal.[23]

Wallis told Cecil that she had been taken by surprise by the Abdication. She knew less than anybody. She revealed to Cecil that the King had been prepared to delay talk about his marriage until after the Coronation and that the Prime Minister had papers signed by her stopping her divorce if necessary. Wallis was not bitter. She told Cecil: 'It has only shown me who among my friends are my friends.'[24] At times she said it had been hard not to hang herself from the antlers in this room. Cecil thought she was very like a man and noted that she admired her future husband. She was 'determined to love him though I feel she is not in love with him. She has a great responsibility in looking after someone who, so essentially different, entirely relies upon her.'[25]

The next day was devoted to photography. Wallis spent the morning with the hairdresser and manicurist from Paris. Cecil decided to take romantic pictures rather than smart ones, so Wallis wore organdie dresses and posed among the daisies in the shade of sunlit trees. Later, having changed at speed, Wallis posed in her bedroom. Cecil found her a 'helpful and sympathetic' sitter and was surprised at how much jewellery she still had. All in all the session proved a success. Condé Nast devoted six pages to this essentially non-fashion feature in American *Vogue* and the issue at once sold out. Wallis too was pleased: 'I have been more than delighted with the pictures – certainly the best that have been done.... It was such fun having you here and I do appreciate all the trouble you took with my strained face.'[26]

Cecil watched the Coronation of King George VI and Queen Elizabeth from a stand in Parliament Square. He found himself overwhelmed with sentimental and patriotic feelings. No tiny detail escaped his eye: the consort of some Commonwealth King, dressed in Paris clothes but looking as if she had come straight from Harlem; the beplumed Field-Marshal who dropped his ticket as he saluted; the pretty little coaches that brought the peers and peeresses from quiet country lives to the splendour of the Abbey. He was particularly impressed by the 'effect of the jewellery, fur and velvet on a startling skin'[27] of the Queen, Queen Mary and the Duchesses of Kent, Gloucester and Devonshire. He thought the King looked 'slightly deathlike with cadaverous face',[28] while the Queen looked 'so much lovelier than in any of her photographs and her unaccustomed pallor was very moving'.[29] When the magnificent ceremony was over, Cecil watched the peers and peeresses emerge:

> It is typical of today that Lady Anglesey and Lady Cholmondeley should squat like old beggar women on the steps outside the annexe, while the crowds peered and pressed. Of those that looked particularly beautiful, the older and bigger women were triumphant. The goatish Duchess of Portland was supreme.[30]

Within a month Cecil was back at the Château de Candé to take the wedding portraits of the Duke and Duchess of Windsor. His photographs were taken on 2 June, the day before the private ceremony. He packed a case on the offchance that he might be invited to stay for the day itself, but this could not be. Cecil was tremendously excited to undertake this assignment, but it was not without complications. He had been sent by *Vogue*, who naturally expected exclusive use of the pictures. But Wallis wanted Cecil to release some of his to the general press. She was adamant about this plan, saying that otherwise she would have chosen Dorothy Wilding. As Cecil noted:

> That was good for me though not good for *Vogue* for it may mean that if *Vogue* choose their batch quickly I may have time to be the first to the general press and America with wedding pictures and thereby gain untold sums of money.[31]

America was more interested in this event than in the coronation. The massive sum of £15,000 was at stake for the first photographs. Cecil began to dream of 'a new roof at Ashcombe, the road done up, presents to Mummie and to all my friends'.[32]

Cecil has published his account of the wedding visit.* He restrained himself from publishing somewhat harsh descriptions of the bridal couple. Wallis, he thought, 'today especially unlovable, hard and calculating and showing an anxiety but no feeling of emotion'.[33] Her face, he noted, 'broken out in spots and not looking her best'.[34] The Duke of Windsor had been reluctant the year before to be photographed by Cecil, whom he described as 'a photographer of women'. Today Cecil observed him:

> His expression though intent was essentially sad. Tragic eyes belied by impertinent tilt of nose. He has common hands, like a little mechanic's, weather-beaten and rather scaly and one thumb nail is disfigured. His hair at forty-five [in fact forty-three] is as golden and thick as it was at sixteen, his eyes fierce blue do not seem to focus properly, are bleary in spite of their brightness and one is much lower than another. Whether or not he will be pleased with my photographs I cannot tell for they will not be flattering to him, accustomed to highly retouched pictures taken many years ago, but I was quite pleased with what I got under very trying conditions.[35]

There was another photographer at the château, a Mr Soper, of Tilney Street. He was an uninspired old hack, formerly in the employ of Vandyk. When Cecil had finished, Soper took a few snaps. Both the Duke and Wallis laughed at his choice of the darkest possible room for no doubt gloomy results. Cecil treated him 'rather superciliously' and forgot about him.

The session over, Cecil dashed back at top speed. The pictures were printed in the Paris office of *Vogue* and Cecil was delighted with them. He flew over

---

* See *Self Portrait With Friends*, pp. 54–8.

the Channel and raced to Mrs Chase at *Vogue*'s London office in Bond Street. Mrs Chase was very excited, but then the story took a sour turn:

> She chose this and that and then when the question of General Press release was brought up she entirely changed her tune. For half an hour, for half a valuable hour, we argued. Wallis wanted there to be certain ones for the General Press. It had been agreed there should be, and now Edna and Condé were loth that there should be. I argued. My eyes shot fire. Miss Joseph at home was bargaining about the price of the pictures I may or may not have. If I could be permitted some the message was to be I would be home for lunch, but the picture and the millions of pounds was dashed by a picture already in the *Evening Standard* – the picture that the photographer from Vandyk had taken after me. This had already been released, had been radioed to USA and on its way on the *Queen Mary*! That took the wind out of my sails. However the pictures now given permission to be released by *Vogue* were in my hands, being dashed to the flat. After a skirmish I was given three hundred pounds for them, felt a wreck and after torturing myself to write an article for *Vogue* went to sleep at long last.[36]

The sequel was unpleasant. Mrs Chase thought the *Evening Standard* picture was Cecil's. She wrote accusing him of selling a scoop: 'I feel you have let us down badly ... now we fear that anything we publish will be an aftermath.'[37] Cecil was livid. He demanded an apology for 'the disgusting letter' he had received, explaining angrily that if he wanted to make a scoop he could have done so on the spot in France:

> Far from letting you down, I doubt if you realize how much I have done for you in impossible circumstances, or what I have not done for myself in the very way you accuse me of doing. From the moment I stepped from the train at St Pierre des Corps, I was inundated with fabulous offers for my impressions and photographs. Naturally I refused them all.[38]

Mrs Chase had not intended to hurt Cecil, as she explained, but he was left bitter and resentful. In his diary he wrote:

> This row has wounded me so deeply that I have taken a great dislike to *Vogue*, know it offers me little more than money and that if I were a brave and courageous person would give it up entirely and start something else.[39]

17

All the Damned Kikes in Town

Mr R. Andrew's Ball at the El Morocco brought out all the damned kikes in town.

One of Cecil's offensive doodlings
(*Vogue*, 1 February 1938)

Ashcombe was the scene of a magnificent *fête champêtre* in the summer of 1937, given by Cecil and Michael Duff. It took weeks to arrange. Salvador Dali had seen bird and animal masks in Vienna which Cecil found in London and purchased for the waiters. Artificial flowers and ribbons came from Paris. Thirty supper tables were adorned to look like ballet dancers 'or how a débutante should look'. Madame Karinska made dresses, and these arrived, as ever, at the very last moment. Buses were hired to convey the guests up and down the steep hill. These were decorated with satirical posters, teasing famous hostesses, such as: 'See Wiltshire on a Corrigan scooter. Goes everywhere. Never breaks down.'[1] John Sutro composed a mock Restoration play: 'John has an alarming brain,'[2] noted Cecil. 'Given a stiff drink he can compose in verse *ad lib ad infinitum*.' The only shadow cast on the proceedings was the death after a painful illness of Desmond Parsons (brother of Lord Rosse) on 4 July.

For the party itself Cecil began by wearing a coat covered with red roses and broken eggs. In the course of this perfect evening he changed at least three times. Guests arrived in relays. There was country dancing and fireworks; the play was performed and received with gales of merry laughter. Then there was dancing in the 'dazzling ballroom', Cecil acting host to his friends from all over the world – Mona Harrison Williams, the Reed Vreelands, and so on. But Cecil did not invite Peter Watson (now in the throes of his affair with Denham Fouts), fearing that his disapproval might cast a blight on the evening. The party went on all night. Nor did the approaching dawn deter the revellers. The band only stopped at 7 a.m. Even then the daylight did not produce an effect of squalor and broken glasses. 'With aching legs, with tortured feet',[3] the happy hosts at length gave in to sleep.

Cecil's summer holidays were spent first with Mona Harrison Williams in

Capri (where he was devastated to hear the news of Marge's death) and then at Schloss Kammer, where he found David Herbert, Raimund von Hofmannsthal,* Margot Asquith and others. There were the usual strange happenings. One guest was told to leave and did so 'exhibiting rudely her behind'.⁴ Toscanini called at the castle one day. Also present were George Hoyningen-Huene and Horst, Cecil's rival as a *Vogue* photographer. Disconcertingly Peter Watson materialized at the castle. Cecil avoided him by writing letters in his room.

Cecil had a new girlfriend now, in the form of Lilia Ralli.† In May that year he had joined her in Paris and noted:

> Lilia was very sweet and gay and I get along extremely well with her the more I know her. Her squeaky, childlike, breathless voice, without timbre, used to irritate me, but now it does not. She is very alert and good company and I am very fond of her. Together we did a lot of shopping.⁵

Cecil and Lilia had gone to Interlaken together, where she helped him in his first tentative efforts to ski. Now, in August, they shared the thirty-four hour train journey to Athens: 'Lilia, in her Greek surroundings, soars in my estimation for she is one in a thousand, one in a million among her country people. They are so niggling and bourgeois. She is a dynamo of subtlety and human understanding.'⁶ Cecil, accustomed to Doris and her piles of suitcases, was nevertheless surprised at the number of tiny little objects Lilia found it necessary to travel with. Innumerable little bags were filled with jewels shaped like roses, cherubs, negroes, tortoises and butterflies. One night sitting beside a pool of still water, her spectacles dropped in. Quite unconcerned she left them there all night and they were retrieved in the morning. After this trip Lilia wrote to Cecil: 'I never feel more completely entertained as by your company and please remember it.'⁷ Lilia Ralli was known to her friends as 'Figgi' because she continually used the expression '*Figure-toi*'. Cecil called her 'Figleaf' and she called him 'Cecilywinks'. The romance was important to Cecil not only because Lilia was intensely chic, but also because she was a close friend of the Duke and Duchess of Kent, and Cecil thus heard news of them from her and was drawn closer into their circle. Later Cecil lost interest in the physical side of their relationship, but a deep friendship remained.

In September, after a two-year battle to find a publisher, *Cecil Beaton's Scrapbook* was published. This was a collection of essays, photographs and drawings, which Bébé Bérard had inspired him to make. Many of Cecil's publications proved irksome to him and this apparently harmless book was no

---

*Raimund von Hofmannsthal (1906–74), son of the librettist Hugo von Hofmannsthal. Married first to Alice Astor, then to Lady Elizabeth Paget.

†Madame Jean Ralli (d. 1977). Born in Athens. A childhood friend of Princess Marina. Later she worked for Christian Dior.

exception. Max Beerbohm, the elegant writer and caricaturist, thought his pictures, taken specially for the book, 'admirable likenesses of me', but complained that he hated the striped curtain in the background of some: 'I am sorry to be so fussy. But I did on the telephone ... say that I must have a quite plain setting.'[8] He went in against a dark backdrop, cane and gloves in hand. Many years later (in 1952 and 1969 respectively) Greta Garbo and Katharine Hepburn punished Cecil for his articles about them. As usual Cecil was advised about his style by Edith Olivier, and in his new publishers, B.T. Batsford Ltd, he found both enthusiasm and originality. They went on to publish ten of his books in the next twelve years.

Batsford was founded in 1843. In an age of mass production, they were staunch upholders of the tradition of good craftsmanship. They were one of the last of the publisher-booksellers. Purchasers of any of their volumes knew that the author had brought his manuscript in through the same front door and that it had been produced above the shop. Cecil's work was always a challenge to them. As Charles Fry, his publisher (once described by John Betjeman as 'a phallus with a business sense'),[9] wrote: 'Cecil Beaton might burst in, elegant, excited, hatless, with more photographs and drawings which somehow had to be crowded into an already crowded book.'[10] The complicated task of layout fell to Brian Cook (now Sir Brian Batsford). He recalled Cecil's 'tremendous outflow of talent',[11] but that Cecil had no knowledge of layout or the technical problems involved. It was Brian Cook who devised the revolutionary colourful wrappers, with a single illustration which encircled the entire book, and attempted very daring colour schemes such as the bright yellow board covers for *Cecil Beaton's New York* (1938). The *Scrapbook* was published 'more for fun than anything else'. The boards and endpapers were hand covered with a Sanderson wallpaper of pink roses. Cecil welcomed its publication:

> If any book deserves not to fail this is one, but the price, 21/-, will prevent its having a wide appeal. However, it is worth all the disappointment for it is something I am pleased with ... and it is time that I can show some of my work outside *Vogue* magazine.[12]

The *Scrapbook* was dedicated to Peter Watson (a distinction it shares with Cyril Connolly's *The Unquiet Grave*). Peter wrote that he thought the book 'really a triumph, a hundred per cent success and *must* have a bigger circulation than the Bible.... And Peter? Who is he? If I don't know him may I meet him – If I do I am very proud.'[13] Peter wanted to meet before Cecil sailed for America, but Cecil decided to play him at his own game. Taking the telephone into the lavatory at Ashcombe (so that his mother would not hear) he dictated a telegram: 'Am really glad you liked my book which naturally was dedicated to you. I miss you very much but perhaps 'tis better so. Signed Cecil.'[14]

Stephen Tennant called the *Scrapbook* 'really so brilliant, such a dry wine', adding later: 'I said it was a dry wine – but it's both sweet and dry, the article on Garbo is so good.'[15] The book was a success and an additional 1,200 copies were printed. Brian Cook and the artist Derek Hill arranged an exhibition of Cecil's work at the shop in North Audley Street. The walls were papered with the book's wallpaper; photographs and sketches were pinned to this, and furniture and artificial flowers from Ashcombe completed the decoration. A party was held there in November, when Cecil was in New York.

One review caused particular discussion in the Beaton circle. Raymond Mortimer, the critic and already a friend, described it as 'not great art, but great fun'. He wrote of Cecil in the *New Statesman and Nation*:

> One godmother gave him the ability of a business-man and another gave him the nature of an artist, but the third gave him a distaste for a business career, and an incapacity for serious art. The consequence has been a remarkably successful life as a photographer, stage-designer and journalist.[16]

Raymond Mortimer explained to Cecil later:

> I hoped you would not mind, for I have a notion that you are immensely less conceited than most of us, in spite of your having been so triumphantly successful. I still think – as my review tried to suggest – that you have not yet used your talents to the full and I'm extremely curious to see what your future is going to be.[17]

Cecil rather welcomed this criticism, which he interpreted as a spur to write rather than draw or photograph. Later Charles Fry suggested he write a book on New York, which he agreed to do as another way of distancing himself from *Vogue*.

Cecil sailed for what would be his last New York winter for some years, in September 1937, rather earlier than usual. He knew many of his fellow travellers, amongst whom were Doris, 'very quiet and alone and sad, under an unlucky star',[18] Douglas Fairbanks Jr 'trying to be everything',[19] Cole Porter, 'very disinterested and uninteresting, tired, aged, snobbish Puck', and Hollywood mogul Louis B. Mayer, 'porpoise, nannie'.[20]

The New York season started slowly but rose to an exhausting crescendo. Cecil succumbed to such a bad cold, causing miscellaneous aches and pains, that he submitted to the ministrations of a famous Assyrian doctor, Dr Wolfe, recommended by his friend, Diana Vreeland. Cecil continued to work but he felt restricted and frustrated:

> The weeks have flown – four of them already or maybe five and all that results are a few pages more of my photographs in the inevitable *Vogue*. The weekly salary is a boon but the *Vogue* influence is now beyond a

joke. It makes me limited more than ever in my interests and encourages me to recover the same old ground. Year after year.[21]

Cecil's disenchantment with *Vogue* had become serious since the unfortunate business of the Windsors' wedding pictures. But there was more to it than that. The previous winter Cecil had been put on the carpet for photographing models in dark glasses, standing 'in angular poses with their elbows crooked and their feet planted well apart'.[22] Cecil had grown bored of elegant, languid poses: 'Instead of looking like mannequins unconvincingly pretending to be ladies of the *haut-monde*, they suggested ballet dancers at rehearsal.'[23] Eventually the pictures were allowed to appear and, as Cecil said, 'they inaugurated a new phase in the history of fashion photography'.[24]

In January 1937 Cecil had written to Mrs Chase to explain the trend of his new photographs. He was bored by the 'technical perfection'[25] of the photographs in *Vogue*. He thought they should lead the way by reverting to old-fashioned photographs: 'I am certain it would add variety and a new note as well as a new look to an issue.'[26] Cecil also wanted to draw with red chalk on grey paper and wondered if it would be possible to have a double-page fashion spread with a pop-up (as in children's books). 'I don't know if it is terribly expensive,' wrote Cecil, 'but it would be sensational to have fashions done in this way.'[27]

Cecil's ideas were opposed as always by Dr Agha, who feared that Cecil was trying 'to deny everything *Vogue* has worshipped for so many years – to substitute ugliness for beauty, dowdiness for elegance, bad technique in photography for good technique which we spent so many years trying to develop'.[28] But Cecil maintained that all he sought was more realism in both photographs and paintings. He was seeking new forms of beauty and distinction. His favourite models were the actress Ruth Ford ('she is intelligent, interpretive, beautiful and exquisite in a not too extraordinary way'),[29] and Mary Taylor (whom 'I could use more often than you wish').[30]

Meanwhile his fortune-teller friend, Bathsheba Askowith, had urged him to do more writing. She said that he had been impatient to succeed but that now his career was well established. It was like a steamer that had just embarked on a long voyage. There was hard work to be done, and it must be done slowly and carefully, not in conditions of stress. She warned Cecil that he was easily influenced.

As the New York winter of 1937–8 progressed, Cecil tried to veer from photography to writing. He also designed costumes for Tallulah Bankhead as the heroine in *Antony and Cleopatra*, his first work for Broadway. He was particularly pleased with a close-fitting oilcloth dress that hung 'in shiny, glistening folds like water'.[31] At the dress rehearsal he was amused at the husky-voiced Tallulah striding about in a paper crown and an unfinished costume that exposed her entire body, exhorting the grey-haired seamstresses: 'Don't you see it's got to cover me here. I can't go on showing my pussy.'[32] Cecil thought the first night a great success, but the critics lambasted it. John Mason Brown wrote: 'Tallulah Bankhead barged down the Nile last night as Cleopatra and sank.'[33]

Soon after this Cecil saw the production of *Julius Caesar* by Orson Welles and John Houseman, and in the New Year, to his great excitement, Orson Welles invited him to do the costumes for his projected productions of *Henry IV* and *Henry V*.

Cecil's health was deteriorating:

> Suddenly I realize how ill I have felt for so long. Every day would be an exhausting one for me no matter how little activity it contained. Every day produced annihilation and at night no pleasure was so great as the relief of sinking into my bed. Every day produced a minor headache and as I rushed along the hotel corridors I sighed and the effort of screwing up my face to produce a grin and good evening to the maid or the elevator boy was a major one. Only after my initial visit to Dr Wolfe did I realize how long I have felt like this. All the time I was in Greece I was incapable of normal energy and would be amazed and marvel at the vitality of others. Here in New York a person like Clare Brokaw [Boothe] Luce would be a being from another planet for her energy and power of concentration is that of an abnormally healthy person.[34]

He not only took medical treatment but paid many visits to Bathsheba Askowith. He believed that part of his problem came from his prolonged separation from Peter. Cecil's mother was worried too. On 30 November 1937 she wrote saying he must ask for three months' sick leave from *Vogue* work. This he did not do.

Cecil continued to work as hard as ever. With Charles Henri Ford he went on expeditions for his New York book. They visited police headquarters to see the daily batch of arrests and called on a Harlem photographer. Cecil decorated parties for the Duchess of Westminster and Julia Welldon. For Loelia Westminster's party on 13 December he raced against time, drawing giant caricatures of famous New York figures. Despite an appalling cold he felt some responsibility in helping make the party a success. He danced the Big Apple when he should have been in bed. In the New Year of 1938 he gave a party for Ruth Ford's debut in *The Shoemaker* and he photographed Helena Rubinstein: 'an old Polish frog ... with a huge casket of jewels. I have never seen such a collection and she clicks her teeth and shrugs "Only Rubbish. Much more in Paris" – but they are jewels that would belong to a Kingdom, not a private individual.'[35] Mrs Patrick Campbell arrived to be photographed with her Pekinese, Moonbeam, and when Cecil felt self-conscious about his voice after hearing it on a recording, he went to the old actress for voice lessons. And so the rush continued and he coped as best he could.

As this time Tchelitchew was still influencing his work. Cecil absorbed many of his thoughts about everyday life too. He told Cecil he must only mix with 'sympathetic people, artists and writers and people who worked and with whom it would be interesting to exchange ideas and problems'.[36] Much of Tchelitchew's conversation consisted in berating the Jews, and Cecil, who had no strong views either way, respected the artist's opinions on this subject too. He even laughed naïvely at a joke about the writer and broadcaster Kay Halle in Berlin. Someone had asked her: 'Who is the man dearest to you who is a Jew?', to which she had replied, 'My father.'[37] At the same time Cecil saw a number of films which he found particularly inadequate. He resented the power that the Jews had over Hollywood, equating this with a lack of artistic taste. Films were very much in the forefront of the popular mind as David O. Selznick was in the middle of making *Gone With the Wind* and no Scarlett O'Hara had yet been found.* Cecil met George Cukor, the director in charge of the search, at the actress Rosamond Pinchot's. He thought him 'exceptionally witty and so accustomed to being funny that he is only slightly amused at his own jokes'.[38] Cecil was delighted when Cukor suggested he might do some film décors.

'I have had wonderful compliments this week,' wrote Cecil soon after his thirty-fourth birthday in January 1938, 'a piece in the manner of C.B. from Parker Tyler flatters me most, Glenway Wescott calls me a philosopher and moralist and last night Mario Panza watching me dance the Big Apple said I was a most civilized being and had the calm sureness of a Chinese. I don't often talk of my prowess, bouquets and seldom write about them I hope.'[39]

Cecil would have little reason for complacency over the next few months for on Monday, 24 January 1938, his world crashed around him in a most unexpected manner.

He was in bed when the telephone awoke him sharply at 9.30. A reporter asked to see him about references to him in Walter Winchell's column. Cecil thought this must refer to a party he was giving for English friends, but Winchell, a staunch anti-Nazi, had another preoccupation. The item, itself a mere two inches long, began:

> The Feb. issue of Vogue, the mag., contains some hidden anti-Semitism!
> ... A magnifying glass is necessary to detect it in Cecil Beaton's lettering
> for Frank Crowninshield's article on New York Society on page 73....[40]

Some examples were then quoted:

> Cholly asks: Why?? is Mrs Selznick such a social wow – Why is Mrs
> Goldwyn such a wow? ...

* Eventually the English actress, Vivien Leigh, was chosen at the end of 1938.

Party Darling Love Kike. Mr R. Andrew's Ball at the El Morocco brought out all the damned kikes in town.[41]

The point was made: 'None of those remarks has anything to do with the Crowninshield text.'[42] The journalist pressed Cecil for a quote: 'Why did you do it?'[43] Later Cecil tried to explain in his diary how the incident had occurred:

I was baffled and ejaculated it was done unconsciously. I am not anti-Jewish and am violently hostile to Hitler, but if there is any possible explanation these quotes contained my subconscious momentary irritation at having seen so many bad Hollywood films. Not only was I trying to make some plausible excuse but I was trying to analyse my sentiments for having done these little scraps of lettering and now having had three days to think the matter over, feel that I felt at the time that these impertinences would only be impertinent as far as the art department where they would be deleted at any rate if not deleted there, they would be innocuous. The drawing had been done at a time when I was suffering from a bad cold. It had been finished late at night when I was sick and tired of the whole thing and irritated beyond control at the pressure put on me by the office.[44]

Margaret Case had spotted the slogans and said to Cecil: 'Oh! they'll have to alter some of those captions in your drawing.' Cecil had snapped back: 'Always the same story. Let them alter the whole beastly thing!' Margaret Case was sure he would want to do it, but Cecil declared that he had washed his hands of the matter and rushed off to his next appointment. Besides, the offending captions were less than the size of half a little toenail. Cecil claimed later that he forgot all about the lettering, but Walter Winchell's story was different: 'So delighted was he with his little trick that he spread the news among his intimates, gloating of how it had put one over.... Naturally, that is how we heard about it.'[45] Another theory is that his persistent opponent, Dr Agha, had informed Winchell. For years he had resented Condé Nast's genuine affection for Cecil.

Cecil telephoned *Vogue* while the reporter clung like a leech. He was summoned at once to the office. 'I was scared but much more scared when I saw Margaret's face, the faces of various editors and the group of lawyers, advertising men and others clustered outside Condé's office.'[46] Cecil tried to explain himself as best he could, promising that he was not anti-Jewish. His only resentments were 'the people that run Hollywood and pretend to make an art of what they know is an industry'. This 'appalling catastrophe' resulted 'from some lettering that might just as easily have been abracadabra for it was never meant to be seen or if seen at all only for submission to Dr Agha in the art department'.[47] He wrote out two statements of apology for issue to the press.

Cecil's offensive Vogue *drawing, February 1938. The controversial words can be seen in the enlarged detail.*

Cecil's nightmarish day continued with his giving a lecture in the morning and a long-planned cocktail-party for Lord and Lady Rosse, and others who had come over from England. Anne Rosse remembered that Cecil was on the verge of tears: 'He was very vulnerable at that time.'[48] Cecil stopped all telephone calls and made sure no journalists could reach him. He dined with Helen Astor, who knew the importance of the Jews in New York, having been unable to have Furtwängler as conductor of the New York Philharmonic Orchestra. Altogether there was a lot of hypocrisy concerning Jews at this time. Mrs Chase once told Madge Garland that while it was acceptable to lunch with Jews in a restaurant, it was not acceptable to dine with them in their homes.

He then went through pouring rain to the Opera, where he found Condé Nast's butler awaiting him with a note from Nast. Typed, it read: 'I would appreciate very much your coming to the house at ten o'clock – before if you can make it. Please be here by ten at any rate.' In his own hand Condé Nast had added: 'I am so terribly distressed over horrible mess – Forgive me for asking you to run away from the opera.'[49]

Cecil went to Odom's box and stayed long enough to hear Alfredo sing 'Libiamo, libiamo ne' lieti calici' in the first act of La Traviata. But the only cups that were overflowing for Cecil were cups of wrath as he discovered when he reached Nast's Park Avenue apartment:

> When after the long wet ride I got to Condé's apartment he was waiting for my bell ring and hurried me into the dining-room where there have been so many gay parties but which now took on a sinister aspect with a decanter of whiskey and two large tumblers on the table. The lines in Condé's face were deeper than usual, his voice dryer and quieter.[50]

Condé Nast had a message for Cecil: 'We're in a tough spot. ... I could not mind more if I were losing my own son but I can see nothing else but to ask for your resignation.'[51] Nast produced a statement he had prepared for the press, which Cecil thought unduly pompous:

> While Condé was out of the room and I paced around I had a feeling of freedom – and I have never more felt as ambitious. I had complained so much about the restrictions of Vogue and now I was free in so far that I would not be able to appeal to the same public that I have had in future – although a certain terror gnawed at me the anxiety was less than I had expected and I felt for the moment very lean and energetic, young and capable of fighting.[52]

His bravado was to suffer many further blows as the seriousness of what he had done was brought firmly home to him. Meanwhile he relied on Kommer, himself a staunch Jew, who at one o'clock that morning tried to persuade Nast that the withdrawal of 130,000 copies of the offending Vogue was an adequate gesture to the Jewish community. But Nast had already released to the world the news of Cecil's resignation. Wearily Cecil returned to his hotel and learned that his great friend, Rosamond Pinchot, had committed suicide. (In London another mini-row blew up when Tom Driberg, 'William Hickey' of the *Daily Express*, lifted a sketch of her from the *Book of Beauty*. This turned out to be in *Vogue's* copyright.) In the days that followed, New Yorkers took sides over Cecil's misfortune. Margaret Case proved a loyal ally, Condé Nast personally took him to one of Mrs Vanderbilt's lunches. Gertrude Lawrence cabled: 'What a bloody shame. Love Gertie.'[53] His friend Lilia Ralli wrote from Paris: 'Prince Paul of Yugoslavia in Belgrade could not get over it, as he said: Democracy the way it's going in USA looks fiercer than Bolshevism and so much more of a hypocrisy.'[54] Cecil was shocked when others congratulated him for taking a brave stand. The playwright Frederick Lonsdale, who was strongly anti-Semitic, telephoned to say Cecil would have 'countless supporters'.[55] But Cecil noted: 'this is far from what I desire. I am *not* at all anti-Jewish and the last thing I wish for is to create any disturbance in an altogether upheaved world.'[56] Raimund von Hofmannsthal, on the other hand, blamed him bitterly for his action, and Clare Boothe Luce, whose husband owned *Life* magazine, declared: 'Henry wouldn't now touch him with the end of a ten-foot barge-pole.'[57] A joke circulated describing Cecil as the 'Heillustrator'. Johnnie McMullin of *Vogue* was right to conclude that Cecil's behaviour on this occasion was stupid rather than wicked, and also right when he declared of Cecil: 'The only alternative is that, like Hitler, he had begun to think himself omnipotent.'[58]

The scandal raged on in the press and there were more consequences to face. None of Cecil's work could now be published. He kept remembering long-awaited pieces that would have to be axed. He heard that *Vogue* lost $36,000 as a result of his misdeed. He received a confused and anxious letter from Edna Woolman Chase, then in Nassau: 'I am frantic. Surely there must be some awful error. I did not see anything but the names on the envelopes which I asked you to change.'[59] His sisters wrote to him ticking him off and reminding him firmly that his mother and her expenses were his sole responsibility. The Jewish stockholders in the Mercury Theatre made it clear that Cecil would not now be allowed to do the *Henry IV* costumes for Orson Welles. 'More and more disturbances seemed to crop up,' wrote Cecil, 'until I was reduced to pulp. I felt as if I had committed a murder.'[60]

It took Bathsheba Askowith, the psychic, to explain to Cecil that his actions were done as a result of 'someone with stronger feelings than I [Cecil] had who had made me their instrument and to be technical I know I would not have been Jew conscious to the extent I have been if it were not for Pavlik's hatred of them'.[61] He also told Eleanor Lambert that Kommer used the word 'kike' to imply, as he understood it, 'vulgar people'.[62]

Robert Forsythe, writing in a New York paper called *New Masses* (2 February 1938), thought that Cecil's attack was more one of a risen social climber than of an anti-Semite. It has been said that when the door opens to admit the social climber, he makes certain that it closes swiftly behind him. From humble origins Cecil had risen to such heights that Mona Harrison Williams ('the best-dressed woman in the world') would pose only for Cecil. David and Irene Selznick were rising stars and Selznick International was backed by Jock Whitney (like Mona, an important Long Island figure). Forsythe continued:

> Among the uppercrust there have been gags around about Dave and Irene and their new society connections, the Whitneys. Quite plainly the Selznicks were climbing, and nothing irritates a man who has climbed more than seeing another trying to climb. So in one place in the Cecil Beaton border, there is a reference to Mrs David Selznick, and in another you get the line about kikes. An interesting study in psychology, if I am right.[63]

During the winter Cecil had had a row with Irene Selznick in a flower-shop. It was much more an anti-Selznick attack than anything else. Unfortunately by its nature Cecil's action was bound to be condemned as anti-Semitic. Condé Nast suggested that it might be a good idea if Cecil left New York. He sailed home in April, noting: 'Never before (and never again I hope) have I left New York with such joy and light-heartedness. There was not one single regret at parting.'[64] Cecil believed his expulsion from *Vogue* was temporary, but a letter from Nast dated 21 April 1938 made it clear that he would not be asked to rejoin the staff. Nast wrote:

> Although I am ready to believe that you have no really anti-Semitic feelings and what you did had in your mind no more significance than a 'prank', nevertheless you chose, most unfortunately for all of us, to play this prank in such a way that you plunged me, as a publisher, into a political and racial situation completely out of character with *Vogue* and entirely at variance with, and distasteful to, my own feelings.[65]

Cecil replied that this letter was 'rather a surprise and an unexpected shock to me'.[66] He then questioned the details of his remaining obligations to *Vogue*. His contract of 1 April 1937 lasted until 31 March 1939 and guaranteed him a salary of $37,000. This was now terminated, though Cecil maintained that he had not breached any agreement and that at his dismissal statements had been issued which were 'highly damaging to his considerable reputation'. For the sake of peace, Nast paid him £3,184 damages, in two instalments, on 5 December 1938 and 5 January 1939.

Vogue found Cecil hard to replace as he was one of their most regular contributors, but he suffered little remorse over the incident and was soon planting jocular references to it in his books. In *Cecil Beaton's New York*, published in London in October 1938, he paid tribute to Condé Nast: 'Mr Nast has employed many people and everyone he has employed becomes a friend for life.' He also wrote:

> In a city made up of so many nationalities and races, dangers lurk in everyday activities. It is difficult not to offend someone present when expressing an opinion in public. One can even reap a whirlwind (as I unfortunately discovered) by using a slang word of which one does not appreciate the full implications.[67]

In his spoof book of royal memoirs, *My Royal Past*, published in the autumn of 1939, Cecil has the Baroness von Bülop write: 'It was here that I met an Englishman, named Cecil Beaton, who had himself found some sort of trouble in America, and he became sympathetic to my story.'[68] And as Cecil recovered his morale, he declared brashly to David Herbert: 'I'm damn glad I did it!'[69]

Cecil's American career was effectively ruined, at least for the time being, by the *Vogue* incident, which continued to persecute him into the late 1940s and even, to a lesser extent, into the 1960s. Gradually, however, it was a story that faded from public memory and it rarely recurred in the press in the years that followed. Its worst effect was the difficulty it caused Cecil in working in the theatre or in films. As his prime victim, the producer Irene Selznick, commented years later: 'He paid heavily, very heavily. He was punished.'[70]

18

Rest and Recuperation

One must find a cool and fresh position on the pillow.

Jean Cocteau to Cecil, diary, September 1938

Even a year after the 'kikes' incident Cecil was suffering acutely from its hostile effects. In certain quarters of New York he was branded 'a fascist and anti-Semite'.[1] His work had to be removed from the US Camera Club annual collection of photographs after protests from a Jewish organization. Massey's, the New York booksellers, took only one copy of *Cecil Beaton's New York*. Cecil's American publisher, Jo Lippincott, was threatened with a general boycott on other publications if he continued to deal with Cecil. When reviewing Cecil's book, Bennett Cerf resurrected the *Vogue* incident and the notorious hatchet-man Walter Winchell and others were quick to do likewise. In December 1938, Edna Woolman Chase wrote to Cecil:

> I long to see you but I think perhaps you are wise not to come over this winter. I am afraid there would be a fresh blast of unpleasant publicity. The Jewish question still being at the boiling point keeps all the memories very acute.[2]

Kaetchen Kommer came to Cecil's rescue. He welcomed the gratitude Cecil expressed for his previous help and explained that he loved helping people: 'The fact is that since my early boyhood I had a deep conviction that none of my friends could ever make a train unless I took them to the station and put them into their car.'[3] He met Winchell with Clare Boothe Luce, and Winchell agreed to a private meeting with Cecil on his next visit to New York. Kommer assured Cecil that the Jewish issue had nothing to do with the bad sales of his book. The handicaps were that 'the book is too expensive'[4] and that 'New Yorkers are not particularly interested in books about New York'.[5] Cecil then proposed putting on an exhibition in aid of Jewish refugees. Kommer disapproved of this, but took the opportunity to give Bennett Cerf 'a quite uninhibited piece of his mind'.[6]

Kommer's efforts on his behalf led to a further monstrous slur in Walter Winchell's syndicated column on 6 March 1939: 'Cecil Beaton sent a specially bound copy of that *"Vogue"* (in which he kicked himself out of the country) to Goebbels who arranged jobs for Beaton with a Berlin mag.'[7]

Cecil contemplated litigation, but many people (most notably Gertrude Stein) advised against this. Frank Crowninshield wrote to Winchell, with the approval of Condé Nast, to explain that the story was untrue and that Cecil had 'taken a pretty serious beating and suffered much (financially, professionally and mentally) as a result of his lamentable indiscretion in the pages of *Vogue*'.[8] Meanwhile Cecil wrote to Eleanor Lambert: 'I am really getting quite sick of Winchell's unfairness. It seems to me so beside the point.'[9] Eleanor Lambert advised him to let the matter rest, but was sorry to point out that Winchell's latest attack reduced the sale price of the Windsor portraits (taken in Paris in November 1938), from about $200 to $95.

Cecil had not appreciated how strong the *Vogue* veto would be. In the spring of 1938 he had photographed the Duchess of Gloucester, and although she had been very shy and the results accordingly disappointing, he was convinced that *Vogue* would want them. They did not. Madge Garland, meeting Cecil soon after his return to London, found him a changed man: 'The difference was so extraordinary. Before that he was a painted young floozie. He came back a serious man.'[10]

Under the terms of Cecil's *Vogue* contract he was not permitted to work for other periodicals until 1939. As *Vogue* themselves were not using him at all, he had an unexpected amount of free time on his hands. Thus in the best traditions of one who had overstepped the mark, he took the opportunity to travel. He went to Paris with David Herbert and stayed with that flamboyant pair, Elsie Mendl and Johnnie McMullin. Cocteau reassured Cecil: 'I only like people that are broken, that are ruined, that have disasters annihilate them so that they must start life new and afresh.'[11] Later Cecil photographed Cocteau while someone puffed opium into his suddenly 'galvanized corpse'.[12] He posed by the ruins of the Paris Exposition and Cecil took what he later considered his best photographs of him. He also photographed Marie-Laure de Noailles there, although he knew she and Cocteau despised one another.

In July 1938 Cecil set off on an extended trip. He began at Maxine Elliott's Château de l'Horizon near Cannes. Then he and David Herbert drove to Cap Martin to board Daisy Fellowes's yacht, the *Sister Anne*. They sailed away to Corsica, Sardinia, Sicily and Malta (where Daisy showed them a strange establishment where, evidently, young British petty officers were 'lured to their doom by continental vamps').[13] Cecil revelled in the space on board but David concluded that 'People who own yachts are tyrants.'[14] Everyone on board seemed to be busy writing diaries, but were inhibited by the real fear of having them found and read. Many had dreams, Cecil's being especially colourful: 'about the upset in my family when my aunt Jessie swallowed an ermine tail off an old yellowing cape'.[15] The cruise continued through the Greek Islands while Cecil took many photographs. When he had to change a film ('always a tedious and laborious business')[16] he invariably got left behind. He noted after one such episode 'an unused film has more magic than any pictures one has ever taken'.[17]

While Hitler's forces were mobilized on the Czechoslovak border, the cruise continued past the Dardanelles and Troy to Istanbul. At Scutari they visited the cemetery, where Cecil blithely arranged a skeleton artistically against a headstone for some photographs. 'I felt I should be only too proud to have my skull and bones used for a contemporary artist's properties when I have lain long enough beneath ground.'[18] The formidable Daisy Fellowes dominated her guests, deciding where they should and should not stop. By luck they hit upon Pettaliae, the home of a rich Greek family, the Embiricoses, and Cecil caught up with Lilia Ralli, who had been cruising with the Kents. At length they arrived in Athens, where Cecil and David resolved to escape to Venice. They invented a telegram summoning them to leave at once. When they broke the news to Daisy, she said: 'You needn't have made up all those lies, darlings, you two have stayed on this ship longer than anyone else!'[19] Cecil considered his hostess, who was a mixture of contradictions:

> Daisy has been impossible. She has bullied one person, keeping the others on her side only until it is time to bully the next person. She is spoilt, capricious and even wicked but she has many generous impulses and often has behaved with the breadth of point of view of a man. She has let us remain to ourselves without any obligations and considering the fact that as a reigning beauty she is accustomed to such treatment she has put up with discomforts in a most sportsmanlike way.[20]

The Venice stay was overshadowed by the growing threat of war. David and Cecil stayed with Juliet Duff at the Palazzo Vendramin, but Cecil resented her penny-pinching and was bored by parties given by rich Volpis and Morosinis. Caroline and Liz Paget, Raimund von Hofmannsthal and Rex Whistler were also staying with Juliet. Brian Cook, Cecil's publisher, came over to check the proofs of the New York book, and Rex was prevailed upon to contribute line drawings of hearts, bells and horseshoes. Odom took Cecil on a short trip to Padua and Mantua. Peter Watson was also in Venice, but Cecil still refused to see him, maintaining his eighteen-month strategy.

In Venice Cecil found Doris Castlerosse installed in the Palazzo Vernier dei Leoni (now the Guggenheim Museum) on the Grand Canal, living the life which inspired Cole Porter to write:

> And Venetia who loved to chat so,
> Is still drinking in her sinking pink palazzo.[21]

Doris had gone to live in America. She divorced Lord Castlerosse and became the protégée of the tough, very rich Mrs Eleanor Flick Hoffman. Loelia Duchess of Westminster recalled: 'You only had to look at her to know what was going on. Doris got more out of her than from any of her rich men, every jewel the size of a cherry.'[22] Mrs Hoffman gave Doris the Venetian palazzo, which Cecil thought 'a very expensive house that contains nothing of any value but might have been as effective if done on the cheap'.[23] In this summer of 1938 Doris* gave a successful ball, at which one of the guests was Princess Aspasia's young cousin, Prince Philip of Greece.

When the summer sun lost its heat, Cecil took the train to Milan and Genoa. Odom, now in Cannes, then sent his car to fetch him. After a few days in Cannes amongst people that Cecil thought 'made of life a tribute to waste',[24] they drove together to Tamaris, near Hyères. 'After learning about this place, the mecca of all the people whose work I am interested in, for so long, it was a great treat to be arriving here at last.'[25]

Tamaris, advertised as *'la station la plus au sud de la côte d'azur'*,[26] was described by John Sutro as 'the artist's Locarno'.[27] Edouard Bourdet, the playwright and director of the Comédie Française, and his wife Denise lived at the Villa Blanche, where many writers came to rest or work, including François Mauriac, Paul Morand, Jean Giraudoux and Jacques de Lacretelle. The irrepressible Cocteau was usually near by at the Hôtel de la Râde at Toulon, often appearing at the Bourdets' with a newly finished poem which he produced like a fisherman with a freshly caught shellfish. Bébé Bérard, on the other hand, settled for several summers in an annexe of the Grand Hotel de Tamaris. It was the presence of Bébé that lured Cecil. He was welcomed at the hotel by Denise Bourdet and Charles de Noailles and found himself dining with a group of twenty, presided over by Bébé, and including Frosca Munster, Georges Auric, the musician, and his wife Nora. Later they went to the little casino (a favourite haunt of Paul Morand, who became fascinated by the life of one of the croupiers). Here Cecil met Sir Francis Rose and his new American boyfriend (a thug inclined to beat Rose up and lock him out of the bedroom). Cecil wrote:

> Rose is someone I have always wanted to meet. A painter who occasion-
> ally produces a really wonderful picture. An Englishman living in France
> and China who looks like Toulouse-Lautrec and in graces is of the Horace

---

* Doris's life deteriorated quickly. On 1 September 1942, Kommer wrote to Cecil: 'Time and the war have not been kind to her. She looks, I'm sorry to report, devastated, and has become an acid misanthrope. She speaks with impotent bitterness of most people, feels herself persecuted and seems to have nothing to fall back upon.... Of you she speaks with startlingly deep affection.' Later that year, on Churchill's advice, she returned to London. She got into trouble over some pawned jewels. She took an overdose of sleeping pills in the Dorchester and died at St Mary's Hospital, Paddington, on 12 December 1942.

Walpole period and in manner like an intelligent spinster. He is in character and tastes very like Miss Stein and Miss Toklas.[28]

He had first seen Rose's works at Gertrude Stein's apartment in Paris in the spring. Influenced by Gertrude, who derived from the painter her motto: 'A Rose is a Rose is a Rose', Cecil believed that after Bérard, Rose was 'the greatest young painter of today',[29] though he was aware that Tchelitchew and Charles Henri Ford 'turned green with fury at the mention of his name'.[30]

Gertrude Stein had told Cecil the strange tale of Sir Francis Rose. He had recently lost a considerable fortune to a swindling boyfriend. From now on he had to survive on the proceeds of selling his house in Cannes, a sum that might last a year. Rose's father was a baronet and his mother was French. A gentle child, he was brought up in Paris where he fell under the influence of Cocteau and his *galère*. Painting was his only interest. Since the loss of his fortune he painted the entire time – 'a typical English story'[31] as Gertrude Stein put it. During his holiday at Tamaris, Francis Rose lost the remains of his fortune at the casino. As soon as he met Cecil, Rose became his greatest fan and took to following him around like a dog. Early each morning he came to Cecil's room to make sketches of him. Sadly Cecil soon discovered that 'his drawings and gouaches are as bad as some of his oils are marvellous',[32] and it tired him to sit for something that was clearly turning out to be atrocious. Later Rose described Cecil as a man of 'remarkable artistic and commercial mind ... the stockbroker of fashion'.[33] He dubbed him one of the leaders of 'the great rococo revival'[34] of the 1930s, along with Syrie Maugham, Elsie de Wolfe and Rex Whistler, all of whom were spreading 'the great white wave of plaster'[35] over everything. He thought that while Cecil had derived his sense of colour from Bérard, he had learned much more from his old friend Charles James. He went on:

> Versatile with his many gifts, as nimble with his talent as with his fingers, he gave the impression, however, of being a Dresden porcelain shepherd; only he was really a shepherd made of steel with a destiny as flexible and solid as Wall Street.[36]

It was not long before Cecil concluded of Francis Rose: 'He is doomed and no one can help him ever.'[37] Nothing made him revise this view during the forty years that followed.

Cecil's stay at Tamaris, 'the happiest of my holidays',[38] began in an atmosphere of anxiety. Hitler was speaking at Nuremberg and Cecil feared a holocaust. Nevertheless he stayed on while Bébé painted his portrait (now in the National Portrait Gallery).

He was fascinated by every aspect of Bébé and the way he worked. He slept on his bed, never in it, always wearing the same dirty clothes. He would wake from a deep sleep of snores, with his dirty little dog barking noisily, and get up without ever washing. He worked in an unfurnished room and depended on regular pipes of opium, yet, as Cecil noted: 'His personality and temperament outweigh all the disadvantages and he is never sordid or unattractive.'[39] Cecil loved the portrait as it gradually developed, but found that any distraction caused Bébé to stop work. Bébé also had a dread of returning to the canvas, having neglected his painting for some years:

> At work on my portrait I notice that each stroke or dab of the brush is made as a result of intense concentration and after each bout of work, lasting perhaps fifteen minutes, he sinks exhausted, to smoke a pipe on his bed. The amount of work he was able to do in the first sitting was quite extraordinary.[40]

John Sutro's arrival at Tamaris was taken as a reassuring sign that the days of peace were not over. Sutro remembers that it was during this summer that Bébé told Cecil, 'You'll never be a good painter.'[41] This depressed and discouraged Cecil in much the same way that Henry James was discouraged from writing plays, and for fifteen years he neglected his painting.

Oliver Messel and Peter Glenville (later a distinguished stage and film director) also appeared. Cecil thought Messel's career was in decline:

> Oliver has become rather a sad figure particularly in contrast to the brilliant promising and already sensationally successful youth of 15 years ago.... He has not lived up to his promise and in fact has continued along the same lines, his work even becoming less good than it used to be. His talent is a monkey's talent. He imitates and picks up ideas from everyone he sees but his life is so disordered that he sees only very second-rate people and he never uses his intellect.[42]

During the evenings at Denise Bourdet's the gloomy fears of war were dispelled by charades, John Sutro making mock 'peace' speeches, Bébé dancing 'like a butterfly',[43] and the assembled company doing oddly assorted chorus-girl routines. There was an evening when some of them went to Marseilles and visited a brothel called *Chez Aline*. Watching tarts receiving visitors through a two-way mirror, Cecil was horrified to observe a young man put out his hand to retrieve an unfinished cigarette the moment the love-making was over. The evening was 'a nerve-racking experience'.[44]

Cecil had to return to London by 24 September to sign 250 copies of *Cecil Beaton's New York*. Before he left he witnessed Bébé painting the second figure in his portrait:

> A little boy who by contrast throws my likeness into dramatic contrast. The work on the eyes produced pools of magic and each day the painting

becomes surer and greater. One feels that only time is against Bébé, whereas most other painters may ruin their work by continuing it one has confidence that each sitting reaps greater glories and it is tragic not to have half a dozen more sittings on this most lovely work.[45]

Bébé now threw away his old clothes, donned a town suit and accompanied Cecil on the train to Paris. As Bébé snored, Cecil realized that 'the summer holiday of shorts, sunburning and the summer fun was as if in a blackout in a film banished in a flash'.[46] The actor Leslie Howard (Ashley in *Gone With the Wind*) was in the next seat and asked both Bébé and Cecil to work in films. As Cecil commented: 'It was nice to pretend that life was going on just as usual.'[47]

He met Brian Howard on the ferry train returning to London, who told him that everyone was living in trepidation about the forthcoming war. At home he found differing attitudes. Stephen Tennant said he liked 'Hitler's mysticism, the way he parted his hair, the mad stormy look in his eyes'.[48] Edith Olivier was busy distributing gas masks in Wilton and Cecil observed trenches being dug in suburban parks near London. However, soon after this, Chamberlain flew to see Hitler for the third time. 'One's heart leapt,' noted Cecil. 'One's gorge rose. The tears welled over my cheeks. As in moments of great emotion I found myself unable to speak.'[49] The indomitable hostess Sybil Colefax fed Cecil with news from the House of Commons, and to celebrate the new peace he took his mother to Dodie Smith's hit at the Queen's Theatre, *Dear Octopus*.

While 'peace in our time' seemed to have been achieved, a new tension broke out at Ashcombe. Cecil's mother complained that she had been left to deal with all the problems during his prolonged holiday. A dreadful row ensued, with his mother threatening to leave by bus the next day, never to return. Cecil regretted her dependence on him both economically and emotionally. In her widowhood she never bothered with her old friends and scarcely read a book. Presently she relinquished 12 Rutland Court, her South Kensington flat.

Cecil still found time hanging heavily. He conceived the idea of collaborating with John Sutro on a play. His inspiration came from a variety of sources – the servants' hall at Wilton, a Cliveden weekend party, Diana Guinness's love for Oswald Mosley, and Ronald Firbank's book, *The Artificial Princess* (which he felt evoked the 'feminine artificiality' of his parents' generation). Nothing came of this and Cecil contemplated his lot:

During the weekend at Ashcombe I read many plays and felt for the first time that I was getting somewhere in my study. And by being quiet and alone for so long I also realized how much time I have wasted in the last ten years working for *Vogue* at such fever pitch that the general or main part of my brain was not able to function at all. During the whole weekend I realized most painfully how appallingly limited my interests have been, and wondered how at the beginning of my photographic career someone even like George Huene had been able to put up with someone so inhibited and small. I have been for years supercilious about superficial people, have judged Noël Coward for his lack of interest in the world in general, and now realize myself as incapable of writing dialogue about any character except certain artificial women for the simple reason that I have never been interested in any normal male being or in his interests. Only in the crisis have I even a superficial interest in the affairs of state.[50]

Cecil Beaton's New York received good reviews in London. Somerset Maugham told Cecil at lunch with Sybil Colefax that he should be very thrilled that James Agate said he had not only wit but genius. Raymond Mortimer telegraphed that it was the best reporting job he had ever known. But in New York even 'gentile' booksellers did not dare display copies, nor was it ordered in large quantities. In Paris, where Cecil was determined to take a winter break, the Duchess of Windsor told him: 'Your New York book makes even the hair drier a pleasure!'[51]

While there Mona Harrison Williams told him: 'I don't like the look of you.'[52] The doctor told him his blood pressure was low and his muscles too weak. Cecil felt that his problem stemmed from still craving for Peter Watson whose life, he believed, was founded on a more solid foundation than his own:

I am very conscious of my limitations and all the time seem to be dragged down into my own sink of froth and scum. David Herbert is by now almost a bad influence on me, for his merit has been to create gaiety and fun and now I feel myself averse and fighting against having his sort of fun! Perhaps I am wrong but I don't believe Peter is and it is like him I am trying to be.[53]

Cecil spent time with Cocteau, Jean Marais and Gertrude Stein. He found when talking to Stein that 'a note of reverence marks one's every sentence.... Any flippancy and childishness that may appear in Gertrude's work has entirely vanished from life.'[54]

His most enjoyable Paris evening was spent with a newly detoxicated Bébé:

He is the most congenial person for me and it is my triumph that he should like me so much as he does. He filled me with such praise, gave me for my book such bouquets that I beamed with gratitude and of course this is not idle flattery.[55]

Bébé told him that Peter had asked after him secretly. Cecil was delighted and grateful:

I now feel I would like to get physically well, my body in good trim, my tummy muscles tightened, my skin a different colour, my hair thicker and then go back to the friendship that has cost me so much happiness, but which on account of its disadvantages I was silly(?) strong(?) enough to relinquish.[56]

Sir Francis Rose had hired an apartment on the Ile St Louis for a year for the same annual rent as three weeks in the Ritz. His group picture of Bébé, Cecil and other Tamaris figures was hanging in the Salon d'Automne. Cecil thought it 'a complete failure'.[57] In January 1939, Rose came to England and painted at Ashcombe and Wilton in preparation for an exhibition in London. Suddenly Cecil fell under the spell of his intelligent and cultivated mind:

Of a sudden I could hardly bear to be out of earshot of this delightful person from whose sibilant tongue such pearls of philosophic wisdom drop. I began to take a most proprietary attitude toward him – and when Juliet [Duff] became as enchanted as I was, I felt very loth to lose out of my sight my precious new friend.[58]

In March 1939 Cecil accompanied David Herbert to Tangiers, where they rented a small house in the native quarter for £3 a week, from the painter Jim Wylie. 'It overlooks the Governor's Palace and is between the prison and the madhouse,' Cecil wrote to Kommer. 'We want to stay here for several weeks and the only thing that is likely to stop us is the situation with Herr Hitler who has given us all a nasty turn again.'[59]

Cecil was soon overcome by 'the beauty of the reality'[60] of Tangiers, the white-draped figures, the flower market, the irises, the gnarled silver trees; but he disliked the tile work, the carved wood and the designs on wood and fabric. Before settling in Tangiers, they toured Morocco, visiting Casablanca, Fez, Marrakesh and other places, but none impressed him as much.

The colours of Tangiers are like sweetmeats to my eyes. They have a great strength and force and yet their contrasts and their effects are created on a much quieter scale than I am accustomed to. Faded pinks suddenly sing out more importantly than any puce and magenta and in a street of blue-washed walls a small child at a well in a faded dress of pastel green creates as much effect as a shrill discord. If I am fortunate enough to be given the Comédie Française production of *Romeo and Juliet* I would utilize a great deal of these pale colour contrasts.[61]

He spent long hours at work on the drawings of his forthcoming spoof, *My Royal Past*, assisted by David Herbert, who drew some of the intricate backgrounds. While Cecil worked at home, David became utterly absorbed in the local life to which he would return years later as a permanent expatriate.

'After three weeks David has become a complete Tangerine,' noted Cecil, 'knows all the local gossip of this oriental Cheltenham and knows every inch of the town. From our roof garden he describes the scenes taking place in the square outside.'[62]

Cecil and David met all the local characters: Jessie Green (a leading figure), Miss Denistoun (the missionary) and Pierrefeu, a mysterious person who built enormous dams, yachts, painted and sculpted and helped Cocteau create *Le Bœuf sur le Toit*. At the end of their stay, in April, Cecil sat on the roof garden, listening to 'the tinkling bells and cries of beggars, the prayer calls from the mosque, someone beating a carpet, a towel flapping in the wind, a child crying and the lunatics moaning and bellowing their hymns of exasperation and impotence', and he concluded: 'I am pleased to go, for I now do not wish to become too embroiled with personalities here, and I feel that the essence has been fully savoured.'[63]

It was now fifteen months since Cecil had done any commissioned work. With spring in the air, he decided to brave a meeting with Peter Watson. They lunched together and visited the Chelsea Flower Show. The meeting went well but left Cecil disturbed and frightened:

> Maybe the interval has helped me to behave less selfishly and I believe he has suffered a lot and been extremely miserable, and he may be more amenable, but in order to preserve something that is so valuable to me I must play a game and it is this game of protection that I hate so much now as ever before and I hanker after the supreme luxury of being honest and acting without thought to the consequences.[64]

Francis Rose was in the East End, researching an article for *Vogue* to be illustrated with his own drawings. Cecil visited the eccentric baronet there, finding him installed at the Seamen's Institute for 8d. a night and dressed like a 'dirty workman'.[65] Needless to say, Rose was suffering another emotional upset. He had become enamoured of a stoker, called John, who had been wandering the streets out of work for six months. While they were together, the stoker's luck changed and he was signed on with his old ship for £4 a month. Rose was about to leave for Paris when John had come running up and said: 'We are going to be together.' He had secured Rose the job of steward (at £8 a month) on the ship's forthcoming voyage to Jamaica. Rose was dumbfounded at this plan and explained, somewhat clumsily, his reasons for declining. The stoker then departed in high dudgeon, leaving the forlorn Francis behind. When Cecil said good-bye, Francis was going from bar to bar enquiring, 'Have you seen my mate?' The story ended in tragic melodrama with the wretched stoker jumping out of a window, breaking his back, and dying in the arms of the bereft baronet. Cecil concluded: 'Francis had told the whole story to a kind Irish priest who said he must leave. So, leaving money for the funeral, ends the story of

Francis's week in the East End.'[66] The story was kept secret, shared only by Stein, Toklas and Cecil (who felt physically sick when he thought about it).

In Paris in June Cecil stayed with Francis (now in the company of a wrestler) and attended the wedding of Liz Paget to Raimund von Hofmannsthal (recently divorced from Alice Astor). It was a gloomy occasion because the Pagets regretted 'this poor beautiful girl being wasted'[67] on the foreigner. The happiness of the couple greatly reassured Cecil: 'I have often dreamt of the horror, the responsibility and anxiety, the shyness of a honeymoon – but these two were so delighted, so gay, that I felt even I one day might enjoy a honeymoon.'[68]

Cecil spent as much time in Paris as possible because in London the line was: 'I'm so depressed. I've got some information about the situation and war is inevitable',[69] while in Paris they said: 'I'm so depressed. After four sittings my wig for the Beaumont Ball has gone wrong.'[70] Randolph Churchill told Cecil that he liked 'the feeling that this was the last lap of gaiety',[71] news which horrified Cecil. There were many elaborate parties in that last season and Lilia Ralli was at hand to help Cecil enjoy them. When Francis Rose became unmanageable, Cecil fled to Bérard. Francis had the habit of taking stimulants to overcome exhaustion. He would then experience a sudden burst of energy and go 'to pass the night in lustful pleasure with a vicar's daughter that had to come to Paris for that purpose'.[72] Eventually he collapsed, but recovered before Cecil left and 'managed to get not only my portrait but another picture out of Bébé for me'.[73] Cecil returned to London with Francis and many new treasures for Ashcombe, found in flea markets.

In London Cecil was assailed by tonsilitis, which left him 'thoroughly embittered and exasperated with life in general'.[74] However, as so often in Cecil's life, his ill-fortune was to be short-lived. Two events affected this: 'Suddenly my fortune was changed. My stars were different and the complexion of my life altered.'[75] The first was that Cecil was invited by Alexander Korda to design costumes for a proposed film, *Manon Lescaut*. This was an opportunity to work with Korda's newly married actress wife, Merle Oberon. Cecil noted: 'This would be child's play, would reward me liberally and possibly get my foot into the world of films.'[76] Eleanor Lambert thought this would certainly be 'a stepping-stone to Hollywood work'.[77] Unfortunately war put an end to this project and Miss Oberon returned to Hollywood.

The second excitement was more fruitful. Prince and Princess Paul of Yugoslavia had been invited to Buckingham Palace by King George VI following their recent state visit to Hitler. Their arrival on 17 July heralded important political meetings. The visit, meant to last six days, was prolonged for over a fortnight because Prince Paul had to have some wisdom teeth removed. Lilia Ralli, a childhood friend of Princess Paul (Princess Olga, the Duchess of Kent's sister), was also in London. Partly on Lilia's recommendation Cecil was suddenly summoned from Ashcombe to photograph Princess Paul at Buckingham Palace. 'It was a great thrill for me to go into the Palace for the first time,' wrote Cecil. 'It was one of the rare times that of late I have been deeply thrilled, and as I walked behind a scarlet liveried page down miles of dark red carpeted corridors I was walking on air.'[78] Princess Paul's suite delighted Cecil in every detail: the huge Chinese vase filled with a mauve flowering plant, the yellow silk brocade, the writing-table with its blotter, paper-cutter and inkstand, the notepaper of the highest quality, even the sherry was 'the very best quality I know and strong as dynamite'.[79]

Cecil began by taking some quick photographs of the Prince Regent, before he hurried off to the dentist. Then Princess Olga reappeared wearing the largest diadem he had ever seen, with diamonds 'like almonds' around her neck. Even so Cecil did not find the Princess dazzling: 'She looked too Royal, too Russian. ... One cannot but see her as a nun.'[80] He photographed Princess Olga against his backgrounds of Fragonard trees and Piranesi ruined arches, which impressed her because previously she had always been photographed against black. Princess Marina joined her sister, walking badly and tripping up over a carpet. When the two sisters began to laugh at some private joke, Cecil found they both became 'gawky' and recorded: 'it is impossible to realize that here are two of the loveliest people today'.[81] Lilia Ralli and Turia Campbell (a Russian friend, later with the BBC) joined in the session and Cecil went on photographing 'even after my own enthusiasm had waned'.[82]

Two days later the telephone rang at Gerald Berners's house and a lady-in-waiting enquired if Cecil would come and photograph the Queen the following afternoon. At first he thought it must be 'a cruel practical joke – as that is the sort of thing Oliver [Messel] might do – but it was not. My pleasure and excitement was overwhelming – a tremendous rush of organization had to start forthwith and I was too highly keyed to enjoy the Indian dancers we went to see'.[83] Cecil could be grateful to Princess Olga for this sitting. She liked her photographs so much that she continued to give them out well into the 1980s. Of the Queen's invitation to Cecil, the Princess recalled: 'we encouraged it'.[84]

Cecil found himself back at the Palace at ten o'clock the next morning to choose the rooms for the photographs and to discuss with Queen Elizabeth which dresses she should wear. He thoroughly enjoyed his tour before he entered the royal presence.

I was full of trepidation to know what would happen when the Queen was ready to see me. I have, by now, such a profound admiration and love for her, that it is inexplicable that before I could have felt it was dreary and dowdy to have the Yorks on the throne.... No one could have done the job as well as she and one knows that there is nothing she could not succeed at if sent out for her country. She might even win Hitler to peace![85]

Cecil had come round to the Queen gradually. Looking at her photo at the time of her wedding, he had thought 'she does look sloppy'.[86] Later in 1923, however, he saw her dancing at the Ritz and noted: 'She really is most delightful with a very fresh complexion and face and charming smile.'[87] Recently Norman Hartnell had begun to design for her, and this, like Cecil's photographs, was an important step in her transformation into a romantic Winterhalter queen. She told Cecil that Hartnell had spotted him in the Palace and had been very intrigued because, 'twinkled the Queen: "I expect he had visions of his lovely dresses appearing again" '.[88]

The Queen was in a pale grey dress with long fur-edged sleeves, which Cecil recognized from photographs of the recent Canadian tour.

> The face looked very dazzling, white and pink and the complexion flawless but as a photographer I was anxious at the lack of definition in it.... She was very smiling and easy. Nevertheless I felt myself standing very stiff and my knees shaking rather. 'It is a great happiness for me, Ma'am.' – 'It is very exciting for me!' ... Her arms and wrists were white and rounded, with diamond bracelets and perfumed with tuberose. She is very short, and her heels are very high. I liked her but feared for the camera results. In the glaring light from the garden windows she looked flat and shadowless but I went away in high spirits and full of expectations for the afternoon.[89]

Cecil then departed to consult Merle Oberon about her costumes: 'It was a question of from the sublime, and having grown accustomed to seeing such lovely things on all the tables and each object of great beauty it was painful to be served some sherry out of a modernistic decanter.'[90]

Cecil has left several accounts of the successes of his afternoon photographing the Queen.* She clearly enjoyed it as much as he did and their enthusiasm infected each other. The sitting, which was meant to last about twenty minutes, continued until well after six o'clock. Cecil ran out of films and someone was sent out to buy more. 'Never have I known such celerity,'[91] said the Queen, who reminded Cecil (and Lady Juliet Duff) of Lady Diana Abdy (wife of Sir Robert, the art connoisseur): 'She has the same subtlety and cultivation, the same twinkle and shrewdness and the same effortless intelligence.'[92] The Queen and Cecil moved from room to room and at length into the garden. Cecil persuaded her to put on eyelid paint,

---

* See particularly *Photobiography*, pp. 131–7, and *The Wandering Years*, pp. 372–7, or *Self Portrait with Friends*, pp. 65–71.

Lady Diana Cooper

Princess Natasha Paley against
the bedsprings

Cecil sketching Mona Harrison Williams

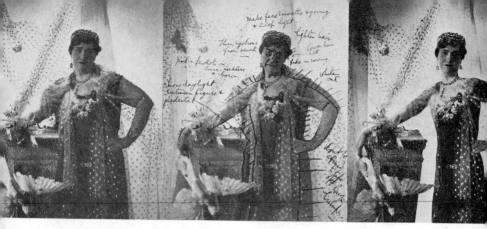

Three stages of retouching

Bébé Bérard

Princess Louise, Duchess of Argyll

Tableau from *My Royal Past*, 1939.
Left to right (standing): Sir Michael Duff, Lady Bridget Parsons, John Sutro,
Sir Osbert Lancaster, Mr and Mrs Barbosa;
(seated): Lady Harris, Lord Berners, Sir Frederick Ashton.

Above left, Wallis Simpson
sketched by Cecil,
November 1936

Above, Cecil photographing
Mrs Simpson, Château de Candé
1937

Princess Paul
of Yugoslavia, 1939

Queen Elizabeth at Buckingham Palace, 1939

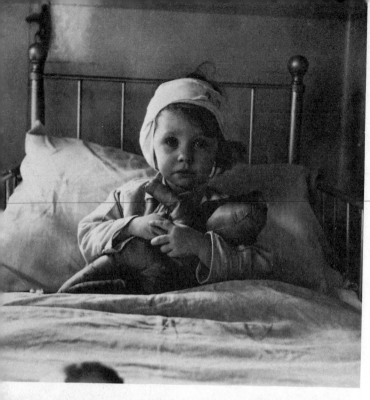

The bombed-
out child,
1940

London bomb
damage,
1940

Patterns of
broken tanks,
1940

Below, Cecil
in improvised
luxury, the
'Ritz', 1942

Lieutenant-General
Adrian Carton de Wiart, vc,
1944

Below, Cecil watching a troop
exercise, Pihu, China, 1944

which delighted him, and he took 'many more lovely pictures that should be very romantic of the fairy Queen in her ponderous palace'.[93] When eventually it was time to leave, Cecil said to the Queen, 'I can't bear to say good-bye.'[94] As a souvenir of his visit he pocketed the Queen's handkerchief, scented with tuberoses and gardenias, which she had tucked behind the cushion of a chair during the photography. This was for Cecil 'a relic of the occasion that will have much more romance and reality than any of the photographs'.*[95] The Queen left for Windsor and Cecil for Ashcombe. He was astonished by how easily the session had been arranged:

> If *Vogue* had tried every means of achieving such a result they would have failed in spite of all their riches and advantage. If I had tried there would have been no response, but suddenly the Queen felt she'd like to have me photograph her and it was all done with such simplicity at only a moment's notice.[96]

This photographic session had important long-term consequences.

Meanwhile Cecil accompanied Francis Rose to Bilignin, Gertrude Stein's house, near Belley, Ain, about six hours by train from Paris. Cecil found himself in a tranquil atmosphere:

> It blows a soft kiss like a breeze to the painter, to the poet and writer. The colours and sounds and smell combine in a unity, simplicity and *recherché* elegance to produce a complete harmony within oneself.[97]

Gertrude told Cecil: 'Your balance is what is important. The balance between fantasy and reality.'[98] She wrote or dispensed wisdom from a rocking-chair, Francis painted, and Alice B. Toklas arranged delicious meals, while Cecil devoted his time to his diary. Quiet days passed with Hitler's threatening presence the only blot, though Gertrude, an eternal optimist, did not believe there would be war. As the news worsened, Cecil became increasingly uneasy. To escape the claustrophobia of the house one evening before dinner, he took a long walk and got hopelessly lost in a maze of apparently identical country lanes. Cecil panicked and knocked on cottage doors:

---

* Cecil kept the handkerchief and it re-emerged in an envelope in one of the Beaton albums at Broadchalke after his death. When Cecil was writing *Photobiography*, he consulted Lord Pembroke as to the advisability of publishing the story. Sidney Pembroke wrote to him on 7 July 1950: 'While dancing with the Queen on Wednesday night I talked about your forthcoming book and related the "hankie incident". She laughed long and loud, and really enjoyed the story and she really has a great "penchant" for you, likes you very much, so seeing that it was going well I said that, funny tho' it was, I had suggested that you leave it out and what did she think? "Well, perhaps you know I think it *had* better be left out, but oh! how delicious and amusing!"' Cecil omitted the story from *Photobiography* (1951) but published it in *The Wandering Years* (1961), p. 377.

The isolated cottagers looked at me with terror and amazement. They were all listening in on their radios, and their President was making a fateful pronouncement. When eventually I was blinded by some car lights and heard Gertrude shouting the nightmare was over. Never have I enjoyed a hot bath and fish more.[99]

While they were out a friend had telephoned to Gertrude to ask if she had heard the latest war news. 'War?' replied Gertrude. 'Who cares about the war? We've lost Cecil Beaton.'[100]

In another version of this story Samuel M. Steward, a young American professor from Chicago, relates that Cecil was completely drunk and eventually found between 'two huge six-feet-four Senegalese soldiers from the caserne' who were walking him home, all drunk and all singing 'L'Alouette'.[101] Cecil did not mention Steward in his diary and Steward himself was to write that Cecil had paid little attention to him. When Steward first related the story in the *Chicago Tribune* of 18 March 1940 he made no reference to Cecil being drunk. If Cecil failed to charm Steward, Alice thought him 'a lovely guest'.[102] Francis Rose looked back on Cecil at this time thus:

He listened and he said his own views; in fact no person could have been more modestly intellectual. With flowers he did wonders, and his manners were so good that even Miss Toklas could not be disappointed. It was, of course, very hard for him to understand serious painting or serious writing, as his observation of everything had up to this period been superficial. The word 'taste' meant to him his craft, as the word 'art' means painting to a painter or music to a musician. At this moment Cecil was making a stupendous effort to explain to himself that there was a difference between Picasso and Rex Whistler. He genuinely preferred Rex, as anything monumental in art is violent and often disturbing, and this upset Cecil....

I loved the barber shop and village sweet shop fantasy of his 1930 taste. It was like a lost pageant or cavalcade of all the toys, toy theatre and mechanical toys, that were no longer to be made after the war had spread plastic glue over all the pretty trivialities of fantasy.[103]

The day after this misadventure he and Francis underwent a disagreeable train journey to Paris *en route* for England. The next day, as Cecil was about to step into his bath, Lord Berners' deaf butler, Nelson, suddenly shouted: 'The war has started.'[104]

On the day before war broke out, Batsford commissioned Cecil's spoof royal memoirs, *My Royal Past*, and this was published in December 1939, the fruition of Cecil's last pre-war effort. Cecil was paid £150. He wrote the

My uncle posing for a statue.

The court portrait painter at work on my aunt.

Two drawings from My Royal Past, *1939*

book as a revenge on the desperate memoirs of 'fatuous, tragic old minor Royalties'.[105] Hailed by the critic Trevor Allen as 'a soufflé of wit and malice',[106] it was a light-hearted endeavour from start to finish. Besides the writing and drawings, a considerable number of photo-montages were put together. Cecil hoped to use the ballet dancer, Frederick Ashton, as 'the Baroness'. Eventually Tony Gandarillas filled this role. Tilly Losch was the beautiful aunt. She had been taken ill at Vaynol in December 1938 and recuperated in Switzerland. Cecil went out to photograph her. He then cut out fashion plates from old editions of *La Mode* and *Figaro*, retouched the photographs to produce minute waists and printed the pictures in reverse. Groups of friends dressed up with relish – Ashton, Bébé Bérard, Lady Bridget Parsons, Francis Rose (with moustache painted out later), David Herbert, Osbert Lancaster, Lady Harris, Lord Berners and others. (Michael Duff and John Sutro can be found in the 1960 edition, of which Marghanita Laski wrote: 'It would be nice to be able to recommend *My Royal Past* for a good, clean laugh. But it isn't quite clean and I didn't laugh'.)[107]

One afternoon a large party of them with laundry baskets full of costumes, uniforms, orders and decorations descended on the studio of Thomas Downey, the Edwardian photographer, in Ebury Street. The old lady in charge had numerous wonderful backdrops and, although at first suspicious, later warmed to the idea so much that she herself agreed to appear as 'My wonderful mother'. The text itself was full of the type of royal joke, so beloved of Michael Duff and David Herbert, in which *double entendres* abound and the royal personage makes much of little. Cecil drew on his own memory, proving that nothing was ever wasted. He had once met Queen Maud of Norway and she had actually said 'we *roared* and we *roared* and we *roared*'.[108] In the early 1920s a dog had been run over and the grotesque Lady Alexander had announced: 'These dogs. They have no idea how quickly one is upon them.'[109] Tchelitchew had spoken of Edith Sitwell being 'in all her states'.[110] The Duke of Windsor had told Cecil of his battle to use his preferred profile on coins.[111] Rex Whistler told him that George VI and Queen Elizabeth waited in the coach at the Palace until the clock struck and thus they departed for the Coronation at the chosen hour.[112] Stephen Tennant had been amused by ladies on a bad sea crossing being 'aided'[113] to their cabins. All these stories and many more found a natural place in the book.

Queen Mary was said to have disliked *My Royal Past*, but Queen Elizabeth, Princess Marina and other 'royals' adored it. One of those particularly impressed was Peter Watson, who wrote:

It is quite one of the best jokes I have ever seen. I really have lots to say about it. First I am agog at your capacity for pains and hard work. To develop a joke into a *chef d'œuvre* of polish and finish is a great feat. The photographs of Tony are really wonderful.

Also I consider the coinciding of publication with the queen's photographs perfect da-da and proof of my old contention, your implacable will to shock. It is in fact a masterstroke even to see the book with its sinister undercurrents of sex, perversions, crass stupidities and general dirt, beaming severely from Maggs Bookshop in Berkeley Square. I admit you are the only person in Europe alive able to put such a thing across and I consider it a remarkable achievement.[114]

Thus ended the seemingly carefree days of social life and crazy enterprises. An era was over for ever and from now on, in common with all Britons, Cecil and his friends had to endure the horrors of war.

Part Five

The War Years 1939–45

19

Winged Squadrons

*And so everything we had dreaded had happened and
it was very undramatic. And nothing had happened yet
that was different and yet life had altered. One had no
appetite for the sort of things that had been fun. They
were now remote. I could not read entertaining short
stories. I could read history. I could not enjoy foregather-
ing and gossiping at Juliet's and the peace of the garden
was something that cut against the grain.*

Cecil's diary, September 1939

The declaration of war effected an immediate change in Cecil's life and to
some extent in his character. He was aware that his previous endeavours
did not particularly fit him for war work. He lacked the skill to drive a lorry
or dress wounds, let alone to fight. At once he renounced his past life. His
diaries were no longer obsessed with personal hopes and wishes, but with
a strongly held patriotic concern for the fate of Britain. His friends were
impatient to be useful. Edith Olivier, previously 'so fantastic and whimsical',[1]
began to organize the neighbourhood, dealing with food control, evacuated
children and Air Raid Precaution units. Sidney Pembroke expressed the
bizarre wish to serve as a private in the Anti-Aircraft Service. Some time
earlier Cecil had considered the possibility that a war might be 'the beginning of a new and less limited life',[2] but David Cecil warned him that many
of his over-enthusiastic friends had enlisted only to find the rigours of camp
life exceedingly unpleasant. Cecil noted that 'it is no use to get into a wrong
job too quickly as it is impossible to extricate oneself'.[3]

Cecil presented himself at County Hall in London, even before Chamberlain's announcement, to ask if they wanted him to drive refugees to Wiltshire. They did not. A few days after war was declared he went to see the
town clerk at Wilton and joined a small assortment of people to man the
telephones in case of air-raid warnings. He succeeded in getting two weekly
shifts of twenty-four hours each. Meanwhile he found creative work futile.
His first session was on the night of 17 September 1939 from 11 p.m. until
8 a.m. Nothing ever happened at these sessions but there was the odd false

alarm. On such occasions nobody knew what to do, but Smith, the Wilton House butler, was the first to act. Once, during an exercise, Cecil accidentally plugged into a genuine station and found himself informing an agonized first-aid officer that two Lewishite bombs had been dropped at the corner of the Shaftesbury–Netherhampton Road and that he must proceed at once to rescue the victims.

Sometimes they had first-aid lessons from a doctor at the Salisbury Infirmary. Overall it was a boring and disappointing job and Cecil dreaded the cold of future months, but he thought his companions, the local farmers, 'showed a much wider sense of understanding of the whole situation than any of the people I have seen since the beginning of the war'.[4]

David Herbert's mother, Lady Pembroke, was also in the station and often Cecil returned with her to Wilton for a good breakfast and a rest. He photographed Edith Olivier in her robes as Mayor of Wilton and also the forty evacuee children who arrived to stay there. Eventually he gave up his ARP work because the petrol rationing made it impracticable.

Cecil's mother spent most of the war at Ashcombe with Aunt Jessie. Francis Rose arrived to stay there too, apparently indefinitely. He disobeyed all the rules by leaving lights on and blinds up. This attracted the attention of the police and terrified Mrs Beaton: finally Cecil had to evict him. Cecil spent weekends at Ashcombe if he could get there, but at other times he took sanctuary at Wilsford with Stephen Tennant or enjoyed lively weekends at Loelia Westminster's Surrey home, Send Grove, where he found Ann O'Neill, and Esmond Rothermere and Ian Fleming (both of whom she later married).

From time to time he came up to London, 'a real town of the dead with rows of empty houses discarded even by the caretakers and their cats'.[5] At night he quite enjoyed finding his way about in pitch darkness. He often saw Peter Watson, now a clerk in a first-aid institution. He thought he had improved enormously as a person. Cecil had shown Peter his first Matisse, but now he was 'the leader in the direction of the arts and I am panting to keep up'.[6] Harold Acton, whom Cecil met with John Sutro at the Café Royal, judged Cecil at this time: 'Under a lackadaisical manner he was a determined dynamo and a stalwart patriot. His seriousness was held in reserve.'[7] When in London Cecil could usually find friends at the Ritz. Later they congregated at the Dorchester, where 'the storm is drowned in wine and music'. Outside Selfridges he caught sight of the Duchess of Windsor seated in a dark car behind a magazine. Cecil terrified her by putting his head through the window and saying 'Wallis'.

In November Cecil went to Buckingham Palace to see the Queen about her photographs. The Duchess of Kent had assured him they were a great success, but he feared that because of the war none would be passed for publication. 'The public is in need of a fillip,' noted Cecil, 'and these pictures would be a sop if they were allowed, but taken in all the full Regalia they are very grand and do not look like wartime pictures as indeed they were not meant to be.'⁸ Cecil found the Queen in her Blue Room in a granite grey dress. She approved all the photographs that were already his favourites, while occasionally pinching a leaf from a sweet geranium and enjoying its scent.

He was allowed a free hand to sell the approved pictures as he wished. A publicity agent, John Myers, a friend of John Sutro, took over the distribution and in due course bulging envelopes were posted world-wide. All the British national papers printed the photographs, the *Daily Sketch* entitling them 'Best Pictures ever taken of Our Queen'.⁹ One appeared on the cover of *The Queen's Book of the Red Cross*, another on the printed Christmas card the King and Queen sent to every serving man in the Armed Forces, and some were published as far afield as the *Leader* in Melbourne and the *Bulawayo Chronicle*. More importantly, *Life* magazine published one. Charles Henri Ford described this as a 'terrific come-back'.¹⁰ Financially the pictures proved 'a boon and a blessing'.¹¹ More were released in March 1940.

The Queen congratulated Cecil on the picture of evacuated children at Wilton (which the *Sketch* had published). She suggested that he get a propaganda job as there was always a new and different angle that could be found for photographing any subject and even war had its pictorial side. In due course Cecil took this advice. First, inspired by a concert that Edith Olivier had arranged, he decided to put on a pantomime for the troops at Wilton, called *Heil Cinderella*. The plan soon escalated and Cecil commented: 'It is like running a war and I cannot think that Hitler feels more unnerved and responsible than I now do.... The Russians bomb Finland and it matters less to us because we have still to find a Dandini.'¹² The pantomime was given in aid of the *Daily Sketch* War Relief Fund to provide cigarettes, games and comforts for the Forces. Cecil put the idea to Lady Pembroke, a committee was formed, and the first night set for New Year's Eve 1939/40.

John Sutro and Cecil wrote the play between them. Then they took the script to Simon Carnes (later Fleet), Juliet Duff's young companion, who was in hospital. He tampered with it, writing down to the men in a patronizing style. Cecil found his changes 'painful' and tried to excise most of his additions. He wrote: 'It hurt me very much to endure these alterations and from the first rehearsal until the last I was anxious to cut a little more of this work which I knew to be of a different calibre.'¹³

For some weeks Cecil lived at Wilton, overseeing the rehearsals and the endless problems of casting. One obstacle was the intense cold, which caused them to drink a great deal. Eleanor Abbey produced enticing costumes, Rex Whistler and James Bailey helped paint the scenery, Lady Margaret Drummond-Hay, having not appeared for days, suddenly materialized to play Prince Charming and disarmed them all with her good health and smiles. Talent emerged in unlikely ways. A shop girl from Salisbury appeared and turned magnificent cartwheels. Their worries over the piano-playing of the local vet's wife were relieved when a Canadian redhead in the chorus turned out to be an ace swing pianist.

The first night was postponed because Cecil lost his voice. Others of the cast then fell ill in twos and threes. However, the show was a wild success:

> It looked lovely. Lady Pembroke made a moving and dignified Queen. Oggie [Lynn] was excellent and so was I. We were thrilled each time to know who was in the house at each performance, what they thought of the show, and the newspaper reports were an unending source of interest. We had rows, bitter murky rows, people would repeat any malice they could, but under cover. On the surface everyone was polite. Unlike real theatricals we had no big flare-ups in public. Simon was too weak as Producer. No one but myself was willing to take the reins and so I came in for a good deal of criticism. David [Herbert] once said after I had been away, 'We all got on so much better without you', and I daresay it was true. The show without me would have been a mess of a much lower quality. It was a quality I was determined to fight for at whatever the cost![14]

Cecil played an ugly sister opposite the squat singer Oggie Lynn, who resented him so much that she once 'threw a temperamental scene in front of the audience'.[15] The company performed at Wilton, then in Salisbury, and later toured the camps on Salisbury Plain from where the Blenheim Bombers set off for Kiel and Kuxhaven. One night at Wilton the lights failed and the orchestra had to fill in for six or seven minutes. Another time a corporal, having scrutinized the chorus line, was heard to whisper, all too audibly: 'That's mine, second from the left.'[16] The audience enjoyed songs such as 'We're going to hang out the washing on the Siegfried Line' and 'Run, Adolph, Run'. Augustus John was at Wilton one night to see Poppet John perform, and wrote: 'You and Oggie were *superb*; you have evidently the true *comédie* spirit and I have never seen Oggie look quite so ravishing. Ugly sister indeed!'[17] Ivan Moffat recalls a backstage flirtation between Cecil and the fiery painter's beautiful daughter.

Another crisis occurred when Lady Pembroke resigned as their president because she was going abroad. David wanted to succeed her, but was not allowed to. Due to such intrigues he and Cecil became somewhat estranged. The show went on tour, first to Brighton, then to Bournemouth. In Brighton, Juliet Duff, now playing the Queen, suddenly fell ill and a Lady Jones (alias the novelist Enid Bagnold, who lived at Rottingdean), stepped into the breach at short notice. Like Cecil, Enid Bagnold was in love with the theatre. 'To find myself on the boards behind footlights was such an ecstasy that I spent all night learning the words of the Prologue,'[18] she

wrote later. Then Juliet Duff got better. 'I could kill her,'[19] declared Enid to
Maurice Baring. He advised her to make a play of it and *Lottie Dundass** was
born, in which the replacement murders the star in order to go on stage
once in her life.

Heil Cinderella then opened at the tiny Fortune Theatre in Covent Garden
after the settlement of a dispute with British Equity, the actors' union, who
opposed its production because there were so many unemployed professional
actors needing work. On the opening night Gerald Berners popped into
Cecil's dressing-room to worry him by saying he had heard there would be
booing from 'left wingers' in the audience. In fact the show went well, the
audience was a chic one, and there were terrific ovations.

> Each night the audience had a Lady Astor, or Kent or Eden. It was all I
> hoped for and the speech I made received a grand ovation and then the
> relief of it all being over and smothering one's face in cold cream and
> saying 'Really do you *really* mean it? Oh, how glad I am.' All the
> dressing-room life I loved.[20]

The show ran for a week in London, the climax of a four-month preoccupation.

As the first long winter of the war drew to an end, Cecil was busy furnishing
his new home, 8 Pelham Place in South Kensington. This late Georgian
building was one of a row of little houses built during the urbanization of
London around 1820, and suitable for modest, middle-class life. Cecil transformed the house into a mixture of home and workshop. He decorated it
boldly, mixing many periods and paintings, placing fine antiques near works
by Picasso, Dali, Bérard and Tchelitchew. In 1940 he bought two Graham
Sutherlands from the Leicester Galleries for £16. Chips Channon, lunching
with him a year later, described Pelham Place as a 'tiny but super-attractive
snuff-box of a house'.[21] It was normally a tranquil street which seemed far
from the turmoil of war. This was to remain his London house for the rest
of his working life.

Cecil began a round of photographing ministers and war leaders. The first
was the Chancellor of the Exchequer, Sir John Simon. Cecil thought him
'pompous and pontifical in the way of a schoolmaster', but 'a good-looking
old trout'.[22] He noted: 'He obviously fancied himself very much indeed and
I was delighted that he had not spotted the prominence I had given his two
bottles of acid drops on the desk!'[23] General Sir Edmund Ironside, Chief of
the Imperial General Staff, inspired immediate confidence, being a rugged
giant of a man with piercing blue eyes and a straightforward honest

---

*Performed at the Vaudeville Theatre, London, July 1943, starring Dame Sybil Thorndike
and Ann Todd. The character of Oscar Garanty bears some resemblance to Cecil, although in
old age Enid Bagnold said it was not based on him.

approach. The General wrote at his desk and smoked a pipe while Cecil photographed him.

> He was filling page after page with rather schoolboyish long hand, writing his daily diary or daily report. I fished around the island of his desk and found many opportunities for a catch, but never did I realize what a big catch there was for by focusing carefully onto the diary I could read, no longer upside-down, in the ground glass of the camera back, every word of his schoolboy's diary.[24]

When Cecil took these photographs to the editor of the *Sunday Chronicle*, J.W. Drawbell, they discovered they could read the General's diary with a magnifying glass. There were lines such as 'Daladier said he would resign if we did not show we were in earnest in our support of Finland'.[25] Drawbell was very excited, but mindful of his *Vogue* drama, Cecil tore the offending piece from the photograph. 'I felt quite cold with anxiety lest any mischief should be made from this situation.'[26] But Cecil got his commission from the *Sunday Chronicle*.

He photographed Sir Kingsley Wood, Secretary of State for Air, 'a bright little wire, like a very intelligent grocer, with sparkling eyes'.[27] Other sitters included Anthony Eden, Ernest Bevin, Lord Halifax and Air Chief Marshal Sir Cyril Newall. Cecil photographed Loelia Westminster and Lady Maud Carnegie cutting out pyjamas, and young debutantes such as Mary Churchill and Judy Montagu playing with evacuated children at Breccles Hall, Norfolk. He sent his work to Sir Kenneth Clark, the Director of the National Gallery, who was currently employed as Controller of Home Publicity at the Ministry of Information, working under Sir John Reith. Clark described his job as 'head of the waste-paper basket department'.[28] Everyone with an ingenious scheme to save the nation came to him with it. On 29 April 1940 he wrote back to Cecil: 'I have talked to Hugh Francis about a chance of your going out as an official photographer, and he seems to think that something can be arranged though it has not been fixed yet.'[29] A permit arrived for Cecil to photograph the Maginot Line, but the authorization came when it was too dangerous, so Cecil missed an interesting chance.

Cecil's secretary Miss Joseph had left to get married and a new secretary arrived in the guise of Maud Nelson. She was Oggie Lynn's girlfriend and had been social secretary to the recently deceased Napier Alington. Maud was unable to type and was often negligent and inefficient. She was possessive of Cecil and profligate with his gin and food; a woman who would display the most jealous and spiteful attributes of the lesbian character, and became a scourge to him. A girl sent to nurse her in old age described her as the most frightening woman she ever met. However, she began well enough. She told Cecil he needed £600 to pay his income tax arrears: 'I have not been in such a state financially since I started my career fifteen years ago.'[30]

Cecil approached C.B. Cochran with a plan to stage a revue with John Sutro, but he received no encouragement, nor did this particular collaboration with John make progress.

Maud Nelson decided that Cecil should accept an offer from Pond's Cream to go to America in May and take some advertising pictures for them for a fee of £2,000. 'I was very loath to go,' wrote Cecil, 'extremely anguished to leave England at such a time and to face an America where there would possibly and probably be, at my appearance, an ignition to the trouble that caused my departure three years ago.'[31] However, this would be his last chance to make some money until the end of the war. As his departure approached, news of German advances became graver. To cover himself, on Diana Cooper's advice, Cecil telephoned Lord Cranborne at Charles Street. The Paymaster General said the news was 'howwid' but that he should undoubtedly 'pwoceed'. On the other hand Condé Nast, Margaret Case and Eleanor Lambert cabled advising him not to come, but the messages did not arrive until Cecil had sailed from Liverpool on the *Samaria* in the company of a lot of 'dark and depressed refugees'.[32]

Cecil spent a month in America, staying with Mona Harrison Williams on 5th Avenue and on Long Island (where he found an uprooted Emerald Cunard). He took on as much work as he could manage without a secretary. He photographed Vanderbilts, Whitneys and Astors for Pond's; he went to plays and saw his friends; and he flew to Boston and later to California.

In Hollywood the placards announced the fall of France. Fred Astaire commented: 'Now I suppose we have no overseas public.'[33] Cecil was reunited with Anita Loos, 'no less young and stringent than she was five years ago',[34] and he flew to Carmel and to San Francisco for the fair. In New York he persuaded Liz Whitney to give him a cheque for an ambulance. He contemplated prolonging his stay to earn money:

> But no, my qualms were over. I felt very definitely that I had been given my chance, that I must not overdo the chances. Each Englishman could say it is more important to make money and give the tax money to England. But no. If many were to do that we should feel the result badly. I was to leave after one month.[35]

Cecil sailed back to England on the *Britannic* in July, another nightmare-ridden trip. 'I find myself returning as if from a health cure, fat-stomached, and nerves fortified from the lapse from possible raids and the horrors a little more distant.'[36]

Back in England Cecil began to photograph extensively for the Ministry of Information, as a result of K. Clark's wish to find an artistic way of recording the effects of war. His commission was unique and he was able to demand special facilities and better fees than most. Hugh Francis, with whom Cecil dealt throughout the war, often found him difficult, but remained aware that the long-term value of his work was likely to be more important than the occasionally less than satisfactory short-term effect. In August, Cecil toured the North Country and found them cheerful in both Newcastle and Jarrow despite the bombing. He was horrified by the deserted streets and the overall damage but was moved by sights such as a headless doll or the scattered remains of a jigsaw puzzle. He visited hospitals and saw a little boy who had lost his foot. He was impressed by the small children sharing the responsibility of behaving well. 'Only those that are unconscious, coming round from an operation by slow degrees, give vent to the stores of unhappiness hidden deep in them,'[37] wrote Cecil.

It was on such a visit that Cecil took his most famous wartime picture. The subject was Eileen Dunne, a girl of three years and nine months, who had been hit by a splinter from a German bomb in a northern village. Cecil photographed her with a bandaged head and a stuffed toy, looking astonished and sad in her iron bed. Hugh Francis was deeply moved by this picture, and so was *Life* magazine, who published it on their front cover of 23 September 1940. It became the poster for the William Allen White Committee in America, and had a profound effect on American public opinion and continues to stir even unsentimental hearts to this day.

This photograph, following his Queen Elizabeth portraits so swiftly, restored Cecil to the favour of *Vogue*. In an interview with Harry Yoxall, the British managing director, in April 1940, he was warned that in these difficult times rates were low. The full-page rate of twelve guineas was raised to fifteen in July and Yoxall believed Cecil could earn £750 a year. In fact he earned more. Condé Nast at first refused to credit his work in America but, when *Life* gave him the front cover, this ban was dropped. A credited fashion photograph appeared in *Vogue* of October that year. A bigger splash was made in March 1941. Margaret Case reported that apart from a small item in *Town and Country* and one or two anonymous Jewish notes, Cecil's reinstatement was marked only by admiration for his work. Soon he was demanding an automatic focus enlarger at the *Vogue* studio, which his old foe Dr Agha promptly vetoed.

Cecil also worked on four films during these early years of war. The first was H.G. Wells's *Kipps* for Carol Reed, whom he liked 'more than anyone I've met through films'.[38] Cecil thought they had made his costumes 'dreams of a bygone era',[39] and the fashion editress of *Vogue* went into 'ecstasies'[40] over them, as well she might since they were recognizable precursors of his later work in *Gigi* and *My Fair Lady*. High praise came from Lesley Blanch, then writing for *Vogue* before becoming the distinguished author of books such as *The Wilder Shores of Love*:

This is Cecil Beaton's first film, and with it he has established himself in yet another new métier. Painter, caricaturist, journalist, satirist, photographer and designer: a dazzling list of talents, which, allied to elegance – *goût*, in the strictest Parisian sense – plus wit, a wide culture, enormous business acumen and the energy of a highly charged dynamo, combine to make him an outstanding figure. I once described him as a coloratura photographer: but as I get to know him better, I find this does not do justice to his expanding, deepening talents. He is no fire-work effulgence, but a brilliance at once mercurial and stable. His work on 'Kipps' has been a *tour de force*.[41]

The eponymous star of *Kipps*, Michael Redgrave, loved the film still Cecil took of him: 'Although it might be said to be deceptive, for in it I look about sixteen, it has – more than any other "still" – the spirit which I hoped I had as Kipps.'[42]

Viscount Castlerosse, Doris's ex-husband, had a small scene in *Kipps* as an irascible fat man in a bath chair at Brighton. He became a close friend of Carol Reed. Lunching with him one day at Claridge's he spilled some port. This put him in mind of Pitt the Younger and he regaled Reed with stories of his life. From this grew the film *The Young Mr Pitt*, for which he contributed dramatic narrative and dialogue. The theme was patriotic, its oft-repeated message: 'In peacetime everything is possible.'[43] Cecil designed the dresses and décor, which starred Robert Donat as Pitt, John Mills as Wilberforce, Phyllis Calvert as Eleanor Eden and Robert Morley as the appropriately corpulent Charles James Fox.

Cecil then worked on Shaw's *Major Barbara* at Denham for Gabriel Pascal, a film on which money was squandered recklessly. It starred Wendy Hiller, Deborah Kerr and Rex Harrison. One of Penelope Dudley Ward's dresses cost £250, and the final clothes bore little resemblance to Cecil's original designs. Filming was often interrupted by the alarm warning of enemy aircraft, at which point actors and technicians hid under the concrete stage until the 'all clear'.

In April 1941 Cecil designed fourteen dresses for Sally Gray in Brian Desmond Hurst's film, *Dangerous Moonlight*. As the film progressed her costumes changed fabrics from crêpe de chine to velvet and went through all the colours of the spectrum. Cecil also designed for George Black's revue, *Black Vanities*, starring Frances Day, and Flanagan and Allen at the Victoria Palace. He created a vision of a 1912 Bank Holiday in Brighton. *Time and Tide* thought Cecil's dresses 'appalling' though 'not exaggerated'.[44] Cecil only saw his dresses on the first night. 'The things people do in one's absence,' he noted. 'I was blinded with fury to see that Frances Day had ripped to bits one of my costumes and put it together the way she thought better.'[45] When Cecil remonstrated with her, the actress explained that she had to put a crinoline under the skirt because until then the skirt had a habit of clinging to the band instruments in the orchestra or suddenly tripping her up and might land her 'on the lap of some fat gentleman in the front row'.[46]

In September 1940 Cecil went to Downing Street to photograph Mrs Churchill with her hair 'set like Pallas Athene'.[47] He greatly enjoyed hearing her version of the war news and seeing how a Prime Minister lived at a time of national strife. When he had to deliver the prints, he went to get them from *Vogue* but found the district evacuated because of a timebomb. He was telephoning in desperation when the bomb went off, the explosion knocking the telephone out of his hand. Then he spotted the messenger boy sauntering along with his photographs, and was able to keep his appointment. Buckingham Palace was bombed and Cecil was quick to record (without any evidence to support his theory):

> It is the genius of the Queen that has caused the Palace to be bombed so that the East Enders should not feel they are alone in their misery. What a *wonderful* person that Queen is, just by being so nice and so good.[48]

Cecil was commissioned by Pamela Churchill, the Prime Minister's daughter-in-law, to photograph her five-week-old baby, young Winston, at the Queen Anne rectory at Hitchin that she was sharing with her sister-in-law Diana Sandys. When the Prime Minister first saw his grandchild, he looked down at him and asked: 'What sort of a world are you being born into?'[49] So much did this infant seem to represent the hopes of the future that Cecil's pictures received enormous publicity and again appeared on the front cover of *Life* (27 January 1941).

He was nervous the night before he went to Downing Street to photograph the Prime Minister, but knew he must do all in his power to 'wear down his grim façade'.[50] It was 10 November 1940. Cecil went straight into Churchill's presence:

> At the centre of an immensely long table sat the Prime Minister, immaculately distinguishedly porcine, with pink bladder wax complexion and a vast cigar freshly affixed in his chin. Fat, white tapering hands deftly turning through the papers in a vast red leather box at his side.[51]

The Prime Minister was angered by Cecil's interruption, but the atmosphere was momentarily lightened when Cecil presented him with the first photographs of his grandson. Time was against Cecil and the elaborate preparations he made proved in vain. Churchill was to be photographed at his table but he objected in barks and growls to Cecil's first candid camera attempt. When he was ready, he stared into the camera 'like some sort of an animal gazing from across the back of its sty'.[52] Later his mood became benign and he walked happily up and down the corridor for some more snaps before going to his Cabinet meeting. He invited Cecil to come again.

The press was clamouring for the pictures but they had to be passed by the Prime Minister. Cecil went to Downing Street to see Mrs Churchill and found himself in trouble. She had wanted all the papers to publish Cecil's photographs of her. *Vogue* had the first bite, and Kenneth Clark thought *Picture Post* might like some, but Clark was idle and after several weeks the pictures were still lying on his desk. A row ensued and the pictures were eventually sent off with the stipulation that Cecil be credited. *Picture Post* later interviewed Mrs Churchill, but at the last minute refused to submit the article for approval or to credit Cecil.

'The Lady of No. 10' appeared in *Picture Post* on 23 November and, though Mrs Churchill did not at first see it, her friends, as always happens in such circumstances, stirred up trouble. Lady Reading said to her: 'You should be protected against such things. The reproduction of the left eye in one photograph is so black and bad you look like a hard-bitten virago who takes drugs.'[53] When Mrs Churchill finally saw the article she particularly objected to the implication that her marriage had been arranged by Lady Randolph Churchill. Never an easy person, Mrs Churchill first attacked Cecil. 'You must have had it kept from me,'[54] she accused. Later the situation deteriorated and Mrs Churchill ordered that all the photographs of her currently circulating among the editors' offices be withdrawn at once:

> She was working herself into an even greater state of nervous hysteria. Her face flushed, her eyes poured with tears. 'Really it's too damnable. It isn't as if my life has been too easy. It hasn't but when I married Winston he loved me,' she blubbed and I held her hand and comforted, 'But he *still* does. We all know that!' She let herself go and for me it is so awful a sight to see someone weeping that I kissed her on the forehead and held tight her hand. But instead of 'coming round' she wept more uncontrollably and confided, 'I don't know why it is, but I suppose my friends are not exactly jealous but they think that other people could do the job better and that I shouldn't have been married to Winston. After all he is one of the most important people in the world. In fact he and Hitler and President Roosevelt are the most important people in the world today.' This was embarrassing for me, but it was no use to argue or split hairs, but now I felt the moment had come for her to behave with more dignity. She was abandoning herself to a complete stranger. It was really rather reprehensible.[55]

Fortunately Mrs Churchill recovered her composure, liked the pictures of Little Winston and also of her husband. 'Yes these should be *published* and published far and wide but that was different! He was the P.M. (She was only his wife.)'[56] Exhausted by his ordeal, Cecil went to a flower shop and sent Mrs Churchill an enormous bouquet of red and white roses, violets, yellow orchids and dove carnations. He received an affectionate telegram in reply and his pictures of the Prime Minister were extensively published just before Christmas. Randolph Churchill wanted Cecil to photograph Little Winston's christening but his mother refused to have photographers.

As the first anniversary of war came round, Cecil noted: 'I hope I may continue to build up something interesting as thus far in this war I have found it possible only to find and make my own war job.'[57] Left to his own initiative he explored London, photographing bomb damage. On 30 August 1940 he visited St Giles's Church and looked at the sun pouring in through the broken stained-glass:

I climbed ladders and was sorry that I had not arrived earlier on the scene to take Milton lying among the sandbags, but he was again erect in a temporary position by the beautiful iron railings. I looked at the freaks of awkward damage, memorial plaques of carved stone blown across the entire width of the church to lie unharmed, the whole frontage of the deserted business premises opposite wrecked, and yet the lamppost stands erect with no pane broken.[58]

Often London's streets were deserted by day, while at night Cecil could not help enjoying the sky:

The heavens sparkling with more stars than ever were patterned with nearly half a hundred search lights. Occasionally coloured flares were dropped but these seemed to die after a short descent. The bee hum of German planes filled the air, the road, the house, the bedroom. Most Londoners were feeling very tired next day.[59]

His own house, 8 Pelham Place, was almost bombed one day. He and John Sutro saw blue smoke curling from the garden, soon followed by magnesium flashes. Three nearby houses were directly hit. In the panic outside some courageous old ladies advanced towards the flaring bombs, known as 'sandwich breadloaves'. Cecil observed: 'It looked like a strange domesticated ballet as these women hurried into the road and heaved up and down at their pumps.'[60]

On his peregrinations through the city Cecil congratulated himself on his idea of photographing the wax head of a woman amongst some rubble. 'To a certain limited public of women who have their hair dyed and waved it would bring the horrors of war very much home.'[61] Unfortunately this caught the attention of an officious passer-by, who demanded to see his papers. He was escorted to the police station before the matter was cleared up. Such incidents often interrupted his work, because the nerves of Londoners were fraught as a result of stress. When he was photographing some more damage, a woman in hat and pearls berated him and gave his companion, Bridget Paget, a hard slap on the back. Cecil explained his plight to Enid Bagnold:

> It is an exciting job I have, prowling around, but dangerous in that the crowd do not believe in any papers and always believe I am a fifth columnist and bosom friend of Unity Mitford.[62]

Presently he collaborated on *History Under Fire* with a new friend, James Pope-Hennessy. During the uneasy months that preceded the war, Pope-Hennessy had wandered round London's landmarks with his teenage friend, Clarissa Churchill, wishing to see, perhaps for the last time, his favourite places. This resulted in *London Fabric* (published by Batsford in 1939), which won him the Hawthornden Prize in 1940. Now he returned to these haunts and others to record the losses with as little bitterness as possible. Cecil liked him at once:

> One of his nicest attitudes is his capacity for happiness. He is really contented. In short I find a new friend, for he likes me as much if not more than I like him. We respect and admire each other and he is what I look for and need. He is an ideal companion. We are so much like one another that no explanations are necessary and complications are not likely to arise because we are honest with one another.[63]

Kenneth Clark approved of this project and Harold Nicolson managed to obtain for Pope-Hennessy two months' leave from the Army. Pope-Hennessy's aim was 'to show the Americans that while certain things are frankly gone for ever, London on the whole is not so badly destroyed'.[64] He warned that their enthusiasm must not get the better of them: 'I can see us getting into the most dangerous mentality about it, can you: irritation that some church or other hasn't been reduced to Piranesi rubble for our purposes?'[65] Pope-Hennessy was surprised how widely known Cecil was: 'all the bungalows and villas everywhere in England know of him', he wrote to Clarissa Churchill. 'Is that fame?'[66] *History Under Fire*, which concluded that from the historical angle the *Blitzkrieg* had failed, was generally well received when it was published by Batsford in July. John Piper, an earlier critic of Cecil's, wrote in the *Spectator*:

> Mr Cecil Beaton is an old hand. The war, he decides, has played enough tricks without the artist and photographer adding to them, and he has taken some excellent, straight photographs of buildings and parts of buildings, selecting carefully, rearranging subjects laudably to make them tell better, interspersing engravings of churches in their early nineteenth-century glory to demonstrate something of what we have really lost.[67]

Through Pope-Hennessy, Cecil made friends with Clarissa Churchill, the

Prime Minister's niece. 'She is quite outstandingly worth noticing and one of the human beings I like and know best in the world,' recommended James Pope-Hennessy. 'I forget if you read *London Fabric*, but it is mostly about her, and dedicated to her and so on.'[68]

Clarissa is also the remote fair-haired heroine of Lord Berners' book *Far from the Madding War*. An intelligent girl, she was to become one of Cecil's most important friends. He came to rely on her advice on intimate matters and their destinies were closely linked. In the late summer of 1941 Cecil invited her to Ashcombe: 'you must see the house as it is so beautifully situated and at the moment – in this Indian summer weather – it is at its most romantic. One breathes in Cardinal butterflies with every intake – and the gardener has managed to produce more flowers than even I could possibly pick!' He continued:

> Your letter amused me so much. It had such an impact behind it – a good clean shot that got a bullseye. You have such a strength for a young person and you do make me feel that I've been caught bending, while the younger generation have not only knocked on the door but taken up residence. As you seem not to resent my presence I am thoroughly delighted and I trust a good time may be had by all together.[69]

Cecil undertook a number of tours outside London for the Ministry of Information. He was surprised to find himself a photographer again but thought this better than 'doing some minion soldier or guard's job which I would hate and alas do so incompetently'.[70] At the same time, the war gave a new fillip to his work. As he told the columnist Peter Stewart: 'I was sick to death of posing people round apple blossom.'[71] Indeed when Cecil tried to take that kind of portrait now, Dr Agha of *Vogue* was quick to complain that with the retouching they compared badly to his 'marvellous war pictures'.[72] Cecil visited 2,000 Wrens at Portsmouth and found them living like sailors, yet eager to be photographed: 'Fat and old, young and thin, they all thought it very amusing and a great excitement and prayed that it would be in the *Tatler*.'[73] He in turn was excited to photograph the Commander-in-Chief, Admiral Sir William James, 'as the Admiral, now over sixty with red face and white flowing hair was and still is the original Bubbles'.[74] In his spare time he went over to Bath to photograph the artist Walter Sickert in the twilight of his days, and in the New Year of 1941 he added Lady Halifax, King Zog of Albania and a uniformed Edwina Mountbatten to the Ministry of Information's files.

Cecil's most important exercise in 1941 was his work with the RAF. In the New Year he set off to Wales with Derek Adkins, of the Directorate of Public

Relations of the RAF, to tour Welsh air stations: 'He was much nicer than I had hoped for and we got along well,'[75] wrote Cecil. This was the first of a nationwide series of visits to RAF stations, which resulted in a variety of articles, a great number of photographs and two books, *Air of Glory* (named after the poem by Vaughan), a scrapbook of wartime photographs published by HMSO in 1941, and *Winged Squadrons* (published by Hutchinson in 1942). Cecil became fascinated by the heroic struggles in the air: 'Never before have battles been fought six miles above the surface of the earth at a speed of over three hundred miles an hour,'[76] he wrote. He inspected the recruitment and training of the young airmen, chronicled the way they lived, and aspects of fitness and health and team spirit. He turned his attention to fighter pilots, the work of Coastal Command and the Fleet Air Arm. He wrote of the typical day of a bomber pilot under the fictional name of Robert Tring.

Cecil found his meetings with the RAF a considerable strain. It was exhausting to meet so many new people one after the other. He found their names and ranks hard to remember and was forever trying to conceal his 'abysmal ignorance' and shyness. He was surprised and impressed by the way the RAF adored their work, how the men even made model aircraft in their spare time and pored over aeronautical magazines. What he wrote about the RAF was well received.

He was struck by the heroism he witnessed and the RAF tradition that if a pilot failed to return to the station, his name was seldom mentioned though his mates looked depressed for a while. 'It is a terrible slaughter that is going on and makes me so very keyed up to think that these people have so little of life left.'[77] At the Air Ministry he kicked up a fuss that the development of his films (at a secret country place) took so long. A group captain had written to say that most of the crews he had photographed were now missing and the pictures would be of value to the next of kin. Cecil worked in a continual rush, which killed any enjoyment he might take in his work, as he complained to Francis Rose: 'I am really very overworked and got rather ticked off last week for undertaking too much and being behind with my work. I've done such a lot of photography that it isn't really funny any more. It's just like being a press photographer.'[78]

Cecil had the ability to record what he saw with sensitivity. Edna Woolman Chase, at *Vogue*, receiving his first account, wrote: 'It is told so simply and so touchingly.'[79] In his book *Winged Squadrons* (which he submitted to the censor at the end of 1941), Cecil turned an eye normally trained for details of theatre and ballet to the work of the gallant airmen. He paid particular attention to the human emotions behind the endeavours and he examined the claustrophobia everyone was feeling. In his photographs he created interesting compositions from the tools of war. He speculated as to how the survivors would cope with life after the war. 'Night after night', he wrote, 'these young fellows, kids many of them, are sent out to pay the price of the follies of old incompetent politicians. They go gladly, but one wonders if the lesson has been learnt, or whether in another twenty years the youth of the next generation must again make these sacrifices.'[80]

When *Winged Squadrons** was published in the summer of 1942 it received universally laudatory reviews. Raymond Mortimer wrote of Cecil's penetrating and informative impressions:

> They have left me with the conviction that if he had been fifteen years younger he would have made an excellent pilot, for his character has enabled him to obtain a great degree of fellow feeling with the men he describes. Consequently his book strikes me as much the best of its sort that has yet appeared.[81]

Cecil went on tank duty on Salisbury Plain and found his ride 'one of the most unpleasant and painful experiences for I had not developed a tank technique with the result that I was most rudely knocked and bruised, my camera hitting me in the jaw one second, an awful twang on the elbow the next'.[82] He spent a short time with the Navy at Harwich. Captain Caspar John, Augustus John's son (later Admiral of the Fleet), thought Cecil should go to sea for a week but there was not time as Cecil Day-Lewis, then also at the Ministry of Information, needed his work too urgently.

The Duchess of Gloucester was photographed inspecting WAAF headquarters and Cecil thought 'she does her stint beautifully – unlike alas the Duke of Kent whom I had to see that night at Feldwell'. Cecil felt that the Duke was bored by his work and did not pay enough attention to the 200 men who were about to set off in great danger, but was more interested in arranging for Cecil to come to Coppins to take family groups.

In July 1941 Batsford published *Time Exposure*, the result of Cecil's collaboration with Peter Quennell. Years later Quennell recorded his opinon of Cecil at this time:

> I became aware that he was a remarkably hard-working man; a dedicated professional, sharply attentive to the smallest details of every image his camera produced. He thought little, I discovered, of leaving his bed between 5 and 6 a.m. rather than leave a piece of work unfinished, and refused to take advantage either of his well-established reputation or of his natural facility.[83]

Time Exposure (Cecil's title) included a selection of Cecil's pre-war work, reflecting a world of which Quennell wrote: 'All we can be sure of for the moment is that it has been lost for good.'[84] The book received much more critical attention than *History Under Fire*. It was the first occasion on which

---

*Photographs of the WAAF by Cecil appeared in *Wings on Her Shoulders* by Katharine Bentley Beauman, also published by Hutchinson.

distinguished critics and friends examined nearly twenty years of Cecil's work. V.S. Pritchett wrote:

Garish in the 20s, bizarre in their varieties of escapism in the early 30s, dramatically incongruous in the years just preceding the war, Mr Beaton's photographs have the truthfulness of the absurd, the underlying grimness of the artificial and highly selective.[85]

Osbert Lancaster described Cecil in the *Spectator* as 'an elusive figure about whom too little is known but who occupied in relation to his age much the same position as the Comte d'Orsay in the preceding century'.[86] In Cyril Connolly's newly launched *Horizon*, Stephen Tennant described the final impression of the book as one of 'charming evanescent gaiety'.[87] Later he wrote: 'Mr Beaton is always explicit, there is no mystery in his art.... In Cecil Beaton's art it is always the birthday morning – the eve of the Ball, the rise of the curtain.'[88] Meanwhile Eddie Sackville-West, best known as a music critic, opined in the *New Statesman*: 'I like Mr Beaton less when he is attempting to compose a still life than when his painter's eye has snatched a piece of pure lyrical beauty from some fleeting gesture or attitude, some forgotten corner, some odd figure passing across the lens between London and Timbuctoo.'[89]

The publication also proved the ideal opportunity for old scores to be settled in a fit of midsummer madness. Osbert Sitwell wrote a seven-page letter from Renishaw, which he began by rebuking Cecil for changing the names in his preface in 1929, and for referring to his father by the family nickname 'Ginger' in his *Scrapbook* in 1935. He complained that in *Time Exposure* Siegfried Sassoon and Anita Loos should not have been published on the same page, and that the publication of photographs of the Sitwells in this book was malicious: 'Nor do I think that either Edith or myself is to blame for the world war, the bombed babies and the maimed men and women: which deduction is to be presumed from the book',[90] he said, revealing a certain paranoia. Osbert Sitwell asked Cecil to write to the *New Statesman*, whose review by Sackville-West ('Lady Clark's ex-chauffeur')[91] had also infuriated him. Cecil replied defensively at equal length, refusing to do so:

It is really a little far-fetched to consider that I have been unkind in placing Siegfried Sassoon (God bless him!) next to Anita Loos. They are both friends of mine, and I admire them equally in their different ways. Permission, where necessary, has been given at some time or other for the publication of all the photographs that are in the book. As the photographs of you all – particularly those of Edith – are ones that I am especially pleased with, I could not imagine that there would be any feeling about their being reproduced again after this lapse of time.

perhaps I have also done wrong in allowing the picture of Edith in bed to be circulated throughout America in a collection of the best photographs since photography began? If I have, I am again sorry.[92]

To this Osbert Sitwell replied:

If you had sent a letter to the *New Statesman*, you would at any rate, even if it had not been published, have made a gesture – As it is, I have only asked you to do one thing, and you have not done it.[93]

Cecil then wrote to Siegfried Sassoon, who replied: 'I hasten to reassure you that your anxiety is needless! ... Osbert's fuss is nonsense.'[94] Nevertheless Osbert and Cecil remained at daggers drawn until 1947.

The last word came inevitably, and very enjoyably, from Gerald Berners at Faringdon, who clearly relished the row:

My attention has been drawn to a photograph of myself appearing in your recently published 'Time Exposure' in which I am represented standing *half in* and *half out* of a door way.

This would seem to imply that my position in the world of Art is not fully assured and that I am merely poised on the threshold of the Hall of Fame.

I have no doubt that the publication of this malicious photograph will do incalculable harm to my reputation as a composer, an author and a painter. It may even prejudice my social standing....

P.S. To say nothing of you having placed dear Anita's picture on the same page as that *dreadful* Siegfried Sassoon – and why include the Sitwells?[95]

In August 1941 Cecil lunched at Windsor with Lily Elsie, his childhood heroine. Seeing his photographs Miss Elsie stipulated: 'perhaps you could just slice off a bit of hip on the one standing by the wall as I look enormous'.[96] 'Dear Lily Elsie,' wrote Cecil. 'Her memory will always have a fragrance that no one else ever possessed for Cecil Beaton.'[97] At other times he enjoyed staying with the Duff Coopers on their farm at Bognor. 'What a lovely world you create,' he wrote to Lady Diana, 'and even in wartime you are not baffled.'[98] He also strengthened his ties with Enid Bagnold at Rottingdean, noting that, with her new cow, Enid was 'very down to earth, earthy, with a healthy appetite for the essentials of life which came out in her conversation by incessant allusions to frogspawn, the mating of horses and the pregnancy of women'.[99] They discussed plays together.

Cecil used to read his first attempt at a play to the Australian actress, Coral Browne, then starring in *The Man who came to Dinner* at the Savoy Theatre.

Cecil went to photograph her in 1941 and they began an affair which lasted until he went to Cairo in March 1942.

Coral Browne had been living with another man for several years when she met Cecil so their meetings had to be clandestine. Sometimes they went dancing but normally they met in the afternoons. Cecil found some costumes that belonged to Doris Langley-Moore and photographed Coral Browne wearing them. She recalled:

> I have been in love with three men in my life, two I married* and the third was Cecil. He was a great enthusiast, tremendously interested in everything he did. We were very compatible and I was tremendously happy. He was a very passionate, very ardent man and quite unlike the way people normally think of him. I used to listen to the play he'd written about the Viceroy of India. It was amateur time when it came to play-writing but we had the same interests at heart.[100]

The romance was frustrated by Cecil's possessive and vicious secretary, Maud Nelson, who conspired to split them up. When Cecil went away to the war, Coral Browne terminated the affair.

In September the Beaton family lost Cecil's cousin Frank to the holocaust of war. Aunt Lilias wrote to Cecil's mother:

> Frank was killed in Syria by the treacherous French, a low-flying plane machine-gunned him while he was picking up the wounded in his Red Cross Ambulance. They are I think much worse than the Germans.[101]

In October Cecil suggested to Brendan Bracken at the Ministry of Information that he might assist in instructing at a proposed new photographic school but nothing came of this. In November he visited Scotland for ten days to combine visiting several aerodromes near Edinburgh with a job for *Vogue*. When he left he was 'heartily sick' of himself and his surroundings. His visit was made enjoyable by the presence of Audrey Stanley (the divorced Lady Stanley of Alderley). The highlights of his trip were seeing Vivien Leigh in *The Doctor's Dilemma* and one night talking to her at his hotel until 3 a.m., and photographing the waxen death mask of Mary, Queen of Scots, at Holyroodhouse.

At the end of 1941 America declared war on Japan and Cecil got wry pleasure from Edna Woolman Chase's card: 'Well we're in for it now. Have just had our first alert. God help us all!'[102]

The New Year of 1942 began with a short break from work. Cecil celebrated his thirty-eighth birthday rather gloomily: 'another nail in my

---

* She married, in 1950, Philip Westrope Pearman, who died in 1964. In 1974, she married the art historian and film actor, Vincent Price.

coffin'.[103] He began to wonder about the past and the future at what was actually the exact half-way point of his life:

> Had it been a good past for preparing for older age? Doubt it? Long to write for stage, perhaps without any talent for it. Have cold feet. Thought about Daddy. How little I had to talk to him about, yet how like in so many recurring ways. Find myself behaving like him. Polite interest shown when obviously bored, childish whimsical look when walking alone, or in the dark. Wondered a lot about my childhood picking daisies. The theatre at Cambridge, Tris Bennett. Wished Peter had rung but not disappointed he didn't. He never even thanked me for Christmas books. Likes treating me badly. Let him. It doesn't smart any more.[104]

In the freezing January of 1942 Cecil's activities included taking Margot Asquith out to dinner and photographing Robert Morley at Twyford. Staying with John Sutro at Denham he spent an evening with Noël Coward, then working on his film, *In Which We Serve*. Cecil had always been jealous of Noël, a state which could not cease at will. Nevertheless as Sutro's cocktails mellowed the two men, Cecil felt that at last they were friends and wondered if Noël had decided that in the difficult years ahead they should stick together. Noël told Cecil he liked *My Royal Past* and he also declared: 'You've done a great job that has got you great respect in the RAF. It just shows how utterly wrong I've been, what a mistake I made. You've been yourself always and how right you've been.'[105]

Randolph Churchill had suggested that Cecil be sent to photograph in Cairo, an idea that thrilled Cecil with the chance to escape from London and achieve something positive. His recent article on the ATS inspired confidence with the Ministry of Information and his prospects looked good. While an enormous collection of his old photographs were pulped for the war effort, Cecil waited on tenterhooks:

> No news yet of remaining here or being sent out to the East. I long to go. It would be stimulating and useful and would give me an incentive that I feel lacking at the moment.[106]

20

Near East

*I had certain qualms about what the next four months
would bring.*

Near East, 1943

The Ministry of Information loaned Cecil to the Air Ministry primarily to
photograph the work of the RAF, and anything that might be of interest for
record or propaganda. His brief was to be as accurate as possible. He left
Euston on 21 March 1942 at twenty-four hours' notice and on the boat for
West Africa he found 300 flashbulbs and films representing 10,000 poten-
tial exposures. He sailed on a former luxury pleasure cruiser converted into
a warship. On board he spent his time drawing or observing the life around
him. One night the commander woke him by flashing a torch in his face
and suggesting he might like to see the bridge. The life of the crew, 'almost
animal-like in its simplicity and cleanliness',[1] he found absorbing and on
Saturday evenings he joined in hearty naval toasts: 'To our wives and
sweethearts ... and may they never meet.'[2] Cecil found the airmen on board
very friendly as long as he joined a group of them. To single one out was
never a success.

Wintry conditions subsided and tropical kit became the order of the day.
In due course they docked at Freetown in the Bay of Sierra Leone where
the blackness of the natives contrasted with the whiteness of the uniforms,
the birds and the hospital ship. The Ministry of Information wanted Cecil to
produce some photographs of the West Coast of Africa but, although he was
armed with the right papers, an official forbade him to pass because he had
a camera.

The pilots, civilians and Cecil all expected to fly down to Freetown. Instead
they were transferred to the ship *Altmark II*. Pessimism set in as its old crew
jeered, 'Oh! boy – I am sorry for you – hope you like cockroaches.'[3] Conditions on board were repellent. The lavatories stank, the water-taps only
worked for an hour a day, the heat was stifling and the food inedible. The
negro stewards were so overworked that they sweated 'large blobs into the
soup',[4] the bar was crowded and the glasses were washed by a dip into a

'small bucket of gruel-like water'.⁵ Cecil found his snoring or groaning cabin-mates too awful to share with, so slept as best he could in a wooden chair on the upper deck.

Eventually, before they sailed, there came a sudden reprieve. Cecil and others were whisked away in an RAF launch. They could not believe their luck. 'The hot beer at Airways House, prior to bed, was nectar,'⁶ wrote Cecil. At dawn they flew along the coast, refuelling at a new aerodrome in the middle of the jungle. Their trip of over a thousand miles led them from jungle to wasteland and in due course to Kano, reputedly Africa's oldest walled city. They crossed the Nile and landed at Wadi Seidl. Cecil's group escaped briefly to Khartoum and enjoyed the luxury of lemon and lime on the terrace of the Grand Hotel. They ran into Gaston Palewski* and the interior decorator Felix Harbord. Cecil had the chance to observe local life: 'women of high quality of incompetence and low standard of looks' performing to a khaki audience of 'masculinity oozing at every pore with sweat and desire for those unappetizing, yet available, pieces of Balkan femininity'. Cecil was grateful not to be one of those bewitched, sex-starved majors who 'tried to kiss the outstretched, veined hands and doubtless entertained hopes of further intimacies'.⁷

Finally, gratefully, Cecil reached Cairo. He presented himself at the office of Walter Monckton, the Acting Minister of State in the Middle East and Head of Propaganda and Information Services, who was away, so he was briefed by the chain-smoking Mr Tweedy, who told him to emphasize 'might' at all times. Cecil was then sent to Charles Bray, a cricket correspondent in civilian life, now a wing-commander at RAF Public Relations HQ. He mapped out an itinerary and issued Cecil with a RAF uniform with the badge 'Official Photographer' on the shoulder. Cecil spent a week in Cairo, during which he photographed Air Chief Marshal Sir Arthur Tedder, the AOC-in-C, Middle East and Prince Mohamed Ali, the bearded heir presumptive to King Farouk, who wore sponge-bag trousers and, on his finger, a vast emerald.

Cecil travelled to the Canal Zone, his first visit into the field. He was put in the charge of Group-Captain John Elton, who had trained with Reggie at Upavon in the 1920s. One evening they dined at Suez, but otherwise Cecil was happy to wander around the station on his own. He took a lot of photographs and saw where loaded 'medium' bombers were kept. The architect Frank Scarlett, then serving as squadron leader in a RAF photographic reconnaissance unit, also met Cecil at this time. He recalled: 'Before he came out, there were lots of jokes about having to keep backs to the wall, but Cecil Beaton got on very well with the toughs and they were very much impressed with him.'[8]

Cecil was delighted that Wing-Commander Bray had arranged for his old travelling companion Derek Adkins to be his conducting officer in the desert. 'I am most thrilled to be here,' Cecil wrote to Derek from Shepheard's Hotel, 'but find it awfully difficult to "get cracking" – the atmosphere and climate seem to conspire against any effort and achievement. Maybe I'll settle down or be got down soon!'[9] Just before setting off for the desert, he noted in his diary: 'Have somehow most unfairly switched all my responsibilities onto Derek and start off without much enthusiasm for he has it all.'[10] In Alexandria Cecil visited the fleet and went on board a cruiser. Field Marshal Smuts, the South African Prime Minister, arrived on the flagship of Rear-Admiral Sir Philip Vian, lately returned from Malta. 'As we sailed past, Smuts in topee and waving a baton was haranguing the ship's company turned out in white uniforms that became translucent in the sunlight. He is a grand old man, always giving more than is expected of him.'[11] In Alexandria he was reunited with Lilia Ralli, who had escaped from Athens to her childhood home after the fall of Greece. Then Cecil entered the desert. As he rattled along in a car piled high with crates of drink and tinned fruit juice, he found his mind 'restless and staccato'. Conversation was disjointed and difficult:

I wondered how on earth warfare could be carried out in this desert. The distances so appalling. The picture of warfare became impossibly confused. No lines could be held. Little pockets of men would become small isolated pinpricks on this vast terrain: We followed along by the sea and in the evening light everything soon became very beautiful, the sea the colour of those Brazilian butterflies' wings. I have never seen the sea so blue before. Then when the pall of light sank behind the horizon we were treated to a show of magic beauty. The sunset was something unimaginable, more transient than a flower, more brilliant than any jewel, more fluid than any architecture, more varied than any landscape was the landscape in the sky, with islands of gold and silver, peninsulas of apricot and rose against a background of many shades of turquoise and azure. The activity of the sky, changing so quickly yet apparently motionless, made the earth look even more barren and forlornly ugly.

So this is the desert, a very different desert from the Sahara, dust desert that I had imagined it to be. . . . I had wondered if it would be possible to find a new slant on the visual aspect of this battlefield but soon realized that at the moments before dark the whole landscape becomes magic and the quality of light unbelievably lovely, turning the sand to powder, the sky to opal and the soldiers' sunburnt skin becomes a living, glowing fire.[12]

Cecil arrived at Bagush and slept in a tent known as 'the Ritz'.

He found the spirit of desert life similar to ship-board camaraderie. The life was primeval and the men were 'sand happy'. The men's possessions were likely to consist of no more than a razor, a sleeping-bag, a roll of lavatory paper and a packet of cigarettes. He was comforted to hear that however bleak the conditions they compared favourably to life in the trenches in 1916.

From his desert travels there emerge some of Cecil's most memorable war photographs. He seldom photographed any action, but he was there to capture the equally important background to war life. He caught the men in lectures and at briefings, ground crews at work and leisure hours in the mess. He witnessed the spadework, the repair work and the endless transport arrangements being made. He was often there as the alert sounded and he made curious and memorable surrealist images of the aftermath of the battle, 'the carcasses of burnt-out airplanes lying in the middle of a vast panorama of burnt-out trucks'.[13] He encountered tremendous problems. Sand crept into his camera obstructing the opening of the shutter or scratching a negative. The sunlight could make a subject merge completely into the background. Daylight in the desert often resulted in men appearing with black faces and only the crowns of heads or tips of noses illuminated. A sandstorm was as bad as a London fog in November. The best time to work was just after dawn or just before sunset.

Cecil travelled in the desert from 27 April until 13 May 1942. He began by feeling that he was not getting a true impression of the desert. He knew that conditions at the front would make the Fleet Air Arm station 'seem like a 1st Class Hotel'.[14] He found the hanging about very tiring. He was chilled by the casual attitude to life and death. The commanding officer said of a pilot who had not returned: 'Well he's either recovered his engine trouble or is in the drink by now.'[15] He worried that many of his impressions were still second-hand from others returning from further afield.

After photographing Scottish soldiers at Mersa Matrueh, Cecil and Derek moved further in. 'I long to see more traffic on the roads, more people, more aeroplanes, more tanks,'[16] wrote Cecil. But all he saw was barren land. Already he found his photographs were 'just repetition'.[17] At Sidi Barrani they visited ruined barracks and an air station with torpedo-carrying Beauforts. Wherever they stayed Derek was always highly efficient and introduced as much comfort into desert life as possible. Sometimes at night Cecil was kept awake by distant gunfire or the flapping of the tent's canvas. They journeyed up the Halfar Pass. Cecil photographed Air Vice-Marshal Sir Arthur Coningham, the Air Officer Commanding, who sat 'like colossus at his desk' and waved his arms 'in broad masculine gestures'. He described the desert to Cecil as 'a tactician's paradise, but the quartermaster's nightmare'.[18] Coningham told Cecil that much of his time was spent preventing the men from becoming apathetic. He also visited Lieutenant-General Neil Ritchie, the GOC Eighth Army (who within three weeks would engage enemy tanks during Rommel's last offensive). Cecil found him 'slightly worried and anxious'.[19]

In Tobruk Cecil had one of his most directly startling experiences. He visited the 62nd General Hospital and was conducted round the ward by the surgeon, a breezy character called Colonel Simpson-Smith. Like a number of people whom Cecil encountered on his trip, the Colonel had heard of him. 'I have never been more grateful to my notoriety or publicity than on this trip when a thousand situations have been saved by my name meaning more than permits and passes and points of view,'[20] wrote Cecil.

The Colonel showed Cecil his burn cases. 'Hullo you old rascal', was his typical greeting for a patient. 'You're getting on fine. We want to have a look at you.'

> The sight revealed really sickened me. Yet I could hardly believe it was human – a couple of eyes blinked out of a terrible growth of vivid blues, greens, purples, blacks and dark greens. On the head a mat of sand coloured hair. The blankets removed, the legs too blistered, coloured rather ghastly and only the stomach remained flesh coloured and since the chest was constricted with burns and paint, the stomach had to blow itself out and in, double time, double measure.
>   'Do you want to take this?'
>   But oh no! This was too much.[21]

The tour continued among cases that looked more like human parrots than airmen. Cecil thought the colonel a kind man, though he had a cold-blooded, dispassionate air. He could not wait to bring Cecil in on an operation. 'My God, you're lucky, Beaton,' he announced. 'This will be a wonderful opportunity for you. You can take your time. It's a complicated operation. May last one and a half hours.'[22] Thus Cecil, who from an early age had delicately chosen a path in life concerned with the contemplation of beauty, now steeled himself to watch the patient's torso being shaved with a Gillette razor ('the worst part'), and then painted orange with iodine. The operation began:

> By degrees one becomes hardened, though I felt a little weak when looking up from my drawing to find the surgeon's gloved hand going down deep in between the coils of entrail through the newly formed cavity.[23]

At the end everyone felt drained of energy.

On a later journey the car broke down and they continued in a khaki lorry. Cecil enjoyed photographing the blimpish Lieutenant-General Willoughby Norrie, who even produced a German prisoner for interrogation in front of them. Cecil called on the Desert Rats and the 5th Royal Tank Regiment. It was a great excitement to lunch with David Stirling's newly formed SAS and the Long Range Desert Group. The dashing Commander took him to see his men:

A more frightening-looking band of chaps it would be hard to imagine. Dustier than you would have thought possible with bloodshot eyes and strange head-dresses or hair standing on end, bearded, they had no connection with this period of history. They were like primeval warriors.[24]

On the flight back a sudden burst of machine-gun fire terrified Cecil: 'So we were caught. Well, that's too bad for Mummie, for the book I would have liked to have done but which would nevertheless just be another book. These are the things that passed through my mind in a flash.'[25] Later the pilot apologized. He was just testing his guns.

From Alexandria Cecil sent a postcard to Juliet Duff:

I feel fifteen years younger than when I left England. Air and life in desert makes everyone healthy and happy (like an advt). I did not want to leave and was particularly contented at Tobruk.[26]

Cecil had missed the German attack by two weeks and regretted that he had not spent more time with the Army. He was not at all pleased with his photographs, 'but much more interested in the prospect of writing about my trip. The writing is to me now of first importance. The photography a means to the writing.'[27]

He spent some days in Alexandria, where Lilia Ralli was recovering from flu. Later, with bright red bows in her hair, she conducted Cecil to the canal banks, the public gardens and the zoo. They lunched at the Union Bar with Derek Adkins, who stayed on when Cecil returned to Cairo by train, feeling queasy with Egyptian stomach. Back at Shepheard's Hotel he spent the evening sorting his large batch of prints.

Cecil now had five weeks in what Eric Hambro called 'The Short Range Shepheard's Group'.[28] Cairo was the height of luxury and hedonism compared with the bleak desert conditions nearby. Egypt had become a refuge for a wide range of characters, 'the final bolt-hole of European refugees', as the novelist Olivia Manning described one aspect of it. Of these characters she wrote:

Existing on credit, or the British Government, they moved in a café society of crowded emptiness, seething with rivalries, petty scandals, squabbles, hurt feelings and exhibitions of self-importance.[29]

On the other hand Mark Chapman-Walker, a major on General Wilson's staff, wrote of the sophistication of some of the city life:

> For instance, polo was played every afternoon at Gezira, and at the Mohamed Ali Club the library and sitting-rooms were exactly like the Carlton Club, and on the roof gardens at night one not only had impeccable food but saw some of the finest jewellery and prettiest women I have ever seen in my life.[30]

Cecil thought Cairo 'a most tatty capital'. Writing to Juliet Duff he said: 'I suppose it has an allure of its own, but it is a pity we have to be here for the war as the climate is not conducive to hard work and long hours.'[31] Nevertheless he began each day by writing notes for an hour. He went to his headquarters promptly at 9. In the afternoon he took the traditional siesta from 3 to 4.30, but at night an open-air cinema under his window kept him awake until after 1 a.m. His work was to sort and caption the desert photographs, and he was assisted in this task by a dreamy, pretty secretary called Pamela Burns, whom young men telephoned continually to ask out. Cecil observed that she 'like many young girls has tremendous sensibilities of sensuous delight: "I *hate* chicken skin. I love smoking a cigarette when I'm wet after bathing." ...'[32] He was sad to hear she had died of a sinus operation in 1944. He also wrote articles and spent some time establishing which Ministry would pay him the subsistence money of £1 a day he had been owed for over a month.

While in Cairo he had an interview with Walter Monckton, who was leaving Egypt 'rather piqued'[33] and disappointed at not being made Minister of State. Cecil very much liked the new Minister, R. G. Casey,* and his wife. With Maie Casey he could talk of modern painting, while he was deeply struck by 'the direct and to the point business-like, energetic'[34] approach of the Minister himself. Dick Casey told Cecil that he must present the typical English soldier as 'a thick strong-set fellow' and not 'a speckled spotty little chap'.[35]

He was entertained by Brigadier John Marriott and his wife Momo (sister of Nin Ryan), who were at the heart of Cairo's social life. He lunched occasionally with Toby Milbanke, formerly an inkstained Harrovian contemporary and the man who insulted him in the theatre in the summer of 1928. He also lunched with Gerry Wellesley† (known in certain circles as 'the Iron-Duchess') in his native Arab house near the mosque. Formerly a *pissoir*, Egyptians habitually came to 'pee up against his door', which resulted in a 'peppery stench that is not very welcoming'.[36]

---

*Later Lord Casey KG (1890–1976), Governor General of Australia 1965–9. His wife Maie died in 1983.

†Lord Gerald Wellesley, architect and aesthete, later 7th Duke of Wellington, KG (1885–1972).

Cecil was amused by events around him. Waiting outside the pay clerk's office he heard a captain say: 'I'd like to sleep with a girl tonight but don't know how to go about it.'[37] Sir Thomas Russell, Pasha of Cairo, in a white uniform with a tame parrot on his shoulder, told Cecil that he had put an end to the smuggling of drugs buried deep in camels' throats. Patrick Kinross told him that Clare Boothe Luce had been allowed too much freedom to interview the British, that her notes had been confiscated in Trinidad, and that she had described the RAF as 'flying Fairies'.[38] Cecil was pleased that, unlike most Britishers, he had seen a number of Egyptians. To Juliet Duff he wrote that he had not been looked down on 'for consorting with a half-veiled odalisque'.[39] He himself then met the formidable Clare Boothe Luce. Later she told Kaetchen Kommer: 'I saw Cecil in Cairo. He is in splendid form, he is doing some superb work and he gave me hell for *Europe in the Spring* [her report on political attitudes to the war].'[40]

Whenever called upon, Cecil went to work. The Ambassador, Sir Miles Lampson, and his young wife Jacqueline, involved Cecil in photographing their weekly tea for wounded soldiers and other events they attended. They took him to the convalescent club for New Zealanders and a hospital which contained special beds donated by Kay Francis and Edward G. Robinson.

As news of the fighting in the desert improved, Cecil was given the assignment of photographing an important prisoner who was arriving. He hoped this might be Rommel. It turned out to be General Crüwell,* Rommel's number two man, the GOC Afrika Korps, who had been shot down while flying over the Gazala line. Cecil found the VIP prisoner sitting in a car smoking a cigarette and wearing dark glasses. With his 'floppy uniform like a Tyrolean beater, covered with red tabs and buttons, he looked like something stuffed and put in a cage'.[41] Cecil was surprised but impressed at the consideration which his captors showed him, especially when they found out that his young wife had died the week before; but later it was discovered that he had ordered the execution of 2,000 citizens in Jogordina in Yugoslavia.

Worn down by the climate Cecil soon felt stale and looked forward to moving on. 'Have got sick of Cairo's indolence,' he wrote to Clarissa Churchill, 'and "Egyptian Stomach" and feel in need of fresh air and change.'[42] At four o'clock on the morning of 7 June he set off to Heliopolis and thence to Teheran:

---

*General Ludwig Crüwell (1892–1958), the British Army's most formidable opponent in North Africa after Rommel. Almost reappointed ten years later as part of the rearmament of Western Germany. Died at Essen.

Teheran as far as we saw it is a charmless poor city with little of architectural beauty. The mountains produce a lovely screen. There were many nice trees. It is fresh and green.[43]

That night he dined with Christopher Sykes, the writer son-in-law of Russell Pasha. Cecil had only one full day in Persia. The Americans wanted him to photograph their aeroplanes being lined up. Cecil found this interesting but after taking six pictures he was arrested by the Russians, who ordered that his film be destroyed. Maddened by this, he visited an aircraft factory and photographed Iranians at work with the British. Then his trip was justified by the news that the Shah and his twenty-year-old wife* would sit for him. After a snooze on a sofa in a tent Cecil set off in the Shah's car for a 'modern and perfectly hideous palace and garden of such bad style and expensive ugliness as would not be found in Hollywood today'.[44] He found the imperial family on the terrace beside their modernistic swimming-pool:

They looked like a gang of South Americans, not of very high standing. The King in an old grey suit looking very young, Jewish and untidy long hair, not much of a shave, jagged frayed collar and dirty black and white shoes. The Queen in a Shaftesbury Avenue dress, very short skirt, very tight-waisted, bright poison green. She was very painted, very common, very pretty, almost very beautiful, but of film star quality, coarsely *photogénique*, a real treat for the afternoon. There were also present a tough-looking sister of the Shah, a real virago† ... a boy of three that looked like a girl, a daughter of the Shah, a pretty little hoof-nosed doll...[45]

The empress particularly enjoyed the session, allowing her skirt to trail in the pool, and posing like a film star 'with tremendous abandon'.[46]

Cecil then flew to Iraq. At Habbaniya, under the auspices of Air Vice-Marshal H.V. Champion de Crespigny (AOC Iraq and Persia), Cecil witnessed war dances and drilling. The highlight of this part of his trip was to fly in an Oxford to Baghdad to photograph the boy King of Iraq, Faisal II. There he was greeted by his old Cambridge colleague, Stewart Perowne, now press relations attaché at the Embassy, who hurried down the steps in a felt hat to conduct him in his car to the Palais des Fleurs. First they visited the Embassy offices 'and when Perowne took off his hat he proved to be absolutely bald! Oh that gave me quite a shock! My contemporary bald made me realize I should worry less about the thinning of my hair – or should I worry more?'[47]

Cecil preferred the palace in Iraq to its Iranian counterpart. The Regent,

*Muhammad Reza Pahlavi (1919–80) and his first wife, Fawzieh (b. 1921), sister of King Farouk of Egypt.
† Princess Ashraf (b. 1919), later the Head of Iranian Delegation to the UN.

'like a dancing instructor', led in the seven-year-old King by the hand: 'The child in white cotton with quite an adult face proved to be an incredible phenomenon, a really touching little boy with tremendous gravity, sense of responsibility, manners, charm and intelligence.'⁴⁸ He told Stewart Perowne he thought him 'very Marie Laurençin'.⁴⁹ Cecil also liked the Regent: 'The Shah of Persia is a garage mechanic turned gigolo. I believe the King of Egypt is an appalling vulgarian, but this man is quietly remarkable.'⁵⁰ He also photographed Sir Kinahan and Lady Cornwallis. He found the Ambassador 'altogether a splendid leader and fighter',⁵¹ but photographing Lady Cornwallis was a problem. 'What am I to do?' he asked Stewart Perowne. 'I don't want to make Lady Cornwallis look like a hag!'⁵² Then Cecil photographed General Nuri-es-Said, the 'shifty' Prime Minister, who was rather highly strung because he had recently effected the hangings of the leaders of an unsuccessful revolt (two of the nooses failed to work at first). In Baghdad Cecil was reunited with Adrian Bishop. Once an all-powerful figure at Cambridge, he was now a burnt-out case. He had taken vows as a priest, but was on loan to the Ministry of Information doing war propaganda. Not long after this he fell to his death from a balcony. Cecil also met the travel writer, Freya Stark, 'just the sort of bumptious woman I detest'.⁵³ Then he returned to Habbaniya.

Cecil motored to Jerusalem and settled into the luxury of the King David Hotel. There was little to be done but sightseeing. He spent an unforgettable evening at Bethlehem, where the Nativity Church was crowded with 3,000 adults and children who had come to watch propaganda films.

In Jerusalem he photographed two patriarchs. The Greek Patriarch adorned himself in black with a tall hat and magnificent jewels on four gold chains. He proved 'a perfect target'⁵⁴ as Cecil steered him around the various rooms of the Patriarchate. The old Greek knew that Cecil was lunching with the Russian-born Princess Peter of Greece and succeeded in delaying her party. Cecil then photographed Monsignor Barlassina, the Latin Patriarch. He looked like 'the wicked cardinal in *The Duchess of Malfi*'. He joked that after all these photos the police would easily catch him. 'He roared,' wrote Cecil. 'His false teeth exposed, I missed a wonderful picture by not clicking.'⁵⁵

He then travelled to Transjordan and was put in the care of the Emir Abdullah (King Husain's grandfather). The Emir, 'a nice old man with painted eyes, who smelt particularly appetizing and looked very starched and *chic* in an immaculate white suit and turban',⁵⁶ entertained Cecil to lunch. He reminded Cecil of Ninnie, the family nurse, and surprised him by unlocking the mighty doors of his palace with a Yale key.

Petra was dominated by Colonel Glubb (Glubb Pasha) who founded the 'scarlet clad' Arab Legion and turned it into a crack fighting force. Cecil was not impressed by him:

I was surprised to find so unimposing a figure, for he is a badly made little man, with teeth that have got knocked together and grow inwards like a beak. His remarkable qualities are not at once obvious and it is doubly unfortunate that he has been built up into the great newspaper figure as the second Lawrence for his merits do not lie in the more theatrical effects erected by the English attitude to the Near East.[57]

Glubb advised Cecil that if he wanted to see the 9th Army he should go to the source, not Damascus but Beirut. In Damascus Cecil arrived at a hotel where the manager told him to choose a woman and take a double room. He took the double room but not the woman. From there he travelled to Beirut, his vitality sapped by the humid heat. He acquired a poky room in a hotel and telephoned Princess Joan Aly Khan, who came to his rescue. 'Joan is a bright nice girl,' wrote Cecil, 'and I'm fascinated by her subtle appearance – a strange paradox of prettiness and misshapen ugliness.'[58] He relished the luxury of her house and caught up with the news. He was amused to hear that General Sir Edward Spears was unpopular and that people said that Syria should be 'French without Spears'.[59] Hardly had Cecil settled in than he had to leave for Fouglass to photograph army demonstrations under the vigilant eye of Lieutenant-General Sir Henry 'Jumbo' Wilson (c-in-c Persia and Iraq command). While at Fouglass news came of the fall of Tobruk to the Germans and Cecil fell victim to a rare bout of self-pity and misery:

> I am not ashamed of saying that I felt absolutely sick with panic. It is one of the most crushing disappointments of the war that suddenly this campaign, which started off so well for us with congratulatory messages from the King and newspaper reports to say that Rommel's plan had been scotched, has suddenly turned into a major defeat and disaster.... My day was a nightmare of brooding, of feeling sorry for myself, feeling that I was trapped out here with all my work gone for nought. I had awful mental pictures of my private diaries being captured in Cairo and read out over the Radio by Lord Haw-Haw.[60]

The next day his panic deepened:

> I had waking nightmares, all very reprehensible, of being taken prisoner, of being marked for life, unable to pick up the former threads if I survived. I felt that I had really been caught this time and was unmindful of the hundreds of thousands of other soldiers in a much worse plight. It made me annoyed to think that I should 'flap' so easily. I had thought I had more courage but the fact is I have selfishly hung on to escape from real war when it means being caught out of England.[61]

But Cecil did not give voice to his panic. He was soon at work in appalling heat, travelling in a car like a 'furnace', with his camera too hot to handle.

He feared for the fate of the negatives within. His work completed he wondered how long he would have to wait before returning to Cairo. The future looked bleak. Meanwhile he stayed with Joan Aly Khan, who took him to the New Zealand Hospital. She was impressed by how sensitive Cecil was with the patients. He never photographed a bandaged man without his permission and when he promised to send copies, these were despatched without charge. Joan Aly Khan was able to announce: 'They can get you on Misery [MISR, an Egyptian transport plane] if you want today',[62] and before he knew it, Cecil was back at Shepheard's Hotel in Cairo.

He called on Randolph Churchill, who had just come out of hospital and who alleviated his panic about the German advance. But Cairo itself remained in a lull, stunned into inactivity by the prevalent bad news. Much of Cecil's time was again taken up with the tedious task of captioning and sorting photographs. 'The second half of my trip has produced much better results than those from the desert. The desert has proved itself unphotogenic.'[63] On the other hand the German advances meant that much of his earlier work would not now be used. The papers wanted only photos of Palestine and Syria.

On 29 June Maie Casey took Cecil to visit the badly burned and mutilated at the 9th General Hospital at Heliopolis. She corroborated Princess Aly Khan's impression of Cecil:

> I had known of Cecil as a photographer of beautiful women which tended to intimidate me. I found a person quite unlike my expectations, a serious man whose perceptions reached with compassion beyond skin or flesh towards the creature concealed inside. His visit was such a success and so long talked of that when General Montgomery came to stay with us at Mena in 1943 I was asked by the hospital if he would consider spending an hour or so there to cheer the patients.[64]

And Cecil himself wrote: 'The visit to the Hospital drains you of much strength. Your sympathy is at work all the time. You buoy yourself up to carry other people's burdens. This was no exception. We were both worn out after two hours tour.'[65]

Cecil was anxious to leave Cairo. Visiting the photographic division of the Embassy he found they were evacuating, with Arnold Smith in his shirt-sleeves working out plans for this. 'I left with my pile of photographs under the arm,' noted Cecil. 'No one would look at them now.'[66] It was touch and go whether or not he would get out, but the next morning at dawn he flew to Lagos. 'With what tremendous relief did I leave this restless corrupt town from which the German army is now only ninety miles away for England with all its disadvantages yet with the Channel which, so far, prevents the Germans from encroaching nearer than twenty miles.'[67]

* * *

In Lagos, away from the dust of Egypt, he contemplated his lot. He had enjoyed taking the war photographs, but felt that as an art photography did not stimulate him: 'this has no future interest or stimulus and I must try other forms of creation'.[68] His spirits rose when his departure for Lisbon became certain. He arrived in neutral Portugal on 9 July and awaited instructions from the Ministry of Information. Meanwhile he went sightseeing in the peacetime atmosphere of a capital which was overrun with collaborators and war exiles. He enjoyed the company of David Eccles (the politician), the well-informed economic adviser at the Embassy, and Marcus Cheke, the author and diplomatist and his former Harrovian contemporary, 'a nice eccentric eighteenth-century character',[69] who proved an inspired and excellent guide. He fell victim to Lisbon tummy: 'Oh Lord how many more sorts of stomachs must one suffer!'[70] He also had the chance to inspect some German propaganda magazines which he thought vastly superior to *Vogue* with a quantity of restrained colour prints and wonderfully dramatic blurred effects. Never keen on anything that hinted of technical perfection, he declared these 'a triumph of contemporary spirit feeling'.[71]

The Ministry telegraphed saying they wanted Cecil to photograph the local celebrities. During the next few days he raced round, photographing the President, General Carmona, a former revolutionary turned *grand seigneur*, and the Cardinal Patriarch (Cardinal Gonsalves Cerezeira), once hailed in the streets of Rome as 'Cardinal Bambino'[72] owing to his absurdly youthful appearance, as well as various generals, admirals and society ladies. Cecil's work resulted in an exhibition of fifty-six photographs held at Estudio do SPN in Lisbon in December 1942.

At his last sitting Cecil dropped his camera on a stone staircase. 'This made me realize with what confidence and good luck I had embarked on my trip with only one camera.'[73] It was time to go home. Still reading *War and Peace*, which had accompanied him through his trip, Cecil began the hazardous and uncomfortable journey home. He flew to Ireland and then to Bournemouth. He relished every sign of the late summer from his train to London and arrived at Pelham Place to find his mother 'thin but well' and his Aunt Jessie 'very bright'. After a quiet dinner catching up on the news, he retreated to the bed 'which I had thought about so much in the desert'.[74]

Cecil's work in the Near East was widely published and acclaimed. Hugh Francis at the Ministry of Information was delighted when *Vogue* used Cairo material in their August issue, though of course Dr Agha complained that there was no Egyptian scene with troops and began Cecil's text with a news picture he found. Cecil published some of his experiences in Cyril Connolly's *Horizon* under the title 'Libyan Diary'. Later he produced *Near East* for Charles Fry at Batsford, who had found that the war opened up a new range of books and who had achieved some success with Paul Richey's

Fighter Pilot (75,000 copies), *Sub-Lieutenant* by the young Ludovic Kennedy, *Wings of War* (with a contribution by Cecil called 'Back to Earth'), *Infantry Officer* and Hector Bolitho's *Combat Report*. Cecil's *Near East* was praised for its vivid reporting as well as its photographs. In a long review the critic V.S. Pritchett wrote:

> One cannot but compare Mr Beaton's talent for collecting the right fragments and letting them achieve their own effect together, with the lovely photographs. His eye for texture and pattern gives something intimate and fresh to all his notes and there is little in this book that is banal.[75]

As he resumed the threads of an English life, Cecil hoped 'to benefit for some considerable time from the added assurance, interest and experience of the trip'.[76] In August 1942 he photographed the baby Prince Michael of Kent at Coppins. Ten days later the Duke of Kent was killed in a flying accident. Cecil told James Lees-Milne that the Duke had 'good taste without knowledge of the arts' and that he had irritated Cecil by treating the war as no more than 'a tiresome interruption of his life'.[77] Cecil had never been an intimate of the Duke's, but his death led to Cecil becoming one of the Duchess's closer friends and escorts. In 1943 he went to Coppins to pose for 'this poor widow, her face strained and furrowed by sorrow and anxiety'.[78] He admired her renunciation of social functions in favour of a true devotion to her children and her art. 'The picture turned out to be a hundred times better than I had expected – a really excellent likeness.'[79]

During the fifteen months that Cecil spent in London in the middle of the war, he undertook Ministry of Information work (travelling to places like Tyneside), royal work, theatrical and film work and he wrote a book.

His royal work was his most important. On 23 October 1942, Mrs Roosevelt arrived in London to stay at Buckingham Palace, to see the part women played in the war effort and to inspect the welfare conditions of US troops. Queen Elizabeth, who had arranged this visit, summoned Cecil to the Palace to photograph the President's wife in the Bow Room with the Royal Family. The King looked nervous, the Queen smiled blandly, Princesses Elizabeth and Margaret gave 'furtive sidelong glances'. To Cecil Mrs Roosevelt appeared 'enormous, over life-size in fact, with a roving smile and eyes that never focused anywhere. She was elephant coloured. No particular stress or emphasis in any feature. Her hair nondescript.' When Cecil confided to the Queen that he thought Mrs Roosevelt had 'no repose', she replied, 'Oh! But she has much *animation*.'[80]

Later Cecil photographed the Royal Family in turn. While he always loved the Queen, he found King George VI a rather peppery character, lacking 'mystery or magic'.[81] Cecil was not in awe of him, but he found that Princess Elizabeth had become a charming, well-brought-up young girl. 'Together the Princesses reminded me of the beginning of my photographic career when I used to photograph Nancy and Baba as schoolchildren.'[82] A week later he returned to photograph the Queen and her daughters again.

He also took the photographs of Princess Elizabeth released for her eighteenth birthday. He was determined to use Windsor as a setting. A Palace car took him down on a cold Monday morning in 1943. While he was excited by the ornate grandeur of the castle, he was a little disappointed that neither of the Princesses seemed 'to have had their hair freshly washed'. As he was to take the King and Queen in the afternoon, he was invited to luncheon and placed on the Queen's right. A large party gathered including the painter, Sir Gerald Kelly, 'who has been in the household painting one bad picture after another for the last four years. Everyone groans at his continual presence but seems incapable of ousting him.' Cecil was not in the least nervous during luncheon and engaged his monarch in loud-pitched conversation about 'nothing in particular'.[83]

Cecil's theatre and film work resumed in Bristol in October 1942, when he spent a week photographing Noël Coward's play *This Happy Breed*. He remained astonished that Coward, who appeared to him so second-rate, could have produced something so outstanding. Coward thought Cecil's photographs 'far and away the finest'[84] he had seen of any stage production. Later in 1942 Cecil designed the costumes for Binkie Beaumont's revival of George Bernard Shaw's *Heartbreak House*.

He has described his problems with Edith Evans at some length* – particularly those concerning her wig. Having been issued with something that resembled a Japanese lady's wig, Edith decided to take it home, back-comb it and then wear it in her chambers in Albany. It turned into something resembling 'a black, wiry mass of the stuff one finds in an Edwardian sofa'.[85] A new wig was produced.

Cecil thought Edith a mass of contrasts: 'She feels beautiful in spite of one of the ugliest faces any woman possesses today.'[86] Though she was a wonderful actress she depended on John Burrell's direction, for whom she had great respect. Ironically (as it turned out) it was to Enid Bagnold that Cecil confided his first experiences with a major theatrical production:

> Each actor is out for all he can get for his part and the ordinary standards of manners and friendship do not apply. It is a sort of desperate factory where all feuds are eventually forgotten. But if they happened in real life there would be law suits and hostile silence for the rest of time.[87]

When the play opened in Edinburgh, John Burrell wrote of the success of Cecil's beautiful costumes: 'Isabel [Jeans]'s dress, on her first entrance, is always greeted with gasps of delight from the audience.'[88] But, overall, the

* See *The Years Between*, pp. 221–32.

play was not a wild success, nor did its aged author enthuse. Shaw wrote to Edith Evans:

> No complaints: the part is too easy for you. But to have to pull the play through against four hopeless miscasts, including a faded maiden aunt [Deborah Kerr] as your youthful rival and a Shotover [Robert Donat], who is obviously a leading juvenile in a stuck-on beard, takes a bit of doing. It should be billed as Half Heart House.[89]

Heartbreak House opened at the Cambridge Theatre in London on 18 March 1943 and ran for 236 performances.

Cecil spent considerable time discussing plays with Enid Bagnold, by now a firm friend. In 1943 he photographed the Joneses, not always with good results. In November 1943 Enid wrote: 'I was not unagreeably surprised at a slight look of a tired Slav that comes out in your photographs.'[90] But then she showed them to Diana Cooper, who asked: 'Darling, are you sure you haven't *wounded* Cecil in any way?'[91] Enid's family disapproved of the greyness of her hair due to overlighting.

There was the possibility that Cecil would work on a Ouida ballet with music by Benjamin Britten. He created designs for a play by Ivor Novello (who in 1944 served a month in prison for breaking petrol restrictions). Nothing came of these, but Cecil's work for John Gielgud was more successful. He designed the sets and costumes for Major Eric Linklater's play, *Crisis in Heaven*, assisted by Hal Burton, later a theatre director. The play opened in Edinburgh (after Cecil went to the Far East). He never saw it, but heard that it had been a success in the provinces but a failure in London and had come off after a month and only thirty-eight performances. His consolation was that 'Dorothy Dickson had looked dazzling and my work much appreciated'.[92] Maud Nelson described it as 'breathlessly beautiful from the word go'.[93] Had Cecil been in London he would have adjusted certain details. He also created the costumes for the film of Frederick Lonsdale's play *On Approval*, starring Beatrice Lillie, Googie Withers, Clive Brook and Roland Culver. This film, which came out in London in the spring of 1944, had a record run in Hollywood of twenty-two weeks.

During this period Cecil had constant problems with his *Vogue* contract and their continuing demand for exclusivity. Unfortunately a portrait of the Marchioness of Salisbury appeared as a frontispiece for the *Sketch* in April 1942. *Vogue* described this as in flagrant and direct contradiction to their agreement. In November 1942 Cecil complained that he lost earnings because *Vogue* gave their sitters complimentary photographs, were slow in selecting their pictures and careless over his credits. He complained about his fees to Edna Chase, who pointed out that his rates were perfectly adequate. She warned: 'I think we should have to feel our way a little carefully because I am sorry to tell you that the old bitterness about the

Jewish episode still rankles.'[94] (One advertiser had cancelled his contract.) Cecil was paid just over £1,130 between September 1942 and April 1943. 'I am pleased to think that this is considerably higher than the sums you earned in either of your first two years of working for us in the war period,'[95] wrote the British editor, Audrey Withers. While at times *Vogue* found Cecil a trial with his demands and complaints, so too they often found his advice extremely helpful. Cecil urged them to be more critical. A piece on the theatre earned the praise of the editor, who wrote that she 'got a lot of pleasure from the sharp tang of your own theatre piece, because here you were reviewing the whole field and threw rotten eggs as well as bouquets'.[96] Cecil welcomed the departure of the awful Dr Agha in October and his replacement by Alexander Liberman. 'Our new man, Liberman, is full of charm and was formerly on Vogel's staff in Paris,'[97] wrote Edna Chase.

Cecil wrote his book, *British Photographers*, for W.J. Turner, the editor of the 'Britain in Pictures' series. When it came out in 1944, Elizabeth Bowen wrote that it was 'as succinct and illuminating as one could wish, or, given his name, expect'.[98] Raymond Mortimer hoped Cecil's challenge to young artists to make colour photography an art might 'persuade some of those who would otherwise swell the already bloated ranks of mediocre painters to divert their attention to this still neglected medium'.[99]

Cecil's work contrasted somewhat with the occupations of his various friends. Cyril Connolly was literary editor of the *Observer* and editor of *Horizon*; Brian Howard an aircraftsman in the RAF; Nancy Mitford was working at the bookshop, Heywood Hill; and Rex Whistler serving in the Welsh Guards. Kenneth Clark extricated Freddie Ashton from his hated life in the RAF to choreograph two ballets, while Francis Rose invited Cecil to join him and a Glaswegian sailor called Ted to see a musical in the docklands. Rose was invalided out of the RAF in February 1943 and married the widowed Mrs Sproul-Bolton (the travel writer Dorothy Carrington).

James Lees-Milne recorded his opinion of Cecil in this mid-war period:

> For one so sophisticated he is shy. And his polished courtesy makes me shy at first. He is very observant, misses nothing, the speck of potato on one's chin, the veins in one's nose, the unplucked hair sprouting from the ear. Yet how sensitive and understanding he is! After ten minutes I succumb to his charm, and am at ease. For there is nothing one cannot say to him.[100]

Lees-Milne was surprised when James Pope-Hennessy confided his longing to sleep with a woman. Cecil had 'told him how easy it was'.[101] But Cecil himself was in agonies of pain from a stone in the gall-bladder, a plight made worse when Emerald Cunard visited him in his recuperation and sat by the bed saying, 'Oh physical pain is nothing. One cannot remember it as soon as it is over. It's moral pain one cannot bear.'[102]

By October 1943, Cecil was suffering from fatigue. Nevertheless he welcomed the decision of the Ministry of Information to send him on a visit to the Far East. His mission was to photograph 'the war effort in India and social services of all kinds'.[103]

Early in December he left London. His departure was uneasy and he had the premonition that he was in for trouble. Deborah Kerr said, 'Cheerio, and if I don't see you again ...'[104] His mother was tearful and anxious. He flew to an aerodrome at Land's End, where a dozen transport aircraft were stranded due to the freezing weather. Even Field-Marshal Smuts was delayed here, warming himself by a stove in the mess. The delay lasted a depressing eleven hours. The waiting passengers were due to fly to Gibraltar in the icy cold of a dark night. Cecil and his companions got into the Dakota and engines began to roar:

> What happened now is something that no one knows. I only know that for me the terror and agony lasted for an eternity from the start of the run. I bowed my head in my hands and prayed very hard. My brain was working peculiarly clearly and I prayed that if I survived my life might be simplified, that I should resist the distractions of so many unimportant things. Then my terror became intensified. My eyes were shut and I was not conscious of anything outside.[105]

Cecil's mind raced back over his childhood and schooldays, to Lily Elsie, Peter Watson, Ashcombe and New York. A voice from behind him said very quietly, 'Yes, that's it. Now we're for it.'[106] Flames ripped through the cockpit. Someone opened the escape door and passengers groped towards it. Cecil did not know if he was jumping from a great height to certain death but preferred the fall to burning. He jumped – and landed head first in a grassy field only a few feet below. Someone shouted 'Get up and run', and they fled from the burning wreck above them as quickly as they could. The passengers were saved and even the Canadian pilot survived though he was seriously injured. All the victims were taken to hospital. After a restless night Cecil made himself fly to London rather than entrain. Only when he was back at home did he fall victim to the full horror of his experience and shock set in. Sir Reginald Dorman-Smith, the Governor of Burma, who witnessed the crash, told Cecil later: 'No one had ever come nearer to death then we.'[107]

Years later Lord Balfour of Inchrye, who was Parliamentary Under Secretary of State for Air during the war, read of the incident in Cecil's published diary and wrote to him:

> You are a brave man and this I know. You refer casually to your crash on the way to M.E. Do you remember coming to my room in the Air Ministry the day before you left. We discussed your trip. I wished you

'Bon Voyage'. Next day a limping and bandaged Cecil came again to see me. You came with just one request. Could I fix as soon as possible another flight passage for you? That's why I say you are a very courageous fellow.[108]

21

Far East

You are the luckiest person in all the world just now.

James Pope-Hennessy to Cecil, 17 April 1944

INDIA

Cecil referred to his misadventure as 'a false start',[1] if he mentioned it at all. After some delays he set off again, this time with none of the qualms he had felt before. After his accident every flight would fill him with terror. His journeys around India and China were to involve many hazardous expeditions in the air. None of these did he try to shirk, though he invariably suffered more than his fellow passengers. He travelled to India via Lisbon, Gibraltar (where John Perry, of H.M. Tennent, was ADC to the Governor and he therefore stayed at Government House) and Cairo. In Cairo he stayed with the Lampsons, who found him 'very amusing as he always is, being a repository of all the latest gossip and scandal at home'.[2] At a military party which Cecil found boring, a secretary who had once worked for him while a student at Queen's College, Harley Street, approached him and told him how she had felt:

> She said she had arrived at the house scared stiff, that I had received her in bed, had ticked her off for using the best notepaper, had dictated a bogus article about ATS, and about Diana Cooper, had marvelled at Maud – 'was Maud my all?' – and what had happened to the maid Dorothy. It was really quite alarming to realize what a lot an ordinary girl like that can pick up about the goings on in the house. This one became more and more drunk, told me that more and more of my things were 'bogus' and I took my revenge by pouring a glass of dynamite cup into her tweed overcoat as she danced.[3]

Cecil then flew the long journey to India and eventually passed over the Taj Mahal, 'very poetical even in the unbecoming haze of midday heat'[4] and landed in New Delhi. Major Peter Coats, the Comptroller of the Viceregal Household, was awaiting him with the welcome news that he was to stay

with the Wavells at the Viceroy's House. Cecil had met Coats and Lord
Wavell the previous summer when he had photographed the Viceroy at
Chips Channon's house. Cecil was extremely impressed by the grandeur and
vastness of the proportions, the length of the marble corridors (the one on
the ground floor was 256 feet long), the number of servants in scarlet and
gold liveries, and the 150 gardeners, many of whom could be seen sweeping
and watering under close supervision. Cecil reported to his mother:

> A family party for dinner, but that means about a dozen, all the dozens
> of red servants salaaming and the English curtseying and bowing. Lady
> Wavell in trailing grey, very simple and easy – and the whole family is
> really rather touching and charming, and it was nice to see Wavell rather
> playfully reacting to his daughter's curtseys. A toast 'To the King Empe-
> ror' and after dinner listening to the news, gossip and early bed. I thought
> I could find my way back to my bedroom, but was mistaken and walked
> along these marble floors for half an hour.[5]

He was soon at home and, in the words of Peter Coats, 'almost an extra
ADC and in a haze of well-deserved escapist luxury'.[6] His mission in India
was to send back reports and photographs favourable to the Empire and as
such he was under contract to the Ministry of Information from 7 December
1943 until 9 September 1944. He was much nearer the line of fire this
time. He would see the casualties being brought back to camp. He would be
faced with dangerous situations. The Ministry was anxious to obtain coverage of typical Indian life in the villages, schools, hospitals and social
services. Cecil found that nobody in the Ministry in Delhi knew of his arrival
or who was responsible for him. In due course a daunting itinerary was
planned. Cecil was aware that he knew very little about India. Meanwhile
he was happy to enjoy the luxury of the Viceroy's House and mixed well
with the ADCs. He admired the way Peter Coats ran the house with efficiency
and light humour and acted as a stooge to the Viceroy, gently reminding
his master of the right anecdote for the right occasion. During Cecil's stay
the ex-Mayor of Bombay, Jamna Das Mehta, complained of a rat in his
room. Coats explained: 'Ah, a rat, sir, those are for our most distinguished
guests, the others only get mice.'[7] Cecil always enjoyed a good ADC joke.
Simon Astley told him that Wavell had been taking a course in Pelmanism.
Having interviewed a Miss Tuck for half an hour he said, 'Good-bye, Mrs
Hunt.'[8] Of the other ADCs, one of whom was Lord Euston (now Duke of
Grafton), Cecil particularly liked Billy Henderson: 'I find him a more delightful companion every day and have seldom come across anyone at all like
him.'[9] Only the previous Vicereine, Lady Linlithgow, disapproved of the new
set-up, and wrote of the ADCs' room as 'the Pansies' Parlour'.[10] Christmas
parties and picnics were the order of the day and Cecil did various sketches
with which he was not pleased: 'My sketches have not improved one iota

since the last ten years and it made me mad to find the sketches were unlike my spirit, in fact as far removed as an advertisement for mackintoshes by Bernard Weatherill.'*[11] On 2 January, Peter Coats took Cecil to the enormous palace of Faridkot, 'recently vacated by some young Royal whose ideas on taste coincide in many cases with those of a brothel keeper'.[12] Here the Mountbattens were living:

> One bedroom has a mirror ceiling. Lord Louis and I lay on the double bed while I photographed the result in the ceiling, all of which sounds high spirited, but maybe on account of my injection I felt very uneasy and slightly appalled by the boarding school atmosphere of the establishment. The Headboy was such a breezy hero, so full of ideas, vitality, health and success. I felt a bit old and scraggy. ... Lord Louis struck me as being very impressive as a dynamo. I asked 'Isn't the climate here a great damper on effort?' – 'We mustn't let it be. We've got to galvanize everyone else by our vitality. ...'[13]

Cecil gathered that Mountbatten did not want to be publicized either as a second Monty or a playboy but as a tough leader. 'Yet he never looks anything but the finished article even when travelling under the roughest conditions.'[14] That afternoon the Viceroy was to be photographed, but his GCSI star was locked up and only after considerable chaos could the key be found:

> The robes are not fitted and the morning coat was not so romantic a substitute, but HE did, nevertheless, look extremely elegant and dapper. In fact he looked so well cut and suave in this dovegray coat [chosen by Peter Coats at Leslie Roberts'], ten years younger. Some of the pictures should be quite romantic – and I trust there will be enough straightforward ones to fill the desired requirements.[15]

Cecil's Delhi life involved attending a VC parade, photographing a conference of war chiefs and dining with the Auchinlecks, the General ('the sort of heavy, clottish male soldier that I don't understand or admire') and his erratic wife, who threw almonds across the table at the Auk and caused him to comment: 'You're very violent tonight.'†[16] On 8 January he was sorry to have to leave on his trip.

Cecil's first stop was Calcutta, where the occasional coarse rose-coloured building loomed amongst the shacks and a crowd of dirty-looking Indians thronged the sidewalks. He stayed at Government House and took an instant dislike to the Acting Governor of Bengal, Sir Thomas Rutherford, whom he thought a charmless rodent. Fortunately for Cecil he was soon replaced by

---

* The tailor, whose son is now Speaker of the House of Commons.

† Lady Auchinleck left the General soon afterwards and married Air Chief Marshal Sir Richard Peirse.

Dick Casey. Cecil set off for a tour of the jungle, which he described in a letter to Clarissa Churchill on his return to Calcutta:

I have determined that the only nice parts of my trip are the rough ones. Living comfortably is hell to one's peace of mind and after two weeks at Viceroy's House I became so soft that I dreaded the prospect of the war fronts. But after the initial shock of discomfort, never being able to sit or lie on anything soft, dirty water for tea and drinking etc, I felt absolutely marvellous, impervious and serene. I was lucky to see the war under ideal weather conditions. It must be appalling in heat or rain. It is strange how little people in England are interested in our troops on the Burma front and those troops feel very badly about it.... I was taken up the River on Sunday to see a colony of Holy Men, all covered in ash and wearing only a scarlet jockstrap, one of the most extraordinary and sinister sights, a boy about ten years old with long flowing hair, grey face and body, reading from the Holy Book and playing a zither twice his size. ... There is a local Sybil Colefax here, a local Picasso. The Caseys have their first dinner party on Friday so I shall see the 'cream of society' which I believe stinks.[17]

To Diana Cooper, he added:

The war itself (though a particularly 'grim affair' of scalping or being scalped by a Jap) had much less horror than the war at home, for everything looked so idyllic, like a wonderful picnic party with mules and jeeps bringing up the tea things and if someone's head got in the way of a bit of shrapnel, well it was just too bad. But accidents do happen at picnics, and the Red Cross van is there in readiness.[18]

Cecil's jungle visit brought him within earshot of the guns. He found the men out there resigned with fortitude to the possibility of several more years trying 'to winkle out the Jap and kill him'.[19] The only advantage of jungle warfare over desert life was the shade and water, and the wide variety of rations. As Cecil reached his fortieth birthday, on a day when he made a sixteen-hour mountain journey, he worried that his life was merely the 'reiteration of a theme'.[20] He hoped in the future to rely more on his brains than his instincts.

In the jungle Cecil met another photographer, Antony Beauchamp, now doing cinematographic work. Beauchamp recalled that the troops cheered Cecil as an unlikely reminder of a forgotten world. He was impressed by the effortless results Cecil achieved, combined with his lack of technical expertise. He told Cecil that he was 'an apostle of the job in England'[21] and that, although he had always disliked the idea of him, he had inspired him to take up photography. They got on well and only when Cecil was tired and therefore appeared 'bored and supercilious'[22] did Tony Beauchamp tick him off for not regaling a new band of soldiers with stories and news from the outside world.

Back in Calcutta, Cecil set to work rearranging every room in Government House for Mrs Casey, who wrote later: 'Cecil taught our gentle and poetic Hindu doer of flowers to vary our decorations by the use of the clear green lettuce leaves which enlivened the tedium of endless cannas.'[23] In the course of an hour he converted the blue drawing-room into a pink one. 'It was like decorating a play,' he wrote, 'with a wonderful array of helpers at my disposal. . . . The room was metamorphosed. It became slightly Edwardian, very feminine and almost human. I strewed many books around, a few sweet dishes and even a dessert plate.'[24] Cecil was pleased to hear that the Military Secretary, Rex Peel, commented to the Governor: 'I must say Beaton earns his keep here,' and Casey's reply: 'Yes, he's a man of parts.'[25]

Cecil fell ill with the very dangerous disease, dengue fever. As he lay in bed he illustrated an adventure story written by Mrs Casey's son Donn. 'I did some drawings for his book,' noted Cecil, 'but towards the end of the day I became careless and he soon ticked me off for diverging from the script.'[26] Cecil liked the Caseys and was aware that the Governor hoped to be Prime Minister of Australia* one day. David Clowes, in true ADC style, passed on a remark he heard Mrs Casey make: 'I married His Excellency eighteen years ago and he's never relaxed since.'[27]

Cecil remained at Government House until 14 February. When he returned to Delhi he discovered that his photographs were not only badly printed but underdeveloped. Because he had changed his dates, he was not allowed to stay at the Viceroy's House, but he lunched there when Joyce Grenfell was one of the guests: 'here for WVS and she has the lovely pale flower looks of a delicate Edwardian beauty that are rarely seen today, a tragic expression worn as a gesture'.[28] In some ways Cecil was glad to escape the ceremonial rigours of Viceregal life. He returned to the house where he was sleeping and that night dreamed 'of Lily Elsie making a tragic return to the stage and doing a quite horrifying dance, and of Oliver Messel, in my absence here, trying to put a stop to my work on the Linklater play [*Crisis in Heaven*] and pretending that he had the option on the designing'.[29]

Cecil made friends with the Swiss photographer Raymond Burnier, who now lived in Benares as a Hindu. He prised from him the theory that his work, his new obsessive ambition to write a play, and Ashcombe were opiates 'that went to compensate for the lack of love'. Burnier was surprised that Cecil never analysed his work after it was done. He said he thought his work 'must be near mysticism' for him 'to have a complete feeling of satisfaction'.[30] In Delhi Cecil joined an art class organized by Billy Henderson, which made him aware of how much he had neglected drawing and paint-

---

*He became Minister of External Affairs and Governor-General, and was the first ever Australian Knight of the Garter.

ing and how unlikely he was to progress. On 22 February he left for the North West Frontier.

Cecil's four-day visit was memorable for terrifying flights. On the way out they flew blind through white mists, and on the way back the automatic release went wrong and the Indian pilot signalled to Cecil to take the dual control stick, while he crawled about on the floor fixing the trouble. This was followed by several false landings. Cecil stayed with the GOC, Major-General Bruce Scott, at Flagstaff House, Peshawar, who told him that while all was quiet at present, trouble could flare up at any time. The terrain was impossible to clear and the tribes were hostile and still living in caves. Nevertheless this was a good buffer between India and Afghanistan. A great menace was the elusive troublemaker, Fakir Ipi, who hated the British. Cecil visited RAF pilots in a local training-school and witnessed a RAF revue organized by the comedian Cyril Fletcher, then a welfare officer, who both produced and wrote it. Cecil was surprised how much he enjoyed it all 'and some of it was so insidious that I kept remembering it with appalling vividness for the next day or two. As I cleaned my teeth I would see Mr Fletcher galvanizing everyone to sing with him.'[31]

At the Khyber Pass Cecil witnessed a battalion of the 7th Rajput Regiment setting off on a tactical exercise in frontier warfare.

In the evening Cecil dined with the Governor, Sir George Cunningham,* 'a very stiff man made of rock', who gradually thawed and even smiled. 'Just the sort of man I would normally never like, but so much less credit to me for not realizing his merit, a good talker.'[32] As so often in India and so rarely during his previous trip to Egypt, Cecil's thoughts turned to himself:

> I was quite drunk in the car after two whiskys and sodas and thought it extraordinary how my father's son should gad about the world in this way, off to dinner with people I don't know at all, have nothing in common with yet have by degrees, in spite of shyness, a certain assurance. My notoriety helps 90%. The nights developing and enlarging photographs to be sent to the *Tatler* have brought in their dividends. It is a great help that wherever I go here, there are English people. I am likely to find things made easier for me from the somewhat childish motive of wishing to help a celebrity.[33]

After a few more days spent back in Delhi, Cecil flew to Bombay on 1 March: 'very sticky and hot', he reported to Clarissa Churchill, 'but I like this place more than any other town I've seen'.[34] He spent twelve days there. Government House was a colony of white trellis-work houses with green lawns, borders of scarlet cannas and tropical trees. The main building was reached by a red carpeted flight of stairs flanked by servants in scarlet

* Sir George Cunningham (1888–1963), Governor of NW Frontier Province 1937–46, and of NWFP Pakistan 1947–8.

and white. Cecil found himself in a pale yellow room with five doors leading to a balcony overlooking the sea, 'an ideal honeymoon place, a wonderful opportunity for relaxation'. The Governor's wife, Lady Colville,* was 'very petite and fluffy, nervous, with bows in her hair'.[35] She conducted Cecil to a meeting with RAF men, and after tea he explored the town.

It was not long before Cecil was conducting Lady Colville and her daughter round the house, suggesting that the black Victorian carvings be painted to look like ivory and the overall decoration be white and red. He was as impressed as he was slightly alarmed to find that the daughter, Mary, had wonderful taste with flowers. 'I felt that the younger generation had caught up with me and I could now go no further than she had, for these were my flower arrangements. It was rather a shock to me: leafless, bright pinks, mauves and scarlet jammed together.'[36]

Cecil visited a hospital and photographed the Colvilles in full dress. The Governor thought the process a waste of time, a sentiment with which Cecil quite sympathized: 'I had no mind left after the rather idiotic photographs.'[37] It was more fun taking Mary in imitation poses of early Nancys and Babas. He photographed armoured cars, trucks and tanks at the great Military Ordnance Depot. He also visited the races with Sir Victor Sassoon and the brothel quarter of the town under the protection of the eccentric bearded ADC, Lord Wharton (the pair disguised in old clothes) and the police. Cecil thus had a first-hand view of the stern way order was enforced.

In Bombay Cecil felt he had an easy time but was praised by the Governor for his diligence. He then took a bumpy flight to Hyderabad and photographed the striking Princess of Berar, whom he had taken at the time of the Coronation in London, and with whom he now made friends. He caught a glimpse of the dirty and unshaven Nizam of Hyderabad and witnessed an old crone of a princess ordering silver ornaments and scarves in wild screams and yells. Cecil examined the mad woman: 'I was enormously impressed by the Patrician beauty of this primitive-looking hag, the aquiline nose, the pointed lips, pouting, the high lean cheekbones and fierce birdlike eyes.'[38] The harridan pointed at Cecil and began to scream. He bowed dramatically to her, but in so doing went too close. Panic followed and she was carried off screaming. Cecil discovered that this was a regular occurrence and that anything she took was later returned from the Palace. He also heard that she was fond of young men and that he might have been abducted.

Cecil concluded that the Europeans had made India suburban and that few people did an honest day's work. He made a list of his own problems for Clarissa Churchill:

---

* Colonel the Hon. Sir John Colville (1894–1954), later 1st Baron Clydesmuir, was Governor of Bombay from 1943 to 1948. He died after scissors were left inside him during an operation.

I have done a lot of work, mostly bad. My brain has become addled by

1) overeating, gorging.
2) the hot wet climate.
3) trying to take in too many things and getting exhausted.
4) getting accustomed to not listening to bores, and being unable to attend when some interesting person talks.

4a) not quite hearing or understanding all that is told one (native English).

5) hearing too much about places, things and people that one has not heard about previously.[39]

Cecil returned to Delhi via Bombay where Major Donald Neville-Willing took him to photograph the Indian dancer, Ram Gopal, and a boy pupil dancing by the rocks of the sea. Billy Henderson then agreed to accompany him to Jaipur:

I have just returned from Jaipur, the first time I have seen India as I hoped it would be, a dream town, all coral coloured, with a brilliant Prime Minister [Sir Miras Ismail], a Persian with flawless taste, tremendous enthusiasm and courage, who is all the time making the most remarkable improvements. ... I hate big European cities, the English types are beyond sympathy, the snobbery *tragic*.[40]

In Jaipur Cecil witnessed a leopard hunt, the bait for which was a tethered goat. He watched with a characteristic mixture of excitement and compassion. He photographed the Maharajah and Maharanee of Jaipur in their palace and then, under the excellent auspices of Raymond Burnier, he visited Benares, a town with too much refuse. That night Cecil enjoyed some hashish and the evening was spent in 'a dazed trance'.[41] The next day he felt 'extremely flaccid and unconscious of my body',[42] which proved a great advantage during their sightseeing. Cecil took a boat down the Ganges, saw some people washing and others burning dead bodies wrapped in cotton.

Cecil suffered 'pangs of remorse'[43] that he had neglected Ministry of Information work. He set off to Benares University and the wise Chancellor greeted him from his bed during a particularly violent rainstorm.

From Benares Cecil returned to Government House, Calcutta, where the film star Paulette Goddard was lunching, having returned from an energetic visit to China.

Cecil was injected against the plague and promptly fell ill as on his previous visit. There were endless delays before he could leave for Chungking and the house was in an uproar due to the imminent arrival of the Wavells. Cecil's leg became more and more inflamed until a famous local character, Dr Denham White, counteracted the serum. Cecil remained in bed feeling sorry for himself until his sudden recovery. He was well enough to dine with the Wavells, but fortunate to avoid the experience of the Viceregal party the next night. They dined with the RAF and ate bad prawns. The primitive sanitary conditions and lack of bathrooms caused the distinguished gathering agonies of pain and humiliation. They returned to Government House the next day in ill humour. In due course Cecil went through the various formalities (obtaining a military permit lest he be conscripted) and on 8 April 1944 he flew over 'the Hump,' the mountain range that divides India and China.

Cecil's visit to India was not considered wholly successful by the Ministry of Information. They were disappointed by the poor quality of Indian developing and printing and felt that Cecil had taken too much 'duplication of subject'.[44] Hugh Francis stressed that the whole trip was 'a long-term venture and it is therefore all the more essential that really first-class negatives well processed and printed should be the result'.[45]

CHINA

Cecil had flown over 'the Hump' before he realized it. It was uncomfortable, he had a splitting headache and he was surrounded by Chinamen. Earlier several had been sick; now there was 'a great deal of throat clearing and guttural expectorations from the Chinese'.[46] It was a relief to land in Chungking and be conveyed to the Embassy in a bamboo sedan chair. Major-General Gordon Grimsdale, the Military Attaché, who had met Cecil in Calcutta and invited him on his tour of southern China, came down the hill to greet him. The atmosphere of Chungking was dreamlike:

> Chungking was very beautiful. The reflection of mountains on river quite wonderful, the trembling lights on the black mountains and the full moon in the cloudless sky. On the roads coolies carrying enormous loads of wood planks.[47]

Cecil arrived at the British Embassy and was greeted by the Ambassador, Sir Horace Seymour,* 'in grey flannels, his wife in dark blue long dress'.[48] Brooks Atkinson, the New York Times drama critic, was staying in the house, which was rather like a small temple with a hexagonal room in the centre. Cecil soon discovered that life here was quite a contrast to that of the Caseys in Calcutta: 'nothing but essentials'.[49] The next day was a quiet one apart from an expedition to tea with Madame Sun Yat-Sen, 'the most loved of the Soong sisters, the widow of the General now almost deified'.[50] Cecil met Stanley Smith, the Australian representative of the Ministry of Information.

---

* Sir Horace Seymour (1885–1978), Ambassador to China 1942–6, and his wife Violet, daughter of Thomas Erskine.

China had been in a state of war with Japan since 1937. In 1942 Chinese forces had recovered many occupied parts and, after Pearl Harbor (December 1941), China had become a member of the ABCD Nations (American, British, Chinese and Dutch) and was waging war on the enemy in the Pacific. There had been little fighting since December and the exchange rate was ridiculous – a coolie was paid $3,000 a month; an orange cost $100. While Cecil spent quiet days sleeping off his weariness, Lady Seymour noted in her diary: 'Cecil Beaton staggered in having slept most of the afternoon.... I like him. ... I am afraid he finds us all rather dim with our ancient garments and my greying unpolished hair and general dilapidation.'[51] The next day she added: 'C. Beaton is amusing with his reactions to Chungking, he thought it felt geared to war – I can't see how.'[52]

On 12 April, feeling a little homesick, Cecil set off on his trip with Gordon Grimsdale and Leo Handley-Derry, a tall major also attached to the Military Mission. They flew to Kunming, a place alive with buzzing aeroplanes, jeeps and cars. After photographing General C.L. Chennault from Wisconsin, 'a sort of Middle Western Heathcliff',[53] they flew the next day over rugged mountains to visit Kweilin. Cecil inspected the work of threshing, watering and carrying undertaken by the old women he saw on the way. Kweilin had wooden shop fronts, people resting under the curved roofs of pagodas, crowds in the streets and people cooking by the roadside. Cecil regretted the intrusion of characterless modern buildings which were already threatening the charm of the city. He wandered round the town while children played games and flocked around him, especially when he changed a film. At the end of the day he returned exhausted to his bare boarded bungalow. The plan was to leave the next morning, but rain prevented this. Cecil was confined to his increasingly damp bungalow while the yard outside became a mud patch. For four days he was stuck in Kweilin, with only his overcoat to wrap over his tropical clothes.

He filled his time visiting the widow of a missionary who ran the local hospital (gathering notes for a play about missionaries), and spending time with Ake Hartman* into whose care he was consigned. They attended a Chinese bath: 'a most pleasant interlude of sensuous delight',[54] dined at the Vitamin Restaurant on delicious chicken, smoked opium (essential for a safe diet) with the owner Mr Wu, and then undertook what Hartman later described as a 'ghastly trek in the rain that I let you in for after our poppy interlude with Wu-ski'.[55] Mud oozed over their boots and Cecil was as lost as when staying with Gertrude Stein.

Kweilin was the top-secret, furthest and most isolated allied outpost of the BAAG (British Army Aid Group). The BAAG consisted of MI9, MI5, the SIS

* Ake Hartman (d. 1977) was later evacuated to Kunming. After the war he lived in Shanghai and finally retired to Italy. He married the artist Vera Southby. ◆

and the SOE. The complicated radio links were operated from Kweilin by a young major in the Royal Signals, Philip Smith, who recalled: 'It was very brave of Cecil Beaton to come and visit us and I can assure you he was very welcome.'[56] Cecil entertained them with hilarious stories of his recent travels and, as so often, proved in reality a better man than his public image implied. Philip Smith also revealed that Åke Hartman was 'a fluent multi-dialect Chinese speaking Swede in the British Secret Service'.[57]

Meanwhile Cecil read Bernard Fergusson's bland and breezy account of his life in Burma and was appalled at some of the castaway remarks: 'Only one casualty. Some poor chap overslept at a halt.' 'The horror of this man's awakening alone in the jungle sent my blood cold,'[58] wrote Cecil. Eventually he became so bored and desperate for reading-matter that he unpinned the pictures from *Sphere* on the walls to read what was on the back. The only time Cecil really came to life was when he explored Chinese theatre, savouring the delicacy of the make-up.

Shortly before 4 a.m. on 18 April, the party departed by truck and then by transport aircraft above the banks of the Kan river to Kanshein. They crossed by ferry and called on Chiang Chung-kuo, ruler of five states and son of General Chiang Kai-shek. The endless delays put Cecil into a cantankerous mood, which was somewhat alleviated by an invitation to spend the night in the dictator's guest-house. Leaving Kanshein, they travelled through lush peasant countryside, arriving at length at Pihu, an outpost not far from the East China Sea. The events that followed were somewhat of 'a Gilbert and Sullivan affair'.[59]

The party was presented to about a dozen generals, whom Cecil thought looked about twenty years old. Similarly they thought he was fifty because of his grey hair. General Li Mo-an, GOC 23rd Route Army, gave a ceremonial tea-party to welcome Gordon Grimsdale. Cecil thought him 'a small fat rubber-faced boy with enormous nostrils and shaven head'.[60] When the two national anthems were played the excruciating noise, 'as if fifty cats had gone mad', broke the strain of the last days and caused Cecil to shake with laughter:

I tried to think of all the most horrifying things that could happen to me, the room suddenly invaded by Japanese who would proceed to slash us all with swords, but even this did not prevent my laughing at this incredible noise.[61]

Cecil went to photograph General Li and his family, his fat young wife 'yawning or gurking'[62] without inhibition. The General himself worried that his decorations might appear to have slipped in the snaps taken at the tea. That morning a lot of preening took place. 'I have seldom known such ill-concealed vanity,' noted Cecil. 'A general in attendance kept patting the C-in-C's tunic, adjusting buttons. It was therefore with a certain satisfaction that I took one picture in which it was obvious to me but not to others that a fly-button was undone.'[63]

With Gordon Grimsdale he visited the British Military Mission to meet soldiers who had been stranded in this lonely place for many years. A tactical exercise was staged: 'The Chinese boys covered in green leaves rushed about a mountainside firing into one another's backsides. How no one was killed I don't know.'[64] The spectators were warned not to laugh, lest the Chinese lose face.

The next day there was a giant demonstration involving about a thousand men and a superlative banquet given by General Li, who with his wife 'could hardly be seen above the table cloth'. As Cecil reeled to bed he thought: 'I cannot feel that the Chinese will relish the dinner given in return in our Mess tomorrow night.'[65] Cecil missed this dinner (at which the wine soon ran out) because he was confined to his hard wooden bed with a gravely upset stomach. He was also fortunate to miss a dinner at which the Chinese generals proposed 'no heel tap' toasts, to which the wretched guests had to respond by draining their glass of wine which tasted like linseed oil. Leo Handley-Derry fell victim to the Chief of Staff's sense of humour several times. The next day Cecil began to sketch but upset one of the boys who carried the water from the river. The boy minded doing this job (which was beneath him), and to have his shame recorded in a drawing was too deep a humiliation and he burst into tears. Cecil's visit to draw the Lis was equally tricky. The General was very precise as to how his stars should be drawn while Madame Li would not sit still and behaved in an ill-mannered way.

When not running to the outside lavatory in pouring rain, Cecil lay on

General Li Mo-an, Pihu 1944

his bed writing letters. The rain came through the bamboo roof and fell on to one he wrote to Diana Cooper:

> I hadn't realized quite what it means for a country to be cut off from the rest of the world for so long. All supplies that come in are flown over the Himalayas, and there is a great shortage of equipment, transport and medicine. But one realizes that nothing unessential is made new, and by degrees all the cushions are worn out, all the springs have gone in the 'easy' chairs, all the sheets are threadbare. It has been quite a shock to realize the poverty of Chungking. Not one person lives in a house bigger than the smallest maisonette and none are properly furnished. I have enjoyed the *wonderful* mountain vistas, more like Chinese paintings than reality, the azaleas and wild roses, the wonderful Chinese cooking and the cheerfulness of the people, roaring with laughter when all else fails and the nonsense, the improvisation. They know the brakes have gone and there are no new brakes to be got so they drive without. Too bad if something fails to get out of the way in time.[66]

He also wrote to Clarissa Churchill:

> By degrees my body has become accustomed to sleeping on an almost bare board. I have had the ignominy of a slight bout of dysentery – all that part of life is particularly revolting out here – and I am a victim of a major firework display within my stomach, rockets, Catherine wheels and a few merciful squibs make my days and nights very unsettled. ... At first I was frantic if a day was wasted, but now I am perfectly calm passing the time cleaning my shoes and talking to the driver. ... I have been very shocked by the poverty of China ... no springs apparent in any seat, teacups with handles broken. Someone complained that the hot towel was dirty. The 'waiter' replied poignantly, 'It's not dirty it's old', and the peasants have to work from the ages of five to eighty in a frantic endeavour to keep alive. It is altogether a very different picture than the one most Europeans imagine.[67]

On 29 April the British party set off for the return journey in two trucks. Cecil paused to take a snapshot and thus missed a serious accident, for thirty minutes later the first truck went 'over the khud', fell forty feet, somersaulted three times and scattered baggage, clothing and passengers everywhere. Mercifully nobody was killed, but Gordon Grimsdale broke a leg. 'Only by a very short snapshot exposure had I escaped,' noted Cecil. 'I am sorry to admit that my reactions were very selfish and I wondered how on earth I would ever get away from this place as arrangements were made to return to Pihu.'[68] Presently they set off again, as Cecil wrote to Enid Bagnold:

There have been delays through bad weather, bridges swept away, and rivers too high, air passage disappointments, and all the time so very far from radio, rail, or the outside world. It has been an experience, but too long. One's senses cannot remain keen for so many weeks on end, and the discomfort has been such that I shall always feel I am luxuriating in future. The smells have been the worst part of all, the bugs, spitting, the dirt and the exhaustion have all been preferable to these revolting dumps of human manure, kept prizedly as being worth its weight in gold, certainly in China. It took us about three weeks travelling to get back to the airdrome and on the last stretch of road, they were fertilizing the rice fields. I feel weak at the remembrance of things passed by![69]

Cecil's discomforts on the trip included headaches in hot sun, pyjamas that got soused in petrol, the skin of his thigh painfully rubbed off, and having to spit superstitiously every time he saw a magpie (and they flew past in profusion). He became pensive, feeling he had only fifteen years of work ahead and wondering if he should get married. However, he thought the trip had done him good:

It has been just what I needed, and the toughness of the trip has been beneficial too. For it does no one harm to get tired and to walk too much, to be either too hot or too cold, to go hungry for a few hours. I am heartened to realize how well my constitution stands up to these tests. But I have become painfully conscious of my limitations and mental weaknesses. My brain is a poor one, poorly trained.[70]

He had found it hard to concentrate or assimilate information. He had learned how to respect his fellow passengers but was conscious of 'their intuitive knowledge that I am not one of them'. He had enjoyed his attempts at being 'a sport about everything', but he clung in secret to his 'selfish interest'. In some ways he wished he were 'more of an all round man, for at the moment I feel my talents are very weak and remote'.[71]

Leo Handley-Derry confirmed later that Cecil had done his best and had put on a good show even when very tired. They felt protective towards him and appreciated that whereas they had been in China for four years, he was a newcomer to this kind of life.

Eventually on 24 May they reached Chungking, where Cecil found letters from home: 'the first for three months, and I now only realize, by contrast, how miserable I have been for the last month seeing no one that is at all near to me or my interests'.[72]

He was anxious to escape home and even the comfort of the Embassy could not dispel his disappointment at learning that he had to stay on. A feature of his second stay with the Seymours was the presence of the rubber merchant Walter Fletcher, then on special service in the Far East, who was ensconced in the better of the guest rooms. Lady Seymour recalled Cecil's antipathy to this somewhat bluff businessman and how on several occasions Fletcher appeared to leave and Cecil at once commandeered his room, only to have to debunk when Fletcher returned.

'Cecil sent a ten-page report to the Ministry of Information complaining about their organization in India. Then on 27 May a telegram was sent from Hugh Francis with his verdict on the final consignment of Indian negatives and the first Chinese ones. He thought the processing much better but wanted more detailed captions. Three hundred SEAC negatives were lost. The Indian pictures showed too many British personalities. Francis trusted 'Chinese material will be predominantly Chinese showing especially life and war effort of the people'.[73] Francis wanted Cecil to spend longer in China and a further six to eight weeks in India, filling gaps, especially 'typical village life scenes, schools, hospitals and social services featuring Indians'.[74] As Cecil took this in he noted: 'I become more and more sorry for myself, considering it unfair that I should be put to such needless efforts in order that the Min's files are stocked but no attention paid to seeing that my work is reproduced.'[75] *Vogue* was also disappointed that Cecil had sent so few articles and that the Ministry released so few pictures.

Cecil drew and photographed many Chinese celebrities including generals, governors and leading educators. He relished the exquisite Mrs K.C. Wu, wife of the Mayor of Chungking (a leading Chinese Nationalist), but was not impressed by the Vice-President's son, Mr Kung ('with a face like a foetus he had all the complexes of a short man together with all the faults of a rich man's son').[76] His father, Dr Kung, 'the arch rogue of the present regime',[77] was portrayed at the Parliament building. Cecil 'could not help admiring the old toad',[78] who was replaced later in the year by T.V. Soong. Then Cecil came face to face with one of the most formidable characters he met on his Far Eastern tour. General Carton de Wiart* had one hand, one eye and a VC won in the Great War. 'Cyrano with assurance'[79] was how Cecil described him to Diana Cooper. Cecil became intrigued by him. The General had no knowledge of politics but spoke on all matters with complete frankness. His temper was legendary and he was known to turn dark purple at the slightest provocation. He was difficult to work for, but as his ADC pointed out, 'He was not given a VC for knitting. He is of the stuff of which the young ones today are not made. He is a blade, the sharp blade of a sword.'[80] Cecil felt sure that he must have his moments of pathos, but his only problems were having to get up in the night (he had been shot through the bladder) and feeling cold in his handless arm. Otherwise, as the ADC said, 'He has a wonderful life and enjoys every moment of it.'[81]

*Lieutenant-General Adrian Carton de Wiart, VC (1880–1963). Churchill's special military representative with General Chiang Kai-shek, 1943–6. Knighted 1945. Author of *Happy Odyssey*, a book of racy memoirs, not recommended for the squeamish.

Most of all Cecil hoped to photograph the Generalissimo and Madame Chiang Kai-shek, but the Head of State was elusive or too busy and his wife was suffering apparently from a skin disease. She had kept one American photographer waiting for ten weeks. Cecil was more than disappointed to miss them: 'It is intolerable that I should come this far to be ignored,'[82] he wrote. Later he discovered that there were matrimonial problems; a Miss Chen was having a baby by the General and Madame Chiang was sufficiently westernized to be taking this badly.

News of the D-Day landings came on 6 June 1944. Then Cecil visited Chengtu to boost the cultural side of his portfolio. He photographed ministers, professors, a hideous bride, and a gruesome amputation at the Canadian Mission Hospital. Back in Chungking he was sent off to photograph two more ministers, two factories and a fire-engine. Cecil became aggravated by a further fierce telegram from the Ministry of Information demanding fortnightly reports on his work. Exhaustion and dysentery brought him low, but he was pleased to hear that the Ambassador would write to Brendan Bracken 'telling him of my prowess and that in the present conditions of flap, I could not be expected to do more'.[83] He bade 'a really deeply affectionate and grateful farewell to the Seymours whom I have come to admire enormously'.[84] As he wrote to Juliet Duff: 'The Seymours have been angelic in ministering to me. But for them I would have found life very hard here. As it is I am leaving without regrets, and having received a terrific series of impressions, one contrasting the other.'[85]

INDIA

Cecil's aeroplane left China in pouring rain. His hand trembled with fear. But gradually the climate changed and he landed in tropical Calcutta:

> At last this was something I had dreamt of for so long! The relief and satisfaction was terrific. I had a headache, was exhausted, but in such teeming spirits of relief. The freedom of escaping from China was like coming out of jail, of being free of the Gestapo.[86]

His sojourn in Calcutta was soured for him by the arrival of a most self-confident Noël Coward, then on a tour giving troop concerts. Despite their reconciliation, Cecil shared the view of Emerald Cunard: 'He's too slick. He's the Artful Dodger of society.'[87] Noël was at his best when singing new songs, and at his worst when discussing politics:

> Noël shouted and said he had become more and more imperialistic and would like to beat the black and yellow buggers down the street. Only way to comply [sic] with them. Why do a lot of intellectuals talk balls

and give them self government. Not fit to look after themselves. Much too sweeping statements and too sweeping a condemnation of Delhi.[88]

The next day Lord Louis Mountbatten arrived and there was a big dinner-party:

> Noël very excited. Supremo looked rattled and rugged, untidy, dirty boots. Did not wish to see some of the generals that had been assembled. Dinner went well, was extremely informal. I sat next to Supremo who was in light mood and only wishing to make jokes. No intention of listening to China's troubles which Mrs C[asey] had asked me to expound upon, but thoroughly frivolous about our photographing in the glass bed at Faridkot House. Noël galvanized almost jumping out of his skin, trembling, face contorted. Determination to be amused.[89]

Later Noël played the piano, stealing the show and leaving Cecil out in the cold. The next day Cecil looked out of his window and observed Coward being photographed with thirty Indian journalists after a press conference: 'This was success and Noël was enjoying it.'[90] It caused Cecil to reconsider his own role with advice from the sensitive ADC John Irwin (who had been on the point of a nervous breakdown on his last visit). Irwin said: 'It is not so interesting to see what Noël Coward has done for the world as it is to see what the world has done for Noël Coward.'[91] Noël talked only of himself. Irwin's Indian friend Bishron thought Cecil naïve and superficial, and that he had no real contact with the outside world. He told him he must put more conviction into his photography:

> I realized that all the pictures I have done on this trip mean nothing to me at all, are no advance, are a wedge between me and my art, that I have relied solely on technique.[92]

Irwin urged Cecil to photograph the difference between factory workers coming on duty and those coming off, primitive forms of worship, sacrifice and superstition. Cecil noted that the talk with John had been 'a real jolt' and that Noël's presence had pulled him 'up to my fullest stature of consciousness'.[93]

After three weeks in Calcutta Cecil flew back to Delhi, where he learned that his London house had been somewhat damaged by bombs and that his childhood friend Gwen Le Bas had died in the bombing of Guards Chapel during a service. He stayed once more at the Viceroy's House and Noël Coward again dogged his path by giving a successful concert to 600 people in the Durbah Hall. Cecil and Noël ended up quarrelling about the designer Gladys Calthrop (whose son had just become a war casualty).

The Viceroy questioned Cecil about his visit to China, but all the stories pointed to the same end: the hopelessness of the situation. On 12 July Cecil and Billy Henderson took the train to Simla, where they stayed in the Viceregal Lodge with the Wavells and their entourage. Peter Coats took him to see the Leave Camp, but otherwise Cecil found himself worn out with fatigue. Even a gossip with Coats about Sybil Colefax left him unmoved: 'maybe it is that I am surfeited with social life that I am now so very much less interested in it than I used to be during the past twenty years'.[94]

Cecil was relieved that he could head homewards and wrote to Clarissa Churchill: 'I can't take in any more impressions. There was a suggestion I go to Australia, but oh no not now please. I long for home even with the flying bombs.'[95]

He left Simla for Delhi on 24 July. Lady Wavell, whom Cecil thought sometimes disliked him, was particularly friendly. And Cecil thought that in the Viceroy he had a firm friend: 'It is really a genuine sympathy that he feels for me and how could I be but flattered?'[96]

A grim flight was to take Cecil from Delhi to Karachi. He would lie on the floor, sweating, feeling frightened and sick, in some pain. There would be endless hanging about, rollcalls, delays and frustrations. But leaving Simla he was alone with his thoughts for the first time in many days. 'This was farewell to India,'[97] he wrote, and the car circled down the hairpin bends taking him away.

HOMEWARDS

Cecil flew to America via Aden, Elfasher, Maidugari, Cairo, Accra, Natal, Brazil, Trinidad, Puerto Rico, not to mention the vulgarity of Miami, and arrived in New York, where he soon picked up the threads of the old life. There was one shock to face – the death of Rex Whistler on 18 July: 'I have seldom felt so upset. ... I sobbed uncontrollably.'[98] Cecil welcomed the photographer Louise Dahl-Wolfe's attack on the prevalent American attitude to the war. She complained to the editors of *Harper's*: 'Why can't I take a picture of President Roosevelt or be sent to Normandy. It makes me sick that we go on taking these awful clothes.'[99] Cecil was horrified that the fall of Paris was hailed with delight 'as a means of getting at Paris fashions quick'.[100]

He was also depressed at his prospects of earning a living. He was bored with the thought of photography, but knew that he could not escape it. The *Vogue* people in New York did not let him forget his Jew row misdemeanour. At a weekend party Edna Chase took him out onto the verandah and told him there had been some adverse publicity. Forty pages of advertising had been lost on his account recently. She discussed with him her worries that he should do any work for them other than war work. Cecil was very depressed, worried and upset. His old ally, Eleanor Lambert, produced some useful publicity for him and, when he asked her how much he owed her, she said simply, 'How would you like to go and jump in the lake?'[101] On 4 September Cecil took his first fashion photographs for *Vogue* for seven years and the next day took portrait studies of 'a fat-faced, well-mannered little college girl',[102] the sixteen-year-old Shirley Temple. Before he left New York he succeeded in clearing the air, and soon after his return to London the new art director, Alexander Liberman, wrote to tell him 'the whole magazine improved ever since we published your drawings and photographs'.[103] Cecil thought of his New York visit in retrospect with great affection: 'It had made me feel ten years younger, had given me more confidence and the knowledge that after the war I can earn money.'[104] He felt even more relief and excitement to return to London than after his Near East trip. He was delighted to discover that his China pictures had come out excellently.

During the remaining months of war, Cecil staged an exhibition of his war work in Paris. Staying at the British Embassy for a month with Duff Cooper (now out there as Ambassador) and Lady Diana, he saw Churchill and De Gaulle lay wreaths on Clemenceau's tomb on Armistice Day 1944. 'I am always near to tears on these occasions,' he noted, 'but this seemed particularly moving. All day long the repesentatives of the Liberation marched past the Arc de Triomphe.'[105] Cecil also toured the front lines with Churchill and the General. He spent the early part of 1945 at work on his book, *Far East*. The war drew to its close and on 4 May 1945 Cecil wrote:

The good news has little reality for me. The one o'clock news which for so long has filled one with a feeling of dread or disappointment now tells of the complete collapse of Germany. No longer is there that dread feeling in the pit of the stomach.... Mussolini dead. Goebbels dead. Hitler dead. Unconditional surrender of the German army, air force and great destruction done to a fleeing navy. Any moment we expect the final word of triumph. Yet Hitler has succeeded in bringing a gloom throughout the world. No one can celebrate in a Europe that must continue to suffer so appallingly. But it is a great boon to think that the great miseries are over, and that the nightmares of the concentration camps are no longer in existence to prove that we are living in a period of barbarism that by far outshines the horrors of any medieval or biblical age.[106]

The King's speech a few nights later was relayed in 'silence so great that only the twittering of the birds could be heard, the birds revelling in the branches of the newly covered trees'.

Cecil was not the same man in 1945 that he had been in 1939. He had become much more of an establishment figure. Whereas before the war he would have dismissed brigadiers as ridiculous old fogeys, he had now had the chance to be impressed by the importance of their work. His values had altered. He would rather despise old friends who had remained in luxury while others had risked their lives. He had made himself useful during the war and on many occasions shown unexpected bravery and inner courage. His war photographs are already judged an extraordinary illustration of the contemporary holocaust. Even in 1946 Peter Quennell was writing in the *Daily Mail*:

> To say that they are among his best photographs is saying a good deal. Beaton (who used years ago to revel in spangled nebulosities and flimsy, fussy whim-whams) is now commendably direct and clear-cut, yet tempers his matter-of-fact approach with an uncommon sense of beauty.[107]

Reviewing his book *Far East*, published in late 1945,* Desmond MacCarthy was one of those who praised Cecil's penetrating writing and his sensitive matter-of-factness: 'His descriptions are those of the painter rather than poet and they are more remarkable for detail than for panoramas or vistas.'[108]

Edith Olivier wrote to Cecil: 'It's a wonderful record of an unimaginable experience and you are a very great man to have endured it without returning a twisted deformed lunatic!'[109]

Years later Cecil found that on re-reading his diaries very little of his experiences had left 'even the slightest residue of memory'.[110] After his death Gail Buckland, the photographic historian, concluded that Cecil's war photographs were surprising, sincere, subjective and a demonstration of the breadth of his talents:

> His knowledge of how to light a face, create a dramatic background, spot a symbolic action, humanize a sitter, see beauty, use abstraction, arouse sympathy and compose a picture ensured that this body of work was varied and stimulating. The mood of the photographs changes according to what Beaton thought proper in a certain situation, according to how he felt. Some of the work combines to produce a coherent statement, as in his series on the Royal Air Force. The Chinese and Indian photographs, however, seem amorphous as a group, but are individually powerful.[111]

*In the same year Cecil published *India* (Thacker and Co., Bombay) and two illustrated works, *Indian Album*, dedicated to Lord Wavell, and *Chinese Album*, dedicated to Clarissa Churchill. In June 1945, Maie Casey arranged an exhibition of Cecil's India photographs in Calcutta.

Part Six

The Garbo Years 1945–52

22

The Passing of a House

*The expulsion from Ashcombe was a great sadness to me.
Love, marriage, death, the passing of a house – these are
the milestones of life and they point a finger to the clock.*

Ashcombe, p. 124

A bomb fell on the hill near Ashcombe on 14 May 1944, damaging the
keeper's cottage, blowing out all Ashcombe's windows and dislodging a
ceiling. This damage had been put right but besides that the place had
fallen into disrepair. Cecil's relations with the owner, Mr R.W. Borley, and
his son Mr Hugh Borley, had deteriorated accordingly. The tennis court was
now a jungle of nettles and many of the statues lay crumbling in the long
grass. A schedule of dilapidations was served on Cecil in October 1944.
Acrimonious correspondence was exchanged from solicitor to solicitor.
Shortly after the end of the war came the thunderbolt news that Cecil's
tenure of Ashcombe was to be terminated when his lease expired on 24
June 1945. His departure date was fixed for 29 September.

In the summer Cecil spent as much time as possible amongst 'the sleeping
beauty, the overgrown weeds, the melancholy trees'[1] of his idyllic hideaway.
He worked on a play, but with such difficulty that he was often tetchy with
his family and too highly strung to sleep at night. Then he began to write
a book about his house:

> In the blue haze of summer heat the trees looked so beautiful that my
> anguish at parting is very acute and I can hardly imagine that I have
> only two or three more weekends here. I have been for long walks in the
> hills and with the yellow tansy like some exotic hothouse flowers and all
> the wild flowers I feel I have never seen it look more lovely.[2]

In August John and Gillian Sutro came down for a last weekend. Afterwards John described his feelings:

> It was kind of you to ensure that I visited ASHCOMBE once more, and so
> many memories flooded my mind of the fragrant times I had spent there.

It is curious that I didn't think of Ashcombe as a house where I stayed, but as the highest point of the life I most enjoyed leading. Your sadness at leaving can be tempered by the thought that you created at Ashcombe for your friends an atmosphere of rarefied aesthetic and physical enjoyment, which they could never have found elsewhere. I don't think you could have repeated this atmosphere at Ashcombe in this decade. Circumstances, you, they – all have changed so much and the ghosts of the past might have haunted you too much. But your genius for bringing out the latest elegance, wit or passion of our circle can continue elsewhere, and perhaps as the times permit no farewell party at Ashcombe I can thank you on behalf of all the hands on the bathroom wall for giving us something so solid and enduring to look back on. I am glad that you will write a book on Ashcombe, for I think it should be made clear that we were not a group of Elizabeth Ponsonby's dressing up purposelessly and I should be sorry to see the sort of distorted legends which have sprung up about the nineties attaching themselves to our innocent and agreeable enjoyments.

You will forgive me as your sincere friend saying that recently I have found a certain melancholy in your outlook; please realize how much you mean to your friends and how much you have done for them; and let us, now that the war is over, endeavour to recreate the reality of the society which was at Ashcombe: for after all it was not *'genius loci'* but you who made it.[3]

Peter Watson, whose visits were once so eagerly awaited, was now in a clinic in Lugano, suffering from jaundice. He wrote:

How sad for you to leave Ashcombe. I am so sorry. It makes such an awful break in one's life changing house especially now, end of war, autumn etc. And oh the horror of getting rid of the stuff and rubbish of years it is like tearing out one's guts.... It is a lesson in improving other people's properties, improvements which will go for little enough with Mr Boredom I suppose![4]

In one sense Cecil's father had been right to warn him not to pour money into rented premises, but in another he was quite wrong. Ashcombe represented the happiest phase of Cecil's life and he never regretted a penny of its expense. Appropriately Edith Olivier was the last guest:

I cried all the way home and heard nothing of Major Harrison's faint babbling which never ceased at my side! It is the end of a wonderful creation.... Dearest Cecil, the brain which created Ashcombe is still creating and I only hope I shall live to see the next thing you do.[5]

In 1950, 5,500 copies of Cecil's book, *Ashcombe*, were published and Cecil was paid £250. One of its readers was Lord Wavell, who wondered shortly before his death:

> Would Ashcombe have seemed the same in these drab post-war years? Can you console yourself at all with the idea that it may be better as a memory of things that were, that it might be more haunted than enchanted for you now? I suppose not.[6]

Arthur Bryant reviewed the book in 1950: 'Mr Beaton is not only an artist; he can write. His account of his wartime visit to China was one of the best of the war. His tribute of love for his lost home equals it.'[7]

Cecil was not there when the furniture was removed and only on one occasion did he ever dare descend again into the valley. He always regretted having to leave and felt that he never again found such magic or such a haunting and beautiful atmosphere. In later life he used to return to the top of the hill and gaze down into the tree-covered valley towards the hidden house. Hugh Borley settled in this house in 1945 and he has protected his privacy with firm resolve. Cecil's era is recalled as a time when the pheasants were disturbed too often by ambling houseguests, and when notoriety descended with rumours of sunbathers in scanty costumes which, though the rage in Venice, were an outrage in this rustic corner of Wiltshire.

The theatre now became the focal point of Cecil's work. He had spent much of the winter of 1944 and spring of 1945 photographing stage productions. For John Gielgud he photographed *Hamlet*, *The Circle*, *The Duchess of Malfi* and *A Midsummer Night's Dream*. He took portraits of stage figures such as Ivor Novello, Diana Wynyard, Emlyn Williams, Margaret Leighton and Dulcie Gray; and Lynn Fontanne in Rattigan's *Love and Idleness*. In the summer of 1945 he photographed *The First Gentleman* with Robert Morley, Wendy Hiller and Rex Harrison, and reviewed it in the *Sunday Chronicle* on 22 July.

Cecil's opportunity to design for the West End theatre materialized in 1945 when Binkie Beaumont, the high priest of H.M. Tennent, put on *Lady Windermere's Fan*, starring Isabel Jeans, Athene Seyler and Dorothy Hyson. Cecil was determined to make the production as lavish as possible in order to sweep away the drab war years at a stroke. John Gielgud was inspired by his ideas for scenery and costumes and thought they justified the revival of this essentially slight play. Cecil was given £200 on account of one per cent of the gross weekly box office receipts. Binkie Beaumont thought the inspiration for the sets should be based on Chips Channon's house in Belgrave Square. Cecil drew on his own experiences for inspiration: the candy-striped silk favoured by the actress Elfie Perry, the dark green walls of a London club hung with prints in serried rows, the gilded garlands of the Bow Room in Buckingham Palace. There were endless complications. One scene at the end of the play had to be transferred to the beginning, and a chandelier was found to obscure guests entering the ball room and had to be removed. Gielgud's doddery aunt Mabel Terry-Lewis had to be replaced by Athene Seyler because she could not remember the names Lord Windermere and Lord Darlington. Gielgud and Binkie Beaumont insisted on having one scene white. 'Can I help at all, Cecil?' asked John Gielgud as Cecil staggered in laden with pink flowers. 'No,' he replied. 'Just congratulate me.' Gielgud recalled: 'He liked to get his way. Both he and Oliver Messel were terrible *prima donnas*.'[8]

The play opened in Sheffield in March and went to Oxford in June. From the start Cecil was deluged with praise:

> The hero of the evening is Mr Cecil Beaton. He has mounted the play in an Edwardian French set which surpasses the richest of Osbert Lancaster's period fantasies. And his costumes must be the most brilliant and striking that have been seen on the stage for years.[9]

In London the reviewers used nouns like 'splendour' and 'gorgeousness', and adjectives such as 'beautiful', 'magnificent', 'enchanting', 'lavish' and 'delicious'. Only Philip Hope-Wallace struck a critical note, considering that Cecil had not been entirely successful in establishing a *fin-de-siècle* atmosphere: 'Much of this is like a walk through a museum and the charm – which is the charm of an old *Punch* joke – fails to come up as fresh as it should.'[10] None the less *Lady Windermere's Fan* played to capacity audiences at the Haymarket for 428 performances. Isabel Jeans again had the audiences gasping as she appeared in a colour Cecil created for her called 'flamingo pink'. The ballroom scene was nothing short of a fashion parade. Cecil gave a ticket to his old patron, Lady Alexander, who duly tottered into the foyer. Her husband, Sir George, had played Lord Windermere in the original production in 1892.

Cecil also produced sets and costumes for Binkie Beaumont's revival of the Pinero farce, *Dandy Dick*, which toured Manchester, Leeds and other places, starring the plump comedian Sydney Howard and the crotchety veteran actor A.E. Matthews. This 'Gothic revival with an ecclesiastical note'[11] gave Cecil great pleasure: 'I think the farce will revive well and the dresses – tartan, piccalilli and ginger coloured – are a distinct contrast to Lady Winderbags,'[12] he wrote to Lady Diana Cooper. His originality and sense of balance were praised by the reviewers.

For some years Cecil had harboured a strong ambition to write a play. As early as October 1942 he records:

> I have come away appalled by the task in front of me but more than ever burning with the desire to write a play – and a successful play – and one that must make a real 'stir' – for though I feel the theatre has eluded me all these years it was my first love and I shall only be happy to go back to it.[13]

To this end Cecil spent part of the winter of 1945 in Enid Bagnold's Dale Cottage. Here he could work peacefully and he and Enid could discuss the manifold problems of an endeavour on which they had both set their hearts. Enid, having had some success with *Lottie Dundass*, was now trying to place *Poor Judas* and *National Velvet*. Diana Cooper who had listened politely to their earlier attempts – 'both *awful*' – described this phase as Cecil and Enid 'yawning over each other's plays'.[14]

During these years Cecil was also a frequent visitor to the British Embassy in Paris. Performing his traditional role he had helped Diana Cooper transform the famous old building into something stylish. He relished time spent with the group she gathered round her, known as 'La Bande'. This included Bébé Bérard, the Bourdets, Marie-Louise Bousquet, Georges and Nora Auric and others. Through Cecil, Cocteau (who had a bad reputation as a collaborator) infiltrated himself into their number. Towards the end of the year there was a revival of the old rivalry between Cecil and Oliver Messel. Gabriel Pascal was to direct Shaw's *Caesar and Cleopatra*, a film with Vivien Leigh and Claude Rains. Oliver consulted Cecil about the proposed fee. Cecil told him to ask for considerably more and then promptly rang the producer to say he would do it himself for considerably less. The attempt to oust his rival did not work and Oliver got the job. This unedifying incident is still quoted to Cecil's discredit by those in the Messel camp.

In February 1946 Cecil sailed on a troopship via Canada to New York. He was irritated to find that *Vogue* had few assignments to offer him, but was pleased to be asked to design the décor for *Cyrano*. He worked on this for three weeks and then suddenly José Ferrer telephoned to say that he had heard Cecil was a Fascist and had an appalling reputation. He refused to employ him:

> So after eight years the old Jewish row had asserted itself again. I was in despair. I could hardly sleep. I felt my career ruined. I spent hours talking about various ways of combating the old difficulties and consulted by the hour my lawyer and new friend Arnold Weissberger. We had a horrible interview with backers of the production who had refused to risk their money in a venture in which I was in any way connected. I did not get the job. I went to see Mr Bernays, a public relations magnate who might help whitewash my reputation. He could do nothing but advise me to keep a 'passionate anonymity'.[15]

Cecil felt that anything he might do would be thwarted. Barbara Payne asked him to design *An Ideal Husband*, but he turned it down. Instead he tore up a letter of refusal and accepted the challenge of doing *Lady Windermere's Fan* in California: 'Perhaps out there there would be less opposition.'[16]

In the spring of 1946 there occurred what Cecil described as 'one of the

greatest events in my life'.[17] This was his second meeting with Greta Garbo
at a party in New York given by Margaret Case. This time Garbo reappeared
in his life escorted by her Russian friend, Georges Schlee. He had discovered
a delicatessen which imported caviar direct from Russia and he and Garbo
had invited themselves round to drink vodka and eat a pot of 'the real thing'.

Greta Garbo

When Cecil saw Garbo he was so taken aback by her beauty that he had
to hold on to the back of a chair. She gave him some caviar on a biscuit.
He examined her appearance: she was much thinner now, her nose spikier.
He knew she remembered him when she said: 'I didn't wear lipstick when
you knew me before.'[18] Cecil told her it looked 'like a child that had been to
the jam cupboard'.[19] There were lines when she smiled. The perfection was
gone:

> The uncompromising beauty of mouse blonde hair, the scrawny hands
> a bit weathered, the ankles and feet a bit poor and bumpy-looking. Has
> no look of luxury. The hat like a pierrot – Callot – the highwayman shirt.
> The incredible eyes and lids, and blue, clear iris. Historic beauty.[20]

Suddenly it seemed Garbo was about to leave. Cecil hijacked her onto the
roof terrace. They were soon involved in a long conversation as the cold bit
through them high above the lights of Park Avenue. Cecil was determined
to blurt out his new-found feelings. She promised to ring him. When they
met several days later, Garbo told him that she hated wearing underclothes
or being restricted in any way. She also told him her vertebrae were easily
put out of line, yet she evidently let Cecil touch them. On their third meeting
she said: 'I follow the fleet. I don't know what it means, but I often say
things that only mean something if you scratch below the surface.'[21]

At this meeting, somewhat prematurely, Cecil proffered a proposal of marriage. It was received with Garbo's characteristic evasiveness: 'Good heavens. Well this is so sudden. I once said to a friend of mine who asked me out to lunch: "But really this is very frivolous of you." I don't think you should speak so frivolously.'[22] One night at a party given by Mona Harrison Williams they danced in 'a blackened room with furniture stacked under dust covers and light coming through windows from street lamps'.[23] Afterwards Cecil waved to Garbo as she retreated homewards down the street.

It was during this springtime of 1946 that Garbo suddenly said to Cecil: 'I wonder ... If you weren't such a grand and elegant photographer ...' Cecil said: 'Then you'd ask me to take a passport photograph for you?' Garbo posed for Cecil and many photographs were taken. As he wrote later: 'The results formed a prized collection – though few of them were suitable for passports.'[24]

Cecil always maintained that Garbo 'put a pencilled cross on those of which she approved and would allow me to publish in *Vogue* magazine'.[25] Accordingly he sent the selection to Alexander Liberman, who was overjoyed. Cecil described the pictures as 'a precious windfall'.[26]

Meanwhile Cecil believed that his romance with Garbo was progressing in a positive way. He felt he had received enough encouragement to write 'bombshell' letters to his mother and Maud Nelson. His mother replied:

Your letter received last evening and I'm not quite collected yet to realize what you are up to. As you say it is a 'bombshell' but I could not be more delighted if it is your happiness and everything turns out for the best and as you wish! You have always loved and admired Greta (her Rose is still framed above your bed) and it seems so strange you should meet again and all this should happen. It's a very big and serious step to take but you are quite wise enough to know what is the best for your future. I am longing to know what the future will tell for you and your financial side which we can't make out in any way.[27]

To this Maud Nelson added:

Your bombshell letters arrived last night and neither your Mummie or I have recovered yet from the news and the various implications. We laughed and cried and hugged each other and finally wanted a whisky and soda to pull us together.[28]

Maud advised Cecil to enjoy his new romance, to be careful not to get hurt and not to dwell too much on 'the marriage side of the whole thing'.[29] She added a note of warning: 'I have had friends in the past who knew her very intimately, so that I am well aware of the secretive and elusive qualities she possesses as well as the greatness and nobility of her character.'[30]

But Cecil's enthusiasm was somewhat premature. The romance went no further than visiting the Paleys' house for Easter and picking dark purple violets, or attending one of Madame (Valentina) Schlee's famous Russian Easter parties. On 21 May 1946 Garbo left for California and Cecil summed up the situation:

> Meanwhile I met Greta and we spent the time together, exchanging badinage, walking in the park while the buds of Spring opened. We spent many happy hours in each other's company and this was one of the greatest events in my life. One day she said she was due back to the coast and I cried at the idea of her departure. As it happened my last weeks were so hectic in N.Y. without her being there.[31]

Cecil sailed for England on 1 June. He designed the ballet *Les Sirènes*, which was choreographed by Freddie Ashton, with music composed by Lord Berners. He found the work exhausting as he reported to Enid Bagnold, from Faringdon:

> I used to whip off these things in a few moments, but I don't know whether one takes more trouble as one grows older, or whether it is merely that one has not so much vitality, but I find it takes me so much longer to get the results.[32]

Les Sirènes was set in an Edwardian seaside resort. When Clarissa saw it, she wrote: 'Your clothes were exquisite. I liked the oddly *sultry* colours, *but* I think the scenery has been abominably painted.'[33]

In the midst of this Cecil telephoned Garbo in Hollywood. She told him that she was upset that more than one photograph was being published in *Vogue*. The blame must rest with Cecil because his mother wrote to him: 'I was afraid you overdid it without her consent. At any rate she may come round when you see her. I hope so.'[34] It was, of course, too late for Cecil to stop publication even if he wanted to. In July 1946 Garbo paid her first visit to Sweden since 1939, a trip ruined by press harassment. Cecil sent her flowers, but for two years she refused to acknowledge them. She was furious about the photos, and when she returned to America she refused to answer any of Cecil's calls, letters or telegrams. At times he resorted to Peter Watson techniques, quoting his letter which read: 'You cannot dismiss me like a recalcitrant housemaid.'[35]

Some time later, on 7 October, when he was back in New York, Cecil telephoned Garbo in California. When she heard it was 'New York' calling she thought it was Schlee and answered. She was quite friendly and said, 'knowing that 2,000 miles separated us "Come on over now." "No, but can I come later?" – "No, only now."' Cecil told her he thought she enjoyed making him suffer and she said: 'I wouldn't do anything to any human being to make them suffer.'[36] Anxious not to be a bore, he left a gap of a month after a series of unsatisfactory telephone calls. Just after Christmas

1946 he telephoned: 'She was frankly delighted to hear me and accepted my advances without reservation.'[37] She urged him again to come right over and talked 'some nonsense I couldn't understand about bringing a pillow when I went to see her – a crimson velvet pillow'.[38] However Cecil and Garbo did not meet again until the winter of 1947.

Cecil sailed for New York in July 1946 and flew to California on the 14th. Whereas he had loved Hollywood in the 1920s, he now found it vulgar: 'There is no standard of taste at all.'[39] He set up *Lady Windermere's Fan* and worked on his play in his spare time, rising daily at 6.30.

The San Francisco production of *Lady Windermere's Fan* was more expensive than the London one. There were many more guests in the ballroom scene and Cecil was able to use 4,000 artificial roses. The absence of Isabel Jeans was deeply regretted, and it proved hard to find English-looking character actors. 'I decided overnight at Cole Porter's after a lot of whisky to step into the role of Cecil Graham,' he wrote to Diana Cooper. 'It's a little plum part and I'm going, God willing, to play it for another six weeks.'[40] Cecil worried as to the advisability of venturing on to the stage, even with such foolproof lines, still wondering if his 'Kike' misdemeanour would catch up with him. His mother and Maud and many others were dead set against it, while John Gielgud was encouraging: 'Your English style will no doubt put all the other gentlemen to bed. I speak figuratively, of course.'[41] So was Clarissa. The play opened in a blaze of publicity in Santa Barbara on 23 August and then in San Francisco on the 26th. Cecil designed the costumes for himself and co-actors, amongst whom were Penelope Dudley Ward, Estelle Winwood and Cornelia Otis Skinner. His sets were given the highest possible praise. Opinions only vary as to whether or not Cecil was a good actor. Oliver Smith described him as 'a very gifted amateur',[42] and his later amanuensis, Waldemar Hansen, said: 'He was not the world's greatest actor but his voice was marvellously Oscar Wilde.'[43] Lincoln Kirstein saw him in New York and wrote: 'I think you yourself were so good, so poised and so professional.'[44] So did Elsa Maxwell, who was very impressed and wrote in her column: 'He has a gay recklessness and abandon which is irresistible. Each Wilde classic delivered by Cecil was beautifully timed and was tossed off casually as *bon mots* should be.'[45] Cecil certainly enjoyed the experience and the thrill of getting his weekly pay packet was immense. He took an hour and a half to put on his make-up. That he ventured on the boards at all was courageous and added a further dimension to an already diverse career.

The *Lady Windermere's Fan* production came in the midst of the long silence from Garbo. But it was at the same time that Cecil heard reports that gossip about them was circulating in London. Emerald Cunard was at the centre of it and most unwisely Cecil sent her a telegram entreating her to have mercy. Alas, this merely fuelled the flames. Every time Cecil went on stage and heard Mrs Erlynne declare: 'What happened last night shall be my secret. Don't let's spoil it by telling it to anyone,'*⁴⁶ he felt contrite. 'Only if the whole relationship is really genuine and whole-hearted on both sides can it survive the intrigue that has now built around it.'⁴⁷ He wrote to Clarissa Churchill, 'Perhaps it will be useful to have such a test. Greta arrives in New York this week – and it will be interesting to know how she will receive me – if at all. She is a most easily hurt and startled creature and Lord Kemsley's reporters have been about as swinish as possible.'⁴⁸ Clarissa was sympathetic:

> Emerald has been terrible. I so understand your desire to tell people – then the sickening remorse and terror once one has told – sickening because it *does* take the bloom off – and terrifying because one may have ruined the thing itself. I'm afraid it's no good appealing to E's better nature.... You must lie about the gossip, and swear you have told no-body (after all it would have got out from you having been together so much anyway) and say you are sickened by it as much as she is – and perhaps suggest you only meet really in secret. Whatever you do you must not consider, either from you or from her, not meeting at all.⁴⁹

James Pope-Hennessy also wrote:

> Clarissa and I still feel you are not conducting yr arrangements with great discretion but then it is your life and you understand it, the tele-gram to Emerald seems to *me* as rash as hysterical – and *utterly* misguided but there it is. I frankly think the presence of the Oggie circle† so near the centre of yr private life an infinite danger ... do for God's sake tear this up.⁵⁰

One day Cecil drove to visit Garbo's house. He found the address, No. 622 North Bedford Drive, Beverly Hills, and was shocked to see photographs of framed celebrities such as Elsie Mendl and Greer Garson. 'With disgust I left,'⁵¹ he wrote, only to discover that this was in fact the house of Henry Crocker, a socialite, used by Garbo as a poste restante. She lived at No. 904.

After six hectic weeks as 'Cecil Graham', Cecil returned to New York to open in the Broadway production. He wondered 'if rotten tomatoes would be thrown at me or the theatre picketed by Jews who were still smarting with indignation at my ten-year-old crime'.⁵² It was a busy time and Cecil was much before the public eye. Two ballets Cecil had designed came to fruition. *Camille* opened at the Metropolitan Opera House in New York with Alicia Markova and Anton Dolin. Dolin was rather surprised that Cecil had

---

*The correct quote is: 'Don't spoil the one good thing I have done in my life by telling it to anyone. Promise me that what passed last night will remain a secret between us' (Mrs Erlynne, *Lady Windermere's Fan*, Act ɪᴠ).

† Maud Nelson, Cecil's secretary, was Oggie Lynn's girlfriend.

not produced a bed for Camille to die on. He raised the matter with Cecil who was blithely unconcerned. 'She'll have to die on the window-seat,'[53] he said. *Les Patineurs*, an Ashton ballet, opened simultaneously at the Ballet Theatre. Both these ballets were praised for their opulence and beauty.

In London *Our Betters* was revived. This had given Cecil his first chance to dress Cathleen Nesbitt, once admired by Rupert Brooke. She starred with Dorothy Dickson and Max Adrian. It was no problem for Cecil to recreate the period authentically. Following the opening, which Cecil missed, Clarissa declared it 'genuinely aesthetically *lovely*, clothes and all'.[54] Cecil also designed costumes for Lilli Palmer in the film *Beware of Pity*, directed by Maurice Elvey.

During this period Cecil did little photographic work. He was particularly disenchanted with American *Vogue*: 'Here I am most useful to them as a photographer who can flatter old women and so they give me all the difficult jobs and after working for them for fifteen years I am still asked to take an elegant photograph of three generations!!!'[55] His financial prospects were looking up. He was due £500 from *Les Sirènes*, £440 from Batsford for royalties, and he had £6,570 in his account. Then one day Alexander Korda, the Hungarian impresario, announced: 'I want to buy you.'[56] Cecil claimed that he had no wish to work in films, having long adhered to the idea that film-makers were vulgar and tasteless. 'But I don't want to be bought and I'm terribly expensive.'[57] However Korda convinced Cecil that he could make good use of all his talents as writer, designer, director and photographer. The contract was duly signed, giving Cecil a good sum and expenses of £3,000 a year. 'It has been a wonderful year for you, dear Cecil,' wrote Maud, 'and I know you appreciate your luck which has been well deserved in every way.'[58] Cecil sailed home in good spirits on the *Queen Elizabeth* on 3 January 1947.

In the end Cecil did two films for Korda, *An Ideal Husband* and *Anna Karenina*, both of them lavish productions designed to compete with Hollywood. He started work at Shepperton Studios on 24 March 1947. The routine caused an upheaval in his life as he had to rise at dawn to arrive at the studios in the cold early morning and often stayed there until eight at night.

While Cecil admired Alexander Korda, he despised his brother Vincent, whom he found sad and disillusioned 'with soul sold to the devil'.[59] Clarissa had been given a nebulous job (along with Penelope Lloyd Thomas, both on salaries of £1,000 a year), and was to find her own niche in the film world. There was a lot of publicity about these girls. Clarissa and Cecil sat together 'exhilarated and interested in Korda's direction, his incredible quickness and perception, subtlety and flair'.[60] The Hollywood star Paulette Goddard, brought over to appear in *An Ideal Husband*, arrived (causing a strike at the studio by bringing her own hairdresser) and, on the transatlantic crossing advice of Noël Coward, attempted to base her role on a mixture of Diana Cooper and Sylvia Ashley – 'really rather painful'.[61] A few lines from *A Woman of No Importance* were laboriously woven into the script in an attempt to justify Miss Goddard's American accent. The imperious Martita Hunt was summoned to improve Michael Wilding's vowel sounds but declared: 'He's too common for the part.'[62] Cecil became increasingly involved. One night he complained that some of the scenery was phoney and inelegant, causing Korda to fly into a rage. There were numerous changes of mind and of plan. Constance Collier (who struck up a rivalry with Martita Hunt) noticed that in between directing shots of *An Ideal Husband*, Korda was reading the script of *Anna Karenina*. His powers of concentration were strong. Cecil was deeply impressed at the memorandum he dictated to a stenographer at the side of the stage:

> In spite of the terrible conditions in which he had been working he had written an absolutely brilliant analysis of Tolstoy's book, of where the script had gone wrong and why and where it must be rewritten. These notes showed sensitivity, appreciation of the literary nuances and a passionate appeal to respect the great Tolstoy. It was a revelation.[63]

Likewise, Cecil did his best to uphold the highest standards but, when filming took place, it was hard not to take against the extras in crowd scenes: 'Whenever there was a bad feature of their costume to show they showed it. One felt one was battling with an army of bad taste.'[64] All in all the technicians were delighted if they achieved a minute of film each day.

In the middle of the heat-wave summer of 1947, Cecil passed from one set to another. On the *Anna Karenina* set he watched them laying down imitation snow, and Vivien Leigh struggling into a velvet suit, overcoat and sable cape. Meanwhile over at *An Ideal Husband* a dining-room table was set for a huge meal. Cecil pointed out that the Venetian glass goblets were not of the period. They were replaced by tumblers with napkins folded in them 'as if for a bourgeois wedding feast'.[65] There was great enmity, rivalry and at times boredom expressed between the two productions. One particularly bad day dawned when the Hyde Park scene in *An Ideal Husband* and the *Anna Karenina* ballroom scene were to be shot simultaneously. The ballroom guests were lined up and Julien Duvivier, the director, snarled: 'They all look like English girls that haven't had enough to eat. Get some full bosomed girls that look like Russian aristocrats.'[66] The wardrobe department that had worked all weekend to dress these extras now had to start refitting. Mary Kerridge, the doyenne of the Windsor Rep, who played Dolly Obolensky, remembered being given a white muslin dress with black spots to wear in the wedding scene. This cost £200 but could only be glimpsed for a few seconds. One day a cape that Cecil designed was dismissed until Prince Wiasemsky supported him and said his Russian mother had had one like it.

Another day Cecil arrived to find the set deserted. Korda had halted filming for a fortnight while he went to America to fight a lawsuit.

Vivien Leigh, whom Cecil found 'so carefree and intelligent in her private life',[67] proved no fun to work with. There were problems from the start. Her clothes were made specially in Paris. The corsets proved so tight and uncomfortable that she went to a doctor fearing broken ribs. Only later did Karinska discover they had been put on upside down, thus pushing in what should have been pushed out and *vice versa*. As the strain of filming intensified, she became overwhelmed by her difficulties. On the day that Olivier was knighted, Cecil burst into the dressing-room to congratulate her. He was greeted by a face 'of furious scorn'[68] and she immediately changed the subject to complain about her dressmaker having been left in London by the studio. Cecil became so exasperated with her that when she complained that her gloves were too small, he cried out: 'No, it isn't that the gloves are too small but that your hands are too big.'[69] Vivien Leigh was particularly sensitive about her hands and the remark was not forgotten.

Cecil noticed that Vivien had developed the technique of not showing her feelings or real self at the studio. Nobody was fooled by this, but Cecil dreaded what must happen at home when she unwound. Vivien disliked the photographs of herself, which seemed to prove that she was not as young as she believed. Those she really hated she prodded vindictively, destroying them. Though still very beautiful, she used to hide in dark corners, muffled in furs and veils. Yet she was completely confident of the atmosphere she would create in the dying sequence. In between shots she read Thurber's *Is Sex Necessary?* and roared with laughter.

There were lighter moments. Korda's mistress, Christine Norden, a buxom blonde with cool Nordic features, badly miscast as Mrs Marchmont, was overheard by Cecil's driver to say: 'That person Cecil Beaton is the most extraordinary person. I don't understand him. He hates the sight of me and yet I've never spoken a word to him.'[70] Cecil designed her a mouse-coloured wig. However, when Korda saw it, he said to Cecil: 'Cecil, dear boy, in Victorian times they still fucked, you know, just the same as we do today. There were blondes then, there are blondes now. Get rid of that wig!'[71] Cecil also created a ravishing outfit for her but Paulette Goddard felt upstaged and ordered the rainbow-coloured tulle bows on the shoulder to be removed.

In June Stephen Tennant visited Shepperton Studios. He was now rugged, grey-haired and unmade-up. He had been in a nursing home in Hillingdon for three months being treated with insulin. He enjoyed his afternoon: 'I *loved* your dresses and hats. They are very beautiful and unusual. Vivien Leigh's toilette, the tart's ensemble, is exquisite and the hairdressing accents her individuality perfectly, extreme though it is.'[72] Another visitor was Diana Cooper's son, John Julius, who got caught in a mock snowstorm on a railway platform between Moscow and St Petersburg. It reminded Cecil of his time in the desert.

Cecil's other work consisted of writing an appreciation of Rex Whistler for *The Masque* (Curtain Press, 1947). Stephen Tennant judged the booklet as 'very sympathetic and brilliantly discerning'[73] and sent a copy to the Queen. Margaret Case thought this 'some of the best writing' Cecil ever did – 'a true artist writing of another'.[74] And then he undertook the décor for *Charley's Aunt* in Brighton (which came to the Palace Theatre, London, later in the year).

This was a period of change in Cecil's life. Old friends were dying and new ones were replacing them. Sybil Colefax now had false teeth and crutches and communicated only by knowing nods and smiles. Aunt Jessie put £300 down for her funeral expenses. Gerald Berners spent a quiet month in the London Clinic. Gertrude Stein died and Alice B. Toklas was 'staying on alone'[75] at the rue Christine. Elsie Mendl declared: 'I've outlived my time',[76] and Ivor Novello: 'I used to be considered a beauty. The only thing left is for me to become a genius.'[77]

The following year, in 1948, Laura Corrigan died and was cremated before her death was announced. 'I suppose she was afraid too many people might be curious to have a look at her without her wig,'[78] wrote Cecil. She was buried in Cleveland. 'Laura had left instructions that she was to be placed next to Mr Corrigan, but unfortunately there was no visibility for two days. As you know there has been snow here for three months on end, and when the storm abated they couldn't find Mr Corrigan. They were digging for him in the snow for nearly a week before they were able to locate him.'[79]

During this time Cecil was in search of a new house. From 21 to 24 February 1947 he stayed at the Daye House for the last time. Edith Olivier, who had found Ashcombe seventeen years earlier, now produced two new possible houses. The first was Hatch House, a seventeenth-century house redone by Detmar Blow, which had a beautiful façade but no charm inside. The house was deserted because the owner had died a fortnight before. The other was Reddish House at Broadchalke, whose owner, Mrs Wood (mother of the artist Christopher Wood, who committed suicide on Salisbury Station in 1930), had also died lately, a fact spotted by David Herbert. Cecil had seen the house years ago and thought it lovely:

Thence to Reddish House. The façade is even more appealing and charm-ing. We were disappointed with the informality of the interior and I could not for some time get to grips with the rambling way the rooms were placed. The snow everywhere made it seem bleak and cheerless. We did not have a very good impression. Nevertheless I was keen enough to insist upon my mother and Maud coming down to see the place. On the

Monday morning the sun shone for the first time. Everyone's spirits soared.[80]

Excitement gradually overcame Cecil and he thought at last that 'the loss of Ashcombe may be somewhat compensated'.[81]

Broadchalke is a small village not far from Wilton and Salisbury in the Chalke Valley. The church dates from the thirteenth century and was restored in the fifteenth. John Aubrey, the antiquary, Rowland Williams, the theologian, and Maurice Hewlett all lived in Broadchalke at one time or another. Edward Hutton wrote that the infamous John Bekinson had also lived there. He flattered Henry VIII for money 'but repented later and confessed his sins'.[82] Hutton judged that 'the renegade who could write a treatise *De Supremo et absoluto Regis imperio* and dedicate it to Henry VIII is no friend of ours or worthy to dwell in this valley'.[83]

Reddish House itself is a Queen Anne house with a steep garden behind. When Lord David Cecil saw it, he described it as a pocket edition of a three-volume novel. It is curious to find that in January 1918 Maurice Hewlett had tried to persuade the hearty poet and publisher J.C. Squire (who first commissioned a book jacket from Cecil in 1926) to take the house* and that the artist Christopher Wood had been a great friend of Sir Francis Rose. Cecil's bid of £10,000 was accepted and he took possession of Reddish on 21 June, to his delight and the great enthusiasm of his mother. He was soon busy attacking weeds, tearing down ivy, and deciding which furniture from Ashcombe fitted the dignity and elegance of his new home, and which should be discarded as frivolous junk. The 'barley sugar columns made of brass that were the posts for my former circus-roundabout bed'[84] had to go.

* See *The Letters of Maurice Hewlett*, ed. Laurence Binyon (Methuen, 1926), pp. 184-7.

23

My Greatest Triumph

He was in love with her. He certainly was. Or infatuated.
A better word really....

Truman Capote to the author, 28 June 1983

There was nothing straightforward about the four-month love affair that Cecil had with Garbo in the winter of 1947 and the spring of 1948.

Cecil's life had changed considerably since his first meeting with Garbo in 1932. She too had sailed a strange course. In 1932 she declared:

I have been like a ship without a rudder, lost and very lonely. I am awkward, shy, afraid, nervous and self-conscious about my English. That is why I built a wall of repression about myself and live behind it.

A film-star's career is a full-time job and I am in deadly earnest when I say that.[1]

Since then her reclusiveness had got considerably worse. In the following years Garbo made her most famous films, *Queen Christina*, *Anna Karenina*, *Camille*, *Ninotchka*. She despised them all, believing she was prostituting herself. This 'great actress with the temperament of an artist',[2] as Mercedes de Acosta described her, was always unhappy when working on a film. She was a perfectionist, yet never looked at the 'rushes' because these depressed her. In the evenings she came home to sit alone locked in a cellar. George Cukor maintained that she reserved 'her real sensuousness for the camera'.[3]

From 1937 to 1938 she had been romantically involved with the conductor Leopold Stokowski, but discovered in Italy that he was sending reports back to American newspapers saying they were to be married. She left at once for Sweden. In 1939 her lover was the health food expert, Gayelord Hauser. In 1941 she made her last film, *Two-Faced Woman*, concluded that malevolent forces were continuing to destroy her career and went into retirement. Hauser brought her to New York where she spent her time hunting around in Third Avenue junk shops. Thinking she needed new clothes, Hauser introduced her to the designer Valentina, who then had a boutique in the basement of the Sherry Netherland Hotel. Garbo tried on dresses and astonished Valentina's husband, Georges Schlee, by her total lack of inhibition. She stood naked before this stranger, awaiting a fitting. Garbo became close friends with the Schlees and a curious triangular ménage was established and worked happily for some years.

Schlee and Valentina were both from Russia, he a figure shrouded in 'a romantic and pleasant air of mystery'.⁴ Coming from a rich St Petersburg family, he had been driven south by the Reds. He endowed a university in Sevastopol and ran a newspaper there. After the collapse of the White Army in 1920 he fled from his country, taking with him a beautiful young refugee girl called Valentina Sanina, with flame-red hair whom, it was said, he met on a railway station. Their travels took them through Greece, Italy and Paris and they arrived in New York in 1923.

She was fifteen and a half when he asked her to marry him. Valentina told him: 'I can't give you love. I don't know how to love, but if you want friendship, then I'll marry you.'⁵ He replied: 'If you marry me, I'll look after you for the rest of your life.'⁶ This he did, after his fashion, for twenty-two years, though Garbo maintained that their marriage only lasted seven years. Valentina opened a dress shop in New York, but it folded when the principal backer disappeared. However, in 1928 they founded Valentina gowns. She designed and Schlee handled the business side. It was an instant success and they went from strength to strength. Valentina's clothes were timeless from a fashion point of view and she had a passionate belief in the freedom of movement of the body. Irene Selznick thought there was nothing grander than a simple Valentina dress. She said that Valentina was the first person to design clothes in which a woman could throw her arms round a man's neck without her dress riding up her back. Valentina designed for private clients and was also a noted stage designer, working with Lynn Fontanne and Katharine Hepburn and doing costumes for plays like *The Philadelphia Story*. Schlee was a trained lawyer and a canny businessman, who invested her money wisely. They became rich and moved into a spacious apartment in 450 East 52nd Street (a block which Dorothy Parker called 'Wit's End' because Alexander Woollcott lived there). At the height of her success Valentina had sixty-seven people working for her.

Garbo and Valentina became close friends. They wore similar clothes and looked rather alike. Schlee escorted his wife one night and Garbo the next, a situation which seemed to work easily, at any rate on the surface. Later Schlee got tired of this. He effected a private coup, took Garbo over and closed down Valentina's business. Thus Valentina lost her friend, her husband and her business at one stroke.* At this time, however, Schlee was not

*Valentina continued to design, however. As late as 1969 she designed a short, black velvet evening dress for Lee Radziwill.

in total control of Garbo. Mercedes de Acosta believed that Valentina was stronger than Garbo and would in two years or so win her husband back. Cecil could never have known into what a tangled web he was now stepping.

Garbo was forty-one when Cecil met her again in 1946. That meeting fuelled hopes of a romance, led to the taking of the so-called passport photographs ('thereby achieving my greatest ambition, and crowning my photographic career',[7] as he put it), but left a position of stalemate since Garbo refused to see him or communicate in any way. When Cecil returned to London in January 1947 he began to write her a series of letters. With some foresight Cecil kept carbon copies of them and these were found in a tin box in his room after he died.

Cecil communicated his delight at finding Reddish House with its rambling rooms and romantic grassy slopes. He wrote:

So then I shall be a country squire. Just for a spell at any rate. So then I am the owner of a country seat. So then I am a man of property. Did you ever think your friend would turn out to be that.[8]

Cecil described the bedrooms and continued:

If you come to be my wife I trust you will allow me to sleep in the sitting-, or dressing-room, if not in the large room.[9]

Sometimes Cecil did not send the letters that he wrote. Occasionally he became annoyed at her refusal to respond to his calls:

There are many reasons why I should be slightly distressed at the seemingly cruel manner in which you have lopped off one of the branches of interest but strange and upsetting as it may be to you, I understand so well what goes on in your curious and even surprising mind, that I am able to forgive a great deal, and to suffer much less than I could have imagined.[10]

He assured her that he never spoke about her to any of their friends. When Boris Kochno saw her in New York (she dined with the Schlees and Bébé Bérard dressed as Sarah Bernhardt), and he reported this to Cecil, Cecil replied in phrases which would appear to be an imitation of the particular idiom of Queen Elizabeth: 'Oh, how charming of her. How very nice for you. And how exceedingly nice for her too.'[11]

All Cecil's letters paint an enticing picture of the tranquil rural life he was now leading and of his lovely new home. He hoped to arouse Garbo's curiosity and lure her to visit him. He seldom received a reply, and as the summer progressed his own letters dwindled, especially while she was travelling with his 'enemy' Georges Schlee, whom he described as 'the second-rate dressmaker-assistant'.[12] From Paris Cecil wrote: 'I dreamt about you the night before last. Perhaps we are our happiest in our dreams.'[13] On his return to London some food packages arrived from New York:

> But it wasn't until bedtime that I unwrapped them, and when I discovered who had sent them I was filled with a rare and deep happiness. Thank you. Thank you. I have been feeling very lonely of late. I hated not being in touch with you and there were times when I felt extremely sad and depressed that so much had happened since we last met. Nevertheless I have always had complete faith in you and I know that whatever you may say to me that we have a very sincere sympathy and love for each other and that it is not something that happens often in a lifetime. I have always held you so very close in my consciousness and however busy I have been have always wanted you to be near and to share the excitements, and your present to me has come like manna from heaven, and I know you are as understanding and true as I have always believed you to be. As for myself I have never before wanted to devote myself entirely to any one woman, but I know one day all obstacles will be overcome and that we shall spend many happy times together. You have the lion's share in all my plans and I am not very impatient for them to materialize, as neither you nor I would be happy without complete trust in one another and I feel you have to see me again to realize how very genuine a person I am if I am permitted to be.[14]

Garbo arrived in England at the end of August in the course of her European trip with Schlee. Surrounded by reporters, she said angrily: 'I had hoped I would get off the ship unobserved.'[15] Cecil wrote: 'It's a great event, as if Venus came to Mars.'[16] He hoped that Garbo would call him but resolved that he would not contact her. However, he became so restless that eventually he left a message. Garbo did ring back but by then Cecil was in the country.

Further aggravation followed when David Herbert announced that he and Michael Duff had met Garbo on the Côte d'Azur. Then he heard that Ivor Novello was giving a party for her in London: 'I shan't be there. But I would like it if you ring up and come to my house for a quiet meal and I could motor you to see one or two things in London that I think you should know before you leave.'[17]

Garbo's London visit was very upsetting and distracting for Cecil. He wrote urging her to forget America and her film career in favour of the more sympathetic Europe. He continued:

> It is really terrible that you should spend your time hiding from imbecilic film fans on Madison Avenue or Sunset Boulevard. All of which is a long way of extending an invitation to you to come and build your nest here at Reddish House.[18]

For days Cecil kept Pelham Place in a state of readiness, bedecked with crimson flowers and blue hydrangeas. He never ate fish for lunch for fear of the smell of cooking. He sat at home, trying to read, alert to every car door slamming. But, though Garbo indicated that she might come, she never materialized. She merely telephoned to say she was delayed. 'Delayed,' wrote Cecil crossly. 'I suppose Heloïse and Abelard were delayed.'[19] He placed the blame for all broken plans at the feet of Schlee:

> It was no good your being here and yet not here, for under the auspices of that Russian sturgeon I could have no chance. I think it was mean of him, though, to allow you so short a time in England, and of course it was intentional.[20]

He was obliged to console himself with the boxes of chocolate that came in the food parcel. They proved she recognized his existence: 'Here is a chocolate filled with nougat, or coffee cream or marshamallow that you have sent to me,'[21] he wrote. But he was depressed: 'The lettuces have lost their hearts and I too.'[22]

Maud Nelson thought Garbo's effect on Cecil was disastrous. She took to slipping into the Brompton Oratory to light candles for him. It was therefore no bad thing when, in October 1947, Cecil took his three-month leave from Korda and sailed to America to fulfil the terms of his new contract with *Vogue*.

There were further complications to this story. Cecil continued to nurture an unfulfilled hope for the good-looking actor, Geoffrey Toone, who had played Lord Windermere in *Lady Windermere's Fan*. In June 1946, shortly after the passport photo session, Cecil had written in his diary: 'Geoffrey Toone showed himself particularly charming to me and I felt that life would hold so many tremendous possibilities if one knew how to seize them.'[23] But presently the young actor wrote to him:

> I'm so sorry if I made you feel very bleak. I probably said much more than I wanted to. ... The point is that there is just no heart in me for any sort of emotional friendship and anyone that seems to make any emotional demand on me just worries and upsets me out of all proportion. Please don't think I doubt your integrity with regard to me for a minute. I honestly don't.[24]

Geoffrey Toone was also in New York for part of this winter and he and Cecil occasionally met.

During Cecil's first week in New York he was in the company of an Australian whom he had met in Bombay in 1944 and of whom he then wrote: 'He is the sort of person I'd like to have in my life. Sad that our ways were divergent.'[25] Only after the Australian had left New York did Cecil try to contact 'the person who has occupied my mind for the last two years'.[26] When he rang, the operator informed him that 'Miss Brown don't live here any more'.[27] But the following day he tried again and this time she did answer. Cecil had not seen Garbo for a year and a half but she was as frivolous as ever. She asked where he was. As during the previous year he was in rooms 249 to 251 in the Plaza. Garbo said she would love to come and see him: 'It may not be before Monday.'[28]

Cecil told Garbo he had a lot of things for her (his unsent letters). She asked if they were matches. He asked if she wore her red pyjamas:

'No, but I look at them sometimes.'

'I'm so glad, Honey.'

'Honey?'

'Honeychile.'[29]

This conversation proved something of a breakthrough as Cecil noted:

> It's all so easy and I'm so relieved. I might have been an avoidance, a terror, a silence, an escape to emptiness. I am now at the beginning of a new campaign. I trust that by being clever and not forcing the issues I may win through to victory.[30]

On Monday 3 November Cecil went to photograph Gertrude Lawrence in the morning. In the afternoon he waited for his reunion with Garbo. He prepared the room with flowers, scattered her favourite cigarettes and put on his second favourite suit, optimistically saving the best one for another time. After a long wait during which Cecil became extremely nervous, the bell rang and he opened the door to admit a thinner, more drawn Garbo than he had remembered. 'What a charming surprise,' said Cecil out of nerves.

'Surprise?'[31]

For a while Cecil stood his ground. Then he began to massage her back. There was a considerable amount of inconsequential chatter and Garbo's traditionally playful answers to questions: 'I'm not going to tell you.'[32] Meanwhile she never referred to the past, nor did she look at an album of photographs near her or any of the magazines. She took in details of his apartment, however. Then she did something unexpected:

> Her practical side came out when touring the apartment she suddenly drew the mustard velvet curtains. I was completely surprised at what was happening. It took me some time to recover my bafflement. Within a few minutes of our reunion, after these long and void periods, of months of depression and doubt, we were suddenly together in unexplained, unexpected and inevitable intimacy. It is only on such occasions that one realizes how fantastic life can be. I was hardly able to bridge the gulf so quickly and unexpectedly. I had to throw my mind back to the times at Reddish House when in my wildest dreams I had invented the scenes that were now taking place.[33]

The next evening Cecil was late returning from cocktails at Gramercy Park. Garbo was waiting patiently outside his door in a sou'wester hat. This time there was 'no swinging on awnings' and 'slight irritation at continuous badinage'.[34] After that the days passed and 'Miss Brown' did not answer.

A week passed before Cecil saw Garbo again. She had been ill. When she reappeared she was 'white but excessively, touchingly, wonderfully beautiful'.[35] She stayed a short while, then a chic friend from Santa Barbara, Mrs Sanson, called for her and they left. But the tense atmosphere had lifted: 'there are no more complications'.[36]

After these intimacies Cecil began a long phase of taking walks with Garbo in Central Park. He would suddenly announce he was going out to his surprised secretary, Miss Cleghorn, and set off in impatient haste. Sometimes as he waited his nose became 'mauve with cold'.[37] When she sauntered along, wearing a dark blue coat and Pilgrim Father hat, with a large black bag over her shoulder, Cecil's spirits soared. Invariably recognized by passers-by, they greeted each other with the feigned insouciance of two spies in a bad film. Cecil enjoyed the subterfuges just as he enjoyed the frivolity of their inconsequential conversation as they ran arm in arm through the gritty parkland. Their walk over, Cecil entered the Plaza alone. He ordered tea from Eugene, lit candles and dismissed Miss Cleghorn. Garbo arrived separately, in anguish at having been caught sneaking up the back stairs by the hotel's public relations director, Prince Serge Obolensky. Still cold from the walk, they drank their tea:

> 'Don't ask questions,' she said. 'Don't scrutinize.' She kept looking at her watch. 'Isn't it awful to be with someone who is always following the clock, who is so strict and won't let you ask questions or scrutinize.' Suddenly as if it were the most ordinary question in the world she stretched out her arm towards the other room and asked with such disarming and natural frankness 'Do you want to go to bed?'
>
> Sometimes photographs are more like people than people themselves. Very seldom when I am walking along with Greta am I able to see her. Occasionally we stop and turn and look at the new moon, and I see her as she has appeared in a prized photograph or on the screen. This afternoon there were many flashes of her in the Pilgrim hat as she was in *Queen Christina*, and later in the half light she was the living embodiment of her 'stills'. Later she said 'La nuit tombe' and outside there was only artificial light.[38]

Cecil found himself in a curious role. He believed that for once he was being used for his body. Accustomed to pining out of unrequited love, he found this unexpected situation rather disconcerting. He confessed as much to his old friend Natasha Wilson,* who said with emphasis: 'It's

---

*Formerly Princess Natasha Paley, who married Jack Wilson.

ridiculous.'[39] She had no advice to offer, but Mona Harrison Williams had plenty. She told Cecil he was 'a dope'.[40] She said he must play Garbo's game back to her. He must not hang around waiting the whole time. 'You've got to get her mind. And her mind's got to worry about what's going on in your mind, and when you see the results working don't have any mercy. It's crucial. You can't afford to be a dope about anything that's important in your life!'[41]

Cecil tried this advice. For four days he was silent. Then Garbo rang him. Afraid that he had been unfaithful, she came round. He told her that he had been out with Mona until 3 a.m. and that he was dining with her again that night.

> That went very well. Questions asked about my other friends, and after certain admissions she said, 'So you are stepping out in both directions?' We talked more like two friends, for we exchanged information instead of mere childish gibberish and she said 'Damn that cocktail-party.* Why do you go? I want you to stay here.' But I was determined to go. The magic was working too well. Why though did it make her smile so much. Was it because she was no longer bored by the faithful admirer?[42]

Cecil continued his campaign of not ringing. When she called him, he made a point of waxing lyrical about Mona's beauty. 'I cannot feel pity, for the battle is still too desperate and on so many points I gave way. But it is quite remarkable what a difference the change of tactics has made.'[43]

On Thanksgiving Day (27 November) Cecil sent round a vase of white orchids with one of his London letters. Then without a word he left for Boston for the weekend. Garbo rang in his absence and then again on Monday. Cecil offered no explanations. That afternoon they met at five. Garbo asked many jealous lover's questions beneath a veil of jocularity. When the mustard velvet curtains were drawn, Cecil felt mesmerized by her huge eyes so close to his:

> Eyes that continued to stare for so long, that never lowered their lids in sleep. For sleep is something that comes to her with great difficulty. We talked of many intimate things that it is difficult to talk about, but managed to achieve a happy understanding and mutual enjoyment.[44]

They dined at the Mayerling restaurant. Garbo told Cecil that he 'draped' himself too much and criticized the way he stood when telephoning, with his hand on his hip. She said firmly that 'She wanted to make a man out of me.'[45] In the theatre – they went to see *The Winslow Boy* – she said: 'I think I'll have to propose to you.' Cecil replied: 'Oh no, that wouldn't work any more. You wouldn't really like that.' 'Throughout the play she stared at me

---

* Cecil was due for cocktails with Loelia Westminster at six.

and I remembered how I used to stare at Peter and how annoyed he became.'[46] On the way home they stopped at Hicks for a drink. Cecil's attitude and Garbo's are nicely revealed in his account:

> I thought that each place that we go to together becomes sacred, and I feel I would like to return and say to the bartender, 'You remember me. I came in the other evening with that lady who wouldn't drink anything except water because you hadn't got any fresh oranges to squeeze.' At Doubleday's bookshop I pointed out a picture of herself in an album of photographs of the last decade. 'I don't give a damn,' she said and laughed. ... It has been a pleasant evening for both but less ecstatic for me for I had to hold onto myself to prevent myself from being devoured.[47]

The next day they walked in the park and kissed. Garbo then had a date with Schlee, which she claimed bored her. On 3 December Cecil went to watch the Royal Wedding colour film* before Garbo joined him. The Princess of Berar came for a drink and Garbo spoke freely and easily with her. Later they went to the cinema and then returned to Cecil's rooms for a talk.

Cecil continued his ploys and they continued to work. Garbo said again: 'I think I shall have to propose to you, make an honest man of you.'[48] After one such discussion Cecil came away 'feeling that there really was a possibility that one day I might get her worked up sufficiently to do a bunk and before thinking it over too long get ourselves married. I have pictured to myself all the possibilities and would like so very much to take on the risk, to take the opportunity of having a really new start in life.'[49]

Presently Cecil's nonchalance made Garbo angry, but it remained effective. One day they spent ten hours together. Cecil said: 'You're so unreliable. I couldn't ever marry you. You're not serious about me.'

'What a rebuff, and I love you, Cecil. I love you. I'm in love with you.'

---

*Princess Elizabeth had married Prince Philip on 20 November. Michael Duff sent Cecil a hilarious account of the wedding: 'The real thing was enchanting, Queen Mary in ice blue, shimmering in the iciest of ice blue, nodding away like a contented potentate so ancient that she scarce held together. You felt that Pussy, Lady Cynthia, and Bertha Dawkins were supporting her with unseen hands. Occasionally this ageing mammel(?) whirled her hand about, as though a plague of flies had been let loose. Edwina Mount B had one too many paradise plumes, while —— positively crawled in what looked like seafood, which clung to her dyke-like hat. ... The King looked unbelievably beautiful, like an early French King and HRH the Bride a dream and like a fairy tale Princess. Princess Marie Louise looked like a bodkin with nothing to do, and Helena Victoria tatty, moth eaten, and throaty looking, wheeled in her bath chair by Marie Lou. ... Michael of Kent punched Cousin William of Gloucester in the kisser during the wedding rehearsal, which alarmed our Duchess considerably, and he received a good talking to from Granny, who with parasol in hand, was prepared for action should it occur again on THE DAY. Michael was far too scared by the whole proceedings to do anything untoward [Sir Michael Duff to Cecil, 10 December 1947].

Cecil noted:

Perhaps my sentiments were too crudely expressed but perhaps in view
of my behaviour for the rest of the night they were helpful. The desired
effect was to make her want what I secretly most wanted. Perhaps I was
tired. I did it badly but it did not seem to ruin the evening.[50]

Later they went to a raucous play and to a night-club, the Blue Angel. Cecil
loved observing Garbo watching the cabaret with childlike happiness:

This was much more my triumph than when she turned to gaze at me
and whisper 'I love you. I love you.' Somehow this was too much for me
to take in. Of all the people I have admired to make a beeline that ends
thus is almost too good to grasp. It is to date my greatest triumph.[51]

That night for the first time Garbo admitted him to room 26c of the Ritz
Tower. As she prepared him a simple meal, he looked around, but she would
allow no lights to be turned on, so it was all rather gloomy. There was
kissing and he left after 3 a.m. The following day was a busy one for Cecil,
ending with dinner with Carmel Snow. 'I was very tired after last night's
activity,' noted Cecil, 'and felt it was perhaps as well that tonight we were
separated.'[52]

One day they discussed their friend Mercedes de Acosta:

Greta said there must be something wrong, otherwise she wouldn't be so
alone, so unpopular and miserable. 'But she's done me such harm, such
mischief, has gossiped so and been so vulgar. She's always trying to
scheme and find out things and you can't shut her up. She's like a Jew.
The more you insult her the readier she is to come back for more.' When
I said she had asked me point blank if I was having an affair with her,
G. said, 'That's just like her. It's so vulgar.'[53]

When Garbo said she had considered marrying William S. Paley, the Chairman of CBS, Cecil said, 'Why don't you marry me?'
'Why?'
'Because I am not rich. I have nothing to offer you but salvation.'[54]
Another day Garbo made her first reference to her friend Georges Schlee.
Serge Obolensky had again spotted her in the Plaza. 'Well I do have the
rottenest luck,' she said. 'I bet the "little man" will see me next and then
my goose will be cooked.'[55] Garbo said that Schlee was not feeling well. He
was tired of having to look after sixty women and did not like going home
at the end of the day. Cecil concluded optimistically: 'This is the first time
she has alluded to the Schlee business. It is obviously a drab necessity
that she must go through with.' Fortunately Garbo also said she would go
back to California when Cecil left: 'There's nothing to keep me in New
York.'[56]

Cecil left for a theatrical weekend with Ruth Gordon and Garson Kanin. Anita Loos accompanied him: 'We are dining on Saturday with their neighbors [*sic*], the Gilbert Millers, so we shall have a terrific time baiting them and laughing at them behind their backs,'[57] wrote Cecil to Simon Fleet. In fact they talked for eighteen hours a day and Cecil hardly dared leave the room lest he missed something. He did not mention Garbo, but added:

> The whole city seems to be very much quieter than usual, or maybe it's just me. I haven't done much work but I am enjoying it enormously and will come back immensely refreshed.[58]

Although Cecil only wrote about Garbo in his diaries at this time, other events went on around him. Cole Porter and his wife, though very rich, complained bitterly about tax worries. The Windsors sent out a Christmas card of the nativity with the caption 'A King was born'. The Duke telephoned Cecil at great length in reply to a note Cecil wrote about the serialization of his memoirs. To add to the jollity of the festive season Elsa Maxwell was being sued by the Waldorf for $800.

As Christmas approached, Garbo became braver. She was going to Tennessee Williams's *A Streetcar Named Desire* with Schlee and said: 'How would you like me to telephone you afterwards and if the devil's in me I'll come right over and spend the night.'[59] But she did not come, nor did she ever stay the night or allow Cecil to do so. But, ever the coquette, the next morning she telephoned and appeared:

> In the brilliant light she was as beautiful as ever. The eyes like an eagle's of pale mauve blue. The skin on the neck and chest of the finest grain and as shiny as marble. Her legs long and like a young girl of fifteen. The skin is deep apricot in colour. We were very happy in our mutual ecstasy. Sunday morning had been put to its ultimate use.[60]

Later, her hair tied with a yellow ribbon, they shared a bath: 'We laughed a lot and I felt very happy.'[61] Cecil began to take his happiness for granted. He wrote to Clarissa:

> As always I suppose I am anxious to try and make these delights more binding and permanent but I doubt if I shall really succeed although my self assurance is beginning to be something quite alarming. I have never before realized the strength of a thought. If one has this little seed planted in one's head it can grow into something that really moves mountains. For years I had put the wrong little seed in my head and it made me very unhappy.[62]

Just before Christmas Cecil developed a heavy cold. Garbo was to dine with Schlee. She and Cecil sat in her apartment. She hated her first name, he hated the pseudonyms, Miss G and Miss Brown. When he joked that he should call her 'wife', and shouted this out, she said, 'No, no, you must be quiet. There's never any sound in this apartment. It's as if no one ever lived here. Never any noises at all.' Cecil noted dispassionately: 'and I can well believe it'.[63]

Cecil was ill in bed all Christmas Eve. Garbo visited him. The next day at noon she was to take him to Mercedes (known to Greta as 'the little black and white'[64] friend because she always wore black clothes and powdered her face white). She would not tell Mercedes who was coming, adding: 'You'll know soon enough so long as you've got the extra plate.'[65] Christmas Day began with Cecil going to the Ritz Tower and out of idle curiosity opening the kitchen door. Garbo cried out with some violence: 'I hate curiosity in people. I dislike intensely if people don't mind their own business.'[66] Cecil felt 'utterly crushed'.[67] Then they went to Mercedes's and a 'rather pathetic and silly chorus boy sissy'[68] called Mr Everly also arrived. Garbo burst into life and entertained the company by singing, reciting poems and bits of Heine. At 3 p.m. she left promptly, accompanied by Cecil. As they neared Schlee territory she walked on ahead urging Cecil to ring her that evening.

Cecil went to see Diana Vreeland, and that evening dined at Mona's. While the women were upstairs and the Duke of Windsor with the men next door, he rang Garbo, and they discussed the pointlessness of the morning's party. She told Cecil not to display the plate she had given him as it was a favourite of the 'little man's'. Mona gave a ball after dinner but Cecil left at 3.30 with a splitting headache. When he awoke next day New York was under snow. He still felt very ill but had to photograph a society bride. Cecil had arranged drinks at his apartment. It was a great adventure for the guests to get through the snow. Garbo arrived in gum boots and a seafarer's hat in the company of Schlee. The other guests included George Davis, Salvador Dali, Alan Porter and Natasha Wilson. It gave Cecil a chance to examine his hated rival:

As for Georges I do not trust him at all. He seemed very ill at ease and his eyes never met mine with any confidence or honesty. He seemed to emanate a very troubled electric atmosphere and even the drinks did not give him a false confidence in me. He made one or two remarks that I did not think in the highest quality. On arrival he said: 'You must have asked an enormous number of people here', and when accepting another drink, said, 'I'll just have a sip to show ——— there's no ill feeling.' I whispered to Greta: 'Is it going all right with him?' and she said with infinite conviction: 'Ooh yaais.'[69]

Cecil told Natasha that he wondered if this would prove his heyday. At the moment he felt confident for the future. As the party broke up and the other guests were leaving, Cecil tried to sneak a quick kiss. A look of terror crossed Garbo's face and she said, 'Don't be so silly.'

People often upset Garbo by coming up to her when she was out walking. She told Cecil that she had seen the Windsors coming out of a gallery on 57th Street and that everyone had stared at them. 'How horrible it is not to have any privacy. I felt so sorry for them,'[70] she said. No one had recognized her.

After another of their long walks they went to the Metropolitan Museum from where Cecil rang Miss Cleghorn and told her not to work any longer. In the dark, cold afternoon they returned to the Plaza:

> We enjoyed ourselves in a quite uninhibited unshy way. We seemed to have great confidence in each other and with each meeting we seem to know a little more of one another – or at any rate I of Greta, and the more I know the more I profoundly admire and respect her. The Mona campaign has worked wonders so far and I feel that by having employed tactics a state of reality has been achieved.[71]

On New Year's Eve 1947/48 Cecil dined with the Harrison Williamses. Suddenly the telephone rang with the message 'It's Mr Thompson on the line'. Garbo was sad after a difficult evening with Schlee and wanted Cecil to join her. 'Mona was sweet and as large hearted and understanding as ever and I soon oiled out of the room without bidding the others good night.'[72] As Cecil taxied down Park Avenue, with its long centipede of brilliant Christmas trees, he observed the other merrymakers and thought himself 'the luckiest person in the world'.[73] Presently Garbo and he were drinking 1840 whisky, the gift of Margaret Case, in his rooms at the Plaza:

> I gave a toast to our marriage, our life together, but Greta did not elaborate on this theme, and smiled a little diffidently. But our embraces were wild and tender and we had neither enough arms to entwine around each other's shoulders and waist.[74]

Later Garbo talked and then the two stood at the window as the sirens sounded and the car hooters hooted and 1948 dawned. After this Cecil got wildly drunk and uninhibited. Garbo was amused and appreciative.

Throughout January and almost all of February Cecil and Garbo were together in New York. Garbo looked at early photographs of Cecil at Harrow and Cambridge. Her mouth opened wide at his early effeminacy: 'Now really! This is too much. Oh the drapery. Now were you ever like that? That's terrible.'[75] Cecil had willingly deserted a party given by the Windsors at the Waldorf in favour of 'the most beautiful woman of our time'.[76] Garbo told Cecil: 'Some people when you were very young and effeminate may have found you most obnoxious to begin with, but then you worked and proved yourself useful. But in general the homosexual life is a "cut up" without a sense of responsibility.'[77] Often Garbo would say 'I must be going' and this would prove the prelude to sex:

> I did not know that so many fancies could be born of the moment and in so many different moods, of sentimentality, playfulness, emotional love or sheer lust. I began to realize how much time I had wasted and how little I had learnt in the sphere of lovemaking.[78]

Garbo liked men who were gentle and sensitive to the woman's reactions. She said, 'I don't like anything rough or staccato.'[79] Cecil could not believe his luck: 'Here I was with someone whom I'd always wanted to love me and here she was loving me.'[80] Cecil was continually surprised at her knowledge of poetry and literature despite her claim of never reading anything, as well as her enthusiasm for sculpture even if this was expressed in an unconventional way. 'Yum, yum, yum,'[81] she would say, gazing at the exposed nipple of a female figure by Michelangelo.

Meanwhile Garbo had to spend a lot of time at the sickbed of her friend Schlee. He had succumbed to a nervous illness, sensing that there was something between Garbo and Cecil. Having devoted his life to Garbo for four years he did not like these developments. He had been unhappy on the European trip and he and Cecil had been at war since Schlee told Margaret Case: 'He made a great mistake and I can do him great harm.'[82]

One day Cecil and Garbo found themselves in a restaurant next to Niki de Gunzburg, Natasha Wilson and others. They all went to Niki's apartment and Natasha began to relate the tale of the French princess who had been caught *in flagrante* with Mr Norman Winston.* At a party given by Kitty Miller, Rosita Winston had announced that she had caught her husband in bed with the Princess that very afternoon. The Princess was packed off home to France on the next aeroplane. Cecil relished this 'really juicy scandal'[83] and shared it with his friends. Diana Cooper wrote from France: 'I'm awfully sorry for her. True in 100,000,000 Americans she was foolish to pick Mr Winston, but poor girl to have to crawl back to [France], tail gripped between those ungovernable legs. Humiliation.'[84] Meanwhile Mr Winston put a note on Mrs Winston's pillow saying 'Are we, or are we not, living together?' As a result Mrs Winston became richer by 'a great block of stocks, platinum mink cape and some emeralds'. When asked why she had spread the story around town, Mrs Winston said 'I have never been not famous for not thinking.'[85] These were the sort of stories that circulated at Niki's apartment. Afterwards Cecil got a wigging from Garbo:

> Greta seemed rather antagonistic suddenly and when we left she said, 'Oh my, I've still got to teach you so much. How can you degrade yourself to

* Norman Winston (1899–1977), builder of middle-income houses in suburban areas throughout the world. Friend of Mayor Wagner. Mrs Winston was a Cherokee Indian.

the level of telling such ordinary, boring details of gossip. Why did it interest you? What's so funny? It was no good to suggest that the characters involved were so curious as to make it into a strange French farce. She thought it beneath me to take such an interest in the fact 'that two people, a man and a woman, were found in bed together'. She held forth violently: 'It's not important. It's a natural thing to do. It's the law of nature. The poor little man has something between his legs and suddenly feels in need of a woman. Then he goes to bed with one. The fact that it gets into the papers is the reason why you're interested but it isn't interesting really. It's a "Biological Fact" and it happens all the time. Behind all these windows it's going on now.' And she waved her arm at the surrounding skyscrapers.[86]

The next day she related a story that again illustrates her independent spirit and Scandinavian attitude to sex. A man had seen her in California and by chance found her address in a tailor's. By stealth he obtained her telephone number and rang her. She thought he had a house to sell and called back:

She decided to go and see him. He answered the door. They talked. They saw the garden together, the downstairs room. And Greta thought to herself: 'Why not?', so she asked: 'Have you a very beautiful view from your bedroom?' Next day he went to the war.[87]

With Cecil, Garbo visited Tchelitchew, who felt at once that she was somebody he had always known and who would never fade from his memory. Just before Cecil's forty-fourth birthday, Garbo was drinking vodka with him and asked: 'You don't write about people, do you?'[88]

He wrote in his diary:

I was really shocked and upset that she should ask me this for it was a hangover of the past that I thought was entirely forgotten and forgiven. I said 'How could you imagine I should ever do anything that hurts you. I love you so much. I only want to do the things that will make you love me more. Surely you trust me?' – 'How would I hang around the Plaza the way I do if I didn't. But people have so often used me, have hurt me by doing things that have surprised me. I've known crooks and they've wanted to use me, and they have, and though I've been shocked and ... I still don't believe they're bad.'[89]

The most worrying aspect of Cecil's affair with Garbo is that his diary is devoted exclusively to her from November 1947 to March 1948. He was anxious to preserve the minutest details as soon as possible. It is impossible to say if he had publication in mind, but there is one telling remark: 'I drank a lot and was sleepy, so I am afraid I am unable to report on Greta's philosophy.'[90]

On Cecil's birthday Garbo gave him a pink enamel saucer painted with flowers, which they had admired on Third Avenue. Margaret Case gave a party for him. Elsa Maxwell made a speech saying the world was enriched by Cecil's presence. 'That is a wonderful thing to hear someone say that they are grateful that you were born,' said Greta. A birthday cake arrived inscribed: 'Cecil – an Ideal Husband'. Later they all went to see Korda's film. Cecil sat next to Garbo: 'my cup of bliss was full'.[91] But still any plans of marriage seemed a long way off.

Garbo succumbed to a cold, but the meetings continued. When they separated, there were great wavings and sometimes Garbo put a white towel out of her window to speed Cecil on his way. But to Cecil's chagrin she continued to attend cocktails and dinners given by the Schlees. The cold dragged on and a constricted chest was diagnosed. Cecil hoped she would go to California and he would follow her there 'as there are so many disadvantages to traipsing around New York and there have been inevitable little quips in some of the Broadway columns'.[92]

One night Cecil was woken by cries of lovemaking in a nearby room of the Plaza. This disturbed him: 'Lust is too revolting if it comes to this, the man a brute, the whole situation just too unattractive.'[93] He told Garbo that it had almost put him off the idea of sex. She replied: 'I know how strange the noises of the night can be, the laughter, the people fighting in the street below. I sometimes lie with my heart beating like mad and it's so awful I feel life can't go on.'[94] Michael Duff arrived in New York. He was allowed to come to Cecil's rooms to meet Garbo again. Later she sat, 'her hair hanging over her face, her legs wide apart, her generous broad smile and lower eyelids. Suddenly she would look at me with lowered lids and one eyebrow raised, a natural and alluring regard which has been copied by the whole world.'[95] Another 'sympathetic English' friend produced to meet her was Loelia Westminster.

There came a bad day when, after a meeting with Schlee, Garbo announced on the telephone: 'I've some very sad news for you.'[96] Schlee had complained of her behaviour. Cecil must not come to California. He was in despair; but relief came when they met and he said he might have legitimate business to discuss with Hitchcock.* She winked: 'Then I couldn't prevent your doing that.'[97]

Cecil was aware that he had a sexual hold on her. He attributed this to the fact that

I am so unexpectedly violent and have such unlicensed energy when called upon. It baffles and intrigues and even shocks her. May this last a long time!![98]

---

* Alfred Hitchcock wanted Cecil to work for him if he could get Korda's permission.

When Garbo asked Cecil to give her Bérard's sketch of him he felt he really had a place in her life.

Cecil received letters from home warning him to make money. He had to telephone Korda, to whose command he would soon once again have to submit. Cecil took more snapshots of Garbo sitting in his apartment. Another day he was twenty minutes late and Garbo told him, 'only half jokingly, "Shan't trust you any more", and this hurt a lot'.[99] Korda was in New York. Cecil began a new line by suggesting that he star Garbo in Jean Cocteau's Elizabeth of Austria play, *The Eagle has Two Heads*. Korda and Garbo met 'and everything was fine and dandy although he refuses to let her see *Anna Karenina* in case she would see how bad Kieron Moore is ...'.[100] Cecil encouraged Garbo a lot and they talked like businessmen, not lovers: 'I was feeling quite ill and tired with my cold and Greta was also feeling ill ...'. Cecil was as keen on the film idea as on that of marriage. He noted that he would 'insist upon designing her costumes and setting'.[101]

Schlee had taken a proprietary role over the film business and he was therefore dubbed 'the second agent'[102] by Cecil. One night he took Garbo to the theatre and Cecil decided to go along and watch them. Garbo looked striking in a black skullcap that covered her hair:

> We indulged in a dangerous game of which I fear her companion must have been conscious though for my part I hid my head from his view behind the heads of other people sitting in front of us. At times I felt that the vibrations sent out from me to her must surely be felt by everyone in the theatre.[103]

Soon after this Cecil told Garbo he might sail back to England, though it was his firm intention to follow her to Hollywood. On 20 February he went to the theatre and decided in the interval to ring her. There was a man in the callbox who seemed to talk for hours. Cecil became aggravated and almost tapped on the door. When the man came out it was Schlee. Cecil was amused at first but then thought: 'But seeing Schlee fly to the telephone as I do, and that after seven years, gives me an indication of how dreadfully devoted he must be, and that here is really something to have to contend with – a really tough battle! But the reward is worth it.'[104]

Garbo was to leave for California on 24 February and Cecil did not know whether he would see her again. He was as determined as she was to appear vague about plans. There was a farewell encounter:

> We went into the other room and I watched her wonderful face staring at me, or turning her head *'profile perdue'* with the chin thrown back and revealing the incredible beauty of the line of her throat. The sun was pouring through the windows and I would have liked to have remained until it was long after dark, but once more a hurry. . . . I heard some

slight scuffling in the room, like the wind blowing tissue paper. It was
Greta dressing herself. When I protested she said she had only remained
so that I might have some satisfaction from her tired little body.[105]

That evening Cecil went to a film with his actor friend Geoffrey Toone.
Garbo rang up sounding a bit hysterical: 'I was not prepared to be launched
into a farewell conversation and Geoffrey's presence embarrassed me.' He
rang back later to hear her say she had been unhappy. She would miss
Cecil, 'but we'll see what Fate has for us'.[106]

'Your departure has created a great blank in my life,' wrote Cecil in a
letter which dealt mostly with his hopes for the film. He had read the script
and felt only she could make it 'romantic and mysterious'.[107]

'Thank you and love'[108] was the unsigned telegram of reply. Cecil remained in New York a few more days, awaiting the right moment to fly to
California:

> To make my winter's conquest complete I knew I must see her in her
> own home. I must be able to spend the days uninterruptedly with her,
> just to stay from morning until bedtime without her looking at the watch
> and saying 'Got to go now'.[109]

Cecil was as vague as possible. Then he telephoned and was convinced that
Garbo wanted him to come. He planned to stay until Sunday, 'thus having
a honeymoon of four days',[110] but fortunately *Vogue* decided he should work
for them and would pay all his expenses. He ended by being there from 3
to 15 March, only working for *Vogue* in the extra week. He wondered if
Garbo would be as welcoming as he hoped or whether Schlee would come
out in hot pursuit.

Cecil arrived at his hotel in Beverly Hills. He was delighted to escape
freezing New York for the bright blue skies and fresh air of California. Garbo
came to meet him at a nearby bus-stop in her little buggy and drove him to
her home. She was embarrassed about the state of it, but Cecil was impressed by the Renoirs, the Modigliani, the Rouault and the Bonnard: 'At
last I was in the Holy of Holies. ... This was magic!'[111] Cecil wasted no
time:

> In a bout of tenderness I gathered her into a series of long embraces. We
> suddenly looked at each other in startled amazement. 'You really want
> to in the middle of the morning?' In a trance I went upstairs through her
> sitting-room up the circular steps to her pale blue, pale grey and bur-
> gundy coloured bedroom. We were very happy in our fervour and some-
> thing very violent had overtaken us both. We had not seen one another
> for so long. Our reunion was most passionate and ended in a serenity
> that was most beneficial. We came downstairs the tenderest of friends.*[112]

*This passage was erased from Cecil's manuscript diary, but copied identically in his own
hand on a separate sheet of paper.

Garbo loved the outdoor life of California (though Katharine Hepburn told her the bugs never die, but went to ground in the winter to multiply and would eventually take the place over). Therefore long walks along the beaches of Santa Monica were the order of the day. Once they saw a pair of young lovers being spied on by a negro. 'For me the negro and the flushed young couple was as weird a combination as any conceived by Truman Capote or his ilk.'[113] In the evening of the first day Garbo cooked for him and then it grew cold: 'My teeth were still chattering as I went upstairs again to Greta's room. . . .'[114] Ever since a burglary Garbo had been very nervous of intruders. 'I'm afraid to be alone,' she had told Cecil. 'I never was like that, but I am now.'[115] But even then Garbo did not let Cecil stay the night.

Garbo worked in the garden, drove Cecil to the market and they met the actress Constance Collier. In the evenings they dined together. Picking the waxy flowers of a blossoming orange tree, Cecil inhaled the scent and said, 'This is everything that I came all this way to enjoy.'[116] The evening was bliss: 'If there is another war then I shall be able to remember that I had the ecstasy of this night.'*[117] Another day Cecil sunbathed, taking off all his clothes: 'Greta seemed today a little less loving and more matter of fact. But the night of bliss cannot be sustained *ad infinitum*.'*[118] When the maid known as 'the Dragon' was away, Garbo too sunbathed naked. Then she washed with the hose. Their passionate affair continued after they partook of 'the usual salads and very good too. . . .'[119].

They saw friends like Charles and Elsie Mendl and Clifton Webb, which Garbo thought a waste of time. When they went out together Cecil found he played second fiddle to his luminary friend. They took mountain walks, though Cecil felt the cold damp air getting to his throat. After dinner he liked to smoke a cigar and lie with Garbo on the cedar-coloured sofa. On Monday 8 March Cecil began work for *Vogue*, which gave him glimpses of Hollywood which were 'vulgar, cruel and relentless'.[120] He welcomed his return to the haven of Garbo's home. Sometimes she became 'like a fifteen-year-old boy and looked more tired and more seriously beautiful than I had ever known her'.[121] Bad news came when Korda wired that he could not do *The Eagle* but wondered if Garbo might like to do *The Cherry Orchard* with Cukor. She sighed. She thought Chekhov a bore. Only on one night were Garbo and Cecil separated. She dined with the Mendls and Mary Pickford while he kept a date with Garson Kanin and Ruth Gordon. Constance Collier invited them together and Charlie Chaplin went through his repertoire of imitations.

On Friday 12 March they went to Metro-Goldwyn to see the Garbo version of *Anna Karenina*. 'Well, well,' she said. 'It takes Beaton to get me to the studios for the first time in six years.'[122] It proved to have considerably more

---

* Another expurgated diary entry.

suspense than the Korda one. Cecil often found himself in awe of Garbo when she philosophized about life. He was conscious of the 'frivolity and superficiality'[123] of his mind. When dining with Salka Viertel and her husband he was sorry not to be able to discuss film scripts with Garbo's favourite director and friend.

Alone with Garbo, Cecil related the story of his friendship with Peter Watson:

> After some time Greta seemed rather jealous and asked 'Do you love me?' but she sensed maybe a slight restlessness. However we went upstairs and enjoyed the opportunity of being together, an opportunity that seems to be petering out now for I have only one day more now before returning to New York, London and the indefinite future. Some time later in the dark, Greta said... that I had never before made love to her as I did tonight. ... I felt very happy and pleased with myself and great satisfaction for my prowess as a lover. Then I must hurry home for Greta was very tired. We waved tenderly to each other in the night. As I trailed my weary body home I wondered if I had made any advance on this trip towards the goal of marriage, towards an arrangement for a film or even a trip to England, and I must admit that I had not. However this has been a most happy, idyllic interlude. I am forever amazed that I have had these long un-interrupted days with my loved one and through all the hours together we have always been sympathetic companions though most of the time we have been besotted lovers.[124]

Cecil wanted Garbo to pose for a drawing but she refused. He wanted to photograph her but 'these were done under protest and she did not look well. Her hair suddenly became fluffy and messy and she looked unlike herself, rather vulgar and middle-aged.'[125] Cecil knew that her appearance swayed his affections considerably and Garbo sensed this.

On the last day they visited Catherine d'Erlanger and the photographer George Platt Lynes. They met the controversial author, Katherine Anne Porter. Later they discussed the power of the press and how it upset her so much. Garbo often said that Cecil was lucky not to have suffered. He thought she did not consider him a serious person:

> In that there is a modicum of truth for I have never until I met her realized how little I am able to scratch beneath the surface of the meaning of things.[126]

Later they returned to Garbo's house:

> I have a picture of her as a sort of Saint Sebastian laid out for suffering with her head thrown back and her arms held high with clenched fists. I have a picture of her profile outlined with a red glow from the heating

light on the wall by the bed. I remember her turning her head and gazing at me very sadly. Tomorrow I leave. This is our last night together. We lingered in each other's clasp in the hall and then the pantomime of the waving from door and window. As I walked home I wondered if I was not in a way rather relieved that I was departing tomorrow.[127]

Cecil was worn out by the intensity of the relationship. Garbo had not had enough sleep. She too was feeling the strain. Cecil felt the urge to work and had been reminded by his mother and secretary of his obligations as the family breadwinner:

I have done nothing for so long and I feel I should now set seriously to other tasks. For the past four months I have done little else but devote myself to my passion for Greta.[128]

Cecil's departure called for an enormous bouquet of mixed flowers. He went round to the house: 'I felt rather as if I were about to undergo an operation, an amputation, but my voice was very clear and cold.'[129] Suddenly emotion overcame him. His chest quivered and shook with sobs. The tears flowed freely down his cheeks. As he got into the yellow cab, he gazed at her 'looking like a tired, sad child of sixteen, looking out at me with such infinite pity and sorrow'.[130]

The taxi driver tried to talk to him but Cecil took none of it in:

I was blubbing like a fool. It was a wonder the driver did not notice in his mirror that he was driving a lunatick [sic] middle-aged man that was convulsed in childlike tears and sobs.[131]

The train journey to New York was a long one. Cecil settled down to the task of recording his bizarre adventures in his diary.

La Dame
aux
Camellias

Garbo as La Dame aux Camellias

24

The Return of the Prodigal

*I'm afraid much as I would like it, I realize the chances
of ever marrying her are very slight. She seems more
than ever in a muddle and can't help herself out of it, and
I don't think even I could influence her not to do the
wrong thing for herself. The emptiness and pointlessness
of her life, as it is, is monumental and Lord knows what'll
happen to her in ten years' time.*

Cecil to Clarissa Churchill, 29 December 1950

Ruth Gordon* and her husband, Garson Kanin, were on the train that
conveyed Cecil back to New York. He tried to tell them about Garbo, and
Ruth Gordon refused to listen: 'Don't,' she said. 'If it's no good, I don't want
to hear it, and if it is, I'll have a problem.'[1]
Back in New York Cecil wrote to his friend:

If Zöe Akins felt she had the entrée to the Vatican when she was given a
glimpse of your swimming-pool you can imagine how I felt at being
allowed to share your existence for that brief but limitless period when
there were long uninterrupted spells and we were living outside clock
time – in another sphere of happiness. It was wonderful for me to feel so
close and attached and I felt we got to know one another much better.
You can rely on me always to feel for you an increasing devotion and
affection. Thank you. Thank you. For the salad luncheons shared with
you and the blue birds, for the walks by the Pacific ocean and in the
mountains and the expedition to the farmers' market and seed shop, and
for the lovely sunny days in your garden. Thank you. Thank you. Merci
infiniment!

Muchas grazias
Dunk schon [*sic*][2]

---

* Ruth Gordon (b. 1896), best known to the present generation for her film roles in *Harold
and Maud* and *Rosemary's Baby*.

Cecil sailed from New York, after hectic days, on 27 March 1948. Four days later a telegram arrived from Hollywood which just said 'Cecil'. Armed with Virginia hams, he returned to a much improved Wiltshire home. He was preoccupied with perfecting Reddish House, the drawing-room of which was inspired by the lavish designs he did for *Lady Windermere's Fan* and is a tribute to the Edwardian era he so loved.

The spring and summer of 1948 are recorded in the letters he wrote to Garbo. These letters are as embarrassing to read as are almost all love letters. They begin as often as not with expressions such as: Mon ange, Le Bébé dort bien, Dear Sir or Madam, Angel, Dear Heart or even Comrade. They ask, 'Please, my dear young man, do scratch a few lines to your ardent suitor',[3] and end 'I remain, dear Sir, your dutiful, humble admirer Beaton'.[4] Occasionally there would be a covering letter couched in formal language that Schlee could see, containing a more intimate one within.

Cecil awaited further developments with Garbo and worked with gusto on his play *The Gainsborough Girls*, which took three years to come to fruition. It was again a period of change as old friends made way for new.

Edith Olivier suffered a stroke and died in May 1948, bringing home to Cecil 'a horrible realization of the nearness of death and of the shortness of life'.[5] At the funeral two ring doves flew from the church tower in unison. As their eyes filled with tears, Cecil and David Herbert cried out: 'Edith soaring through tracks unknown!'[6] Edith's death was followed by Emerald Cunard's on 10 July 1948. Cecil deeply regretted the loss of one 'who had pointed a finger to the future for me for twenty years'.[7] He asked permission to visit her remains – 'Emerald had become like a medieval sculpture with uncompromising definite features carved out of ivory'[8] – and he placed a rose by her bed.

Bébé Bérard came to stay and one evening they were talking quietly when the telephone rang and Cecil was asked why he was not at the Duchess of Kent's costume party at Coppins. It sounded fun and so, although it was late, they set off. Cecil mistook how far Coppins was from Broadchalke. His headlights did not work, a ground mist descended and he got thoroughly lost. He asked the way of a policeman, who asked why he had his car out at this time of night. Nearing Iver he enquired at various cottages where Coppins was and found villagers cowering with fear at their doors. They finally arrived at 3 a.m. fearing the party was long since over:

What a joy to hear the strains of a band, to see lights and cars and people moving about. We had the most wonderful welcome which recompensed us for many of the horrors of the journey, and soon we were in the midst of riotous gallops and polkas. The atmosphere of the party was enchanting, very friendly and small. Only the Duchess's intimate friends and relations.[9]

The Duchess had become a close friend of Cecil's and had lunched at Pelham Place in the summer of 1946. She now 'commanded' Cecil and Bébé to spend the night on sofas and stay for luncheon. She and Princess Olga came down in their dressing-gowns for a post mortem on the party. Cecil and Bébé breakfasted and lunched in their dinner-jackets. Later that month there was a showing of *The Eagle has Two Heads*, Cocteau's film. The Duchess of Kent was present, though annoyed that a private visit was made unexpectedly pompous and formal. The 600 guests hated the picture, though Bébé's costumes were very chic. The Duchess dined with Cecil and about a dozen friends after Bébé's ballet based on Haydn's *Clock Symphony*. All this caused Alice B. Toklas to write to the Chicago professor, Sammy Steward;

> Do you remember Cecil Beaton – he's desperately in love with Greta Garbo and the Duchess of Kent equally so with him. Do you like my gossip – everybody tells me a little – eventually I hear it all. . . .[10]

Needless to say, the Duchess was just a friend. Cecil was only granted the privilege of kissing her on the cheek in 1964.

Bébé Bérard died in the theatre in Paris, like Molière, suddenly, in January 1949. He was attending the final lighting rehearsal of his latest production

Christian Bérard

and a crowd surrounded him. He was only forty-six. 'For many years now he was one of my best and most loyal friends,' wrote Cecil, 'and one whom I was always excited to see. He was so stimulating and such a brilliant person that I needed only to be with him a few moments before my imagination was fired.'[11]

Shortly before this Cecil paid his penultimate call on Elsie Mendl at Versailles. He expected to find her at death's door but she made a triumphant entrance for dinner in her wheelchair even though she only weighed forty-two pounds. The next day she entertained twenty-four for Sunday lunch, including the Lunts. Two years later, on 12 July 1950, Elsie died aged ninety-four. Cecil wrote: 'In spite of her fantasies and frivolity [she] was a very remarkable character with great qualities of loyalty and kindness and a shrewd realistic approach. RIP.'[12]

Cecil was always ready to acquire new friends. In New York he had become an acquaintance of George Davis, the fiction editor of *Harper's Bazaar*, who, until 1945, ran a co-operative house in Middagh Street on Brooklyn Heights where people working in the arts could live or stay at reasonable prices. The brilliant group that gathered there included W.H. Auden (who enforced the rules of the house and collected the rent), Christopher Isherwood, Carson McCullers, Paul and Jane Bowles, Benjamin Britten, Peter Pears, Oliver Smith and others. Oliver Smith recalled that Cecil was 'a hunting-dog for talent' and they met 'in the forest of New York'.[13] Cecil was already a celebrity who would arrive on the scene 'like a marvellous old comet and then disappear'.[14] He was the first person in New York to speak about people like Lucian Freud and Francis Bacon. One of the people whom Cecil met through George Davis was Truman Capote. In the summer of 1948 Truman came to stay for a night at Broadchalke. 'I found him a very remarkable person, a genius and although only twenty-three years old has the maturity of a man of sixty,' reported Cecil to Garbo. 'I like him a lot, as well as being impressed and think if he lives (his blood doesn't flood easily in his veins – or some other such awful thing happens to him) he will make a contribution to the world.'[15]

Lucian Freud also became a friend at this time when he came to Reddish to draw Cecil:

I sat in the barn for hours on end bored stiff and not knowing what to do with my mouth, and the boy did a most wonderfully careful likeness of Vincent Sheean. I wasn't very pleased but tried to overcome my inferiority complex. The boy is charming and unexpected and it was nice to have him about the place for several days sketching the dog, the summer house and the branches of apples in the kitchen garden.[16]

And in September 1948 Clarissa Churchill became Cecil's delighted neighbour at Rose Bower Cottage, Bower Chalke. She would never be far away now until the day he died. 'I am so excited that I cannot sleep,' she wrote. 'I have never owned a bit of the earth before.'[17]

Cecil undertook more stage work. Responding to an sos he designed the décor for St John Hankin's *The Return of the Prodigal* in November, starring Dame Sybil Thorndike and John Gielgud (and directed by the latter). This Cecil created in his favoured Edwardian style, working at a frantic pace, but the results disappointed him and he found the play somewhat thin. It was not a success, running for only sixty-nine performances at the Globe, but as James Laver wrote: 'the Beaton décor and costumes provided a feast for the eye such as we have not enjoyed since the same artist's *Lady Windermere's Fan*.'[18] Binkie Beaumont thought it was unsuccessful because 'it is caviar and something that only appeals to us and the small group who are still interested in style, convention and manners'.[19]

In the midst of a certain amount of to-ing and fro-ing between London and New York in the autumn of 1948, Cecil devoted his time to the Olivier production of *The School for Scandal*. He had originally been commissioned to design this in the winter of 1947. After some preliminary work he left the Hogarth engraving designs in the care of his assistant, Martin Battersby. In December 1947, Battersby reported to Cecil the many problems he was having with Vivien Leigh. Cecil had ordained mother-of-pearl buttons. She did not want them:

> A hard glint came into Miss Leigh's eye, a hard tone in her voice and a very hard line in her jaw. 'We won't bother about that and I *don't* want buttons.' Round One to Miss Leigh with Battling Battersby retiring to his corner snarling hideously, and feeling that it is better to win the last battle than the first.[20]

However Battersby did not win the last battle. He did his best to put in as many Beaton touches as possible. He clashed with the wardrobe department who had their own ideas of design and presented him with costumes which, on the point of completion, bore little resemblance to Cecil's original plan.

In January 1948 he had a sticky interview with Laurence Olivier and John Burrell and had no choice but to resign 'as a matter of expediency'.[21] Soon after this Maud Nelson detected that the Oliviers were turning against Cecil 'especially V.L. and I am beginning to hate her in consequence and to feel quite definitely that she may be at the bottom of the A.K. [Korda] difficulties – a Siamese Cat and very hard and grasping at that'.[22] Since these original problems the play had travelled the world, during which time the marriage of Laurence Olivier and Vivien Leigh had crashed on the rocks.

Before the London opening at the Old Vic, Olivier bombarded Cecil with new ideas and demands for alterations. Cecil became irritated: 'I just don't like theatre folk. They're too self-centred and spoilt.'[23] However, the results were lavish in taste and money. Ivor Brown wrote: 'Vivien Leigh's beauty was perfectly framed by the dresses and hats arranged for her, and Gainsborough himself could have rejoiced in the portrait of Lady Teazle thus provided.'[24] Dennis Arundell, his erstwhile Cambridge colleague, called Cecil's work 'a revolution'.[25] Cecil was in America on the first night but the Oliviers cabled: 'At the very mention of your name you received the most wonderful of any acclamation last night.'[26]

Back in London in March 1949, Cecil went to see *The School for Scandal*, which he found thrilling. 'The Oliviers rather grudging in their generosity and I fear they are not good friends behind my back.'[27] This episode, so lightly brushed aside at the time, was eventually magnified into the highly exaggerated account that Cecil gave in *The Strenuous Years*. In that version neither would speak to him other than in monosyllables and Cecil ends by declaring: 'I would have no further interest in them – let alone feel that we were friends. They were both out of my life for ever.'[28] On the other hand contemporary evidence relates that in May 1949 Cecil went to see *Richard III*, sat in the front row and offended the Oliviers by not going round to congratulate them. 'They were absolutely furious.'[29] Even so in April 1950 he lunched with both of them, writing to Garbo: 'I didn't like her. Oh dear no, she has lost her looks, very fat in the face. It's very sad and it makes her very unhappy and bad tempered.'[30] Again he wrote to Garbo in November 1950: 'I should be very jealous if you had even met the Oliviers. They aren't real friends of mine though they may now pretend to be.'[31] Furthermore in 1956 Olivier telephoned Cecil to ask him to design *The Prince and the Showgirl*. Though Cecil did not do this, he certainly considered the idea and it was all perfectly amicable. 'I was impressed by L.O.,' he wrote then, 'his solidity and maturity, seriousness.'[32]

Soon after this episode, Cecil was caught up in the 1949 revival of *Apparitions*, which caused endless problems. This time they scrapped the painted scenery and caused effects to be projected onto an enormous cyclorama from a lantern. On the first night there were twenty-one curtain calls, Cecil tripped up in full view of the audience and the Duchess of Kent threw him a rose from the Royal Box. Cecil's old aunts sat in the dress circle 'in all their old moth-eaten bits of fur, and bits and pieces of old-fashioned jewellery and they were thrilled to be taken to the Royal Box and presented and given champagne'.[33]

Cecil's photographic career came to another important climax at the end of 1948. Prince Charles was born on 14 November and after an agonizing silence from the Palace, where everyone was preoccupied with the King's illness, he was summoned to record the Prince's arrival in the world in an irresistible series of portraits, most notably of mother and child. They were taken on the King's birthday, 14 December. Queen Elizabeth ordered forty-eight copies and was charged two guineas a picture.

Unfortunately there was an unpleasant sequel to this. Overseas newspapers broke the Palace embargo and the *Evening Standard* reproduced the front cover of *Samedi Soir* with a picture of the Prince, causing consternation among its rivals. The *Standard* also printed a snide article about how much money Cecil would be making. John Gordon attacked the Palace Press Office in the *Sunday Express* and objected to Cecil having a world monopoly in pictures of the Prince. Cecil was obliged to sue the sanctimonious Scotsman.

In June 1949 Cecil went to Paris to photograph the Windsors in the house which Paul-Louis Weiller had loaned them. 'The Duchess's face in repose has a tragic look,' noted Cecil. 'His face now begins to show the emptiness of life. It is too impertinent to be tragic.... The eyes do not correspond. He looks like a mad terrier, haunted one moment and then with a flick of the head he is laughing fecklessly.'[34] He stayed with Lilia Ralli, 'my little Greek friend who was very hospitable and sweet', he reported to Garbo, 'but no bedding out together any more because I am faithful to you in my own fashion ... I am faithful to you darling in my way'.[35] When the Duchess of Kent flew to Paris for a charity ball, Cecil escorted her and Lilia on a round of Paris night-clubs.

In London Cecil invited the Duchess of Kent to a small party which expanded to include so many people from different worlds that the Duchess was swamped. Then the Palace rang and summoned him to photograph Princess Margaret for her nineteenth birthday:

> The photography at the Palace was hard work and didn't give me enough opportunity to talk to [Princess Margaret]. She had been out at a night-club until 5.30 the morning before and got a bit tired after two hours' posing. But she is witty and seems quite kindly disposed towards humanity.[36]

The photographs were taken of her in a white Hartnell dress embroidered with sequin butterflies. The press thought she had a look of Queen Alexandra. Later in the year in London Cecil photographed Princess Marie Louise, Queen Victoria's granddaughter, which proved highly comical. Cecil had always thought the Princess 'an old gaga absurdity', but he ended by finding her 'absolutely enchanting'.[37] Later, at the time of the Queen's Coronation in 1953, she was the subject of one of his most striking photographs, in her diamond tiara, pearls and fur wrap, one hand outstretched as if in blessing. He did not dare show her the more dramatic results of the sitting, which she might not have found sufficiently formal or dignified.

Cecil was able to travel in Europe in 1949. In April he spent some days at the Villa Mauresque with Somerset Maugham. He found the Côte d'Azur a little forlorn and not living up to his *Merry Widow* dreams. He was interested in the way the ageing author fended off fans, press and visitors with letters of introduction. Juliet Duff was the only woman of the party.

Graham Sutherland was at work on his memorable portrait of Maugham, and Chagall came to lunch.

In the summer, at Broadchalke, Tilly Losch came to stay, soon followed by Peter Watson. In his diary Cecil noted:

> Peter came to stay at Reddish House for the first time. We have seen one another very little during the last few years but after three days with him I feel all the same emotions and now he has left I feel quite a void in my life.[38]

To Garbo he wrote: 'He is a strange, warped individual.'[39]

In August Cecil set off for Tangiers, after a summer ruined by dreadful rows with his mother. He went so far as to wonder if he should not seek his own place of retreat and independence, giving up the country house he now loved so dearly. He left home in a state of nervous exhaustion for the luxury of his first summer holiday since the war. He drove with David Herbert via Paris and Vézelay to Vienne, Nîmes ('still as romantic in memory'),[40] Arles and on to Marseilles. They sailed to Tangiers, which after an interval of ten years seemed more sprawling and less sharply coloured. The French writer Jacques de Lacretelle described Tangiers as a town without a soul. Cecil saw at once that it was full of 'black-market gangsters, Spanish crooks, French expatriates, the different Legations and the old eccentric English, the old ladies who have lived here all their lives and the decadent ones who come here merely for louche reasons'.[41]

Tangiers life was as suffocatingly parochial as ever and Cecil was soon busily taking notes to turn the inhabitants into characters for a play. No small detail of the lives of Ferida, Ada and Jessie Green, Mrs Wildbaum, Ira Belline and others was too trivial to record. David Herbert announced excitedly: 'we know so little of what goes on here'.[42] Unhappy Arab wives cut hands off corpses, morsels of which they put in soup to poison their husbands. Tarts got excited when the fleet came in and drunken rows ensued. Truman Capote was living on a mountain top, occasionally coming down to the town to add 'a shot of good sense'.[43] He was an exaggerated figure with his shopping basket filled with Listerine, white chocolate, tins of butter, candies and books from the American library. The novelist Jane Bowles, Truman's hostess at the Hotel el Fahar, previously a stranger, became 'more wonderful and alluring and brilliant and surprising'.[44] One night she found herself in unexpected danger. A party had been drinking at David's house. There was dancing and, in a moment of exuberance, Cecil picked up the tiny novelist and swung her round, narrowly missing some marble. Oliver Smith recalled: 'He could have killed her.'[45]

Cecil and David stayed at Loel Guinness's house, the Villa Mektoub. There were two memorable parties. One was given by the eccentric Comtesse de Lafaille, who ran what Etienne de Beaumont called a concentration camp for animals. She gave a fancy-dress party in a room with Aubusson carpets on the wall and straw on the floor. The party was a fiasco and both host and hostess passed out from alcohol. Cecil then helped arrange a masquerade in a grotto he decorated to which people came dressed as errants and were served champagne, cooled in the sea, and hashish. Truman, claiming a fear of scorpions, was carried down the cliff-face by a group of Moroccans and the guests lay about in the moonlight on cushions spread out on the sand. Inevitably the real party took place when the post-mortems began the next day.

Tangiers was not entirely to Truman Capote's taste. 'Cecil Beaton is here,' he wrote, 'staying in a house owned by the Guinnesses. Wouldn't you know that we two iron-winged butterflies would find ourselves in the same hollyhock? If not for him, I'd move on....'[46] Cecil remained in this sultry atmosphere until September, after which he was glad to escape. He and Truman sailed to Marseilles. 'Well, at any rate it's a real town,'[47] said Truman. From there Cecil went at once to Paris where he rang Garbo. 'Is that you, Beattie?' she asked. 'Well I never.'[48] Hearing that, he knew she was in a good mood.

Cecil's last brush with Garbo had begun badly but ended well. At the beginning of a six-week visit to New York in December 1948 he had telephoned and she had refused to take his call. He was furious and when she rang back pretended not to recognize her, asking, 'Is it some Japanese?'[49] He found her very restless. When he asked her 'Will you marry me?' she replied, 'Oh what a brutal question.'[50] She worried about returning to films and was critical of everything around her, including Truman Capote. She told Cecil:

> Truman Capote isn't first class, believe me. He wouldn't say the things he does if he were and he's so outrageous, such silly behaviour. He's not a person in the round. Nobody criticizes people for their private life. That's each individual's own business, but why make everything so obvious. It's offensive. You should always allow people the benefit of the doubt.[51]

On the other hand Truman described Garbo's face as 'the peak face of humanity, nothing short of perfection'.[52]

During Cecil's stay, he met Garbo each day and believed they were developing 'in even closer intimacy'. But when Cecil asked her to reserve a particular Monday evening, she said she could not. Clearly she was seeing Schlee, which angered Cecil. However, the visit ended on an optimistic note.

Cecil had not seen Garbo since then but he had seen Georges Schlee in Paris in June. 'The little man' was friendly and they had discussed the film Garbo might do with Josh Logan. Cecil suggested that Schlee bring Garbo to Reddish and Schlee had responded by inviting Cecil to come and see her in Paris:

> So if you feel like it do get him to send a wire and try and mention my name to him glibly from time to time. It only makes me seem like a ghoul if nothing is ever said. It may be wrong but I think my visit to him cleared the atmosphere quite a bit, at any rate for the time being and I'm very glad I went, and thrilled it turned out well.[53]

Since then Garbo had been to Italy on her abortive, though seriously meant, plan to make a film called *The Duchess of Langeais* opposite James Mason. The project came to nothing because the company had no money and their attempts to persuade Garbo to undertake the fund-raising were soon squashed. The paparazzi had besieged Garbo in her hotel where she spent long days with the blinds drawn. Thus the last chance of Garbo making a film was lost for ever.

In Paris Schlee told Cecil how clever he had been in extricating her from her dealings with the producers. Cecil concluded:

> The way he has managed to take control of Greta's interests is quite alarming, and I see no possibility of her getting free of him, for although they are no longer stimulated by each other's company and they are apt to eat in silence, she gives a feeling of importance to his dreary existence and he is not likely to let her slip from his clutches. She, meanwhile, is touched by his loyal devotion and his efforts on her part, and thus they are bound together.[54]

Diana Cooper suggested that Cecil might like to take Garbo down to Chantilly, the love pavilion near Paris to which she and Duff had retired after leaving the British Embassy in 1947. The Coopers were not there at the time and so Cecil, Garbo and Schlee set off on their day trip. It was the first time that Schlee had had the chance of observing Cecil and Garbo together. Cecil was to Schlee 'a ghoulish unknown quantity always to be contended with and never seen'.[55] On this day all went well, though Cecil admitted that occasionally 'I looked at him with a steely glare of hatred in my eyes but I do not know whether he detected it or not.'[56] Schlee never left them alone except when he went to the lavatory before the drive back to Paris.

> Then Greta whispered, 'Can't you come to America now? I know of two people who would lend us their house in the desert. They're in Europe now.' But before we had time to whisper more than a few urgent sentences, the ghoul was back and I rustled some thousand franc notes pretending that we were discussing how much to tip Jean.[57]

That night Cecil took Lilia Ralli to the theatre. On his way home he caught a glimpse of Schlee and Garbo in their blue car. He was upset to see how happy they were in each other's company, their heads quite close together,

Garbo smiling affectionately. In December Garbo backed out of the desert scheme.

Cecil was again in Paris in November 1949 to design a ballet for Boris Kochno at the Théâtre des Champs-Elysées. *Devoirs de Vacances*, by John Taras, starred Leslie Caron (later the star of *Gigi*), with music by William Walton. Cecil was horrified at the way everything was left until the last moment. He stayed at Chantilly with Duff and Diana Cooper witnessing the scenes so well captured by Enid Bagnold in her novel *The Loved and Envied*.*

In 1949 Cecil was only forty-five, yet he felt he was ageing alarmingly. Ever since Temple Court days he had been having his hair cut by Mr Massey at Selfridges. Even in those days Cecil thought Massey looked old. This time it was his turn to flinch at the image in the glass. However, worse was to come. When a handglass was produced to show him the crown of his head, he discovered for the first time that he was almost bald. 'I felt quite sick, as one does when an elevator rushes too quickly through space.'[58] Cecil appealed to Massey, hoping it was not true, but Massey made the situation more 'tragic' by adding: 'I shouldn't have let you see it. Should I?'[59]

In January 1950 Cecil sailed for New York on the *Queen Mary*. He was lunching with Ann Rothermere when the telegraph boy gave him a wire. It came from Maud and stated: 'Dear Aunt Jessie passed peacefully away 2.30 a.m. Friday.' The news was not unexpected. 'I am filled with regret that I did not take more opportunities of really talking to this wonderful old bird,' wrote Cecil to Juliet Duff, 'as she had a great philosophy and wisdom and it's so silly not to avail oneself of the benefit of the experience of people like that. Family relationships are very tricky things and after a bit one sees only a certain side of a person and habit and self-consciousness prevent one from starting off on a different tack.'[60] Aunt Jessie would have been eighty-seven on the 12th. Cecil wrote eleven long pages of diary about his aunt, whose last days had been painful ones. Years later (in 1971) he published *My Bolivian Aunt*, a eulogistic tribute to this important early influence on his life. The last time Cecil saw her, Aunt Jessie drank two glasses of champagne with him and said: 'You can never be repaid for all you've done. We can't do without you, Cecil.'[61] She waved with her shrunken hand and blew him a kiss. He left the room in tears.

The year 1950 proved to be one of heavy responsibility for Cecil. Still battling on with his play and still getting nowhere, his first assignment was in New York. He redecorated the thirty-seventh-floor tower apartment at the Sherry-Netherland for Serge Obolensky who gave him a fifty per cent discount in these rooms and twenty-five per cent off in the restaurant. Thus for some years Cecil based himself in the Sherry-Netherland Beaton suite whenever in New York. He took snapshots of Garbo smiling over a coffee-

* Lady Diana Cooper is 'Lady Maclean' in this book. See also *The Strenuous Years*, pp. 62–72.

pot and was annoyed that silly gossip articles appeared about the romance in New York papers. He was even more annoyed when Ed Sullivan printed a piece stating that Cecil had not been cleared by the Anti-Defamation League of B'nai B'rith, another brief resurrection of the *Vogue* row of 1938.

Cecil's stage work included designing *Cry of the Peacock*, by Cecil Robson, based on a Jean Anouilh play. This production is mainly memorable for the atrocious way the director and chief backer, Leonora Corbett, was ousted, despite doing an excellent job. Robert Coleman wrote: 'The best thing about *Cry of the Peacock* is the stunning rococo setting and period costumes, circa 1912, by Cecil Beaton.'[62] Cecil and Lincoln Kirstein worked on the Ashton/Benjamin Britten ballet, *Les Illuminations*, which opened at the City Centre, New York, in March 1950. Kirstein never had any problems working with Cecil because of their shared love of ballet. Each day he arrived at Cecil's hotel with more books and ideas in order to give it a childlike quality. Cecil also consulted John Myers, the art dealer, who suggested he study Paul Klee's work for dour skies and crazy churches. Cecil dressed the characters as clowns. One day there was a row over the costumes and Cecil and Freddie Ashton were heard in heated conversation. Lincoln Kirstein commented: 'Cecil and Freddie are once again at needlepoints.'[63] *Les Illuminations* was badly received when it opened at Covent Garden on 20 July. The highbrow critics called it 'decadent, nasty, chi-chi and chic'.[64] Cecil was surprised as he thought it 'a lovely work and very near to Rimbaud'.[65] But John Piper, an early critic, wrote formally to say that his designs were 'among the finest I have seen on the modern stage at all'.[66] When it was restaged in New York in 1967, Lincoln Kirstein wrote: 'It was even too brilliant for Mr Barnes as per the enclosed.'[67] Clive Barnes, the distinguished critic, was normally a thorn in Cecil's flesh:

> Mr Beaton is a designer I have more often despised than not – he is a kind of rich man's Christian Bérard. But in this *Illuminations*, with his speckly black-and-white backcloths and Aubrey Beardsley-like white figures floating around in a *fin de siècle* inferno, Mr Beaton has created a pastiche that somehow enhances the genuineness and validity of the ballet's statement.[68]

In March Cecil came home to design *The Second Mrs Tanqueray*, one set of which was based on the tapestry room at West Wycombe, the seat of the Dashwood family. Cecil liked neither the play, nor its audiences, who made him feel out of touch with the public's taste. Cecil could not have known it at the time but there was at least one member of the audience who was impressed – the young Roy Strong, then a pupil at Edmonton County Grammar School:

> Heroes of childhood remain heroes for life. I was fourteen when I saw my first set of scenery and costumes by Cecil Beaton. The play was *The*

Second Mrs Tanqueray, memorable also for Eileen Herlie's marvellous portrayal of Paula with her stunning final exit in the last act. At the time I was extremely stagestruck, passionately wishing to design for the theatre. I still remember the impact of those sumptuous sets and costumes, the magic Beaton touch bringing Edwardian opulence to the greyness of post-war London: rich swagged draperies, huge potted palms, trailing, heavily fringed tablecloths and an explosion of bijouterie. Every costume caused a gasp in a world just embracing the extravagance of the New Look. Then and ever since one has recognized that the art of Cecil Beaton stood for something important – *Style*.[69]

Truman Capote craved the orange-lined cloak that Cecil created for Eileen Herlie. Before the play opened in London in August, 'Herlie Burly', as Cecil called the star, was given a new husband and a new dress. The Duchess of Kent attended the play with Cecil on 31 August.

Later Cecil redecorated the Duke of York's Theatre in London, restoring the red plush, the gilding and the debased rococo. He earned the plaudits of Cecil Wilson in the *Daily Mail*: 'For Cecil Beaton's artistry in transforming the shabby old Duke of York's into an elegant Christmas cake of a theatre there can be only praise.'[70]

In April 1950 he endured his first major row with Maud Nelson. Maud was not particularly well, nor was she particularly helpful to Cecil. She wrote offering her resignation, which Cecil accepted. Then she wrote again, pointing out that she had worked loyally since 1940 on the same small salary, had got Cecil important jobs through her contacts and had taken the brunt of a particularly bad row he had had with his mother. She had not meant to resign and so for three more years Cecil had to suffer her inefficiency, prolonged absences and occasional hysterical outbursts.

The following month Cecil went to photograph Queen Elizabeth for her fiftieth birthday. Cecil was again overcome by her charm and took hundreds of pictures. He was amused to hear that a woman painter who had been at the Palace, doing a portrait of the Queen, had fallen victim to her delicious iced cakes and put on an extra stone in weight. Later in the year his telegram on the birth of Princess Anne on 15 August 1950: 'Respectful Congratulations',[71] was followed by an invitation to photograph the baby Princess:

> Babies are difficult at the best of times and this one was one of the worst times because the baby only wanted to be allowed to sleep. Who's to blame her? I was not allowed to take a jack along with me to keep her eyes open so we had to make bird noises, rattle keys, clap our hands, jump up and down. The more idiotic the performance the more bored the baby. Only a drop of glycerine on the tongue seemed to bring any favourable reaction.[72]

Cecil was pleased with his picture of Prince Charles kissing his sister, which travelled far and wide.

In the summer Cecil spent two weeks in Taormina, where he swam for hours absorbing all the details of marine life:

> The whole bed of the sea is so littered with surprises that one would not be amazed to see a drowned sailor lying with pearls in his mouth, but when I was exploring on my own beneath the water I got a terrible shock when an enormous white object shot in front of me. I thought this was the end and a vast octopus had got me, but no it was the leg of the American Janie Pansa.[73]

For part of the time he stayed in Truman Capote's pink house on the hills covered with olive groves. Truman, now a supportive friend, encouraged him over his two ambitions, the play and his romance. At difficult moments Truman would write: 'Cecil, what would the world do without you? You are one of its few bright fixtures.'[74]

Cecil certainly emerged as a bright fixture in the elegant photographs taken by the American photographer Irving Penn, in September. Penn had served in the Eighth Army and greatly admired some of Cecil's North African photographs. He was anxious to photograph Cecil with the 'most dramatic effect'.[75] He suggested evening dress and opera cloak. This was by nature of a present. Irving Penn recalled: 'I didn't want to hurt him. I tried to think what he would like. When he came into the studio, he took a black ball-point pen and began to draw his hair back on at the front. That was Cecil. It was theatre. He didn't mind who knew.'[76] The handsome results of this sitting were much admired in New York: 'They are pictures of another Cecil Beaton than most know,'[77] wrote Penn. The two photographers came from different backgrounds but were fellow *Vogue* workers. At one sitting Penn arrived feeling very different from Cecil:

> I thought once that you must be making fun of me since the instructions you gave me were almost directly opposite to the things I say during a sitting, but in retrospect I realize it was all a piece – the vague clairvoyance, the gentleness of not meeting the subject too hard on, the charmingly smooth relationship you have with your assistants.[78]

Later Irving Penn commented:

> He invented the Cecil Beaton woman. She was rather English, rather distant, the sort of woman that has roses falling at her feet. He could take a store girl from Texas or New York and transform her. Photography is projection. He projected them. Sometimes Cecil would come into the studio, giving the impression that he'd had too much wine at lunch. He'd seem not to have thought about it all very much. He'd tear a bit of paper

on one side, he'd talk to the model. He'd go behind the camera. Out would come the Cecil Beaton woman.[79]

Penn suspected Cecil's inner loneliness, wondered what happened after the last guest had left and wished that he had known him better. 'I showed him a professional face too,'[80] he said. On the other hand he thought Cecil's portraits of Garbo particularly poor: 'He never got anywhere with her. It was a troubled brother and sister relationship.'[81]

Meanwhile, Garbo was in America, making a year's work out of becoming an American citizen. Cecil received several letters from her in which she said how much she wanted to see him in America, how out of sorts she was, how she was cramming 'poison' down her throat, unable to travel, but hoping they could perhaps later have what she called a fling at Paris. Cecil bumped into Schlee when they were both in Paris and he told Cecil that Garbo was not ill at all. Cecil rebuked her:

> Fine! I am so glad!! It's thrilling news: I wish you had sent me a wire saying 'Ulcer vanished' and I should have had no more mental pictures of you eating blue grey cauliflower.[82]

Garbo continued to write, reminding Cecil of a visit they had paid to a fortune-teller, Nella Webb. Garbo said that she was contemplating entering a home for overwroughts. She assured Cecil that she missed him very much. Cecil replied: 'I am sad to think we are both going through such a static, frustrating period and I feel Nella Webb must be wrong with her dates. However she did tell us not to worry and that all would come out well.'[83]

In November 1950 Cecil saw Mercedes de Acosta in Paris. She told him she thought it was now too late for him to marry Garbo. On 30 November Cecil sailed on the *Queen Elizabeth* to New York. The Duke of Windsor was on board and so was the ghost of his memoirs, Charles Murphy, who regaled Cecil with gossip about the problems of the Windsors. In New York the Duchess saw Cecil's suite at the Sherry-Netherland and was so impressed that she declared she wanted to move from the Waldorf at once.

Curiously Cecil was fearful of the outbreak of another world war. Nevertheless when Garbo arrived unexpectedly from California to see a doctor about a rash, his spirits soared. Garbo, described by Mercedes at this time as 'a complex mixture of greatness and pettiness',[84] was at last an American citizen. She had taken to wearing a spotted veil to protect her identity in the streets. When she and Cecil attended a new version of his *Camille* ballet and he went to take a curtain call she was livid. 'I realized how vulgar my self-display had been,' noted Cecil, 'and how once again all G's instincts are the right ones.'[85]

Whereas 1950 had been a static year with no progress made, 1951 saw the realization of Cecil's two dreams about his play and Garbo's visit to England. Alas, however, both these were to end in disappointment.

Meanwhile Cecil created the décor for Balanchine's ballet *Swan Lake*, which was staged by the New York City Ballet at the end of the year. It proved a colossal success: 'It is the most beautiful thing we have ever achieved, and the house is sold out every time we do it,' wrote Lincoln Kirstein. 'Karinska's tutus were applauded the moment they arrived on stage. She even managed to find some real swan's feathers.'[86]

On Cecil's last evening in New York he discussed marriage with Garbo. 'I probably will,' she said, and then Cecil waved a sheet from his Sherry-Netherland window and she flashed a light from Hampshire House. 'It was a lovely farewell gesture and I feel that with the years our friendship has been cemented even firmer.' She said: 'With me that generally happens. I have few friends but they always stick.'[87]

Cecil went to Florida, Miami and Jamaica. Ann Rothermere reported news of the trip to Diana Cooper:

> This remote tropical island has become a playground for that fraternity of gentlemen in whom I find most pleasure – the joy of putting Cecil and Oliver Messel in underwater masks and introducing them to a new world of fish and coral design; Cecil was tremendously brave and seeing a sneezing dangerous barracuda chased it 'because it looked like a disagreeable dowager'.[88]

Later he went to Spain. In England he designed *Our Lady's Tumbler* by Ronald Duncan, placing eight tall black candle-holders in Salisbury Cathedral, and *Casse-Noisette* for Freddie Ashton at Covent Garden. 'Some of Cecil Beaton's costumes are among the loveliest I have seen,'[89] wrote Richard Buckle.

Cecil finished his books *Ballet* and *Photobiography*, which he hoped would round off his career as a photographer. When he photographed Princess Margaret for her twenty-first birthday, Queen Elizabeth made a point of coming from her rooms to thank him for the book, saying she had laughed at the descriptions of her lady-in-waiting in maroon wool. Osbert Sitwell wrote that he and Edith were touched by his mentions of them: 'They brought many delightful hours back to us.'[90]

Tchelitchew, on the other hand, was hurt not to be mentioned. Diana Cooper thought the book 'proves photography to be a true and living art. And what a life it has given you, what a war, what courage? ... The Queen's conversation is a photograph in itself. Some fool said to me, "Why does Cecil do that. The Royalty will be furious", but they'll be enchanted.'[91]

25

*Man Proposes, God Disposes**

I feel my life very empty and lonely. I really want very much to get married and make all sorts of radical changes. I feel hemmed in by my secretary and don't feel my life is at all as I would wish it.

Cecil to Garbo, 31 July 1951

The curtain rose on *The Gainsborough Girls* at the Theatre Royal, Brighton, on 16 July 1951. This was the culmination of three years' work and weeks of preparation, with the attendant share of frustrations, excitements and disappointments.

The idea for the play was buried deep in Cecil's past. In his diary of 11 November 1928, Cecil wrote:

I thought it might be fun to write a story with times and periods jumbled together so that some fabulous woman would be sitting to have her portrait painted by Greco to Gainsborough simultaneously – enter celebrities of every period to a large dinner.[1]

On his train journey from California to New York in March 1948, Cecil mentioned the idea of writing a story about Gainsborough's daughter going mad through snobbishness. Ruth Gordon and Garson Kanin suggested he should make a play out of this.

Cecil set to work, busily writing and rewriting: 'Do hurry it along because we are so anxious to see it,' wrote Garson Kanin on 6 May 1948, 'and just see that it is terribly pretty and sexy and romantic and filled with clashes of all sorts.'[2] Having buried himself at Broadchalke for some weeks, Cecil braved a first reading to Hal Burton, who gave him 'about the coldest douche I think I have ever suffered', he told Garbo. 'I have not yet recovered from the shock and I am pretty resilient as you know.'[3] Cecil was told that his play lacked dramatic form, there was no conflict between the characters, no suspense, no direction or sense of purpose. Cecil asked if he should continue and was answered with silence. Nevertheless, when he recovered, he threw himself back into the task.

* A line quoted by Garbo to Cecil.

Enid Bagnold thought Cecil would be on stronger ground if his play was based on the rise of a young man: 'You know all about what it is like to be poor and unknown and what it is like slowly to shine out till one is known and loved. *That* is a universal subject and you have sometimes let fall to me such exclamations of reality that I know you could do it.'⁴

He persevered with *Gainsborough*. In New York in November 1948 he risked reading it to three highly professional friends – Anita Loos, and his first encouragers, the Kanins. Cecil was reinspired by their rapturous reception of his work and was so excited that he could not sleep for several nights. Nothing, not even the lesser enthusiasm of later readers, could dampen his wish to pursue the career of playwright, as he explained in a letter to his mother:

> I have felt that it was the one chance for me to be able to alter my profession, since I really don't think that photography will hold me in good stead during my middle age, and I feel I have more or less skimmed all the cream off that particular activity.⁵

On his return voyage to London in February 1949, Cecil discovered that Somerset Maugham was on board. Monroe Wheeler, a curator at the Museum of Modern Art, was travelling with Maugham. He invited Cecil to join them for meals.

Maugham asked if he could read Cecil's play. At first Cecil lied and said he did not have a copy with him, but then decided to seize this wonderful opportunity. Maugham read the play and announced: 'I have read your play but I will tell you what I think of it at some more suitable time and in private.'⁶ Monroe Wheeler fuelled Cecil's anxiety by telling him that Willie was worried about what to say. Maugham met Cecil at 3.30 that afternoon. His conclusion was that it was well written, very dramatic and the characters were excellent. However, Gainsborough and Christie spoke in an eighteenth-century idiom while other characters used expressions such as 'giving someone a lift'. He felt the final curtain was too arbitrary and advised Cecil to read Fielding and Sheridan in order to absorb more of the eighteenth-century flavour. Then Maugham said: 'Now I'm going to leave you for the cinema',⁷ and bolted for the door.

Cecil placed his play with Binkie Beaumont, who talked of tempting the formidable Tyrone Guthrie to direct it, and of starring Ralph Richardson and Vivien Leigh. Guthrie was not forthcoming, so Beaumont drew up a new shortlist of first-class directors – Michael Benthall, Peter Glenville, Anthony Quayle or John Gielgud.

The Kanins came to stay at Broadchalke to give Cecil further advice, as Cecil reported to Garbo:

> I then came down here with the Kanins whom you don't like but at the risk of putting myself in the wrong I liked them more than ever and

enjoyed their visit enormously. They were so appreciative of all the things English and were like two very cultivated and clever children never missing a trick.[8]

Binkie Beaumont then announced that he disliked the play in its revised form because Cecil had turned a domestic play into a stark tragedy. Diligently, Cecil rewrote to order, but in April 1950, after two years of prevarication, Binkie Beaumont gave up on the play. Cecil then had to find new agents in the form of Richard Aldrich (husband of Gertrude Lawrence) and Dick Myers (Aldrich and Myers). At last in 1951 Cecil was told the play was ready for staging. He had not had an easy time. Although he was an expert at decorating a set and creating magnificent costumes he found dialogue hard to make convincing. As always his approach was visual. He wanted more than anything to express himself as a serious artist. The efforts he put into this play were ill-rewarded in every way, not least financially.

Directors came and went before Norman Marshall took charge. Actors were sought, won and lost. Laurence Hardy was signed: 'I am so grateful for his youthfulness, and for his enthusiasm and his deep strange coky-crackle voice is a deep asset.'[9] Henry Sherek, the producer, leaped about like a dynamo. As rehearsals progressed Cecil noted: 'I am entranced by my own play and try not to laugh at my own jokes but I find it terribly hard not to cry at the emotional scenes.'[10] Though there were the inevitable set-backs, Cecil looked forward to a first night of triumph and dreaded how he would survive a disappointment. He began to feel the strain when Ronald Howard walked out of his part and Martin Battersby resigned as his assistant set designer, never to be forgiven. Even Angela Baddeley* threatened to depart when Cecil suggested a little padding to hide her thinness. At home Cecil's mother fell and broke her wrist, causing serious worries over her health, and Maud proved as hopeless as ever in the general strain. Garbo was in Bermuda with Schlee, who had come out of hospital, and beginning to plan her escape to join Cecil. Tension mounted before the first night:

In a taxi going to the [Festival of Britain] exhibition I find myself returning to a certain scene and my bosom heaves. Heaven knows how I will ever survive the disappointment if the whole thing flops. I am banking so much on its being a success that if it is not my whole career is in a hell of a mess. I can't, after the excitement of the last few weeks, just go back to taking photographs and yet I feel at the moment I would never be able to achieve another Gainsborough. The months in my bedroom, the help from various people, have all added up to something that surprises me. But conjectures are dangerous and I must try not to think too much of the future during the next three days.[11]

---

* Angela Baddeley (1900–76), later the far from sylphlike cook, Mrs Bridges, in *Upstairs, Downstairs.*

Deep unhappiness was to follow. After the rehearsal Cecil's agent Laurence Evans 'looked extremely glum'[12] and the producer's wife, Mrs Myers, when asked if she would like a sandwich, said, 'I would like a taxi.'[13] Maud Nelson had unwisely primed the first-night audience with too many friends and London critics. 'Half of them were on tenterhooks for me and very tense and unresponsive,' wrote Cecil, 'and the other half were equally tense with friendly enmity.'[14] There were no laughs in the first act and not enough in the second. At the dinner afterwards Diana Cooper rushed round stirring up friends to applaud Cecil when he emerged, but when the reviews came the worst had to be faced, 'and all my day dreamings of people saying "this is a new dramatist – this a good play" were dashed.'[15] Dick Myers did not give up at once but the critics stamped the play a failure: the evening was declared insipid. Nevertheless the grey-haired Brighton ladies enjoyed it in its fortnight there and it went on to play at Newcastle ('a terrible week'), Leeds (which was 'mad about it') and Manchester. 'A sickening cable'[16] came from the management in Paris squashing any hope of going to New York.

The day following the first night Duff Cooper wrote to say he thought much of the criticism unfair and some of it 'deliberately malicious'. He went on:

> Having won distinction in other fields you have naturally aroused jealousy and there are many obscure scribes whom you have never seen and who are delighted to have a chance of throwing dirt at you. I thought it a good play and I enjoyed it. What is more, I am sure you can write a better one.[17]

Constance Collier and Katharine Hepburn came to see it and were enthusiastic, Kenneth Tynan wrote that he expected more of Cecil. This play revealed that he had 'a simple and sentimental heart.... It was as if an avocado pear had been squeezed and discharged syrup.'[18] Cecil felt gloomy: 'I am sad at the idea of having to go on being a photographer. I feel I have had the best of that career.'[19]

The ballerina, Lopokova, whom Cecil visited at Firle, told him it took three weeks to get over bad press notices. James Pope-Hennessy was in awe of Cecil's determination not to be defeated. After a short break Cecil was back at work on rewriting with his collaborator, Hal Burton.

Cecil also concentrated on his determination that Garbo should come to visit him in England. From Hampshire House she wrote that she was on the verge of breakdown but that if Cecil still wanted her to come, it might be possible. Meanwhile Schlee was trying to make up his mind whether he was still ill or getting better. Whatever happened she would have to make a surprise departure at the last minute.

Cecil went to Venice in September when, in a rare and successful collaboration, he and Oliver Messel dressed Diana Cooper as Cleopatra for the Beistegui Ball. Then in October he awaited Garbo. Proving that anything was possible if she so wished it, Garbo arrived at Southampton in the middle of October 1951. Cecil came on board, whisked her away from Schlee before either of them really knew what was happening, and took her to Reddish in the boneshaker car of a local old character called Len Gould.

Garbo now began a stay of two months. It was an outstandingly beautiful autumn and she took to country life instantly. Cecil watched with pride as she regained her self-assurance, health and happiness.

Hal Burton was staying with Cecil at this time, helping with the play. He did not meet Garbo for some time but they soon became friends because his quiet unthreatening personality appealed to her at once. He recalled her happiness at Broadchalke, despite the pressmen that jumped out of hedges from time to time. He was also able to help her through a difficult evening when all Cecil's family foregathered to help celebrate Mrs Beaton's seventy-ninth birthday. Cecil described Hal as 'such an asset during Greta's visit'.[20] Meanwhile Maud Nelson showed her habitual signs of jealousy while Mrs Beaton felt an exile from the moment Garbo arrived. She began to refer to her as 'that woman',[21] and when Garbo was at Reddish, she went to London and vice versa. Had Mrs Beaton taken the initiative and quizzed Garbo, she would have said they were 'just two bachelors',[22] and had they in fact married, they would have presented her with a *fait accompli*. Bravely Cecil introduced Garbo to Peter Watson. Garbo was jealous of Peter, but he was at ease with her, and almost mockingly amused that Cecil should be pursuing this course. Clarissa Churchill fell immediately under Garbo's spell. 'Who can resist the fascination of Greta when the allure is turned on,' wrote Cecil, 'and it was certainly turned on for Clarissa's benefit.'[23] James Pope-Hennessy was so infatuated that he could do no work for five weeks.

> She has the most inexplicable powers of fascination which she uses freely on all and sundry; but whether it is deliberate or not nobody knows ... she is only explicable as a mythological figure. And then it gradually dawns on one that she is entirely uneducated, interested in theosophy, dieting and all other cranky subjects, has conversation so dull that you could scream.... Cecil Beaton guarded her like an eagle, and nobody was ever allowed alone with her.[24]

The Marquess of Bath failed to recognize the glamorous lady Cecil brought to Sturford Mead and when he asked Cecil who she was, Cecil exclaimed, 'It's Garbo, you clot!'[25] Augustus John, however, was likewise captivated. He wrote to Cecil:

> I fell for her of course and hoped to see her again in these parts but I hear she's gone to America. *Quel oiseau!* Will you send for her? I really

must try to capture that divine smile but to follow it to the USA would kill me. I wouldn't mind so much dying *afterwards*.[26]

Diana Cooper wondered how Garbo occupied her time each day and thought in conclusion that Cecil was more interested in struggling on with his play. One journalist, John Rydon, got more than he bargained for when he questioned old Len Gould as to whether or not he had observed any sign of romance on the journey from Southampton. The old countryman looked up from his dibber in the fields and said: 'Well, he didn't finger her.'[27]

Lady Pamela Berry invited Cecil and Garbo to her election party. Garbo, in plunging neckline, surprised the male guests by entering the dining-room and summoning them from their port with the words: 'It's time to go now.'[28] Later she laughed happily, throwing her head back despite press cameras, while Lord David Cecil surprised Lady Pamela by the enthusiasm with which he announced, 'I touched her.'[29] On Guy Fawkes Night, Garbo pulled a giant cracker with Lady Pembroke, 'a sight not to be missed'.[30] Diana Cooper wrote to Cecil beseeching him to bring Garbo to Chantilly at the time of Princess Margaret's visit to attend the British Hospital Ball in Paris. Diana was then in the middle of her battle with the 'horrible Harveys',[31] who had succeeded Duff at the British Embassy. Her invitation was not relayed to Princess Margaret; nevertheless when Diana met her at the hospital, the Princess said that she would love to come to Chantilly for the day. The American writer, Susan Mary Alsop, writing of this party, described Garbo as looking 'exactly as she did in *Anna Karenina* ... talkative and gay'.[32] Princess Margaret sang 'The Bonny Earl of Moray' and Garbo slow hand-clapped her performance at the piano.

Cecil did not enjoy this *mondain* Paris phase, despite their 'great intimacy and happiness'.[33] He found it rather pointless. He hoped to take Garbo to Vaynol for Christmas with Michael Duff but she suddenly decided she had to return home. Cecil left her in Paris with the knowledge that in three weeks he would be in New York. Later, he would describe Garbo's visit to him as 'a long and emotional autumn' which, with the work on his play, 'had reduced me to a jellied pulp'.[34] Part of the strain was keeping everything to do with Garbo a dark secret from everyone else. In his diary even later he wrote: 'Greta was a full-time job and an anxiety as well as a pleasure.'[35]

From Paris Cecil went to Vaynol for the New Year. He was so tired that he felt 'like crying all the way here'.[36] The year ended with revisions on *The Gainsborough Girls* well under way and two other plays in the pipeline (*The Feathered Nest* and one about a changeling). Hal Burton expressed his respect of Cecil's tenacity and determination to carry on despite the disappointments of the year.

Not unnaturally, Cecil telephoned Garbo the moment he arrived in New York. He was devastated that the situation had suddenly reverted to the switchboard announcing: 'Miss Garbo don't answer.'[37] Garbo wrote to Cecil saying she was not going to call him for a few days for several reasons. He thought this monstrous since they had 'been three months together as man and wife'.[38] He felt he had been honest with her, never pretended to be anything that he was not and felt he deserved more respect. 'She has been in a bad and silly state and needs a talking to,' Cecil confided to Clarissa. 'She is very different from the person we knew at Broadchalke.'[39]

When Cecil finally saw Garbo, she hinged her anger to the remarks Cecil had published about her in his *Scrapbook* in 1937:

> She is not interested in anything or anybody in particular, and she has become as difficult as an invalid and as selfish, quite unprepared to put herself out for anyone: she would be a trying companion, continuously sighing and full of tragic regrets; she is superstitious, suspicious and does not know the meaning of friendship; she is incapable of love.[40]

These perceptive remarks were not likely to advance Cecil's chances when they were referred to in a gossip column speculating as to whether or not the pair would marry. Cecil had the chance to air the matter at a rather drunken lunch at the Colony and the tension eased somewhat. He was left thinking her 'a strange unaccountable person who should not be given a free rein to make her own disastrous mistakes'.[41]

The root of the cooling down between Garbo and Cecil was of course Georges Schlee; he had been seriously worried by Garbo's two-month stay with Cecil and for the first time considered him a serious threat. Presumably it was as a result of some action of his that Garbo suddenly fled back to New York before Christmas. Certainly Schlee was determined to keep a firmer grip on Garbo in the future.

Cecil undertook three major projects in 1952. His first, the ballet *Picnic at Tintagel* for Freddie Ashton at the New York City Ballet Center, was generally felt to add nothing to Cecil's work on *Les Illuminations*. Cecil himself confessed: 'I'm rather tired by now and haven't great enthusiasm for it.'[42] Nevertheless the morning critics gave him 'wonderful notices'.[43]

The second project, *The Grass Harp*, on the other hand, proved an enjoyable challenge. Truman Capote was determined that Cecil be commissioned to do the sets and costumes. Saint-Subber, the producer, proved 'an angel',[44] and Cecil at first welcomed the firm approach of the director, Robert Lewis, though later he felt he was too dogmatic. The play was not a success in New York because, as John Malcolm Brinnin pointed out later, 'a gentle lyric conceived in the checkered shade of a remembered childhood was too frail a thing to survive the impositions of show bizz razzmatazz'.[45] Virgil Thomson, who composed the music, blamed Cecil, declaring *The Grass Harp* 'a fragile play sunk by scenery'. He went on:

An interior by Cecil Beaton full of bric-à-brac and china, a tree-house and a tree that filled the stage, were beautiful, all too beautiful. I tried to compensate for their luxuriance by using music sparsely, not too much of it.[46]

Cecil himself believed that with more work the play could have been a smash hit. When Truman put on his second play *The House of Flowers* in February 1955, Peter Brook refused to use Cecil. But Truman did not want him either and pressed Irene Selznick to employ Cecil on *The Chalk Garden*, thus keeping him busy and letting Truman off the hook.

At the time of the death of King George VI in February 1952, Noël Coward and the Lunts decided that Cecil should design *Quadrille*. Binkie Beaumont settled the worry that Cecil might be extravagant and expensive by a 'take it or leave it' offer of twelve per cent royalties against a £200 down payment. Cecil accepted because, 'It is one that I am particularly anxious to do as I adore the play and think it most important in every way that I should be associated with it.'[47] Recalling his Cambridge days, he wrote to Noël to say: 'It has always been my ambition to do scenery and costumes for one of your plays.'[48]

Cecil sailed to England at the same time as the Lunts. He set to work, assisted by Hal Burton, who undertook the technical jobs that Cecil found difficult, such as making plan elevations and scale drawings. It was a new experience for Cecil to work professionally with Noël. From the start it was a case of 'nothing but smiles all round'.[49] Alfred Lunt brought the best out of Lynn Fontanne, even though this devoted couple behaved in a self-centred and competitive manner on stage. Noël remained extraordinarily calm and Cecil asked, 'How is it you're not harassed and pulling out your hair?' Noël replied: 'It doesn't do you any good and it's bad for the hair.'[50] But Cecil still could not become fond of Noël, even when after the station act, Noël met him at the pass door, put his arms around him, kissed him and said: 'If I've written a beautiful play you've also done a perfectly wonderful job.'[51]

The play opened triumphantly at the Phoenix Theatre in London (only a few days after the death of Gertrude Lawrence). Though popular with the first-night audience it was roundly abused by the critics. Nevertheless it ran

Noël Coward, Cecil's bête noir

in London for 327 performances and, when it opened in New York in
October 1954, it soon became a Broadway hit second only to *The Boyfriend*.

Noël Coward thought some of Cecil's sets 'a bit over-elaborate',[52] but Cecil
himself remained proud of his work for this play which he jokingly called
'The Lunts Vehicle'.[53] His vigilant critic and friend Stephen Tennant
considers that 'his *Quadrille* sets and dresses are a thrill still',[54] but Peter
Daubeny, the distinguished West End impresario, was so aggravated by
them that he delivered a broadside to Cecil in his book *Stage by Stage*:

> Man of fashion, writer, theatrical designer, photographer, painter and
> now playwright, will he not rest till he has built a cathedral and written
> a mass for its consecration? Nevertheless I must confess I deplore this
> dissipation of a special talent into alien channels where it can hardly
> hope to shine.[55]

Cecil's private world was not dull. He, Noël and Clarissa became godparents
to Ann Fleming's son, Caspar: 'I wonder what the child will grow up to
be?'[56] wrote Cecil to Garbo on 4 September 1952. (He died of a massive
overdose in 1975.) His friend Clarissa married Anthony Eden on 14 August.
For weeks this was a secret he guarded closely, so much so that later Ann
Fleming said to him in surprise: 'And we knew all about this before any of
the others and never even told one another about it.'[57] Cecil wrote to say
that he was 'deeply thrilled'[58] and welcomed the opportunity Clarissa now
had to expand her interests and gifts and play an important role in national
life. Some time before this he and Lady Pamela Berry had encouraged the
union. Though he was delighted that his friend had become the Foreign
Secretary's wife (and would in due course occupy 10 Downing Street), he
had reservations. These he confided to James Pope-Hennessy, who replied:

> I am glad you feel as I do about C: I am quite truthfully in *dreadful despair*,
> far more than I could have imagined; she is as effectually translated as
> if she had died, and to see one's oldest friend become the centre of all
> that obscene publicity, and exploited by that vulgar family [the Chur-
> chills], is unbearable to me.[59]

Garbo, who was now to be spotted in America walking hand-in-hand
with Baron Eric Goldschmidt-Rothschild, expressed her delight at the little
blonde Mrs Eden's good news. She added that if Cecil could see how badly
her own state now was, he would be grateful that he had not married her.

Cecil attended the Opening of Parliament in November 1952, viewing it
entirely as a theatrical production. 'At all times I love looking at human
beings,' wrote Cecil, 'and here they were seen in such extraordinary perspective in their traditional fancy dress that has been developed and tried
and improved through the centuries until it is found to be perfect.'[60] Lynn
Fontanne, another witness to the ceremony, said: 'Isn't it lovely to be in

a crowd that doesn't push?'[61] Cecil thought the men were better dressed than the dowdy women, but the Queen struck him as 'a real personality' with her erect stance and rigid little head. Cecil must have caught the Duke on a bad day:

> As for the Duke of Edinburgh he seemed nothing more than an adequate consort. He looked extremely ill, his eyes hollow, his complexion green and his pale hair already beginning to thin. I doubt if he will live long.[62]

These were difficult days for Cecil. His mother suffered a heart attack in the summer but was well again in time for her eightieth birthday on 14 November. Cecil felt that they had nothing in common any more and he was always relieved to escape to the luxury hotel life in America. Yet he pitied his mother and conceded that his life centred around hers more than he cared to admit. Cecil's family gave Mrs Beaton a Cartier gold link bracelet with a heart-shaped fob, on which were engraved her initials, her birth-date and their names. From New York Cecil telephoned his mother, and then collapsed in uncontrollable sobs:

> Perhaps it was for some of these reasons that I wept so bitterly, so that when the waiter came in with a breakfast tray of tea I had to look away from him sightlessly out of the window.[63]

Cecil delayed telephoning Garbo lest she refuse to answer. Truman Capote had recently sent Cecil a letter of warning and this he had taken to heart. Truman wrote:

> Darling, I hope you have an easier, or at any rate less neurotic, rapport with Greta G. this winter. But I'm afraid she will never be a satisfactory person, because she is so dissatisfied with herself, and dissatisfied people can never be emotionally serious. They simply don't believe in anything – except their own limitations.[64]

In due course Cecil and Garbo met, but he was now more critical:

> [Gayelord] Hauser had telephoned to her: 'You're not still just wandering the streets,' he asked her. 'Haven't you taken a house? Haven't you done anything about anything?' 'No,' and she laughed at her inability. But it is no laughing matter. Ten years ago she was so beautiful. Those ten years have not been kind. The next ten years are not likely to be less cruel.[65]

Cecil feared that Garbo would have 'a very empty, lonely and unhappy old age'[66] – and these fears proved founded. She convinced Cecil that Schlee was the most important consideration in her life and that Cecil must never rely on her. At Christmas she came to the Sherry-Netherland. Cecil opened the door full of seasonal glee: 'Why Merry Christmas to ye,' he cried with open arms. Garbo looked dazed. 'Now you cut that right out!'[67] she said.

Part Seven

The Victorious Years 1953–65

26

Tunnelling Towards Something New

I still have not found my true forte and am looking for a new career.

Cecil to *Daily Mail*, 6 March 1953

Cecil had a friend in New York called John Myers. His wide-ranging career included being an art dealer of the American avant-garde, an editor, publisher, puppeteer and stage producer. He met Cecil in the 1940s and was amazed at how well-groomed he looked considering the amount of work he did each day: 'He rises at seven o'clock, writes letters, works on his diaries. The bed is covered with papers, water-colour sets, brushes, pencils, notebooks, photographs, newspapers, magazines, whatever he needs for the projects he is pursuing.'[1] Cecil would then spend the day at *Vogue*, lunching somewhere, and fulfilling crowded afternoon schedules before emerging to take a full part in New York's social life:

> He loves high society and moves in this watery element like a dolphin, since he's certain as to who he is, Cecil is without snobbery; he is at home with a boxer, an impecunious dancer, a charwoman, 'coloured' people, or dressmakers as he is with his duchesses and field marshals. There's another reason for this: he's totally non-intellectual, and below his crisp surface is a childlike nature. Only a naïf could believe that the eccentrics and monsters he deals with are creatures of glamour.[2]

John Myers liked Cecil's character and enjoyed going to his parties. In turn Cecil enjoyed discussions with Myers about Jackson Pollock and other figures of the contemporary art scene.

In the winter of 1952 John Myers came to see Cecil in order to give him a salutary talking to on the subject of *Vogue*. He warned him that they thought his work completely out of touch with modern times and only retained him because he was Edna Chase's favourite. Myers said that if Cecil wanted to work seriously for the theatre, he must devote himself full time and not just give it his left-over energy. He must also consider how much he needed to live in luxury hotels as photography represented a major source of his income. Cecil consulted Diana Vreeland, who spurred him on by saying: 'You have been these last years tunnelling towards something new. You are just about to come out to the light.'[3]

Cecil then set off on his first lecture tour, visiting Minneapolis, Chicago, Kentucky, Cleveland and Toledo. He concluded that the *New Yorker* cartoonist Helen E. Hokinson had said the first and last word on the world of women's clubs. Cecil did his best to get through his performance despite nerves that often gave him an upset stomach, and the discomfort of the hotels he stayed in. He was kept alive by the amusement he derived from observing the ladies and by what they said about other guest speakers. Sacheverell Sitwell had mumbled so that they could not understand a word he was saying; he rubbed one leg against another, picked his nails, skipped through his notes and when asked about his sister, merely said, 'Oh horrors.'[4] Gertrude Stein had offended the Cleveland Museum by telling a reporter that the best things in Cincinnati were the river and the cakeshop. Cecil found the talking a great exhaustion and, always a pessimist, never failed to notice the one man who had dropped off to sleep through boredom.

Truman Capote was amused by Cecil's excursion on to the rostrum: 'Was so happy (and relieved) to have your letter, for I'd begun to wonder if perhaps one of those mid-west club ladies hadn't kidnapped you for her very own.'[5] Overall the tour was a success. 'Perhaps it will become an annual event,' predicted Truman. 'The club ladies will await you like the spring swallows.'[6]

Cecil repeated the experience the following year, after a bout of intestinal virus known as 'green death'. In January 1954 he found himself at the Beverly Hills Hotel where, six years earlier, he had been so happy, walking back from Garbo's house in the small hours of the night 'in a cloud of love'.[7] Cecil felt rather sad in Hollywood without her: 'And now I am here, she is far removed. She is ill, she is sad, infinitely pathetic on the end of the wire in New York.'[8] The second tour gave Cecil the opportunity to photograph Grace Kelly and to include in his lecture a description of her as a contemporary beauty. At the time she was living in a mustard yellow apartment with paper-thin walls. 'It was clean,' recalled Princess Grace, 'because it was new.'[9] Cecil arrived on her only free day from filming *Rear Window*, a Sunday. The Princess recalled:

> I remember this elegant Edwardian figure coming in, so stylishly dressed, and what a contrast he made to this mustard yellow flat. He came with his Rolleiflex and there was not enough light. I sat on the floor under a lamp and he took his pictures.[10]

Afterwards she wrote to Cecil: 'They are the best that have been made of me – and so beautifully mounted.'[11]

Cecil also endured the shock of undergoing his fiftieth birthday, 'a very quiet and rather depressing birthday alone in Chicago'. He minded this acutely: 'I'm too old to be allowed out in public. I must retreat into a darkened shell,'[12] he wrote. He spoke in Seattle, San Francisco, Los Angeles, Milwaukie, Louisiana, Wisconsin, Norfolk (Virginia), Atlanta (Georgia) and Cleveland (Ohio) amongst other places. Then he went to Montreal before finally returning to New York. This tour was a mixture of horror and reassurance. Often alone, Cecil had time to observe the depressing but safe lives of the citizens of these American towns. Part of him despised the ladies to whom he lectured, but the other part of him needed their accolades and admiration. He was called a poet and a genius: 'Now really that last was going too far,' he noted. 'But it was agreeable to be a success. That's what I wanted and here it was. Silly to scorn it.'[13] He was surprised to find that he had fans who had followed his career in detail. Through his books people like Lady Juliet Duff and Lady de Grey had their followers. And he was often able to discuss the problems of life with strangers who entertained him in a way he would never have done at home. More seriously, Cecil came to certain conclusions about life:

> I was forcibly struck by the fact that has reoccurred like a theme during this trip, that the only important things in life are the fundamental ones – selflessness, devotion, love, affection – that radios, newspapers, decorated cubbyholes do not impinge beneath the surface level ... in all these towns with their great wealth, business activities, entertainments that endure only a few moments, the great artists of the world are the only ones who speak the universal language, that in these museums (visited each day by thousands) the message of Fantin-Latour with a pot of wall flowers is stronger than that of any highly publicized public figures whose clarion call is silent so soon.[14]

It was a good overall experience but an average of $500 for an hour's talk was a far from princely sum after the agent took half and taxes were paid. He could have earned much more by photography. Later he extracted the maximum advantage from these tours by writing a book on his experiences entitled *It Gives Me Great Pleasure*, which was published in 1956 (in New York it was called *I Take Great Pleasure*). Enid Bagnold read it and thought Cecil expressed 'a sort of ignorant talent'[15] as a writer. She thought him much funnier in conversation.

After his first lecture tour in 1953, Cecil returned to London and finally plucked up the courage to dispose of Maud Nelson. This he did in a letter announcing that her services were at an end. For years now he had been unhappy with her. There had been rows between Maud and his mother. She had committed terrible crimes. She sold his Picasso for a mere £200, ordered her drink with his and, during the time of rationing, she purloined

The Queen's Coronation sketched in the Abbey

a fresh salmon destined for his mother. She both aggravated and frightened him. Lately he had taken to walking round South Kensington and not coming home until she had left in the evening. He was more than relieved to have written his letter: 'I groaned with a deep groan of satisfaction. I felt suddenly as if I had wings.'[16] His slight fear that Maud might commit suicide was not realized.*

In her place, in August 1953, Cecil engaged a friend of Hal Burton's. 'I have decided to take on Miss Hose and think she should be really good and a great help,'[17] he wrote. Eileen Hose had worked as the personal assistant to General Sir Frederick Pile, GOC-in-C Anti-Aircraft Command in the war and later a Director-General of the Ministry of Works. Therefore she had been present at many of the important meetings concerned with the country's air defence and had been awarded the MBE. Hal Burton had no doubt that she was the person for Cecil and he was right. Eileen was the perfect personal secretary in the tradition of Berenson's Nicky Mariano. Cecil was soon writing to Hal: 'I must tell you what a success Miss Hose is being. It makes all the difference to my life! I can't thank you enough for helping me to get her and I only trust she'll stay for ever. It makes me realize too what

---

*In 1957 Maud Nelson attacked a High Sheriff's daughter to whom she was attracted, striking her with a broken bottle. She came to trial and Cecil courageously went to court in April that year to give her a character reference. This well-meant gesture was not helpful. Maud went to Holloway prison. Years later she turned up in Tangiers, where David Herbert found himself entertaining what he described as 'a bald-headed old man with a few grey hairs sprouting unwillingly on his pate'. She died more or less unmourned in the spring of 1969.

a terrible drag poor Maud has been. It was a nightmare now I look back on it.'[18]

Cecil was anxious to take a full part in the Coronation on 2 June. Therefore he made a particular point of asking if he might photograph the Queen Mother. She agreed and he went to Buckingham Palace where she was living before the move to Clarence House. Cecil was worried about the sudden rise of the photographer Baron, who was a friend of Prince Philip. Fortunately, however, the Queen settled on Cecil and he was appointed to take the official portraits at the Palace. He was allocated a seat in the Abbey so that he could sketch the ceremony.

He always worried inordinately before a commission of this kind and official cards and instructions confused and worried him. He felt as though he were going to his execution when he attended the rehearsal in the Abbey. It was a curious fear of officialdom that caused him to dream up a situation in which the military figures attacked him. He might have been back at school:

'You've got a sketch book 14 × 16. Don't you know you're not allowed anything larger than 10 × 8?' The book confiscated. 'What is that bulge in your coat pocket? Indian ink? Do you think Indian ink is allowed in the Abbey? Go on! Move on!' Again I would be robbed of my possessions. 'You know no pencils are allowed!'[19]

But all went well and Cecil was soon engrossed. His gimlet eye took it all in, a shaft of light that caught a gold sequin on the white satin dress of a maid of honour, or a jewel in a bishop's ring, or a diamond in the tiara of the Mistress of the Robes.

I was enthralled watching a million details and as I did my drawings, balancing my Indian ink precariously, I found I could not listen or think, I became purely an instrument of my eyes. Neither did I find it easy to switch from the usual spectator to the listener. I found it more natural and easy for me to draw than to take in thoughts.[20]

There were old friends in the Abbey: Lord Salisbury bearing the Sword of State, Randolph Churchill, improbably clad in black velvet, calling himself 'Big Lord Fauntleroy', and the former Lord Gerald Wellesley, now Duke of Wellington, one of the four Knights of the Garter bearing the canopy for the Queen's anointing:

It was all very dignified but I had a moment of private amusement to see Gerry Wellington so serious as he held the lances of the canopy. I would like so much to have seen his face if I had shouted to him that Sidi Azaid had a message for him, for during the war in Cairo Gerry used to behave very badly in an Arab Bath which was subsequently closed down.[21]

Cecil had too much wine at Grace Radziwill's dinner-party the night before the Coronation, so started the day with a low vitality count. He filled his grey top hat with sandwiches and Indian ink and set off to the Abbey at first light. He enjoyed seeing the guests in other cars in their ceremonial costumes and particularly 'Sir James and Lady Dunn with mouths dropped at the corners, having nothing to say to each other'. In the Abbey there were further vignettes: 'the encounter of Lady Wavell and Peter Coats (he looked like the last of the Principal boys)', the Fairbankses 'sitting next to an entirely black man in gold. From my sparrow's seat I could see all the Peeresses' bald spots, and their surreptitious nipping out of a flask, or arranging of a train.' With all the glamour and the recently-honoured war leaders, Cecil concluded that nevertheless 'the old aristocracy was really in charge'.[22] The ceremony itself he has described in *The Strenuous Years*,* likewise his visit to the Palace to take the official portraits.

Cecil had to click away as best he could but 'had only the foggiest notion of what I was doing, if taking black and white or colour, if giving the right exposure'.[23] He found the Queen Mother as ever the most helpful and encouraging, while the Duke of Edinburgh (who would have preferred Baron) ragged the proceedings somewhat. His grin ruined several shots taken with the Queen, but when Cecil turned his attentions on the Duke alone 'in spite of his preconceived notions he was flattered by my attentions'.[24] The Kents behaved like schoolchildren, 'mother nagging children, children nor mother ever still',[25] and the Duke of Gloucester questioned Cecil's every stage direction: 'His eyes popped and lips bulged as if he might explode.'[26] The results were much better than Cecil had dared hope and were presently circling the globe.

Soon after this great event Cecil was in his garden when the cook, Mrs Murdock, asked him accusingly why he had attended the Christie† trial. He did so because he had never been to a trial and thought it would be useful for the playwright's eye. Cecil only went for one morning and in that time concluded that Christie was mad. He thought his pained expressions were those of an actor giving a brilliantly spontaneous performance. Christie enjoyed the attention he was getting and yet Cecil felt the sympathy one feels for a diseased dog:

No matter how polite and ingratiating he has something very inimical about him. Like a schoolmaster at a preparatory school, punctilious, refined, vindictive, he can be hated as only a preparatory schoolmaster can be hated.[27]

* See pp. 141–50.

† Christie had murdered his wife and three other women and plastered them into the walls and floor of his house, 10 Rillington Place. He was sentenced to death on 25 June 1953 and hanged on 15 July.

Cecil observed his every gesture, applying the shrewd technique of one trained to note every visual nuance:

> For days I was haunted by this sordid story, amazed and baffled that such things could be, and it was very disturbing to see Christie everywhere. Each ordinary man having a cup of milky coffee in a café might have been Christie and I felt that even if this man hadn't murdered four women the odds were that he wasn't just the ordinary meticulous person leading a humdrum, conventional life that he seemed to be.[28]

Cecil published *Persona Grata* in 1953, a selection of portrait photographs with text on each by Kenneth Tynan. Then he created *Aren't We All?* for Binkie Beaumont. This was a Frederick Lonsdale revival starring Ronald Squire, Jane Baxter and Marie Lohr (who had made her film debut in the rôle in 1932). When Cecil first saw his work at Brighton his ear was so sensitive to criticism that he overheard a woman describing his sunny Henley Regatta décor: 'It's all blue this time.'[29] The play opened at the Haymarket on 6 August 1953 and ran for 123 performances. It was chosen as a gala to be attended by the Queen, the Queen Mother and Princess Margaret. Cecil later published an ill-considered account of this occasion in *The Strenuous Years.**

His summer holiday was spent at Portofino with Truman Capote. He maintained that Truman filled the gap left by the death of Bébé Bérard four years earlier, but judged that he was perhaps 'more deeply reliable and understanding'.[30] Cecil was surprised that a twenty-six year old should have such wisdom:

> In some ways I feel anxious lest this phenomenon may be too extraordinary to last, and that like Bébé he may not survive to old age. There is something almost frighteningly violent about the way he sleeps so soundly, enjoying sleep so sensually; he gets such violent reactions to everything in life when once he has come out of his drowsy, slumbrous wakenings. He is so surprised, so full of wonder. He is so conscious of the deliciousness of rare and expensive things as well as the simple things. I feel slightly scared that someone who lives so intently, so warmly, so generously may be packing into a short span, more than most people are capable of enjoying or experiencing in a long lifetime.[31]

In Rapallo they called on Max Beerbohm, who wrote: 'It was a very great pleasure to commune with you, and with Truman Capote.'[32] John Gielgud appeared and amazed Cecil with his tunnel-vision dedication to the theatre. Cecil went to Venice and photographed the aged Countess Morosini, whose letters from the Kaiser were said to have been addressed: 'To the most

*See pp. 112–15.

beautiful woman in the most beautiful house in the most beautiful city in the world.'[33]

On 5 October 1953, Cecil took another brave step in his career. He was admitted as a student at the Slade School of Fine Art (part of University College, London) to study for two days a week. Thus instead of rushing by taxi late to a lunch engagement after a morning working in bed, Cecil found himself in the underground at 9.30 sharp. This was the first time he had been given any art tuition since Harrow and he described the exercise as an attempt to 'bury the ghost of W. Egerton Hine'.[34]

Cecil was quite shy amongst the young art students, some of whom treated him with veneration. 'You don't know what you mean to our generation,' said a twenty-three-year-old youth, explaining that Cecil embodied the exuberance of 'a life that we all admire'.[35] He was pleased that going to the Slade provided a link with the young and found it a salutary contrast to his normal, tired world.

As Cecil contemplated an enormously fat nude with 'a mouth twisted to one side in the most exaggerated pout I have ever seen',[36] he found he had problems calculating the proportions. He began by feeling inadequate, but this state led him through humility and self-abnegation to a position where he felt able to absorb new ideas. He learned that 'painting is not a question of colouring but rather of drawing with paint in the round';[37] he learned to think rather than to dabble and became aware of the importance of the relationship between one space and another. The students spoke of their work as making 'a statement' and the teachers were encouraging and inspiring. As always Cecil responded well to criticism. One day the model was 'a juicy young blonde bombshell and the sight of her lying nude on an improvised sofa was quite sensational'.[38] Even this experience isolated Cecil. The young students thought of anyone over thirty as old and at once launched into capturing any hints of approaching middle age.

Cecil found this work very tiring and often frustrating. By the end of term he worried that the experiment was not going to be a success. Looking back later he concluded that his studies had 'a tremendous, profound influence' on him and had brought home 'with an appalling cruelty the difference between the quality of the work I have been doing and that which it will be necessary for me to do if I am to succeed by serious standards'.[39] As so often other commitments preoccupied Cecil and kept him away. In the spring of 1954 he put in another appearance, writing to Diana Cooper: 'I feel I must clock in, otherwise it would be a major defeat. But I'm *hating* it, making no progress.'[40]

Lucian Freud thought that Cecil never escaped the influence of Eggie Hine, and his then wife Caroline Blackwood pointed out that Cecil was never fully integrated into the Slade because of his neat pack of sandwiches and the press attention he attracted. He was photographed at work and eating his lunch on a bench. Nevertheless this course set him towards the goal of becoming a painter.

Much of Cecil's diary at this time concerns his life lived between London and Reddish. He believed that 'all good work is done in the country. One should only come to towns to market one's produce.'[41] On the train journey down, he would read the *New Statesman*, the *Spectator* and foreign fashion magazines. He left London on Fridays and came back on Tuesdays. Beside him would be the long boxes in which he would convey every opening bloom to London to brighten Pelham Place. Sometimes, later on, when the historian Sir Arthur Bryant moved to The Close in Salisbury, he would be sitting opposite Cecil writing away in silence, his secretary beside him as Eileen might be beside Cecil.

Time somehow followed a different pace in the country. Cecil could doze or read in the afternoon, but he was usually busy. He seldom took a walk or left the precincts of his house. Arriving at Reddish he would waste no time before throwing open the door to the terrace to survey the garden. Leaving his cases in the hall he would make several energetic forays into the garden to gather beautiful flowers for the house. He found this a way of regaining his energy before he settled down to more serious work. Though aware that at times he was a hermit, he was in no doubt that he led a healthier life than that he led in London or New York. In the evenings another of his relaxations was to work on his scrapbooks (these are now collector's pieces). His ultimate joy was the leisurely smoking of a cigar.

Cecil was considered a fastidious dresser and his name appeared frequently in lists of best-dressed men. In 1952 he was in *The Tailor and Cutter*'s first eleven along with four-year-old Prince Charles. He was always entertained by this as he considered it a myth. He only had a second bath in the day if he was really tired. When he was not seeing anyone he wore old clothes and did not shave. If his first engagement was lunch then he shaved just before going out, so that he looked as fresh as possible. Eddie Sackville-West, now a neighbour at Long Crichel, was astonished at this, declaring: 'My dear, I dress just as carefully if I'm going to see no one. I dress for my own satisfaction, not for the doubtful pleasure of others.'[42] Cecil liked to vary his guise from the scruffy to the ultra chic. Sometimes he appeared at dinner at Reddish in a London suit. At other times he wore outrageous clothes, so that his collaborator Waldemar Hansen said: 'It was embarrassing to be seen with him.'[43] And at about this time Evelyn Waugh joked to Nancy Mitford about teddy boys, who dressed like Cecil in 'braided trousers and velvet collars'.[44] He wrote with more hope than truth: 'Poor Cecil is always being stopped now by the police and searched for knuckle dusters.'[45] Cecil himself joked in speeches that a teddy boy had approached him and said: 'The job's on tonight with razors.'[46]

Waldemar Hansen was a young American intellectual of Danish and Welsh origin whom Cecil met through John Myers soon after the war. An enthusiastic traveller with first-hand knowledge of almost every country in the world, he was later the author of *The Peacock Throne*, a comprehensive study of the Moghuls in India. He helped with his revised version of his book, *Portrait of New York*, and other work, and from 1950 until 1958 acted as his amanuensis, virtually ghosting the five books Cecil published at this time, helping him with articles and with the revisions to his play. Cecil was forever astounded at Waldemar's wide-ranging knowledge:

> He is fascinated by the countryside and knows the names of more wild flowers than I do. Yet he was brought up in a poor quarter of the city of Buffalo (upstate New York). His knowledge about science, philosophy, literature, music and general matters is such that my head spins and I realize how abysmally ignorant and undedicated my life has been.[47]

Waldemar recalled: 'Cecil would call: "I need you in two months' time." Fine. His nets were out.'[48] Waldemar did not always admire what Cecil did but he was in awe of his capacity for work: 'He had an unerring instinct for what was chic and fashionable: he knew whom to cultivate. He was the right kind of snob. He had his stethoscope on the heart of society and when there was a change in the beat, he wanted to know why.'[49] Waldemar was aware that Cecil derived ideas from people like Charles James but he said: 'He knew how to extract the marrow from them and had a canny eye for what his ideas would turn out to be.'[50] He concluded: 'As a photographer and designer he used his pasticheur talents. His failing was that he wanted to be successful in all art fields.'[51]

Waldemar was a considerable influence on Cecil, particularly in his written work. In June 1954 *The Glass of Fashion** was published. The title of the book was the same as a play by Sydney Grundy first staged at the Globe Theatre in the 1880s, and in which his father had acted in the 1890s. Cecil had worked long hard hours on this book, which is the first to relate the changing fashions directly to those who created and wore them. As the dress designer Digby Morton wrote: 'Undoubtedly *The Glass of Fashion* is Mr Cecil Beaton's most important opus so far.'[52] Cecil's old friend Anita Loos added in her review: 'my personal reaction is one of amazement over the growth of his talents, both as an artist and a writer'.[53] The book is an inspired chronicle of the twentieth century in which Cecil was nobly assisted by Waldemar:

---

* It was also published in America, in France (translated by Denise Bourdet with a preface by Christian Dior and a profile of Cecil by Violet Trefusis), and in Japan, all in 1954.

Drawing of Gaby Deslys from The Glass of Fashion, *1954*

Cecil could not write. He was too fecund in his ideas. He overloaded his sentences. I had to say 'You'll exhaust your reader'. But fashion (that which creates an age) was his cocaine. He could make it happen. He sought the eternal in fashion, true fashion, not the comings and goings. He was interested in the high practitioners of it – like Balenciaga and Madame Errazuriz.[54]

Waldemar gave Cecil particular help with his classical allusions. If it is a surprise to find Cecil writing about a 'celebrated Taoist dictum', referring to 'Renaissance individualism' and 'the golden age of Plato and Phidias', then the answer is that it came from Waldemar, who, as a New York intellectual, was better versed in such matters than Cecil.

The Glass of Fashion gave Evelyn Waugh a chance to attack Cecil to his friends. To Nancy Mitford he wrote: 'You may also be surprised to learn that the great leaders of fashion were Alice Obolensky, Phillis de Janzé, Diana Vreeland and Cecil's Aunt Effi* (a new character). There are gross historical misstatements on every page. I was asked to review it. Ten years ago I should have romped into it.'[55] To Lady Mary Lygon he wrote: 'Mr Beaton's book is a veritable congeries of factual error.... He gave two balls in its

* Au ssie. ·

374 · *The Victorious Years 1953–65*

honour. Most appropriate ha ha ha. I suppose he is unhinged by sexual excess ...!'* [56]

In January 1954 Cecil was at the Ambassador Hotel in New York when he heard the news that Duff Cooper had died at sea, that Truman Capote's mother had committed suicide and that Natasha Wilson had taken to the bottle. In April 1954 he was with the Abdys at Newton Ferrers to meet Henry Moore:

> It is always a joy when one is in the presence of a highly individual artist and can see the world through his eyes. To be with Dali is to discover that the fire irons are strange spiderlike objects. In the company of Jean Cocteau one finds that almost everywhere, even in the most prosaic atmospheres, there are curious magi-romantic phenomena. On this walk one suddenly realized the strange Henry Moore boles and holes in the thick trunks of trees, the trees themselves becoming like Moore figures and he would pick up a small gnarled root with a shape that interested him for possible future use.[57]

In the summer Cecil visited Portofino, Ischia and then stayed with Mona (now married to Prince Eddie Bismarck) in Capri. He shared a bathroom with a 'dangerously good-looking' Adonis who inspired love from several of the female guests and nine pages of descriptive diary from Cecil, who seemed always to be peering in on him from the bathroom, 'lying asleep and squashed flat in his blue pyjamas, the long horn feet splayed out beyond the bed end, his head turned in his shoulders', and there, despite the noises of the morning, he would sleep his fill 'until he awoke completely refreshed much later than the rest of the household'.[58] When he left, the Adonis crumpled up a love-note from one of the ladies. This Cecil later uncrumpled and copied into his diary. The gist of the message was to suggest a rendez-vous at the Palace Hotel in St Moritz. Because he took a number of photographs for British *Vogue*, Cecil was able to submit expenses to cover accommodation, entertaining, fares, gratuities, excess baggage and sundries such as flowers for Mona: these totalled £180.

In October 1954 Cecil attended the opening of his first Shakespearean production, *Love's Labour's Lost*, at the Old Vic with Ann Todd, John Neville and Eric Porter. His work delighted John Gielgud: 'The simplicity and ingenuity of the whole design serves the play most admirably, and the clothes are most beautiful, striking and poetic.'[59] Anthony Quayle, the director of the Shakespeare Memorial Theatre, thought them 'one of the most stylish

---

* Not long before Waugh had complained to Nancy Mitford of Cecil's jacket for *Madame de Pompadour*: 'Beaton's drawings always give me goose-flesh but the wrapper is easily disposed of.'

and beautiful pieces of designing I have ever seen – original, always under control and quite ravishing'.[60]

Then in New York he designed *Portrait of a Lady* with Jennifer Jones and Robert Flemyng. The play opened in Boston and failed to interest him much because he thought it was run by a bunch of amateurs. This gave him a chance to give them detailed advice as to how the world of Henry James could be captured faithfully and for this they were grateful. Cathleen Nesbitt had the best part as Countess Gemini and the most elaborate costumes. 'One gets a wonderful sense of authority and poise from just seeing oneself in one of his creations,'[61] she wrote. She recalled the applause that greeted her on her second entrance when all she did was stroll across the stage:

> I say *I* was greeted, but it was Cecil who was greeted and with real enthusiasm, as well he might be. He had designed a riding habit from top hat to boots all of such an elegance, and such a glorious true emerald green, that the effect was dazzling. Long after the rather dull play was forgotten and even the names of those who had played in it gone with the wind, people remembered that green riding habit and that hat. What a fortune Cecil could have made if he had abjured all his talents and just set up as 'the Greatest Man Milliner in the world'.[62]

Later Cathleen Nesbitt also concluded how important a setting by Cecil was to the overall effect of a play.

The path of Cecil's friendship with Garbo had been an uneasy one ever since Schlee had firmly reclaimed her after her happy stay in Broadchalke. In 1953 she moved into the same block as the Schlees, 450 East 52nd Street, overlooking the East River. Her apartment is a few floors below that of Valentina Schlee and both ladies still live there. Garbo decorated her apartment in what Cecil called 'a dreadful hotchpotch of colours'.[63] Cecil was almost brutal in his criticism of it and its sad unfulfilled occupant when he saw it that year:

> But saddest of all is the fact that she is leading here such a futile life of frustration, and that all this comes from her own character which seeks to destroy herself and which in spite of her miraculous beauty, sensitivity and talent she has almost succeeded in doing successfully and completely in spite of the world still clamouring for the effects of her genius.[64]

One day late in 1954 Garbo arrived for lunch in his sitting-room, as uncommunicative about her life as ever:

> We were very happy together. I was somewhat appalled by the thinness of her body. She seemed half the size of the person that I had known ten (?) years ago. She complained that she was far from well, that nothing

could be done about it. She sighed *'C'est la vie'*. I thought that, considering the intimacy of our relationship, she left somewhat abruptly. I was almost hurt that she seemed determined to visit, of all people, the Gunthers* whom she pretends to be bored by. But the times when I am deeply hurt by her offhand or elusive behaviour are happily over. I no longer have the capacity to suffer the pangs of an insensate lover.[65]

One day Cecil went to her apartment, where visitors were extremely scarce. Schlee rang down intermittently but they went on drinking. Suddenly, out of the blue, Garbo accused Cecil of being a 'flippant person'. He was enraged and demanded an explanation. Garbo cited his book *My Royal Past*. She called that flippant, adding, 'and only a flippant person would write about me as you did, without knowing me, in that *Scrapbook* that someone gave me'. Cecil exploded:

'May I talk to you for four minutes without your interrupting me? May I tell you that I think it outrageous of you to judge me today, a man of fifty, by something I wrote when I was half that age?' She interrupted: 'A person is always the same. Only a flippant person would write about me that I smelt like a baby.'†[66]

Later he said:

'Would I have succeeded in the way I had all these years if I had been flippant? My work would not have gone on being appreciated if I was a flippant person.'
  'You have many talents.'
  'I have no talents. I merely have character and it's the seriousness and determination of my character that has made me continue – not my flippancy. Yes, I used to be glib and facile. I was a late developer and fighting to assert myself in life [and] I was a very wild erratic person when young.'[67]

Cecil then reminded Garbo that he had protected her and had always been loyal and devoted, never indiscreet and never exploited her as other friends had. He now considered that he had been deeply hurt emotionally when, after her year of silence, Garbo had visited him in 1947, 'had gone to the bedroom, pulled the curtain cords, had turned down the bed. I had fulfilled what was expected of me, but my feelings had not been those of a flippant person. I had been deeply shocked and wounded.'[68]

  Cecil said all this and Garbo tried to kiss him, but he turned away: 'No, I don't want to kiss you.' She then said: 'Don't you want to come and live

* John Gunther (1901–70), American author and journalist, and his wife Jane.
† Cecil had written: 'Her hair is biscuit coloured and of the finest spun silk and clean and sweetly smelling as a baby's after its bath' [*Scrapbook*, p. 53].

in this apartment when we're married?' – 'No, I don't want to live in this apartment.' Cecil looked 'with horror at the pink lampshades, the evidence of Schlee taste'. Cecil summoned the elevator and the elevator man observed Garbo hanging onto Cecil's coat collar. He returned to his hotel and walked about his rooms 'like a caged lion fuming with fury'.[69] In the end he concluded that the scene had had a salutary effect on both of them.

He sent her a stiff letter shortly after his return to London in January 1955:

Dearest G,

Was sorry we didn't have an opportunity to talk again before I left. I expect you were extremely busy and I had rather a lot to do. I was sorry because I think, maybe, we both drank too many vodka martinis when we last met and parted from one another's company without certain explanations while at the same time perhaps we both said a few things that had been better left unsaid: However 'in vino veritas' and I think I should explain that my high state of emotion was caused less from anger than from the decisive acceptance of failure that I felt for myself; a failure that, after all these years, I am incapable of bringing out in you your qualities of trust, intimacy and unselfishness.

I am afraid I had always only half admitted this to myself, but had gone on hoping that one day you might be somewhat touched by my continued loyalty.

Alas! By harping back to the fact that I, among a thousand other writers, saw fit to print something about you over twenty years ago and that this somehow has more importance to you than anything I have done or felt for you in the years since we got to know one another – it was a cruel revelation.

I realize, of course, that you were not, at this time, feeling your best, and again I believe I have made allowances on that score for you as on so many other scores. I hope I shall hear that you are soon feeling much better and that you are able to take up some interest, possibly like Madame [René] de Becker, and working in a hospital or doing any little job for other people that will also have the benefit of taking you 'out of yourself'. If this sounds impertinent it is because I feel that only those who haven't your future interest at heart could encourage you to continue to lead the listless and ingrained sort of life you do in New York. Only your real friends are willing to risk causing you displeasure by trying to adopt a more charitable attitude towards life.[70]

In February 1955 a row with British *Vogue* brought his contract to an end by mutual consent. Cecil had recently picked a quarrel with American

Vogue over an item about his taking elocution lessons with Constance Collier. He had fanned the flames in *The Glass of Fashion* and Edna Chase had felt obliged to remind him yet again of the 'unfortunate episode in which you were concerned'.[71] In 1954 there had been another row and connexions were severed. Cecil hoped that he would have more freedom, but he also hoped that as a freelance *Vogue* would pursue him with offers of work.

Cecil was not interested in his *Vogue* work at this time and there is no doubt that he pushed them to the limits of tolerance. 'I have unpleasant news for you,'[72] wrote Audrey Withers, the London editor, on 10 February. She explained that Cecil's April lead pictures were unpublishable. Cecil had altered the compositions, he had rushed his work and failed to concentrate. She concluded that he seemed bored with fashion work. Cecil had his own complaints to raise about the disorganization of the sittings. He defended his interest in fashion and his integrity, but he was glad to escape.

Cancelling his contract, Harry Yoxall wrote that he hoped they could still use Cecil occasionally and in effect this is what happened. In his memoirs Yoxall wrote that his most exacting task had been the periodic renewal of Cecil's contract. Evidently Cecil played extremely hard to get. But Yoxall was generous in his conclusion:

> Yet despite all our conflicts of opinion and occasional ruptures (particularly as his fame developed in the field of stage design), Cecil was an inspiring collaborator. He was the only one who was able to write, draw and photograph. He made, I think, a greater contribution to the reputation of *Vogue* than any other artist.[73]

Edna Woolman Chase, now retired, begged Cecil not to drop the fashion field altogether: 'You have such an innate understanding of what is really fashion and really smart that I feel that part of your talent should not lie completely idle.'[74] When she sent Cecil her memoirs, she inscribed it to one who had 'brought me many happy editorial moments – a few distracting ones perhaps'.[75]

Cecil now took a mass of portraits. In February 1955 he went to Portugal to photograph the wedding of King Umberto's daughter, Maria Pia, to Prince Alexander of Yugoslavia. 'The nuptials were very picturesque,' he reported to Diana Cooper. 'Ruritanian, nostalgic, comic, tragic, touching. I love the Queen of Italy, a romantic-looking embryonic *Folle de Chaillot*.'[76]

He photographed Queen Helen of Romania, who wrote: 'all I can say is that I hope they are good as I consider myself very flattered by them'.[77] Mary McCarthy, receiving hers, wrote: 'I seem to have my lipstick on crooked – will this appear in the final product?'[78] From the villa I Tatti in Italy, Bernard Berenson joked: 'Returning after two months I find the photos of my senility that you were good enough to send me.'[79] These were pub-

lished in American *Harper's Bazaar* and Audrey Withers was nice enough
to write: 'I was very envious!'[80] Rose Macaulay thought hers were 'just and
deserved', but asked that the hair be made to look less white 'in the interests
of truth to life'.[81] Nancy Mitford, on the other hand, pleaded: 'Oh Kek this
is *me* begging *you* not to put that photograph that makes me look like an
American beauty-product-seller.... I know you'll say but the catalogue. One
mistake in a catalogue against a life-time of shrieks?'[82] A blow to Cecil's
photographic work was the death of Mr Herbert of Jeffrey & Boarder and
the folding of the firm that had printed his work for many years: 'now the
struggle for good prints must continue, and quite possibly it will lead me
into despair, frustration or taking pictures only with a big camera'.[83] Another aspect of portrait photography which annoyed Cecil at this time was
the habit of sitters to choose pictures which were the most flattering to
them, but the least interesting. This he would have encouraged early on in
his career. Cecil was delighted to hear that Sir Winston Churchill would
allow him to take his photograph again. He promised to do this with the
minimum of disturbance. Such was his status now that Lady Churchill
invited him to lunch. Unfortunately due to a technical hitch only one of
these photographs came out.

While in America doing stage work, Cecil earned $15,000 for designing
the costumes for the Zachary Solov ballet, *Soirée*, at the Metropolitan Opera
House. His work was well rewarded for the time he devoted to the project.
'I did it one evening late here and it's pretty if undistinguished,'[84] he confessed to Eileen.

Back in London, Cecil was granted an important commission to photograph the Queen prior to her state visit to Nigeria. He went for a preliminary
meeting with Martin Charteris, then the Queen's Assistant Private Secretary,
and, while waiting, helped himself to a wad of Buckingham Palace writing
paper so as 'to write letters to friends in America'.[85] While Cecil admired
the good taste of the Queen's equerry, Patrick Plunket, and the high-spirited
efficiency of Martin Charteris, he took the traditional line of finding the
Press Secretary, Commander Richard Colville, hopelessly unhelpful. Colville
would happily sanction an afternoon of the Queen's time for a Christmas
card or presentation photograph, while being obstructive in every way to
the general press.

Cecil was allowed to put forward his own suggestions for this sitting.
With his usual imagination he found the throne under the vast Delhi Durbar
canopy in the Ball Room. Martin Charteris was enthusiastic but wondered
if the Queen would be self-conscious. Cecil won him over by saying: 'If she
can't sit on that throne who can?'[86] Cecil asked for two evening dresses to
be worn and the robes and plumed hat of the Order of the Garter. This was
approved. Cecil himself had to paint the sky-blue background for the Garter
photographs. This he did in the Blue Drawing-Room on the day of the

sitting, an event he approached with a much more calm disposition than on his first visit in 1939. At this time royal photographs did not have the advantage of special make-up men such as those who glamorized Princess Anne for Norman Parkinson in 1971 and 1973. The Queen wore only a little lipstick and no mascara. With the ugly artificial lighting, Cecil had a hard job to achieve the result he was seeking. However he was a skilled operator and he had one other advantage over other photographers:

> Luckily it seems that the Royal Family have only to get a glimpse of me for them to be convulsed with giggles. Long may that amusement continue for it helps enormously to keep the activities alive. Throughout the afternoon I found that it was very easy to reduce the Queen to a condition of almost ineradicable *fou rire* and this prevented many of the pictures being sullen and morose.[87]

Cecil's enthusiasm mounted when they got to the Ball Room 'and the Queen, at my bidding, and with no trace of self-consciousness sat on the enormous throne chair under the crimson canopy'.[88] Thus Cecil obtained a particularly apt image of the young monarch, a tiny dignified figure, modest as a woman, young and attractive, yet in no sense overawed by the rich ceremonial trappings that surrounded her. Before the Queen left to entertain the Princess Royal to tea, Cecil obtained some lovely portraits of her in Garter robes before a backdrop of Windsor Castle.

27

Magpies Against a White Drop

> *A gardener not wholly herbivorous*
> *From wilting was out to deliver us.*
> *With blood, sweat and toil*
> *She composted the soil*
> *And made even the lilies carnivorous.*

> Joke limerick composed by Cecil
> for Irene Selznick but not sent

Cecil described his participation in *The Chalk Garden* as 'one of those misbe-
gotten ventures that one makes through a mistaken notion of helping a
friend'.[1] The result, he said, was 'not only the loss of that friend and – worse
– a whole summer, but the birth of a conviction that no theatre success
should be gained at the cost of so much acrimony, chicanery and ruthless
cruelty as had gone into bludgeoning this charming, but rather fragile little
comedy into a Broadway near-hit'.[2] That Cecil wrote these words nine years
after the event demonstrates the depth of his bitterness.

Enid Bagnold and Cecil had discussed plays together ever since they became friends in the *Heil Cinderella* epoch in 1940. At first Cecil was Enid's
only link with the theatrical world. She fed on his stories of stage life. 'All
my plays are yours,' she wrote, 'I shall stipulate that with the manager';[3]
and later: 'I always feel a deep play binding with you.'[4] They advised each
other over the plays that they wrote and encouraged each other when
enthusiasm flagged. While Cecil was buried deep in his rewriting Enid suddenly had some success. Three of her plays were produced and in 1944
National Velvet became a highly popular film. In January 1952 Enid's play
Gertie opened in Boston with 'full house, good audience, good notices on the
whole, but, oh, is it good enough?'[5] It was not. When the play was axed in
February, Enid responded valiantly by announcing she would write a play
based on her recent experiences. This became an article called *The Flop*.
Cecil found her exuberance almost too much: 'America has done something
quite curious to her in that she is so self-assured and convinced that she
is miles above every American she meets.'[6] Then Enid wrote *The Chalk*

Garden. Cecil read it with more than excitement, as he reported to Diana Cooper:

> She had a tough time here with her nose to the grind, never saw the bright light, but it was all worth it. She has made her play into a little masterpiece. I am deeply impressed and touched by it, a real work of art and it should be enormously effective in the theatre.[7]

In December 1953 Enid had made a pledge to Cecil: 'I should needless to say be honoured if you would do the scenery if ever it gets done.'[8] Since then the distinguished director, Irene Selznick, had become involved with the production. Ever fastidious, she and Enid worked away on the play, going over every minute detail to the point of tears until *The Chalk Garden* was ready to open in America. The last person that Irene wanted to have any part in all this was Cecil. The serious slight in the *Vogue* drawing of 1938 which was directed at her still rankled and she was foremost among those who refused to work with him. It cannot have helped that Cecil was working concurrently on *Portrait of a Lady*, starring the second Mrs Selznick, Jennifer Jones (though this did not worry Irene). She expressed her distaste by telling Enid that Cecil was 'dilettante', but Enid was adamant and Irene agreed to take him on. Of these problems Enid wrote: 'Irene simmered: Cecil flashed. Both had the same carved eyes. His missed no personal eccentricity (Irene had a million) that he could mock. Their tension was like a bright wire pulled tight across the sun!'[9] Irene rebuked Cecil early on, asking him: 'Do you hate me? So many have repeated such awful things you've said. I do wish you'd keep them to yourself until *after* the play is over.'[10] Enid had her own predicament to face. 'Irene and I stand together,' she wrote to Cecil. 'But I stand on one leg and she holds me up with a spear.'[11] From the start it was an impossible triangle, with Cecil and Irene disliking each other intensely, Irene and Enid perpetually at loggerheads, while Cecil was undeniably envious of Enid's success. Enid was aware of this but Cecil began his involvement by giving generous advice and encouragement. She wrote to him:

> You react to art (to use that grand word) with all the gallantry and rush of heart that is so often absent in artists. You yourself have so many difficulties (for instance unlike me you have to earn your living), and you have the major difficulty and bitter disappointment that, in spite of your passion for the theatre, the play you care so deeply about isn't yet on. And yet you have the generosity to give me all this letter, all this praise, all this understanding – in fact all this unselfish joy in what you believe will be my success. I shall never forget it of you; but all the same it is what I have always known about you.[12]

Work began in earnest. To Diana Cooper Cecil expressed his early fears: 'I doubt, though, that it's going to be an easy experience working with so many violently strong characters.' When Cecil accepted a commission, he was able to assess how much time and energy his contribution would take. This time besides the costumes there was only one set. Once again Hal Burton was at hand to give advice and Alan Tagg to create a model. But Cecil counted without Irene. She began to question minute details of the set as early as December 1954, long before the play was even scheduled. She summoned him to numerous exhausting meetings, many of which he felt to be a waste of time. By May 1955 she was complaining to Enid that there was not enough 'conspiratorial intimacy'.[14] She brought Cecil to heel, suggesting he had too many diversions and was not giving enough of his time and talent. So did Enid:

What has worried me is that you didn't seem to be taking it seriously. ... You have that power of work and sense and directness which marks you out from those who only vapour out their beauties. ... Turn on that tap now for my play, please dear Cecil.[15]

But Cecil had had enough. He resigned. Only Enid's plea: 'The play to me just simply won't be the same without you',[16] brought him back. He produced some new drawings and Enid was delighted. More and more instructions came from Irene. Cecil missed his annual holiday, and then yet more instructions came before Irene returned to America. Enid sailed on the *Queen Elizabeth* on 11 August and Cecil followed on the 14th dreading the prospect of 'battling with tough Broadway producers'.[17]

There were many other rows and complications in the production of *The Chalk Garden*. Enid upset Gladys Cooper, Irene sacked George Cukor, Enid quarrelled with his successor Albert Marre. Irene took steps to keep Cecil under control, aware that he put his side before all others. 'It was always costumes by Cecil Beaton, the play by ...' she recalled. 'The tail wagged the dog.'[18] She appointed Laura Harding, the American Express heiress and close friend of Katharine Hepburn, to help Cecil with the costumes. She had a good eye and knew where to find bargains. Likewise Johnnie Johnstone was employed with the sets. Both of these were in effect Irene's spies. She gave them precise orders and budgets and, while Cecil took an afternoon nap, they reported exactly what he was doing.

Cecil became increasingly exasperated. In the late summer heat he wrote to Diana Cooper from Fulco Verdura's apartment on East 60th Street:

Have been shut up in this awful muggy heat with only occasional glimpses of the rest of the world; if lucky a weekend off, but now things are about to boil and not a minute to be spent away from the grind. My admiration for Enid is very great although on matters of taste she maddens me. But she has not 'let go' for an evening, an hour since she arrived. She has done some valuable rewriting and the play is really beautiful, touching, funny, marvellously written, the cast excellent, [Siobhan] McKenna a triumph. I am sure it'll be a big hit, and my God Enid deserves it. I have not learned to love Irene Selznick. Perhaps I am particularly conscious of her dictator-complex at this moment. With luck I should be free of her claws in two weeks' time, and I think the chances of my ever signing on for her again are quite infinitesimal.[19]

Within a week Cecil's tone had taken a turn for the worse. Again he wrote to Diana:

The terrific liaison between Enid and I.S. is more perfervid than ever. They've tortured one another and everyone else in sight for six weeks. Enid looks haggard and pale, working from five in the morning, Irene wild-eyed. They discuss, discuss, *discuss*! Never has there been such a volcano of words, and we've all worked so hard. . . .

It was a sad day for me when I signed with I.S. I've been badgered and bullied and had no summer holiday and I'm furious! My friendship with Enid has survived and I'm really fond of her, but she has lost her head completely and I'm afraid a return to grim reality will be an awful anticlimax.[20]

At this point, the New Haven opening, Cecil feared the play might fail. Real drama was to follow in Boston. Irene thought Cecil's set was too white, causing the light to bounce, and ordered it to be sprayed. 'It was too white,' wrote Enid later, 'and once sprayed, it was never the same.'[21] This was to be the cause of great bitterness later, but curiously Cecil took it well at the time. 'I altered the set a lot,' he reported to Eileen, 'took the production photographs till 2 a.m., then fitted the new actresses.'[22]

Enid's play opened in New York on 26 October. A week later Cecil paid a quick visit to London and on 12 November Truman Capote wrote:

You'll be amused to know that *Chalk Garden* has become the rage: people can't afford *not* to see it. Your article was in the *Tribune* today and the play itself is getting terrific publicity.[23]

Cecil returned to New York in December. He attended Irene's party for Binkie Beaumont, but refused to kiss his hostess.

In January 1956 he heard the news that he was not going to be asked to do the London production of *The Chalk Garden*. Then 'the juices of anger'[24] flowed in him. The excuse given was 'aesthetic and ethical reasons'.[25] And so while the reviewers praised his décor, Cecil seethed: 'I practically invented the way the play should look. Enid had no visual sense at all.'[26] All the protagonists passed the blame on to one another. Irene said later: 'It was Enid's decision; Binkie was only too pleased not to use Cecil.'[27] She thought the trouble stemmed from Cecil's jealousy over Enid's triumph: 'He poisoned her paradise.'[28] Meanwhile friendly letters had passed between Enid and Cecil with no mention of this business. At length, however, Cecil wrote bitterly to Enid, delighted with his jibe: 'It's sad that so fragrant a blossom as your play should have been nurtured in such a stench.'[29] Cecil continued to castigate her:

I felt once more that my friendship for you, and my admiration for your work in general, and my enthusiasm for this play in particular, had cost me dearly.[30]

Enid tried to explain:

It's all been out of my hands. Too long and too psychologically involved to go into that. (Not psy-inv. between you and me!) Expense came into it. Irene came into it. Binkie came into it. I alone kept outside it. Probably for my own sake.[31]

Enid concluded: 'I am terribly sorry you aren't doing the décor here. It will be nothing so distinguished. I am sorry about the whole thing, your experience in America and everything. But never sorry that I begged Irene to ask you to do it, or that you agreed.'[32]

By the time Cecil returned to London he had had the greatest success of his life with *My Fair Lady*. Enid congratulated him and told him the news of the new sets:

So disappointing. It's *so* bad. Serve everybody right. Joyce Grenfell lamented loudly when she saw it. Quite right. I'm so glad you're back. You have had tremendous triumphs.[33]

Still Cecil did not relent. He even wrote a mean letter to the *Spectator* which, in view of his *My Fair Lady* triumph, John Gielgud thought 'unworthy of him'.[34] Cecil referred to the way the London managements 'give the public a cheap run-of-the-mill production with sets that would have been considered worthy of a touring company before the 1914 war'.[35] Enid was upset that Cecil thought she had hurt him. Again she disclaimed responsibility:

Irene was always revengefully desirous you shouldn't do it in London. If that had been all I could have dealt with it.

On arrival here Binkie didn't want to have to pay your high fee, or percentage. (He never told me: Irene told me.) On top of that John came down here and saw pictures of the set and didn't want it. I think not that he *disliked it* but wanted ideas of his own as Director.*[36]

* John Gielgud said later that he was never allowed to see the New York sets. Neither Binkie nor Enid wanted Cecil. Gielgud too was ostracized by Cecil for many years.

She ended: 'I have very few friends, and you, to me, are one of the nearest.'[37] To this Cecil replied:

> It isn't just that I am hurt. I am shocked and angry at such cowardice and underhandedness, to say nothing of the poor taste involved in this seedy business. . . .
>
> From the moment Mrs Selznick defiled my London house by her presence in order to pave the way for driving a hard financial bargain (Truman Capote, whom she admires and respects, was here at the time and was aghast that she could demean herself to put on such an act) I realized that I had got myself into a situation that was not going to be easy.[38]

Cecil thought Enid should have supported him after *The Chalk Garden's* great success in New York:

> But your position was now very strong. Since I cannot believe you have much respect for Binkie's appreciation for literature or the arts of decoration (see his Essex cottage), you could have demanded of him how any fair-minded or sensible person could believe that a set of distinction, accepted and praised in New York, by an English designer should be thrown out for the London production in favour of an ordinary suburban set.[39]

Cecil concluded that he had never known 'so much vileness and turmoil as over this production' and thought Enid should have fought harder 'because friendship and loyalties must come first, since self-respect comes before compromise and convenience'.[40] Enid was wounded by this and realized there was no hope of appeasement: 'Well you have many friends. You can afford to lose this one, I suppose. I have very few, a handful, and don't like losing one.'[41] Irene thought the London set by Reece Pemberton 'so terrible it should have given him sufficient revenge',[42] but for many years Cecil waged a war of silence against Enid. Whenever he saw her he bowed exaggeratedly, what she called 'a deep bow, very startling, out of Dickens',[43] and passed silently by. Cecil thought that if Herman Levin 'had not brought Lerner and Loewe into my life at this psychological moment I firmly believe, so great was my fear of finding myself again bound by contract, that I would have given up designing for the theatre'.[44]

My Fair Lady was the first successful musical in which there was not so much as a single kiss. Alan Jay Lerner has related how the film producer Gabriel Pascal acquired the rights to film it along with other George Bernard Shaw plays. He arrived at Ayot St Lawrence and Shaw's maid asked who sent him. 'Fate sent me,'[45] he replied. Shaw came down to greet the stranger and listened to his plan to bring his works to the screen. 'How much money do you have?' Pascal pulled out some loose coins and answered, 'Twelve

Above left, Diana Wynyard
in *Kipps*, 1941

Above, Isabel Jeans
in *Lady Windermere's Fan*,
1945

Left, Vivien Leigh
in *Anna Karenina*,
1947

Clarissa Churchill

Cecil in *Lady Windermere's Fan*, 1946

Edith Olivier

Cecil by George Platt-Lynes

Zerbe's photo of Frank Chapman, Valentina, Gladys Swarthout
and Georges Schlee (The Little Man) at El Morocco

Cecil's sketch of Garbo as *Queen Christina*

Garbo in New York, 1946

Above, Garbo in her garden, California, March 1948

Cecil and Garbo in London, October 1951

The Queen in Garter robes, 1955

The Queen and Prince Charles, 1950

The Ascot scene, *My Fair Lady*

Marilyn Monroe,
New York, February 1956

Cecil with Leslie Caron,
Gigi, Hollywood 1957

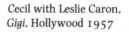

Above, June Osborn

Above right,
The dying
Isak Dinesen, 1962

Cecil photographing
Nureyev and
Margot Fonteyn

shillings.'[46] Convinced that this was the first honest film producer he had ever met, Shaw released the rights, including those for *Pygmalion*. It would be wrong to suggest that a short or easy path lay ahead, but in time Alan Jay Lerner and Fritz Loewe set to work with Herman Levin as producer. They were determined to have Cecil for costumes because 'his very look is such that it is difficult to know whether he designed the Edwardian era or the Edwardian era designed him'.[47] Oliver Smith had already been commissioned to do the sets and Cecil normally insisted on doing both. However, Herman Levin was persistent and Cecil was greatly attracted by the show: He signed. Herman Levin recalled: 'I've done hits and I've done flops. One thing I can tell you is that if it's a hit you get your first choices. You want Rex Harrison, you get Rex Harrison.'[48] Similarly Oliver Smith noted that to work together was a great test of the friendship that fortunately existed between him and Cecil:

> We were both internationally acclaimed scenic stars, both extremely ambitious and aggressive.... He wanted to work enough to go in. It was an enormous compliment to me. Once the tug of war was over, he was friendly and collaborative. If there were scenic difficulties he pitched in and helped me. Designers of real talent such as Cecil can collaborate. It's the untalented that make the difficulties.[49]

Julie Andrews confirmed this:

> I was so pleased that the two of them were co-ordinating so much with each other. It wasn't as if one or other of them were being the star about it. It was the most wonderful collaborative effort ... they seemed to want to work out colouring. And the general projected look of the show they both worked on as a team, as much as Cecil made the most enormous personal contribution.... It showed in the final result.[50]

To the collaboration both men brought their particular skills. The overall design was based on a two-hour meeting at the Plaza. They set the palette scene by scene. The play is such that most of the drama is over by the time Eliza has learned to enunciate her vowels. Thereafter the effect is largely visual, with the Ascot gavotte, the Embassy ballroom, flower scenes at Covent Garden, and Mrs Higgins's drawing-room. For his costume designs Cecil was able to draw on an enormous vista of early experience. The past decade of his theatrical triumphs also stood him in good stead. From *Lady Windermere's Fan* onwards his talent had unfolded like a young bloom in each successive production until it burgeoned in full splendour in *My Fair Lady*. He had been drawing Ascot fashions since he was a child. He had even published sketches in an article called 'Ascots of the Past' in *Vogue* on 28 May 1930. His black and white scene – the 'motionless frieze of ladies like magpies against a white drop'[51] – upon which the curtain rises towards

Cecil's first Ascot drawings in Vogue, *May 1930*

the end of the first act brought a gasp of astonished wonder night after night, combining all Cecil hoped for – elegance, beauty, surprise and wit. Even thirty years later, particularly abroad, if Cecil's name and photographs do not seem at once familiar, mention of this scene normally brings instant recognition.

Following the great visual display of the Ascot clothes, Cecil complemented a grey ballroom with costumes the colour of sherbet ice-cream. He threw in daring and original bright oranges. Cathleen Nesbitt was signed as Mrs Higgins for three months at $1,000 a week. Cecil dressed her in vivid yellow. Cathleen wrote: 'When I heard I was to be dressed by Cecil Beaton, I really wouldn't have minded having no lines at all.'[52] At first Cecil ran into problems. When he selected his colours in delicate pastels, Abe Feder, the lighting man, subjected them to the bright lights in his studio. The colours disappeared, so Cecil had to choose stronger ones to achieve the effect he wanted.

From the start Cecil found working on *My Fair Lady* a great contrast to *The Chalk Garden*. 'The management is very agreeable, professional and easy,'[53] he reported to Eileen in October 1955. They liked him too. Herman Levin recalled that Cecil put himself across as a *grand seigneur*. Once they

Design for an opera-goer in My Fair Lady, *1956*

were hungry and the only possibility was a hot dog stand. Levin had a hot dog while Cecil ordered a *pizza* (which he mispronounced). The onlookers gazed in wonder as the elegant figure stood there, eating it happily. Helene Pons, who had first recommended Cecil to Herman Levin, made the costumes for the play. At first he deeply regretted not having had Karinska and felt he had to keep a close eye on all Miss Pons did. The hats were a particular problem. Cecil lost his temper when one had to be redone for the third time. He was delighted to find that the pearl buttons on his curtains at Ashcombe still existed. Eileen sent 3,000 over and he sold them to Miss Pons. Thus those buttons that rattled so nostalgically at his beloved retreat took on a new lease of life on the costermongers' coats in Covent Garden. For his inspiration Cecil recalled the cartwheel hats of Aunt Jessie. He gave Mrs Higgins his mother's grey ostrich-feathered hat and Eliza wore a striped dress inspired by the first actress he saw, Mrs Perry. When faced with a pear-shaped girl he consulted the director of design at the Brooklyn Museum and was shown a coat with seaming all the way across the back. Rex Harrison's clothes – and certain head-dresses and liveries – were made specially in London and Cecil ran up a bill of £830 7s 6d (then about $2,332).* At all times he had to maintain the balance between a Shaw play

*Rex Harrison was annoyed that Herbert Johnson supplied William S. Paley with a hat identical to that of Higgins.

Julie Andrews as Eliza

and a musical. One hundred and fifty costumes were seen at a dress parade towards the end of October. 'It will be very exciting,' Cecil wrote to his mother, 'and I think some of them are going to be unlike anything I've done before. Here's hoping the play will succeed. The five weeks' run in Philadelphia is already sold out and they have two million dollars advance sale. The music is really pretty!'[54]

Julie Andrews, who had made her name in *The Boyfriend* and was to star as Eliza for three and a half years, recalled the endless fittings in the heat of Helene Pons's studio. Once she fainted and awoke to find Cecil fanning her and calling, 'Oh somebody please get her a glass of water. Do something with her.'[55] She found Cecil 'quite a taskmaster in terms of what he wanted',[56] but recalled that despite the size of the hats (which meant that the ladies often had to come through doors sideways) the clothes were well designed and well made and throughout the long run there were never any problems with them. Even the ball dress, which she wore for effect coming down Higgins's stairs all alone before the ballroom scene (and which thus received another gasp of delight from the audience), was easy to wear despite its considerable weight. Julie Andrews used to joke with Cecil in a cockney accent and thus established some rapport with him though they were never close friends. She said: 'This little smile used to be there. I think it's because I used to tease him rather a lot. Something about him made me do that to him.... I don't think I could ever come up to his level of knowledge and style so I used to try and bring him down a bit and he kind of liked it, I think.'[57]

Simultaneously with his *My Fair Lady* work, Cecil was designing *The Little Glass Clock*, an undistinguished play recommended by his lawyer, Arnold Weissberger, because the money was good. There also came an offer which indicated Cecil's current prestige, but he turned it down, writing to Eileen: 'I think my name on a scent is going too far.'[58] Cecil made tentative friends with Garbo again, but kept his feelings in check: 'I had put a brake on my emotions. I would not let myself love her without restraint. I was still deeply wounded by her lack of unselfishness, by her harbouring old suspicions. I wouldn't allow myself to suffer so much again.'[59] But Garbo's sadness won him round in due course. By the time he left for home she was verbally answering the tough letter he had sent the year before:

> I do love you and I think you're a flop. You should have taken me by the scruff of the neck and made an honest boy of me. I think you would have been the Salvation Army.[60]

These words thrilled Cecil. For a while he wondered if perhaps it was not too late to make more permanent plans.

Meanwhile, in the temporary absence of Waldemar Hansen, Jim Benton, 'with dark monkey fringe for hair and a nice deep voice',[61] came to work for Cecil at the Ambassador. He began by being frightened, but was soon impressed by Cecil's dynamism. Jim Benton confided to Eileen:

> Incidentally I stand in absolute awe and envy of C.B.'s vast energy! I'm not with him all day, of course, but certainly see his activity in the morning and helping to set up his schedule for the rest of the day! The man is truly a genius, isn't he?[62]

As rehearsals progressed Cecil became increasingly exasperated with the Helene Pons studio and Rex Harrison was 'very tiresome' with the director, but all around the signs showed that a major hit was imminent. Julie Andrews attributed this to 'a combination of a book and lyrics and music and performance and all the other talents as well'.[63] All these united simultaneously and were beautifully controlled by Moss Hart. Jim Benton saw the dress parade of the chorus: 'The costumes ... are unbelievably beautiful.

... They are truly the most daring and at the same time most glamorous that have appeared on the American stage, at least, in years.'[64]

As the play ended on the first night in New Haven, Alan Jay Lerner noticed Cecil rushing from the audience 'a look of fury in his face'.[65] His wrath had been caused because Julie Andrews had worn her yellow boat-shaped hat in the 'Show me' scene the wrong way round. The leading lady had been doing her best to cope with Rex Harrison who was 'pretty much a basket-case of nerves as were we all'.[66] Now, after all the crises, the revolving stage that had broken down, the dreadful snow-storm and the general tension, she was back in her dressing-room:

> I was sitting absolutely dazed and wondered what had hit me at the end of the performance. There wasn't a soul around and suddenly my door burst open, Mr Beaton came in, grabbed the hat in question and said, 'Not this way round, that way round.' I nearly burst into tears because it was the first thing anyone said after this mammoth evening.... I needed someone to say 'well done' not 'How could you get that wrong?'[67]

It still seemed surprising to think that the show would run two or three years and Cecil wondered if he might make as much as $20,000 out of it. He described the opening night in New Haven:

> It's been a big job and the last nigglings are maddening to all. Had difficulty with Julie's hairstyles and in the end discarded her wigs. We now have to make over a new balldress for her. She couldn't wear with enough dash the perfectly marvellous jewelled sheath we have given her.* The scenery is not bad but Oliver Smith is the most casual person I've ever known and I can't think how he gets any jobs. He didn't turn up until two days before the opening and his sets are only done in the most slapdash way. No attention to detail. It's been desperately hard work for all. Everyone except Rex Harrison has behaved impeccably. He is beneath contempt and refused to appear at the first night saying he was unprepared and would not go on and make a fool of himself. So the management decided to call the whole audience off. Harrison relented at four in the afternoon† and after frantic telephonings the show went on again and had a miraculously smooth opening night considering there had only been one disastrous Dress Rehearsal. Levin and gang have behaved better than any management I've ever known, such politeness and consideration and heart, and no vengeance or malice at all, a real experience to find people behaving so decently in difficult circumstances.

---

*Julie Andrews did eventually wear this. The Drury Lane version was sold to the Victoria and Albert Museum for £500 in 1982.

†In his autobiography, Rex Harrison explained: 'I don't think I've ever been as frightened before or since in my life' [*Rex*, Macmillan, 1974, p. 170].

But for the patience of Moss Hart, the director, the show would never have got on. I caught a cold and a bad throat, like half the members of the cast.[68]

Meanwhile the pace of life continued at a hectic rate with difficult photographs to be taken for *Modess* advertisements. And while Cecil basked in the knowledge that the police were now keeping back the crowds outside *My Fair Lady* as the lucky ticket-holders emerged, thrilled to a man, he achieved the wish of photographing Marilyn Monroe, for which he had striven amidst much negotiating for three months.

There had been the possibility that Cecil might design Marilyn's dresses for her latest film, *The Prince and the Showgirl*. The 'tornado visit' took place at the Ambassador Hotel on 22 February. Marilyn flounced in an hour and a quarter late but Cecil spotted at once her splendid quality. 'She was instantly forgiven for she has a completely disarming childlike freshness and ingenuity and her mischief is irresistible.'[69] He followed her round the room, clicking away:

> She romps, she squeals with delight, she leaps on to the sofa. She puts a flower stem in her mouth, puffing on a daisy as though it were a cigarette. It is an artless, impromptu, high-spirited, infectiously gay performance. It will probably end in tears.[70]

When some of the results were published in the *Saturday Evening Post* (netting $3,000), she claimed they had not been approved and there was the inevitable exchange of letters of rebuke and explanation. Later *Harper's Bazaar* published an article written by Cecil (with Waldemar's help) on Marilyn.

The Little Glass Clock opened in Princeton with Cecil delighted with Karinska's work on his 'absolutely ravishing'[71] scenery and costumes. But overall it was a disappointment. He thought his own play would have done better:

> The play is awful and the acting is worse. [Eva] Gabor [sister of Zsa Zsa] gives an opera singer's performance but without ever bursting into song. Rather she screeches in Hungarian singsong that is enough to drive the audience mad.[72]

Cecil was also hard at work compiling his book, *The Face of the World*, with Waldemar Hansen. At this moment of triumph in his life, he still had two great worries. The first was the expensive rate at which he lived (Noël Coward told him that he was saving £30,000 a year by being domiciled abroad), and the other was to ensure he had enough time to paint seriously when he came home. Then there was the visit of Joan Crawford on 13 March. Waldemar suggested she would be good for *The Face of the World*, but Cecil had replied: 'What the hell do I want her for?'[73] He thought her just a five-foot carrot-top redhead. But Jim Benton's excitement at the imminent arrival of his favourite star restored Cecil's faith in the glamour she held for the outside world. She came in the afternoon and sat on the floor. As with Marilyn Monroe, Cecil spotted something beneath the surface. He set about getting her to show different emotions – fear, anger and love. At one point he asked: 'Joan, could you hold that pose?', and the old professional replied: 'I can hold it for two minutes if necessary.'[74] When she had gone, Waldemar commented: 'Why, she hasn't had such a distinguished work-out in years!'[75]

All this was suddenly eclipsed by the Broadway opening of *My Fair Lady*. Cecil wrote to Eileen:

> It was really a thrilling first night. The audience gave as good a performance as the cast. The show is really wonderful, solid, professional. Shaw comes out unscathed, lyrics excellent, whole casting and conception admirable, and people cheered for ages. It was an electric evening, everyone in agreement that it's the best thing since *South Pacific*. It will surely come to London. I am grateful and overwhelmed. It was such fun in the apartment during the lull before the storm, messengers bringing flowers and telegrams and a huge palm tree [sent by Bill and Babe Paley]. All we needed was a pug to bark. Today I've been answering dozens of telegrams and listening to praise. It's very warming. Next week is going to be filled with interviews and photograph sittings.[76]

Cecil decided at this point to employ a press agent 'as I think and Weissberger does too that it is useful to plug away now when "Fair Lady" is in the news, and it's extraordinary how important people are impressed by the silliest little squib in the papers'.[77] Fan letters poured in, one of which read:

> Oh! Mr Beaton, if you are ever in Albuquerque, N.M. again, my husband and I would love to have you come and take a snap-shot of our little ninety-room cave.[78]

My Fair Lady was chosen unanimously as best musical of the season, the first time all the judges had agreed for twenty-one years. After Truman Capote had seen it three times, he wrote: 'It's probably the best show I've ever seen and I was so proud of your work: you, Rex and Moss (and Shaw!) are heroes of that production.'[79]

In no way did Cecil relax his pace and bask in glory, nor was he deceived by the effects of success:

> I find I'm almost tired of having compliments, and last night I went to see my old ballet *Illuminations*, and felt that it was really such a work of art that it's *unfair* that this should have been so much better received by the general public.[80]

Cecil threw himself at once into the business of reviving *The Gainsborough Girls*. He did four more *Modess* sittings, causing Carmel Snow, the editor of *Harper's Bazaar*, to comment that he achieved in one day what most photographers would in five. She invited him to do a considerable amount of fashion work the next winter. He did three pages of the Ascot scene for *Vogue*, one of which included him in a frock coat (a Rex Harrison discard). Waldemar and Jim slaved away on *The Face of the World*, and Cecil described his hotel room as a factory. He gave two cocktail-parties. When Moss Hart saw Cecil's list of engagements hanging in the bathroom 'he almost had a fit. There were so many to dovetail.'[81] He also did ten fashion designs based on 'Pyggers' for Samuel Winston at $750 apiece. As Winston was Charlie James's arch-enemy, this provoked an unwelcome bout of hysteria from his old friend. Cecil caught a bad cold and retreated gratefully to the *Queen Elizabeth* on 4 April for a recuperative voyage home. On the way home he concluded:

The success of the Pygmalion musical was beyond all expectation. It made success seem easy and now, when I am stopped on all sides to receive compliments, I wonder why it never happened before.... It has not come too late, but I am perhaps a bit bitter that some of my friends in the theatre (if there is such an anomaly) did not spot my talent twenty years before (though I must admit my touch is firmer now than ever it was).[82]

Two years later, on 30 April 1958, *My Fair Lady* began its run of 2,281 performances at Drury Lane in London. The quality of the costumes was considerably higher, thanks to Bermans, and Cecil altered the styles somewhat because, as he pointed out, his New York ones had been a little ahead of fashion but fashion had now caught up with him. The New York version of the play had popularized pointed shoes, billowy blouses and established a craze for chiffons.

The show opened in an unprecedented blaze of publicity, because its New York triumph was now a widely known *fait accompli*. Looking back, Cecil wrote that it had been an easier operation for him:

There were the usual difficulties with Rex Harrison at the theatre but fortunately I had little contact with them. He did, however, give me one or two unpleasant moments though war was never declared between us.

The success of the production here was even greater than one imagined. This made everything rosy for me and the *Sunday Times* put me in their series of profiles, the Queen came and we talked in the back of the box ... all sorts of people that had paid no attention before now became ingratiating.[83]

28

The Crest of a Wave

*I was on the crest of a wave, must enjoy the ride, must
be careful not to be careless and fall off unexpectedly, but
must look to the furthest horizons, and not fail to explore
any possibilities – a most exhilarating state of affairs.*

Cecil's dairy, April 1956

Cecil did not enjoy his success for long, because tragedy struck within a
month of his return to London. On 3 May Peter Watson suddenly died. Cecil
had lunched with him a few days before, while Peter took time off from
hanging an exhibition of Brazilian garden schemes at the ICA. They talked
happily and with gusto. Predictably the only difficult part of the conversation was when Cecil tried to talk of his great success with *My Fair Lady*.
Peter 'looked startled, as if I had lost my head and then he realized what I
was trying to explain, a popular success and what it means'.[1] Cecil thought
him 'a completely fulfilled, integrated person: someone who has now discovered himself'.[2] Cecil wanted to invite Peter for the weekend with his
blind Aunt Cada, but failed to find time to ring up. Then Tony del Renzio of
the ICA called to announce the death. As always on hearing bad news Cecil
'let out a moan that was like that of a bull in agony, a great volume of
grief'.[3] It transpired that Peter had gone to the country to throw off a cold,
and had returned to the flat he shared with his sinister friend, Norman
Fowler. After a long drive he had taken a hot bath. The bathroom door was
locked. Whether he fainted or had a heart attack (or indeed whether, as
some have suggested, he was murdered by Norman),* Peter was dead and
lost to Cecil for ever. In his grief, as again so often, Cecil judged the effect of
the shock by his own visual image caught by chance in the looking-glass:

> The shock was enough to want to make me die as well, for my face was
> contorted, swollen, mauve, my hair white, untidy and almost bald. I
> looked like the most terrible old man, and it was appalling that this

---

*Norman disappeared to Jamaica where, a few years later, he was found dead in the hotel
swimming-bath. Like Peter he had drowned.

terrible old man was grieving for the love of his life. It was unworthy of Peter that I should continue to behave as I did when I was twenty-four [twenty-six], and yet I still felt as I did then and tears coursed down with the same intensity as when for other reasons, still on account of Peter, I have been uncontrolled in my frustrated misery.

But there are no regrets in my amorous friendship. I am sad and sore that it was never a mutual love affair, a friendship only for him, yet perhaps his instinct was right and that if ever he had allowed it to be put on a different plane it would have lasted less than a lifetime.[4]

In his misery, Mrs Cartwright, the 'nice cleaning woman',[5] tried to comfort him, holding his head like that of a child. Eileen was 'tactful and sweet'.[6] Cecil retired to Reddish to burst into tears at Juliet Duff's table and then more sensibly to mourn quietly and to fill the pages of his diary with the tale. He tried to share his sorrow with Garbo, in a letter that began frivolously before relating the news. 'No one has really made quite such an impression on me,' he wrote. 'I can't bear to think there's no further link. I don't even have the consolation that other bereaved people have that there is an afterlife. The void is utter.'[7] But Cecil was a survivor. He concluded: 'Of course I shall continue tomorrow morning with my active life.'[8]

Peter's history is not without interest. After Cecil had been more or less cured of the worst obsession of his love, Peter fell into the hands of Denham Fouts, who persecuted him mercilessly. Cecil used to hear of 'the appalling dogfights that Denham had with Peter. They were just what Peter needed.'[9] Cecil hated Denham Fouts with what Truman Capote described as 'an unconsumed passion'.[10] Subsequently Denham got into trouble with little boys and dope. He died of a heart attack, the result of his addiction, on a lavatory in Rome on 16 December 1948. Another friend, Michael Wishart, wrote that it was not known whether death came 'by invitation or as a gate-crasher'.[11]

Tchelitchew fell in love with Peter and so did Marie Laure de Noailles, his introduction to the world of French painters, writers and musicians. Bébé Bérard, Markévitch, Henri Sauget, Emilio Terry, Jacques Février and Jean Hugo became his friends and, through Peter, Cecil too entered this world. Peter surrendered his place in the fashionable world completely. He became a serious patron of the arts through *Horizon* and the ICA. He was respected by artists such as Lucian Freud, Francis Bacon and John Craxton, and he became completely Bohemian, with strong convictions based on careful thought. Cecil wrote:

He wore awful mackintoshes, his hair once so sexily lotioned was on end. He became thinner and more gaunt and, in spite of bad colour and wrinkles and scraggy legs with huge knees and feet, he seemed to be more beautiful and covetable than ever.[12]

More seriously, Cecil concluded:

> Without caring about this he became respected by the most intelligent writers, his judgement revered, his fairness impeccable. With his feet in the gutter, he had indulged in every vice, except women, but he was really like a saint.[13]

Meanwhile Norman became hysterical and was taken to hospital, as Cecil explained to Waldemar Hansen: 'Lucian and someone else said that Peter had become not only disillusioned about people but also about things. I didn't feel this to be so. I'm *sure* it was an accident, but I will let you know further developments.'[14] The coroner's verdict of accidental death was followed by a depressing cremation in Golders Green. Cyril Connolly, Stephen Spender, Graham Sutherland, Roland Penrose, Lee Miller, the friend Norman Fowler and a handful of others bade him farewell. The process lasted a mere quarter of an hour. Cecil went to London Airport and flew to Paris to stay with a rather depressed Diana Cooper.

Truman, a good friend to Cecil if not to Peter, tried to reassure him:

> He loved you, Cecil: you were his youth, as much as he was yours. The last time I saw him, in Rome, 1954, he told me you were more marked by 'tender honesty' than anyone he'd ever known. I remember because I liked the phrase 'tender honesty' and knew what it meant.[15]

While in England Cecil was determined to work quietly, but presently he was bidden to America once more, this time to attend a fashion show at Nieman-Marcus in Dallas, based on some of his *My Fair Lady* designs. He went there in the height of the August heat and received a much coveted Nieman-Marcus fashion award (a fashion Oscar).

He was subjected to a succession of television and radio interviews and several impromptu speeches (for which his lecture tour stood him in good stead). Marie Louise Bousquet, the French editor of *Harper's Bazaar*, was with him and kept him in continual fits of laughter. She used to pull her Balenciaga dress up and ask: 'Are my stockings straight?' As Cecil noted: 'They are but her legs aren't!'[16] Another joy of Dallas was that he could photograph the oil millionairesses for $1,000 a session.

In September Cecil went to Paris to join Garbo. He found her with Cecile de Rothschild in a sitting-room at the Crillon full of dying flowers: 'her face wrinkled, her hair terribly untidy. She has absolutely no vanity about being seen like a gypsy.'[17] Garbo was to come to London but only when she felt well enough: 'It's all very difficult,'[18] wrote Cecil to Eileen. Meanwhile he had time on his hands.

It was on a Saturday evening that Cecil smuggled Garbo into London:

> She was not spotted by strangers even, and there was no photographer.

My feelings throughout the journey were mixed, hopeful that all would go well and smoothly for her, and that she would not be made unhappy, and yet enjoying secretly the excitement of the press onslaught. I felt very clever at arranging the whole thing so discreetly.[19]

Cecil dropped Garbo at Claridge's and arrived at Pelham Place, 'looked at myself in the glass and my deep set eyes told of my exhaustion'.[20] The next day Cecil was in for a surprise:

She is like a man in many ways. She telephoned to say, 'I thought we might try a little experiment this evening at 6.30.' But she spoke in French and it was difficult to understand at first what she meant. But soon I discovered although I pretended not to. She was embarrassed and a certain *pudeur* on my part made me resent her frankness and straight-forwardness, something that I should have respected.[21]

Cecil was puzzled by Garbo. She tore up her letters because it was a waste of time to answer them. 'But', wondered Cecil, 'what is time being preserved for?'[22] Her hotel room had no books, just a few old magazines and some bruised fruit. She expressed no wish to meet Eileen or to hear about Cecil's family. She expressed no sympathy on the death of Peter. Rarely did she come to life. Her most lively moment was the childlike enthusiasm with which she watched the Guards on sentry duty. Another excitement was a visit to the Edens at No. 10 on 17 October. On this occasion Garbo made light of her problems as Clarissa, Cecil and she drank iced vodka. Then the Prime Minister arrived and opened the conversation with the two topics Garbo disliked most: her film career and her native land. However, Garbo gave 'one of her marvellously timed, completely spontaneous performances, as natural as breathing and as refreshing'.[23] Later she met Harold Macmillan. 'He looks after all our money,'[24] said the Prime Minister.

On the way out a press photographer, lying in wait for the President of Costa Rica, got the unexpected scoop of Garbo and Cecil together. Thereafter Cecil's life was made hell. The press rang him until two in the morning. They pursued the pair to Covent Garden where they attended *Romeo and Juliet*, performed by the Bolshoi Ballet, and the next day they took Pelham Place by siege. The star ballerina, Ulanova, was dining with Oliver Messel opposite, while Cecil was entertaining Garbo, Cecile de Rothschild and Hal Burton. The doorbell began to ring during dinner. Cecil looked out to see a crowd of photographers lurking on the pavement. The besieged guests tried every trick, even turning the lights out, but in vain. Nor was it possible to escape over the garden wall. Finally Garbo and Cecile made a run for the taxi:

The effect was like a storm of atomic explosions. About twenty flashes went off again and again. It seems strange, now, that I should have been so upset. But my stomach was completely upsidedown. I was unable to sleep. Greta was very firm, and if not suspicious that I had in some way been directly responsible for such a scene said, 'The boys do too much talking. Maybe it's normal, but I shouldn't perhaps see so much of Mr Beaton for a few days.' This horrified me and I wondered whether or not the visit to the country would be ruined by the presence of a loitering photographer.[25]

Press speculation was fuelled by the fact that Garbo was wearing a ring on the wedding finger. She came down to Reddish with Cecile de Rothschild and they had a peaceful time, dining with Juliet Duff, walking near Ashcombe and visiting Salisbury Cathedral. Cecil had set aside a clear month to look after his elusive friend, but suddenly she became restless and decided to go back to Paris and then to New York:

She didn't feel able to cope with anything but a quiet life, of going to bed at seven o'clock. I was terribly dejected. I had hoped she would come and stay in the country for quite a long time, that perhaps even we might get married. I told her that she had recently blamed me for not taking her by the scruff of the neck and marrying her. How could I now prevent her from making another mistake? 'Oh! I always make mistakes.'[26]

Cecil was very sad when she left.

Towards the end of November an exhibition of his drawings was held at the Sagittarius Gallery in New York. Cecil's old flame Adèle Astaire bought a design for *Lady Windermere's Fan* for $950: 'The prices are high but the snob appeal has been plugged.'[27] While in New York he photographed Maria Callas. He also did some work for a fierce editress which brought him to a pitch of rage. When, two years later, the photographer Louise Dahl-Wolfe suffered a similar experience, it provoked from Cecil a letter of sympathetic venom:

Circulars should go out against that vile woman! She is not only mad she's malevolent. WHY, why did you and I both finish the job? *Why* didn't we walk out half time? I can never forgive myself for not teaching her a lesson. I've never had a worse experience. Same as yours no doubt, but I'm a meaner character than you and I want my REVENGE!

I loathe that gurking genteel bitch. She is low in the fashion world and that's saying a lot.

I look forward to seeing you in the New Year. Meanwhile if you see [——] please spit in her eye.[28]

In similar vein, as Christmas approached, the question of Christmas cards arose. Cecil wrote to Eileen: 'we had better send an affectionate one to the

Oliviers, but not to Beaumont or Gielgud or the new face-lifted Jones'.*[29]
Meanwhile, following the success of *My Fair Lady*, Cecil found he was
approached by 'manufacturers of curtains, Christmas cards, women's pyjamas and table mats to do designs and I've been rolling in contracts and
done quite a lot of designs'.[30]

On 17 December Cecil received a telephone call from the British Consul
with a message from the Prime Minister asking if he would accept the CBE.
Jim Benton was in the room when the call came and observed Cecil:

> He hung up the phone and sat in a somewhat bemused stance, puffing
> his cigar. (He had just come in from an exhausting afternoon sitting.)
> And then he began to smile. It was terribly charming.[31]

To Anthony Eden, Cecil wrote:

> I was quite taken aback that I should have been thought of in connection
> with any honour as the sort of work I do doesn't seem to fit into any of
> the accepted categories. It is for this reason that I am so especially
> proud.[32]

To his ecstatic mother he wrote:

> I was very pleased and said yes like a shot. I expect the Waverleys have
> put a spoke in my wheel [*sic*] or perhaps Clarissa. Of course it would be
> nice to have a knighthood† and one doesn't generally get both but a
> stitch in time.[33]

Cecil's mother replied: 'I feel this is the greatest moment of your life. I only
hope and pray success will *always* follow you. (It generally has.)'[34] On the
other hand Ann Fleming wrote:

> The general reaction amongst your friends was that you should have
> received a knighthood. They were just as excited as the soccer fans are
> about 'Matthews‡ the dribbler'.[35]

As Cecil suspected, the honour had been Clarissa's idea: 'I am glad you were
pleased and that we could do that small thing before we left,'[36] she wrote
from Otehei Bay, Northland, New Zealand, where Sir Anthony was resting
after resigning the premiership on 9 January.

In January 1957 Cecil went to Japan with Truman Capote, who had been
commissioned by *Harper's Bazaar* to write an article about the filming of
Sayonara, Josh Logan's production, contrasting American and Japanese

---

* Enid had paid a rewarding visit to the plastic surgeon Sir Archibald McIndoe.

† Cecil was put out to find Chips Channon knighted in the same list.

‡ Stanley Matthews, the veteran footballer, also received a CBE.

methods – Hollywood versus Kabuki. Already Hollywood was living in fear of what Truman would write about them. They reacted with panic, and two-faced hypocrisy. Truman 'roared with dry laughter at the picture his approach created'.[37] Cecil's flight was paid for by Japan Air Lines (arranged by *Harper's Bazaar*) and he would pay them back by taking certain photographs for them. He and Truman flew to San Francisco on 27 December. The trip started badly. Truman's head was stuck in the elevator door at the St Francis Hotel and both had problems over Japanese visas.

A lady from Cecil's book Japanese

Cecil tried to read Japanese novels to overcome his ignorance of Japan. In Honolulu Truman lost his luggage for three days. However, the weather was blissful and there was a funny incident when Truman was taken for a child at dinner with a local couple, the Dillinghams. He was ordered to the children's table on the patio:

The retreating figure emanated a dynamo of hatred, scorn and fury, a figure out of a strip cartoon that would have had a bubble of sophisticated but censorable expletives coming from its mouth.[38]

Truman was not by nature a traveller. 'I think Cecil enjoyed it more than I did,' he said. 'The one thing in the world I'm *not* is a sightseer.'[39] Nevertheless Cecil was impressed at how quickly Truman found his way about town and where the best martinis were served.

Cecil loved the cleanliness and the colours of Tokyo. Even so the wife of the president of JAL, whom he was obliged to photograph, managed to produce 'the only ugly kimono materials I have yet seen'.[40] The job took almost a whole day and was uninspiring; however, 'the deal was done – my pictures, god willing, should be the best that Madame has ever had and the ticket is partly paid for'.[41] Before departing for Hong Kong and Thailand, Cecil took in the details of the colours of artificial flowers, the vivid cinema signs, and the raw fish and other specialities of Japanese food, not all of which he found 'palatable to the sight if eaten with Western prejudice'.[42] To begin with he found Japanese aesthetics too precious and mannered, but he came to like the swinging lanterns and their obsession with cherry blossom, a season he missed because it only lasted about ten days a year. But this contrasted with the hideously coloured junk toys that were then a feature of Japan.

After Hong Kong (which Cecil found thrilling with the bay and all the Chinese junks even if he hated Government House, thinking 'one reception-room might be that of a powder room in a night-club'[43]), they went on to Bangkok. Again Cecil knew nothing about Thailand, nor did he expect the blazing heat. They loathed the hotel and they were exacting to their guide, determined to make the most of their few days. Cecil tried to help Truman operate his new camera when they visited the Floating Market, but even he found it hard to capture what he wanted from the moving launch. As they explored the sights, Cecil became enthusiastic. At the Temple of Wat Po he was interested to see geese wandering about, while scruffy dogs and minute cats lay sprawled on the feet of statues of Chinese dragons. It was 'a haunting, peaceful spot'.[44]

The Ambassador in Bangkok was Berkeley Gage, whom Cecil had met in China during the war. He arranged a display of Thai dancers in the grounds of the Embassy. Cecil met Group Captain Peter Townsend, who was on a world tour and writing about it as part of the process of creating a new life as the Princess Margaret furore died down. He found Cecil in the midst of the dancers and wondered for a moment if Cecil was taking part in the dance:

> It was a fascinating performance,' both by him and the dancers. During a moment's rest between dances, he would call one of the girls over into the shade of a tree. 'Hold that branch', he would say, arranging it so that she held a leafy spray close to her enchanting face. Click went his camera and click went mine.[45]

Thanks to this the Group Captain obtained some excellent poses. Cecil saw more dances at Angkor Wat in Cambodia and compared the dancers to the Duchess of Windsor 'in their posturing attitudes wearing tall head-dresses, jewellery and elaborate tight dresses'.[46]

Back in Tokyo, after a flight during which Truman and Cecil spoke incessantly, Truman came to Cecil's room and, although physically worn out, continued to regale him with stories. 'His interests encompass the world,' noted Cecil. 'He has a really good brain, well trained and well fed, continuously employed and refurbished.'[47] Cecil wrote to Eileen:

It's been an exhausting, interesting and curious trip. T. very brilliant, a ham as big as a ballroom and he is overcrammed with sweetness and affection for me – can be brutal to others. We have got along well for one month.[48]

Cecil photographed Utaemon, the female impersonator, in whose alarming presence he was forbidden to wear a hat. Other distinguished sitters included the writers Yukio Mishima and Yasunari Kawabata, the André Gide of Japan.

They went to Kyoto, very much the high spot of their visit though Cecil wished it were spring. (Nevertheless a mink-lined coat kept him warm.) They took part in the tea ceremony, the exact purpose of which remained unclear to him. Here they met Helena Rubinstein and her travelling secretary, Patrick O'Higgins. The latter, a friend since just after the war, described the encounter. The concierge of the Miyako Hotel told him: 'Two very fine English ladies waiting for you in bar. Both dressed like gentlemen.'[49] O'Higgins continued:

Cecil Beaton and Truman Capote rose to meet us. Cecil had doffed the wide Thai straw hat he had been wearing; but, still swaddled in a number of happy coats, scarves and other unrelated garments, he did present an unusual sight, while Truman had also removed his racoon fur cap and a voluminous ulster of bold design.[50]

Helena Rubinstein questioned them closely about their travels, after commenting: 'Intellectuals can dress as they please.'[51]

Cecil and Truman joined Josh and Nedda Logan and Bill and Edie Goetz (Irene Selznick's sister with whom Cecil was friends). Josh Logan, the director of *Sayonara*, was also in a state of panic that Truman was going to debunk his film. At this point, following a rebuff in Tokyo, Truman had given up the idea of the article, but both he and Cecil saw the sport in pretending it was going ahead. Cecil liked the Logans, who invited him onto the set, while Truman fell into a rage and hissed, 'Don't photograph them. It's demeaning.'[52]

The star of *Sayonara* was Marlon Brando, whom Cecil had spotted at Tokyo airport on 8 January:

> He has lost his looks in ten years, looks like a heavy-set businessman, podgy hands, a thick build, a Guys and Dolls hat. But his behaviour is all that could be desired, courteous, co-operative, good humoured, but quiet and restrained smile, a tongue flip an occasional reminder of his embarrassment at giving spontaneous performances for camera and microphone.[53]

Meeting Brando on the set, Truman sat down to talk to him as conspicuously as possible. This incited more paranoia in Josh Logan, who rang Marlon Brando later to ask what they had talked about. The star replied 'Buddhism', and then revealed that Truman was in the room. Logan rang back three times and finally Truman answered the telephone on the pretext that Marlon Brando was in the bathroom. One of the problems of this film was that Japanese heroines had to be deterred from saying 'I rub you' when they meant 'I love you', and Marlon Brando was extremely worried when a Buddhist monk asked for his autograph: 'I thought he'd given up all worldly ideas!'[54]

Later, on 9 November 1957, 'a very audacious piece'[55] by Truman appeared in the *New Yorker* (later republished in *The Dogs Bark*). Cecil predicted: 'A lot of people are not going to talk to him as a result of it.'[56] Truman wrote to Cecil:

> Brando told the papers he was going to sue me for libel; but I have good reason to doubt it. I had a telegram from the Logans telling me how much they 'loved' the piece. What a pair of hypocrites![57]

Years later Marlon Brando was still upset about it. In 1963 he gave Cecil his version of the story:

> He told me he was not going to do a *Sayonara* piece. He'd arrived too late. He told me a person very close to him [his mother] had committed suicide and I kind of went along with him.[58]

Other aspects of Japan that Cecil enjoyed were his attempts at Japanese flower arrangement and the strange ceremonies of a Noh play, though he thought the music was 'slow torture'.[59] He was confused by his three new cameras: 'It is time I took myself more seriously as a technically expert photographer.'[60] While they led an active life during the day, both Truman and Cecil managed early nights and an average of nine and a half hours' sleep. While Truman began work on a novel about finance exchange set in the places they had visited, Cecil read through the latest version of his play. He was surprised how much time Truman wasted and how many of his

projects were abandoned. Then, as the inevitable bad stomach upset overcame Cecil, he became restless to get back.

He went to Nikkō in the snow and had perhaps his most successful
Japanese day. On 8 February he and Truman returned to Honolulu. At this
point Truman's spirits soared because he loved anything American. Cecil
thought Truman had not liked the Japanese. His own opinions were hazy
and paradoxical:

> I liked the excessive formality of the Japanese, their toothy grimaces and
> their bowings, their polite giggles.
>
> I can see they can be maddening (less so than the Chinese – less
> complicated and time wasting), they can be cruel, that is true. I dislike
> their ideas of democracy and the Americanization of Japan is to be re-
> gretted. . . .
>
> Their children are adorable, quiet and pretty and gay, with ruddy
> cheeks. Their aged are beautiful and distinguished.
>
> They have great respect for beauty and yet many have absolutely no
> aesthetic sense whatsoever. Side by side is the best in taste together with
> the worst.
>
> The colours are the brightest, most garish (puce pink the favourite
> colour) and yet the best colours are more subdued than any. The real
> colours of Japan are the grey misty blue browns of Kyoto. They are slaves
> to cleanliness. Every part of them and their living is faultless. . . . Yet the
> mess after a Kabuki performance is unbelievable, the auditorium a
> mound of tangerine peel and trash of every sort.
>
> They are kind in a cold formal relentless way. They have in many
> things a cold clinical approach to life.[61]

In Honolulu Cecil recorded 'the horrid experience of finding my [Tiffany's]
watch stolen'.[62] However, there was worse than that. Cecil had become
involved in a high-spirited encounter with some sailors, which took an ugly
turn. Truman saved the situation by showing a surprisingly forceful side of
his character and sending the assailants on their way. However, both he
and Waldemar Hansen (to whom Cecil later related the tale) went so far as
to say that Cecil might have been murdered. The next day Cecil was 'a bit
too restless to enjoy the bathing as much as I'd like',[63] but was restored to
his normal self in time to dine with Doris Duke, the Lucky Strike heiress,
who was being more successful than most heiresses in her attempt to flee
conventional life, living in 'her really fabulous Arabian Nights Dream Persian House'.[64] Cecil left Truman in Honolulu and flew back to San Francisco,
to 'pick up the threads of my usual life',[65] with the help of shopping expeditions with Ina Claire and a lunch-party with the Lunts (still in dressing-
gowns). Back in New York Cecil thought the trip 'well worth doing . . . the
photographs alone seem to justify the trip',[66] but doubted he would ever

return. He and Truman found themselves exhausted. Later, in England, Cecil gave Stephen Tennant a gloomy account of his trip: 'Rain never stopped and Cecil said "We were so bored sitting night after night in smart restaurants." I said: "You took letters of introduction with you, surely?" I forget his very terse reply.'[67] With Waldemar's help once more, Cecil wrote his book *Japanese*. Weidenfeld's young editor Mark Boxer gave this a revolutionary design with pages that folded out so that the captions to each section could be seen at a glance. There were delays that angered Cecil but the book was finally published in 1959. Meanwhile *Harper's Bazaar* was overwhelmed with the quantity and quality of Cecil's photographs.

In New York Helena Rubinstein decided to capitalize on her meeting with Cecil and commissioned him to redesign her picture gallery in the Japanese manner for a fee of $5,000. Gradually the penthouse room 'metamorphosed under Cecil Beaton's light-hearted touch into a verdant, pseudo-Japanese winter garden'.[68] But there were endless quarrels and Cecil was not sorry to escape back to London. His parting words to Patrick O'Higgins were: 'Tell your boss that it's very difficult to make a silk purse from a sow's ear.'[69]

In London in March 1957 Cecil photographed the Queen Mother, Princess Margaret, the Kents and the Princess Royal. On 23 April it was announced that his *My Fair Lady* costumes had won a 'Tony' award. He also won another Antoinette Perry award (the previous two were for *Lady Windermere's Fan* and *Quadrille*). In May he worked on costumes for the film *The Truth About Women*, directed by Sydney and Muriel Box and starring Laurence Harvey, Julie Harris, Diane Cilento, Mai Zetterling and Eva Gabor. His old costumes were seen in a revival of *Apparitions* and described as old-fashioned. New beautiful ones were designed for Samuel Barber's opera *Vanessa*, directed by Gian Carlo Menotti, which was shown at the Metropolitan Opera House in New York in January 1958. This proved 'a smash hit', but because Cecil had had a difficult time he refused to take a curtain call. *The Face of the World* was published in October. This was another book in the tradition of the *Scrapbook* with photographs and articles and sketches covering all aspects of Cecil's career. Many had been photographed specially, including T.S. Eliot. The prickly poet found the poses somewhat theatrical but wrote: 'I have had many photographs taken in this particular room, but no one before has thought of making use of the glass partition; and with such astonishingly successful effect.'[70] *The Face of the World* was criticized for the bad quality of the reproductions. Nancy Spain (whom Evelyn Waugh had recently sued successfully for £2,000) was as rude as ever in her *Daily Express* column: 'But in spite of the fact that it is intriguingly dedicated to G.G. (his friend Greta Garbo I presume) I must admit I found it a really desperate bore.'[71]

Also in 1957 Cecil was appointed a Fellow of the Ancient Monuments Society and Vice-President of the Broadchalke Cricket Club.

*   *   *

As soon as Cecil came back from Japan in 1957 he was invited to do the décor and costumes for the Lerner and Loewe musical of *Gigi*. 'MGM – Hollywood – means being there in August – oh dear!'[72] wrote Cecil to Eileen, but he accepted.

The Gigi *logo*

Colette's novel, first adapted for the stage starring Audrey Hepburn, was a relatively daring topic for a musical, as it concerned courtesans and *cocottes*. Colette had based her story on the real-life love affair of a tall and handsome Frenchman called Constant Lee (of the sugar family) and Marthe Davelle. Alan Jay Lerner only agreed to do it on condition that Cecil did the sets and costumes and that Maurice Chevalier had a part. Some of the film was to be done on location in Paris and some in Hollywood. Cecil flew to Paris to reconnoitre suitable period spots, such as the Palais de Glace, the Musée Jacquemart-André, the Place Furstenberg and Place Palais Bourbon. While Maxim's had retained its Belle Epoque splendour, the Palais de Glace had become what Alan Jay Lerner called 'as tattered a relic as the hotels on the broadwalk of Atlantic City'.[73] Cecil and Vincente Minnelli managed to restore it to something of its previous grandeur. Cecil concluded that he had exhausted his Edwardian ideas in *Lady Windermere's Fan* and *My Fair Lady*. Thus he read all Colette's books and set about recapturing the *Belle Epoque* with a fresh and, this time, unsentimental eye. His initial work was done in the peace of Reddish, but when he reached Paris the usual dramas began. Karinska could only make a few costumes so he had to work with Madame Toussaint. As August was approaching many of the costumes had to be sent out to unknown and dubious tailors. Cecil had to bear in mind that on the screen bright red became claret, grey turned into Russian blue, chartreuse yellow into jaffa orange while turquoise blue looked like a vile medicine. Rarely would a costume be seen in full, so all interest had to be focused above the waist. Likewise eye-level was the focal point for the sets. Nothing could be left to chance, however, and zips had a habit of catching the light. He feared that Leslie Caron showed signs of being 'difficult and pernickety'.[74] He feared trouble:

> On celluloid Leslie Caron's mouth seemed vampire red, while her nut brown hair took on the shade of an old beetroot. Louis Jourdan, our hero, arrived from the South of France with a sunburn that defied all make-up disguises and the most uncontemporary of crew-haircuts.[75]

Just before filming began, Cecil had to rush back to London to sell serialization rights for *The Face of the World* to the *Observer* for £1,500. He returned to Paris, worn out, and slept lightly in a loaned apartment, having to leave several doors open in order to hear his distant early morning telephone call. He went to the Bois de Boulogne where an impressive array of *calèches* and women on horseback were gathered but, despite great activity of cameras and megaphones, there was no 'take'. The next day as the sun continued to shine, a 'take' was made and reshot fourteen times. Eyeing the weather nervously, Cecil became anxious and impatient. While Arthur Freed watched quietly, Vincente Minnelli was perched up a tall crane crying out technical instructions: 'His concentration and quickness of perception make him a master of this very difficult and new *métier*. If such a thing as a genius of a director is possible he is such a one.'[76] Meanwhile there were earnest cries such as 'Get the extra man who lost his moustache by the Serpentine to change places with the extra with the moustache this end of the picture', and 'Send a dozen *cocottes* over here at once'.[77] The weather deteriorated, the branches of the trees swayed nervously, and leaves fell. The extras became hungry and fractious. Some waiting women dozed off while one lay asleep with her mouth open. A bee flew into her mouth and stung her on the end of the tongue. Tiny scenes worth a moment's laugh absorbed the director completely. The glamorous model, Monique Van Voren, was determined to be in the film and she was to be Gaston's lady in the carriage at the Battle of Flowers. A bouquet was thrown in her lap and she had to sneeze. For this scene Van Voren sneezed energetically at rehearsal and for ten 'takes'. She sneezed into a microphone for the sound track. As Cecil wrote: 'Her whole soul was put into her Hatishoos.'[78] The director became frantic as he watched this scene, 'his expression was the wrapt concentration of some scientist watching to see if his Atom Bomb was to annihilate the whole world'.[79] Suddenly the heavens opened and a deluge came down. All the flower-decorated carriages were soaked, all the extras took sanctuary under trees in Perspex mackintoshes. Van Voren went on sneezing. All the costumes then had to go back to the wardrobe to be dealt with.

The skating scene created other problems. The sporting extras would do anything for an extra brooch or flower. Jacques Bergerac (one-time husband of Ginger Rogers) was signed up to play the skating instructor. This 'dark Adonis about eight feet tall, a toothy smile and Spanish eyelashes'[80] was duly sewn into his costume. Even the flybuttons were sewn up. He then announced he wanted to go to the bathroom. Minnelli said to him: 'No, no, and if you don't mind we'd like you to sleep in this suit just as it is.'[81] Unfortunately it was then discovered that Bergerac could not skate, so a device was constructed to stop him falling over, while a long scene was considerably shortened and he was only filmed above the waist. While Eva Gabor chatted happily to everyone, Cecil's only thought was of how to escape.

Tempers began to fray, the extras demanded more pay. Cecil was observed in a restaurant approving an imitation diamond necklace which a white horse was to eat at a ball (an episode that did not reach the film), the scenes at Maxim's were shot, the restaurant having been commandeered for four days. After the heat and then the rain in the Bois, and after the 'ordeal by ice'[82] at the Palais de Glace, Maxim's was again uncomfortable: 'The confusion, noise and heat in this inferno continued until all participants were prostrate from exhaustion.'[83] Having accustomed himself to swapping the jewellery of the extras from one to the other, Cecil had to restrain himself from doing likewise when, a while later, the other diners were genuine customers.

In this scene the top model Anne Gunning (later Lady Nutting) was hired at huge expense to be Uncle Honoré's guest in the scene when Gaston and Gigi dine. She is only seen for a moment, bedecked in plumes. This scene and the skating one Cecil thought particularly exciting. The whole adventure of the Paris filming was curious. Cecil had found old actresses to look like Sem caricatures. This last scene was filmed first so Leslie Caron's début was in her most extravagant mauve outfit. Thereafter she reverted to being a child.

Cecil returned to London to fit Isabel Jeans's costumes and, when he came back to Paris, was told sharply: 'You can go home tonight and be in Hollywood next Friday.'[84] Before he knew it Cecil was in Hollywood, and thrilled to be a member of the MGM personnel where he had first come in the hope of photographing Garbo in 1929. Howard Strickling, who had given Cecil some much-valued stills of the elusive star, was now head of the publicity department. Cecil became a regular at the canteen, eating his Elizabeth Taylor salad or Cyd Charisse sandwich. He lived in a bungalow and drove to the set in a large automatic Ford wagon loaned to him by Eva Gabor. He learned his way but once drove to Santa Monica by mistake. He enjoyed the studio life and the technical expertise with which his every command was carried out. He enjoyed digging up costumes from old films and was thrilled to find Garbo's *Queen Christina* outfit on a special hanger.

He found the five-day week routine very stimulating and relaxed well at weekends. His work to October 1957 grossed $20,000 and he was paid $2,000 a week until the end of filming. At parties in the evenings he saw Clifton Webb, Cole Porter, George Cukor, Christopher Isherwood, the Gary Coopers and others. He found the expense and luxury of the houses quite extraordinary but observed: 'there isn't a decently furnished house here. Some people have lovely pictures but the decorating is entirely suburban. It's like a tropical Golders Green.'[85]

The decorating of the sets was followed by more filming and more retakes. Isabel Jeans, who began by being very nervous but looked set for a big success as Aunt Alicia, had to spend two days in a bath for one scene. This was then reshot with her lower down in the tub. She spent a further three days awaiting her carriage. The cat in Gigi's apartment ran off the set at a critical moment. They retrieved it and put sunshine oil on its paws: it settled down to lick itself clean. Later it clawed at Leslie Caron's face and dress when she was singing 'Say a Prayer'.

Cecil particularly liked Uncle Honoré's *art nouveau* apartment. He was forever on hand to cut stuffed peacocks down to size for hats. He once trimmed thirty hats in an hour and a half. Conscious of the decorum of a Hollywood film he stuffed nets into any over-exposed cleavage he spotted. Leslie Caron was generally unpopular though always sweet to Cecil. One night in the absence of her husband, the director Peter Hall, Cecil escorted her to a film première and faced 'squealing fans and photographers'.[86] She impressed him:

> Through sheer intelligence she has become a very good actress. She is tiresome, argumentative, stubborn, delays activity of the film, but there is nothing glib or slipshod about her. She has to have everything clear in her brain before she proceeds. Otherwise she is incapable. It is because she is so close to each little scene that she can improvise when the camera turns and create something new and fresh even when the script calls for conditions or situations that might be considered banal.[87]

Leslie Caron had made many enemies in Hollywood in the past, but was not conscious of hostility. She was furious, though, when informed that her songs were to be dubbed. Furthermore, Cecil noted, not without surprise:

> She cannot bear M. Chevalier for his easy charm and superficial good humour. She feels it cannot be true and has seen him be himself to his valet. It was, she said, 'very shocking'. But, she said, if you give out a performance all the time you either become nothing or reveal yourself occasionally as the real monster who is the antidote to the saccharine person that you present to the world.[88]

Alan Jay Lerner recalls that Cecil himself took a sudden dislike to Louis

Jourdan. Driving along the set one day, he was about to stop to greet Jourdan, when Cecil insisted that they drive on.

Gigi ran into further problems when it was ready to be shown in January 1958. A certain amount of reshooting and editing was carried out to excellent effect. It was released in the United States in June 1958 and in London in February 1959. Beverley Nichols wrote to Cecil: 'The colour and swagger and invention made me feel as though I were assisting at some delightful flower show to the sound of music.'[89] Mike Todd cabled: 'I think your contribution was one of the greatest I have ever seen.'[90] And Diana Vreeland: 'It was such a joy, galloping gaiety, absolutely flawless fun all the way.... I can see how completely happy you were last summer in Paris, working with French people on this delightful piece.'[91] Amidst the main reviews, Stanley Kauffman wrote:

> Gigi is consistently pleasant but is extraordinary in only one way. Do not be deceived by the advertising. The real star is Cecil Beaton, who designed the costumes and scenery.... His work in this film is gorgeous.[92]

Dilys Powell wrote that Cecil's designs 'both costumes and settings, are at once elegant and exhilarating'.[93] Cecil won the annual award of the American Institute of Decorators for his work on *Gigi* and *My Fair Lady*. He also won his first Oscar for 'best costume designs'. *Gigi* won nine Oscars in all and Maurice Chevalier received a special award for his services to the screen over the years. Cecil was disappointed at not receiving another Oscar for best art direction. This went to Preston Ames, who had been credited as set designer to fulfil the complicated union rules. He had worked under Cecil, who complained to his lawyer:

> I don't grudge Mr Preston Ames his Oscar, and know it will be of great 'prestige value' to him, but I somehow feel it is the head of a department and not his associate or even his assistant who should receive recognition for the work done, even if he has been given it in another category on the same film.[94]

29

Noses to the Grind

*I knew this sudden popularity was based on the hysteria
of success of MFL and possibly had little to do with the
merit of my work. Yet to see so many rows of red tickets
gave me much pleasure.*

Cecil's diary, summer 1958

A popular exhibition of Cecil's *My Fair Lady* designs was held at the Redfern
Gallery in London to coincide with the London opening of the show in April
1958. Forty pictures were sold in the first hour. Daisy Fellowes (another
unsuccessful suicide attempt safely behind her) paid fifty guineas for a design
for Eliza's ball dress. Cecil was asked if this exhibition would make him a
nice nest-egg and he replied: 'Yes, but only for a sparrow's nest.'[1] The
success of the exhibition gave him particular satisfaction because he always
lacked confidence in the merit of his paintings.

Simultaneously Cecil gave an enormous party at the Café Royal on 29
May. It was attended by the frustrations and rows that habitually precede
party-giving. But on the night the roses opened nicely on cue. 'The list was
star-studded,' noted Cecil. 'Perhaps it represented a lifetime of social climbing. Anyhow on paper it looked very impressive to me.'[2] It was certainly a
contrast to those early parties at Hyde Park Street. Agnellis and Brandolinis
arrived in private aeroplanes and stayed at Claridge's. The guests included
the Duchess of Kent, who arrived from the Old Vic and while dancing with
Cecil gently expressed the wish not to meet Elsa Maxwell. Elsa sat 'a huge
billowing rhinocerous mass in Roman draperies covered with oversize straw-
berries'.[3] Later as Lucian Freud became a bit drunk, sitting between Lady
Lambton and the Duchess of Devonshire, he threw nuts at the huge old
harridan, who pretended to welcome the attention.

Reviewing the party later, Clarissa Eden wrote: 'It was like a good fruit
cake – all plums. With a few nuts from the continent.'[4] Other guests included the Philippe de Rothschilds, Julie Andrews and her husband, the
designer Tony Walton, the Gilbert Millers, Loelia Westminster, Margot Fonteyn and her husband Dr Arias, John and Momo Marriott, her sister Nin

Ryan, Binkie Beaumont, the Duchess of Buccleuch, Yves St Laurent, Antony Armstrong-Jones, Lord Kinross, Paddy Leigh Fermor, Oliver Messel, Sally Poole (now the Begum Aga Khan), the Swedish Ambassador and Hardy Amies. Rex Harrison arrived with Kay Kendall, who was already ill and died of leukaemia the following year, aged thirty-two. This possibility did not occur to Cecil who, judging her purely visually, thought her too thin: 'She has passed her prime.'[5] Eugenie Niarchos got full marks for remaining tender despite her riches: 'She is a gentle sweet soul, untouched by her husband's ambitions';[6] so did Lilia Ralli, and Lady Cranborne, 'the most beautiful of all'.

Georgia Sitwell irritated Cecil:

> Later she looked at me and made a strange hooting laugh at me: 'Whoo, whoo, whoo.' 'What's biting you?' I asked. 'Whoo, whoo, whoo!' To which I replied in a horrible hoarse 'Ha, Ha, Ha.' Later I relented of my cruelty and asked her to dance.[7]

Cecil was very touched when his sister Baba said, 'Do dance with me', and felt warmed by this. But trouble was brewing.

Simon Fleet, distinctly the worse for alcohol, was making the most of escaping from Juliet Duff. He became tiresomely amorous. He rubbed his face against Grace Radziwill's, then he ran his fingers through Bindie Lambton's hair. This annoyed her and surprised Esmond Rothermere. David Somerset commented: 'No one's likely to do it to him. If they did, it'd be like pulling your hands through a very old moulting lavatory brush.'[8] Fleet then made a disagreeable pass at Daisy Fellowes and put his hand up Pam Churchill's skirt. Cecil remonstrated with him several times. But he got worse.

Much later Cecil was at the Milroy, a night-club in Hamilton Place. His wild tango was interrupted by a call from Michael Tree who with his wife, Anne, and her sister, Elizabeth Cavendish, had observed the wretched Fleet being marched into a Black Maria and thence to Savile Row police station. Cecil prevailed on Eric Dudley to help. Dudley was by now hopelessly drunk but in a friendly mood. After falling down all the stairs of the Milroy he attempted to ring his solicitor with the aid of a torch. He asked Cecil: 'Is this Fleet a man of means? It'll cost him fifteen guineas at least if I get this fellow out of bed at this time of night.'[9] Finally Dudley rang the police station:

> Hullo – this is er – Lord *Dudley* speaking. I believe you've got a chap there named Simon Fleet. Well I don't really know him but he's a decent enough sort of fellow – and you know we've all been to this party given by Mr Cecil Beaton. And what – er – are you going to do to him?[10]

Eric Dudley stumbled out of the telephone box with the news that when Fleet had sobered up he could go home. Such incidents were almost essential to a party like this, though Cecil felt 'for me there had been something missing and that had come from within myself'.[11]

Once Cecil had enjoyed the *My Fair Lady* publicity to the full, he retreated to the country to paint and to work on Leslie Caron's costumes for *The Doctor's Dilemma*.

He did not relax for a moment. Though he had now achieved success at a very glamorous level, there was to be no basking in glory. *The Doctor's Dilemma*, rather a ponderous production, was not to prove an important milestone for him. It starred Dirk Bogarde, Alastair Sim, Robert Morley and Felix Aylmer. Cecil dressed Leslie Caron in aesthetic loose-flowing garments. 'It's only fairly good,' he wrote to Eileen when he saw the film. 'Caron is really rather miscast and although she is charming it shows her limitations. She becomes a bit monotonous. Ridgeon [played by John Robinson] is a stick and unattractive but all the other doctors are excellent.'[12]

More importantly, while *My Fair Lady* and *Gigi* were keeping his name in the public eye, he knew he must revive *The Gainsborough Girls*. Ever since its failure in 1951 Cecil had been working away quietly on it. He had presented it without success to Leland Hayward, the New York producer. In 1954 he wrote to Garbo: 'Suddenly I realize how right the Leland Haywards were in their criticism. ... It *was* overwritten and verbose. Maybe persistence will be rewarded in the end. I've worked on the bloody thing for nearly five years already!'[13] He was helped by Waldemar Hansen, who came to stay at Broadchalke. Cecil faced the fact that he could never write a play without a collaborator:

> The fact that I cannot invent oblique lines of dialogue, lines to order, lines to fit a certain situation or mood or character is something that has been brought cruelly to bear during the last four to six weeks.[14]

In 1954 Binkie Beaumont rejected the play for a second time.

Cecil tried in turn to get Grace Kelly, Lilli Palmer, Mary Ure and Julie Harris to star. They all declined. He tried to interest Glen Byam Shaw, Anthony Quayle, Peter Hall, Peter Glenville, Charles Laughton and Mel Ferrer. He failed. In New York in 1958 Waldemar Hansen finished polishing another version of it and so Cecil summoned him to come once more to England.

Waldemar duly arrived for what evolved into a very happy visit. Suddenly Allan Davis (later famous as the producer of *No Sex Please! We're British*) showed interest in the latest version. When he had read it he came down to see Cecil and Waldemar and gave the verdict that it still required a lot of work. His advice was to make the part of Gainsborough considerably more important. Cecil was horrified at the thought of yet another rewrite, but he knew that he must either press on or abandon the project for ever:

It needed strength to face the project once more. The hollyhocks were now out, and we calculated that we had only a little over a fortnight in which to work on the new draft. I would cancel all visits to London. We have noses to the grind for eight or nine hours a day (implicitly felt by W. that to work longer was in the long run impossible).[15]

Work pressed on, exhaustion set in, but Waldemar never ceased to have new ideas. Cecil sometimes found it hard to concentrate. The most danger-ous of his diversions was when in his mind his ear became 'tuned in to the applause and echoes of success at last'.[16] He also felt guilty that he contri-buted so little to the collaboration. It heightened his awareness that in photography he depended heavily on technical assistants and, in his stage work, on more professional people like Hal Burton and Alan Tagg. He asked himself: 'I wondered in what branch of activity I can work alone?'[17]

In the midst of their work Mercedes de Acosta rang to ask Cecil to invite Garbo for the summer. He was considerably relieved when she decided instead to go aboard Niarchos's yacht and spend an unexpectedly lively summer in casinos and at parties. Work on the play was completed two days before the deadline. Later Waldemar wrote: 'I think that I, more than anybody else, respect the dogged tenacity with which you have stuck by the play through endless rewrites. I feel certain that something is going to happen on it, sooner or later.'[18]

When Cecil and Waldemar were not busy with the play, they polished the text of *Japanese* and some articles for the *Observer*. During spells of work, while walking in the garden and even while Cecil was lying in the bath, they talked incessantly. Waldemar seldom drew breath and Cecil's only complaint was that his own brain was incapable of the necessary concen-tration to give full attention to all his ideas. He felt inadequate when con-fronted with Waldemar's 'analytical intelligence'.[19] Cecil wrote: 'He is not, like myself and so many other "art lovers", swooning in an ecstasy that is founded on nothing firmer than instinct.'[20] Thus, having achieved his goal in the world of theatre design, Cecil now made a conscious effort to absorb intellectual ideas. Success gave him the chance to develop in hitherto unex-plored areas, and Waldemar was on hand to spur him on when, not un-naturally, his energy flagged through sheer exhaustion.

After Cecil's initial flurry of work on the play, there were no immediate results. He continued to earn his living in his established manner. In the summer of 1958 he stayed with Truman Capote and the night after he left Truman's normally irascible friend, Jack Dunphy, said: 'Cecil is a wonderful man.' Truman commented: 'High praise from him; but not a tenth what you rate from me.'[21] Cecil went to Venice to stay with the Brandolinis but found that having achieved his ambition 'to penetrate the grand world', the glory was 'less than it was and it is too late for me to be satisfied with the chatter of the insignificant ones'.[22] The Brandolinis gave him a substantial cheque, which saw him through his remaining holidays. Similarly, when he lunched at Pratolino with Prince and Princess Paul of Yugoslavia he was able to photograph Princess Maria Pia of Italy (the wife of Prince Alexander of Yugoslavia) with her twins and sell these to Italian magazines. Onassises and Agnellis encountered and photographed in the summer were also of value.

Nothing equalled the sums he could earn by photographing glamorous models in grand settings for *Modess*. In October 1958 he earned $6,000 in a morning's work at Londonderry House, but even this did not equal five gruelling sittings at Broadchalke. In one long day he earned a record $15,000.

Even so Cecil never handled his profits very well. He tended to spend gross sums on improvements in the house or garden and was forever being caught out by back tax. Money poured in from *My Fair Lady*, and he suddenly found himself the victim of supertax. From New York, in January 1959, he wrote to Eileen:

Doesn't it mean that after the first bad year I'll be in the court? I don't think I can go on working at such pressure for ever (around me I see people having heart attacks, strokes, ulcers, etc.) and I know that I'm lucky in that most of my trips and air tickets are part of expenses.[23]

Eileen pointed out that Cecil was rich by most standards: 'You have two houses, both run as complete establishments, with seven servants, four full-time and three part-time, all well paid, and then there's me. You live as you want to live and entertain a good deal, and you do it all out of the money you earn: you have no capital behind you.'[24] In 1958 Cecil's net overall profit was £20,000.

Cecil was in America in January 1959 to oversee his designs for Noël Coward's version of the Feydeau farce, *Occupe-toi d'Amélie*, which was to play under the title *Look After Lulu*. Coward thought the designs 'brilliant', but despite the flattery Cecil still found himself uneasy in Coward's presence. He had hoped that the job of producing four sets and various costumes for 1908 tarts would not be exacting, but it required an entire week in New Haven (longer than for *My Fair Lady*), and many hours of work late into the night.

When the play opened Noël Coward and his camp followers congratulated themselves on a success, but Cecil felt Noël had let the audience down. When Noël asked him if he thought it would be a success on Broadway, Cecil said: 'No. Not unless there is an enormous amount of cutting and polishing. Unless it's *enormously* improved I don't think you'll get away with it in New York.'[25] Nor did he, for after savage reviews by the all-powerful Brooks Atkinson and Walter Kerr, the play floundered. Cecil was disappointed as he hoped it would at least run for the season. His work was praised as usual. 'Cecil Beaton's settings are like a brilliant tropical aquarium with a lavish flora of swirling, colorful gowns and hats,'[26] declared *Time* magazine. In London, the play starred Vivien Leigh, lately deserted by Laurence Olivier, following bad rows. Thus, unwittingly, Cecil was once again involved with an Olivier. As in New York the London run was short. The play closed before Christmas 1959.

Then, at a dinner at the Plaza, Cecil accepted the Elsie de Wolfe Memorial Award. The citation read 'for his outstanding contributions in various areas of the visual arts'.[27]

Back in England, Jack Minster took over *The Gainsborough Girls* (now rechristened *Landscape with Figures*), so by April 1959 Cecil's greatest hopes were fuelled once more.

Now that Gainsborough was a more substantial part, they could seek a more important actor. Roger Livesey, their first choice, turned it down, so they sent it to Sir Donald Wolfit. Jack Minster warned Cecil: 'if you like the idea of him and can be bothered to battle against that wodge of pompous complacent self-importance, I think possibly he might be talked into it. He takes flattery like cows eat grass!'[28] Cecil went round to see Wolfit and hooked him: 'With all the energy that I could summon I tried to sell Wolfit the part. By flattery of the basest kind I was able to convince him that it was his charm that we needed.'[29] Wolfit, a prize hypocrite, wrote of the play: 'It's a big dignified piece of work and the London theatre would be all the healthier to have it in its midst.'[30] Cecil was thrilled when Mona Washbourne agreed to be Mrs Gainsborough as he had always envisaged her in the part: 'this dream player that I'd been so covetous of when first I'd seen her in *Ring Round the Moon*'.[31] Douglas Seale became the director, 'a great stroke of good fortune',[32] Henri Sauguet wrote the incidental music. However, endless problems still loomed and the play lived in daily danger of collapse. In the course of an eight-day trip to New York Cecil had to raise half the backing. $1,000 came from Helen Hull, and his mother, whose condition was fast worsening, contributed a generous £500. Cecil then had to write to friends in London. When one rich lady declined money but looked forward to being at the first night, Cecil wrote 'Pig' on the letter. He again sacrificed a much needed summer holiday, rehearsals began and Waldemar was summoned once more from America to help with the final touches.

Complications abounded. Cecil and Wolfit could not have been worse matched. Wolfit would not wear clothes made by Bermans, nor a Wig Creations wig. The company began to loathe him because he hogged all the scenes and tried to persuade Seale not to rehearse scenes other than his. He had still not signed his contract and at several points threatened to walk out, thus jeopardizing the future of the play. Mona Washbourne, who recalled that it was a charming play if not a great one, had a scene in which she was dying. Wolfit hated the attention and sympathy she elicited, so made an enormous fuss at his easel splashing paint about in order to divert the audience to him. She amused Cecil by saying she had christened him 'Donald Wolfshit'.[33] Ann Firbank, who played Margaret Gainsborough, one of the daughters, said Wolfit was very clever at mischief-making. He could rehearse in one way and then perform in completely another on the night. He sentimentalized the role of Gainsborough, which enraged Cecil. He bruised the other daughter's* arm by gripping it tightly. On the first night he sent Ann Firbank a quarter bottle of gin with the note: 'tell the others it's not poison'.[34] Cecil got into such a rage that he confessed in his diary: 'I hated him so much that I could hardly look at him on stage. Not only did he vulgarize the part but interpolated modernisms and crudities that stuck out of the text like a sore thumb.'[35] Wolfit was an aggressive and tiresome old monster: not for nothing was he the inspiration for 'Sir' in the play *The Dresser*. He also loathed homosexuals and thus Cecil was anathema to him. Ann Firbank recalled that Cecil got his own back by making Wolfit's stage photograph look awful, the line of the wig very much in evidence and blemishes wherever possible. Cecil objected strongly to Wolfit's behaviour in rehearsal and asked Jack Minster to get rid of him before any London opening, and demanded an assurance that Wolfit would not change his lines.

When Waldemar arrived there were a lot of fiddly pieces of rewriting and improving to do. Work took place in the customary fever of exhaustion and then the play opened at Newcastle on 7 September. On this occasion Wolfit inserted two or three big speeches of his own invention, interpolated banal comments and made the play run ten minutes too long. He threw down a portrait to divert the audience when Mary's face was being slapped; he scraped the canvas loudly during Christie's speeches; he repeated the lines of other actors; he moved about during Mary's mad scene, and took a drink at inappropriate moments. Nevertheless the notices were not bad. Wolfit, however, was not satisfied. At lunch with Cecil, Wolfit announced that he wished to leave the play at the end of the week or to make substantial changes to his own lines. The lunch ended with him storming out of the dining-room, threatening to get a doctor's certificate to say he was ill. The next day he telephoned the press and all hell broke loose.

A battle was now waged on three fronts. Wolfit and Cecil made statements about each other to the papers. In Dublin Cecil demanded that Wolfit apologize publicly, on stage or in front of an audience, and he refused to shake hands with him at a press conference. Acrimonious letters were exchanged between solicitors. Yet the play ran on in Newcastle, Dublin, Brighton and Wolverhampton and to the disappointment of the audiences no sign of the

* Mary, played by Christine Finn. The young Samantha Eggar was also in the cast.

row could be detected on stage. At times after a particularly bad crisis, Wolfit would suddenly become docile and say, 'What about the Savile for us in London?'[36] Then he would flare up again. In Newcastle the play lost £847, in Dublin it made £533, and in the last week in Wolverhampton lost a further £640. In despair Cecil concluded he would never again write a play: 'For I must face the fact that I have not yet got the necessary under- standing of the craft and my instinct is not strong enough to guide me. Yet the longing for that form of success will never die.'[37] He wished he had devoted the same energy to serious painting. He concluded: 'I fear it will be some time before I can recover from the wounds of the last month.'[38] On 22 September Jack Minster declared the venture 'a near-miss'[39] and said they would close after Wolverhampton.

Cecil did not leave the matter there. He wrote angrily to Wolfit: 'Following your initial indiscretion, you continued to feed distortions to the Press. I will not enumerate them, since you are scarcely the person to appreciate objec- tive truth. ... I feel that there will be less opportunities for you to create these disturbances in future. And I, among countless other hundreds in the theatre, will have little sympathy for you.'[40] Curiously, Cecil instructed Eileen that in the event of a reply he did not want to read it. The answer came on 16 October 1959 from Wolfit's solicitors, Theodore Goddard. They warned Cecil that if he impugned Sir Donald's standing in his profession, the actor would certainly 'consult' them.

Cecil prepared a long statement to the northern press, declaring: 'His action in attempting to scuttle the ship was completely unethical.'[41] Cecil's attitude to all this was defined by his assistant Jim Benton:

> Cecil is still determined to punish Wolfit even if it does cost money; however, he realizes how very much has been lost with the failure of the play to come to London and he doesn't want to spend a lot of money to get back at Wolfit.[42]

Cecil wanted to report Wolfit to Equity, but was deterred by fear of a libel action. He considered suing for damages but his solicitor said that as he had no direct contract with Wolfit, it would be impossible to prove. On the other hand, he was able (via Jack Minster) to send his complaint to the Society of West End Theatre Managers, though nothing came of it. Later, in New York, Cathleen Nesbitt told Cecil that Wolfit had cut her part as Lady Macbeth so as to make his own more important. Cecil was aghast: 'He was up to all the same dirty tricks with Shakespeare as he was with me!'[43] Needless to say, despite what he thought, Cecil was soon pressing on with new plans to promote the play. In 1969 and 1973 he completely rewrote it and began to circulate it once more. He also wrote other plays and he continued to preoccupy himself with the possibility of staging them almost until the day he died.

* * *

Following the collapse of *Landscape with Figures*, Cecil left England 'with the slate wiped clean of something with which I have lived for ten years'.[44] He had to reconsider his career. Photography was by now only a means of earning a living and recording events that interested him. He knew he was not a serious painter or writer, nor could he live by his drawings. Was he, he wondered, just a costume designer? Certainly *Gigi* and *My Fair Lady* had kept him in the public eye while he pursued other things:

> The answer is that success in one or two fields has buoyed me up for some time into believing I was able to indulge in several art forms and this cruel event of this summer has knocked me off my perch and I am grovelling in self-pity without knowing which way to go when once again I regain my feet.[45]

The musical *Saratoga* was Cecil's next project. For some time he had been working on designs though he felt he had not put his 'personal stamp' on them. *Saratoga* opened in Philadelphia and Cecil was delighted that it was a romantic musical. He described the cast at great length, noting that 'Keel* is a bit heavy and doesn't look quite young enough. My contribution almost overloads the rest: scenery is lovely and dresses too (though some of the singers are fat and gawky). Everyone in raptures about them.'[46] Diana Vreeland, who came to the benefit performance with Margaret Case, Eleanor Lambert and Truman Capote, wrote:

> I feel what you have done for *Saratoga* is stupendous, the sequence of tones and colours are simply amazing. Your prolific quality which never is in danger of becoming quantity is staggering. In many ways I believe this is your most out put.[47]

When the play opened in New York, John Chapman wrote in the *Daily News*: '*Saratoga*, which opened last night at the Winter Garden, belongs to Cecil Beaton, being the most beautifully costumed musical I have ever seen.'[48] But apart from that the reviews were very bad and Cecil concluded: 'I'm sorry that nothing really comes up to my contribution, and I don't mean this in a conceited sense.'[49]

On 14 November 1959 he rushed back to England, more drained than ever, to take on six tortuous weeks at Stratford, designing *The Two Gentlemen of Verona* for Peter Hall, the new Director of the Shakespeare Memorial Theatre. He found it hard to cope with the busy young director, who rejected some of the sets because they were not of high enough technical standard. Cecil became exhausted and retired to the health farm, Enton Hall, for a

*Howard Keel (b. 1919), beefy singing star of *Oklahoma!* and other musicals; best known today as Clayton Farlow in the television soap opera *Dallas*.

week. Then there were more changes of plan until he became fed up and walked out. 'We don't know what Peter Hall is going to do in the circumstances, because everything is so desperately urgent now,'[50] Eileen reported to Jim Benton. 'However, I am afraid that is not my worry. What is so awful about the whole thing is the wicked waste of Cecil's talent, time and energy.'[51]

A year later, in September 1960, Cecil worked on the sets and costumes for *Tenderloin*, a Hal Prince musical about brothel life. It soon became clear that this was not going to be another *My Fair Lady* and generally Cecil found it too much hard work for someone of his age. The play misfired, but Cecil was impressed by the tenacity of its seventy-four-year-old director George Abbott:*

> He's an inhuman old goat with a gibbering speech and cold eye, but one must hand to him the clarity with which he says what he wants and how he sees in a flash everything that has to be done. He is incredibly experienced and knows how to brook all interruptions. He is a lone goat, with pincer-like approach snipping bits off here and there mercilessly and if people's feelings get in the way it is 'too bad' but he doesn't care or notice.[52]

When the stage manager twisted her ankle with a howl, rehearsals continued without a word of sympathy from him. Cecil found the chorus-girls tiresome. When he remonstrated with a girl with enormous bosoms that he called 'the erstwhile stripper',[53] complaining that her false eyelashes were as big as her hat, she said, 'As big as my what?', and Cecil fled 'in terror'. Cecil concluded that *Tenderloin* was 'what the expense account hosts will call a fun show'.[54] Besides two rave notices, the play was badly received. Walter Kerr wrote in the *New York Herald Tribune*: 'Cecil Beaton has done the costumes, but he has spent all of the attractive flourishes of his designer's crayon on the settings. Those poor inmates haven't an indecent thing to wear.'[55] Alan Jay Lerner thought Cecil had cancelled out his costumes with his sets. *Time* magazine wrote of Cecil's 'inspired bad taste'.[56] Hal Prince, in his shock at not having his customary success, was generous to Cecil: 'You've done a marvellous job for us. You're a kind of genius and I'm only sorry the show wasn't better for you.'[57] As Cecil commented: 'What more could I hope to hear.'[58]

Cecil also held another exhibition of his theatrical designs at the Sagittarius Gallery. Monroe Wheeler, the art curator, upset him by staying for precisely two minutes and pronouncing that he should do more in the manner of his oil copy of Gainsborough. Nevertheless thirty-seven pictures were sold by the time he left New York, and in the end he earned about $5,000.

* George Abbott (b. 1886); in 1984 he directed *On Your Toes* in London.

Returning from Boston, Cecil might easily have been on the aeroplane which the theatrical impresario Bronson Albery saw fall into the sea by the airport, drowning sixty people. It took off an hour after Cecil's flight. Cecil had to some extent overcome his fear of flying but now he speculated as to how his death would have been received. In his musings he wrote pessimistically:

> My diary would come out with a certain posthumous interest and soon the ripples of my existence would subside and I would be forgotten and all my labours in vain.[59]

This trip made Cecil feel old for the first time. At the age of fifty-six, he thought Cyril Connolly's adage about fat men and thin men should be expanded: 'Inside every old man there is a young man signalling to be let out.'[60]

In the New Year, 1961, Cecil had his first opportunity to work at the Metropolitan Opera. To design sets and 400 costumes for *Turandot* had been hard work, but rewarding. This was the Met's first performance of Puccini's opera for thirty-one years. The idea arose as early as December 1959. Cecil entered into correspondence with Yoshio Aoyama, who was originating the production. He was given complete freedom and found that in itself quite hard. A basically barbaric opera, full of bloodshed, it was nevertheless based on Gozzi's rococo fairy story. Sacheverell Sitwell directed Cecil to Boucher's Chinese tapestries made at Beauvais and Cecil churned out drawings at a great rate. A number of vital oil sketches were lost in air transit between London and New York. Fortunately, however, Cecil had kept a set of colour transparencies.

There were problems with the star singers. Rudolf Bing, general manager of the Met, nicknamed the tenor Franco Corelli 'the Gorilla', and Cecil followed suit by calling Birgit Nilsson 'the Hippo'. Cecil was terrified at the first fitting:

> Miss Nilsson is certainly ugly, squint eyes too close together, a crooked hooked nose almost meeting a vast chin with only a small lower lip between. Her bosoms are of the Peter Arno cartoon variety but she is better than her photographs. She is young. I gathered up all my energies and boldly said, 'Why you're a good-looking woman. You're tall and svelte. You have got a good figure. What were all the messages about? I've been receiving so many alarms that I thought I was coming here to meet a hippopotamus!' Miss Nilsson teetered on high heels and looked nervously from left to right, then realized she was cornered and let out the most terrific laugh that has been heard since Caruso died.[61]

The 'Gorilla' turned out to be 'a fat, greasy ice-creamer with dark black curls in the nape of his neck'.[62] He created endless problems, not least by refusing to wear the prescribed purple as he deemed it unlucky for him. Rudolf Bing himself got fed up with his performers:

> I'm sick of these ghastly people! They're not artists! They have no respect. They're just waiters or horse-stealers with some disease of the throat so that they make extraordinary noises, and command enormous sums of money and think they can behave just as if they were – well, what they are – waiters and horse-stealers.[63]

According to Elsa Maxwell, some of the cast wearing contact lenses could not see through the beads and various head-dresses they had to wear. Then at the final rehearsal Cecil had a blazing row with 'the Hippo' over her make-up. She complained that her dress made her look fat and wanted it to be sprayed down the side. 'There, for ever,' wrote Cecil, 'ended a short friendship.'[64] On the first night the atmosphere was electrifying. The seventy-nine-year-old Leopold Stokowski was greeted with a thunderous standing ovation as he entered on crutches (due to a fractured hip) to conduct. However, trouble was afoot. Cecil had chosen the colours of the costumes with great care. The first act was to start with drab indigos, greys and blacks. Gradually, act by act, it would crescendo into the last scene of Chinese pinks, yellows and oranges. One 'trespasser' of a chorus girl came on in the first act in orange when she should have been in drab blue. Inevitably she was forever at the front of the stage. When the women lay on the floor 'her orange bottom was the biggest and most prominent, a full sun that never set'.[65] Suddenly it was too much for him. He left his seat and thundered backstage. With exaggerated gestures Cecil beckoned her off-stage. Eventually she came and Cecil pulled her skirt in rage. His efforts were rewarded with the sound of rending material. He pulled the torn skirt down and left the bewildered girl in her BVDs with the skirt in tatters at her feet. Unfortunately this caused a major incident. A strike loomed and the show was threatened. Cecil was frog-marched to the dressing-room by the management and forced to offer a public apology in front of forty angry half-naked chorus-girls. For the next hour he felt remorse tinged with outbursts of nervous laughter: 'I realized how easy it would be to commit murder if one was enough enraged. The orange woman had ruined my first night. But by degrees I realized what a success the evening had been for me as well as for all concerned.'[66]

Cecil had always felt a special fondness for *Turandot*, which was described as 'the biggest opera hit in ten years'.[67] Noël Coward thought his costumes 'quite lovely',[68] and Winthrop Sargeant wrote in the *New Yorker*: 'The sets and costumes, by Cecil Beaton, are lavish and absolutely ravishing.'[69] When Cecil was asked to do the production for Covent Garden in October 1962, he asked Rudolf Bing's permission to repeat his designs. Bing agreed to this reluctantly and insisted on a credit line. He explained: '*Turandot* was one of our most successful productions, largely thanks to you, and incidentally also one of our most expensive ones, both in designer fees and everything else.'[70] Unfortunately in the London production the designs were reduced in scale so that the performers almost had to duck to enter the stage.

Soon afterwards Rudolf Bing invited Cecil to do *Adriana Lecouvreur*, which was to be performed in February 1962. Cecil started to research, listened to the music and even read a dreadful novel by an American lady about the loves of Adriana. He reported to Bing: 'By now my enthusiasm is of a high temperature and I have done quite a lot of preliminary work.'[71] Having been paid $6,000 for *Turandot* and $1,000 expenses for an assistant, Cecil's fee now went up to an all-in fee of $9,000. He slaved away and sent the models over to Ed Wittstein. He in turn delivered them to the draughtsman, Dick Casler, whose maid mistook one of the boxes for refuse and dumped Cecil's prized work into the incinerator.

After four months of hard work Cecil was absolutely enraged: 'I *know* accidents can happen, but this has just got me on the raw. . . . I don't really think I have ever been quite so exasperated as I am to have your news.'[72] The production was clearly ill-fated. In August Herman Krawitz, the Met's business and technical administrator, told Cecil that due to problems with the Musicians' Union the 1961–2 Metropolitan Opera season was cancelled. Cecil's contract was therefore terminated. Krawitz described the situation as 'absolutely hopeless'.[73] Cecil was paid a second and final instalment of $3,000. In May 1962 Rudolf Bing told Cecil they were reviving *Adriana Lecouvreur* but copying the Naples production in order to save costs.

At the end of 1961, Cecil's rich friend Mary Lasker secured a production of *La Traviata* at the Met by promising them $75,000 on condition that he did both costumes and sets. This was finally achieved in 1966 at the new Metropolitan Opera House under the direction of Alfred Lunt. It took two years to produce and was beset by new problems, such as a turntable that collapsed. Anna Moffo (Violetta), the leading lady, was photographed in inappropriate black gloves, and Cecil wrote: 'It makes one want to spit!'[74] He had to veto Lunt's wish to have live mice in the last scene. Cecil's plan with the costumes was to purvey 'the latent desire in the feminine bosom to be romantic – to go against the grain'.[75] Waldemar thought the sets were too grandiose: 'Violetta's house was done like that of a duchess not a tart. He erred on the side of opulence.'[76] Reviewing the opera, John Chapman declared that the sets and costumes outclassed even *My Fair Lady* in beauty and elegance.

Meanwhile, romance was in the air once more.

30

June

I cannot go on into old age in such an independent way.
It would be wonderful to have a child, to have someone
other than myself to consider.

Cecil's diary, autumn 1958

Cecil's mother became an increasing burden to him at the time of his success with *My Fair Lady* and the failure of his own play. Ever dutiful towards his family, he was aware that they took little interest in his work and even less in the mechanics of it. Once he asked for vital drawings to be brought to London. These were left in the car, jeopardizing an important deadline. His mother was unconsciously an expert at putting him in the wrong. If Cecil wanted to entertain guests that he deemed 'unsuitable company' for her, she would magnify the incident by insisting on going out to dine alone in a cheap restaurant. Many of Cecil's friends she judged 'a dirty lot', and while he was prepared to overlook bad manners in the rich or talented or even in their less worthy hangers on, she was not. Admittedly it was unfortunate that she had once observed a guest at Reddish lurch drunkenly from the library, enquiring 'Where can I get a pee?'[1] as he undid his fly buttons.

Recently a new problem had intensified. In her lonely and introspective old age, Mrs Beaton would often have two dry martinis before lunch. Her breathing would then become bad and her complexion blotchy. As this situation deteriorated, Cecil felt the time had come to tell his mother that one drink was enough. It was not easy, but the situation was aggravated when he inadvertently removed the cellar keys from Reddish. This provoked a letter from Mrs Beaton which upset him greatly:

I'm sorry you have such a poor opinion of me. I can't think I've ever let you down. I've always been proud of what you have done. However from now on I hope to be a *reformed character*. If I could only find a small flat I would not trouble you, or be in your way. I hope you will remember I am eighty-five years now. Not many years or months left so I think you should be considerate. However let bygones be over.

> I still love you. I am very proud of you. ....
>
> [PS] I find there is no gin in the decanter so I've sent out and paid for a bottle. I hope there is some left for you.[2]

Cecil responded dramatically, as he recorded in his diary:

> The tears gushed down my cheeks. I didn't know I could weep so co-piously. I wept for the appalling sadness of life. I wept for the loneliness of old age, the pathos of pretence, the emptiness, the rushing by of life, and the fact that soon I would realize things too late. I marvelled at the simplicity of expression of my mother's letter, its complete lack of guile and its force.[3]

Cecil knew that his mother could not live much longer and he knew that, despite everything, he would miss her very deeply. It was therefore with some interest that Cecil responded to a telephone call from Diana Cooper, one morning in the summer. However busy he was, Cecil always set aside the work in hand for a call from Diana and he seldom regretted so doing. This time she referred to the recent visit to his house of an attractive young friend of hers, who had arrived one day with her son to collect a picture for a charity sale. Cecil had been in the bath and he came out on to the landing to have a few words, dressed bizarrely in short pyjama trousers. The pretty mother was June Osborn, widow of the pianist Franz Osborn. She was born in 1920, the posthumous daughter of Captain Arthur ('Boy') Capel, and his wife Diana (later Countess of Westmorland), the daughter of Lord Ribbles-dale. Her Capel aunt was Bertha, Lady Michelham, a noted beauty in Paris. This is how Cecil recorded Diana Cooper's conversation:

> 'Oh, June's mad about you,' said Diana. 'She told me all about coming to see you, and you wore short pyjama trousers. She was very impressed. Why don't you marry her and have a child?'
>
> 'It's a good idea. How interesting. Tell me about her.'
>
> 'Well, she's a saint. I've always adored June. She's so funny and so good.'
>
> 'But you see it would be so difficult to marry just now – with my mother.'
>
> 'But June would look after her. She's an angel and she loves you.'
>
> 'But then you see I'm a swine and put off if everything's too easy.'
>
> 'But she's difficult too, because she's mad.'
>
> 'I like that.'[4]

Cecil began to think about June, and to relinquish the last vestiges of his hopes for Garbo: 'Greta by now really an impossibility. Ridiculous to think one can go on too long.' He liked June enormously without being in love with her. He found her witty. He respected Diana's wisdom in these matters and the idea of marriage appealed.

A rather nervous lunch took place at June's house. Diana was there and Cecil felt self-conscious and old. (At fifty-four he was sixteen years June's senior.) Thereafter he trod a careful path, sending her postcards from his holiday and generally keeping in touch. He feared a rush courtship, or making a mistake: 'for someone to give up the habits of a fifty-year-old lifetime is a difficult thing – for both parties'.[5] Presently Cecil took June to the Old Vic and they had supper afterwards at Pelham Place: 'We got on marvellously well. The evening was full of laughs and sympathy. By slow degrees the possibility has been growing....'[6] Poor June was then put through a number of tests by Cecil, all of which she passed. The first was a dinner-party at Pelham Place with Ann Fleming, Lucian Freud and Francis Bacon. This evening was ruined by Lucian who, on this occasion (though never subsequently), was extremely offhand to June and refused to speak to her. This upset Cecil considerably, though he thought June behaved wonderfully:

> It made me closer to her. I could hardly sleep that night for fury of Lucian. I considered all his bad faults and came to the conclusion there is every reason for those who do [for] saying he is a wicked character.[7]

There was a weekend at Bruern in Oxfordshire with Michael Astor, during which they asked each other a lot of slightly self-conscious questions about past history and interests. She appeared bright, kind and lively in this country group, who were not her normal friends. But, noted Cecil, 'June looked extremely unchic and I'm sad to have to say this worried me.'[8]

Another evening Cecil painted June's portrait, but was suddenly overcome with irritation. Though he felt her becoming closer to him, he felt strained and in need of independence. He recalled that the same thing had happened with Lilia Ralli: 'We had even been happy lovers for a time and then this withdrawing on my part was irrevocable. I wouldn't want this to happen again.'[9]

Most of the time they enjoyed happy jokes and relaxation, but in no sense were either struck by a *coup de foudre*. Cecil also felt slightly class conscious with her:

> There is another aspect of her which I don't feel easy about for the moment. Maybe it can be overcome. But for all my admiration of the aristocracy there is a certain quality of impermeable assurance that is very admirable, but which somehow, perhaps through envy at not possessing it myself, I feel hostile about in certain aristocrats. June has this quality. She can be made sad but she can never be vanquished. She knows she is the salt of the earth and this is sometimes annoying.
>
> There is also a sympathetic twang in the voice that in other aristocrats sounds affected. With her it is sincere, but riles a little none the less. These things have to be faced and overcome.[10]

June recalled: 'The trouble was we were both so terribly shy with each other.'[11]

Cecil continued to perform his 'living autopsy' on the kind, shy, slightly sad, widowed mother that he contemplated making his wife:

> June is good, she is kind, very delightful of appearance (not what I would have designed but perhaps she will let me take a hand in dressing her according to my taste). In fact June seems to me to fit the bill in a general way and since I am no longer headstrong enough to rush into a love affair and abandon all willingly she seems, in cold blood, to be the sweetest, kindest and altogether most suitable person that I could find before it is too late to find anyone who will put up with my beastliness in my increasingly beastly old age.[12]

As so often the brake was put on the romance for a time by the need for Cecil to go to America to design *Look After Lulu* for Noël Coward.

This winter visit of 1958-9 gave Cecil time to think over his predicament. On his fifty-third birthday Garbo took him out to lunch and he told her he was contemplating marriage with June. 'I'll be right over to stop it,' she said. 'I'll come over to cut her head off. Well, well, well, so you've got a girl have you?'[13] It was no time before Garbo had worked out that Cecil was not in love with June, but she detected a cooling of Cecil's interest in her. When Cecil invited her to meet Lord Rothschild and the peer was offhand to her, she left early. Back at home she rang Cecil and said in a sad voice, 'Give me another chance. Good night, Beattie.'[14] Cecil wrote: 'My heart broke.'*[15]

Before he came home Cecil presented his problem to Truman, who said that if he married it must be from 'strength of character'[16] because he did not need marriage. He would never be lonely and even in old age would still be interested in young people and the activities of the world.

It was in the summer of 1959, as his mother drifted further into a world of her own, that Cecil again thought of marrying June:

> If she would have me and be clever with me I should be very fortunate. June has just been to stay at Reddish for the first time. She brought such gaiety and fun to the house. We laughed such a lot.... She looked so pretty and summery and her personality was so strong that she brought her own idiom to Salisbury platform where she arrived wearing gloves with her luggage in a Diana-esque basket. She was a star. I suddenly

*Cecil's disenchantment did not decrease. Garbo came to London in November 1960 and stayed at Reddish. She was sensitive to his lack of interest: 'Mr Beaton has such a severe look and it isn't at all as he used to be' [Cecil's diary, November 1960]. Cecil told Hal Burton that the scales had at last fallen, and Hal said that he had noticed a certain hardness in her. She was no longer 'the helpless, hopeless waif, but knew perfectly well that she was heading for perdition' [Cecil's diary, November 1960].

realized this and wherever we went she found a natural place for herself.[17]

In June 1959 Cecil had to return to New York for a few days. Before that he panicked in a letter to Diana. The situation was so volatile that Diana had even heard a story that Cecil might marry Eileen. He wrote:

> Eileen is marvellous, considerate and ebullient. I admire her and don't know how I'd continue without her, but she's my friend and secretary and the other would be *impossible*. I do want to have a long talk with you about June. There are so many advantages and it could be such a wonderful idea, and I think it could be worked, but I have fears of it going wrong by June being too nice to me just when I needed her to be off-hand. I can be such a swine and don't want to be given the opportunity to behave badly. After living for myself for so long it would be difficult for someone to housetrain me (though I see it will be my salvation ultimately) and I do think it would be ghastly if June found I was less of a person than a career. However there must be terrible qualms (rightly!) on her side – but in any case would she 'have' me?[18]

It was not until Christmas 1959, after the drama of his play and after his autumn visit to the States to design *Saratoga*, that Cecil contemplated the question again. Cecil's wish to marry, to have someone to be his centre, to 'give presents to',[19] to share Reddish with and to save him from the feared loneliness of old age, had become 'an *ideé fixe*'.[20] He dreaded becoming 'a pernickety old bachelor bothering if the Louis Seize was out of place'.[21] By degrees Cecil's heart was 'touched' and after a luxurious weekend in Kent with Michael and Anne Tree at Mereworth, he became 'utterly entranced'.[22] He admired June for her many qualities: 'Her eyes so bright and blue have that wonderful quality of seeming to become dewy when one looks at her in or for sympathy, and her graces are utterly delightful.'[23] Cecil only worried that 'the sexual attraction'[24] might go wrong. Cecil thought June fitted into the pattern well. She was an amateur who 'gave the artist the magic quality that only an uncreative person can'.[25] He also mused: 'From the hint that Diana dropped about June having seen me in short pyjamas I knew I was not physically unattractive to her!!!'[26] Over the months he had only discussed his hopes with Diana and Truman, who warned him that marriage was a legal undertaking, meant to last for ever. For weeks he was racked with indecision until he reached the point when he wanted to 'talk about the possibilities'.[27]

Although Cecil and June talked on the telephone every day, they did not often meet. Just before June's son came home for the Christmas holidays, Cecil invited her to lunch with Bertie Abdy. She accepted and then Sir Robert 'chucked'. This then was Cecil's chance, 'the occasion I had chosen to "pop the question"'.²⁸ Not unnaturally Cecil panicked: 'Good Lord! This was my last moment of freedom. How could I ever give up my independence, give up that most precious thing of all – my own time?'²⁹ Lunch took place with superficial chatter and then time began to run out because June had to take her son to the cinema.

Coffee was brought in and suddenly with appalling business-like ferocity and determination not to let the chance pass, I said *à propos* Susan Rose's wedding, 'Well, what about our getting married? For a long time I've been wondering if I dare ask you if you would marry me, as I think it would be such a good thing for me although there is every reason why you shouldn't want to.'

June looked most terribly frightened. Her whole figure was shattered. Her eyes bluer, more tragic, her features became more sensitive and delicate. I felt terribly coarse and insensitive and her reaction surprised me too. But I must go on. I must explain. I must buffer the shock, for June had received a shattering shock. She looked very pained as she said in a deep and halting, jerking and lisping voice, 'Oh no, Sissil, I *don't* think it would be a good idea, not for us. I don't know why, but I don't think I can ever fall in love again. I *don't* think it would work.'³⁰

Cecil then began to produce reasons why she should not marry him – his age, selfishness, independence, 'a great queer streak which might make things very difficult'.³¹ He told her openly about his unrequited love for Peter Watson. He talked of Garbo, of his lack of solid money. He became nervous and started to tug at the knot of his tie. He went on talking and his voice became intent: 'It was like continuing an argument when you know you have lost. For I began to realize that, for the moment, most unexpectedly I had lost.'³²

Suddenly June remembered her son and the cinema and hurried to leave. Cecil clenched her wrist in a spontaneous gesture and tears prickled in his eyes. He urged June to think it over, and with a nervous haunted smile from her, and a few light quips from Cecil, she drove away to her family responsibilities. Cecil came back into the house, puffing at his cigar:

Although I had been turned down I felt extremely elated. I felt as pleased as Punch with myself. I had popped the question and suddenly all my forebodings were things of the past. I felt relieved even if I did not know why. I certainly knew in a much more forceful manner than ever before that I had done right, that I had chosen a rare and remarkable person and that all was not lost even if for the moment she had said no.³³

Cecil took the afternoon off. He sent June a wonderful hothouse bunch of lilacs and freezias, and a note apologizing for giving her a shock. Then he went to the National Gallery to look at Italian Renaissance pictures.

In the days that followed, Cecil talked a lot to Diana, who said: 'I *can't* advise. It's *too* difficult. Anyhow you wouldn't be broken hearted if it didn't happen, would you?'[34] Diana also smoothed an afternoon at the pantomime with June and her son Christopher. On Christmas Day 1959 Cecil rang up just as June was about to have her Christmas pudding. He said: 'I hope you get the sixpence and I don't draw the bachelor's button.'[35] That afternoon June wrote to Cecil to explain why marriage between them would not work. She wrote that she was touched and flattered that he loved her enough to consider marrying her and 'I was also touched by your sweetness and frankness of the proposal'.[36] She felt that they only met on a social level 'to giggle at the passing show' and that this was not the basis for marriage:

> But I truly feel I would dement you at closer quarters. We have scarcely talked alone together – there is so much you don't know about me. Pathological untidiness, birds nesting in the bed, sometimes weeks plunged in deep depression (ask Diana), over-attachment to Xtopher to mention just a few horrors. The queer streak which I love in you as a friend would torment you as a husband. Imagine if it *did* worry you – that would be an agony for me and I always would know. You said so engagingly at the proposal that the thought of completely changing your present way of life sometimes filled you with horror. Could it be that you might feel a tiny sense of relief at what I say?[37]

June concluded that she thought Cecil a complete person in himself and hoped that his life at Reddish would be happier after his mother's death and that they could still be friends.

Cecil turned for advice to Truman, now embarking on the research in Kansas which led to his runaway best-seller *In Cold Blood*. Truman replied:

> I am surprised that 'this person'* was surprised when you 'popped the question'. And amazed that she hesitated; but think this speaks *very* well for her; and if it eventually works out, I'm sure it will be a better and happier thing for the thinking-over. Actually, to me it sounds more promising now than earlier, However, we shall see.[38]

Meanwhile Cecil retreated alone to St Moritz to marvel at how the British were 'still the first enthusiasts to rush down a mountain on their stomachs with their nose one inch from a wall of ice'.[39] For the time being he was obliged to continue with his old life of work, travel and parties. The first part of 1960 was packed with royal photography, the first pictures of Prince Andrew, and Princess Margaret's wedding, but still thoughts of June preoccupied him. He kept wondering if she could be persuaded to marry him. He felt that they had grown closer in the months since his Christmas proposal and yet there were still doubts on both sides:

* Cecil and Truman always referred to June anonymously in letters.

I wonder if, after all, I am suitable for marriage, but the more I consider the potentials the less reason there is to believe that I would not be tremendously lucky if I was given the chance of sharing my later life with someone as intelligent, as amusing, as serious and above all as good as June.[40]

There was a certain amount of gossip and even an item in an Irish newspaper. Truman was beginning to hear stories:

Have had several letters from various sources making mention, mostly flattering, of That Person: 'Everybody in London knows that he (you) is in love with her, but she has several suitors and seems undecided; her friends think she will wait awhile.' So I gather matters are still where they were.[41]

On his return from holidaying in Capri and Spetsai, June came over to Reddish to see him. Cecil was on the point of departing for his American winter. Time was against him once more. At any minute Mrs Beaton would stir from her rest and Mrs Talbot would ask when to serve tea. In a terrible rush Cecil's second proposal burst out: 'Have you thought any more about our being spliced?' Cecil was decisive, but June was not. 'Oh don't put it like that,' she said. 'Have you?'[42] She said she did not know if she ever wanted to marry again. She left Reddish on a sad note and Cecil packed his case and fled for his train, a 'knife shooting in the stomach'.[43] He longed to cancel his departure but there was work to do.

Arriving in America Cecil received a letter from June in which she said, 'my mind remains unchanged'.[44] Cecil showed this to Truman, who thought it 'sensitive and warm and honestly troubled'.[45] June had said she had a deep instinct that marriage would not work. And yet the door was left open. Truman warned Cecil that if he won her over, he would start with the disadvantage of having to prove continually that he was right and she was wrong. 'However,' wrote Truman, 'if that is what you want, you must try; but please do not want at *any* cost.'[46] Cecil accepted by degrees that no marriage would come, but the set-back saddened him more than he expected:

It has not been long since the idea had formulated that this was the ideal person with whom to share my old age. But nevertheless the broken idea gave me a certain feeling of loss. Nothing seemed quite so exciting without this prospect. Here I have my longed-for independence and where does it get me? To a very few promiscuous encounters that are completely without importance or reward.... I began to fear for a futile old age.[47]

June's friends continued to match-make for her. Lady Diana Cooper recalled that at one time Rhoda Birley hoped June might marry Edward Heath while June advanced the cause of Rhoda Birley in the same direction. Mr Heath was no doubt oblivious of these goings on. While June did not entirely renounce the idea of Cecil, Diana Cooper wondered if she was not already in love with Jeremy Hutchinson.* He was then married to the actress, Dame Peggy Ashcroft, but in 1966 they were divorced. Later that year he married June. She explained to Cecil: 'We have been secretly in love for a long time. ... I don't know what you will think. I pray it is not a frightful shock.'[48] She was greatly relieved when Cecil wrote her a touching letter full of good wishes for the future, and they all remained friends, including Dame Peggy.

*Jeremy Hutchinson QC (b. 1915), son of St John Hutchinson. Created Life Peer as Lord Hutchinson of Lullington in 1978.

31

Royal Photographer

Cecil Beaton is one of the latest in a long line of royal iconographers which stretches back to the Norman Conquest of England.

Peter Quennell, *Royal Portraits*, 1963

Cecil loathed being described as the royal photographer, but he was equally unwilling to cede the position to another. And of all those who might threaten him, he feared Antony Armstrong-Jones the most. The threat had become more serious when he was commissioned to photograph the young Duke of Kent in 1956, and later the Queen, Prince Philip and their two children in the grounds of Buckingham Palace in 1957. Seeing these pictures, Cecil wrote to Eileen: 'I don't think A.A. Jones's pictures are at all interesting but his publicity value is terrific. It pays to be new in the field.'[1] Cecil was nevertheless considerably relieved to hear that Princess Margaret wanted more photographs by him early in 1958: 'Am very pleased to hear about Princess Margaret sitting and must really make every effort to take the best yet! Just to teach others for being so disloyal!'[2]

Cecil returned from New York in February 1958 longing only for the peace of the English countryside. Suffering from a bad cold, he retired gratefully to bed. But when Princess Margaret invited him to lunch to discuss her session with him, he rose from his sick-bed, noting: 'It was perhaps the first cold I have cured by snobbery.'[3]

The Princess told him that she had just been 'Epsteined' and described how the sculptor had given her eyes as large as goggles, very cadaverous cheeks and a long Jewish nose. Cecil thought her very clever to have thought of sitting to him. He found her at her best and talking well:

> Conversation was of plays. P.M. liked *The Entertainer*, but loathes T. Williams. 'I like angry young men. They're not nearly angry enough. If they're angry, I'm furious. But I hate squalor! Tennessee Williams makes me feel ill.'[4]

The photographs were taken in front of her Annigoni portrait 'and her likeness in the portrait looked like a spiritualist's materialization'.[5] Cecil was quite optimistic about the photographs: 'They show her as a personality, as someone with sex appeal, and a certain growing likeness to her mother.'[6]

Over the next two years, Armstrong-Jones became more and more successful and Cecil became accordingly more annoyed. It was ironic that it should be Oliver Messel's nephew who posed this threat. Cecil had been Oliver's rival for years, not only in his emotional tangles with Peter Watson but also in the ballet and theatre world. Cecil thought, however, that he had now vanquished Oliver. He noted: 'his ideas seemed to have run out, and he repeated himself getting weaker and weaker until his decorations looked like those of his poorest imitators.'[7] Cecil was relieved that his CBE had been gazetted a year before Oliver's.

Cecil nurtured a preoccupation with Oliver's sister, Anne, especially when she married the Earl of Rosse. Cecil was not wholly unsympathetic to Armstrong-Jones. He liked some of the portraits he had taken of Prince Charles and Princess Anne, but not those of Princess Margaret, which nevertheless 'certainly put the seal on the success of my rival'.[8] He noted:

Tony Armstrong-Jones had suddenly enormous success and indeed deserved it for his photographs were vital and he himself was a young man of great liveliness and a certain charm. The fact that he moved in the second-rate world of magazines and newspapers sullied him a great deal, but when I lunched with him in his little studio basement I thought personally he survived with his freshness pretty well intact.[9]

However there was a worse shock in store. On 26 February 1960, Clarence House announced the engagement of Cecil's rival to Princess Margaret. The bombshell news reached Cecil while John Sutro was staying with him. 'Not even a good photographer!'[10] was his bitter anguished cry. He telephoned Sidney Pembroke, who responded by declaring: 'Then I'll go and live in Tibet.'[11]

Cecil lay awake for two or three nights running, trying to analyse his distress. He concluded that the root of it was envy: 'that nothing so momentous as this would ever happen in my life, that all my excitements and interests paled in comparison'.[12] Only by marrying Garbo could he have outstripped what he called 'this Cinderella-in-reverse story'.[13] Curiously the engagement had two important positive effects. Cecil had the field of royal photography safely to himself again while the social status and glamour of photographers soared (exemplified presently by successful lensmen such as the guardee Earl of Lichfield and the trendy cockney David Bailey, part model for the amoral photographer in *Blow-up*). Nor was Cecil excluded from the excitement of the engagement. A week after it Tony Armstrong-Jones invited him to lunch at the house of his prospective best man, Jeremy Fry, in Bath. In the afternoon, on a whim and in order to escape the press, the royal party came over to Reddish for tea. Eileen and Alan Tagg had to remove Cecil's *Turandot* designs in a hurry, while Eileen had to cover up as best she could Mrs Beaton's disparaging stage-whispers on the diminutive stature of the royal bride. As the royal party drove away, Eileen summed up the scene: 'Well now that I've seen them together I'm happier about it than I was.'[14]

Cecil was also invited both to the Queen's reception before the wedding and to the Abbey, and he was the official photographer at the Palace after the ceremony. The reception was the first occasion on which Cecil had been invited to the Palace socially. He felt he had earned his invitation and was pleased to be in the Dowager Duchess of Devonshire's party. While he loved seeing the Palace filled with guests and flowers, he was by no means overwhelmed. He was highly critical of all the royal dresses and he cast a cold eye on the poor bridegroom:

> The man of her choice looked extremely nondescript, biscuit-complexioned, ratty and untidy. He fidgeted with his large hands as he held them behind his back, leant forward, and smiled a tired smile. The fact that this man is of little standing, that he is in no way romantic (even as Townsend was) makes no matter for he is the man the Princess has fallen in love with, and so all must be made perfect in the eyes of the world. The fact remains the young man is not worthy of this strange fluke fortune, or misfortune, and because he is likeable and may become unhappy makes one all the sorrier.[15]

Cecil sat for a while with the Duchess of Kent, whom he found the warmest and friendliest person there, and reflected: 'how awful it must be having a succession of dreary people coming up to make their non-stop obeisance'.[16] The wedding itself impressed Cecil for the radiant happiness of the bride and groom, whose eyes seldom left each other. Princess Margaret's dress he thought badly designed for such an unsuitable hair style. But the Queen's outfit appealed to him enormously. The Duke of Edinburgh wanted the photographic proceedings completed as soon as possible while the Queen Mother was helpful and encouraging and later, despite irritating behaviour from courtiers, gave Cecil permission to release the best ones to 'the dear public'.[17] Even so the press photographers got their pictures out first. In a rushed day Cecil also wrote an article for the *Montreal Star* and later a piece for the *Sunday Times*.

For Cecil 1960 was very much a royal year. In March, despite the new prominence of Armstrong-Jones, he was summoned to photograph the infant Prince Andrew, the third of the Queen's children to be thus welcomed into the world. He took the session very seriously, believing once more that his reputation as a photographer 'was in the balance'.[18]

In those days Palace formality and stuffiness needed careful handling, but

Cecil had an ally in the Queen's equerry, Patrick Plunket, and obtained permission to photograph in the Nash rooms. On the appropriate day Cecil's 'cheerful friend' Sister Rowe arrived with the baby and the two elder children. Cecil said: 'Oh well, I suppose we'd better start photographing right away if that would be all right.'[19] To this Princess Anne announced: 'Well, I don't think it will be.'[20] Cecil loathed her on sight. Presently the Queen and Prince Philip arrived and Cecil did his best to get something inspired out of a very conventional group:

> I felt as if I were being chased in a nightmare when one's legs sink into the mire. The family stood to attention. I said something to make them smile, so clicked. I clicked like mad at anything that seemed even passable. The baby, thank God, behaved itself and did not cry or spew. It sometimes opened its eyes. But even so I felt the odds tremendously against me. The weight of the Palace crushed me. The opposition of 'this hearty naval type' must be contended with, and due deference to the Queen. ...[21]

Prince Philip found it impossible to come to terms with Cecil. He began by making irksome suggestions: 'Take it from here. Why not there?' Cecil told him why not quite firmly. Then the Prince wanted to take pictures himself and asked: 'Do you mind my using your lights?'[22] Cecil thought Prince Charles very overawed by the atmosphere 'as if awaiting a clout from behind, or for his father to tweak his ear or pull the tuft of hair at the crown of his head'.[23] But Cecil spotted that he was a kind boy and 'got more sympathy from him than from any of the others'.[24] Finally Prince Philip broke up the session:

> Surely we've had enough. If he's not got what he wants by now he's an even worse photographer than I think he is! Ha! Ha!' That sort of joke is admirable for the mess or an official review but oh the boredom today.[25]

The royal parents left and Cecil steered ten-year-old Princess Anne to the window:

> The wretched little girl shrugged her shoulders and 'pulled a face'. 'Yes,' I said like a demon. 'You hate it. I know. But hate it by the window there. Hate it looking this way, hate it looking that way, hate it in profile. Now *detest* it looking straight at the camera.'[26]

Cecil went on clicking until Prince Philip returned unexpectedly and said in amazement: 'Now he's started again. He's taking Anne now!'[27] After that Cecil was left alone with Sister Rowe and the baby:

> I then threw myself upon the mercies of Sister Rowe. She was splendid and would have done anything to help me get good results. She would

have even given the baby a vodka cocktail to keep it awake. As it was she pinched it, jerked its hand, thumped its back and it was while she nursed it by the window that we got what I felt were the best results.[28]

Cecil had asked the superintendent for some Philip de la Salle silk to be sent up. He photographed Prince Andrew lying on this surrounded by speckled carnations, lilies of the valley and spring flowers. The Queen passed nine photographs for publication but to Cecil's chagrin these last ones, which he deemed the best, were not released. Press coverage was the greatest that Associated Press had dealt with to date and their handler had to take a holiday when his work was done. At the weekend Cecil could hardly remain awake. His only grudge was that *The Times* printed his photograph of Prince Andrew without acknowledgement, which was then their standard practice.

In 1960 Cecil made a deal with Camera Press, who thereafter distributed his pictures, normally on a 60:40 fee basis. The sums he earned varied considerably, but royal events were always lucrative. In 1964 a set of royal portraits brought in £1,125 3s. Two beautiful fledglings, Victoria Heber-Percy and Charmian Montagu-Douglas-Scott, netted £37 16s in April 1960, Edith Sitwell earned him £103 in 1962, while Eugenie Niarchos only fetched 4s in Brazil in May 1962.

Another royal event occurred when Cecil decorated Covent Garden for a gala performance of the Royal Ballet in honour of President de Gaulle. Cecil recreated the effect of the gala for President Loubet in 1903. He used 600 yards of silk, and 25,000 pale pink carnations, supplied by ten florists. He announced proudly: 'Nobody will be able to buy a pink carnation in Covent Garden for three whole days.'[29] The evening was made dramatic by a Yeoman of the Guard collapsing on the steps. Though tended by Lord Evans, the Queen's doctor, who was a guest at the gala, he died later in the evening. The President honoured Cecil by appointing him Chevalier de la Légion d'Honneur. Covent Garden paid him 250 guineas.

Cecil was also called upon by Michael Duff, now unhappily married to Lady Caroline Paget,* to help lighten the stiff, royal atmosphere when the Duchess of Kent came to stay at Vaynol in connection with a visit to Llandudno in May 1960. Cecil found that in the Duchess's presence the guests became unnatural and either made silly jokes or descended into sycophancy. Her lady-in-waiting only became normal on the croquet lawn, when she was prepared to send the Duchess's ball 'flying into the rose bushes'.[30] Cecil re-examined the Greek Princess, whom he had so much admired when young:

As for the Duchess herself she fought valiantly to be considered an

---

* Caroline Paget (1913–76), daughter of 6th Marquess of Anglesey. Plas Newydd is opposite Vaynol, across the Menai Straits.

ordinary entity and succeeded in being sympathetic, beautiful in a still romantic way in spite of her beauty having been so marred by unhappiness and the cruel damage of years. Sometimes, with her head tied up in a chiffon scarf she gave the impression of a real Romantic Queen of legend, like an Elisabeth of Austria, doomed and glamorous.[31]

In December 1960, Cecil was further absorbed into the royal circle when the Queen Mother invited him to a farewell dinner for the Whitneys (the retiring American Ambassador and his wife). Cecil was surprised because, meeting the Queen Mother at Maureen Dufferin's, he had said out of stage fright: 'I've been thinking it's time you saw me again.'[32] Needless to say, Cecil described the dinner at considerable length, analysing in particular the integration of Antony Armstrong-Jones into the family.

The Queen Mother was about to be painted by Graham Sutherland. Cecil advised her that the result would be better if he was not allowed to work from snapshots and had to rely on sketches. He went home in a haze of brandy and cigars. Finally in the spring of 1961 the Trees invited him for a weekend at Mereworth at which the Armstrong-Joneses were guests. Thus the man who had once stood on the outside became, by the means of photography, one who mixed freely with royalty on a social level. But on one point he still watched from the outside. Observing the happiness of the royal couple, he noted: 'Love is a miracle.'[33]

From now on Cecil's attitude to royal photographic commissions was somewhat different. Though bored by the red tape that surrounded such work, he was still reluctant to cede his favoured position to another. This landed him in some exasperating situations. In the spring of 1961 he was summoned to photograph the young Duke of Kent. The Duke proved a difficult sitter as he tended to hang his head unhelpfully on one side. He contrasted badly with his father, Prince George: 'The father had such charm and great good looks. The father was smiling,'[34] noted Cecil, when some of his portraits were produced. The Duchess came in and made faces to try to help the sitting. Cecil tried his 'dentist' line: 'Let's see the molars. I'm a dentist and I want to file away on the nerves zzzzzzzzz!'[35] This produced a slow grin. When the results were ready, Eileen was summoned and admonished: 'Now you're under oath not to tell anyone what I'm going to relay to you. Not a word to anyone for two hours. Not even Mr Beaton must know!'[36] Then Eileen was told that the Duke was engaged, but even then the bride's name was not revealed. If Cecil felt the whole performance was a bit overblown, he appeared equally unreal to the Kent family who, though very fond of him, used to do imitations of his way of talking for their private amusement. Indeed several of Cecil's friends became adept at carrying off his particularly distinctive voice. Antony Armstrong-Jones inherited Oliver Messel's flair for mimicking Cecil and John Sutro was another expert.

In June 1961 Cecil was summoned to Yorkshire to photograph the Duke's wedding to Katharine Worsley. The ceremony in York Minster was impressive with fanfares competing with the organ to send shivers down the spine. At Hovingham, the Worsley seat, Cecil was taking 'the only good picture of the day, one of the bride alone'[37] when Richard Colville, the officious press secretary, shouted at Cecil to do as he was told and take groups. This prevented Cecil from providing the bridal pair with anything more of interest, the sad result of a misguided devotion to duty. Having taken the groups, Cecil enjoyed the passing show, especially when Princess Marina and the Duke of Kent handed their cigarettes to Sir Philip Hay 'who became a mobile human ashtray'.[38] Cecil concluded that 'a very nice ordinary girl, with an unusual strength of character, had become a Cinderella princess'.[39]

Clearly the Queen's Hanoverian uncle, the Duke of Gloucester, and Cecil were unlikely to be in sympathy with each other. If the Duke's butler is to be believed, the Duke greeted the news that Cecil was to photograph him in the spring of 1961 in a disgruntled voice: 'That's the fella with the floppy hat, isn't it? Can't stand the man. Never stops talking in a funny voice. Bloody suspicious, I think.'[40] Certainly the Duke sent a message via his equerry that 'Mr Beaton would not have to photograph HRH looking through a whole lot of flowers.'[41] The session was made difficult because the Duke had made an appointment to go to his doctor on the same morning. Cecil wrote: 'The Duke then glowered into the camera with wild, mad eyes, walrus moustache and his smooth hairless head and hands shone in the camera lens.'[42] But he achieved a good result. The Duchess was very nervous, though Cecil thought she 'really looked extremely well in a grey spotted little crinoline with good jewels and orders. She has improved with the years because the bones have come out and her cheekbones are high and architectural.'[43] Cecil felt the York House atmosphere was 'so unlike anything that is happening today.... It has nothing to do with Kennedy, the Atom bomb....'[44] He came away bemused. On another occasion Cecil went to Barnwell to photograph the Duchess with her sons. Just as Cecil had them posed, one of them let off a gun which caused Cecil to jump with fright, to the restrained amusement of the Duchess.

Cecil's career as royal photographer continued into the 1970s. On many occasions he was obliged to point out to the press that Buckingham Palace had not created him and he was not, as such, the 'Court Photographer'. However, he admitted that when he was first summoned in 1939, it had given him a considerable respectability. In exchange, he freed them from the stiff formal poses of yesteryear and created for all of them a more glamorous and popular image.

Sir Roy Strong judges:

He contributed to the creation of a new mythology of monarchy after

Edward VIII and Mrs Simpson. It drew on 1930s neo-romanticism but had its regal roots in subconscious visual allusions to Winterhalter, Gainsborough, Van Dyck.... Before that the Yorks had no image. It is his visual perception that is so important. He had the most incredible eye. He always cared about the monarchy with tremendous passion. To the end he remained deeply patriotic.[45]

In 1963 Weidenfeld and Nicolson conceived the idea of publishing a now rare and impressive volume called *Cecil Beaton: Royal Portraits*. Naturally Cecil sent the Queen Mother a copy and her words of thanks say much for Cecil's contribution to the field of royal photography:

I find it very nostalgic looking through the pages. The years telescope, and I suddenly remembered what I felt like when I wore those pre-war garden party clothes – all those years ago. It is absolutely fascinating to look back and I feel that, as a family, we must be deeply grateful to you for producing us, as really quite nice and *real* people![46]

32

The Severing of Links

*I'm a hangover of my youth, without the charm or the
vitality, without the eccentricity of youth or the wish to
fight convention.*

Cecil (depressed) in his diary, August 1962

The publication of Cecil's first volume of diaries, *The Wandering Years*, in
July 1961 was the result of a sustained bout of hard work, undertaken
concurrently with all his other activities. The editing took over two years
and there was much rewriting by Waldemar Hansen, who had to be deterred from adding too many words like 'bespeak' and 'quintessential'. The
result was a highly polished version, far from faithful to the original text.
When he first undertook the task, Cecil consulted friends for advice. Anita
Loos liked them, Peter Quennell thought them repetitious and dwelling too
much on early struggles, and Cecil's editor Barley Alison thought them
snobbish. Truman Capote warned Cecil not to cook the books, but in vain:

> But the virtue of the diary is in its honesty; if you tinker with it it will
> become something other than yourself. These critics are simply asking
> you to be something other than you are: something that conforms to
> their idea of what is proper, tasteful, interesting etc. I say fuck them;
> such people would never like the diary regardless of what you did.[1]

At last he was able to put the finishing touches to his work. He did not
spare the dead in his past but he was cautious of old friends such as Francis
Rose and Daisy Fellowes, who, he thought, would sue at the slightest
provocation.

Cecil knew that his diaries would be the perfect excuse for his enemies
and critics to 'let forth a volley of slings and arrows'[2] and he was not
disappointed. Inevitably there were attacks, most notably in *Punch* and the
Irish press. Evelyn Waugh took what Cecil called 'just another opportunity
to overthrow his bile',[3] and opined: 'he can't write for toffee'.[4] On the other
hand Cyril Connolly wrote an important piece in the *Sunday Times*, Raymond Mortimer's reaction was more favourable than hitherto, while Lord

Birkenhead was eulogistic, and Simon Raven pointed out the dilemma between Cecil's 'cherished vision of Beaton the artist and man of sorrows with
his vulgar if excusable desire for the love and applause of top people'.[5] Cecil
was a bit surprised to find 'what ire I do provoke in the bosoms of people
who know me only from my work and by reputation'.[6] As always he tended
to side with his direst critics. He believed his work would not last, that he
was fashionable, superficial, underdeveloped mentally. He chided himself for
his ignorance of general knowledge, politics, religion and philosophy and
his inability to learn new things. He thought he had only achieved success
'by working fantastically hard and by dint of my driving ambition'.[7] He
knew he was considered funny and amusing in New York, but put no value
on the opinions of Americans. Cyril Connolly had written: 'although I have
always liked him I have looked upon him as an artist with mixed feelings
of pity and admiration'.[8] Cecil agreed. He still believed that Peter Watson's
career was worth more than his. Worst of all, he noted:

> That I have not inspired love in anyone enough to take me under their
> wing and insist on my mending my frivolous ways is a serious self-
> condemnation. That I have not inspired real love at all is a very pitiable
> lacuna, and that is the awful realization I must face. I wasn't able to
> inspire enough feeling in Peter and certainly Greta only superficially was
> intrigued – not enough. June is interested but not enough to marry me,
> and others have merely been phenomena of the flesh.[9]

Certainly Cecil's ambition was his driving force, but it is curious to find him
so unaware of the high popular esteem in which he was now held. He had
witnessed the delight of the *My Fair Lady* audiences, he had an Oscar to his
name, he had taken many a bow on a first night. He knew he could
command high prices for his work. He could see a certain fascination for
him growing in younger people. He was now entirely accepted by the people
he had sought from childhood. And yet he lacked the confidence to relax
for one minute. He drove himself so hard that the end of each week found
him exhausted. He had injections and ray treatments from Dr Gottfried who
told James Pope-Hennessy that without these Cecil would have collapsed
years ago. Though Cecil had enemies and there were some who despised
him, by and large his friends loved him and felt that he brightened a room
the moment he entered it. When he told Juliet Duff his plans for the summer,
she commented: 'What a season! You must reserve some time next weekend
to tell *all* about it.'[10]

Yet there was also a cold streak. In public he adopted a formidably aloof
persona which he had long found useful in intimidating those he worked
with. George Cukor said later that he had found it hard to give orders to an
English milord. Cecil's West Country neighbour, Michael Pitt-Rivers,
observed that Cecil was a different person in London than in the country.

The more natural Cecil came to life at Broadchalke, where he dropped his more exaggerated mannerisms. 'We wouldn't let him get away with it,'[11] observed Lady Pembroke, and Cecil was more than aware of the fact. Continually developing (despite his fears on the subject), Cecil would continue to strive for the new (which was not necessarily the fashionable). Earlier in his career he once put off the Graham Sutherlands to go to the Edens because he thought it grander. Later in life he might have done the opposite. The dilemma suggested by Simon Raven in his review was resolved by Cecil advancing on all fronts, and as soon as he had overcome the social barriers in his path he threw himself with humility and determination into a more artistic world.

The publication of the diaries brought old friends out of hiding. Sachie Sitwell thought the diaries justly and truthfully written. He continued: 'I do admire the use you have made of your talents and the way you have worked.'[12] Alice B. Toklas wrote: 'the two notices of Gertrude moved me deeply. Your appreciation, understanding, sensibility of her quality are rare.'[13] On the other hand, Marie Laure de Noailles tried to stir up trouble over Cecil's mention of Tony Gandarillas and drugs, but failed. Angry letters came from the close relatives of one or two old friends from Hampstead days, to whom disparaging references had been made. No critic mentioned that the Bérard portrait on the jacket was printed in reverse.

Once this excitement was over, Cecil visited Tangiers to attend Barbara Hutton's ball. This event was an opportunity for much intrigue. David Herbert ensured that none of his arch-enemy David Edge's friends were invited and there was concern as to whether or not the hostess would be sober. In the end 'she was too far gone in euphoria to be able to articulate except by pantomime'.[14] Cecil went on to Venice for a Volpi ball, hoping the dramatic hostess would send some uninvited guest away. Instead he found Charles de Beistegui complaining that everyone had left before he could give a dinner for them. Cecil also joined Michael and Anne Tree in Spetsai and immersed himself in millionaire life amidst Niarchoses, von Thyssens, Paleys and Wrightsmans. He felt that by so doing he had played safe, 'closing the doors on the haphazard'.[15] Back in London nothing was so astounding as the dramatic arrival in London of the dissident Russian ballet dancer, Rudolf Nureyev. Dame Margot Fonteyn invited him to take part in her afternoon gala at the Theatre Royal, Drury Lane, in October. Cecil went along with Diana Cooper. The dancer was annoyed only to be doing a *pas de deux* in *Sleeping Beauty*, but he had the stage to himself for Scriabin's *Poème Tragique*. His performance was hailed by one critic as that of a wild animal in a drawing-room. Cecil felt rejuvenated by the experience as though an electric current had been switched on: 'My very blood stream was altered by the thrill of what was being performed.' That evening at Margot Fonteyn's party, Cecil met Nureyev for the first time:

I kissed him on the cheek and forehead. He was very surprised but I felt the consistency of his smooth, poreless, vellum skin, and was pleased that I had made such a public fool of myself. When I talked to Freddie Ashton about the dance I could not keep back the tears in spite of kicking the door hard behind me. Perhaps it is something other than this afternoon's experience that reduced me to such a state of hysteria.[16]

The following January Cecil went to photograph the dancer, but Nureyev did not remember him. He was in a furious temper and Cecil noted: 'It was lucky that this trapped fox did not bite me, but merely glowered into the lens.'[17] Nureyev's pride and wrath could not be melted by Cecil's charm. In a long career of photography he had never encountered such an unresponsive sitter.

One of Cecil's recurring endeavours during these years was to submit himself for a portrait by a leading artist. In November 1957 he had made his first journey to the red-brick block of flats in Battersea where Francis Bacon was at work. Cecil was undeterred when Bacon studied him and declared: 'Your face is pink and blue. I can't make out if it is pink on top of blue or blue on top of pink.'[18] After two hours the session was over and it took Cecil over two years before the sittings were resumed in February 1960. When the portrait was finished, Cecil hoped to emerge as 'a sort of floating Sainsbury* in stygian gloom'.[19] He mused as to whether his portrait would bear the pigmentation of a Vuillard. Instead, to his horror, he found a strip-cartoon of a bald, aged, senile figure disintegrating before his eyes. Cecil was profoundly shocked. He knew he could never hang the portrait in his house but thought that he might acquire it as an investment. Bacon suggested £300, Cecil £150. He left the studio 'crushed, staggered and feeling quite a sense of loss'.[20]

Presently Francis Bacon announced that he had destroyed the portrait. Even this worried Cecil:

Perhaps he feels that I am not the sort of person he wants to have in his exhibition, that he would dislike the publicity. Maybe he doesn't really like me at all, in spite of his professed friendship, in spite of, or perhaps because of, my desire to please him.[21]

The incident is typical of the contrasting wishes of Cecil's character – the quest for true art versus the need for flattery. Like many others before and since he was saying: portray me truthfully as you see me, warts and all, only to be deeply upset by the result. Soon after this Cecil went over to sit to Augustus John and told him of the incident. 'You deserve it, for sitting to him,'[22] said the old roué. Then he added sarcastically: 'These idiosyncrasies are the prerogative of genius.'[23] Cecil had a clear image of how he liked to

---

* Sir Robert Sainsbury (b. 1906).

look. The Bérard portrait always pleased him. So did a drawing by Augustus John done in 1952. Yet Hal Burton remembers that as soon as Cecil got this drawing home, he rushed to the studio, seized an eraser and altered the mouth.*

In the summer of 1960 Cecil paid several visits to Fryern Court in Hampshire to sit to John. Nothing was easy. Once he posed despite a stomach ache while his trousers dried in the sun. Shortly afterwards he almost fainted and had to return home to bed. Cecil found that John often ruined his work by haphazard over-painting. He was too old to decide whether Cecil should be cricket pavilion green, or vivid blue, and so tried both. The sittings ceased when Cecil went to America and the uncompleted portrait was bought by a Californian tycoon after John's death in October 1961.

By Christmas 1961 it was clear that Mrs Beaton was dying. She was in no pain, otherwise Cecil confessed he would willingly 'slip her a deadly pill'.[24] She was well enough to come down to dinner and Cecil never forgot that although supported by Baba and the cook Mrs Talbot, she lifted her arm and beckoned to him 'in desperate supplication':

> She looked like King Lear and for a moment her kind attendants were transformed into the Elizabethan characters of this great tragedy, and her gesture, quiet, slow-motioned had all the authority and nobility of the aged king.
>
> All the years of my life seemed to be cast away as I ran towards her; and tried to give her the support that she had given me as a child.[25]

Cecil braced himself for the inevitable. He did not want her to go on suffering, yet he knew he would face the end itself 'in the most terrible state of hysteria'.[26] He was glad to be at Broadchalke, able to look in on her frequently and bring fresh flowers. As death approached, Cecil was upset when, uninvited, 'a huge black bat Mephistopheles appeared in the form of the vicar'[27] to read Mrs Beaton the 122nd Psalm. The first snowdrops from the garden were brought in and a pot of nurtured hyacinths taken from the darkness.

In the midst of his vigil, Cecil had to go to London to take part in *Face to Face*, a gruelling television interview with John Freeman (a forerunner to the 'trial by television' interviews by David Frost later in the decade). The technique used was to ask tough questions. The camera stayed on the subject and only the interviewer's back was seen. John Freeman declared that 'what one is trying to do is to relax a man enough so that he will show himself as he really is'.[28] Occasionally they went too far as in an acutely embarrassing interview which reduced the television personality Gilbert

* It was used as the author's portrait in *The Wandering Years*.

Harding to tears, shortly before his death. Cecil hardly slept for several
nights before the ordeal, which he overcame by talking frankly, amusingly
and disarmingly. When Freeman asked him why he wore a hat, he took it
off with a sweep, declaring: 'I don't like to exhibit myself quite bald, you
know.'[29] He revealed his enmity for Evelyn Waugh and said: 'I'm still looking for the end of the rainbow.'[30] His performance was well reviewed. John
Gross wrote in the *New Statesman* that Cecil emerged 'as a considerably
tougher personality than the last celebrity I saw in the same series, John
Osborne'.[31] Angus Wilson described him as coming over 'rather like Zena
Dare playing in the unmasking scene of some society play like *The Second
Mrs Tanqueray* or *Lady Windermere's Fan*'.[32] Friends were equally delighted.
Ali Forbes cabled: 'Well, they can wrap that programme up for good because
nobody will ever do it better.'[33] Raymond Mortimer wrote: 'I think that he
did not realize beforehand the steel beneath your velvet',[34] and Laura Can-
field (now Laura Duchess of Marlborough) wrote:

> I don't like Mr Freeman's *back* – to face him for half an hour must be
> ghastly. You looked wonderful (I loved your hat) and you were so much
> better than anyone I have ever seen on that programme.[35]

Cecil then went to Paris for two days of hectic work. There Eileen rang him
to tell him his mother was dead.

The severing of this link with childhood and the loss of the person he
loved most in the world caused Cecil lasting grief. At first he was shocked
and ashamed by his reaction to the news. That very night he continued
with his plan to escort Marie-Louise Bousquet to dinner with Balenciaga,
announcing the death when the party was over. Only in London, on his
way to choose flowers at Felton's, did he begin 'howling like a dog'.[36]

At Reddish he sobbed miserably in the garden but went in to see his
mother in death, her face like 'a medieval waxwork'.[37] Describing her every
feature over several pages of diary Cecil concluded:

> It was so awful to think of this lovely statue being committed to an
> eternity of loneliness. She looked so very vulnerable and trusting. To
> leave her to the mercies of the ghouls from the funeral parlour was so
> cruel.[38]

He could not bear to see her in her coffin, so bade farewell before that:

> The tears I dropped onto the freezias and violets by her side were like hot
> tropical raindrops. Mrs Talbot said, 'Don't get upset. Look how beautiful
> she is. Kiss her. Kiss her.'
> Her forehead was so cold.[39]

The funeral was a further ordeal. Cecil bolted from the church and rushed shivering to bed. Mrs Beaton left her money equally to her three children. To Cecil she bequeathed a single diamond ring and all her furniture. The letters of friends were a comfort and all praised Cecil for having been a wonderful son. Ava Waverley wrote:

> When one reflects on your work and your magnificent achievement and all it meant to her – in pride and also in the beauty of the surroundings with which you were able to endow her – there can be no regrets.[40]

Presently Mrs Beaton was buried in the Beaton grave at Hampstead. Later in the year the other important link with Cecil's childhood was suddenly severed with the death of Lily Elsie. Cecil had only seen her a few times in his life, but her magic remained with him. In 1957 news came that she was behaving in a strange manner, turning on those closest to her and inventing imaginary grievances. She was put into a home in Regent's Park and finally moved to St Andrew's Hospital, Dollis Hill, NW2. She attended *My Fair Lady* with her nurse once and in June 1962 Cecil collected her and took her to tea at the Mitre Hotel, Hampton Court. He was extremely disillusioned with her appearance, finding her 'wrapped in a cocoon of elderly fat'.[41] The afternoon freed him from his romantic notions of the past and from many of his dreams, 'much that was second-rate'. It must have given him a moment of pleasure when she wrote: 'What a lovely day you gave me on Wednesday and for taking my face on your camera I was really thrilled. Just imagine you taking a picture of me, well! I almost cannot believe it!!!'[42] Certainly he felt a deep sense of loss when he heard of 'the death of one's first love, one's first stage heroine'.[43]

A trip to Nigeria to stay with the Heads (Lord Head was High Commissioner) and Diana Cooper in Lagos helped Cecil forget his mother's demise. They were joined by others. Everyone took photographs. Lord Head had the theory that the only reason that Cecil's excelled was that his were more professionally printed. Cecil greatly enjoyed the *Salla*, the bi-annual celebrations held by the Emir of Katsina to mark the end of Ramadan. Diana proved an energetic and eccentric guest, wishing to bathe naked in the moonlight, and once falling into a particularly unpleasant main drain.

On his return to England Cecil felt lonely for the first time in his life. Old friends like Francis Rose had fallen on hard times and become pests. Francis seemed to expect Cecil to pay all his debts, his rent and his hospital bills. He got Cecil tangled up with his rather dubious private life. When Francis took up with a labourer called Sheamus O'Toole, Cecil admonished him: 'Your friends don't want to see you any more.'[44] Nevertheless he always relented out of loyalty to the old days, and used to send him his old suits. Eileen, too, suffered torments as the dejected artist turned up all too regularly at Pelham Place demanding, as if by right, the wherewithal to see him through the weekend.

*　　*　　*

Mercifully Cecil had important work to preoccupy him. The Comédie Française in Paris had bestowed upon him the signal honour of inviting him to design *The School for Scandal*, the first time they had chosen an Englishman for nearly three centuries. He adored Paris and he found his collaborators efficient and inspired. Altogether his work was a contrast to the theatre in Broadway or the West End. Karinska was at hand once again to bring his designs to perfection. Besides a few histrionics between the stars, all went smoothly. Cecil believed secretly that this was his best work yet. He hoped for praise from the French. *Gigi* had not won him this because the film was made by Americans and because Maurice Chevalier was hated in France at the time. The accolades duly came and Cecil was delighted: 'It is a first success, and there is never again anything like a first success.'[45] When the play opened Cecil was delighted that 'a tribe of bitches who do their best to make things difficult on first nights'[46] remained generally silent. On the other hand huge enthusiasm flowed from those Cecil respected: Cocteau, Marie-Laure de Noailles and Denise Bourdet. Cecil was praised for his combination of wit, taste and audacity and for his knowledge of the theatre. Likewise the dressmakers, Yves St Laurent and Marc Bohan (of Dior), were thrilled. Gérald Van der Kemp, curator of Versailles, said: 'The *mise-en-scène* is English, your taste is English but the execution is French.'[47] Maurice Escande, the administrator, waved Cecil to a seat in his box and said: 'You are *chez vous* with us now. And we hope there will be many opportunities when you'll work with us again.'[48] Best of all, Boris Kochno said: 'I adore what you are doing. You know it. But I want to talk to you for *hours* about it.'[49] Later Kochno told him that he had been unable to sleep for the beauty of the production. Cecil noted:

> This allusion to my work as carrying on in the tradition of Bérard touched me very much. In fact the surprise was such that I had got more from Boris than I had bargained for. I found myself weeping as I went off on my day's round.[50]

While in Paris Cecil photographed the aged courtesan, Cléo de Mérode. At the time of the *Belle Epoque* her graceful dancing and flawless beauty had made her the toast of three continents. She was a friend of Gounod, Massenet, Proust and Reynaldo Hahn. She wore her hair parted in the middle and combed over her ears. Boldini painted a striking portrait of her. Now in her late eighties, she still gave dancing lessons and lived in a spacious apartment on the rue de Téhéran. Cecil was delighted to photograph her, but she made it clear that she counted on his '*galanterie de gentilhomme*'[51] not to publish anything without her permission. She asked for a little retouching to be done. When she saw the results she congratulated Cecil on being the only person to have delighted her with his work. At the same time she astonished him by being entirely up to date with music. At this time she was fascinated by the work of the energetic modern pianist, John Ogdon. Later Cecil lodged some unretouched versions of these portraits with Camera Press for use after Cléo de Mérode's death. He was aware that if she saw them she would be most upset and he also knew that she would sue as she had done successfully on several previous occasions. Then Cecil set off by train to the South of France. His spirits were high and he felt 'more determined to be fancy free than I have for a long time'.[52] He fulfilled a long-held wish to meet and photograph Edward Gordon Craig at his refuge in Vence. He was an innovator in scenic design, the illegitimate son of Ellen Terry and one-time lover of Isadora Duncan. Cecil described him as 'like a huge bird that had lost many of its feathers'.[53] Craig was busy reading A.L. Rowse on Walter Raleigh.

The summer in England took Cecil to Blenheim in June. His first visit had been in 1925, and he had worried himself inordinately about giving a story about it to the papers. Now he was a guest of the 10th Duke, whose ribald humour Cecil relished. Bert Marlborough announced: 'I'll show you my private parts, you know where the public aren't allowed. They're rather pretty, my private parts, and they've got a lot of colour.'[54] The unlikely pair plodded off round the Duke's private garden. While Cecil derived some satisfaction and amusement from these visits and came away with saleable photographs of the Duke's debutante granddaughter, Serena (now Mrs Neil Balfour), and of Tina Blandford, he concluded that if he had to make a choice, the snobbishness and vapidity of the 'vulgar rich' would willingly be sacrificed for 'the lure of the kitchen sink around which conversation is likely to be more lively and vital'.[55]

In this category he did not include Jakie and Chiquita Astor who, though very rich, welcomed an exchange of ideas. Jakie Astor teased Cecil mercilessly but he loved it. He also boosted his ego from time to time. Cecil was delighted that he thought him classless. 'Oh you've no idea how hard I've worked at that,'[56] he confessed. Jakie Astor also assured him he would never be a bore because of his sense of humour. He diagnosed that Cecil's trouble was his 'dancing feet'.[57] With the Astors Cecil met Jackie Kennedy. He was amused when at the end of dinner in June 1961, Jakie, an old beau of the President's wife, said, 'When you bugger off we're going to have a wonderful post-mortem.'*[58]

Cecil also enjoyed going to stay at Chatsworth with the Duchess of Devonshire, whom he thought 'a great individualist'. He relished such eccentricities as the Duke standing back and saying, 'Privilege after ability.'[59] He loved it when the Duchess pointed out a doorway cut through a portrait in the dining-room. Defending this action to shocked guests, she explained delightedly: 'Well, you wouldn't get any food otherwise.'[60] And he loved her

---

* In *The Restless Years* (p. 131) Cecil took credit for this line.

Mitford idiom, the greeting of her sister, Jessica: 'Did you have a good night? ... Oh you are clever at sleeping!'[61] On the other hand Cecil was fed up with the London season: 'the vulgarity, the inane chatter and false bonhomie. I am really wasting the valuable months and I'm getting too old to do the things I don't need to do.'[62] He had to do a certain amount of social photography to pay his bills, but thought 'there are other ways of keeping the wolf away than by putting up a hideous pale mauve boudoir-tent for the fourth Lady Beatty's twentieth [in fact twenty-first] birthday party!'[63]

Much of the time he cast a cold and discerning eye on any party he attended, assessing its merits as though he were valuing it for Christie's. An example of this was an elaborate Epiphany party to which he escorted Mona Bismarck a year earlier in Paris (in January 1960), given for the Duke and Duchess of Windsor by the wife of the owner of the *Folies Bergère*. His eleven-page diary account brought out the best and the worst of Cecil.

He began by scrutinizing the guest list and was delighted to observe that several feuding factions of Paris social life would be gathering under one roof. Then he turned his attention to the vast bouquets of lilac and dark red roses, soon detecting a number of false flowers in their midst. The Duchess of Windsor was announced as 'Her Royal Highness' and many ladies gave deep curtseys. The Duke of Windsor spoke of Patrick Kinross's book *The Innocents at Home*, about his tour of America in a Greyhound bus. The American-born wife of the Italian Ambassador said: 'I was only once in a Greyhound bus and it was *tur*ribly unattractive!'[64] At dinner lilies sprayed out of gilt candelabra, but the effect was ruined for Cecil because 'these were attached to their gilt base by the crude means of a large lump of putty or plasticine. This would have been all right on the stage or at the *Folies Bergère*.'[65] The menu was written in terms of a sea voyage: 'sailing ships of lobster and prawn bring you to the land of amorous quails where we see the dawn in salad'.[66] Cecil examined his dinner partner, a French duchess, who was better at conversation than 'the silly little ballerina on my right':[67]

> I looked at the danger points to see how old she might be, but the line of the chin is good, the hands are not veined or blotchy, the fat bulges just a little over her lightly fitting corset, but her figure is remarkable even for a girl. Only her walk is heavy and old. She moves without a springing gait, flat footed and cumbersome like an old peasant woman.[68]

At this party two of the guests were to be crowned for Epiphany. Not surprisingly, the Duke of Windsor looked rather nervous as one crown narrowly avoided him. A little sequin crown was then popped onto the Duchess's head, 'a moment that would have been a flashlight photographer's scoop',[69] but the Duchess smiled with her mouth down-turned at the corners and thought she saved the day by shouting across the table, 'Uneasy lies the head that wears a crown.'[70] The festivities became even more bizarre after dinner. A pink perambulator was pushed over to the cigar-smoking Duke. When the pink curtains were opened, a kitten was discovered within. The Duke 'puffed a mouthful of smoke at the kitten who collapsed sideways and seemed to faint'.[71] At this point Cecil had had enough. He and Mona were the first to leave.

In the 1960s Cecil often photographed the young debutantes. One of his favourite models was Charmian Montagu-Douglas-Scott.* He used her in his new spoof, *Quail in Aspic*,† along with Elsa Maxwell disguised as Count Korsetz, and Mae Murray (who failed to see the joke and threatened to sue Cecil). In 1962 Cecil experimented with photo-montages of the debutantes. Anne Faber,‡ one girl thus depicted, wished he had just taken straightforward ones: 'To us he was a God. It was such a missed opportunity.'[72] Cecil also experimented with overprinting his photographs, which led to a curious and not very successful book called *Images*.¶ Another way he earned money was to fly to Detroit to photograph the Chrysler New York Salon. He also designed the interior of the Shell Centre theatre. Most of all he enjoyed commissions such as photographing the spring fashions of Balenciaga and Givenchy.

All this work was undertaken in a general condition of bad health. He worked so hard that his resistance was often low. Any strong alcohol gave him a bad headache. He frequently suffered from colitis (which was to become a more serious problem later), and he found his stomach ached either badly or slightly all the time. And yet his interest in life drove him to forge on and face yet another London traffic jam in order to take in an exhibition or meet some new people whose work interested him.

At the same time Cecil felt older. Photographs that appeared of him – particularly the one of him and Freddie Ashton at a rehearsal of *Marguerite and Armand* – caused him to wince with horror:

> Thank heavens that now I think little about the way I look, for if I did other, or if I thought people saw me as I see myself then I might as well do away with myself for I don't think I'd be the type to be happy in a monastery.[73]

He continued to move in royal circles. At Wilton he dined when the Queen Mother was a guest: 'For the first time I did not find that I was making

---

* Now Charmian Stirling. A niece of Princess Alice, Duchess of Gloucester.

† *Quail in Aspic* was published late in 1962, a poor version of *My Royal Past*, the best bit being a witty spoof introduction by John Sutro. Michael Hogg wrote: 'the text quite often leaves a remarkably disagreeable taste without any compensatory wit' [*Daily Telegraph*, 9 November 1962].

‡ Granddaughter of Harold Macmillan. Now Mrs Anne Cockerell.

¶ Published in 1963 with a preface by Edith Sitwell and an introduction by Christopher Isherwood.

conversation.... I felt we were able to converse as two human beings who have a certain admiration for each other and we both chuckled quite a lot as we skipped from one topic to another.'[74]

Cecil spent as much time as possible at Broadchalke. Clarissa Avon paid a rare visit to lunch and they toured his garden. Significantly he wrote: 'Such a tour is perhaps designed to strike envy in the newcomer's heart. It certainly succeeded with Clarissa.'[75] She was soon asking the names of various plants and where he had found them. The spirit of competition into which it seems that gardeners must enter caused a certain amount of light-hearted anguish to the other distinguished gardeners in Cecil's vicinity. Just as he had often derived ideas for photographs from old friends such as Stephen Tennant, similarly he was quick to spot features in their gardens he could adapt at Reddish. Nevertheless Clarissa Avon and Anne Tree (who was a neighbour at Donhead St Mary in the 1970s) were continually told unfairly: 'You are so lucky to have Cecil Beaton near by for inspiration.'

Just as Cecil liked to inspire envy, so he suffered from it. During the summer he analysed this: 'It does not take the form of envying people their particular talent so much as envying them the success their talent brings them.'[76] Years ago he had made a room laugh by saying that Tchelitchew was so jealous that he was even jealous of Shirley Temple. He made a list of those he envied and it was by no means a predictable one: the Queen, Prince Philip, the Armstrong-Joneses (especially Tony 'for stultifying as much of his present life must be, his is the Cinderella story of our time'[77]), Graham Sutherland, Barbara Hepworth, John Betjeman, Noël Coward and John Osborne. He had hated it when boring journalists came to interview Truman Capote in Japan. Now he was resentful that Laurence Olivier had been appointed head of the National Theatre. Knighthoods were another source of irritation. Cecil told Steven Runciman that he could not bring himself to write him a letter of congratulation out of pique. Freddie Ashton and Laurence Olivier were both knights now. Mercifully due to a tax felony and residence abroad, Noël Coward was not. Cecil felt it was unfair that he should have to work so hard for any little reward that came his way:

Whereas Freddie Ashton can dream away in his summer house in the trees or blink at the ceiling and eventually be rewarded with pomp and ceremony, Sir Laurence can booze away and be out of the running for an age, only to be surprised by the arrival of a messenger bringing him the greatest good news of a personal nature.[78]

One Sunday, while reading a newspaper piece on British Guiana by Evelyn Waugh, Cecil reacted in a curious manner for a man of fifty-eight: 'I was delighted to find it dull and had much pleasure in gouging out his eyes with a pencil, then his nose and mouth and finally destroying his whole head before getting gleefully into my bath.'[79] On the other hand Cecil greatly

PANSY
FORGET-ME-NOT
PRIMROSES

Flower drawing from First Garden

admired selflessness in others and was the first to look aghast when he recognized people becoming victims of their egos. In the worlds in which he worked there was no dearth of egomaniacs.

But Cecil was not unhappy with his own lot. He was at his best in his garden at Reddish and he found picking flowers the most beneficial therapy. As old friends became less important, so was he fortunate in meeting new ones:

> I do feel that the technique of life that I have evolved is in many ways that which I have always wanted to attain. There are few feelings of restriction, I am free, I am protected by the golden quality of Eileen from the most unattractive aspects of my existence, and my domains are filled with drink and laughter and flowers.[80]

On 14 August 1962, Cecil flew to Denmark and spent luxurious and stimulating days with Philippe and Pauline de Rothschild* on the island of Fyn. They wandered by moonlight round the lilyponds, or took a boat out amongst the ducks and reeds. Talk ranged from Kennedy's policy and the Common Market to films, theatre and a wide span of history. On his return to Copenhagen, Cecil recalled a promise to telephone Isak Dinesen. He had not known that she was dying and did not feel he would have time to see her. But when she said, 'Well, you won't see me ever again, that's certain', he knew this was a rare opportunity:

> I wondered if I would have a chance to photograph this marvellous old woman or whether she felt she was now beyond being documented. I wondered if she would have some wonderful things to say about how she was facing the imminence of death. Her remark on the telephone must surely be alluded to.[81]

The Baroness made it easy for him and he successfully captured her sweet, sad beauty. A sufferer for many years from syphilis acquired in her marriage to Baron Blixen, she was now a waif-like skeleton with wrinkles 'like lacework'. Her face was pale, her hair the colour of lavender and she had very black eyes. Cecil was on the way to see Truman, who had upset the Baroness by writing that her mouth was paralytic and that she looked like a scarecrow. Now she was generous to him:

> He's a nice chap and a good writer and he's improving all the time. His last books are the best. Tell him that I have evaporated my spite and that I wrote a preface for his last book translated into Danish. He's a friend and I'm fond of him. Give him my love.[82]

---

* Formerly Pauline Potter. Cecil admired her because in the days when she had little money she did not sell her Bonnard.

At the end she came bravely to the door to wave Cecil good-bye. Within a fortnight, on 7 September, Isak Dinesen died. Afterwards her secretary, Clara Svendsen, wrote to Cecil:

> You were one of the chosen few who understood about style in the same way that Tania did. How she enjoyed the flowers you brought her, they were one of the last joys of her life. When they were gone I tried to copy the bold gay colour-scheme with flowers from the garden, and put my bouquet in the hall, and she told me, 'Put your Cecil bouquet in here so I can look at it.'[83]

In 1962 there were several meetings with Edith Sitwell, who was now confined to a wheelchair. Cecil took wonderful photographs of her wearing a floppy hat and four giant acquamarine rings for her seventy-fifth birthday. 'It is such a comfort *not* to appear as a cross between a turkey that has been insufficiently fattened up for Christmas and an escapee from Broadmoor!'[84] she wrote. Dame Edith invited Cecil to her birthday concert at the Royal Festival Hall on 9 October and he appeared for her in *This is Your Life*, which she called 'Mr Andrews'* Inquisition'.[85] Thanking Cecil for his words she wrote:

> I *am* grateful to you, dear Cecil, for what you said of me during the Inquisition, and for *all* the *great* friendship, most truly valued, and over so many years, you have always and unfailingly shown us. Every time I see you, I feel young again.[86]

Dame Edith was one of Cecil's guests at Pelham Place on Thursday 29 November, an occasion he described as 'another milestone – the biggest yet perhaps – in my social rise'.[87] Cecil had met the Queen Mother at the American Embassy and had imbibed enough to pluck up courage to invite her to tea. 'Tea?' she laughed. Cecil converted the invitation to luncheon and presently it was accepted.

Cecil had redecorated Pelham Place, converting the downstairs room into a large salon, with black velvet walls, and converting his former study into a bedroom with strong red colours. He proudly mixed primitive and modern styles, with works by Larry Rivers and a gouache by Denis Hawkins, Giacometti lamps and Japanese cushions. Cecil, Truman and Eileen watched Dame Edith's dramatic arrival. Suddenly she emerged from her ambulance with the help of two stalwart men:

> Two gold pointed feet appeared, then the glitter of brilliant acquamarine rings sparkled in the wintry climate, then Edith's gold melon crown appeared, and under it, looking very vague and far away, as if she hardly noticed what her courtiers were doing, Edith's pale, calf-like face.[89]

* Eamonn Andrews, then, as now, the presenter.

The other guests were June and Freddie Ashton. They all had a drink, which Cecil ordered to be hidden when his royal guest arrived. The limousine drew up and the Queen Mother stepped out in brilliant crimson. Dame Edith overwhelmed the Queen Mother with apologies for being unable to rise, Truman looked like a schoolboy, Freddie Ashton played a *grand seigneur* rôle and June was 'to the manner born',[90] though she upset Cecil by drawing attention to her cocktail glass. Dame Edith spoke of her recent concert and gave 'a cruel imitation of the man who had distorted her poems' [the actor Sebastian Shaw];[91] they spoke of the Elizabethan period, Truman told the Queen Mother about baseball and held her attention with tales of the Clutter murders and his book. A delicious lunch was served and Queen Elizabeth enjoyed Truman's 'shout of joy'[92] when the summer pudding appeared. Afterwards she sat in the drawing-room. 'It gave me a frisson of pleasure to see her sitting there,'[93] wrote Cecil. '(My mother would have been so proud) and my heart went out to her.'[94] Cecil showed her round the house and when saying farewell the Queen Mother wound down her car window to say 'she thought Mr Capote quite wonderful, so intelligent, so wise, so funny'.[95] To this Cecil replied, 'Yes he's a genius, Ma'am.'[96] Unfortunately this went to Truman's head. He made up the story that the Queen Mother had told the Queen about him and that he had been summoned to Buckingham Palace. In her letter of thanks the Queen Mother praised Cecil's choice of guests and added: 'to complete the pleasure, a most kind and witty host'.[97] Edith Sitwell wrote: 'The Queen Mother has a kind of genius for making everyone feel particularly happy ... it was sad going back to work after your lunch-party.'[98]

Soon after this Cecil set off on a new adventure, a safari in Kenya with Raymond Mortimer and Lady Lettice 'Duchess' Ashley-Cooper. Cecil was soon absorbed by the suspense of waiting for the animals, many of which put him in mind of mythological creatures. He also compared them to creatures on more familiar territory. He wrote of an impala which leapt 'like Nureyev'[99] and, in extolling the beauty of a leopard, noted 'only Cartier could make something so exquisite in finish'.[100] He regretted his stupidity in not bringing with him a telescopic lens, because he had not yet mastered this unfamiliar gadget, acquired in Japan.

The little travelling group was an unlikely one. Lady Lettice, aristocratic and deaf, was not noted for her punctuality. The two aesthetic gentlemen, Cecil and Raymond, were hardly the average tourists. Raymond Mortimer wore a bow tie and when particularly impressed would be heard quoting, 'We have sipped the milk of Paradise.'[101] Cecil got more than worn out by the ceaseless intellectual chatter of this eccentric Bloomsbury figure. At Ngorongoro the party joined a Swedish botanist for a trip in a jeep. Cecil was rather proud of his pink shirt and scarf and his new suede shoes. Alas the botanist proved as bad a driver as navigator. He succeeded in getting the jeep stuck on the edge of a bridge in 'a mass of black blancmange'.[102] While Raymond Mortimer puffed his cigarette in some dry grass, Cecil made himself useful by gathering some boulders to lodge under the jeep's wheels. Mud oozed over his ankles and dirty water crept up his calf. His shoes were ruined. Later the jeep tried to move and the wheels turned wildly to no avail other than to splatter Cecil with mud. The situation looked desperate and they wondered if they might fall victim to some preying rhino. They made a last effort to escape. Cecil threw his weight into pushing the jeep to safety. Suddenly it rushed forward and Cecil followed, landing head first in the mud and water, with the real danger of the jeep rolling back on top of him. All was well in fact, but back at the camp Cecil gave vent to his pent-up feelings by treating Raymond to an onslaught on the character of the botanist, using all the foul language he could muster. Unfortunately Lady Lettice proved not so deaf as Cecil hoped and missed not one of his many four-letter words. From Kenya they went to Madagascar, where Cecil offended Raymond by drawing evil caricatures of the local chancellor of the exchequer's wife, with whom Raymond had been proud to dine. One evening Cecil was colouring these in his room, when he heard Raymond's knock on the door. He hid the sketches hurriedly and then in the panic of their departure carelessly left them in a lower shelf of his desk. Later he agonized in vain over the situation. Lady Lettice laughed and said: 'Forget it. If we have a war with Madagascar, you'll know you're the reason for it.'[103] They visited Mauritius before returning home.

Cecil was about to depart for Hollywood to create the film of *My Fair Lady*, before which he designed *Marguerite and Armand* for Fonteyn and Nureyev at Covent Garden. He was inspired to set the ballet in a semi-circular gilded cage, derived from a Second Empire gilt firescreen that caught his eye as he began work. He put red camellias on most of Margot Fonteyn's gowns, but she was embarrassed to wear them. Nor did she like her hat and as soon as Cecil was out of the way she jettisoned it. 'Margot does not wear her hat,'[104] wrote Cecil to Eileen, 'and, of course, I could have kicked her.' He projected distorted blown-up photographs onto a backcloth to accentuate the hallucinations of the dying Marie Duplessis. This last idea was generally deemed pretentious. The production received an enormous amount of publicity with a gala attended by the Queen Mother and Princess Margaret in March. Cecil earned £750 for his work. Peter Williams, writing in *Dance and Dancers*, compared it to *Apparitions* which had shared the same choreographer, designer, composer and period, and almost the same situation. He wrote:

Ashton has matured like good vintage wine, Beaton has remained in the same vintage almost as bottled, and this was particularly noticeable in

460 · The Victorious Years 1953–65

his costumes, all of which could be put into a revival of the twenty-seven-year-old work without anyone noticing much difference.[105]

Cecil himself had a difficult time with Nureyev before the production. Nureyev cut his coat-tails to a size that did not make him look like a waiter. Then there was an ugly scene at the rehearsal and Nureyev almost refused to wear Cecil's costume, but Dame Ninette de Valois managed to calm him down. He thought the Opera House had given a story to the press. A journalist relayed an untrue version to Cecil, then in Hollywood, and he was aghast at the thought. One afternoon in January 1963 he invited Nureyev to see his new photographs, 'a ruse to get him to the house, show him friendliness and perhaps strike up a relationship that might make our working together more agreeable – or even more satisfactory'.[106] Nureyev created a bad impression. He was impolite and surly, never showed enthusiasm for the pictures he liked, only disdain and anger for those he hated. He was only drawn to the full-length portraits of himself:

> In many ways Nureyev reminded me of Greta, the same wild untamed quality of genius, of not fitting. But Greta is subtle and sensitive and has a sense of humanity, even if she is utterly self-centred. He has no pity, no concern for others. He is ruthless and says, 'If they were dead I not mind.' I felt very much as if I had brought an animal from the woods into my room. I felt at any moment the furniture might be violently kicked, tables and chairs turned upside-down, the whole place reduced to a shambles. It was quite dangerous.[107]

Though Cecil felt at the end of their meeting 'I had played him like a fish', he also felt he had failed to establish any rapport with him, and Eileen had disliked him. 'I couldn't go along with him,'[108] she said.

Princess Margaret lunched at Pelham Place and then Cecil was hijacked to Hollywood.

33

Cecil Goes to Hollywood

Descriptions of the making of a movie, either in fiction or as fact, are histories of betrayal, ineptitude, tantrums, chicanery, and bitter personal disagreements.

Irwin Shaw, *American Vogue*, 1 September 1963

Cecil will surely be remembered for his work on *My Fair Lady* more than for anything else. It was a coveted job secured for him by Bill Paley, Chairman of CBS, who sold the movie rights to Warner Brothers for $5.5 million and added as an afterthought: 'I want Beaton to do the designs.'[1] It meant ten months in Hollywood, a prospect which would have thrilled Cecil in 1929, but now appalled him. From his first day he felt imprisoned and even Freddie Ashton's advice to think of every bored ten minutes as another dollar bill did little to console him. His work on the film was the means of making a considerable sum of money. His agent, 'Swifty' Lazar, hoped Cecil would have no financial troubles for some years to come. At this point Cecil owed £5,000 supertax. He earned $500 a week on the film, which was reduced to $300 after tax and other deductions. He also had a small percentage in the film, but none of this compared with Audrey Hepburn's salary of $1 million for twenty-four weeks, or Rex Harrison's $10,000 a week, or even Stanley Holloway's $7,000. On several occasions he considered breaking his contract and flying home.

In his first weeks Cecil worked closely with the director, George Cukor. He was in admiration of Cukor's professional, if not always disciplined, approach and his intense concentration as he examined old movies, no detail of which escaped his purely technical eye. Cukor fired off instructions to left and right in a stream of bad language and badinage. He began talking before entering a room and seldom completed a sentence. 'I can't think how I will feel about George at the end of it all,'[2] wrote Cecil to Eileen with some foreboding.

Alarmed by Cukor, Cecil was impressed by Alan Jay Lerner, who suddenly materialized with a completed film-script. The three men lunched by Cukor's pool and 'sparks of brilliance' emerged from Lerner amidst endless digressions. 'Alan is a real man of the theatre,' noted Cecil. 'He has gags and laughs galore. We seem to trigger him off and he enjoys our help after working in solitary confinement.'[3] Out of such meetings came the inspired moments of the film. Cecil's heart 'jumped with delight'[4] when Lerner thought of the idea of opening with a flower sequence. He devised the Ascot sequence in which the brims of ladies' hats narrowly miss each other, two identically dressed ladies confront each other with disgust, and champagne glasses pass over heads in imminent danger of spilling.

Cecil's first job was to design the sets and costumes and oversee their creation. He established himself in an office at Warner Bros, decorated with certain items to impress any visitors – his invitation to Princess Alexandra's wedding (which to his chagrin he would miss), a photograph of himself with Jackie Kennedy, one of his photographs of the Queen, and some of Garbo. He worked closely on the sets with the art director, Gene Allen, who happened to be an ex-policeman. The sets were derived from Cecil's past. Professor Higgins's house was based on the Wimpole Street rooms of Cecil's doctor, Dr Gottfried, to which he added Charles de Beistegui's spiral staircase from Groussay. The end result with its Cole wallpaper was an interesting construction of bad architecture with endless nooks and crannies. It was so realistic that whenever Cecil saw it he felt 'I am going any minute to have an injection.'[5] Cecil made the Covent Garden sets look like a Gustave Doré engraving. He sent for photos of the racing tent he had designed for the film *Anna Karenina* and the marquee he had decorated for Lady Lucinda Lambton's ball in 1959. These inspired him for the Ascot scene, which he created as a pastiche. It is also possible that he recalled the white wickerwork of the presentation stand when the debutantes paraded before Edward VIII in the garden at Buckingham Palace in 1936. Cecil remembered a rock-like grotto from his Korda work which found its way into Mrs Higgins's winter garden. At all times he kept a close eye on the work in progress, because he was horrified by the sets for other Warner Bros films. It gave him 'an insight into the Himalayan mountains of bad taste and artificiality that we have to combat'.[6] He was also very disappointed that there were to be no location shots in London, partly because it meant he could not go home, but also because he thought this American film would compete badly with the realistic films now being made by the Italians and Russians. When built, the sets were enormous. The 'Street where you live' scene was at least as big as Wimpole Street, while Ascot, a curiously cheap construction of linen, painted wood, and yards of plastic carpet, seemed to stretch to eternity.

From the very start Cecil was deeply in awe of the research department and the work of the set-painters and costume-makers. Lesley Blanch recalled Cecil's delight at the way they painted stained glass onto windows. One day he exclaimed: 'Do you realize they've got a whole room full of buttons and button-holes?'[7] For the costumes Cecil spent hours delving deep into old-fashioned periodicals and visiting the Los Angeles Museum. He was thrilled to discover he could evolve new styles simply by reversing dresses and using the back as the front. 'It really works,'[8] he wrote to Diana Vreeland. Diana Cooper sent him descriptions of what her mother wore at Ascot before the First World War and drew him some small sketches. Aubrey Ensor, his Heath Mount schoolmaster, sent him postcards of early actresses. Cecil conjured up visions of Julia James and Forzane. He sent for a photo of Baba's coming-out dress (a copy of a Poiret). While Cecil ordered embroidery 'recklessly, regardless of expense',[9] one woman in the wardrobe department bought a collection of wholesale dresses and converted them into 1913 versions. Another woman found a huge carton that had not been opened for thirty years. This yielded a treasure-trove of 1910 materials, straw, odd flowers and other items they could never have dreamed up. The work of making the different outfits was in professional hands. Cecil noted:

> Some of the dresses are such exact realizations of my drawings that it is quite a shock. So many of the materials remind me of adolescence. I can almost smell the thrill of watching grown-up life at a distance.[10]

When Cukor saw the costumes for the first time, the normally very critical director was enraptured. Cecil felt a mixture of relief, joy and pride. Tears welled in his eyes. Work continued and Cecil converted upturned buckets, black straw hats and chauffeur's caps into extraordinary Ascot visions. Audrey Hepburn's Ascot hat was a masterpiece of architectural construction. Cecil had to make endless last-minute changes. A pink dress looked garish on its own, but perfect under grey chiffon. One of the girls said to Cecil: 'What does it feel like, Mr Beaton, always to be right?'[11]

Cecil thought very carefully about each of the stars he dressed. Cukor wanted Audrey Hepburn to look clean, slightly comic, but not chic (which was a great problem). He emphasized that at Ascot she should be slightly overpowered, so Cecil at once turned to Gaby Deslys for inspiration. Audrey's ball-gown, copied from one in the Los Angeles Museum, reminded him of Lily Elsie and the Snow Princess: 'It is quite as beautiful as snow and ice on trees in Switzerland.'[12] He had hoped that Isabel Jeans might be chosen for Mrs Higgins, but Gladys Cooper was signed. She arrived in Hollywood full of professional vitality, if erratic in everyday life, 'forging ahead, interested in every new aspect of her profession'.[13] Cecil decided to dress her like the actress Lillah McCarthy, rather pre-Raphaelite and arty with long necklaces and buns over her ears. She insisted on wearing a wig. Her ball-dress had to be changed and so Cecil gave the black-beaded creation to the Ambassadress, Lily Kemble-Cooper, a friend of Cukor's. Isobel Elsom was chosen as Mrs Eynsford-Hill. She was a childhood heroine of Cecil's, and he feared he would be confronted with a wreck. Instead he found 'a very fat and distinguished woman'[14] sitting bolt upright, holding a stick.* Cecil wrote:

> Suddenly confronted with this beautiful nose and line of chin I remembered holidays at Arley and Sheringham when I was ravished by her profile thrust towards a wad of hydrangeas in a Rita Martin photograph.[15]

Cecil never established much rapport with her, but in memory of those early days he resolved: 'I must work on this monster to make it look its best.'[16] For her Covent Garden appearance he dressed her as Oggie Lynn, but when she altered her hairstyle Cecil was enraged. Mona Washbourne, as Mrs Pearce, was given the hairstyle of Michael Duff's old nanny. Stanley Holloway was impressed by Cecil's idea that his wedding button-hole should be 'outrageously outsize' in an 'unspeakably vulgar' glass stem 'to set quite brilliantly the somewhat brassy, ostentatious vulgarity of the whole conception of Doolittle's marriage'.[17]

Rex Harrison's clothes were another problem. 'He had been difficult before,' wrote Cecil. 'This time he might well be worse. Six years later his nerves are worse.'[18] Cecil ordered seven suits from Sullivan and Williams in London and they were so delighted with the commission that Cecil received a free suit for himself. By ordering shirts and ties from Washington Tremlett, Cecil looked forward to further handouts. The suits were cleared through customs and Cecil presented a hat similar to that in the play but with a brim wider by half an inch. Fortunately Harrison liked his first suit, adored his evening cape and conceded that the new hat was an improvement. He went so far as to thank Cecil and the wardrobe for their work. Later Cecil had to wrestle with problems such as where to put the parting in Harrison's hairpiece, whether he should wear a double-breasted waistcoat (which made him look fat) and how to keep him from getting too sunburnt.

Designing the clothes was one problem, finding suitable extras was another. Cecil listed types that might appear at the Embassy ball, under headings such as Ava Waverleys and Mrs Cushings. George Cukor was tough:

> I don't want anyone covered with lipstick saying: 'I've got no make-up on.' Kick their ass out. They must look naked, scrubbed. Take everything off them. If they've got false teeth, take their false teeth out.[19]

In due course it fell to Cecil to inspect the candidates. He found them 'unbelievably boring and anonymous'. Cecil felt dreadful as he rejected them one by one. Out of the first hundred he chose only ten women and eight men. The extras presented problems new to Cecil. They were either too pretty or too exaggerated. Some were favourites of key people on the set. They pleaded, promised, confided, cajoled and sometimes resorted to hys-

---

* Isobel Elsom had permanently damaged her leg in a bad motor accident.

teria. A girl who had set her heart on a blue dress burst out sobbing when
it went to another. When Cecil relented, she sobbed again. Another girl
promised she could dispose of 10 lbs in no time. Cecil was angry that protruding stomachs and the intersections of suspenders threatened the fine
lines of his creations. He became a familiar figure amongst a lot of naked
girls (some wearing nothing but an Ascot hat) and he exclaimed: 'Will you
cover yourself up. I want to look at your face.'[20] In the final selection Cecil
had to pass down the line of girls four times to satisfy the Guild rules. By
this time his heart was hardened to pleading or insolent looks. The em-
barrassingly un-English extras were the greatest disappointment of the film.
The aggressively healthy beach-girl faces looked most inelegant under Cecil's
ravishing hats.

Cecil also had a scheme to try to persuade the Austrian singer, Fritzi
Massary, to play the Queen of Transylvania. The old star asked a fee of
$20,000 and refused to drop below $10,000, so an interesting opportunity
was lost. The part finally went to Bina Rothschild,* whose height put her in
good stead. Cecil dressed her in Parma violet embroidered with silver bangles
and $1,000-worth of specially designed jewellery. She wore a three-winged
head-dress rather than a tiara.

Cecil's work was exacting. Each morning he braved the Freeway in his
car, 'a Kafka-esque nightmare',[21] after his morning swim rescuing drowning
ladybirds at the Hotel Bel-Air, where he lived. In the evenings he enjoyed
his dinners with Christopher Isherwood and Don Bachardy and went sometimes to Cathleen Nesbitt and Gladys Cooper, and often to Edie Goetz, where
after dinner the lights were dimmed, a screen came down in front of the
Impressionists and a theme song was relayed before the latest film was
shown. At weekends he was delighted to paint Betsy Bloomingdale to earn
an extra $1,500, or to photograph Cyd Charisse or Merle Oberon. He was
grateful when Merle's masseur arrived to end the session because 'Merle is
almost a nymphomaniac. She makes love because she likes it, because of
the money, she is as promiscuous as a man enjoying a quick one behind
the door.'[22] In order to ensure maximum flattery, he ordered the pictures
printed 'out of focus for a third of the exposure during enlargement'[23]
(perhaps revealing more technical knowledge than normally he admitted).

Otherwise Hollywood social life was a nightmare of vulgarity. In March
Cecil had to attend a luncheon at which Jack Warner, President of Warner
Bros, made a speech welcoming visiting French dignitaries. He proposed the
health of the American President and not the French one and then got all
the names wrong. Hervé Alphand became 'Harvey Allfong', the Baronne de
Cabrol 'Baroness Cabbrule', and Gérald Van der Kemp 'Mr Vann dercumph
of Versailles gardens'. The speech was peppered with inconsequential public

*Baroness Bina Rothschild, wife of Eric Goldsmid-Rothschild (one-time ally of Garbo). Born
Henckel-von-Donnersmarck. Lived at Mandeville Canyon, Hollywood, since the war.

relations rubbish and bad quips: 'Nobody's invented an onion that makes you laugh instead of cry, but I'm trying.'[24]

The dinners were even worse, the meal often served at ten o'clock after two and a half hours of drinking. On one evening a retired footballer was asked, when in the presence of the painter he lived with, 'Do you love her?', and replied brazenly: 'Well, I fuck her.'[25] There was a dinner for a man who staved off old age by pinching girls' bottoms. His son honoured his birthday with an ice-cream in the shape of a woman's breast with a cherry as a nipple. There were jokes that the old lecher might sponsor Gilbert and Sullivan in Los Angeles so that someone could serenade him with 'Tit Willow'. One guest said in front of his elegant wife: 'Well now I'm going home to fuck my cook',[26] and Cecil was able to shock the party by enquiring the colour and the sex of the cook. Joan Collins entertained Cecil in her 'vulgar *nouveau riche* house' and he thought: 'She is nice enough in spite of her pretensions. At the end of the evening she said: "I'm carrying on a romance and it takes all my time."' She then played a record of the lover reciting a poem to music. 'Naturally nobody wanted to listen and the evening, always formless and jellified, ended in a mess.'[27]

On the other hand Lesley Blanch was a godsend. Cecil had known her since the late 1940s and she thought: 'There was more to Cecil than people realized. They saw the tinsel image and they looked no further.'[28] Cecil used to ring her before these dinners:

'Are you getting dressed?'
'Yes.'
'Isn't it awful?'
'There'll be good grub.'
'It's not enough.'
'The women will wear Balenciagas.'
'They've no idea how to put them on.'[29]

If Cecil had not had the adventure of meeting and falling in love with a young American called Kin in San Francisco in March, his life in Hollywood would have been intolerable.*

One weekend he escaped to New York, commissioned by Jane Englehard to photograph her for $2,000 plus expenses. Garbo refused his call and he noted that she 'would not be hearing from me then for another year'.[30] He dined with Diana Vreeland, now editor-in-chief of *Vogue*, and, accompanied by Truman, visited a night-club to hear 'a new singer, Barbra Streisand, a brilliant young Jewess who looks like Cleopatra with a good voice and a great talent'.†[31]

---

* See Chapter 34.

† On 7 October 1963 Cecil expended two reels of film on her in five minutes and ushered her to the door: 'I had got what I wanted: this strange Cleopatra-like profile with bold flow from forehead to nose.'

On 18 May Audrey Hepburn arrived in Hollywood and Cecil at once described her as 'an angel of goodness'. He worried that she was terribly thin, 'but her mouth, her smile, her teeth are enchanting, the expression of her eyes adorable and her whole quality overcomes any deviations from the norm of beauty. She is a phenomenon.'[32]

Cecil had first met Audrey in July 1953 and hailed her as 'a new type of film star'.[33] Now Cecil had the chance to learn more about her from her mother who was also in Hollywood. She told Cecil that Audrey lived on her nerves, but was never any trouble: 'She just floats through life and learns everything herself.'[34] The Hepburns had been trapped in Holland during the war and afterwards were rationed to a 1s 4d-worth of meat per head. They had almost starved in their London flat in South Audley Street, which explained why Audrey was so thin. Audrey had practised ballet and appeared at schools and in cabaret and was later in the chorus of *High Buttoned Shoes*. At one point she gave as many as twenty-eight performances a week.

On 29 May Audrey came to see Cecil's work for the first time. She recalled:

> The picture shows the result of it and the photographs and things like that but the *work* that went into the work was such art, because I remember the first time I went to the studio to see all the workrooms – they're miles long and wide and I'll never forget the sight of the enormous laboratory with hundreds of women sewing and doing and the beauty of the costumes which were on stands, of embroidery being done, of masses of beautiful aigrettes and feathers and velvets and ribbons, and violets, which had been made I don't know where.
>
> It was so extraordinary. That was worth the movie just to see that.[35]

To Cecil she exclaimed: 'I don't want to play Liza. She doesn't have enough pretty clothes. I want to parade in all of these.'[36] This she proceeded to do, giving new life to each of Cecil's creations in turn to gasps of delight from the wardrobe and the thrill of Cecil himself:

> She is the darling of the best Parisian designers and is accustomed only to the best and here she was giving me the highest honours, filling my cup to overflowing with her words of praise.[37]

Enthusiasm spread throughout the whole studio and Jack Warner ordained that Audrey could spend two days being photographed in the extras' clothes. The sessions took place on 5 and 6 June. Audrey let Cecil come into the make-up department and said: 'You see I have no eyes.'[38] Cecil thought this quite a discovery. She had become 'a star, a beauty by putting black around her eyes'.[39] Hard work now began in earnest and it was tiring but Audrey never showed the slightest sign of impatience. Cecil had never taken so many pictures in one day and thanks to the studio he was able to see the results before they went home. They were fine, despite the assistant giving him film for daylight instead of artificial light. On the second day the results pleased him more. There were 350 exposures in all. Audrey saw them and wrote to Cecil:

Dearest C.B.

Ever since I can remember I have always so badly wanted to be beautiful. Looking at those photographs last night I saw that, for a short time at least, I am, all because of you ♡ Audrey.[40]

Cecil wrote to Eileen that the clothes would never be worn with the same style again: 'The results are straightforward fashion. But she looks marvellous and they should make a splash in the magazines.'[41] The next excitement came ten days later when Audrey wore her Ascot costume for the first time. Seeing it, Cecil 'yelled with laughter', a reaction that surprised him, but he was pleased that the dress was 'funny, elegant and just right for the scene'.[42]

Meanwhile Cecil was becoming increasingly hostile to George Cukor. In the early days he had gone to parties that Cukor gave, but was sickened by the obscene language amongst the Impressionist paintings, and a scene when 'a fair young Adonis massaged the back of George's shoulders so violently that his grey-haired-covered breasts wobbled like jellies'.[43] The next day he discussed Cukor's paradoxes with Don Bachardy: his love–hate relationship with Britain, with homosexuals and with intellectuals. Cecil was ready to take offence. He was slighted when, on a particularly busy day, Cukor passed over one of his favourite designs without comment. It was worse when there occurred another discussion about going to London. Rex Harrison and Alan Lerner wanted Cecil to go with them, but Cukor said: 'No, Cecil can't be spared from here.'[44] It now dawned on Cecil that Cukor had the power to prolong his Hollywood exile, and this he deeply resented.

Cecil was tired, and admitted in a letter to Eileen that he was 'in a bad mood due to exhaustion'.[45] As usual he had added to his normal responsibilities at the studio. Extra photography, and painting the principal stars in oils, would earn him an additional $8,000 and he was permitted to keep all his original drawings for later use. He photographed every aspect of every set and there exist files of photographs in black and white of stars and extras in various costumes. At the same time Cecil was surreptitiously keeping a lengthy diary out of which he created his book, *Cecil Beaton's Fair Lady*; he wrote a well-paid piece about the film for *Ladies Home Journal*; he led a full social life and at weekends he usually went to San Francisco.

Cecil complained to his agent that he was being used by Cukor 'like an IBM machine'.[46] 'Swifty' Lazar gave him a bracing talk, reminding him of his obligations:

I'm sorry you don't feel more in accord with George, but perhaps you're just overwhelmed with work and you should certainly take a week off – or ten days when you feel you must.[47]

Cukor told Cecil that he had no idea he was unhappy, but it was too late. The power that Cukor could wield brought the same reaction from Cecil as he had felt for Irene Selznick and others. The homosexual side of both men was in competition and their respective vanities were at stake. Cecil had not helped by mentioning his friend in San Francisco. Cecil craved for an English summer 'savouring the smells of grass, mown grass, hay, and being conscious of every nuance of twilight turning into evening and evening into night'.[48] He was also missing a particularly scandalous summer of vice in high places, the Argyll divorce,* soon eclipsed by the Profumo affair, details of which were relayed to Cecil by well-informed friends.

At the end of June Audrey appeared on the set without mascara. She looked young and appealing and Cecil felt he had earned his salary. The screen tests proved the effect and Audrey said she would wear no black mascara in future. 'This will be quite a revolution,' wrote Cecil, 'and the end of all those black-eyed zombies.'[49] Cecil was just about to photograph Audrey when Cukor arrived and sent a message over that Cecil must stop holding up the expensive proceedings. Both men lost their tempers.

Cukor and Cecil fumed quietly for nearly three weeks. Then on 17 July matters came to a head. Cecil was again on the set and had adjusted a ribbon in Audrey's hair. He took a few photographs between filming. Suddenly Max Bercutt, the director of publicity, came over and took Cecil by the arm. Nervously he told Cecil that Cukor did not want him taking photographs on the set. It made him nervous. Cecil saw red:

> Did George resent the still man taking the photographs for Wardrobe and Hairdressing? No. Then why did he resent my taking them of the 'effigy' that by the sweat of hours' work and a lifetime of experience I had been able to create. It was obvious that in some way that he may not know about he resents my presence.[50]

Cecil shouted at Bercutt in 'white hot fury'. He complained to Audrey, who said: 'Everyone's nerves are explosive.' All afternoon he smouldered and when Jack Warner asked him how he was at a meeting with Cukor and others, Cecil barked: 'Oh! It's been a bad day for me.'[51] Steve Trilling, Warner's number two man, tried to appease Cecil, but in vain: 'I was in a mood to do anything desperate even to throwing up the whole job.'[52] Instead he drove back to his hotel and plunged himself and his wrath into the swimming pool.

The next day Cecil composed a bitter letter, complaining about Cukor, but

---

* At Drury Lane one line in the stage version of *My Fair Lady* now raised an unintentional laugh: 'You've got to learn to behave like a duchess' [Higgins to Eliza, Act One, Scene 3].

'Swifty' Lazar intervened to prevent it being sent, saying that it would mean the departure of one or other and Cecil was the more dispensable. The protagonists met at one of Edie Goetz's dinners and she telephoned to pacify Cecil. He took in her words and explained his position to Eileen:

> I have the feeling he feels a deep resentment of me. If someone laughs at a joke I make he looks very sore, if I get a bit of extra praise he doesn't seem pleased. In a curious way I don't think he even realizes I think he's really jealous of me. It all comes from his deep sense of insecurity. This is his biggest job since *Gone With the Wind*, and he's very on edge.... The important thing is I should feel compassion for George. I really do. He is fundamentally a good person. But I can't feel this if I am *too* exasperated and the only way not to be too exasperated is to see less of him. I am going to stop our lunching together and I feel this will hurt him to begin with but I'm sure it'll be better in the long run.[53]

A new week began with Cukor bumping into a chair in Cecil's office. 'Oh, so you've barred the way, have you?' he quipped.

Shooting, as with the grouse season, was set for 12 August. Before that Cecil had endless problems to resolve. He found that black and white often became green and yellow on celluloid. Some clothes had to be dyed as much as seven times. Audrey's hairstyles were difficult, while Rex Harrison lost his temper during toupé tests. There were good moments too. Audrey appeared looking 'unbelievably delicious in her pale pastel mauve confection'.[54] This outfit, Cecil's most romantic for the film, was so beautiful that even the rugged Joe Hiatt, the man in charge of the wardrobe, telephoned to say: 'You know I'm generally taken by how much a dress costs. This time I'm hypnotized by the dress. It's great.'[55] Stanley Holloway, telephoning Cecil who had succumbed to a sore throat, said of Audrey: 'It is remarkable that this scraggy little girl has a green face and then on the screen looks like a million dollars.'[56]

Wilfrid Hyde White arrived, fresh from seeing his horse come second at Goodwood. Hyde White's attitude was refreshingly casual. When sprayed with rain, he complained: 'Isn't that enough? After all this is only another film!'[57] Jeremy Brett flew in. Cukor had chosen him for Freddy as soon as he discovered they would have to buy him out of his Chichester Festival contract for £2,000. André Previn, looking like 'an ant eater', was quietly dealing with all the musical problems. Rex Harrison had said: 'Why, the musicians will have to follow me. They are my servants.'[58] As Cecil wrote to Eileen: 'Audrey is just as marvellous as he [Rex] is awful!'[59] And as the full cast gathered, Cecil only longed to escape. 'I dare say I'd bellyache about much if I were at home,' Cecil wrote to Hal Burton, 'but at any rate there there'd be a stimulus of competition, wit and a challenge that I don't find here.'[60]

The Cukor atmosphere was no better, nor was it helped when Cukor asked Cecil to supervise the studio's still photographer, while he had to stoop to ask permission to take his own pictures. Max Bercutt and Mort Lichter, of the publicity department, came to see Cecil to butter him up and encourage him to be more co-operative 'I was very sorry for myself,' wrote Cecil. 'Innocence had been badly treated.'[61] But in no time Cecil was preparing to take surreptitious shots of the girls in the rainstorm. Cukor exploded and Bercutt rang to say they had nearly lost a director. 'I thought this was going to be my dream,' he said, 'having you on this picture. So many beautiful photographs, but it's all gone wrong somewhere.'[62] Facing the fact that he might be sacked, Cecil was overcome by contrition. He telephoned Cukor to apologize. Cukor said he had no idea why Cecil was so testy. He begged him not to get in the way of the production nor to take pictures in 'these first anxious days'.[63]

When filming began, Cecil was observed wandering among the heaps of vegetables 'easily distinguishable under a sloppy, wide-brimmed straw hat'.[64] Chaos abounded as a lamp fell on a hackney carriage and Audrey's coat was soaked by studio rain. A new coat was created in five hours. Then Cecil complained to the publicity department that Gene Allen had been credited with the décor. They took offence. Cecil reported to Eileen: 'I'm altogether slightly on the warpath.'[65]

A retake was ordered when Rex Harrison said 'French letters' instead of 'French lessons'. He commented: 'That is a different sort of play!'[66] Audrey hated the pea-shelling scenes as she had to eat so many raw peas (and was of course given peas for dinner at home). The steam got into her eyes in the bathroom scene and she frowned all day, and when Higgins put marbles in her mouth, she ruined several takes by laughing. Looking at the rushes Cecil was disappointed that the lighting compared so badly to the work done in Italian films. There was always a spotlight on Audrey. To Eileen he wrote:

> But Rex is surprisingly good. He has learnt how to project on the screen. Audrey is surprisingly cockney sparrow, tough and really dirty, and W. Hyde W. is an inspiration.[67]

Cecil was in a temper again when he saw that the wrong hanging baskets had crept into the Ascot scene, reminding him of window-dressing at Saks. They were removed on Cukor's instructions. Cukor even suggested that Cecil should take a snapshot. Cecil was cheered up by a visit from Givenchy, who habitually dressed Audrey: '*Quel travail!* It's like half a dozen collections!'[68] On 10 October came the excitement of the Ascot scene. One hundred and fifty women and 100 men were steered onto the set, unable to sit down because their costumes were so tight. Gladys Cooper gave new zest to the role of Mrs Higgins, while Cecil prowled about wearing a notice announcing: 'Laryngitis – Can't speak.' A rare communication came from

Cukor's office: 'Mr Cukor sends you his message that the effect was "beautiful", "breath-taking", "thrilling".'[69]

The next day Edie Goetz wrote:

> I have just returned from the 'Ascot' scene at Warner's and I am literally in a daze. These costumes are without doubt the most breathtakingly beautiful, exquisite creations ever wrought by man. And as you are the man, I bow low in your direction.[70]

But it was too good to last. Filming was again on the Ascot set, and Cecil found Audrey resting between shots in her Ascot outfit. He asked her to pose and she agreed readily. David 'Buck' Hall, the assistant director, told them not to get in the way, so Cecil moved Audrey to the side amongst the trellis work. He took a roll of black and white. But Cukor had seen them and sent Hall over to say that Audrey must not be taken from the set, nor must she be tired while filming. Cecil felt dejected and, though Audrey tried to pacify him, he complained of his treatment to Max Bercutt and to Steve Trilling.

The weekend intervened, so on Monday Cecil arrived at the studios with some foreboding:

> I had at the back of my mind the possibilities that could eventualize if I went out to bring things to a head and was as impetuous as I would like to be by nature.[71]

Max Bercutt and Mort Lichter bearded Cecil in his office. There had been serious developments. Cukor had been so cross about the photographs that work had ceased for an hour on Friday. He had complained to Jack Warner and Steve Trilling, and they were worried about their $17 million investment and determined to pacify him at all costs. Cecil listened patiently:

> I felt very calm. This is the end of a beautiful association, and if George ever comes with some bogus wistful regret that I have withdrawn my friendship I will spit in his eye. It is just too bad that because of his love hatred of England, I should have fallen into his trap, and been victimized for so many of the lacunae that he is lacking. I suppose he is a deeply jealous person and, as such, he must suffer the torments of the damned. Long may he roast.[72]

'Swifty' Lazar breezed in to see Cecil. He did not discuss the matter but said: 'I'll get you out of here all right.'[73] The week passed by quietly. Cecil did his work promptly and efficiently. But he avoided the set and missed the Ascot tea-party scene, on which he had worked so hard. He was reduced to asking Wilfrid Hyde White whether it had looked all right. He counted the days till the end and convinced himself that he was Cukor's victim. However, the truth remains: Cecil had broken the rules.

Cecil was permitted to photograph the part of the Ascot scene when Eliza made her gaffe. Even now he sneaked some more pictures of Audrey, while she sat looking down diplomatically so that she could not be accused of posing. He also witnessed Bina Rothschild's arrival in the ballroom and thought how 'suited' Cukor would be 'to the rôle of Karparthy'.[74] Again he took photographs 'in extremely difficult and dangerous conditions'.[75]

Cecil's last duty was to paint the principals – Stanley Holloway, 'a very lovable person and in his way a real gent, whereas Rex H is the phoney',[76] Jeremy Brett, busy learning *Euripides* to overcome an even greater hatred of Hollywood than Cecil's, Wilfrid Hyde White, as unruffled as ever, Mona Washbourne, who asked him about Garbo and thought him unhappy, Audrey, looking tired now, and at the very last moment a suddenly co-operative Rex Harrison. Cecil's final days at the studio were made hectic by the arrival of the Brandolinis (involving late-night parties) and of Truman, who was permitted on the set despite Cukor's fears that he would repeat his *Sayonara* article. Now that part of the film was safely in the can, Cecil was aghast to find the Ascot set already torn down and burnt and the ballroom stripped of its décor. Truman observed some of Cecil's work and declared it done 'with the attitude of an artist'. He said: 'Don't do any more. You've earned your money.'[77] On a brief visit Cecil paid to New York, Margaret Case had begged him to make it up with Cukor. This theme was now echoed by David O. Selznick, and by Truman, who had swiftly gathered the details of the row from a variety of different quarters. Truman told Cecil that a reconciliation would be popular on all sides. Cecil therefore penned the following not wholly generous note:

Dear George
My contract expires next Friday. I am hoping that the Mrs Higgins set will be finished in a very few days. Is there anything else you would like me to do, as I am quite anxious to get back to where I belong particularly in view of the unhappiness of the last weeks?

I would like to thank you for all the lunches and entertainment at your house and for the many kindnesses you showed me until things went wrong between us. I would also like to say how much I regret the present situation and how pleasant it would be to leave here with the feeling that our friendship was not permanently damaged.
    Yours C.[78]

The following Tuesday evening Cukor rang up:

This is George. I got your letter and I think as you haven't got anything else to do it would be all right for you to – er – there's nothing more, is there? No more costumes. No more sets, and I too am sorry, am baffled. I just don't understand and I have regard and like you I hope [*and then a wild laugh*] that all will be as before when we meet on another plane.[79]

With this, Cukor hung up, leaving Cecil feeling he had not been given a very satisfactory absolution.

The last day came and Cecil lunched with the publicity department, a lunch overshadowed by the shock of Kennedy's assassination: 'One's blood turned to a pale blue liquid ... one could only grieve for Jackie.'[80] There were emotional farewells and words of gratitude from the wardrobe department, and then Cecil summoned the courage to bid farewell to Cukor:

> I went up to George, boldly, to say 'I've come to say good-bye and to say good luck'. George looked embarrassed but hard. Not for one moment did he thaw. 'Yes. Why – er – good luck to you' was all he said. Then he slipped out of the picture.[81]

Audrey was dressed in apricot and the Dolly Varden hat, looking sweet and sympathetic, about to film her return to Covent Garden. Cecil crossed the piazza of St Paul's to say good-bye. She was wrapped in a Shetland shawl and looked sad that Cecil was leaving in such an unhappy frame of mind. Cecil flew back home via New York, where he saw on television the dramatic shooting of Kennedy's assassin by Jack Ruby. On 28 November he was at home in his 'oasis of luxury and civilization'.[82]

The film of *My Fair Lady* had a considerable success. In 1979 Bill Paley wrote with pride that it had by then earned CBS more than $33 million.[83] However, the row with Cukor did not end there. Just after Christmas Hedda Hopper quoted Cukor saying of Cecil:

> He doesn't know how to work in a studio. He imagines he's an island to himself. He bored me to death with all that high falutin' finagling. The wardrobe people liked him very much, but he's an amateur when it comes to movie making. He was taking pictures of the stars when we needed them for scenes. Even wanted Audrey Hepburn to pose for him on Saturday. She's very polite, but Mel Ferrer put his foot down and said: 'She's worked day and night and has to rest.' I think Beaton broke his shovel with her.[84]

Then Cukor tried to prevent Cecil publishing photographs taken on the set, but Jack Warner intervened and gave him *carte blanche*. There was an easing from 'non-speaks' to 'mutual distrust' when Cecil and Cukor met in Hollywood in connexion with the opening of the film there. Cecil commented: 'If only some clever person had been able to arrange an understanding between us of the difficulties at the outset, how different the whole atmosphere would have been during the making of the picture!'[85]

In 1972 Cukor had a dig about the execution of Cecil's sets in conversation with Gavin Lambert:

> Beaton's a man of great taste and knowledge and an expert on the Edwardian period. However, his sets were technically very difficult to create, and Gene Allen certainly did the lion's share of the practical work, as well as a lot of designing. I think it would be fair to say that Gene executed the sets and made a very important contribution to the conception of them.[86]

Unfortunately in a BBC interview in 1973 with Barry Norman (*Film '73*), when asked to expand on his row with Cecil, Cukor replied:

> No. No. It's a boring subject. I'm sure he's bored with it and so am I. No, no. Except he did pick my pockets, and he attempted to strangle me (LAUGHS) and he's a forger – and no, no, we just didn't get along very well and I was right.[87]

Encouraged by Alastair Forbes (who described himself as 'a journalist mindful of the pitfalls of libel and slander')[88] Cecil sued the BBC for libel. As for Cukor – until the day he died, in the words of Irene Selznick: 'Cukor went white at the mention of Cecil's name!'[89]

As for the film itself, released in New York in October 1964 ('Everyone wildly enthusiastic about my work')[90] and in London in January 1965 (three days before Churchill's death), it was an immediate and dazzling popular success. Cecil, Alan Jay Lerner and others were a bit disappointed. Lerner wrote: 'There's no doubt in my mind it would have been a far better film had it been an Arthur Freed production.'[91]

Cecil deeply resented any anachronisms that crept in while his back was turned or after he had left. The most serious of these was the modern watering-can that Eliza holds in Mrs Higgins's winter garden and the fact that the horses at Ascot raced from right to left instead of vice versa.

Cecil was basically 'touched' when he saw it, grateful 'that not more damage had been done in my absence, struck anew by the ugliness of the girls wearing the Ascot clothes and a lack of experiment in the photography. It will make 1,000,000,000s of dollars but Cukor's direction not good.'[92] He thought Stanley Holloway's scene less effective than on stage. He regretted that for commercial reasons the film had been finished in a rush.

Alastair Forbes thought that Cecil's slides of the costumes were so exciting that the film could never match them. Alistair Cooke wrote of the impossibility of reviewing such a film: 'You cannot criticize the Changing of the Guard or the Beatles; you either stay and worship or sneer and decamp.'[93] Nevertheless he praised 'the genius of Cecil Beaton, who must have lain awake for years concocting an Edwardian dream that never was on land or sea but is now on view at Broadway's Criterion Theatre'.[94]

Cecil won two Oscars (for 'color costume design' and 'color art direction'). He was not at the ceremony in Hollywood, but Audrey Hepburn was, though because she did not sing, she was not even nominated. Her letter to Cecil is therefore all the more touching:

Darling C.B.,
Just to say how happy happy happy happy I am that you received your Oscar. I wish you could have heard the applause.
All my love
Audrey xxx[95]

34

Kin

*Kin is a godsend. I am so lucky that this should happen
to me.*

Cecil's diary, 15 June 1963

*Everything that has happened to you, Cukor, the film, the
year out here, nothing matters so much as the miracle of
your having met Kin. He is so exceptional and such a
rare person.*

Christopher Isherwood to Cecil, 25 July 1963

Cecil's meeting with Kin was to be his salvation during his *My Fair Lady*
year. Cecil almost missed his flight to San Francisco on the weekend of 23
March 1963. He was glad to escape into the rich world of his friend Whitney
Warren, of whom Cecil wrote: 'He knows his mind even if it is a small one.'[1]

Cecil had formed no lasting attachments over the years. His approach to
sex was somewhat cautious, especially in England, where he had seen
friends fall foul of the law. In America he was more adventurous, but even
so, sex was often an item to be fitted into a crowded day. Occasionally when
working in New York he would receive a young man in his room, sent to
him by a friend. Usually his visitor had departed within twenty minutes.

On the evening of Saturday 24 March Cecil went out on the town in San
Francisco:

> We went to louche bars. At one called the Toolbox the decorations were
> of men in black mackintoshes with tin hats, and on the walls still lives
> of parts of motorbicycles. The atmosphere was quite frighteningly tough
> until one realized that the jeans and leather jackets were in many cases
> a fancy dress. Among these thugs and faggots one tall Scandinavian boy
> struck me as being particularly sensitive and gentle. He had the most
> sweet smile and eventually we talked with one another.[2]

Aged nearly twenty-nine, the 'boy' was exactly half Cecil's age. He had
smiled at Cecil in a friendly way but when a friend they both knew came

over to offer Kin a drink and an introduction, he declined politely saying that he had come to California to avoid 'such coteries'. 'But', he said, 'if he wants to talk to me I'll be standing right here.'[3] Cecil walked over and they talked until the bar closed. He refused to go home with Cecil but offered him a lift. On the way he suddenly wheeled the car round abruptly, braked and said: 'This is where I live. Come up.'[4] Unaccountably he had changed his mind.

Cecil wrote:

> I discovered by baffling degrees that he was an art historian, working for his degree, studying and lecturing at Berkeley University. A chain of coincidences revealed that he had studied Denham Fouts (as seen by Chris I.) and had cut up the same Picasso book that I had desecrated to hang on the walls of his lavatory. His apartment had dried grasses on the window-sill and eight daffodils were very charming in a black pot. There was everywhere evidence of little money but pure taste. This person turned out to be someone of the utmost simplicity and honesty and intellectual integrity. He presented a tremendous challenge and although essentially a difficult character, lone, solitary and seeing too far he inspired me to the sort of gentle emotion that I have not felt for a long time. This adventure had certainly made my trip worthwhile.[5]

Kin was a six-foot-four Californian, born in 1934, a self-exile from the East Coast. As a child he had always been on the move, always a newcomer. After graduating at Princeton University he had fenced in the Olympic Games in Australia in 1956. On the way home he made what was intended to be a brief stop to see San Francisco but never got on the plane again. After undertaking graduate work at the University of California at Berkeley, he took a variety of jobs – working in the office of a small construction company, representing a manufacturer of prefabricated industrial buildings and working in an insurance firm. While undergoing psychiatric therapy he discovered he wanted to teach in college, so returned forthwith to university to obtain another degree.

Back in Hollywood, Cecil's spirits soared when he received a letter from Kin. For two days he tried to telephone San Francisco without success. When he got through they enjoyed gentle badinage. Kin spoke of the library where he studied and Cecil said, 'Oh! but you have the wisdom of the world at your elbow', to which Kin replied: 'Not the wisdom. Just the facts.' Cecil warned himself: 'A gay, agreeable friendship is possible. Don't let it get out of hand.'[6]

Thereafter, whenever possible, Cecil slipped away to San Francisco or Kin came down to the Bel-Air, and they went on many mutually enjoyed adventures. The nature of their first meeting in the Toolbox gave a *frisson* to the relationship, which would certainly have been lacking if they had met socially. In retrospect Cecil believed it had been an uneasy beginning. There were incidents to which he was sensitive: a time when Kin wanted to pick up the bill, when Cecil was recognized by a boy who asked if he could take his photograph, the stares of fellow diners at a '6ft 4 Adonis with someone who is old enough but not the sort of person to be his grandfather'.[7]

The second time he saw Kin he found him 'even more golden and pure than I had thought'.[8] Both his youthful enthusiasm for life and his intellectual leanings appealed to Cecil, particularly the latter which had already drawn him into taxing discussions with Waldemar Hansen and others. Cecil hoped Kin would help him become 'a little less fatuous and flaccid'.[9] When Christopher Isherwood met Kin he wrote: 'somehow I had expected someone more slender and angular – perhaps because I superimposed the image of Peter Watson.... Our conversation was mostly about you and Denny [Fouts] – what an exotic couple!'[10] Cecil and Kin always talked intently. Kin said: 'He never demeaned our relationship with gossip.'[11] Instead they talked of art criticism, while listening to Schubert. Kin's conversation was peppered with words like 'conditioning' and 'relating'. Cecil told him about Coward, Capote and Picasso, 'not trying to show off but feeling I could really inform him on these subjects'.[12]

In New York in May, Cecil showed some of his new friend's letters to Truman, whose considered verdict was: 'He is someone you can trust.'[13] Relaxing on an outing to Mount Diabolo, Cecil told Kin about his life, and thought that in comparison he had a stack of past experiences but had never 'sought the truth beneath the fact'.[14]

Kin offered Cecil the taste of a new outdoor life, the Yosemite valley 'where we camped out in a tent',[15] waking with the birds. Cecil genuinely enjoyed these expeditions even if, after a gruelling week at the studio, he found himself hiking four miles up and down a mountain path at Big Sur at night, following the narrow beam of an electric torch. Kin was impressed by Cecil's stamina and his willingness to undertake such a hike.

Some aspects Cecil did not enjoy, such as communal shaving in the men's room at the camp, but his admiration for Kin overcame all. Curiously many of the traditional traits in Cecil's character were now called into question. He had been sincerely sorry to have been recognized by the stranger 'because it robbed me of the privacy that our relationship has so far had. I wanted to be Kin's friend and break with all the ties that are so intricate and involved and often contradictory.'[16] He liked the absence of smalltalk in Kin, was pleased that he had never seen the play of *My Fair Lady*. He welcomed his talk dwelling solely on serious writers, artists and musicians: 'this freedom from dross is the most perfect antidote to all that I have to suffer in Hollywood'.[17]

One June morning in 1963 Kin had to leave Stockton Street early to conduct an ocean study course in Carmel. Cecil dozed, watching the naked Kin go about his packing. Then Cecil was alone:

I find the flat fascinating in his absence, the untidiness and dirt of his study is unbelievable, but everything has vitality. ... I came across Kin's paper comparing Vasari with some early art historian. It had been marked very good, a most perceptive piece of work, by his professor. It struck me, little that I saw of it, as being brilliant. He is brilliant. I looked at his Plato with the private markings in the margin and decided to borrow this. Then I enjoyed his schoolboy jokes pinned to a bulletin board, a pile of Health and Strength magazines and the cutting describing how a woman took a slug of whisky with cyanide as she realized bad luck was on her side and things had gone wrong for her for just too long. This gesture strikes Kin as being great and wonderful.[18]

In July Kin came to visit the studio, looking very young, 'a great hunk of collegiate good humour'.[19] Kin seemed impressed by the minute details on the set such as the bird droppings on the columns of St Paul's, Covent Garden. When he knew him better Cecil asked Kin if he had ever heard of him before they met. Kin had not. 'I felt this was the case and I was pleased,'[20] wrote Cecil, despite the fact that a considerable part of his life had been devoted to acquiring fame. In fact Kin had to ring a friend for information: 'I've just met Cecil Beaton. Who is Cecil Beaton? Have you ever heard of him?'[21] His friend had. Kin had not heard of Chanel either. 'No wonder I like him so much,'[22] noted Cecil. By August Cecil felt they had become relaxed friends and the period of discovery was over. Isherwood was firm with Cecil: 'Don't let your return to England be the end,'[23] he said. Cecil recalled camping out with Kin one night by a river in a wilderness area:

During the night I watched the moon swerve from left to right and at one moment the effect of its light on Kin's sleeping profile was extraordinarily beautiful. I slept well in the fresh, aromatic air and when he got up early to fish I turned over and slept heavily, dreaming of Freddie Ashton, Oggie Lynn, my mother, the Royal Family – all very interesting physiological situations so far removed from this charming Robinson Crusoe life.[24]

The next day Cecil again observed Kin:

Kin took his clothes off and the sight of him fishing and moving on the rocks was wonderfully beautiful. His body slightly sunburnt against the rocks, and every movement so athletic and pure. It was a rare sight and of all time.[25]

Kin continued to discourse on Donatello, Beethoven, Botticelli and Tintoretto. Sometimes his mood changed and his language became rough. 'I loved him in this mood,' wrote Cecil. 'It was dangerous, kept one on toe points.'[26] Physically too he could change from day to day. Cecil's photographs of him covered the spectrum. Kin could look boyish or tough or like a white negro. He could look gaunt and spiritual or fiercely athletic. He could even give a quizzical look and wry smile that evoked Peter Watson. Stephen Tennant, meeting Kin in England in 1964, described him as 'a great buffalo of a man'.[27] Later Cecil decided he was an astronaut. Eventually they had to broach the question of the future. Cecil hoped Kin would come to London. Kin discussed this frankly and openly: 'He said he thought I was an honourable man and would not let him down without a roof over his head.'[28]

Twenty years later Kin still described Cecil as 'the most honourable man I've ever met'. He continued:

He never sold himself out not even making concessions in his dress though in California his hats and neckscarves often attracted unfavourable attention. But the great scope of his appreciation enabled him to get the point of – and accommodate himself to – a variety of environments.

It was perhaps this quality that led to his being called superficial. Cecil minded the charge badly for when I took him somewhat to task on the subject Cecil said: 'That's what Peter and Greta said. I can't bear you thinking that too.' Later I changed my opinion. I now see that the opposite is true, for it was Cecil's genius to make his living by working constantly with superficiality without losing himself in it.[29]

Kin admired Cecil's incredible eye and artistic sense. When they saw Fellini's $8\frac{1}{2}$ Kin was 'dazzled and confused',[30] while Cecil knew at once that it was a great work. Kin also admired his extraordinary energy and how Cecil had made his way in life under his own steam. On the other hand he felt Cecil was not analytical and he was inept mechanically. He never learned how to close the door of Kin's Volkswagen and sometimes, to Kin's amazement, asked for help attaching lenses or changing films. Kin thought Cecil's development had been restricted by the middle-class values of his family, and said:

He sought every means to expand his life. He was repelled by the mundane. He knew what was a good investment of his time. He had to look at things eye to eye, but he enjoyed looking over his shoulder at the world of art and literature. He had a good sense of humour and though he could be wickedly witty he was never mean-spirited. And he was quick to enjoy a joke on himself such as when we ran out of money in some California back-water and were taken for dead-beats. He never took himself too seriously and what others saw as snobbery was only a firm refusal to conduct his life in a shoddy way. Once when a cook at Reddish had not done well with the evening meal I felt he was unduly irritated. 'There are only 365 suppers in a year,' explained Cecil [quoting Duff Cooper]. 'Why should I have a bad one?' He was right of course.[31]

Kin felt that Cecil had 'in the highest degree' the English virtue of finding and enjoying the best in people and situations. 'He was so wonderful. You couldn't help loving him,'[32] he said.

In October 1963 Kin laughed and said, 'I like you and we get along together.' Cecil wrote: 'Great sobs of gratitude welled up for all that he has given me.'[33] He also observed: 'The difference between my relationship with Peter and Kin is that the one could never have worked.'[34]

When Truman Capote visited Cecil just before he left Hollywood, he said: 'When all your film troubles are over, you'll think of this as one of the happiest periods in your whole life. And I think it is. You may not realize it, but all these trips you've taken are so romantic and you know you look better than I've seen you for years.'[35]

In due course the last weekend arrived. Kin and Cecil stayed in a bungalow at La Quinta at the foot of a boulder-strewn desert mountain. 'We did aquabatics and roared with fun and glee and I wondered if when in two weeks time I look back on such things I shall believe that this escapade in the palm-fringed desert oasis has taken place.'[36] Cecil soon became nostalgic and then pensive. He was upset when Kin left, but pleased that he telephoned the moment he arrived in San Francisco. Two days later a letter arrived from Kin that made him weep: 'It was one of the most intelligent, tender and utterly delightful letters that I've ever had.'[37]

Back in London Cecil was soon reintegrated into the life he had missed. He relished his return to Broadchalke, but looked at it immediately through Kin's eyes. Alan Tagg helped him make the effect less crowded, the grisaille paintings on the landing were replaced by drawings, the *haute école* screens in the hall were despatched to Sotheby's. Cecil now gauged his reactions by what the absent Kin might think. One day he wrote of himself: 'I was another person than the one Kin knows.'[38] He was by no means unhappy to relax and laugh with his old friends and he welcomed new experiences such as attending 'a young Beatnik party'[39] given by Lucy Lambton for the painter Michael Wishart. However, he entered a phase of preparation for the absorption of Kin into his English life. He knew that Kin loved Donatelllo and when staying with Michael Tree at Mereworth he found two long-searched-for rare and expensive volumes on that artist. Clearly he could not steal these books, so he swopped them for a series of devilish caricatures. He was delighted with this deal for two reasons: he could not have afforded to buy the books, and in his present mood he was happy to divest himself of work which Kin would have found discreditable. For Cecil and Kin's relationship was to be lived on a stimulating but demanding level and much of the old Cecil was to be repressed. With joy Cecil sent these two fine volumes as an offering to his new friend. Donatello, incidentally, was a new discovery for Cecil. At the first opportunity he studied his work in the Victoria and Albert Museum. After his second visit he wrote: 'I am beginning to feel some sort of reaction to him whereas before it was blank.'[40]

With the help of Alan Tagg he altered his image from one in threadbare tweeds to one in coats, trousers, boots and ties, all in suede.

Cecil was obliged to wait until 11 June until Kin arrived in London to stay with him. They kept in touch by letter:

> Letters from Kin brought me my only real interest and I realized how important this friendship can be, and hope it will be the one thing that I should bank on making important to me in my old age.[41]

Meanwhile the old life had to continue in what he called 'the fallow period',[42] an opportunity to get as much work done as possible. He needed to work. Eileen had recently reported on his financial situation: 'Your no. 2 account is in credit to the tune of £6,985; Your no. 1 account is in the red to the tune of £9,738, making an overdraft of £2,753. . . . We are up against pressure, but not insuperably so.'[43]

In Paris Cecil photographed the 'deeply *maquillé*'[44] Prince Felix Youssoupoff, the scent salesman who made such a meal of murdering Rasputin. The Prince wrote to say that the photograph Cecil sent 'is very successful and everybody likes it'.[45] During his visit, Cecil noticed a book on Pavlova. The following year he returned 'and luckily the Prince asked if I would like to borrow it. To all intents and purposes it is mine, so my mission was successful.'[46] Diana Vreeland commissioned Cecil to photograph the ballerina Plisetskaya, in an atmosphere of intense enthusiasm:

> Please send me a wire after you finish photographing Plisetskaya. That is the only thing on my mind. Naturally, I see a long, exciting folio, and I feel sure she will do anything for you so long as you have a Russian interpreter in the studio, some music (perhaps something that she is dancing in), and the air charged with excitement – everything lovely, and making her feel like the enormous star which she actually is. This would be our greatest coup, and I cannot help but feel that you are as interested as I in bringing this off.
>
> I hope that all goes well, as she is rather mad and wild, and can be sullen. On the other hand, when the lights go on and when she knows that she has a full audience of everyone in the studio (and she knows audiences –), then she has everyone rapt and spellbound, and she adores every moment.

I have written to Susan Train* to have everything ready and laid out, but I think you and the interpreter will have to do the laughing and the 'excitement-building'. I also suggest that you have champagne, or perhaps she would prefer vodka, and caviar. Do ask Susan to get you whatever you need to put on a really big show.

And wouldn't it be terrible if she behaved like a mule?[47]

This letter was followed by more excited telegrams: 'wildly happy Plisetskaya posing for you. ... Have sent full length sable coat which thought could be thrilling. ... Plisetskaya in my opinion greatest living star and ought to wear what and how she likes but not in theatrical make-up or clothes but as dazzling personality. ... Do her sensationally as her arms, head, throat, gestures etc are so fantastic.'[48] Cecil duly photographed the somewhat overawed star, 'a red-haired little mouse with a long jaw and long nose and sad eyes',[49] in a sable coat worth $18,000. He had never seen her dance and felt accordingly somewhat at a loss.

Cecil had to face his sixtieth birthday on 14 January. There was what he called 'a wake' at Pelham Place during which Diana Cooper presented him with a sword. Cecil's old rival Oliver Messel (who had lived opposite in Pelham Place) had attained his sixtieth birthday the day before and his picture had appeared, an annoyingly youthful face, by Francis Goodman in the *Evening Standard*. Cecil presented them with a photograph of himself as a baby:

I really am not ready yet to launch out as a sixty-year-old. Why don't you find a very young looking photograph as you did for Oliver Messel yesterday and print that? With plenty of touching-up.[50]

In March Cecil stayed with Michael and Anne Tree in St Moritz, but he was not in tune with rich life: 'Frivolity is fine,' he wrote. 'I am good at throwing in the witty phrase, at getting a laugh. I enjoy developing this taste and it amazes me sometimes how glib and expert my technique is. But I have always felt the need of a guy rope, someone who can keep me disciplined to the straight path. ... Such a person is Kin.'[51] Cecil thought about the future:

If Kin comes over this next summer I must preserve the privacy of our friendship. I must not show him off and show off my friends to him. I must try to be as much like myself as I was in the anonymity of his apartment in San Francisco.[52]

Cecil went on to Lucerne to meet Audrey Hepburn and Mel Ferrer, now returned from Hollywood. He stayed with them in their chalet and they walked in the mountains. Later, in Paris, he photographed her in Indian-

* American *Vogue*'s representative in Paris.

inspired clothes. Cecil earned £120 for a fashion feature with top model Jean Shrimpton.

On a visit to America to discuss *La Traviata* with Alfred Lunt, Cecil was able to meet Kin in South Carolina. Again he found him 'everything I hoped he would be and more'.[53]

In April Cecil had to contend with the bad news that his last three books, *Quail in Aspic*, *Images* and *Royal Portraits*, had sold badly, despite the optimism of his publisher. George Weidenfeld had no faith in *Cecil Beaton's Fair Lady*, which he dismissed as nothing more than a eulogy of Audrey Hepburn. Cecil asked himself: 'Oh dear. Is this the beginning of the end?'[54]

In May he went to Morocco to photograph the King, which involved a lengthy chaos of delays and changes of plan. As for the King, 'the little runt looking like Frank Sinatra arrived just after the sun had gone down. We took horrible pictures in semi-darkness for eight minutes.'[55] He stayed with David Herbert, but the Tangerine life which satisfied David now left Cecil absolutely cold. He only went there to see his old friend. He went on to Madrid for more Audrey photographs. In London he took his final group of photographs of Princess Marina, whose graceful ageing struck Cecil as nothing short of a tragedy.

A recent photograph of Princess Marina in the *Daily Telegraph* Cecil described as that of 'the most horrifying old frog'.[56] Cecil's attempts to photograph her were only adequately successful. His attempts at amusing her by falling into the lake at Vaynol were rather more so. He was subjected to a variety of practical jokes by Princess Marina and Princess Olga at the end of which one of the guests told Princess Marina: 'If this goes on you'll give him a persecution mania.'[57] Prince Paul of Yugoslavia stood by, bemused: 'I've spent half my life not being able to understand what those two sisters are laughing about.'[58]

Cecil photographed Princess Alexandra's baby son, James Ogilvy, and was greatly relieved to be invited to be the first photographer to take Prince Edward, the Queen's youngest son. 'It meant that my career was still high, that the inevitable successor to me had not yet been found, and that the evil day of bitterness and retirement had been warded off.'[59] Curiously, Cecil found the four-year-old Prince Andrew 'cheerful and polite and willing to please'.[60] Cecil described him:

> He is a boy with quality that shines out with his niceness, and goodness and good spirits. He is trained to behave well, to be polite, and amenable, but he has the right instinct. Whatever tests one puts him through he comes out well. 'May I take some more? or would you be bored?' – 'I'd like some more.'[61]

All this was secondary to the excitement and trepidation Cecil felt before the arrival of Kin. Two weeks before his arrival Cecil confronted the predicament. Kin was giving up his apartment in San Francisco, selling his furniture, preparing for a new existence quite unknown to him.

> Can it go wrong? I am determined that as far as I am concerned, the opportunity of having someone so valuable to me should not be treated lightly or carelessly. There is no apparent reason why we should not benefit from each other's company to mutual advantage. But the ways of life are full of snares and surprises, yet I am feeling confident, and as far as I have any religious instincts I am terribly grateful to God for having brought about this quite miraculous happening at a late stage in my life, at a stage, in fact, in which such possibilities become rarer.[62]

Kin arrived on a student flight from Montreal. 'I felt an electric current run through me when suddenly the sign told me that the student flight had landed at 19.27.'[63] It was a perfect high summer evening. 'We motored to Pelham, talking hard, so much to laugh about including my house.'[64] Cecil showed Kin his bed, which was far too small, and after a healthy dinner he drove him round London to see St Paul's, the Monument, the Wren churches, Covent Garden and St James's Park. But jet-lag overcame Kin and he fell asleep. They returned to Pelham:

> He slept the sleep of the dead. But he was sleeping here under my wing, and it was as though I had brought back the original Apollo Belvedere, or stalked the unicorn. This difficult, strangely untrained, yet high quality American had seen fit to give himself into my trust and accept my offer to make a new life for him over here.[65]

Kin had to integrate himself into a house where Eileen worked each day and where there were periods of frenzied activity from which necessarily he would be excluded. He admired Cecil's method of working and the way he paced himself: 'In the course of a morning he turned out more than any ordinary person in a whole day. By noon he was up for lunch and could enjoy himself. He hated to be bored.'[66]

Kin had come to London ostensibly to undertake a two-year course at the Courtauld Institute. His arrival never meant that he would stay for ever but there was no time limit. He entirely respected Cecil's choice of whom he should or should not meet. 'Why not?' said Kin. 'He knew the people better than I and he chose only for my good. He kept me away from what Melville called land sharks.'[67] It was never a question of class, more one of sympathy. Kin met Princess Margaret and was fond of Pauline de Rothschild and Christiana Brandolini. On the other hand, in San Francisco, he was never introduced to Ina Claire. Her only knowledge of him was as 'some louche friend of Cecil's on the hill'.[68]

As the friends met him, so they either accepted Kin or they did not. Diana Cooper said: 'If Cecil came along, then Kin came too.'[69] Clarissa Avon found him intellectually pretentious. Eileen accepted the change in the house with good grace, recalled the beauty of Kin as he lay stretched on the lawn at Broadchalke, but regretted the intensity of his conversation. She said: 'He made no concessions. He had no small talk.'[70]

At one time Kin commented on the 'over-civilized' surroundings at Broadchalke and Cecil drove him to see Ashcombe. Kin loved the wild countryside but saw that Cecil was unhappy looking down on lands where once he had been free to roam. Kin said: 'Cecil was genuinely drawn to the outdoors and to isolation, to the terrain. This was another way that he was a very different man than the image presented to the world.'[71]

Cecil was determined to use Kin's stay as an opportunity to see parts of England he did not know. Their first excursion opened Cecil's eyes to the horrors endured by the average British holidaymaker. He was relieved to return to Broadchalke 'and the welcome of a cold supper left on the dining-table made me grateful for the joys of home after even such a brief glimpse of all the outside world of hostelries and lounge bars'.[72]

Then panic set in:

Maybe I was exhausted. Maybe we have tried to do too much. I did not realize that I am so martyred by my moods, but suddenly I wondered if I had made a mistake, if bringing Kin into my English life had not been too ambitious. He had asked me too many questions, about number plates, driving licences, the government, county council. He had pinpointed my ignorance. He seemed suddenly so very rough and ready, hearty and unhousetrained. Alan Tagg seemed to take a dislike, or why else was he so silent? Eileen was slightly spiky. The three of them were willing for me to wait upon them and Kin even left the crusts on the dining-room floor. I was deeply appalled. Was this like a marriage that suddenly proved itself a mistake?[73]

Cecil's mood soon lightened, though secretly he wished he had had more time to work on the *La Traviata* sets with Alan. In London Cecil ordered Kin a suit and invited John Pope-Hennessy to lunch so that the two art historians could meet. Cecil lunched with the Queen of Italy and attended producer Gilbert Miller's eightieth birthday party: 'Kin on the town, not in when I returned, but this must be faced.'[74] At the end of three weeks Cecil wrote, perhaps a little nervously: 'the addition to my life has only been an advantage and a pleasure'.[75]

Cecil finished an onslaught of work in a state 'of extreme nervous stress'.[76] Then with Kin he set off on a two-week tour of Britain, starting at Stratford and continuing via Stanway, Coventry Cathedral, Kedleston and Haddon to stay at Chatsworth. Kin relished the grandeur of the Devonshire seat. He laughed at his bed with a gilded dome and thought that Cecil's reminded him of a funeral casket he had once seen. They continued to Lake Windermere and Cecil paid his only visit to Temple Sowerby, the birthplace of his mother. 'Tears were close,'[77] he wrote. Kin's happiest day was in the wild scenery of the Lake District. They progressed to Edinburgh and on to Cortachy to the Philippe de Rothschilds. Their tour also took them to Glamis, the haunted childhood castle of the Queen Mother. Cecil thought it a frightening place. 'This morning we could hear bellowings from within – possibly from the present Laird suffering from a hangover.'[78] They stayed with Lady (Fitzroy) Maclean before coming down to stay with Lady Lambton and her six children. More homes, stately and otherwise, were encompassed on the return journey. At Houghton Lady Cholmondeley offered them tea with the Queen Mother but they felt too travel-worn to accept. Nevertheless, calling on the Marchioness, they were so overawed by the Palladian palace that they got out of the car and changed their trousers, hoping that this roadside vignette would not coincide with the arrival of Her Majesty's party. In conclusion Cecil thought it 'a very happy holiday'.[79]

Within three weeks they were off to Munich where 'the ghost of Peter'[80] haunted Cecil. They visited Florence, Siena, Bologna, Padua and arrived at length to stay with the Brandolinis in Venice, a city Kin already knew and loved – 'Kin's face wreathed in smiles at the light, at the crumbled façades, the water traffic, at Venice itself'.[81] Cecil tried to show Kin the sights, but found his memory bad: 'A face I never forget, a church I never remember.'[82] The beauty of Venice once again made Cecil melancholy:

> I am seldom a victim of depression but today and yesterday too felt as if I didn't really want to go on living much more. I've been very happy this summer, but perhaps it's being with someone thirty years younger than I am (yet that is so invigorating, keeps one in touch, alert, alive to new ideas) but suddenly I feel old, not in body or mind, but in enthusiasm. I feel my work so inadequate (being in touch with the great masters gives one to despair). I feel there is not time or energy left for me to improve, the old life outmoded and done for. What's to take its place?[83]

The summer holiday took them on to Rome and Athens and to Turkey, which they toured. Kin had the upper hand because he knew about the places they would see, their history and culture. In comparison Cecil felt ignorant and often at a disadvantage because he tired sooner and needed a mid-day rest. There was some danger from the political situation in Cyprus and the fear of imminent war. They were often quite close to student demonstrations and riots. One strenuous day left Cecil 'covered with dust, sunburnt and tired'[84] and he was depressed that his photography was too much influenced by the particular requirements of *Vogue* (who had paid him £380 for an article on Turkey). Cecil's exhaustion sometimes led to a feeling of tetchiness with Kin. Once again his thoughts turned to death:

The death of younger people, and of all those I had known, and wasn't it about time that I settled down to a less hectic life, and read a little and prepared myself more for the unknown?'[85]

At the end of the trip Cecil was both sad to leave and glad at the prospect of Broadchalke. By the time they reached Athens, he was depressed. He got food poisoning and the return trip was agony.

Hardly was he back than Cecil had to throw all his energy into *La Traviata*.

Fortunately he and Kin were relaxed in each other's company. Occasionally there were misunderstandings and Kin did not make friends easily. Cecil thought Kin was happy but he felt 'the responsibility of bringing him far out of his own climate'.[86] He was happier with Kin than when, on Lord Snowdon's recommendation, he was summoned to photograph the Duchess of Beaufort (wife of 'Master', the most ardent foxhunter in Britain) at Badminton. This visit convinced him that 'Ducal homes and ducal life is not for me'.[87]

On 9 October Cecil was the host at the unveiling of a 1771 bust of Catherine the Great by Fedor Shubin. This was to go to the Victoria and Albert Museum in memory of Syrie Maugham, who died in 1955. The gift was inspired jointly by Cecil and Dame Rebecca West. Cecil had been enraged by 'the false impression'[88] given of Syrie in Maugham's book, *Looking Back*. The shrewd Dame Rebecca felt that rather than attack the old boy for his 'senile indecency', friends should do something which made a 'forcible gesture of loyalty to Syrie and ignored Willie'.[89] Two thousand pounds were raised and Dame Rebecca gave her eulogy in the presence of Diana Cooper, John Pope-Hennessy, Noël Coward, Beverley Nichols and others. By that time Maugham was ninety and about to enter the last year of his life in the South of France. Soon afterwards Cecil flew to the States for extensive *My Fair Lady* celebrations and for the opening of his exhibition at the Rex Evans Gallery in Los Angeles. By 11 November his designs had earned him $2,850.50. George Cukor did not come to his opening, nor did Audrey Hepburn, who was staying at Cukor's house. Cecil had also designed special *Fair Lady* costumes for Marshall Field & Co. In September these were the finale to the Presbyterian St Luke's fashion show in Chicago. This was hailed by the *Chicago Sun-Times Family Magazine* as the 'Greatest Fashion Show on Earth'.[90] In New York (and later in London) Cecil did a lot of interviews in connection with his *Fair Lady* diary. He could not wait to get home.

After three weeks away, he was greeted by Kin at London Airport. Cecil decided to have a further exhibition of *Fair Lady* designs at the Redfern Gallery, which meant doing a dozen 'after the event' drawings. He did this, as he put it, 'in a fit of greed, in a desire to squeeze the old MFL lemon until the pips squeaked'.[91] His publicity was not all favourable. Keith Roberts in the *Burlington Magazine* opined:

> He is a slick draughtsman but in his drawing, as in his conceptions, there is a serious weakness. Stylistically, Mr Beaton is an opportunist, with a dash of Sickert here and a spot of Boldini there (a good deal of Boldini come to think of it) and he would seem to have become increasingly satisfied with what is *effective* on the very first – one might say on instantaneous – impact.[92]

The exhibition earned Cecil about £1,200, and for part payment he took a Picasso drawing and an Elizabeth Frink sculpture.

His last excitement of 1964 was to lunch with the Queen Mother. Two of the Royal Household there achieved a greater national celebrity in their later lives: Ruth, Lady Fermoy (the grandmother of the Princess of Wales) and Sir Anthony Blunt (denounced as the 'Fourth Man' and stripped of his knighthood in 1979), Kin's principal at the Courtauld.

In the New Year of 1965, Cecil was unanimously elected Honorary Fellow of the Royal Photographic Society of Great Britain 'as a tribute to the outstanding manner in which you have employed photography in connexion with your distinguished contributions to stage and film design, in your own books and in illustrating the work of others'.[93] Audrey Hepburn congratulated Cecil on 'a humdinger of an evening'[94] after the preview of *My Fair Lady* in London. Princess Margaret and Lord Snowdon attended it and Jack Warner was obliged to remind his tarty girlfriend, 'Don't say shit in front of the Princess.'[95] Warner thanked Cecil for his 'valuable contribution'[96] to the film. Hal Burton, seeing it later, commented: 'I think the Ascot parade surpassed all you have ever done before – but oh those faces under those lovely hats!'[97] But as so often with his family, Cecil's sister Baba, whom he took as his guest, made no comment as to whether she or her daughters had liked the film. Cecil was hurt: 'It is preposterous that a man of sixty should be upset at the lack of bouquets from persons of close blood but far tastes, yet it dunches.'[98] When this last of many premières was over, Cecil decided: 'Now it is time I forgot the whole bloody business.'[99]

Cecil photographed the wedding of Lucy Lambton and Henry Harrod on 16 January, relishing a gathering of 'so many eccentric personalities'.[100] This was a rare excursion in an essentially quiet life. He was happiest painting at Broadchalke, and Kin happiest alone with Cecil – 'we have jogged along quietly together from day to day with nothing to do but read, listen to music, watch television.'[101] But Cecil had plans:

> Kin's image must be changed. He is no longer the romantic fey creature met in strange circumstances in San Francisco. He is a wholesome good person who is identified with my life, with my interests completely. A

good, sterling character who makes allowances for my weakness but encourages me only along the paths of Righteousness. He is a great influence on me though I try consciously not to let him take complete charge of my tastes and inclinations.[102]

Cecil was hopeful for the future: 'We talk as if we are to be together for some while yet. His course at the Courtauld goes on for two years.'[103]

At the time of the *Fair Lady* opening Cecil was delighted to photograph the North Country actor, David Warner, whom he found 'intelligent, alive, energetic' with a face that could change from being 'gaunt, ugly, cretinous [to being] beautiful in a sensitive ivory-carving manner'.[104]

With Kin, Cecil watched Churchill's funeral and 'shed lotions of tears'.[105] Kin was less moved, but impressed by the perfection of all the details. Cecil concluded that he had never much liked Churchill. Now in his diary he confessed that a devil lurking in him had once made him consider winking at the aged statesman, who might well have still been capable of a stern rebuke. As Cecil said: 'This devil must not be encouraged.'[106]

Otherwise his days were peaceful. He would cross the courtyard to the studio dressed in old clothes with holes at the knees of his trousers. He loved to work hard all day, then relax in a hot bath and enjoy the best that television could offer. Weekdays passed into weekends and there was more and more evidence of work done. These Cecil called 'reminders that time is running short'.[107] One sitter was the Bradford artist, David Hockney. Kin came down at weekends from his course at the Courtauld:

> He is funny, full of laughter, unspoilt, enchantingly young and coltish, and carelessly beautiful. In every light, in movement or in static pose, in sport or sleep, he is a continuous delight to the eye, and as an adornment to my house and my life he is the most prized possession.[108]

In April Cecil went to France, to see Chanel in Paris and to photograph and paint Picasso in Mougins. Picasso told Cecil that he had 'the eyes of a painter'.[109] He said that when working late he would pee out of the window rather than walk to the lavatory. He also confessed that he was a great admirer of Princess Margaret. Cecil stayed with the ebullient art expert, Douglas Cooper, and saw a lot of the Graham Sutherlands. Cecil sent them photographs and Graham Sutherland wrote:

> We think they are absolutely splendid and my only regret is that the passing of the years makes it less possible to do justice to your flattering lens.[110]

Cecil painted Jackie Kennedy's children when the family came over for the unveiling of the Runnymede memorial. Their mother felt Cecil had caught Caroline's sensitivity with a tinge of sadness and how much John resembled the late President at the same age.

Cecil always got on well and easily with Eileen. It was only as a result of his debilitated condition due to overtiredness that he flew off the handle and lost his temper with her about the route home they were taking after visiting Ann Fleming.

> It was a very great shock to me. I love Eileen and only want to make her happy and this not from selfish reasons, although if she were to lose her enthusiasm and sympathy for me it would be a cataclysm of such dire magnitude that I could not imagine anything more awful.[111]

The incident cast a pall over the late spring and Cecil felt deeply repentant.

Cecil's diaries at this period are less informative than usual, due no doubt to his sharing as much time as possible with Kin. If there is an underlying theme it is of his general happiness and contentment. Yet as the months went by the diaries give less impression of Kin and more of the outside world, which Cecil had tried to lay aside. Whether Cecil had in a sense become bored with Kin or whether he took him for granted as one of the household is not clear. Certainly he would never have admitted to the former.

However, in the summer of 1965, not long after the outburst with Eileen, matters came to a head. It had been a disappointing summer with a major flu epidemic, which caused even the Household Cavalry to parade without horses. Kin caught flu. So did Eileen and finally Cecil. On a Monday morning Kin came to Cecil's room and asked if they could have 'a little talk'.[112] It was almost exactly a year since he had arrived. He explained to Cecil:

> I feel I haven't made any progress here. I make no contribution and I can't go on playing a rôle where I just sit back and count for nothing. I listen to the talk and I don't participate and no one wants me to. They're really all very friendly and kind but they don't connect. You're the only person that I've come here for, and you're the only person that I like. I make very few friends in America, but here not one. I don't understand the people. They're so busy being clever and pleased with themselves and they've got a lot to be pleased with, but they don't give a damn about me. England bugs me. People say this country is beautiful. It's not, and the climate and the rain is depressing. You can't go for a walk without coming across a bungalow. It's too small. When I shut my eyes I see the hills around San Francisco and the light. It isn't just being homesick. It's missing what I need. I don't like the East Coast of America. I'd rather live in England than in the East but something happened when I discovered San Francisco.[113]

Cecil protested that Kin was much liked and fitted in well. Slowly it dawned on him that Kin was intending to leave. Kin explained later: 'I was uncomfortable depending on Cecil but, more important, I wanted to return to

teaching which I loved and where I felt I had an excellence of my own.'[114]
Cecil was deeply upset:

> Everything had dropped out of my world. I saw my life suddenly so
> unfulfilled with all the inadequate makeshift friends, the activities and
> affairs that mean nothing. I saw all the things that I would be missing.
> Kin's playing Schubert or Bach or early morning music, his schoolboy
> gangling, loping into the room, nose-wrinkled smile, his untidiness and
> the liveliness and high quality of the books in his room, our discussing
> all our pleasures and enthusiasm, sharing every situation, analysing
> every friend and event, the good companionship on motor tours. I became
> in the extremes of grief. I wept so much that breathing became difficult.
> My whole frame shook in an orgasm of misery. I moaned, 'There's no-
> thing to look forward to now!' Kin, a cry from the heart, said, 'Oh Kek!'[115]

During this crisis the telephone remained curiously silent. The outer world
left the two protagonists alone. As time passed, Cecil reconciled himself to
the loss, aware that something worthwhile would now be replaced by the
former extraneous frivolities of his life and that it was very unlikely he
would ever find a new friend. Twenty years later Kin commented:

> He told me that he had not expected more than two years but he only
> got one. I knew that to many people to be under Cecil's protection and
> share his exciting life would appear enviable. I too recognized the quality
> of the gift I had been given but it was not what I needed.[116]

Choosing a metaphor to explain this, Kin concluded: 'It was as though he
had given me the world's most beautiful cat for a pet, but I loved only
dogs.'[117]

He looked back on Cecil's influence and admitted happily that he had
absorbed more than he expected. His San Francisco garden in 1983 with
its profusion of old-fashioned roses was a perpetual reminder of Cecil's taste.
But it was 'Cecil's knack of keeping his priorities clear'[118] that Kin most
admired and from which, since then, he has tried to learn. Kin believes that
though Cecil's professional ambitions and successes were strong, they were
'only a means to a greater end. His real goal was to create for himself the
life he wanted. He did. That was real success. He was a very special person
and I miss him a lot.'[119]

June Osborn thought the failure of this friendship was a great sadness.
Truman Capote went further: 'It broke his heart,'[120] he said.

The summer cheered up a little with some grand parties and then in July
the summer holidays approached. Cecil always felt sad to leave England, but
not this year. The climate had remained bad, and he had to avoid being
alone moping over Kin's departure from Pelham:

As it was he and I both left early on the same morning. His early call and exit down the stairs was as if to the execution. I watched him go from the front door, I in my pyjamas. He had two heavy bags to carry. He gripped his lips very tight and looked very serious. It was as bad a moment, I like to think, for him as it was for me. The taxi turned in to the Crescent. His outstretched hand was stiff and taut. I went back to bed for an hour, not to sleep, but to moan at my loss and to feel desperately sad.

The long journey to Athens was something to keep my mind occupied with new impressions.[121]

Part Eight

The Swinging Years 1965–70

35

Rip-Van-With-It

I am thrilled that Balenciaga and St Laurent love your clothes, and have expressed themselves. Expression has suddenly become extremely important.

Diana Vreeland to Cecil, 7 January 1964

Cecil was quick to discover that, in the words of the poet Dylan (Bob, not Thomas), the times, they were 'a-changin'. As editor-in-chief of *Vogue*, Diana Vreeland instructed Cecil as to what was needed to keep the magazine in tune with the 1960s. She wrote that society itself was no longer interesting, that 'today only personality counts, with very few exceptions unless it is a "new beauty"'.[1] She asked Cecil for 'some very young, raky types that would be amusing for us also etc. Youth is the best thing we can get.'[2] In May 1965 she was in pursuit of beauties and big-time stars 'and only you can give the super duper quality and make the choices'.[3] She commissioned from Cecil an article on noses: 'giving your reasons for "The Nose" ...'.[4]

Cecil was ever eager to immerse himself in the new culture. During his Hollywood year he had regretted missing a party given by Andy Warhol on a merry-go-round on a pier. Warhol had 'staged a fantastic orgy with people making love on the revolving horses and being photographed betimes for an advanced movie'.[5] Later Warhol had visited Cecil at his hotel and stolen a glass 'as he thought it nice'.[6]

Cecil also looked back at the past. He published his war diaries, *The Years Between*, to critical acclaim: 'How you succeed in bringing home those extraordinary years,'[7] wrote Cecil Day-Lewis. From Florence, Harold Acton wrote: 'Apart from reviving fantastic memories it is so vividly, freshly written, no sense of artificiality or fatigue.'[8] Noël Coward wrote an important letter:

It is a very, very good book. Aside from the observation and the indestructible humour which, from you, one gratefully takes for granted, what struck me most was your compassion. It is there, steadfast, all through the book and it moved me more than I can say. Also your vivid use of the English language is a treat for sore eyes. I, who usually pride myself on my psychological judgement, cannot believe I was such an ill-mannered clot to you so many years ago. Happily it *was* many many years ago and time and a great many tides have obliterated it, but oh dear! It's a sharp lesson![9]

The critics too were generous. 'Like anyone else he may be allowed his limitations,' wrote J.W. Lambert, 'but no page of his book is without its flash of beauty, fun or understanding.'[10] Peter Quennell described it as 'an uncommonly readable, and generously entertaining book'.[11] In an interview later in 1965 Cecil said he had been criticized by one of his sisters for being much too outspoken. 'There's no point in the whole thing unless I'm frank. It's going to be even harder in the next volume as I get closer to today.'[12]

Cecil was confronted with the reason for this statement when, following Kin's departure in August 1965, he embarked on a cruise on Cecile de Rothschild's yacht. The party included Friedrich Ledebur, an Austrian giant and one-time actor formerly married to Iris Tree, Princess Jeanne-Marie de Broglie (Christie's agent in Paris, now Chairman of Christie's Europe) and Cecil's old flame Greto Garbo.

Cecil had not seen Garbo for two years. She was sitting on the quayside at Vouliagmeni, her hair tied in a small pigtail with a rubber band. Cecil confided the loss of Kin. 'One whole year. My! My!'[13] she said. And that was all she said of this matter and of her own recent bereavement.

At the age of sixty-three Georges Schlee had died on 3 October 1964, his death the precursor of complicated and lasting repercussions. Cecile de Rothschild had returned to Paris a day early to find Garbo and Schlee at the Crillon, on the point of returning to New York. They all dined together and Garbo left with Schlee at 11.30. While she went back to the Crillon, Schlee went for a walk. Suddenly he had a heart attack, staggered into a bistro and asked the proprietor to ring Garbo. On the way to the hospital he died. Garbo received the call from the stranger but did not understand what he was saying. She referred him to Cecile, who then had to take charge of the situation. Garbo, fearing the inevitable onslaught of press interest, fled the scene at once and even the stringers from *Time* magazine could not establish where she was. On Monday 5 October Schlee's widow, Valentina, arrived in Paris to collect her husband's body, departing with it the next day. The funeral service was held at the Universal Funeral Chapel on East 52nd Street and Lexington Avenue. Among the eighty-five mourners, headed by Valentina, was the author John Gunther, who told the press: 'It is hard to talk about Georges for he leaves no public record. He was just a dear and delightful human being, and a connoisseur of the art of living, a warm and sincere man.'[14] It was a Russian Orthodox service and Valentina handed tapers to the mourners in the front row. Garbo was not at the funeral. Valentina declared that she never wished to set eyes on her husband's friend again. She had tolerated the situation for long enough (Garbo had been present at a farewell party Valentina gave for Schlee as recently as June 1961) but Garbo's selfish desertion of Schlee at the hour of his death was the final humiliation. The rich friends waited to hear the details of Schlee's will. He left everything to Valentina, thus keeping the promise made at the time of their marriage that he would always take care of her. Soon after this Valentina summoned a priest to exorcise her New York apartment and the villa at Cap d'Ail. She loaned this villa to Diana Vreeland in the summer of 1965, saying, 'I have had it exorcised. There will be no trace of that woman!'¹⁵ Mrs Vreeland and her husband duly went to stay, but, Diana commented later: 'It was so full of spooks you could hardly move.'¹⁶ Valentina then sold it.

The feud between Valentina and Garbo continues to this day. They live in the same block on East 52nd Street, but they must never meet. Occasionally by accident their paths cross and pockets of New York life buzz with the news. Nor will Valentina as much as mention the name of the woman she has all too many reasons to despise. On her thirty-seventh consecutive summer visit to Venice in 1983, the name suddenly threatened the conversation. Valentina crossed herself dramatically and said: *'On ne dit pas le nom! Elle est insortable!'*¹⁷

Cecil had sympathized with Garbo at Christmas 1964, receiving in return a telegram saying: Love and thanks G.G. Since Schlee's death, Garbo had commandeered the rich Cecile de Rothschild as her 'jagger'* when she travelled. Cecil felt she treated her as a mixture of 'Schlee and Mercedes combined',¹⁸ because she succeeded in making Cecile feel she was doing wrong, though she was Garbo's kind, considerate and generous hostess. Cecile's attitude was: 'It's G's childish side that should be encouraged. People have always tried to take from her, not give to her.'¹⁹ On this two-week cruise around the smaller Greek islands, Garbo was as difficult as possible. She was demanding, tiresome, spoilt and selfish. She complained if the party talked after she had gone to bed, she complained that a shepherd's voice on land had woken her early in the morning. A nocturnal visit to the loo became a perilous expedition, lest Garbo's sleep be disturbed. Cecil felt that of those on board he was the most critical: 'not because I have any resentment or prejudices, but just because having loved her so much it is a nightmare for me to see to what inevitable paths her negativeness and selfishness have brought her'.²⁰ And yet she could still be alluring and beautiful and Cecil was amazed by her sympathy with children and her childlike reactions to new situations.

He sometimes lay beside Garbo on board, writing his diary. As he

* An Evelyn Waugh expression for one who runs errands or organizes events for another.

scratched away in the 124th volume of manuscript books, he wondered how much he dared publish in the future. He wrestled with his conscience for many years before publishing *The Happy Years* (which includes details of his liaison with Garbo), and this explains the seven-year gap between the two volumes. Meanwhile Garbo lay on deck beside him 'restless and bored'.[21]

Cecil did not think that Garbo ever learned the name of Jeanne-Marie de Broglie. She referred to her as 'this lady'.[22] When they went ashore she was more interested in being spotted by American tourists than in what she was seeing. She would not tell Cecil whether she liked his *Marguerite and Armand* ballet (which she saw in New York in May 1963), nor would she say a word about *My Fair Lady* (which he also knew she had seen). Yet in rare moments of high spirits she could keep a room in gales of laughter. There was one funny incident, when Cecil, Garbo and Friedrich Ledebur went to a deserted cove:

> No sooner had we arrived, stripped naked and stepped into the sun than a distant boat roared towards us. It was a funny scene. Greta trying to get to shore in time on her behind. I, bare assed, walked out. Friedrich was marooned with his white patch of skin and huge hanging balls an embarrassment to him and all who would study the unusual sight.[23]

Cecil found the cruise 'a marvellous rest cure'.[24] Garbo might have come to England later, but she decided it was time to go back to 'the corner' again, and Cecil was unmoved. He went on to the Brandolinis in Venice, which he found too nostalgic. He, Diana Cooper and Simon Fleet accompanied Serge Lifar on his annual August pilgrimage to Diaghilev's tomb at San Michele. He was horrified when Lifar pointed out that he was now older than Diaghilev at the time he was laid to rest amid the cypress trees. This visit to Venice left him with pangs of sadness.

He was reasonably happy at Broadchalke, though lonely without Kin. He enjoyed painting in his new studio and was inspired by the news that the Lefevre Gallery would show him in January. Cecil knew that he should be content with being 'one of the top stage designers'[25] and getting good reviews for his latest volume of diaries, but thought 'it would be a marvellous move to switch from the frippery of *Fair Lady* to the more serious attempts at painting and to feel that in future I can work at less speed and without the distractions of people and a closing date'.[26] Still, he found painting hard work. He identified his problems as maintaining a consistent brush-stroke, of placing the emphasis, of achieving calm or brightness, but most of all attaining an effect of simplicity. He was frustrated that he could not obtain good results easily. The worst was when a painting started well and then went wrong. The best side was that he enjoyed it, found he did not crave company and that in the evening he was happy to read Charlotte Brontë or Proust. He turned down an invitation to accompany Queen Ena of

Spain to the theatre without a shimmer of regret, in order that he could press on with this more rewarding work.

One of Cecil's favourite weekend expeditions was to call on Stephen Tennant at his haunting house, Wilsford. This was always stimulating, usually eccentric and certainly memorable to any guest staying at Broadchalke for the weekend.

Stephen Tennant had endured a long spell of melancholia and depression before coming back into Cecil's life in the summer of 1960. 'I wonder if you really are fond of me,' he had then written. 'I think you would vibrantly seek me out, if you *loved* me. You used to say to Hoyningen-Huene that I was such a lovely person! and I miss your affection and love very much. You once touched me deeply by saying that I *appreciated* and *delighted* in you before anyone else did, in London long ago.'[27] Cecil invited Stephen over and they talked in what Stephen described as 'the *inoubliable* June dusk – June the time of lilies'.[28] Stephen was greatly in awe of Cecil's energy and tirelessness. Again he wrote: 'I do so admire your *outlook on* and grip of life; your tolerance and *greatness* of *outlook* make you remarkable in a world of petty values and cheap standards.'[29]

When Christopher Isherwood and Don Bachardy came to stay in the summer of 1961, Cecil brought them to Wilsford. No guests had crossed the threshold for six months because Stephen had been resting. Wilsford had been so important to Cecil in his formative years. Now after many vicissitudes the house had become extraordinary. Behind the yew trees and the grey stone exterior, the panelled rooms of Lady Grey's era were now papered pink and tinsel. The oak stairs were hung with fish-nets. A miscellany of shells, beads, soap-boxes, Italian straw hats, lampshades, Japanese lanterns and even pyjama tops were strewn about in careful juxtaposition. Sketch books, diaries and posters were displayed on the floor amidst gloves, fans and masks. Stephen himself, once a youthful willowy Shelley, reclined fat and surprisingly healthy, painted with make-up, his hair greasy and dyed. He was extremely excited that Isherwood had come to his house. He asked Isherwood to sit by him on the bed. 'Is it really true? Can I touch you? I'm one of your greatest fans!'[30] Later Isherwood told Cecil that that sort of talk terrified him.

Stephen then launched into an impressive performance, proving that his brain was in no way addled by his long seclusion. He remembered almost everything Isherwood had written (including an article in *Horizon*). He philosophized, reminisced and quoted Aldous Huxley – that 'an artist and a scientist were the only true practitioners of the spirit'.[31] Cecil was very surprised:

I had imagined his brain had rotted with introversion, but it is still a remarkable instrument, and he showed himself to be a real and true eccentric with deep passions for the things he loves, living in a world entirely of his own making with a frenzy and zeal that makes me feel my own existence is quite humdrum.[32]

Taking Mark and Arabella Boxer there in the dark twilight after dinner a week later, Stephen suddenly emerged, a garden twig of syringa in his hand. Cecil had been told he had a headache. Asking Stephen about this he said: 'It's *allegro con moderato*.'[33]

Stephen lived in a world frozen in time. He was not interested in Pinter or Osborne but he could enthuse for an hour about a Pearl White movie. The visits Cecil paid him added a lustre to his Wiltshire life and always lifted his spirit. Gradually those that once flocked to Wilsford now came to Reddish and the former roles of Stephen and Cecil were to some degree reversed.

Juliet Duff was for years a feature of Cecil's weekend entertainments. She often irritated him and Cecil thought she did not like him. However John Perry, a director of H.M. Tennent and friend of Binkie Beaumont, pointed out to Cecil: 'She liked you very much but she was frightened of you. She thought you thought she was silly. She was, but in a very original way.'[34] On Thursday, 23 September 1965, Juliet died aged eighty-four, leaving a bigger gap in Cecil's life than he imagined possible. She had dined with Cecil the previous Sunday bringing Simon Fleet, Christopher Gibbs and Dicky Buckle, the ballet critic, with her. Cecil had long worried about the financial provision to be made for Fleet. He was left the contents of the house but little time to enjoy them. In December 1966 he fell down the stairs of his little house, 'the Gothic Box', in South Kensington, fractured his skull and died. Juliet's death set morbid thoughts alight in Cecil:

> Though I am not yet ready to 'go', I begin to realize how lucky I am that so far I've had no great illnesses or accidents, that I've really been let off scot free, but that I haven't made many preparations or given thought to the mystery of what happens after the human condition is at an end.[35]

Meanwhile Cecil went to Monte Carlo at the suggestion of Princess Grace to design a poster for their centenary celebrations in 1966. 'I asked him', recalled the Princess, 'because he was the epitome of Edwardian elegance.'[36] Cecil was impressed by the richness of the principality, but again haunted by memories. He photographed the Princess with her baby, Princess Stephanie:

> One could not fault Princess Grace and one realized what a great stroke of fortune it was that these two should have met and fallen for one another, for she is first-rate at the job, beautiful, efficient, hard-working, energetic and full of ideas.[37]

Cecil's October visit to New York was overshadowed by Truman's sudden success at the time of the serialization of *In Cold Blood*. In April that year

Truman had witnessed the execution of the two murderers. 'I was there because they wanted me to be,' wrote Truman. 'It was a terrible experience. Something I will never really get over.'[38] He finished off his book in June, after years of work, tension and agony. It proved worthwhile as he became the front cover of *Life* and *Newsweek*, did non-stop interviews and received (apparently) an astonishing 60,000 fan letters. Cecil found it hard to forgive success in others and this marked a gradual diminution of his friendship with Truman. He felt that Truman was wasting his talents in social life:

> The triumph of Truman is salt in one's wound. The man of the moment is greedy for all aspects of his success and never has there been a greater success. He says only the words masterpiece and genius will suffice and must be repeated every moment.[39]

While in New York Cecil received encouragement for his painting from Alexander Liberman of *Vogue*, but criticism that his photographs were non-commercial. He photographed the aged poet Marianne Moore, who liked all the results: 'You make me tailored despite my hideous way of wearing my clothes ... neither a hag nor a combatant.'[40] To Eugenia Sheppard, women's feature editor of the *New York Herald Tribune*, he promoted the revolution in men's clothes. He welcomed longer hair and velvet jackets: 'I wouldn't say it's Victorian but there's certainly a romantic kind of high-wayman quality.'[41] Cecil said he now favoured Rupert Lycett Green's tailoring establishment, Blades. Ever a man to be in the right place at interesting historical moments, he was caught in his hotel during the famous New York power cut. He did not eat for thirty hours. He was not prevented from having a quick 'matter of fact talk'[42] with Kin on the telephone.

Cecil was thrilled to get back to Broadchalke. However, now that he had enough pictures for his exhibition, he could paint no more. He still could not turn down a photographic commission, but he let many theatrical ones pass by 'because each production can become such a millstone'.[43] For this reason he sped to Paris to photograph three Proustians, Céleste Albaret, the novelist's stalwart housekeeper, Jacques Porel (son of Réjane), and Marthe Bibesco. He found each fascinating in their own way and without photography he would never have had the chance of talking to them. Alas, as so often, his three-day trip to Paris took its toll. He fell victim to shingles and was laid low for four weeks. He spent his time reading and watching television. He was ill for so long that he even moved to the blue and white bedroom by the winter garden in the hope of a change. He felt aged by the illness:

> The shingles from which I have been suffering for the past sad six weeks must be used as a warning. At my age it is not possible to thrash oneself

as in earlier days. Some sixty-year-olds when they get over-exhausted have a heart attack or a stroke. I am perhaps fortunate to have had the red light flash in the form of this painful, exasperating depression disease which is said once it leaves to leave no ill effects. Nor is it likely to recur.[44]

Ill-health preoccupied Cecil for the first quarter of 1966. Nevertheless he pulled himself together to attend the opening of his exhibition of over-life-size paintings in intense, strong colours (staged at the Lefevre Gallery 27 January to 26 February). The catalogue gives little clue to the identity of the subjects, who included John Russell, the art critic (Cecil's favourite), David Warner, Sir Alec Guinness, Picasso and Queen Victoria. Cecil wrote nervously:

> I have my first exhibition coming on. This is the high excitement. I am feeling very on edge lest the critics ignore the exhibition entirely, or if their darts find my Achilles heel. But the first of anything is always an event and I am enormously excited to know what will happen this next week.[45]

The prices ranged from £100 to £700. Cecil basked in the professionalism of the gallery and they were equally delighted by the enormous amount of publicity he drummed up, seemingly without effort. He wanted to hear the opinions of Kenneth Tynan and Cyril Connolly, but the exhibition was treated as a news event rather than an art one. The most serious review came from Keith Roberts in the *Burlington Magazine*. Detecting the influence of Dobell and Bacon, he wrote:

> Mr Beaton is anxious to explore seriously the possibilities of oil painting and his aim is highly commendable, but what he has achieved so far is marred by a fatal slickness. It is as if there is, embedded in his talent, a vein of cork, which impels him irresistibly towards the surface of things, no matter how hard he strives to go deeper.[46]

He revelled in Hockney saying he had painted Queen Victoria 'as Van Gogh would have painted her',[47] Sir Nicholas ('Miki') Sekers saying that he was no longer indulging in prettiness and that he was the opposite to Oliver Messel, and Jakie Astor admiring his guts and courage. His friends seemed to like the funny ones best. The embittered Francis Rose tried to say that the fuss in the papers had been out of all proportion. Instead he spluttered out: 'Well Cecil, your exhibition shows that you have made a very great endeavour.'[48]

Twelve paintings were sold, making £2,370, and twenty-eight returned. Looking back, the gallery owner Desmond Corcoran described it as 'a gallant effort'.[49] Afterwards Cecil asked him for his frank opinion of his work. Corcoran gave this and Cecil never spoke to him again.

In February 1966 Cecil took his health into consideration and left for a prolonged rest in the Caribbean, staying with Ronnie Tree, and the Avons, cruising near Grenada with Fulco Verdura and the interior decorator Tom Parr, and ending up in Palm Beach with the rich Wrightsmans. In Barbados he found himself in the company of survivors of a forgotten age all playing bridge for enormous stakes. Laura Canfield took him to see Oliver Messel's house. 'He is building it almost with his own hands,' Cecil wrote to Eileen, 'and it will be delightful, very pretty outside, but indoors no decoration at all, no charm or personality. Strange.'[50] When asked at Heron Bay for an opinion of the house, Cecil said: 'Well, really, Oliver ought to employ a decorator!'[51]

Cecil turned down Kenneth Harper's offer to design the film *Prudence and the Pill* and Rudolf Bing's to do *The Marriage of Figaro*. He worried about a boil on his lower lip. From now on his diaries would be peppered with depressed references to death, disillusionment, disappointments and keeping up the struggle:

I have a mass of stuff like the rind of an old Stilton cheese covering a large patch of my chin. Its psychological effect is incredibly depressing. I feel as if the game was up. I begin to wonder if I *want* to go on, whether the trouble is worth it. Each morning I look again at my lip. No improvement and I wonder if it will ever be right again, and it is just this small detail that can weight the balance.[52]

In public, however, Cecil did a noble job of being the first to decry himself in an amusing way: 'It is a trick I excel in,'[53] he noted.

Cecil found his way to New York in March. His old friend Serge Obolensky commissioned him to decorate an apartment at the St Regis. While there he was amused when a new friend, Sam Green, a man 'with half a beard', invited him to a party given by an 'angry lesbian sculptor Kyrssa', saying: 'There won't be many people. Not too crowded, as she's not all that popular.'[54] He also tried, without success, to arrange a reunion between Garbo and Mercedes de Acosta, her ill-treated and now dying friend. He failed and Mercedes died in 1968, unforgiven for her book *Here Lies the Heart*.

In April he designed gowns for the Chancellor and undergraduates of the University of East Anglia.

Cecil became more closely involved with the young 'swingers' of the 1960s. He relished the wedding of the Pembroke heir, Henry, to an upper-class 'beatnik' girl, Claire Pelly. At Sheridan Dufferin's party for them he was surrounded by open-necked shirts, blue jeans, sweaters, shoulder-length hair on men and women, and the model Jean Shrimpton in football boots. 'Will they, at last, bring their David Hockneys and Pop art to the Single Cube?'[55] he asked hopefully. He became a friend of the painter Michael

Wishart: 'I'm tremendously impressed by your paintings,' he wrote, 'and do want you to let me come and see your latest work.'[56] He made such a successful speech for Mary Quant at a Foyle's luncheon that every copy of her book was sold. 'Dear Uncle Cecil,' she wrote, 'a lunch in *my* honour is the last place I would ever have hoped to meet one of my greatest heroes.'[57] Asked later to describe himself, Cecil declared: 'I like to think of myself as a pioneer, a trail-blazer.'[58] Small wonder that Cyril Connolly was soon calling him 'Rip-Van-With-It'.[59]

At other times Cecil was content to spend time at Broadchalke, enlivened by inspiring if exhausting weekend visits from Diana Cooper. Ray Gurton, the new butler, arrived fresh from the turbulent establishment of Peter Sellers and his Swedish wife, Britt Ekland. So did Timothy White, the white cat, who hunted at night and slept on a velvet chair by day. He would be with Cecil almost to the end.

Whereas the first part of the year was relatively peaceful, the second brought Cecil to a new fever of exhaustion. He redesigned *Lady Windermere's Fan* for Binkie Beaumont. He had achieved such a success with this in 1945 that he was reluctant to allow any other designer to take it on. Cecil was determined to be simpler in detail and bolder in design. He was equally determined to be different. The set included a Turkish corner and the overall effect was red, white and blue. Cecil originally hoped that Vivien Leigh might play Mrs Erlynne. The part went to his wartime girlfriend, Coral Browne. Influenced by reading Proust (and still deeply impressed by a meeting with his biographer, George Painter), Cecil designed her a dramatic scarlet satin outfit reminiscent of the Duchesse de Guermantes. When she saw it, Coral Browne rang up in tears and said she looked like a fire hydrant. She recalled: 'I didn't want to play a scarlet woman in scarlet.'[60] A meeting took place with the director, Anthony Quayle: 'Coral looked very well – after all these years,' wrote Cecil. 'No trouble.'[61] And Coral Browne recalled: 'I was just as attracted to him then as when I first saw him.'[62] Cecil won a victory with the colour, but the satin was changed to net. Similarly his adored Isabel Jeans did not wish to appear in a *poudré* wig. Stanley Hall, of Wig Creations, saved the day with a strand of nut-brown hair.

Unfortunately there were endless last-minute problems and alterations with this production. Binkie Beaumont congratulated Cecil on having 'created a completely fresh production which in no way copies or resembles the original',[63] but later fell foul of Cecil by demanding a new last-minute sketch for the repainting of one scene. The revival was not the huge success everyone hoped. The first night was eclipsed by Peter Brook's anti-Vietnam war play, *US*, at the Aldwych. Cecil slated Wilfrid Hyde White's performance: 'He improvises, won't learn the correct lines and puts in gags about spaniels that conjure up the late George Graves.'[64] He also thought Juliet Mills 'without grace or glamour'.[65]

In Paris there was an exhausting visit to Chanel, inveighing against *Vogue* and jealous of Bardot's latest marriage, tiring fashion sittings with Fiona von Thyssen and at Roger Vivier's, and a lucrative *Modess* sitting at Broadchalke. Cecil was dead beat again. Occasional long-distance talks to Kin revived his spirits. Kin told him: You've strength and energy! It's as if you had three balls.'[66]

Cecil also designed Julian Mitchell's play *A Family and a Fortune*, based on Ivy Compton-Burnett's novel. When this opened in Oxford, an sos arrived asking him to alter the set which the company found too open. This never went further than the Yvonne Arnaud Theatre in Guildford. It was Cecil's last play.

After a cruise with the Wrightsmans, Cecil went to New York. On his return Eileen showed him a letter from his Heath Mount master, Aubrey Ensor, which read: 'I hope all goes well with Cecil – it usually does!'[67] As Cecil commented: 'Little does he realize!'[68]

A further unexpected honour befell Cecil when he was appointed Honorary Fellow of the Institute of Incorporated Photographers. Cecil accepted a certificate from these worthy men, but not without misgiving:

> None the less the proceedings lasted long enough to make one feel a bit of a fraud, for accepting this honour which means so much to these people when I know so little, according to their terms, about the whole problem of photography. It is true when I say I know so little about the technical side which each year becomes more important. Here were middle-aged robust fathers of family earning their living by running large businesses purveying pictures of wedding portraits, social gatherings, buildings, cars, engineering plants. One elderly woman present was a specialist in photographing motor cars, the man next to me at lunch had come from Edinburgh where he is the police photographer. As soon as a crime is committed he is sent to photograph all the evidence. Bloodshed, horrors, buckled motor cars, murder, all have to be carefully and clearly put on record by him. He must have no failures – there is no second sitting for him. 'Isn't it rather an upsetting job?' – 'Only if you know the people involved.' ... A cheery extrovert group. I wonder if they thought anything about me, about what I was thinking of them.
>
> Truth to tell it was hard not to let one's mind wander – and to ponder about their home life, their sexual and other appetites. They seem to have few inhibitions, but who can tell what dark secrets were here lurking, just as in my mind my thoughts were flying in all perverse directions.[69]

Whenever Cecil passed a photographer's studio in a suburban high street, he would exclaim: 'There but for the Grace of God, go I!'[70] He was happier in his own world, dining with Patrick Procktor, whom he described as 'a fellow painter (a chap with hair worn like a Renaissance nobleman)'.[71]

With the doomed Simon Fleet, Cecil attended the Peter Brook play, *US*. He hoped to be 'horrified, shocked, stunned', but instead concluded that it was as though Brook 'had merely misbehaved in public. Ugly, nasty, amateur. The evening was over by the first interval.'[72] It was enlivened by Simon who was suffering from Juliet's death, stress, sadness and a surfeit of alcohol, and cried out: 'Why don't you Americans occupy Gibraltar so that we British can keep it for ever and ever?' This brought the proceedings to a halt and Cecil was concerned at the ugly atmosphere that developed. Voices from the stage replied: 'Can't answer that, Sir. We're only the actors.'[73]

In November Cecil returned to New York. He disapproved of the £10,000 black and white ball that Truman was giving and yet he dared not miss it. He thought it a waste of Truman's time and money and yet 'a master stroke of publicity, though of the wrong sort'.[74] He set off brewing for trouble: 'It is going to be very hard for me to hide my feelings.'[75] He described the party to Eileen:

Well, the party's over. It was a very good one, particularly by NY standards. Every sort of world represented by one or two though the intellectuals in a minority. No personality, as indeed impossible in a Hotel, ugly effect. Very amusing masks and most people had taken a lot of trouble. The Paley dinner beforehand very rich and fashionable but no real quality. Disgusting food.... The publicity, the Radio, TV, cameras etc, was frightening, really out of hand, and I suppose this is really what the whole thing was for. Otherwise it seems a lot of money to spend on a lot of dreary people who have no interest for him. I sat next to Mrs Alvin Dewey, wife of detective. It is extraordinary the effect all the shenanigans have had in the little home town, and will continue now they are going to make the film on the spot, even using the Clutters' house for backgrounds.[76]

Cecil went on to New Mexico to photograph Georgia O'Keefe in the wilds, another person he would never have encountered but for photography. He surprised the old artist by bringing white carnations (in fact sent to his hotel by Diana Vreeland's son). 'You must have had such difficulty in finding them,'[77] she said. As with Edith Sitwell, Cecil found it was impossible to take a bad photograph of her.

Cecil flew home in time for Simon Fleet's funeral, which he reported to Clarissa Avon:

The horrible cremation chapel was disguised by Buckle, etc. in just the way Simon would have done it. The catafalque and altar steps covered with imitation green grass which was scattered, Botticelli-like, with expensive spring flowers, masses of trees of mimosa, a strange 'bande' of faithfuls all with red noses and red eyes.[78]

Iris Tree stayed with Cecil when Simon's ashes were scattered at Bulbridge.

36

Growing Old, Staying Young

Don't let's talk about old people looking young, but about young people looking old. It's so much more interesting.

Zena Dare to Cecil, February 1967

Cecil was so intrigued by Mick Jagger that for his Lefevre Gallery exhibition he painted him from a David Bailey photograph. Soon afterwards they met at the Boudin Ball, at Christie's. Cecil, dressed in a white broad-lapelled coat, was heard to say: 'I'd like to meet Mick Jagger. Marvellous face. Reminds me of Nijinsky.'[1] However, after ten minutes he was back, declaring: 'No conversation at all. Marvellous face – but strictly for photography.'[2] Later, when asked by the *Daily Express* for a quote about Mick, he offered: 'He is one of those calf-like creatures who never seem to have been young. Like the Mona Lisa he knows everything, has seen everything, and has never lost his arrogance. But then he knows he is doomed to be a has-been by the age of twenty-five.'[3] Not surprisingly, the editor rejected this.

Over a year later Cecil was given a second chance. 'I was sorely tempted to get off the plane on Saturday with Robert Fraser and a beatnik friend and to have a weekend of dope with them and the Rolling Stones,' Cecil wrote from Morocco. 'One way of getting Jagger to pose. I lost my chance.'[4] Cecil went to Marrakesh to stay quietly at the Es-Saadi Hotel. Driven from this establishment by piped American choirs singing 'Three coins in the fountain', he moved to the Mamounia Hotel. Suddenly, to his delight, three Rolling Stones arrived, surrounded by 'their vast entourage of hangers-on etc'.[5]

Cecil was oblivious of most of the Stones' current problems. He soon learned that Mick Jagger, Keith Richard and others of their party had just been 'busted' for being in possession of drugs at Redlands, Keith Richard's home near Chichester. They had come to Morocco to escape the ensuing publicity. Mick Jagger was absorbed in his affair with Marianne Faithfull and had flown from Paris. Keith Richard, Brian Jones and his girlfriend Anita Pallenberg had driven together through Europe. Unfortunately for him, Brian Jones had contracted pneumonia in Toulon, giving Keith Richard and

Anita the chance to consummate their passion for each other in Valencia. Brian Jones, arriving later in Morocco, reacted violently by beating Anita up, a fact only partially disguised by her 'death-white, kohl-black sixties make-up'.[6]

Cecil observed the group – Robert Fraser 'wearing a huge black felt hat and bright emerald brocade coat', 'Beatnik dressed Anita Pallenberg, dirty white face, dirty blackened eyes, dirty canary drops of hair, barbaric jewellery, the drummer (?) Keith of the Stones, an eighteenth-century suit, black long velvet coat and the tightest pants'.[7] That Cecil could name neither Keith Richard nor Brian Jones (to whom he referred in his diary as 'Brian Forbes') demonstrates his lack of interest in them. In fact he only wanted to photograph Mick Jagger, who fascinated him because he still could not decide 'whether he is beautiful or hideous'.[8] After a few drinks Cecil found himself in a Bentley with 'the most tremendous volume of pop music'[9] to which Mick and Brian responded rhythmically, while Anita tried to tell him she had just played a murderess in a film. Cecil had the chance to examine Mick in the Moroccan restaurant where they dined:

> He is very gentle and with perfect manners. He considered the Moorish style of decoration gave little opportunity for individuality to the artist. He indicated that I should follow his example and eat the chicken in my fingers. It was so tender and good. He has much appreciation and his small albino fringed eyes notice everything.... He has an analytical slant and compares what he is seeing with earlier impressions and with other countries.... I was fascinated with the thin concave lines of his body, legs, arms, mouth almost too large, but he is beautiful and ugly, feminine and masculine, a 'sport', a rare phenomenon. I was not disappointed.[10]

Mick even referred to the Christie's evening the year before and apologized that they had been unable to converse. They discussed drugs. Cecil spoke of enjoying bhang in India in 1944. Mick said LSD made the brain run on 4,000 cylinders instead of four. He said: 'They can't stamp it out. It's like the atom bomb. Once it's been discovered it can never be forgotten.'[11] Cecil enjoyed the evening: 'It did me good to be jerked out of myself.'[12]

It was an exhausted Mick with white podgy face who emerged at the pool the next day. Cecil hijacked him for a photographic session in the trees and midday sun, thus affording him some much-needed shadows: 'He was a Tarzan of Piero di Cosimo. Lips of a fantastic roundness, body white and almost hairless. He is sexy, yet completely sexless. He could nearly be an eunuch. As a model he is a natural.'[13]

Cecil and Mick Jagger were natural friends, both keenly drawn to the lure of success. The understandable vanity of the young star welcomed the laurels of the older one. The result was what Mick Jagger called 'some nice pictures'.[14] Having befriended Cecil, Mick was prepared to break away from the others and join him and Ira Belline for lunch. Ira, Stravinsky's niece, thought he was like Nijinsky, on whose lap she had sat as a child.

Cecil stayed on to observe the Stones and their dedication to their music. He was sorry they had got into 'bad Hash-habits'. Brian Jones 'tripped off' before dinner and there was a long session in Robert Fraser's room during which cookies were eaten and pipes smoked. Cecil thought they looked healthy enough on this diet of drugs but, as he wrote: 'We will see.'[*][15] Cecil went on to Tangiers to David Herbert, persuading him to write his memoirs (*Second Son*) and they drove together over the Atlas Mountains. Diana Vreeland loved his photos from this trip: 'In my opinion your Moroccan pictures – "the abstracts" – are the most beautiful mirage of form and colour – they are triumphant photographs – every possible congratulation.'[16]

Cecil was finding the new age difficult to cope with from a technical point of view. New cameras, with their possibilities of new perspective, he found hard to load. He liked a wide-angled lens which gave 'a more contemporary look'.[17] Because Cecil was bored, he did not take his camera to the Harlechs for tea and missed the chance of 'poignant documents' because Lady Harlech was killed in a car crash within twenty-four hours. He forgot to load his camera so missed 'Ma'am Darling' (Princess Marina) in the window-seat at Vaynol, Stephen at Wilsford, Lady Emma Tennant in the evening sun at her cottage, and Cyril and Deirdre Connolly staying with Anthony and Tanya Hobson. At this time Cecil also experimented with a bizarre psychedelic lighting in colour portraits of Suzy Knickerbocker. The *Weekend Telegraph*, publishing similar versions of Irene Worth, Michael Hordern, Victor Henry, Isabel Jeans and Vivien Merchant, described the effects as 'similar to those in hippies' light-shows'.[18] Nor was Cecil practical in everyday life. Hermetically sealed plastic covers and sellotaped parcels caused him frequent vexation. He was restless in the country, unable to settle to his work, while in London there was too much office work to allow time for anything else. He went to Ascot partly because as a child he had minded deeply the many times his mother's application to the Royal Enclosure had been turned down. When the doors opened to admit him, he knew it was too late. Loelia Westminster asked him: 'What *are* you doing here?'[19] and he knew he would never go again. He also found the theatre 'another form of enforced entertainment that I am finding hard to enjoy',[20] with the exception of Roy

---

*Shortly after this (in June 1967) Mick Jagger, Keith Richard and Robert Fraser were sentenced to imprisonment for possessing dangerous drugs. Jagger and Richard were freed on appeal but Fraser served four of his six months' sentence. Brian Jones was drowned in the swimming-pool of Cotchford Farm in Sussex in July 1969. The verdict was 'death by misadventure'. The Stones' photographer, Michael Cooper, whom Cecil met dressed scruffily in a green velvet blouse open to the navel, committed suicide in 1972, after his addiction left him in a wheelchair.

Dotrice's one-man show as the Wiltshire antiquary John Aubrey (who had lived at Broadchalke) and *Rosencrantz and Guildenstern are Dead*.

If anything it was the Swinging Sixties that held the most appeal. Cecil was a past master at bridging the generation gap and he prided himself on being among the first to spot new talent or new waves in culture. Christopher Gibbs, perhaps the most articulate survivor of those mercurial times, recalled:

> Cecil was longing to leap into something more glamorous. Obviously with each new decade it became harder. He was a true opportunist in the best sense of the word, and a constant and loyal friend. He was jolly kind to us youngsters.[21]

Cecil was in no way a joke figure among the young trendies. Others who were immersed in Sixties' life in different ways, Henry Pembroke, Roy Strong and Michael Wishart, recall Cecil's interest in them as genuinely kind, helpful and flattering. Many had yet to prove themselves, but Cecil was already the encourager. Christopher Gibbs recalled that when Cecil entertained: 'He wanted to bring out the best in us. He was the director and the guests were the actors and they had to shine. He took credit as the director, of course.' Christopher Gibbs admired the way Cecil developed all his talents to the full, 'and that is what we are here for.'[22]

Cecil took some puffs of dope at Chrissie Gibbs's party in the company of Jane Ormsby-Gore (daughter of the recently deceased Lady Harlech) before she left with Michael Wishart ('freshly out of a nervous nursing-home').[23] Then they awaited the arrival of Mick Jagger and Marianne Faithfull. At 10.15 the exotic couple appeared and Marianne made 'groovy' conversation. Prince Stanislas ('Stash') Klossowski de Rola (son of the artist Balthus, about whom he later compiled a book) was also there, dressed as a Hamlet, with stripes of sequins on his blouse and shoes. He had recently hit the headlines by being 'busted' with Brian Jones at his flat in Courtfield Road. At 11.30 the unlikely group made their way to the Baghdad Restaurant in Fulham Road. There they found Jane Ormsby-Gore, her husband the trendy draper Michael Rainey, Michael Wishart, Robert Fraser and others. Cecil found that none of them ever concluded a line of conversation. A few disconnected remarks was the best he could hope for. 'This does not make for stimulating discussion.'[24] Worn out by the long wait, Cecil declined Robert Fraser's invitation to come back and view Andy Warhol's three-and-a-half-hour film, *The Chelsea Girls*. Instead, at 1 a.m., he wandered home alone through the Chelsea night.

Cecil went to Venice to decorate the Palazzo Rezzonico Ball, the biggest ball since the 1951 Beistegui. It was a masked ball, the theme of which was seventeenth-century Venice in red, white and gold. Then there was another Wrightsman cruise, a repetition of the previous year's 'incredible luxury, a complete igloo of escapism'.[25] A highlight of this cruise was the arrival for lunch on board of Queen Frederica of Greece, King Constantine and Queen Anne Marie, Princess Sophia and Princess Irene. Queen Frederica told Cecil that LSD was 'like taking a glimpse of Heaven but paying with shoddy money'.[26] Cecil photographed all but the King against a Japanese panel in the dining-cabin. He thought Queen Anne Marie 'nothing very special to look at, but when puppy fat goes she'll stand a chance'.[27] Much of the time on board Cecil thought of himself as an aged adolescent: 'How can they make allowances for me appearing each day in a different set of stunning pink and blue clothes?'[28] As always he took a dim view of his own achievements:

> I don't really feel that I am going to come into my own, and justify myself and my existence by some last great gesture. I am likewise certain that nothing I have done is likely to live long after me.[29]

A feature of travelling with the Wrightsmans was that they allowed each guest in turn to pay for dinner when they landed. Cecil's turn came in the South of France and cost him £60. For all the rich living, Cecil continued to love Reddish best. One morning he described the waking scene:

> The curtains in front of me were pulled to reveal a bright summer morning, the sun casting shadows across the lawn picking out the high points of the distant trees, the newly planted orchard and the garlands of new dawn roses still flowering without cease, the green and pale pink show in great contrast against the cerulean blue of the cloudless sky.
>
> I was too delighted to be able to tear myself indoors. The morning went by doing all sorts of things that prevented work. I could not have been more happy.[30]

Soon after this there was a burglary at Reddish and some silver was taken, an act which Cecil thought of as 'a defiling of one's own nest'.[31] It also meant that a sitting with Twiggy was constantly interrupted by telephone calls from police, press and insurance.

Twiggy came to Pelham Place to be photographed and soon decided that Cecil was so elegant that she should have been photographing him. Of her Cecil wrote: 'She is an easy little marvel of photography. Can't look wrong.'[32] To the *International Herald Tribune* he confessed: 'No one else has her look. She's asexual and being asexual she's got great sex appeal. If I say she's got the sex appeal of a child I'll probably get run in.'[33]

In July 1967 Cecil was fascinated to talk to eighty-four-year-old Princess Alice, Countess of Athlone, in the relaxed croquet atmosphere of Wilton. He thought her 'a jolly little woman having a lot of fun out of life up to the end'.[34]

He and Sidney Pembroke went to Stockholm together. Back in London he

Above, Cecil photographing
the Duchess of Gloucester, 1961

Victoria Heber-Percy

Audrey Hepburn
in one of her
My Fair Lady
costumes, 1963

Below left,
Cecil with
Audrey Hepburn
on the set
of *My Fair Lady*

Below,
George Cukor and
Audrey Hepburn
before the ball scene

Above left, Princess Marina at Vaynol, 1964

Above, Kin and Cecil, 1964

Garbo on the yacht, Greece 1965

Cecil greeting
the Queen Mother
at the
National Portrait
Gallery, 1968.
Roy Strong looks on.

Truman Capote

Sir Francis Rose

Mick Jagger and Anita Pallenberg about to perform in *Performance*, 1968

Barbra Streisand in *On a Clear Day*, 1969

Jane Birkin at the Rothschild Ball, 1971

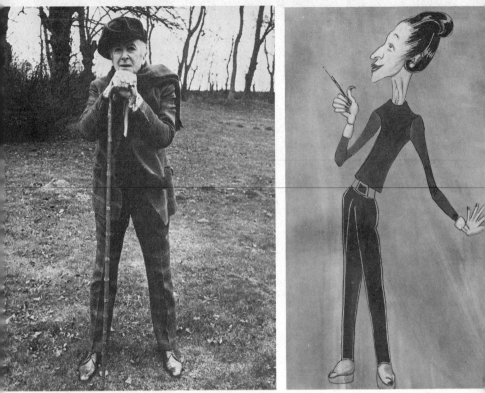

Cecil after the announcement of his knighthood, 1972

Diana Vreeland

Katharine Hepburn with Cecil, New York 1969

Eileen Hose
with the cat Timothy
in the winter garden
at Reddish House

Below, The drawing-room
at Reddish House

Lady Diana Cooper at Reddish House, 1972

Sir Ralph Richardson and Cecil at the National Theatre, 1979

was photographed in 'a mysterious group' for the *Queen* by 'a very go-getting tough Lord Lichfield who had been out so late at Annabel's in the company of the Pill, Miss Lynda Bird Johnson, that he had no time to shave'.[35] The group was meant to show that 'you can judge a man by the company he keeps'. Devised by Jon Bradshaw and Nigel Dempster, Cecil had little in common with the other nineteen people, besides perhaps Lady Anne Tennant, the Marquess of Bath, Osbert Lancaster and David Mlinaric.

There were visits to the decrepit Harold Nicolson at Sissinghurst, and to Duncan Grant in his ramshackle house at Charleston. In September Cecil went to Paris to photograph Rex Harrison, then starring in the film *A Flea in Her Ear*. Cecil beat his own record for the number of pictures taken in such a short time and thought they all had 'a certain freshness of approach'. He found the essentially difficult Harrison in a mood of enthusiastic co-operation, 'his vast ego flattered to the fullest'.[36] Then Cecil undertook a *Connaissance des Arts* tour with twenty others, amongst whom he knew only Liliane de Rothschild. They visited Poland and Czechoslovakia. The trip proved an exhausting one, first because the agenda was packed with sight-seeing and, second, in Cecil's case, because once again he assumed addi-tional responsibilities. Every few days he wrote notes for a *Vogue* article and sent them in letter form to Diana Vreeland. Before the others were up he would spend an exhausting hour photographing the stables at Lancut before a rushed cup of coffee and then a new bout of sightseeing. This meant that he was able to charge *Vogue* $1,336 in fees and expenses.

The usual headaches began to come and Cecil feared he had absorbed too much too quickly. At the same time the suffering of Poland depressed him very much. It is not surprising that he was too fatigued to complete the trip by continuing to East Germany. After a fortnight of 'deep delving into the past' he longed for 'the most violent manifestations of modern art'.[37] In his relief at escaping, he wrote to Diana Vreeland:

> Already I was worn out, very depleted by emotion and the general feeling of malaise that one feels in a satellite country. There is always the risk that, without explanation, one is tapped on the shoulder. I got into such a state of nerves that I felt I was living in a Kafka world. In fact one cannot fully understand Kafka until one has been to Prague.[38]

He came home to England and Ray said: 'You do look ill and tired.'[39] In conclusion Cecil felt that Poland could offer great inspiration for stage and interior decorators 'for the ideas that can be copied are to be seen by the dozen. I can't wait for the opportunity of copying a trellis room done in pale greens with convolvulus that we saw at Jaromerica.'[40]

He followed his visit with a letter to *The Times*, complaining that the Czech writer, A.J. Liehm, had been shorn of the privilege of belonging to the Communist party. Cecil continued:

> When more and more eyes were turning towards Prague for inspiration, this latest suppression of the liberty and freedom of the individual is nothing short of a major tragedy just at a time when the future had come to look bright, and it forebodes a return to the dark days of Stalinist terror.[41]

In England Cecil was swept into the latest problems of Sir Francis Rose. He had remarried, but his new wife had chucked him out, leaving Francis full of strange recriminations. Once again he was destitute, a situation to which he was quite accustomed, but as the years went by fewer people were willing to help him. Inevitably he turned to Cecil and to Eileen for help. 'He is a man who causes such extraordinary violence around him,' noted Cecil. 'His life story is a long succession of suicides, killings, fatal accidents. In his wake he brings chaos.'[42] By the end of the following week Rose had been taken into a monastery, chucked out of it, spent three nights with a stranger and then been taken back by his wife.

Cecil continued to worry about the silence of Kin. He prevailed on Christopher Isherwood to help him. At a meeting with Kin, Isherwood explained what Cecil was feeling. Kin took this to heart and thereafter there was more communication. He even came for Christmas. Isherwood wrote: 'He *is* a strange complex creature but very charming and very intelligent.'[43]

In November Cecil went to New York for the first time for a year. He found that the young had broken completely from their conventional parents, dancing had become like an African jungle rite. The contrasts were extreme. 'The Astors make me feel so young by comparison,' wrote Cecil. 'The Beats make me feel old and square and a sightseer.'[44] Truman gave Cecil a Christmas present of a course with a doctor who removed skin blemishes. Cecil got on slightly better with him this time. 'He is so intelligent in life that I feel envy of him for his capacity for finding new people, new interests, new sources of work. Nothing remains static with him.'[45] But Cecil began to wonder how truthful Truman was. 'What he thinks is the truth is often so far from the actual fact.'[46] This led to an unpleasant incident which blighted their friendship and threw Lord Snowdon firmly into Cecil's bad books.

Cecil had been walking down the King's Road in July in search of clothes for the Wrightsman cruise, when he heard his name called from a taxi brimful with Lord Snowdon, Derek Hart and a team of cameramen. He assumed they were making a film about King's Road types and pointed out the Procul Harum pop group (who were passing by) as better subjects. Lord Snowdon was adamant that it was him they wanted. Cecil asked what the film was about and received garbled answers. They first said London, then senior citizens, then experience. It dawned on Cecil that it was to be about growing old, a subject he enjoyed discussing self-deprecatingly. The team came to Pelham Place in the afternoon and set up a camera in the garden. Cecil kept asking what it was all about. All this and more they filmed.

Now Truman revealed that he had seen Peter Glenville and that the film was about geriatrics. He told Cecil that this would harm him considerably:

> They'd done horrid things to me without my knowing it, had sent me up, and had kept the camera rolling long after I'd thought the shot was over, had shown me behind the scenes. Yes, Peter had laughed about it. Now I must at once see that the film was stopped.[47]

The affair continued to distress Cecil for some months. The immediate repercussions were that Snowdon telephoned to say that Glenville had behaved badly and that Truman was just stirring up trouble: indeed Cecil entertained well-founded suspicions about Truman's health and mental condition. Obviously Cecil wanted to see the film. Alexander Liberman saw it and said: 'You are frank and charming, but I doubt the wisdom of your having done it.'[48] Neither Lord Snowdon nor Derek Hart would show Cecil the film until the night before it was released on television:

> I was appalled to find myself at sixty-four as taking a large part in a film that had to do with senility, old people's institutions, old people being injected with youth hormones and glands, or being massaged, shaken, fitted for wigs. The fact that I looked extremely young and attractive helped, but the fact that under false pretences I'd been brought into this particular setting made me extremely angry.[49]

Other celebrities in the film included the doddery Sir Alexander and Lady Patricia Ramsay,* aged eighty-six and eighty-one respectively, rising with difficulty from a bench at Ribsden Holt, their Surrey home, and bickering as they made their way up the lawn.

The film was shown on 4 April 1968 and drew reactions from many of Cecil's friends. Princess Marina wrote: 'I thought you were very good in *Don't Count the Candles*. The range of the film mixing the poignant with the tragi-comic was clever.'[50] Diana Vreeland thought Lord Snowdon's film had been done 'with thought and heart'. She added:

> And I think you are WONDERFUL outside of the fact you are much too young and gala and I mean it you really are far and away the best thing in, it. Certainly not an atom of the problems Truman was mumbling about. All your part EXCELLENT and very professional.[51]

Anita Loos was less impressed:

---

* Lady Patricia Ramsay (1886–1974), granddaughter of Queen Victoria. Formerly HRH Princess Patricia of Connaught.

This a.m. everybody is reacting to the bad taste and morbidity of that nauseating t.v. of Lord Snowden's [sic] last night. Only you and Twiggy come through as being humans. The broadcast left one with the feeling that his Lordship's power and prestige have given him too much opportunity to be a public nuisance.[52]

As a result of the film, Cecil found his age became a general topic. *Time* wrote that he had dentures (which was untrue). Worse, he himself dwelt more on the subject. It gave him little satisfaction to telephone Snowdon and tell him that he had pulled a fast one, 'for I know that T. was only pleased to think that he might have found himself in a lot of trouble but had just managed to get away with it'.[53] Cecil's line was that he had been conned into appearing in his film 'under false pretences'.[54] Even when Princess Margaret tried to put matters right, she got nowhere and Cecil's venom included referring disparagingly to Snowdon to his mother, Lady Rosse, at the opera. But Snowdon was pleased because Cecil had made the point that by continuing to work, people remained young.

One of Cecil's missions was to photograph Margot Fonteyn. It took many frustrations to arrange the sitting but finally she arrived in New York:

Her spirit shines through. She is like a blade of young grass, but she is still the genteel middle-class little English girl grown scraggy and lean. This is something audiences are not conscious of. They see only the artist in her and this is as it should be. The artist is the important and all rare phenomenon. It is the reason for her becoming a legend, and that is what she will be to future generations. To us who have known her so well it is hard to disassociate ourselves from what we have seen in early stages, developing via Constant Lambert and others into the ballerina *assoluta* who with time will have nothing on Pavlova for such is the case of Mrs Hookham's little girl.[55]

At Reddish Cecil made alterations on the landing and discovered that his house was in bad repair. The cisterns in the attic were on the point of bursting and when removed they were found full of the 'bones of rats, birds, bats and other animals whose decomposing bodies we had been drinking for years'.[56] All this cost money at a time when Harold Wilson and his government were making everyone feel the pinch. Cecil was aware that, as ever, his financial status was 'pretty precarious'.[57] Meanwhile he sacked the cook and, in due course, Ray, the butler, came up with the idea that he might assume extra duties. This proved a good solution. Eileen reported: 'I only wish he had spoken up before; before you went away, and before I had alerted the agencies and brought forth this stream of dreary people who either only want a home or imagine they are going to be cooking for the Queen every day!'[58]

Cecil was soon off on prolonged travels once more, first to Palm Beach where an exhibition of his paintings was to be shown at the Palm Beach Galleries. 'Well, the exhibition yesterday evening was a riot!' he wrote to Eileen. 'I really enjoyed being such a success even among such ghastly people. I felt well and rested so could cope, and you can't *imagine* the stupidity and vulgarity of those rich people. However, they bought all the forty-one pictures in three days.'[59] Otherwise Cecil found Palm Beach life a bore.

His diaries refer to the 'warm bath companionship' of certain well-known hostesses and he concluded: 'It is not the right atmosphere for an artist.'[60] Cecil stayed with Truman and was again vexed by the changes in his old friend. Success meant that Truman knew the weekly returns on his books and the exact cinema attendances at the film. Cecil predicted that he could never reap such a success again and resented the condescension he showed to his friends. 'He has begun to believe his own press agent,'[61] Cecil noted not without worry. He was as bitter as ever about Truman's success:

> He knows that I must resent his being the Elsa Maxwell of his day and did not mention his forthcoming ball, which can only be a poor reflection of the first.[62]

At the same time Cecil was delighted that Truman had written a perceptive introduction to a forthcoming volume entitled *The Best of Beaton*. In this Truman was the generous old friend of the past. Sending in his piece he wrote:

> Listen, my darling friend, if this seems hopelessly wrong please just discard it – or edit as you like. I love you as a friend and admire you endlessly as an artist and your book deserves the best.[63]

Then Cecil flew to San Francisco, Bora Bora and on to Australia. The tropical tourist-ridden island of Bora Bora afforded him a view of the wonders of the deep in a glass-bottomed boat. Then after a troubled journey, he arrived for the first time in Australia and was swept away in the Rolls-Royce of his wartime colleague, Dick (now Lord) Casey, the Governor General. Cecil found life with the Caseys at Admiralty House comfortable but too conventional. From this isolated haven Cecil and the other guests set out to explore Sydney: 'We would have liked to get to grips with nature in the raw but back to the depersonalized dining-room.'[64]

In Sydney Cecil found a number of old friends, including Nin Ryan and Rory Cameron. 'Can't think why so many old hacks have come out here at this time,' he wrote to Eileen. 'Bev Nichols, Robin Maugham, and Sir Robert [Helpmann], who is in a state of euphoria with mauve dyed hair and balletic gestures. He came to cocktails last night and was more viperish than ever.'[65]

Lady Casey gave a cocktail-party at which the novelist Patrick White was present.

The Government House party with Cecil and Nin Ryan went to Canberra on 31 January. There he found Sir Charles and Lady Johnston. He photographed Natasha Johnston in a turban and painted their old Egyptian servant, Mo. Cecil loved his portrait and awaited cries of delight from the Johnstons. However, it was greeted in a non-committal way, which depressed him. The Johnstons did like the portrait though, and it hangs today in Sir Charles's London flat.

Cecil's tour also led him to Melbourne, where he photographed Joanna Baillieu, 'a nice exotic-looking girl wearing much too much eye make-up and too much base'.[66] Back in Sydney he was looked after in style by the rich newspaper owner, James Fairfax, at Darling Point. However, Cecil was sure he would never come back:

> This is certainly a country of a great future, but at the present time it is still extremely jejune and there is nothing that appeals to me. I wonder if really my trip was worthwhile and it has been an experience to see these new places, like, yet unlike any others. Different people, very different accents but it has made no lasting impression.[67]

Cecil returned home via San Francisco, where he witnessed Kin hold a class at the university: 'This was a revelation. Mighty impressed I was. I could not understand how all the students did not fall in love with the teacher.'[68]

He stopped off in New York and escorted Jackie Kennedy to the Nabokov–Balanchine ballet, *Don Quixote*. This included dramatic scenic effects – steam, smoke and occasionally a shot. 'When a couple of revolver shots went off Jackie nearly jumped out of her chair and over the rail of the Dress Circle. I felt sorry for her still in such a state of nerves.' There was also a docile horse which suddenly 'decided to let loose a mountain of mustard coloured droppings' on the centre of the stage. Nabokov came to pay his respects to Mrs Kennedy and impressed Cecil by saying: 'Tonight the horse stole the show.'[69]

In England Cecil wanted to paint, but was the victim of endless interruptions. The prospect of photographing Elizabeth Taylor upset an entire week: 'She's everything I dislike.'[70] Cecil asked for a fee of $5,000 and was delighted to be turned down. Instead he took Barry Humphries for an under-the-counter fee of £50.

In April the Queen Mother lunched at Pelham Place for the second time, a much calmer occasion than the first. The guests were Roy Strong in a psychedelic tie, Lady Hesketh, Leo d'Erlanger, Jakie Astor, Irene Worth and Diana Cooper. The party discussed portraiture and Cecil suggested that Graham Sutherland should paint the Queen. 'Why not you?' asked the

Queen Mother. At the end of the luncheon, as Cecil saw the Queen Mother into her car, he was able to say: 'I want to thank you for always being such a support and good friend to me.'[71] Roy Strong recorded in his diary that later in the day he attended an ICA *soirée*: 'everyone there – CB not recognizing me with Procktor and train'.[72]

In the early summer Cecil worked hard designing white tulip spring bouquets for an American firm. He became exhausted again and when revising an article on Australia with Eileen he suddenly flew off the handle. She wrote him a note: 'What a pity you were in such an ugly mood on such a lovely day.'[73] Cecil was surprised by this: 'A year ago I wouldn't have shown my ugly mood and Eileen would certainly not have remarked upon it. As she did she made a mistake. I was extremely offended.'[74] Again Cecil was surprised when a pretty girl from the *Sunday Times* came to interview him. She asked him how he reconciled himself to his public image:

> The answer is I never think about myself at all in terms of a celebrity. Admittedly I like a certain dignified publicity but myopically I do not give any thought to the impression that this must make on others. I certainly do not feel that the public is conscious of me. I am not a celebrity.[75]

Cecil hoped her article would for once not show him as 'a rather glib fop wearing startling Edwardian clothes and appearing as if my work came without any effort'.[76] The profile was in connection with Cecil's show of theatrical designs at the Wright Hepburn Gallery in May. Eighteen designs were sold at the private view, celebrities like Olivier, Margot Fonteyn and Nureyev being particularly popular. So Cecil came home for a cold supper and by one in the morning had completed seven more. To coincide with this exhibition he gave a cocktail party at Pelham Place, but found most of his seventy guests unexciting.

After London the exhibition travelled to New York. Four of the paintings sold there were returned by their owners on the grounds that Cecil was anti-Jewish. 'This recurrent threat has continued with me for over thirty years now, and it isn't as if I had been anti-Jewish at any point in my life. Amazing how one mistake ... can have such repercussions!'[77] The two exhibitions raised £955 and £1,070 respectively.

Meanwhile Cecil worked quietly at Broadchalke, editing Volume IV of his diaries (before the fate of Volume III was decided) and having strange dreams. One was 'an awful situation in which the Duchess of Windsor was present while I was being humiliated wearing a toupé that would not behave itself'.[78]

The social round continued apace with a dinner at Wilton with Princess Marina and a ball to celebrate Esmond Rothermere's seventieth birthday. Patrick Procktor came to stay bringing a disobedient dog that disconcerted him, wreaking havoc in house and garden. And Cecil dined with Lee Radziwill on the day of Bobby Kennedy's assassination and Lee spoke freely about Jackie. Cecil noted the death of Randolph Churchill: 'He would be furious and perhaps it's typical of his bad luck that he expired on the same day as Bobby Kennedy and that in the newspapers he rates second billings.'[79]

In London, after another Wrightsman cruise, Cecil had an encounter with Madame Yevonde, who had been a pupil of his childhood favourite Lallie Charles. She took some portraits of him but observed worrying traits in him: 'I am rather concerned about your sadness,' she wrote. 'Your splendid career should have made you happy. Old age attacks us all and when you look at your beautiful work you should not repine over much.'[80]

In August Cecil went to New York to meet Kin and to design the Raffles* club. Kin had brought some mescalin tablets and Cecil tried these for the first time. As he succumbed to the drug, Cecil relished the colours most of all:

> All the strong colours became phosphorescent and the pale pastel tones had a stronger glow. The colours were changing all the time, flickering like a fire and one watched in amazement at the various effects. They were so dramatic. Even the ceiling became a playground of changing pale greens, and lavenders and cerulean blues, the net curtains an organ with pipes of slightly swaying rainbow colours that changed according to the light outside. One takes for granted the changing gradations caused by passing clouds, by the changing position of the sun. Now the rooms were different every moment of the day.[81]

It was the same when they looked at *The Best of Beaton*, whose pictures were mainly black and white: 'The Wyndham sisters really seemed to be sitting in front of us, and the Lambton wedding group became deep and lush in textures of many varieties.'[82] Cecil did not feel the lack of control that an excess of alcohol induced. He was very happy. These were new experiences for a man of sixty-four, an age when many of his contemporaries would have been content to walk their dogs in the country.

The drugs even helped Cecil come to terms with himself as an old man. He thought he looked 'like King Lear in the last act', but if Kin liked him like this then 'why shouldn't I like myself too'.[83] Kin, looking at an old photograph of Cecil, had said he liked him better at sixty than at thirty. He was glad he had not met him when he was younger. Cecil came down to earth: 'I had a very long hot bath. I felt warm at last. I felt rather smug and pleased about my secret day as I went out to dinner with Diana Vreeland.'[84]

---

*Now Doubles (in the Sherry-Netherland Hotel). It opened as Raffles in October 1968. The 'initiation' fee was $500. There were signed portraits of beauties such as Princess Grace and Irene Castle (who died in January 1969). Overall the atmosphere suggested a gentleman's club in London.

While in New York, Cecil received a message from Frank Giles, deputy editor of the *Sunday Times*, asking for an appreciation of Princess Marina. She had died at Kensington Palace on 27 August. Cecil had not known she was seriously ill, so the news of her death shocked him deeply. Kin was still in New York and Cecil kept recalling memories of the past:

> Excuse me but I do remember so vividly her talking about her interest at my romance with Greta. She thought it so surprising that I should feel this way. She thought more about one and one's problems than seemed apparent. She had a formal manner but a conspiratorial gift for intimacy and in later years I really felt she was a true friend.[85]

Cecil wrote a touching piece about her, which was clearly heartfelt, but it was not easy:

> All the time I was writing I felt extremely sad, not so much for Princess Marina, for her death was sudden and painless and she did not know she was seriously ill. Moreover her life was an empty one and she had little more to live for. But for people of my age the loss is great for she was so much a part of an era and she added so much to the early days. She was always so vividly around, even until now, so that with her going she leaves a very great gap.[86]

Princess Alexandra wrote to thank Cecil for writing at this 'bewildering' time:

> Thank God my sweet Mama knew no pain or suffering. And now she is at peace. The Sunday article I liked so much as it was humorous and unpompous and she would have enjoyed it![87]

Princess Marina from The Glass of Fashion

37

Forty Years On

I hope you will be crowned with well-deserved laurels. Oh dear that wicked face on the invitation took me back 100 years. Thank goodness you haven't mellowed. Nor I hope have I.

Nancy Mitford to Cecil, 24 October 1968

Roy Strong, who had so admired Cecil's production of *The Second Mrs Tanqueray*, was now the energetic director of the National Portrait Gallery. He conceived the idea that an exhibition of Cecil's photographs would be a wonderful means of bringing the gallery, hitherto a neglected repository of distinguished portraits, into the very mainstream of London's artistic life. It was the first exhibition of photography there, the first time living sitters had been exhibited, and the first time that non-British faces were included.

Cecil lunched with Dr Strong at the National Portrait Gallery in the summer of 1967 and judged him 'such a nice odd character, a real addition to my acquaintance, owl-eyed, funny, calm, and so unimpressed with his success at half my age'.[1]

The idea of the exhibition, together with a plan to lodge an archive of Cecil's photographs at the gallery, was presented to the trustees and accepted on 19 June 1967. Cecil and Eileen were soon busy unearthing old photographs and negatives. On 26 September 1968 Lord Kenyon, the chairman of the trustees, wrote to Cecil: 'This exhibition ... will be a real landmark in the Gallery's history.'[2] His hopes were fully justified. It also proved a landmark in Cecil's career. He began to refer to it jokingly as his 'forty years on'[3] exhibition. He also chose this as the moment to un-retouch some of the photographs, feeling that this was more in the spirit of the late 1960s.

The task of designing the show fell to Dicky Buckle, whose previous enterprises in this field included the Shakespeare 400th anniversary at Stratford in 1964. There were of course the inevitable difficulties when artistic men collaborate. 'Dicky was somewhat intransigent on the telephone this morning,' wrote Roy Strong, 'but I hope you won.'[4] The director prepared his *homage à Beaton*: 'Got all your books out of the London Library – how ever did you do it all? One needs at least two footmen to carry them.'⁵ Plans progressed swiftly.

Cecil was also busy gathering topical sitters for the exhibition and for *The Best of Beaton*.

At the age of ninety-six Bertrand Russell declined to be photographed: 'I must resist firmly the encroachments of this occupation, even when the suggestion comes from yourself.'⁶ The model Verushka was another who did not materialize. The Queen was more co-operative, using the occasion to be immortalized by Cecil on a set of Channel Island stamps (earning Cecil £340). Sir Martin Charteris wrote from Balmoral with characteristic good humour:

> The Queen will be glad to give you a session when you can get under the black velvet and press your bulb at 2.30 p.m. on Wednesday 16 October.⁷

He added:

> I am under legal obligation to remind you that under the terms of the Copyright Act of 1956 the copyright of all photographs taken at the sitting belongs to the Queen. So watch it!⁸

Cecil persuaded the Queen that she should wear a navy blue serge admiral's cloak in contrast to the endless crinolines and tiaras. Cecil liked its clean line and simplicity.

He found the Queen in a good mood: 'She has also developed a manner of making quite a lot of faces, grinning and showing vitality.'⁹ The Queen was amused when Cecil said that he always tried to take photographs without enough light. He said people looked better that way and then wondered if he had been tactless. He found that the Queen looked particularly good if she tilted her head. Later he wished he had climbed a step ladder to emphasize that effect. At the end of the session he had highest hopes from what he called 'the poor man's Annigoni'.¹⁰ He was never pleased with the results but welcomed 'the rapturous cries of others'.¹¹ He wondered if the photographs would prove 'the latest milestone in my career – or is it a nail in the coffin?'¹² It was the former.

Cecil also netted Alec McCowen as Hadrian VII, the novelist Patrick White, whom he had met in Australia, Benjamin Britten, Lord Goodman, Christopher Bruce of the Ballet Rambert, and Mary Hopkin, 'an old-fashioned doll type who has suddenly emerged to be head of the charts'¹³ (with 'Those were the Days').

Cecil went to Paris and hoped to photograph the reluctant Cartier-Bresson, who had sold his private aeroplane and his car and took no incoming telephone calls but did answer letters. Cartier-Bresson agreed to meet him again for the first time in twenty years. Cecil resorted to the ruse of photographing him surreptitiously as he crossed the courtyard. Inside he asked formal permission as he wanted to include him in his show as the photographer he most admired. Cartier-Bresson told him: 'There are three categories of people who should never be photographed – prostitutes, private detectives and photographers.'[14] When he left, Cecil, having in turn forbidden him to take his photograph, wondered 'if I would, under the circumstances, dare to use the pictures I had snooped'.[15] In the end caution overcame him.

As the opening approached, Cecil reviewed his reactions to it:

> My feelings about my 'life's' work are very mixed. I am proud and pleased that this honour is being conferred and I'm pleasantly surprised that a number of the old pictures stand the test of time. But certainly I do not have the euphoric joy that such things would have given me at an earlier stage in my life. The fact that I look so awful myself is something that prevents my enjoyment of the publicity angle.[16]

Cecil also defined his attitude to the future:

> I give a great deal of thought nowadays to my old age. I notice so many inevitable changes taking place so that the usual will happen. My interests are more in the garden, in quieter things of the mind, much less interest in people, and even a disdain for what is known as society. This used to be important to me. Now I am dreadfully censorious, can't be benign about these idiotic women who spend so much money on tastelessly adorning their hideous bodies – the men so desperately climbing the ladder of snobbery. I can't pretend or console myself with the knowledge that I learn anything new, or that my intellectual powers work on any but the most sluggish basis, but fortunately I still have my work to do.[17]

The exhaustion before the exhibition was intense. Cecil was stuck in a traffic jam on his way to Princess Marina's memorial service. He had to run the last three quarters of a mile to the Abbey. From the magnificent service, he rushed to the National Portrait Gallery, feeling ill. 'Here a tremendous thrill, a real *cri de cœur* of joy went up when I saw Dicky had almost finished the exhibition and it was *marvellous!* The first glimpse of the studio made me exclaim with joy.'[18] The excitement gave Cecil a new vitality.

One of the last sitters was the Prince of Wales before the Opening of Parliament on 30 October:

> The sitting with the P. of Wales was dull in comparison to the recent one with his mother. I blame the lousy London climate more than the Prince who incidentally is a simple, nice, cheerful adolescent of nineteen years. He has a gentle regard, a disarming smile and the tip of his nose

is delicately modelled and like a Gainsborough ... his hair is long and this is a triumph of independence over the influence of his father and others at court.[19]

Vogue gave a party for Cecil later that day amongst the white lilies and smilax. He was delighted that the guests paid attention to the photographs:

It was a rewarding sight to see the enthusiasm of June, Diana C, Noël C, Gladys C[althrop], looking at catalogues and the exhibits on high. All our little jokes seemed appreciated and the effects were working. The 'studio' a very lively spot with the revolving P.C. stand of M. Monroe,* the flashing lights, the huge plaster hat and stove, a lively scene enjoyed by all. Django Reinhardt and [Julian] Bream playing Dowland, the incense burning, the lights flicking, the flashlight held the eye, going off every second. Only the toy theatre was on the blink.[20]

All Cecil's worlds were represented. Besides old friends like Freddie Ashton, there was Evangeline Bruce (wife of the American Ambassador), Lee Radziwill, David Bailey, Penelope Tree, Patrick Procktor, David Hockney and Normal Hartnell. That inveterate gallery visitor, Charlotte Bonham Carter, going round, overheard a girl say to her fiancé in a hushed voice: 'I should say this is a real cross-section of English life.' Lady Bonham Carter disagreed. Her verdict was that the pictures were of 'the great and the beautiful'.[21]

On the next day, 31 October, there was a press show and Cecil took Princess Marina's bereaved sister, Princess Olga, around privately:

She was at her worst, her manner so brusque that Roy felt he was *de trop* and retired like a stricken deer: 'Och those are hippies. Great Heaven! So they've taken their clothes off!' She nevertheless telephoned the Queen Mother and said she had been touched. The show was very nostalgic.[22]

The Queen Mother's visit at 5.30 that afternoon crowned the event. Roy Strong said, 'Oh, the excitement. I think this is the most thrilling thing that has ever happened to me!'[23] The Queen Mother made her tour. When they reached the war section, Dicky Buckle took over and told her that Cecil had not known the difference between an RAF badge and a Grenadier's. 'Jolly, girlish, sympathetic, darling Q.M.,'[24] commented Cecil. Due to pouring rain and heavy traffic she left by the back door, passing the Gallery's milk bottles on the steps.

Next morning all the papers (except Mother *Times*) carried huge pictures of the Queen in the boatman's cloak. They created a big stir and were incidentally good publicity for my exhibition to which Roy Strong, always an optimist, said 1,000 people had come in the first public morning.[25]

The good start continued. Thirty thousand people came in November. (Cecil was delighted that this equalled those who went to Henry Moore's.)

* Cecil derived this from Stephen Tennant's idea of a revolving postcard stand at Wilsford. Even now his influence had effect.

Queues stretched into Trafalgar Square the first two weekends. Roy Strong announced that the appeal was very varied. Odd beat types vied with the more normal gallery goers. One man stood weeping in front of the portraits of Gertrude Lawrence declaring that times had changed. The exhibition was extended until the end of February, when the grand total was 80,000. The press gave Cecil full glory. 'In another age he would have been a Lely, a Kneller or a Romney,'[26] declared the *Tatler*. 'To walk into the current exhibition of *Beaton Portraits: 1928–68* at the National Portrait Gallery is to enter a time-capsule of the utmost fascination,'[27] wrote Ainsley Ellis in the *British Journal of Photography*. His old friend Madge Garland declared that his work had now taken on historical importance:

> If he does not care to show his sitters 'warts and all' few would quarrel with him for this omission. Today, his superb technique, hidden behind an apparent facility which belies his serious purpose, can make careless studies of the new generation which reflect the distraught 'sixties as clearly as did his many-faceted portraits of the undecided 'thirties.[28]

Keith Roberts wrote in the *Burlington Magazine*:

> Beaton is, I would have thought, an equivalent in photography to Sir Joshua Reynolds in painting with sitters from every walk of life and an eclectic talent for borrowing visual ideas from a wide variety of sources. Like Reynolds (and, indeed, most professional portraitists), Mr Beaton grasped from the very beginning that portraiture is not so much about likeness as about imagery.[29]

In December the Prince of Wales toured the exhibition with Cecil. Later he wrote to thank Cecil:

> It was immensely kind of you to interrupt your morning to show me round and I very much enjoyed seeing your exhibition and all the familiar faces staring back at one from the walls. Particular pleasure was to be had from the frieze of beauties and one of my favourites was the little girl suffering from bombing – it brought one up with a jerk.
>
> By far the best way of seeing an exhibition is to the accompaniment of music and yours was superb.[30]

Cecil was amused that Jennie Lee, the Minister for the Arts, hated his show, 'and when asked if she didn't concede the war pictures were good barked back: "But they were fashionable then." '[31]

Needless to say, Cecil did not then retire gracefully from the scene. Within a week he was on the set of *Performance* photographing Mick Jagger, James Fox and Anita Pallenberg. This film was the cause of more friction between the Rolling Stones, because, during what should have been a simulated love-scene in a canopied antique bed supplied by Christopher Gibbs, Mick

Jagger and Anita Pallenberg 'began to make love in earnest',[32] unwittingly providing the raw material for an award-winning blue movie in Amsterdam. Meanwhile Keith Richard sat outside in the car, sulking. When Cecil arrived at Lowndes Square with his camera, he was asked if this was not a surprising contrast to his normal work. 'It really is all part of a day's work to me,'[33] he replied.

A week later he flew to Hollywood to meet twenty-six-year-old Barbra Streisand and discuss her wardrobe for *On a Clear Day You Can See Forever*:

> The meeting with Streisand was an event. Her publicity is so bad that I feared she might be the tyrant, the virago, the bitch that she is said to be. Instead she was particularly ingratiating and amenable. From the moment she appeared, late, at the rehearsal, it was evident that she has star quality, is a natural. She is above all else intelligent. Her brain works so clearly, so healthily. She could be a lawyer. She is never hurried. ... She has flair, natural taste. ... As for her looks they are fascinating. Her complexion is poreless, immaculate, shiny. Her eyes a grey blue are beautiful but for the fatal fault of a slight squint, teeth pearly and large.[34]

Cecil was surprised to find someone 'so young who had such an awareness and knowledge of herself'.[35] Speaking shortly before his death, he described two types of superstar: 'the coolly detached and the fanatically involved'.[36] Audrey Hepburn was the former and Streisand the latter. They shared the same regal quality when they wore their later grander costumes.

Although Cecil was only in Hollywood for a fortnight he felt as bad again as in his *My Fair Lady* days five years earlier. He was glad to snatch a weekend with Kin before retreating to England. On 5 December he flew to Tangiers to buy gauzes and spangled tissues in the souks. These he would use in the Brighton sequence of *On a Clear Day*.

At home for Christmas he worried about his health. He had suffered from six weeks of colitis, which distressed him greatly. He never knew when next he would be struck: 'My entrails felt as if they were the bubbling waters of a Dante's inferno.'[37] Besides this he worried about his finances, contemplated leaving Broadchalke for the stables at Wilton (this a recurring idea until his death), and found he was making scant progress with his painting. As always he gained no lasting confidence from his recent important success.

The year 1969 was to be a busy one with Cecil's work on both *On a Clear Day* and *Coco*, Frederick Brisson's musical production about the life of Coco Chanel, starring Katharine Hepburn. Both productions had lyrics by Alan Jay Lerner and both had been in the pipeline for three years. In April 1968, Cecil had been in despair: 'Really Alan is beyond a joke. He has three big projects [the third was *Paint Your Wagon*] on hand and is running round in circles creating havoc in every part of the world at the same time.'[38] Now that they almost coincided, there was some question as to whether Cecil could manage both. This situation was aggravated by the possibility that he might design *Nicholas and Alexandra* for Sam Spiegel. Paramount settled that Cecil would receive a total salary of $25,000 for his services on *On a Clear Day*, which were specifically defined. When in Los Angeles he would be given $750 living expenses. Later Arnold Weissberger wrote that on the basis of $400 a costume, an increase in work meant that Cecil should get an extra $38,400. Howard W. Koch replied: 'To say your letter was a shock to me is putting it mildly.'[39] However he was happy to pay an extra $15,000.

On 30 December 1968 Cecil paid his second visit to Hollywood. He stayed twelve days and resolved that that would be his last visit. He was pleased to escape to Phoenix, Arizona, to the ranch of Jimmy Davison and Nicky Haslam. Here the ever-adventurous Cecil went riding: 'It is quite an event for me to have got on to a horse and enjoyed, in the last rays of the sunshine, a canter along the dried river-bed.'[40] Not having ridden since Ashcombe days, he was at first alarmed by the canter but he remembered the correct reflexes and was soon in control of the situation to the welcome applause of his hosts.

In January 1969 Cecil was listed as one of the best-dressed men in the world:

> What a farce. If only people knew! I spend comparatively little on clothes, an occasional good suit but most of my suits are made in Hong Kong or Gillingham, Dorset, or bought on quaysides during my travels abroad. I do not own a clean pair of gloves and my shirts are mostly frayed. I suppose I should realize the list is entirely phoney when Prince Philip, one of the worst most 'square' ugly dressers, is top of the list.[41]

Lady Anne Tree observed that she considered that Cecil always wore his clothes a size or so too small for him. He was aware that comfort and elegance were seldom combined. Similarly his beautiful winter garden at Reddish contained no comfortable chair to sit in.

At the end of January, Cecil retreated alone to the Bühlerhohe Sanatorium near Baden-Baden. He stayed there for a fortnight, indulging in pine bubble baths and massages, hoping to emerge in better health. Herr Willy Brandt was a fellow patient and about the only break in routine was when Harold Wilson's foreign secretary, Michael Stewart, arrived to confer with him. The other was the announcement of Fritzi Massari's death. Cecil was enraged that he was not allowed to stay up and watch a late programme about her on television.

Cecil had Gibbon and Thackeray to read, but he was soon at work again, polishing his fourth volume of diaries, *The Restless Years*. He had too much time to think and inevitably this depressed him. His thoughts turned to his father (who died two years older than Cecil's present age) and to Peter Watson, whom he concluded, at this time, had been more important to him than either Garbo or Kin. Despite the years of frustration and misery, that relationship had remained 'pure and more magical than anything that has ever happened to me'.[42] He also experienced vivid dreams. Alone, he thought: 'Quite probably if one continues long enough one will regain one's health at the expense of one's sanity.'[43]

Suddenly Cecil was enthused by the idea of reviving his *Gainsborough Girls* play, a copy of which he had brought with him. It was ten years since the last production and a new generation of actors and producers had grown up. He threw himself with customary vigour into the endeavour, working to the point of overstrain. If this was contrary to the aims of the sanatorium, at least he no longer awoke thinking of death. He resolved to present his effort to Patrick Procktor or Patrick Garland. Cecil endured the fortnight and was more than happy to return to Pelham Place.

The play was not revived. In July Patrick Garland, a rare heterosexual in the theatre world, wrote a 'frank, honest and rather butch assessment'[44] of the play and turned it down. Cecil was very disappointed but still did not admit defeat.

He was soon back in his old life, rushing around London, taking twelve taxis a day. He was soon exhausted anew. His exhibition was going to New York but Dicky Buckle was in a rage about not being sent. Aunt Cada's ninetieth birthday was celebrated at Pelham Place in February. His brave old aunt, who had been blind since 1953, was delighted to have attained this age (which her sister Etty just missed). Old friends like Dame Eva Turner, Bertie Watson and Cecil's Heath Mount contemporary, Dudley Scholte, were there to hear Cecil propose an emotional toast.* The spring witnessed Dicky Buckle's failed Isadora Duncan party at which Vanessa Redgrave passed out, more Francis Rose dramas, a dinner with Nureyev at Richmond and Cecil's kind vigilance at the prolonged dying of Sidney Pembroke. The Earl died at Wilton on 16 March. Cecil wrote a heart-felt tribute which was published in the *Salisbury Journal*. The new Earl, his son, wrote in thanks to Cecil: 'I did not realize that such beauty could flow from anyone's pen in the twentieth century.'[45]

In March 1969 Cecil settled in Tom Parr's comfortable and chic Brighton flat, with Ray in attendance, to do his location stint on *On a Clear Day*. T.C. Worsley took him over to break the ice with Enid Bagnold at Rottingdean.

While in Australia in the spring of 1968, Cecil had been moved to send Enid a note wishing her success with her play, *Call Me Jacky*, which opened in Oxford that February. Thus a silence of twelve years was broken to the great relief of Enid: '*How* I stared – with what a hoping heart – almost

* Aunt Cada died in January 1970.

unbelieving at your letter – Dear Cecil – I have missed you like a great chunk of my life.'[46]

Cecil found Enid sitting arthritically in the drawing-room, the house unchanged but now covered in dust. He was fascinated by her, but concluded that he did not like her any more than he had imagined he would. She was too self-centred. Later in the year he found her *Autobiography* very absorbing: 'it is a remarkable legacy for her to leave, an important and profound reportage in depth of a strange, remarkable, original and warped life'.[47]

Before Cecil read the book Enid wondered if he would be furious about her description of the *Chalk Garden* row. Cecil was not furious: 'all is forgiven, if not forgotten, and I am touched and pleased by the nice things you say about me. I can't quite recognize myself as being the wonderful person you make me out to be, but I not only give you a Dickensian bow for the bouquet but a kiss on each cheek.'[48] Enid replied: 'What I said of you is what I think of you and if you only partly believe it, it's the same virtue, ironic intelligence.'[49] Thereafter the two were friends, but always a little guarded, neither wishing to cause another row. As Enid said in old age: 'It was always rather a cold friendship.'[50]

Cecil also ended his *Chalk Garden* vendetta against John Gielgud. Sir John wrote: 'I have missed the pleasure of your friendship over these last years. I have always valued it and regret our long estrangement.'[51] He gave his version of the *Chalk Garden* drama, ending:

I dislike having to blame other people, even at this late date, but as you obviously thought it was all my doing I feel I must give you the facts. It was no use my going into them at the time, but anyway that is how it was.[52]

Cecil then gave his justification but ended:

It is strange that, hating rows as much as I do, I should have found myself on 'non speaks' with half of the London theatre, but perhaps I should have learnt to throw off lightly the disloyalties of those in the theatre whom I have been under the impression were my friends. I have learnt however that there is no benefit in harbouring hard feelings and have even accepted an olive branch from Enid, so I am very glad to feel that we are friends again.[53]

Thereafter the two were friends to the end.

Cecil 'sauntered off'[54] for the first day's shooting at the Brighton Pavilion. Felix Harbord, his designer friend, was there trying to put some authenticity into the banquet scene. Meanwhile Cecil created an instant costume for Irene Handl to wear in an exterior shot. A calico glove bag was transformed into a cap and sprayed dirty. A piece of canvas sacking became an apron and the rug that her chihuahuas usually sat on in their basket served as a shawl. The whole outfit took five minutes to assemble. At the end of the day he found he was much more tired than he would have been six years before. As ever Cecil enjoyed odd vignettes. The extras at the banquet were seated in front of mounds of delicious food. Vincente Minnelli shouted suddenly: 'Eat up. Devour everything in sight. Shove it all in. You're gourmets.'[55] The next day the banqueting table was almost deserted. Either the food had gone off or the extras had overeaten. Cecil's mind pictured the scene: 'in theatrical boarding houses a night of much vomiting'.[56]

In the afternoon Cecil had a photographic session with Barbra Streisand, who liked his hit or miss approach. He continued to marvel at the star. Howard Koch told him:

> She used to be a waitress in a Chinese restaurant and then an usherette in the cinema. Now she has her own companies. And she's just started. She's going to be responsible for her own pictures in future.[57]

Cecil was in Brighton for Easter. On the Sunday he wandered about with his camera trying to take Cartier-Bresson-style photos and finding it far from easy. Then he went to the studio to see Barbra Streisand film in the kitchen. Having suffered an upset stomach following a visit to a kosher restaurant with Howard Koch and a secret date with the new James Bond, George Lazenby, she found the kitchen decorated with 'great sides of beef, geese, chickens, pies, fish, sugar cakes and every sort of giant banquet food, not the most congenial atmosphere for someone with a weak stomach. The smell of the food, now becoming a little high, had to be sweetened by atomizer sprays.'[58]

On Easter Monday they filmed scenes with Barbra Streisand meeting the Prince Regent. Cecil tried to influence them into making the dialogue more elegant, but in vain. He discovered that Barbra's best costume, the purple street dress, would not be seen full length in the film. However, he was pleased to learn from a questionnaire submitted to Barbra that she thought him 'a beautiful man and a beautiful talent'.[59]

Cecil photographed Barbra Streisand in her costumes, having successfully ensured that neither Lord Snowdon nor Lord Lichfield were invited on to the set. Diana Vreeland wanted these exclusively for *Vogue*, which gave Cecil an excuse to point out that he had received very little money from *Vogue* in recent months. Diana Vreeland replied:

> You have always been the most faithful and wonderful contributing editor which we deeply appreciate and you make many suggestions, some of which as you know are not possible for us to use.[60]

Diana Vreeland sent a memo to Alexander Liberman, saying that, though they both thought Cecil unwell and had been trying to spare him, clearly he needed more work and they must make a joint effort to find him some.

In October 1969 she allowed Cecil to sell some of his Katharine Hepburn pictures to *McCalls* which thrilled him:

> When I first went to *Vogue*, Mrs Chase did everything she could to make me feel imprisoned in the CNP organization with the result that I was always chafing to get out. It is obviously so much more humanitarian to let people feel fairly free to do the right thing, but it is also much more intelligent.[61]

As for the photographs, Barbra Streisand liked these better than a series that Cecil took in New York the following May. At this later session, she had felt unwell. She would only approve the photographs after retouching when lines, marks and a spot on her chin had been brushed out.

Cecil's work on the film ended more happily than usual. Howard Koch wrote: 'The Brighton dailies are breathtaking, your costumes are smashing, and everyone is thrilled with the way our film is looking.'[62]

However, Cecil was determined that he would not return to Hollywood for any extra work, and his lawyer assured him this would not be necessary. The film itself was a failure at the box offices, but Cecil's contribution made an enjoyably rich Regency splash in the middle of it. Perhaps the happiest outcome was Cecil's verdict on Barbra Streisand:

> I like B.S. very much; she is a good, fine girl and if we do not speak the same language we are at any rate in sympathy with one another. She is very clever – and meticulous.[63]

On a Clear Day opened to bad notices, deservedly so in Cecil's view. He did not see it until 1971. He thought the over-spending more than explained the collapse of Hollywood as a film centre. He noticed that many expensive scenes had been cut:

> It may be said that I was well paid for the job and that is all I should worry about. But that isn't the whole story. I really sweated to see that things were perfect and that is the only way I can work. But if another job comes along that I don't really believe in, will I remember the lesson of *On a Clear Day*? I rather doubt it![64]

On 1 May Cecil's exhibition, entitled '600 Faces by Beaton: 1928–69', opened at the Museum of the City of New York. Cecil was 'honored' at a benefit. New York society came out in force to give or attend dinners, including the Alan Lerners, Brooke Astor, the Leland Haywards, Mary Lasker, Janet Rhinelander Stewart, the Josh Logans, Mrs Oscar Hammerstein, Irene Selznick, Charlotte Ford Niarchos, Ruth Ford, the Bill Paleys, the Louis Auchinclosses, and so on. As 'Suzy' said:

> Why, if the Queen herself were here tonight I'm sure she'd do something

a little gala for Cecil. He's the sort of chap one feels like tying on one's hair ribbon for, the clever thing.[65]

Lincoln Kirstein recommended new sitters that Cecil could add to this show to give it a modern New York flavour. In the end he chose Charles Ryskamp, the new director of the Morgan Library, McNeil Lowry, of the Ford Foundation, Lincoln Kirstein himself with his sister Mina Curtiss, Peter Mennin, director of the Juillard School, David Hockney, Anthony Dowell and Andy Warhol, 'the Zombie, more dead than alive since he was shot':*

At first the mercurial groups of strange people sitting around in silence or moving pointlessly around his huge factory were difficult to capture. But eventually I felt I had a valuable addition to the exhibition. In fact I had.[66]

As in London, the exhibition was mainly treated as a news event and there was no shortage of profiles of Cecil and crowd-drawing publicity. The most serious criticism was written by Hilton Kramer in the *New York Times* in a long article entitled 'Comedies of Manners', in which he decried the art of 'intellectual condescension and inverted snobbery' prevalent in so many museum exhibitions:

In fact the exhibition (600 Faces by Beaton: 1928–69) seems almost designed to encourage our sense of its superficialities, to underscore the photographer's attachment to the vicissitudes of fashion, celebrity, and the vagaries of publicity. Certainly no photographer who cared deeply about the aesthetic integrity of his medium would have permitted the inclusion of so many indifferent prints or sanctioned an installation – complete with campy musical sound tracks – that invites the blurred vision of nostalgia to take such overwhelming precedence over the appreciation of individual images.

But in all this Mr Beaton has only been true to his own sense of vocation – a vocation that has always ministered to the well-lighted stage on which established figures in the arts, mannequins from the world of high fashion, and the elegant human detritus of the *beau monde* cross each others' paths and engage temporarily in mutual promotion. In his role as photographic courtier to this milieu, Mr Beaton has occasionally displayed a kind of genius – a genius for precisely the form of sociability I have been speaking of. His entire vision is circumscribed by the values of the clients he has so shamelessly flattered over a long stretch of years. There is never a critical note, though there is occasionally some very

* Andy Warhol had been shot in the side at the Factory on 3 June 1968 by a feminist who headed SCUM (the 'Society to Cut Up Men'). Ironically, like Randolph Churchill's death, the story was overshadowed by Bobby Kennedy's assassination.

gentle humor. There are even some very arresting moments – the photograph of Gertrude Stein and Alice B. Toklas is one of them – when he takes a holiday from the world of chic feeling and gives us a glimpse of something infinitely more fundamental. But such moments are rare. He is, in the main, a prisoner of the superficial, making the most of the freedom he enjoys in that realm. ...

Mr Beaton is not a great photographer, but his career is an essential datum in the history of an era.[67]

The exhibition went to the de Young Museum in San Francisco in June and July 1970 and then to the Joslyn Museum in Omaha, Nebraska, for January and February 1971. It might have gone elsewhere but Cecil had insisted that it be hung as in New York. The adventure ended in a row and threats of legal action when it appeared that the entire collection might be destroyed in Omaha in June. Eventually, however, it was transported back to New York.

While in New York Cecil visited an Astra analyst, whom Sam Green assured him had been responsible for the success of *Hair* by advising the producers of the most auspicious astral time on which to open. Cecil thrived on his talks with such people and came away with a new surge of confidence because she told him that 'the next two years would be those in which I made my final contribution of beauty to the world, and thereafter I would retire from the worldly scene to enjoy life in my garden and home'.[68] Perhaps she was more on target when she described Cecil as 'a bachelor married to the public'[69] for his life since the 1950s (and even earlier) had been a long series of delights for the public with very little private happiness for him. Cecil hoped that what he called 'the struggle' would prove worthwhile and did not in the least mind the prospect of 'the garden' later. However, life was not to prove kind to him in this respect. Nor in the more immediate situation did he think he could leave New York in a happy mood. He had suffered months of silence from Kin, who never answered his letters. Literally at the airport Cecil's call to San Francisco was answered and he was relieved to find that, after all, this friendship was not over.

Cecil spent the summer in London. David Hockney came down to draw him. It took eight appalling sketches before Cecil was in any way content. Meanwhile 'poor Roy Strong did not seem to have much attention paid to him and he had recourse to doing bad water colours in the conservatory and garden'.[70] When Hockney's drawings were done Cecil suffered in the same way as he had over Francis Bacon: 'How *could* he see me thus and still like me?'[71]

The summer passed with many visitors to Reddish and a concert evening with the Queen Mother, Cecil enjoying riding with her in her Rolls-Royce. He had an exhausting few days in Paris, but it is characteristic that Cecil should observe and act upon the plight of Madame Dilé, who was being removed from *Vogue* after forty-three years in the *Vogue* studio. He wrote to Alexander Liberman asking that her services be rewarded in some way. Later he also wrote to Diana Vreeland. She responded to his plea. 'I'm so glad you sent Madame Dilé off in flying form,' wrote Cecil. 'She is such a staunch support and has been for so many years. It wrenched my heart when she was turfed out of her little office for some vulgar magazine and had to sit out the rest of her time at CNP in a draughty line-up.'[72] Without his intervention a loyal servant to Condé Nast would have slipped away without notice.

Cecil revelled in the moon landings with Irene Worth and James Pope-Hennessy (the latter suffering from DTs). Meanwhile design after design for *Coco* was drawn 'like a Japanese on a conveyor belt'.[73] In August Katharine Hepburn arrived in London for *Coco* fittings. Cecil's dilemma was to make her look more like Chanel than Hepburn. He went through many reactions to the star. After Barbra Streisand he found her distinguished and was impressed by her directness. She found herself uneasy with Cecil and never responded to his invitations to the country. He began to think of her as 'a complete egomaniac. I see a school ma'am, a Victorian sportswoman or suffragette. I see a woman without a vestige of humour.'[74] However, the clothes looked good. 'Why are you smiling?' asked Katharine Hepburn. 'I didn't tell her it was with relief,'[75] noted Cecil.

Nevertheless, while relaxing at Henry McIlhenny's sybaritic Glenveagh Castle in Ireland, Cecil noted: 'I don't remember a period when I have so hated my life.'[76] One of his perpetual worries was the colitis which caused him many indignities and the ever present fear of public embarrassment. Now he relaxed, enjoying the luxury, but not the Americans:

> Some of Henry's guests were intolerable. I put up with Americans willingly only when I am on business bent. On holiday they are too trite. One old trout from Charleston was bemoaning the way the world was going.[77]

He went on to the house of Derek Hill, and upset the artist by describing it in his diaries as a clutter of untidiness and shabbiness. Then he set off to New York for a three-month stint on *Coco*.

38

Little Black Dresses

I am hating the Coco experience. I feel very depressed about its prospects. The book is as lousy as I thought it was, the music old fashioned. The bright spots are too far between and the bad over banal and beastly. K.H.'s singing voice is really pitiful and I can't think the show will get anything but appalling notices.

Cecil to Eileen Hose, November 1969

Plans to bring the musical *Coco* to the New York stage went back as far as 1966. 'I do think the Chanel piece would be a wonderful opportunity for me,'[1] wrote Cecil to his lawyer on 6 May 1966. However, by August 1969 his attitude had somewhat altered: 'The only reason I am involved in *Coco* is simply and only a question of hard cash.'[2]

Cecil was again working with Alan Jay Lerner, who asked his advice about the script. In 1967 Cecil wrote him a letter giving his detailed criticisms. Alan Lerner judged this letter an example of Cecil's professional

The Coco logo

approach to the theatre. He accepted many of the points made and acted on them. The producer was Frederick Brisson, the son of the Danish actor Carl Brisson, and producer of such shows as *Pajama Game* and *Alfie*. *Coco* had been his dream since 1960. Chanel had finally agreed but wanted to design the clothes herself. Brisson insisted on Cecil being used to create theatrical versions of her fashions. She said she wanted to be played by Hepburn. When Katharine Hepburn was signed, there was a theory that the eighty-six-year-old harridan had really meant Audrey. For Katharine Hepburn it was not only the first time she had been in a Broadway musical, it was the first time she had seen one other than *My Fair Lady*.

Cecil, Alan Lerner and Freddie Brisson had several meetings with Chanel over the years. In February 1967 Cecil wrote: 'Chanel is slowly going mad in a rather interesting way.'[3] In June 1969 he spent five gruelling hours with her while she flew into a rage with her secretary. She started her day slowly, but by 3 p.m. was 'galvanized and can be the great personality she was'.[4] Nevertheless Cecil could not understand why she wasted so much energy reviling modern styles: 'After all she did start the trousers which she now hates with such bitterness.'[5]

There were the habitual discussions about Cecil's contract, particularly the percentage he was to receive. There was an additional problem this time. Just as Garbo had been annoyed by what Cecil wrote about her in his 1937 *Scrapbook*, so too Katharine Hepburn had borne a long grudge about her entry. Some of Cecil's phrases were not perhaps the most flattering:

> Katharine Hepburn creates a bad first impression ... the rocking horse nostrils and corncrake, cockney voice had become the new heroine in succession to the spangled glamour girl.... Her strident voice is like a blade of new grass and she looks as if she had jumped into a stream for her morning bath.... She has tousled, beetroot-coloured hair, protuber-ant cheekbones, and an angry, hungry look, with strong shining teeth; she is joyously healthy and undoubtedly eats an apple a day....
> ... she is in close proximity very like any exceedingly animated and delightful hockey mistress at a Physical Training College.[6]

Katharine Hepburn took steps to ensure that she should suffer no further aggravation from Cecil's pen or crayons. Not only did she insist on the right to approve her costumes, but in her contract with Brisson she added the clause:

> Actor shall also have prior written approval of any written material, photographs or other material written about, or likenesses of Actor issued by or under the control of Mr CECIL BEATON.[7]

In Cecil's contract with Brisson Productions, Arnold Weissberger amended the clause as follows:

Designer understands that Miss Hepburn shall have prior written approval of any written material, photographs or other material written about, or likenesses of Miss Hepburn issued by or under the control of the Designer, while Miss Hepburn appears in the Play.[8]

To be on the safe side, Cecil did not mention Katharine Hepburn in his published diaries. However, in his private diaries he wrote about her and she was also the subject for one of the caricatures in which he indulged when he needed to let off steam.

Cecil was never very happy with the show, which in his opinion compared so badly to the *Zeitgeist* expressed in the film *Easy Rider*, *Midnight Cowboy* and even Warhol's *Lonesome Cowboys*.

As far as Kate was concerned Cecil went through the spectrum of feelings. He began by being moved by her intensity and she seemed pleased to see him. Meeting at rehearsal one day they kissed on the lips, 'a sensational gesture watched by all the management'.[9] Brisson later described this as 'the act of Judas'[10] because he knew she disapproved of many of Cecil's clothes. Photographing Kate, Cecil noted: 'She is blessed with a structure that is made for the camera and this is at least ¾ the reason why she has twenty million dollars in the bank.'[11] He disapproved of the way she wanted to play Chanel as a mousy Mary Poppins; nevertheless he was taken by her 'dynamic Yankee'[12] performance in rehearsals.

As always Cecil had a bogeyman in the production. In the absence of George Cukor, his resentment was focused on Alan Jay Lerner. Cecil shouted at him because the coromandel screens on stage which should have been hidden were exposed. In due course Lerner telephoned about some hats that needed to be changed and Cecil lost his temper as badly as ever he could recall. This provoked a hurt letter from Lerner, wondering at Cecil's mystifying attitude to him on this show. At the same time Michael Benthall, the director, was 'again smelling of whisky to such an extent that he was a fire danger'.[13] After *Coco* opened, he succumbed to a further bout of drinking, a problem which had dogged his career.

Above all Cecil was preoccupied with Katharine Hepburn. He admitted he was terrified of her. She resented the prominence of his name on publicity and hated his ingenious poster for the show. Sometimes she worried that she had taken on too much, particularly with the singing, but she need not have feared. Night after night she received thunderous applause. Cecil observed: 'I can't think she will be willing to leave this for a solitary life for as long as her health holds out (again at this matinée she had another nose bleed). I'm told the show is bringing in more money (at $15 tickets) than any other Broadway show ever has.'[14]

He shared Anita Loos's view of the show itself:

We saw the show last Tuesday … and found nothing to admire except your job. There were two spontaneous bursts of applause in the whole evening – for the black dresses and the red ones. Except for the latter, there would be no climax at all.

Your sets are superb and they work without a hitch – like a movie. In fact they are so absolutely right that they'll probably be taken for granted without any justice to you.

I could write on for an hour about the show but it's just as well not to put such things down on paper.[15]

Meanwhile New York society women telephoned Cecil in ecstasies of rapture. Sometimes these calls were followed by lavish bouquets of flowers. On 25 November Cecil's work on *Coco* was attacked by Marylin Bender in the *New York Times*:

Beaton's Chanels are as much like Chanel's Chanels as a jar of gefilte fish on a supermarket shelf is to *quenelles de brochet* at Grand Vefour. There's a circus pink sequin Chanel, worn by Noelle, the model, that must have been copied line for line on Division St.[16]

There was universal sympathy and a feeling that it was unfair. Even Kate shouted: 'Cecil, I hear you've been roasted!'[17] Cecil felt roasted on all sides, especially when Kate objected to some new costumes or when he discovered that she had allowed another photographer to have the first bite at publishing pictures of her in *Life*. At their worst moment, Frederick Brisson declared that he thought Hitler was alive on 51st Street, and Alan Jay Lerner, who had taken the brunt of Kate's displeasure about the clothes, was heard to say in a mixture of humour and despair that in case she was put off her performance someone should tell her that the man in the box office was wearing a pink tie.

At last the date of the grand first night arrived and Cecil escorted Lee Radziwill to his seats in the second row. He enjoyed the choreographed numbers and was thrilled by the cheers for the little black dresses. The red dresses were also cheered and the star received a standing ovation. Cecil gave a dinner for twenty-two at the St Regis and then went on to the Brissons' party. Here the reviews were circulated and Clive Barnes's was worse than even Cecil had feared. He praised Kate and denigrated the sets and costumes:

Mr Beaton has never struck me as a particularly accomplished designer – although his dresses were often pretty – and nothing in *Coco* causes me to revise that opinion.

There are only three settings in the show – the salon is ugly, the dressing-room is nondescript and Coco's apartment is rather pleasant and restrained in an early Oliver Smith mode.[18]

But the show was far from dead. Kate Hepburn played on until August 1970 and the dollars rolled in for everyone. By March 1970 Brisson was saying that $22,135 was the largest sum he had ever paid a designer.

In April 1970 Cecil won a 'Tony' award for his work. Julie Andrews read out his name to the joyous assembly. Kate Hepburn, who lost to Lauren Bacall, wrote to congratulate him. His old boss, Jack Warner, was delighted, and Joan Crawford also sent heartiest congratulations: 'And it was sheer joy to see your happy face on Sunday night at the Awards Show.'[19] An immediate $726 arrived for the use of the costumes at the ceremony.

By May, Arnold Weissberger was predicting that Cecil could make as much as $60,000. In August Danielle Darrieux took over from Kate, sang beautifully and also received a standing ovation, but without Kate, the show lost its impact and soon closed. Kate went on tour and the show ran until June 1971. In the meantime the death occurred of Coco Chanel, who had let Brisson down by not attending the New York opening. On hearing this news, Kate's next question concerned the weekly takings.

When the show opened in Cleveland, Ohio, Arnold Weissberger's friend, Milton Goldman, cabled '*Coco est morte.* I didn't think the musical was that bad.'[20]

Cecil was left astonished at the audience's enthusiasm for Katharine Hepburn. When his stint on *Coco* was over he concluded toughly:

> She has no generosity, no heart, no grace.... She cannot smile, except to bare her teeth to give an effect of utter youthfulness and charm.... Garbo has magic, but Hepburn is synthetic.... I hope I never have to see her again.[21]

When not working on *Coco*, Cecil had time for friends and the theatre. He visited Kenneth Tynan's *Oh Calcutta!*:

> I found the sketches extremely unattractive and it revolted me to see a row of people on cocktail stools masturbating themselves. Worse to hear young actresses describing their sexual experiences in the most basic and banal ways. Altogether though I was pleasantly surprised and though occasionally disgusted, even angry at the idea of Tynan becoming rich by such means, the evening was more enjoyable than most spent in the present season's theatre.[22]

He witnessed Kenneth Clark (whose *Civilization* was showing) receive an honour at the Metropolitan Museum with the Freudian slip: 'I'm very conscious of this horror.'[23] He attended Mrs Lasker's dinner for President and Mrs Johnson and he undertook work for *Bloomcraft*, earning over $7,000 for some fabric designs, which were received enthusiastically by Charles Bloom Inc.

Cecil was back in the United States in January 1970 to stay with Loel and Gloria Guinness at the time of his latest Palm Beach exhibition.

He began his stay by painting various rich strangers to boost local interest in the show. Afterwards he returned to New York before setting off to Hollywood to photograph Mae West and Danny Kaye. The latter loved it when Cecil said that *Vogue* had made as much fuss about him doing Chinese cooking 'as if the Rocket had been let off'.[24] Cecil found Mae West's apartment thoroughly synthetic and rather small. Anything not on immediate view was covered with dust. His sitter was 'rigged up in the highest possible fantasy of taste'.[25] As ever Cecil marvelled at the lengths to which an aged star would resort to preserve her image. But he stayed well within the bounds of propriety and dared little. He certainly did not dare to voice Sam Green's request for a wisp of her pubic hair. 'That would have been considered outrageous. This great sea queen is a goddess, an empress and there are only certain ways she must be spoken to.'[26] Cecil discovered that the seventy-six-year-old star still had an alleged lover, currently an ex-boxer.

This photo session enabled Cecil to fly to San Francisco to stay with Kin and an article on Mae West earned him $750 from *Vogue*. He found Kin sporting a beard, which he hoped might not be permanent. This particular stay was Cecil's happiest. It included a drug trip (during which Cecil trimmed Kin's beard to a Czarist effect) and a visit to a Methodist church service which was a mixture of Negro Revivalist and Hippy. It also brought Cecil a long-awaited fulfilment.

In a back room at Emilio's restaurant, 'the strange bearded man beside me' talked more freely than hitherto:

> He is much more at peace with the world, more friendly to all, less inhibited and more outspoken and demonstrative. He said that he loved me very much, that he was always afraid that one day the scales would fall from my eyes and I'd wonder why I'd ever thought him intelligent, reliable, lovable or beautiful. This was something I'd waited many years to hear.... I was incredibly happy.[27]

Kin accompanied Cecil to the ranch shared by Jimmy Davison and Nicky Haslam at Phoenix. Horst and his friend Nicholas Lawford were staying. In the afternoon Cecil and Kin went riding. The horses galloped strenuously and sixty-six-year-old Cecil was soon out of breath. After Kin left, he succumbed to a bad cold.

All too soon Cecil set off with Sam Green for 'a rather tentative peep at South America'[28] (a free trip organized by Braniff Airlines). This adventure proved fraught and tiring in many ways. It also involved a certain danger. Sightseeing in a truck, Cecil had to cling grimly to the roof as it veered perilously near a precipice. On arrival the passengers complained, 'We did not come here to be killed.'[29]

It was on this trip, in between his exhaustion and piercing headaches, that Cecil decided to write the life of his Aunt Jessie. He was able to visit the house in Sucre where she lived for some years and to meet two old sisters who had known her. They revealed to him that Aunt Jessie's marriage had ended in a marital separation when Uncle Pedro fell in love with the very young housekeeper. Out of this story Cecil wove the plot of *My Bolivian Aunt*, published in 1971.

Returning from the trip Cecil again visited Kin. This time Kin told him about the problems that had dogged him throughout his life and even led to the contemplation of suicide. Cecil was very concerned about the unhappiness of his friend, even though it seemed that through therapy he was beginning to come to terms with them. As so often in such matters, Cecil was left wondering why someone with so many talents, interests and intellectual curiosity should make himself suffer so much.

There was suffering, both mental and physical, in store for Cecil in the summer of 1970. For some years he had been obliged to rise at intervals in the night and plod off to the bathroom. Returning from America he had a thorough examination and, on the threat of what the specialist called 'ambulance bells in the night',[30] he was booked into Sister Agnes (King Edward VII's Hospital for Officers). He faced the prostate operation with a sense of deep morbidity. Referring to this in her perceptive obituary of Cecil, Clarissa Avon wrote:

> When comparatively late in life he had to undergo a not uncommon surgical operation, the experience became a saga of such vivid drama and detail as to give a shock of revelation to anyone who had ever lain on an operating table.[31]

A letter from Enid Bagnold can only have worried him further:

> Though it's idiotic one keeps saying good-bye to everything ... doctors and nurses for all their smiling compliments are quite indifferent ... only my astonishment that the bedpans haven't changed in seventy years – same old dented metal – and they ought somehow – to come up through the mattress, from below the bed.[32]

Cecil revisited his old haunts, even venturing down to Ashcombe. Then he went into hospital. His diary records every aspect of the affair: the visit from the specialist 'who would cut me open in the morning',[33] the ritual shaving, the anaesthetist who reminded him of the Queen Mother, his last smile from the stretcher. Then, as he came to, he recorded his pain and discomfort, the blood, the saline drip, the catheter, the removal in due course of both and so on. His visitors ranged from Diana Cooper to David Hockney and Patrick Procktor. Gradually he regained his mobility, and his recuperation in the countryside with Ray's cooking was a great joy to him.

Cecil left the country briefly to take his final set of photographs of the Queen Mother in the garden at Royal Lodge.* As he lunched with her *à deux* he felt at last that one day he would get back to normal. He wrote to Diana Vreeland:

> I suppose I've rather enjoyed 'belly aching' about it all, but although the operation would have been an emergency one if I'd left it for another two years, it does seem hard to go into a nursing-home feeling fit, to find on one's release that all the stuffing (as well as other things) has been taken out.[34]

Unfortunately Cecil did not recover well from this operation. Gravel in his kidney caused acute pain and he was soon back in the nursing home. Assailed by every possible ache and pain, he was recommended female hormone tablets, which affected the physical appearance of his body. Cecil considered that the release from pain had been achieved at high cost. For one who was so exacting on the physical appearance of himself and others, this was an horrific state in which to find himself. Cecil also found that he lost the last vestiges of sexual desire while still having to get up often in the night. As if this was not enough, he also lost a lot of his remaining hair.

On his second visit to hospital Cecil watched young people on television and was exhausted by their vigour. He could hardly believe that they 'could lead the violent athletic sexy lives they did. I felt bereft.'[35] His only nice interlude was when doctor and matron permitted him a night out to attend the ball at Windsor on the night of Edward Heath's 1970 election win. The ball was to celebrate the seventieth birthday of the Queen Mother and other members of the Royal Family. Here the old Cecil came back to life as he described the appearance of another of the guests:

> Good God! She had really worked a miracle. Her appearance must have taken the full three weeks of planning since the invites arrived. She must have got up at dawn to start her witches brew, to dabble with the pots and pans of liquid paint with which she disguised the ravages of age ... the little lips were rosebudded in the darkest black red, and on top of all was the triumph of her wig ... the neck was then opened to reveal two highly perched bosoms ... a sorbet wouldn't melt in her cat-smiling mouth.[36]

His enjoyment of this overcame his annoyance at Prince Philip's mock surprise at his leaving hospital specially for the occasion.

When Roy Strong stayed with Cecil in July he noted: 'He needed lots of sleep that weekend and there were rests in the afternoon and early to bed.'[37] Then it was holiday time. Cecil began in 'the incubator sterilized atmo-

* These were issued on her seventieth birthday.

sphere'[38] of a Wrightsman cruise and spent a night in Venice, where Nancy Mitford thought he looked very old suddenly, and some days with the very relaxed Diana Phipps at the 'dilapidated' Villa Albrizzi at Este. To Eileen he wrote: 'Diana P has *real* style and talent. She manages all, improvises, gets her guests to help out and with the least possible trouble manages to do the cooking.'[39] Diana Cooper arrived, soon followed by George Weidenfeld, who did a magnificent impersonation of the American Ambassador, Walter Annenberg. Cecil contrasted this holiday with those of his youth. There was no hope now of even an unrequited love affair. Instead he welcomed it when one of the children ran upstairs to find him his towel. But still he regained some of his lost health.

In August, back at Reddish, Cathleen Nesbitt came to stay for the first time. 'She embellishes the garden and every room she sits in,'[40] wrote Cecil. At the age of eighty-two, Cathleen became at last a real friend. Cecil had admired her since early Cambridge days. Now she became a regular visitor to Reddish House and she was the last guest to stay with Cecil in 1979. He was thrilled to have her in his life, but it was admiration on both sides. Not long before she died Cathleen Nesbitt recalled this first visit to Reddish: 'When I woke up and looked out of the window at the garden I felt I had been crowned. Here I was staying with Cecil Beaton.'[41]

Later Cecil took further holidays at Mouton with Baron Philippe and his wife Pauline, and then he joined Sam Green in Paris to set off on a tour of the Dordogne. While in Paris he paid his last visit to the Windsors to thank the Duchess for sending a Dior dress for his collection. He found them both considerably aged and only now, when so many of his cronies were dead, did the Duke call him Cecil. Nevertheless Cecil thought: 'they are a happy couple. They are both apt to talk at once, but their attitudes do not clash.'[42] The Dordogne tour was only a qualified success as Cecil's health was not ready for such an excursion. At times he became exasperated with Sam Green, and eventually he was impatient to return home.

In the autumn David Bailey began his film on Cecil's life, *Beaton by Bailey*. Lord David Cecil thought Bailey looked like Edgar in *King Lear*, while Bailey's girlfriend, Penelope Tree, he thought like the fairy Blackstick in *The Rose and The Ring*. As part of this first stint of filming, Cecil pursued Penelope with his camera as she went through her paces on the lawn at Broadchalke. The effort cost Cecil chest pains. His doctor told him that there was a small dent in the artery leading to his heart. Though this was not serious in itself, Cecil worried about his increasing headaches, 'and I'm not in a mind to quieten down and slacken off before the grave engulfs me'.[43]

At the same time he found the invasion of the camera crew with 'their wires and lights, their cigarette butts and dried sweat'[44] very tiring, as were the endless delays of filming. Bailey and Penelope lunched with Cecil and there were long silences, possibly because they were high on pot. As Cecil

Cathleen Nesbitt, Cecil's first Mrs Higgins

cleared away some cigarette ash, Penelope asked him: 'Are you a neat freak?'[45] He had to admit he was.

On 22 October there was a supper party at Pelham Place which Bailey filmed. As Roy Strong noted: 'If in twenty years' time one was listing the in-set of the period there it was.'[46] The guests ranged from Diana Cooper, Cathleen Nesbitt, John Betjeman, Irene Worth, David Herbert and Ali Forbes to the young Pembrokes, Ossie and Celia Clark, Edna O'Brien, Patrick Lichfield and David Hockney. After this first bout of filming there was a long gap before further developments.

Cecil ended 1970 in poor health but rich company. He was again at Mouton with the Rothschilds. Also enjoying the fine wine and luxury were the Sachie Sitwells, Prince (Johnny) de Faucigny-Lucinge, Raymond Mortimer, the Stephen Spenders, Glenway Westcott, Monroe Wheeler and others. Pauline lived a life of intellectual luxury. After reclining in the bath listening to Elizabethan lute music, she would summon certain guests for tea in her room at 6.30. Cecil recorded:

> I had a delightful talk on the house telephone with my hostess about how women can have the will to change the shape of their bodies. Since Pauline has taken to wearing tight silk below-the-hips trousers for dinner, her waist has become larger but her hips are much flatter and smaller. I was not among today's favoured for tea.[47]

Looking back on a bad year, Cecil also examined himself:

> The upper lip has become longer. The mouth a thin bitter line, the eyes tragic, old and wild and of a great sadness. Were there no redeeming features? No. Even my complexion has suddenly become covered with large brown spots, toad-like freckles that were not there six months ago and surely those on my forehead had appeared only in the last week? I stood in a trance of horror.[48]

His only consolation was a nice set of Norman Parkinson portraits of him that had lately arrived, which Cecil really liked.

The New Year of 1971 began on an ominous note. 'I wonder if I am really ill,' wrote Cecil, 'and that people won't tell me.... Altogether I am feeling sorry for myself and sick of being brave.'[49]

It saw the resurrection of new Francis Rose problems. The wayward baronet had sunk to residing in digs in the Portobello Road, and later taking sanctuary in a priest's cottage in Wales. On a visit to London he was robbed; back in Wales he threw bricks through windows to ensure arrest and a roof for Christmas. Rose felt that as a friend called Bob was on the point of dying he had no wish to go on. He told Cecil that he had appointed him his heir and intended to commit suicide. The dreadful deed would be done in front of an ancestor's portrait in the National Gallery. Needless to say the suicide was not carried out, but Cecil suffered a splitting headache out of worry that even in an indirect way he might be responsible for it. He was left wondering how it had been that this weird man whom he did not really like had succeeded in becoming his cross for nearly thirty-five years.

In February 1971 Cecil set off via New York and a photographic session with Rose Kennedy to Rio de Janeiro. He went to Brazil in the hope that it would restore his health: 'I feel a bit drained and depleted.'[50] His time there was a mixture of parties, sightseeing and resting, and during much of it he was depressed or beset by headaches. He flew to Buenos Aires where he was reunited with Aunt Jessie's protégées, Bea and Carmencita. A meeting with them, the first for over thirty years, proved a great emotional strain and Cecil was overwhelmed by the sadness of life. Back in his room he collapsed in utter misery:

> I was weeping not so much for silly sweet Bea as for my own lost youth. I was weeping for the dead people I had loved. I was weeping for Aunt Jessie and perhaps for my mother and my brother and all who had been part of my childhood. I was weeping for the whole of a lost era, the Edwardian era of large cosy family parties and holidays and treats, and evenings by the fire. I was weeping for the demolition of 74 Compayne Gardens, and the atmosphere that once that magical house created. Bea was just an excuse for me to weep for the mysterious sadness of life.[51]

The next morning he bought Bea and Carmencita £30 worth of gloves and handbags. He went on to stay with the Carcanos and wrote a glowing account of their happy married life. Reading this later, their daughter Chiquita Astor told him: 'Didn't you realize they were only kept alive by rowing with each other?'[52] After this much enjoyed visit, Cecil returned to Buenos Aires where his Rolleiflex and Nikon were stolen. As usual he was pleased to get home.

Cecil and Eileen viewed the first rushes of the Bailey film: 'It was as if I was looking at my obituary.'[53] There followed another week of filming in London in which he sang 'If you were the only girl in the world' with Cyril Connolly at the Ritz, and was filmed in the spring garden at Reddish. This time the process was much calmer and Cecil felt quite bereft when the film crew departed.

Following his Snowdon experiences, Cecil was anxious to see the film before it was released. He concluded that it was entertaining but disappointing. He regretted that good material from David Cecil, Cyril Connolly and Audrey Withers had been sacrificed in favour of nonsense from Jean Shrimpton and other Bailey groupies. He resented the bitter words of Truman who annoyed him by saying he wanted to be Noël Coward and that he gathered enemies like some people gather roses. Cecil wrote: 'He really does seem to have gone round the bend in a very unattractive way.'[54] To Diana Vreeland, one of the participants, he wrote:

> My heart went out to you last night in a great big swell of mountainous water.... You were so strong and bold and utterly wonderful.... I only wish it had been better. It gave the impression that I never do any work or have anything but a plush life. It was not serious, and the serious

things that anyone said were on the cutting floor.... This *could* have been good, if he'd collaborated with me. I could have helped so much.[55]

David Bailey was aware how much Cecil could have helped and this was not in his plan. With a chuckle he recalled: 'He wanted to be Leonardo da Vinci and Marco Polo wrapped into one.'[56]

He spent Easter reorganizing Reddish with Alan Tagg. Since Babe Paley had taken up blue and white Delft china pots, he knew that his must go. He now recreated the dining-room 'as a monastic cell with pewter – and somehow I don't think Mrs Paley will ever copy that idea'.[57] The winter garden was freshened up with 'a layer of lily of the valley leaf green paint'.[58]

There had lately been some more complaints from Cecil about his payments from *Vogue*. His normal rate was $450 a page, but when they wanted some Gertrude Steins from him in 1970 he suggested that as these were such 'historic documents'[59] he should receive more. His letter was not answered. Cecil felt his Katharine Hepburns should have been better rewarded since *Woman's Journal* paid him $5,000 for the second pick, but still the same old sum arrived. However, in March 1971, Diana Vreeland commissioned Cecil to photograph d'Annunzio's rather sinister house, Il Vittoriale, on Lake Garda.

Cecil was rather fascinated by the house and by the old caretaker who still tended it, and who had served d'Annunzio himself for seventeen years: 'I am sure it will not be long before he is found dead on his master's bed or sunk in a pile of fifty cushions,'[60] he predicted. Sadly this was one of the last jobs Cecil did for Diana. She was dismissed from *Vogue* (as from 1 January 1972) in an atmosphere of financial crisis. This was a shock for all concerned, but Diana rose like a phoenix and by August 1972 had been appointed Special Consultant to the Costume Institute of the Metropolitan Museum (a position she still holds in 1985).

At the end of a Broadchalke summer (enlivened with the occasional visit from Stephen Tennant), Cecil took a holiday with the Trees on Spetsai. Here the news came that Margaret Case was dead. Only now did Cecil realize what a good friend she had been to him since his very first visit to New York in 1928. Much of this had been overshadowed by her long maddening telephone calls to his hotel when he was trying to start a hard day's work. Presently he learned that she had jumped from the fifteenth-floor window of her apartment at 550 Park Avenue. Cecil was haunted by this and could not sleep at nights. Margaret Case had been very upset by the Vreeland dismissal. 'Never more unhappy or frightened in my whole long existence,' she had written to Cecil. 'The joy and inspiration of work has gone. Life in its most cruel terms seems closing in on me.'[61] On 1 August she left *Vogue* and on 22 August she wrote Cecil a further letter:

Dearest Cecil

Forgive what I am about to do. I have a cancer and do not wish to live any longer to become an object of pity poor Maggie and a care for my friends. You are one that I loved the most. Thanks for your love, loyalty and friendship and always being the best companion in the world.

      Margaret.[62]

Cecil went on to Capri to see the widowed Mona Bismarck. He thought this once great beauty looked a wreck. In Paris he visited the ailing Nancy Mitford.

In the autumn Cecil was in the public eye for the publication of *My Bolivian Aunt*, the *Beaton by Bailey* film and the opening of his fashion exhibition at the Victoria and Albert Museum. The first brought him the most pleasure, since no one had expected much of it. Cecil was unduly overjoyed by a glowing review in the *Sunday Times* by Raymond Mortimer: 'The review was so brilliant and incisive, so perceptive, was not only a marvellous piece of work but the ultimate in praise for me. It was a crowning triumph.'[63] When Cecil finished reading the piece, he exclaimed aloud 'Divine, divine',[64] without considering whether perhaps old Raymond, now a benign seventy-six, had not mellowed with the years, or accepting the piece as the tribute of one old travelling companion to another.* However, Cecil derived so little happiness from the many triumphs of his later life that it is good to find him for once rejoicing. *Beaton by Bailey* was not reviewed glowingly. As Nancy Banks-Smith wrote in the *Guardian*, it 'told you more about Bailey, David, than Beaton, Cecil'.[65]

The fashion exhibition at the Victoria and Albert Museum was the result of over two years' work by Cecil. He was the originator of the idea of collecting the clothes in the museum, a third of which were now put on show. His contribution represented what the director, Sir John Pope-Hennessy, called: 'this incomparable enrichment of the Museum's resources'.[66] It had been hard work but aspects of it were rewarding as Cecil tapped every available source he could think of. Dresses came from the Queen, the Queen Mother, Princess Anne, and other members of the Royal Family. He also received donations of all sorts and sizes from all ages and types, from Sybil Marchioness of Cholmondeley to Ossie Clark, from Madame Grès to the hosier Michael Fish, from Audrey Hepburn to Twiggy. Lord Harewood gave

---

* Raymond Mortimer's reputation took a knock when Evelyn Waugh's diaries were serialized in 1972, an event described by Cyril Connolly as 'a fart from the grave'. Waugh described him in 1928 as 'a second-rate young man' [*The Diaries of Evelyn Waugh*, p. 197]. Even Cecil was alarmed when in 1973 Mortimer bowed to the Queen Mother without taking his hand out of his pocket: 'We don't want *any* evidence that that swine Evelyn Waugh was right in accusing Raymond of being second rate' [Diary, June 1973].

him six of Queen Mary's toques. 'Never would I have imagined that the hall at Pelham Place would one day be littered with these majestic creations,'[67] wrote a delighted Cecil. Sylvia Henley gave him a 1918 dress specially made for her by Chanel for the Peace Conference at a time when Chanel was 'Boy' Capel's mistress. The actress Ruth Ford gave prized Schiaparellis that Edward James had given her during their otherwise unfruitful courtship. Jean Shrimpton donated a mini-skirt and Bob Lavine 'some faded jeans, thick socks etc etc, all that is worn by the casual American'.[68] In a sense the exhibition represented Cecil's own life in the clothes that were shown. These included the Hartnell presentation dress worn by Cecil's sister Nancy, and the Charles James wedding dress of Baba, a Beaton black and white Ascot number, the outfit worn by Edith Sitwell on her seventy-fifth birthday, twenty dresses that had belonged to Eugenie Niarchos (who had died tragically in 1970), a Balmain ballgown of Diana Cooper's, the Duchess of Kent's wedding dress by John Cavanagh, a little black Dior worn by the Duchess of Windsor, and the white crêpe evening dress worn by Eleanor Lambert at Truman Capote's black and white ball. Mixed in were pop-art T-shirts by Mr Freedom and clothes by Mary Quant, Thea Porter and Susan Small.

Whilst in New York in April 1970 Cecil had visited Valentina Schlee in her apartment a few floors above Garbo's. He noted how alike the two apartments were before Valentina showed him the dress she would give him for the exhibition. It had been made for Tammy Grimes in *High Spirits* (the musical version of *Blithe Spirit*). Cecil then watched in wonder as Valentina packed the dress:

> It was a work of art to see her wrapping the wisp in some rather crumpled pieces of silk paper. 'They are not new but they are clean.' This folded that way, that folded this way, up and over. She was leaning forward for a considerable time in an agonizingly painful position (she has lumbago) but she noticed nothing except what she was doing, preparing a work of art for posterity. As she manoeuvred the final gesture with the baby-like sleeves folded into a little roll, she leant down and kissed it. 'Goodbye,' she said. It was really very touching because absolutely genuine.[69]

There were a few disappointments. Chanel talked so much that Cecil never got a chance to get something from her (though she was of course represented in the show), and Zena Dare sold the only possible dress she could have given a week before Cecil's letter arrived.

Sir Roy Strong, director of the Victoria and Albert Museum since 1974, describes Cecil's collection of dresses as 'enormously important'.[70] He inherited some of the exhibition's problems. A number of donors had thought of themselves solely as lenders. The Duchess of Kent's wedding dress was one that had to be relieved of its acquisition number and returned. At the time Cecil wrote to Diana Vreeland: 'I'm afraid we've made a lot of enemies. However it's great to look at.'[71] The most vociferous critic was Lord Mountbatten, who complained that Edwina's outfits were not properly displayed. Later Cecil reported further to Diana Vreeland:

> The exhibition is a huge and beautiful success. Lichfield's photographs give no suggestion of the exhibits, except Queen Alexandra, but I suppose he went to photograph the people, not the clothes. Balenciaga has come out tops. Schiaparelli very sensational and the 20's vitrine is mysterious and beautiful with Poiret, earliest Chanel and Mr Erté. Queen Mary's toques (six of them revolving) and Pss. Mary's wedding dress are very touching. It has been a long niggling job and now I'm off to the Rothermeres for the weekend to forget it all and start life again.[72]

Part Nine

The Declining Years 1971–80

39

Garbo Reviewed

*Yes, I have decided for better or for worse to publish and
no doubt be damned by many.*

Cecil's diary, April 1971

Cecil had vexed himself over the question of publishing extracts concerning
his affair with Garbo ever since he finished work on *The Years Between*
(published in 1965). In the summer of 1967 he showed the typescript
to Peter Quennell, who told Cecil that he found it 'deeply interesting'.[1]
He warned Cecil, however, that the story of his relationship with Garbo
would come as 'highly provocative news'[2] to the public and journalists. He
continued:

> If you decide to publish and it would seriously be a pity to sacrifice such
> good material, you *must* remember the kind of journalistic commentary
> to which you will be exposed, and imagine a review by Robt. Pitman, for
> example, in the *S Express*, and the unpleasant headlines that might
> accompany it.[3]

When in New York in December 1967, Cecil telephoned Garbo to ask to
see her: 'I thought I ought to speak to her about the diaries and to confess
that we were living on borrowed time. But she had renegued on our night
out plan and since she did not call me back ...'[4] No meeting took place.

Although Kin advised him that if it pricked his conscience it was silly to
add to the troubles of a busy life, contracts for *The Happy Years** were
exchanged with Weidenfeld and Nicolson in January 1968. But the fate of
Beverley Nichols (who had to go to Australia for some months following the
publication of *A Case of Human Bondage†*) gave Cecil cause to rethink the
matter. So did press reaction to Lord Moran's book, *Winston Churchill, The
Struggle for Survival* (Constable, 1966).

In September 1968, Cecil confided to his diary his feelings of disillusion
about the woman he had once loved:

* In the U S A it was called *Memoirs of the 40s* (McGraw Hill, 1972).
† (Secker & Warburg, 1966). This defence of Syrie Maugham was advertised thus: 'This book
is not an attack upon a dead man: rather it is the refutation of a libel upon a dead woman.'

I am still not able to make up my mind to publish the Diary Vol. III which Greta would no doubt resent so bitterly. Yet in my mind she does not appeal to me any more. All the nicest things about her are lost in a haze of her selfishness, ruthlessness and incapability to love. She has nothing against me, yet is as elusive as ever. The fact that I am not really interested any more makes it difficult to bother to see her. Let her stew in her own loneliness. I know she enjoys life – even the life that she leads – alone and full of petty regrets. But to me it is appallingly vapid. I feel angry that she never made a gesture of forgiveness towards Mercedes* and I know she would not give any generous help to me if I were in need of it. Perhaps I am just manufacturing a situation wherein I would feel it possible to go ahead and be damned. But the years are slipping by and the situation will remain essentially the same until either of us dead.[5]

Another weight on Cecil's mind concerned his consultation with an astrologer in New York in 1969. He had asked when Garbo was least likely to mind publication. No firm conclusion was reached and so in January 1971 he steeled himself against the onslaught. In April he took the plunge and, in the midst of the fashion exhibition work, he and Eileen sent off the proofs. As early as November he had to face the consequences. *McCalls* in America had published an extract from the Garbo diaries and this had been picked up by *Newsweek*. Then the London papers obtained the story.

Now that this bombshell has exploded, all my comfortings about a seven-day wonder and what is an article in a newspaper anyway? seem quite ineffectual. I am disturbed and deeply so. I know it could have been avoided and I am to blame but I decided to be brave and damn all.[6]

Cecil found that if he tried to sculpt, the figure became Garbo. If he tried to paint, again she haunted him. Headaches beset him and he could not sleep. Just when he thought the matter had died down, he opened the *Daily Telegraph* and there was a two-column piece with photos.

Oh no! My stomach went to water. I rushed to the loo. I could not wait till Eileen would arrive at the house to ask if I should take a train up to London or a plane to Tangiers in order to escape my own self-recrimination. Eileen as usual came up trumps, light, airy, girlish, cheerful. Yes, she'd seen it. Don't worry. Have a glass of champagne. When I told Ray not to tell any reporter that I was here because there'd been a nonsense

---

*Mercedes de Acosta had published her life story, *Here Lies the Heart*, in 1960. One of the incidents was the time they spent together in a shack at Silver Lake in Sierra Nevada: 'How to describe the next six enchanted weeks? ... Six perfect weeks out of a lifetime. This is indeed much. In all this time there was not a second of disharmony between Greta and me or in nature around us ...' (p. 224).

about me and Garbo in the papers he made me laugh by saying, 'Yes, Mr Isaac (the wonderful part-time gardener) had seen something in the paper.'[7]

Cecil stayed at Broadchalke, keeping a low profile. If final proof be needed that Cecil had no easy life, the very next day Eileen rang to say that a formal letter had arrived offering him a knighthood.

Oh this was almost too much to take in. I felt this poor human brain was at bursting point. ... Secretly I had hoped for such an honour for many years. Although knights come down low in the scale it would be a great feather in an individual's cap to be thus rewarded. It is not as a result of having friends at court (Weidenfeld with Wilson) or being gradually upgraded in some huge organization (Fred at Covent Garden Opera House). This was a question of Alone I done it. I was sad my mother had not known of it, or even my Aunts Cada and Jessie. But I felt suddenly a good deal more elderly and eminent. Still it is a very nice tribute and I feel I have deserved it, not for my talent, but for character, tenacity, energy and wide-reaching efforts.[8]

Hardly had Cecil expressed the thought than he began to worry that the Garbo revelations might cause the honour to be squashed. He was intimidated by the official tone of the letter: 'The Prime Minister has asked me to inform you, in strict confidence, that he has it in mind ... to submit your name to the Queen with a recommendation that Her Majesty may be graciously pleased to approve that the Honour of Knighthood be conferred upon you.'[9] Cecil resolved to respect the confidence lest another letter arrive saying that 'after all, possibly on account of the Garbo revelations, I will not be thus honoured'.[10] He had to wait until the New Year – 'with fingers crossed I am biding the time patiently'.[11]

Cecil photographed the Rothschild ball at Ferrières, with results which *Vogue* thought 'remarkably beautiful'.[12] Dressed as Nadar, Cecil set up a small studio. One sitter was Elizabeth Taylor, whom Cecil loathed, while Princess Grace was 'very pretty' and the Duchess of Windsor 'behaved like a mad Goya. ... Her face so pulled up that the mouth stretches from ear to ear.'[13] He also took Marisa Berenson as Casati, Audrey Hepburn, and the teenagers' heart-throb, Jane Birkin, with her fierce-looking husband, Serge Gainsbourg. Before the year was out, Cecil had to face the death and memorial service of his childhood heroine, Gladys Cooper, at which old Stanley Holloway read beautifully from *The Pilgrim's Progress*.

He also had a row with Horst, whose book, *Salute to the Thirties* (Bodley Head, 1971), he had reviewed rather spikily for *Books and Bookmen*. In October Cecil wrote to Horst: 'I have been a bit pert, but I hope the praise outweighs the pinpricks. It is meant to.'[14] Horst judged otherwise and in December Cecil was writing:

Raymond Mortimer was right when he said one should never review the books of friends. I sent you the magazine with my article in it thinking it would please you, but it has made me realize that it was a mistake, that I shouldn't set myself up in judgement and so won't be writing any more reviews. I only hope you haven't turned against your album which is really terribly good and as I said I am thrilled to own a copy. The 'pinpricks' were meant in jocular vein and I'm sorry if they hurt you.[15]

Midnight struck at the end of the year. Cecil was drifting off to sleep when the local doctor, Christopher Brown, hurried from his radio to ring up in great excitement. Even then Cecil did not dare ask if it was really a knighthood.

The following morning the good news was confirmed. Eileen, Alan Tagg and Charles Colville came in bearing branches of laurel. The telephone rang joyfully and messages arrived from Malta, Hong Kong (Derek Adkins), Florida and even Melbourne. All his friends rejoiced:

Enid Bagnold:
Oh I'm so glad, so delighted. You've worked so hard at your art so single-mindedly, amid all distractions.[16]

Jane Clark:
I don't congratulate you but the Gov't for at last recognizing that you are an international figure of great importance to British prestige as aesthete, elegant designer and imaginative photographer. We have all felt it was a disgrace you weren't knighted years ago.[17]

Nancy Mitford:
What's this I hear? Very splendid and none too soon and not nearly good enough but still a beginning.[18]

Lady Pamela Berry:
To say we are pleased about the knighthood is putting it too mildly; for years Michael and I have felt increasingly indignant that your greatness and incessant distinguished contributions to the world of arts should not be publicly recognized.[19]

Sir John Gielgud:
What a nice beginning for the New Year, especially for you. I am delighted.[20]

Hal Burton:
Congratulations on your knighthood and well deserved may I say. You have certainly added a measure to the gaiety of nations by preserving and perpetuating the best of everything we look at with our eyes.[21]

Dame Sybil Thorndike:

It was lovely to see your name in the Honours. You've done so much for people both in the world and theatre.[22]

Cathleen Nesbitt:

I confess I find a little of the same reaction as I did to Noël's – 'So what?' It should have been done so long ago that it ought to be an OM by now, but still it's as far as the arts ever get and if ever one was richly deserved! (I would have thought your war record would have been ample grounds even if you didn't happen to be an artist.)[23]

Sir John Betjeman:

Oh I *am* pleased, about time too![24]

Clarissa Avon:

This is grade 1, the end of the line. Now you just sit back, distinguished, successful and accoladed. Much deserved.[25]

Sir Martin Charteris:

Gay assures me that we have already written to shout hurrah! at your knighthood. Just in case she's wrong I'm bloody glad.[26]

James Lees-Milne:

We are overjoyed to be able to add yet one more aesthetic Knight to our acquaintance. It is always satisfactory to read that someone has been honoured for making life more beautiful instead of for making the world increasingly hideous. .... I only wish you had been made a Duke (poor Gerry* in today's paper) which is what you deserve.[27]

Kathy Sutherland:

It will be difficult for some: 'Sir Cecil' – like the old tongue-twister of my youth about Sir Theodore Thistlethwaite the successful thistle sifter'.[28]

Amongst more formal congratulators were the Queen Mother, Princess Margaret, Princess Alexandra, Lord Mountbatten, Sir Alec Guinness, Dame Margot Fonteyn, his old Heath Mount master, Aubrey Ensor, and Binkie Beaumont. As Cecil's life returned to normal, so he set about replying to all the letters. To Diana Vreeland he wrote:

It's been great fun and I've had letters from ancient fishmongers and long forgotten school-friends and all sorts of unexpected people. It makes it all the nicer that they seem pleased.[29]

After a ten-day health break in Arosa, Cecil fulfilled his latest date at the Palace. The investiture on 3 February 1972 was filmed as part of a royal TV film. Cecil was glad to find Cicely Courtneidge there on her way to

---

*Cecil's old wartime colleague, the 7th Duke of Wellington, had died.

becoming a Dame, though later she diverted some of the press attention from him.

His sisters, Nancy and Baba, accompanied him to the ceremony. When his turn came he stepped forward and looked 'very piercingly' at the Queen. He heard her say, 'This is a great pleasure.'

> Since she didn't have anything to impart to me, I felt bold enough after she had shaken my hand to say that I never thought taking her photograph in the little girl's pink taffeta dress that it would lead to this honour.[30]

To this the Queen said: 'It's a pleasure', and Cecil duly retreated. He then returned to his seat and watched the Queen address each recipient in turn. He asked the knight next to him if she had said anything particular to him: 'Oh yes. She asked how long I had been at St Thomas's Hospital. How she knew I worked there I don't know. It was not in the citation.'[31] Either Cecil had been so nervous that he failed to hear his question, or his piercing stare had intimidated the Queen who, though an assured monarch in every way, is essentially modest and shy as a woman.

The knighting of Cecil represented the last accolade in a long career. He did not cease to strive but in many ways his efforts merely harmed his health without bringing new rewards. Headaches, already a worry to him, became a serious preoccupation and minor set-backs took a major toll. In Egypt with Raymond Mortimer in March 1972, Cecil was as interested in the Winter Palace Hotel at Luxor and the Cataract Hotel at Aswan, where the Edwardians had wintered, as in the treasures of the Pharaohs. Headaches made reading a strain, and a pain often came above his eyes. 'Today I became very worried lest this affliction is going to dog my later days.'[32] Plans were frequently disorganized and Cecil found that Raymond was 'very absent-minded, loses things and panics, worries a lot in advance and it is a lesson to me to guard against so many things that old age has brought to him'.[33] Staying in the new Winter Palace, Cecil suffered the harassing experience of being trapped in the lift when an idiotic German pressed the alarm button by mistake. He panicked badly and had visions of being enclosed there for days. When mercifully they escaped, Raymond came to his room and announced: 'My dear, this hotel is really *not* what it sets out to be. I had to come up by the service elevator.'[34]

A high spot of the tour was meeting Peter, an old Copt guide who had worked with Howard Carter. He told them that the story about the curse of the Pharaohs was ridiculous. After all he was still alive. Leaving Egypt Cecil concluded:

> Altogether I *loathed* Egypt and nothing would ever make me return. We saw marvellous things, unforgettably beautiful, and the sunsets were beautiful and the dry heat was a help but the Egyptians are the lowest

of the human race, and they are fast destroying the beauty of their land with cheap cement skyscrapers and all the worst elements of European squalor.[35]

Cecil retreated to Micky Renshaw's in Cyprus, suffering 'one of the worst colds I have had for many years'.[36] Here he worked on a short story about Egypt, which was never published. He also picked up his *Gainsborough Girls* once more and began another rewrite.

In May he undertook a *Connaissance des Arts* tour of North Germany. Cecile de Rothschild, Garbo's loyal friend, joined the group late, having stayed on in Paris for the Queen's state visit. She was not long in lashing into Cecil for his Garbo revelations. Seeing him take a snap she asked sarcastically if he was photographing for *McCalls*. 'She is rude and rough but I must be tough and take it,'[37] wrote Cecil. The real onslaught came two days later at lunch. 'Let me ask you how much you made out of Garbo on the *McCalls*, *Times*, *Oggi* etc world circulation. I mean how much with *Vogue* photographs *et tout ça* during the past twenty years have you made?'[38] Cecil thought for a moment and gave her a straight answer. He thought it was about £4,000. The Baroness rebuked him:

'Not bad is it? I mean I wouldn't mind being given £4,000 to spend on the kitchen.' She laughed that nasal choking voice. 'Not bad eh? For someone who didn't need the publicity. Even Stokowski didn't sell his story to the papers.'[39]

If Cecil can be accused of trying to make money out of Garbo, then he must also be praised for some articles he wrote at this time. *Plays and Players* can hardly have paid him much for the five profiles that appeared with Beaton photos in the first six months of 1972. These were actors and actresses that Cecil particularly admired – Irene Worth, Fenella Fielding, Isabel Jeans, Alan Webb and Paul Scofield. Irene Worth said later: 'Nobody tried harder than Cecil to make me a star',[40] and Isabel Jeans wrote to him:

I am so *deeply* touched and so happy about it. I really don't know how to thank you. You have so understood and caught my moods and thoughts, anxieties and difficulties, about my own particular feelings, both personally and professionally. ... Having had my full share of kicks, your article now is a wonderful recompense and healing balm.[41]

Similarly the actor Geoffrey Toone recalled that Cecil was consistently kind. If ever there was someone that Cecil thought he should meet, either for interest or to help his career, he would be invited to Pelham Place for dinner. 'I have tremendous admiration for his loyalty,'[42] he said.

As he grew older (he was now sixty-eight) Cecil devoted as much space in his diaries to village happenings – the story of a kingfisher or the opening of his garden – as he did to events such as the Windsor Castle banquet for Queen Juliana. Perhaps he had been to one party too many. But it was in his role as 'a serious diarist'[43] that he attended the funeral of the Duke of Windsor who had died on 28 May 1972. At St George's Chapel he met Diana Cooper, and Lady Alexandra Metcalfe said to him: 'Do you realize that you and I are about the only survivors of that wedding at Candé?'[44] As Cecil absorbed the splendour of the occasion he noted that one line of the processional hymn rang out rather poignantly: 'Perverse and foolish oft I strayed ...'

At no time during the service did I feel pity for the dead Prince, only a great emotion that the strength of the monarchy was something that could not in spite of all today's rebels be overthrown. It is as important [an] ingredient in the life of Britain as ever it has been – or so this simple service gave me the conviction.[45]

The subjects for his photographs during these years proved he was as much in the swim as ever. They included Edward Woodward, Edna O'Brien, Borges, Edward Fox, Irene Worth (in Chekhov) and the beautiful Lady Caroline Cholmondeley.

The Happy Years was published in June. Lesley Blanch wrote to Cecil:

It is most beautifully done, so delicate, so full of humour and sadness too, such a perfectly romantic record. But then, I have always thought you essentially a romantic person.... Your portrait of Garbo is marvellously subtle.... We must be grateful to you that you have captured, so marvellously, this enigmatic and legendary creature.[46]

At first Cecil refused to read the reviews. Those that mattered included Beverley Nichols in the *Spectator*:

This is either a true story or it is nothing. I believe it to be true from the first line to the last.... Beaton has given Garbo a new dimension and greatly increased her stature in the history of our times.[47]

Cyril Connolly judged: 'I do not think he has behaved any worse than a painter who exhibits an astonishingly life-like portrait, without permission, of an *incommunicata* sitter.'[48]

However, E.S. Turner in the *Listener* opined:

To this reviewer the picture of Mr Beaton fondling the vertebrae of *La Divina* is as near-sacrilegious as that of Eric Linklater bussing Botticelli's *Primavera* when he found her in her wartime hiding-place.[49]

Auberon Waugh had two cracks at Cecil. The first in *Harper's and Queen* concluded:

For all the fact that it has plainly been most carefully revised and edited, and for all the fact that it seems studied and over-cautious in places, this volume is warmly recommended for its account of some dismal years of British history, most engagingly told.[50]

A year later he tackled the American edition of the book for the *Chicago Tribune*:

The saddest and most bizarre part of the Beaton story comes in his description of a love affair which apparently blossomed between himself and Greta Garbo. As these two social and emotional waifs act out their chosen parts – he as the flamboyant but sensitive extrovert in the throes of an ideal passion, she as the startled fawn – we see the Beaton predicament in a hideous, cold light: first we see that beyond the affectation and the false values there is an emotional desert of sadness and loneliness; then we see that beyond the sadness and loneliness there is an object of the cruelest and most unutterable comedy.[51]

When Cecil was undergoing a most gruelling publicity tour in the States, in April 1973, this piece was used as a weapon by two interviewers – 'a review of my book by – of all people Auberon Waugh* – the son of my old arch-enemy. He seems to have inherited the spleen of his father. A devastating attack aimed to reduce me to a shred. It hurt.'[52]

Cecil began a new obsession with Garbo, seeing a woman on an aeroplane and wondering if it was her. At times he suffered deep remorse, but in his diaries he reaffirms that given a second chance he would repeat his crime. There is no doubt that his deed played into the hands of his enemies, who felt this was the last evidence needed of his unworthiness. Friends such as Diana Vreeland, Clarissa Avon and Diana Cooper were ashamed of his action. Several people cut him in the ensuing years. In conclusion he might have saved himself a lot of anguish had he left the story alone, shifting any responsibility onto his as yet unchosen biographer.

As for the reactions of Garbo herself, there is only a third-hand report from Cyril Connolly. He wrote that Drue Heinz lived in Garbo's block in 450 East 52nd Street, and, seeing her in the hall, asked her point-blank what she thought of the diaries.

She had laughed, waved her hand and muttered something non-committal. Mrs Heinz said she was old and lonely and obviously delighted by the reminiscences.[53]

*Cecil had read Auberon Waugh's first novel, *The Foxglove Saga*, in November 1960. He judged: 'It is clever and he could develop into a brilliant writer. It is already experienced. But what a little swine he must be, even more cruel and wicked and more loathsome than his father. It is awful to see talent go so devilish' [Cecil to Eileen Hose, November 1960].

On this letter Cecil noted: 'Interesting but I fear her way of being non-committal or quotable.'[54] He was relieved when Patrick O'Higgins told him in 1973 that he had seen Garbo in an Italian greengrocer:

> She had two bags in which she put the vegetables she was buying. She wore dark glasses but was full of smiles and everyone very solicitous of her though respectful of her wish for anonymity.[55]

During the summer Cecil worked away on the new version of The Gainsborough Girls. Again it was rejected, but again he did not give up.

Kin came for a week. Then Cecil went to Majorca to stay with Chiquita Astor. Worse headaches afflicted him: 'It is such a damper on activity. I live by my eyes.'[56] Nevertheless he worked on another play, The Chickens Come Home, based on Kitty Miller, Anne Tree, David Bailey and Penelope Tree. Only once did reality strike when Lady Mary Dunn attacked him about a totally different story in The Happy Years. She referred not to Garbo but to Robert Heber-Percy:

> She said to my surprise that it had shattered him. I was surprised how quickly I recovered from the attack and thought myself lucky if worse does not befall me.*[57]

Cecil went on to Austria to Zell-am-See to celebrate Diana Cooper's eightieth birthday and presented her with a beautiful album of his favourite portraits of her taken over a period of forty-five years. He arrived at Munich and wept in the car for the memory of Peter Watson. In September he went to Les Avants to see Noël Coward. Diana was there too with her granddaughter, Artemis. Cecil found Noël greatly aged, but wrote to him afterwards:

> I think it is rare to find someone facing the later years with such added zest and interest and wisdom. Without losing any of your pepper you have become so kind.[58]

Back at home Cecil fixed on his last but long-felt deep ambition to have his play produced. He was optimistic almost to the end:

> God alone knows if this is to alter the course of my life by making it possible for me to spend the rest of my life writing plays which perhaps Truman was right in suggesting was always my ambition, or whether it will be another very bitter disappointment. Here's keeping fingers crossed.[59]

There was more sadness in store. From November 1972 until March 1973 Cecil was aware that his sister, Baba, was dying. The news first reached him when he was in America to decorate the Crystal Ball in Dallas.

* The offending passage is in The Happy Years, p. 130.

Nevertheless he spent six weeks in the States and raised another $4,500 at a Palm Beach Exhibition.* Cecil saw his sister before she died from cancer. This was to be a lasting sorrow. Enid Bagnold wrote:

> Not only I suppose you were children together but I know you were also father and preceptor to them and shared the world you were then attacking so that they had their bit too. I think it was very gallant of you. One (oneself) is enough to manage![60]

Binkie Beaumont died, Noël died. Enid and Diana came to stay. Ina Claire came from San Francisco and David Herbert from Tangiers. Nancy Mitford died in Paris and Cecil wrote:

> I cannot *really* admit that my heart went out to hers, but then her heart was a very peculiar one, and not at all like other people's.[61]

There was an unpleasant incident with Patrick O'Higgins who, having recently published *Madame* (the life of Helena Rubinstein), wrote a fictional account of a weekend at Reddish for *Town and Country*. It purported to be true and included a scene where the Queen Mother dropped in for a pre-lunch drink. A cartoon by Hirschfeld sealed the calumny. Cecil was excruciatingly embarrassed. He rebuked O'Higgins:

> It puts you on the level of a cheap gossip writer and it's not at all pleasant for me to be faced by the Salisburys or the QM who have every reason to say 'CB must have peculiar friends'. The point you made about Garbo was far off the mark. I was responsible for everything that was published and everything was absolutely 100,000% true.[62]

Hardly had this row died down when Charles James, the dressmaker, burst into life to complain about references to him in Cecil's diaries.† He was enraged that Cecil described him as 'embittered'. He wrote ominously: 'I'm sending you a long letter, which may not entirely please you, but you will recognize true when presented.'[63] Eight pages of vitriol crossed the Atlantic the next day. Cecil had Felix Harbord and Mary Hutchinson staying when it arrived. He braced himself and asked the latter to read it to him. The gist of James's bitterness was that he was a creator while Cecil merely made 'a visual rapportage' of what others had created, 'every expense borne by others'.[64] He had not forgiven Cecil for having accepted work from Samuel Winston at a time when he and Winston were involved in expensive litigation. He claimed to have saved Cecil's career by introducing him to Johnson & Johnson after the 1938 *Vogue* drama, leading to the valuable *Modess* contracts. He accused him of being primarily commercial and reminded him of his social rise:

* An exhibition of early work at the Sonnabend Gallery raised a further $4,737.
† *The Happy Years*, pp. 67–8 (*Memoirs of the 40s*, pp. 97–8).

Had you NOT, for instance, escorted women like Lady Alexander to charity dances, which made a fool of you in the eyes of others of our generation, you would never have 'made your way'.[65]

Cecil's comment at the end was: 'Such a pity he is so difficult because I would like to like him and feel he is a genius *manqué*.'[66]

Cecil's work in 1973 consisted of editing an important history of photography, *The Magic Image*. His task was made the more difficult by the knowledge that if he worked too hard, he would be beset by violent headaches. Assisted by Gail Buckland, he added the role of art historian to his many other careers. The book was described as 'a personal selection of photographers we most admire'.[67] After an introduction on the history and definition of photography, the chosen photographers were dealt with chronologically, examples of their work being illustrated. Cecil was modest about himself, quoting only two lines from Truman's introduction to *The Best of Beaton*. He chose the shell-shattered ceiling, Tobruk 1943, as the sole example of his work. The book was well received and given serious reviews. It was even welcomed by the critic of Cecil's major exhibition, Hilton Kramer, as 'quite the most interesting and capacious general survey this season'.[68]

In the late summer he returned to Diana Phipps in Padua with Sam Green. Diana Cooper, now an agelessly beautiful eighty-one year old, was staying. Later Sam and Cecil toured Tuscany and went to Venice for a Volpi Ball, attended now by young luminaries such as Audrey Hepburn, Andy Warhol, Helmut Berger and Bianca Jagger as well as old friends, Diana Vreeland, Serge Lifar and Lilia Ralli. While in Venice he found himself walking towards the dark-spectacled figure of Valentina.

This was the first time I'd encountered her since the publication of the Diaries with so many allusions to the little man (her husband) in them. Would she slap my face? Would she give me the cut direct? We passed nearer and nearer. She eyed me coldly. As we passed one another I very exaggeratedly doffed my straw hat. 'Oh my Darlink Cessaile. Oh my Heavens!' We kissed, laughed, made banal observations. Was she having a holiday, I asked. 'Are there any holidays any more?' she asked.[69]

The Strenuous Years, the fourth volume of Cecil's diaries, was published in September 1973 to a glowing review from their wild Irish reviewer, Maurice Richardson, in the *Observer*: 'One could go on reading him for ever.'[70] Only Osbert Lancaster, whom Cecil described as 'the greatest bore in private life while being one of the funniest cartoonists ever',[71] cast a little acid in the *New Statesman* due, Cecil maintained, to jealousy over the knighthood.

One day at Reddish, Cecil made a list of all those who worked for him. He sent it to Eileen with the note: 'for one solitary person ... almost a round dozen'.[72] Eileen added four more to the list and handed it back with the comments: 'Interesting. Thought provoking. What caused the comment now? Were you: pleased? appalled? bemoaning? regretting? gloating? self-aggrandizing? fearful? sobered? Are you sensible? sure? solvent?!!'[73] Cecil's secret answer was that he loved the activity around him, but hated the amount he had to spend on upkeep. Cecil was well served. Apart from Eileen, his favourites were Mr and Mrs Jack Smallpeice, who were at Broad-chalke for nearly twenty years. Smallpeice, a third-generation gardener, tended the garden with efficiency and imagination. Eileen recalled:

> Cecil established a strong rapport with Smallpeice. He was always sympathetic to Cecil's ideas, not only with regard to what plants to plant, but with any alterations to the structure of the garden. He was patient, faithful and loyal. Most of all, Cecil enjoyed sitting on the terrace with him each autumn, planning for the following year.[74]

Mrs Smallpeice worked in the house. Though she was shy, Cecil liked talking to her. She tended his clothes. Eileen recalled seeing her arrive each morning 'with a pile of silk scarves beautifully ironed and folded'.[75] Meanwhile, firmly fixed in his mind was his dream that something would finally come from his play. He sought Hal Burton's help once more:

> No doubt there will be more rewrites, but if it will eventually lead to a London production, then I will feel that one of my most gnawing ambitions will have at long last, at the age of seventy, been achieved.[76]

Cecil did not take the wedding photographs for Princess Anne's wedding in November 1973. Ever anxious, he wondered if this was because he had baited her as a child. Nevertheless he welcomed Norman Parkinson's 'breakaway photographs which with a good deal of help from *Vogue* made her into a beauty'.[77] He was invited to the ball at Buckingham Palace and to dine beforehand with the Queen Mother:

> Generally when I go to the Palace it is to take a photograph sitting and the burden of the job hangs like a sword of Damocles. Tonight I felt free to enjoy myself, and I realised that at long last I have acquired a certain self-confidence. In my early years it was always a strain to go into a crowded room and come face to face with people whom I know disapproved of me. Now to hell – I disapprove of a lot of them.[78]

When the Queen saw him and her face lit up with genuine pleasure, Cecil's delight was complete.

It is interesting to find Cecil in full admiration of the Prime Minister, Edward Heath. In the difficult months that followed, with the miners' strike and the three-day week, Cecil's adherence to Heath's courage never wavered. At this ball Cecil noted: 'He has shown such courage and strength and the manner ... has become easier and may I not be damned for saying he exuded a certain amount of sex appeal. This is more than Macmillan did as he sat complaining that he knew no one any more.'[79]

At Christmas 1973 Cecil was struck down with mumps. Then in January 1974 came the grisly news of the murder of his old friend, James Pope-Hennessy. He had sent his servant, Len, to buy a carving-knife when the assailants arrived to bind and gag James and search for the advance money he had boasted of receiving for his projected Noël Coward biography. The servant tried to stab the murderers and a blood-bath ensued. Pope-Hennessy died in hospital due to an inhalation of blood. Cecil was left with feelings of despair. Reviewing the murder he wrote:

> One only hoped that he had been drunk or unconscious and one wondered why oh why James with such talent, charm and good looks had gone the way he had.[80]

The tragedy was made more poignant by a letter arriving from James, written the day before the murder, asking for help with Noël's biography.

In February 1974 Cecil went to Mexico and later on to Guatemala with Sam Green. It was a time to wind down and take stock of himself, though inevitably this led to depression. Cecil was now seventy.

> Yet I find that, accepting the inevitable, and 'being my age', and sticking to my generation, the young seem so different, so beautiful, so energetic. They are like creatures from another planet and are as difficult to understand as young fowls or other animals.[81]

As for Mexico, 'the Mexico I first visited with Peter Watson has vanished'.[82] Nor did Cecil wish to return to Guatemala. He ended his break in Palm Beach, where he heard with horror 'that that swine Wilson has taken power again, that that good man Heath with his courage and determination for fairness has been pipped by a whisker'.[83]

As the spring turned to summer, Cecil's days of active life were running out. Sadly these last days were marked by ugly incidents. In March Cecil attended a party at 26 Cheyne Row to celebrate Peter Quennell's sixty-ninth birthday. As he was leaving, he greeted Laura Duchess of Marlborough. He kissed her. She was in the company of Robert Heber-Percy, still smarting from the attack in *The Happy Years*. Ironically Cecil had feared retribution in some way from Garbo, but it was Robert who now wreaked revenge, delivering a sharp blow to Cecil's jaw and sending him reeling into the street. In a long, rather over-dramatized account, Cecil wrote: 'he had waited his chance to take the law into his own hands, break it and give me my come-uppance'.[84] Cecil had been taken totally by surprise. He had felt that perhaps the one advantage of old age was that 'one was likely to escape this sort of violence'.[85] The next day found him cold and shivery as a result of the shock. His masseuse, Charlotte Gaffran, insisted he saw a doctor. Cecil also consulted a lawyer, who wrote presently that though he surely had a good case, he was pleased that Cecil would not be proceeding. The lawyer wrote: 'May I suggest you give a party for all your friends, show them this letter and then forget the whole thing.'[86]

Within a month Cecil was present at the opening of a Kodak exhibition in Holborn to celebrate his seventieth birthday. He made a speech in which he said how happy he was that one of his earliest models was there that afternoon. But his sister Nancy was late and when she arrived she 'came up with a pursed grin of pleasure to tell me that I had post-dated by ten years the early photograph of herself'.[87] Cecil boiled over with rage, feeling that he had been put down once too often. A 'really horrible row'[88] ensued and many long-held grievances were voiced.

For much of the summer Cecil was at Broadchalke, preoccupied with the garden being opened, local happenings such as Derek Hill coming to paint Lord Avon, a visit from David Herbert and the arrival on his doorstep of Stephen Tennant after a rapturous visit to Bournemouth (this followed by a shower of illustrated letters, one of which urged him: 'Do rest a lot, dear Cecil, you are such a marathon worker'[89]).

In London George Weidenfeld gave a party for him and he attended the lunch the Charterises gave for the Queen Mother. He went to Berlin with Ann Fleming to be duly horrified by the Wall:

My greatest hope is that one day during my lifetime the Soviets will crack, that the subjugated 'satellite' countries would regain their freedom. I asked our military guide if he was optimistic. He said: 'Something must change.'[90]

Cecil found these years sad for several reasons. Intensely patriotic and loving the established world of country houses and society, he regretted the fall of Heath, the end of huge parties and grand dinners, the curtain falling on an era he had known and loved. It was a world that he had romanticized and glamorized, but as a conspirator. George Weidenfeld recalled:

Cecil was like Dr Coppelius in *The Tales of Hoffmann*. When the glasses were on, everything was beautiful. When he took them off everything was tawdry. There must have been Cecil Beatons *mutatis mutandis* at the time of the collapse of the Holy Roman Empire, recording the decline.[91]

Similarly Cecil was isolated from some of his friends due to his relentless and unforgiving eye. There are numerous examples of his despair at seeing former beauties reduced to middle or old age. Perhaps the saddest example was Paula Gellibrand, his childhood vision. Although to anyone who had not known her when young, she was a beautiful old lady, to Cecil her appearance was a tragedy. He was generally unsympathetic to the causes of a girth allowed to spread or elegance and style sacrificed to the requirements of country life. In his view his victims were letting the side down. This had the effect of painting Cecil into a corner. The last person to whom the former heroines wished to submit their plight for scrutiny was Cecil. His condemnation knew no limits.

The more intelligent friends rose above this. But even his favourite neighbours, Clarissa Avon and Anne Tree, took note of Cecil's eye. Lady Avon recalled that he would come into her winter garden at Alvediston and declare: 'Ten out of ten, Clarissa.'[92] Lady Anne Tree, when asked if she would cast a quick eye around the house before Cecil arrived, admitted: 'reluctantly, yes'.[93] Another friend, Gillian Sutro, remembered her clothes being scrutinized by Cecil: 'If there was a safety-pin somewhere he'd find it.'[94]

Because Cecil had achieved the fame he sought, his last active year was made harder by the distance from the world that fame imposes. His high standards meant that he was not someone that friends would casually invite on a last-minute excursion to the cinema. Eileen remembers his frustration at facing many long evenings alone. Much of it bored Cecil too. Stephen Tennant recalled him saying: 'We are all stretcher cases now, worn out by the social mish-mash.'[95]

In May 1974 Hal Burton gave his verdict on the latest version of the Gainsborough play:

I just can't analyse my reasons for feeling that there is an air of unreality running through the play. There is a good story line, it has shape, and yet the characters for the most part appear to be going through the motions rather than *being* actual real people.[96]

Cecil accepted the verdict with sad resignation, but only as far as this one play was concerned:

At long last I have accepted defeat. It must be nearly twenty years [in fact thirty] since I started on the play. Have rewritten it God knows how many times. It has twice been tried out. I loved 'Gainsborough'. I loved many of the characters. They have all become part of my life. But perseverance must be recognized as stubbornness if one goes on against all odds. Now I realize there is nothing more to be done about it. And this is very painful; and it makes the period of waiting to hear the verdict on my new play even more excruciating.[97]

But none of these plays were ever brought to the stage.

The summer came and from time to time Cecil turned to his diary to record a pleasure or a pain:

> Midsummer Day. It is the supreme moment of the year, the countryside at its most lyrical and the weather has been of the sort that we dream about during the interminable months of winter. The village people in cotton, the men often stripped to the waist. The garden here is at its best.
>
> Yet the whole country is in turmoil. We wait for the worst economic crisis to happen as if the next war was to be declared.
>
> Three rotten headaches in a row. I begin to get worried.
>
> Most unexpectedly, after a quiet day, I woke up yesterday morning with another headache. Not too bad but enough to make me feel uncomfortable. I could not read or write.
>
> I went on with weeding. Irene Worth was reciting Shakespeare on the garden seat where the first *candidum* lily is out. Her devotion to the arts and to Shakespeare is all-consuming. Later she did much to help, clearing up the borders and petals and the weeding of the rose borders.
>
> The 'Gardeners' Sunday was not the success of the Easter opening for the rain which had held off had prevented the usual numbers from arriving in their hundreds. We clocked apparently 600 which was good though the flowers were dashed by a three-day rain.[98]

Irene Worth was staying the weekend with Cecil in July 1974. Driving together, she was alarmed when he clapped his head in his hands and complained of a sudden blinding headache. They returned safely to Broadchalke and in due course she returned to London.

A few days later, while taking his morning bath at Pelham Place, Cecil felt his limbs getting colder, one by one. He was incapacited by a grave and serious stroke.

40

The Stroke

I thought I had had it. I never thought I'd recover.

Cecil in an interview, 1978

Cecil's stroke was a cruel tragedy, which ended his working life at the age of seventy. A cruel revenge on a man who valued his personal dignity and independence, it brought out the qualities of courage and determination which his life exemplified.

The stroke deprived him of three things. First he could no longer use his right hand. Therefore he could not write, paint, draw or use a camera. Secondly he lost his random access to names. He knew who he was talking about but could not always find the name. Curiously, he could point and say: 'You'll find the name in the front of that book.'[1] If someone else said the name, he would recognize it. He once described the Queen Mother to Michael Duff as 'that friend of yours, whose daughter does a very important job'.[2] Eileen he referred to as 'my best friend'. Finally he lost the dignity of his appearance, though as always in this respect he was tough on himself, for in old age he wore an air of distinction, even venerability, which had been lacking in youth.

Cecil was rushed to the London Clinic for treatment. Then he returned to Pelham Place. As soon as he was well enough he moved to Reddish and this became his permanent home.

It soon became clear that Cecil was not going to die. He began by being very tired and deeply unhappy. 'But', reported Eileen to Jane Abdy, 'the doctor says he will get better, and I am sure it is true if his strength of will is anything to go by!'[3] He was set to work as soon as possible learning to draw and write with his left hand, learning to walk and to speak. By coincidence, shortly before the stroke, he had received a letter from an illustrator called Gladys Peto, whom he had mentioned as an early inspiration in *The Glass of Fashion*. She had had the same stroke in 1970 and had learnt to draw with her left hand. She sent Cecil a good example of her work.

Kenneth Clark's wife, Jane, had suffered a stroke in December 1973 and

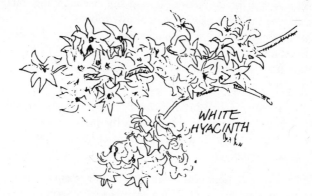

WHITE
HYACINTH

A white hyacinth drawn with Cecil's left hand after his stroke

was now in a nursing-home near Saltwood. Until her death in 1976 she
and Cecil exchanged little notes about nurses, melancholia and other shared
miseries. 'Dearest Cecil,' she wrote, 'I have thought of you every day since
God struck us both. . . . I long for your news.'[4]

Encouragement came from the writer Roald Dahl, who did not know
Cecil, but whose wife, Patricia Neal, had almost died of her stroke, and
Professor Hugh Glanville told Cecil: 'Your talent comes from your brain not
your right hand. You must send the same messages to your left hand.'[5]

Cecil was lucky to have Eileen, who continued to care for him and for his
work and who, in due course, settled in a small sixteenth-century cottage
in Broadchalke to be near by. By this time Eileen could represent Cecil to
the world in the best traditions of the personal secretary. Not only could she
write letters in Cecil's style and even sign his name if necessary, but she
could also review a book for him or write an introduction. In these instances
they would both read the book, they would chat about it and Cecil would
approve the final version.

There was no question of Eileen deserting Cecil in his hour of need. If in
the hectic overworked years since 1953 she had ever considered leaving,
then there were always too many loose ends to tie up, and then a new fever
of work would begin. It was a fulltime job with long hours, and without
Eileen Cecil's work would soon have dissolved into chaos. Now she was also
housekeeper and friend, at hand to keep a lunchtime conversation from
flagging if Cecil could not cope, ready to call a halt to a meeting when he
became tired. And there remained his business life to run from her office in
the studio where he used to paint.

Cecil's friends kept in touch by letter, postcard and telephone, and as he
improved he had many visitors. Clarissa Avon recalled that she and Anne
Tree used to tell him gossip, anything to get a rise out of him. She thought
she was safe with these indiscretions, and sometimes wondered how much

Cecil took in. When he got better, he had the disconcerting habit of occasionally referring to things he should not have known.

In August 1974 Kin wrote: 'I am appalled at the news. For one so active and careful of his health as you are it seems unfair.'[6] On 14 September Jane Abdy called for tea. Saddened by his slowness, she was encouraged by Cecil's reaction to her gift:

> Some pinks which I had brought as a present were wrapped in newspaper. Cecil seized the paper rather than the pinks in an incoherent way and said, 'Give me this.' It was an account of Marlene Dietrich's cabaret. I said: 'How marvellous.' He agreed.[7]

In October 1975 Pelham Place was sold. Its new owner, Robin Raybould, preserved the black velvet walls of the drawing-room, and the red bedroom, and bought some of Cecil's chairs and lamps. At Reddish Eileen now employed a manservant, a cook, a gardener and two dailies. A qualified nurse came on the man's day off and the physiotherapist came once a week. Eileen was able to report to Patrick O'Higgins:

> Cecil is in good form and goes on improving but slowly. He is busy on his diaries, he has an exhibition of his sketches and paintings on down here in Blandford and we are planning another exhibition in London in the New Year.*
>
> This activity keeps his brain working all the time and we all make sure that he has plenty of rest and sleep in between. This is not to say that deep down he is not feeling despair, but he puts on a brave show of camouflaging it.[8]

It is no surprise to find him fighting gallantly to regain his lost faculties. He showed the same strength of character as Aunt Cada when she went blind. Cada was determined to do as much as possible in the ten last years of her life despite her affliction.

The book on which Cecil and Gail Buckland had collaborated, *The Magic Image*, was published in June 1975, and Irving Penn wrote:

> You were too modest in allowing so little of your own work to appear, and all too generous in the words you wrote about me. But I am certainly grateful to you for that, and for the incredible piece of work the book is as contemporary history.[9]

A year later he wrote again:

> I doubt that you have a full idea of the amount of interest young people are showing in your work. They bring an entirely new point of view to

---

* 148 works by Cecil were shown at the Parkin Gallery in June 1976. The prices were kept low to encourage buyers and cheer Cecil up.

it, and great admiration for you as an artist and curiosity about you as a man.[10]

The last two volumes of Cecil's diaries were published in 1976 and 1978 and a composite edition of all six edited by Dicky Buckle came out in 1979. *The Parting Years* contained the story that Cecil Beaton had tried LSD. A reporter from the *Western Daily Press* had the inspired idea to create a little trouble. He telephoned Chief-Inspector Frank Lockyer of Salisbury police, who said he would study the matter. Then he telephoned the vicar of Broadchalke, the Rev. Niale Benson, who had formerly been the headmaster of Russell Harty at Blackburn Grammar School and his boss when he was a housemaster at Giggleswick. The vicar commented: 'If Sir Cecil said it, he was foolish; and if the publisher published it, he was irresponsible.'[11]

Gradually Cecil resumed the reins of life and was able to write letters. To Ali Forbes, he wrote: 'You are an angel. I don't think I really ever will be the same again.'[12] To Paul Tanqueray: 'I don't know why one has to suffer so! Maybe one had it too good, and yet it seemed uphill.'[13] He also struck up a correspondence with a young teacher from New Jersey called Wayne Radziminski whom he never met. Letters went back and forth for three years, each one answered promptly in Cecil's (left) hand.

In April 1975 Cecil was well enough to fly to Tangiers with Eileen to stay with David Herbert. The sketches he did of David's garden were later published in *Vogue*. He also worked on drawings for Cee Zee Guest's book, *First Garden*,* which had an introduction by Truman Capote. Cecil became sadly more and more disillusioned with Truman, especially when extracts from *Unanswered Prayers* began to be serialized. He felt Truman had wasted his talent. 'Have just seen revolting pages of Truman's published in *Esquire*.† Think they are gaga and horrible. He should not be forgiven easily,'[14] he wrote to Patrick O'Higgins, his American friend, who engaged Cecil's sympathy because he was slowly dying of cancer.

In October there was a visit from Garbo, brought to Wiltshire by Sam Green. She hesitated at Salisbury station, wondering if Cecil might have photographers in the trees, but she had no choice. He was delighted to see her and she sat on his knee and snuggled up to him like a child, her steel grey hair tied with an old bootlace. As Cecil made his slow progress to the dining-room, Garbo turned to Eileen and said: 'Well, I couldn't have married him, could I? Him being like this!'[15] When it was time to leave Broadchalke, Cecil made as if to hug her and said: 'Greta, the love of my life!' Deeply

---

*G.P. Putnam's, 1976.

† There is a story about Cecil in these articles. President Kennedy had laughed at the tale of Cecil saying his private parts had shrunk. To this Gloria Guinness replied: 'I wish mine had' [Diary, 6 December 1964].

embarrassed, she spotted the visitors' book. To escape the embrace she broke the rule of a lifetime and signed her name in full. She never saw Cecil again.

Roy Strong also called on Cecil in October. He noted: 'C pulls himself together for a front but in off moments looks pathetic and old. The glimpse of him standing in a green cape-coat with a brown velvet cap on his head, a sad furrowed tragic bundle, waiting to go into the garden.'[16] On the other hand, the producer Allan Davis was in full admiration of Cecil standing in the library and at once extending his left hand. He reassured Cecil: 'No one is as well looked after as you are.'[17] Whether sad or bold, one thing is sure: anyone who had a good story to tell would get an enthusiastic and sympathetic hearing from Cecil, followed by close and interested questioning. These visits to Cecil's warm dark-green library are missed now by his friends and neighbours.

All this cost money and as early as February 1976 plans were put in action to sell Cecil's archive of photographs and ensure him an income of £20,000 a year. In due course Sotheby, Parke Bernet purchased all the negatives and positives (other than of royalty), his pictures by other photographers and his scrapbooks of snapshots and pictures cut out of magazines. On 21 November 1977 the first studio sale was held at Sotheby's and, for example, William Walton (1928) fetched £280, Edith Sitwell (1927) £750, and Irving Penn's portrait of Cecil £700. Bianca Jagger herself bid £200 for a photo of Mick. The sale total was £25,955. It was the first such sale of vintage prints in which negatives were retained by the seller.

Meanwhile Bob Lavine worked with Cecil on a play about his life. Herman Levin, the producer of *My Fair Lady*, was again involved, but nothing came of this. Nevertheless in June 1977 Bob Lavine reported to Diana Vreeland that Cecil was thriving on life once more, 'very bright and smiling and pink-faced'.[18] Diana Cooper said that Cecil had at last accepted his illness. Bob Lavine quoted: 'Resignation is the key to a contented life.'[19]

In November 1977 Cecil broke his retirement and photographed a Bill Blass creation for an advertisement to run in *Vogue*, *Harper's Bazaar*, *Town and Country* and the *New Yorker* in February 1978.

In that month Cecil went to New York accompanied by Grant (his manservant until he died). Cecil saw old friends such as Diana Vreeland, who was extremely impressed with the way Grant looked after him. 'No society lady in the 1930s had her things put out with the care and devotion he had,'[20] she said. On the trip Cecil went to Mexico to stay with Sam Green. Here he became thoroughly overtired and ill. Sam had a problem because Garbo was due. Eventually he flew Cecil to New York and then flew back with Garbo. Meanwhile Grant tried in vain to ring Garbo in New York and Cecil was very sad when she would not answer. 'Cecil is slowly getting back his strength,' Eileen wrote to Patrick O'Higgins. 'He was pretty tired but, as far as I can tell, the trip was a qualified success. Still it was worth doing, even to get him out of a rut; and he loved seeing his buddies in New York.'[21]

There he took a number of portraits. The *Sunday Telegraph Magazine* published five – Diana Vreeland and Anita Loos, his old friends, Louise Nevelson, the sculptress, Joe Papp, the theatre producer, and Carol Bouquet, the actress and star of *That Obscure Object of Desire*.

Later Cecil went for another holiday to Tangiers with Eileen. In May Oliver Messel wrote from Barbados that he was enjoying *The Parting Years*. 'After the ordeal that you must have been going through, the courage and resilience that you have shown is just so wonderful, dearest Cecil.'[22] In July Oliver died. In the diary that Cecil had resumed in July, he wrote:

> I had the news that Tony Snowdon had telephoned with the news of Oliver's death. This gave me a great shock as I always thought of him as a peerless match to me.[23]

He would now turn occasionally to the diary to record a thought, explaining that he had neglected this habit for three and a half years: 'I suppose I didn't enjoy my agony updated. I put down no word in astonishment or fear.'[24] Thus he recorded the deaths of Tris Bennett – 'His health had turned against him, he was no longer a celebrity as he was at school and his friend had long given him up'[25] – and Charles James: 'He was impossible to use* as a friend for his misfortune of some strange sort would soon upset the apple cart.'[26] Reporting this to Patrick O'Higgins, he wrote: 'I suppose I shall be the next to pop off.'[27]

One of Cecil's later joys was to be driven around the countryside. Stephen Tennant, who had kept in constant touch in the 1970s, was concerned at the fate of his friend. 'All your friends miss you so much,'[28] he wrote, sending drawings to amuse Cecil in his plight. But when Cecil visited him at Wilsford and Stephen saw him on a stick, the experience was too much for him. He wrote a sad valedictory letter:

> I *don't want to see* any friends or neighbours ever again. I am a total sad recluse alas. I'm a complete failure in every way. How sweet you are. Infinitudes of Blessings to you.... What a *vile* HELL of Boredom the country is! no more fun now – ever.... I'm so frail now....[29]

Thereafter if Cecil called, the message was that Mr Tennant was unwell. The doors of Wilsford, so often closed in the face of friend, foe or stranger, now rejected Cecil for ever. 'It is an end of an epoch!' noted Cecil. 'A very frail one, but still it held forth a lot for me during the time I spent with him when he filled his birthday bright-day in London surrounded by people of his eye and temperament. Oh dear.'[30] And behind the closed doors lay Stephen amidst his jewels and paints. Indeed he still lies there in 1985.

* He meant 'keep.

In the summer of 1978 Cecil photographed Lesley-Anne Down, who had become famous as Georgina Worsley in *Upstairs, Downstairs* and 'with whom', wrote its script editor, Alfred Shaughnessy, 'male viewers fell in love by the thousand'.[31] She wore romantic fashions by young British designers in the garden at Reddish.

In August Cecil was commissioned to photograph Bianca Jagger. She came down to Broadchalke and posed on the lawn. 'Most photos of Bianca make her look ugly, beastly,' said Cecil. 'But mine make her look more fairy-like. She is a very inspiring-looking woman with real quality to her which is difficult to photograph.'[32] When these were published the retouchers forgot to airbrush the nipples under the see-through Emanuel lace dress.

At the end of 1978 Cecil received the exciting invitation to take forty-eight pages of black-and-white and colour fashions for Paris *Vogue*.

I was enchanted and at liberty! Come hell and high water! I learnt very little about the job except that all prices were arranged, that the hotel and all expenses would be paid. Right! I could only think of the vagaries I was up to. My brain was full of new ideas. I worked at my ideas until I was exhausted! Nothing is more pleasurable than this. I must keep cool and cool off. I should keep all energy for forgotten ideas.[33]

Paris *Vogue* devotes its spring and autumn couture issues to a distinguished photographer. In 1978 Cecil's old rival, Horst, had fulfilled the role. To him Cecil wrote:

It is quite a fluke that I have been asked to do the same thing for French *Vogue*. I am quite nervy as you can imagine, but my efforts won't be worse than the usual prints.[34]

To Diana Vreeland, Cecil added: 'How nice it is to do work for people who understand what one is fighting for.'[35]

Cecil went to Paris with Eileen and Grant. He was there for ten days from 29 January to 8 February and in the *Vogue* studio he took all the Paris beauties: Princess Caroline of Monaco, Paloma Picasso, Olympia de Rothschild, the musical Duchesse d'Orléans, Ines de la Fressange, Isabel Goldsmith, Jane Birkin, Dayle Haddon and others. Meredith Etherington-Smith wrote a glowing tribute to Cecil to introduce the feature. She recalled:

I arrived in Paris *Vogue* one raining Sunday and Jocelyn Kargere pulled all these black and white prints out of a drawer and said, 'Who do you think took these?' I said, 'Well, I may be mad but they look like Cecil Beaton or someone taking him off.' Jocelyn laughed and took me over to the *Vogue* studio and there he was, photographing, in the hat. It was very weird, like seeing a ghost almost.

They had tried to keep it a bit quiet – to spring it. Suddenly everybody in Paris got wind of it and they all desperately wanted to be photographed by him. It was the big thing: Beaton's back! They got all the prettiest girls in Paris. Normally people like Madame Samir Traboulsi don't pose for magazines. They're too grand. It attracted enormous press coverage, proving that Cecil was still news-worthy. It was probably the most successful thing Paris *Vogue* have ever done.[36]

Back home Cecil wrote to Patrick O'Higgins:

It was simply marvellous. I did forty-five sittings in the ten days offered. They were all successful, no exceptions. The quarry was drawn by everybody social and anti-social.... It was really worthwhile doing. I have never worked with such speed and there was even time to see [three collections and the Chardin exhibition].* I seem to have lost my head talking of such matters.[37]

The results were published in the edition of March 1979, and thereafter Cecil became something of a protégé of Paris *Vogue*. In London he photographed Patrick Procktor, Henry Pembroke, Mervyn Stockwood (the controversial Bishop of Southwark) and Diana Quick, about to star as Lady Julia Flyte in Granada Television's *Brideshead Revisited*. He also photographed Sir Ralph Richardson at the National Theatre. Attending the performance of *The Double Dealer* that night, the theatre paid him the signal honour of holding the curtain down until he reached his seat. He also photographed 'the woman who makes strange clothes [Zandra Rhodes]',[38] and the punk rock group, Little Bo Bitch. Plans were made for further commissions in the spring of 1980.

As he returned to the swim he attended various parties, including Diana Cooper's annual luncheon for the Queen Mother, where he met Freddie Ashton. He was one of those who had not visited him in his illness. A week later, staying at Princess Joan Aly Khan's, Ali Forbes said how nice it was to see them embrace. 'Well, I haven't *really* forgiven him,'[39] said Cecil.

In the summer Cecil and Grant went to Italy. To Diana Vreeland Cecil wrote: 'I went to Italy and was gloriously happy staying with a wild man'[40] (his description of his host in Siena, Lord Lambton). On his return he travelled in a wheelchair. Grant recalled that they met Diana Cooper at the airport, also in a wheelchair. On the aeroplane she borrowed £3 for a taxi. 'We never saw that again,'[41] said Grant.

Cecil did his best to keep up with the times. 'I don't like the look of *Now*,'† he wrote to Jane Abdy. 'It is most scrumptious! It has very little beauty. At least says I. I will not go mad if I don't receive a copy, will you?'[42]

---

* Words written by Eileen.
† Sir James Goldsmith's ill-fated magazine.

On Saturday 27 October Claire Pembroke gave a ball at Wilton to celebrate the birth of a son and heir. Cecil reported:

> The Pembrokes are giving a huge ball. I don't know who hasn't been asked, but practically anybody is considered above the salt! I think it will be fun to watch.[43]

It took place on a day made traumatic by the *Daily Telegraph* describing Cecil as the 'late'. In contrast to his first appearance at Wilton when unruly guests had marched him into the Nadder, Cecil was now the honoured guest. A vision of him remains seated in the Double Cube under Van Dyck's enormous portrait of the 4th Earl of Pembroke and his family, between two distinguished ladies, Diana Cooper on the one side and the Dowager Marchioness of Salisbury on the other. When *Vogue* published David Bailey's photographs of the evening, Cecil was pictured with the young Pembrokes as the main spread. In retrospect he thought the ball overlit and the tiaras inadequate, but liked the garden urns filled with candles.

Cecil's last commission was at Kensington Palace on 13 November 1979. He photographed 'the girl, now safely delivered of a child, who made two marriages. She is now [Princess Michael of Kent],* and has got a hand in most steaks. She is quite regal in her manner. Very surprising as a commoner.'[44] These were not published in Cecil's lifetime.

Sir Francis Rose, whose misfortunes had caused so many headaches, dropped dead in Charing Cross Road on 19 November. 'I haven't felt a tear drop for Francis Rose,' wrote Cecil, 'yet he died yesterday.'[45] He was more interested in the fourth man. 'Blunt† is the new word in spying lingo. I only met him on three occasions. Then I did not care for his matter of fact manner of talking.'[46] Nor was Cecil affected by Kitty Miller's death: 'I feel absolutely *nothing* about Kitty's death.'[47] On the other hand he was horrified by the cancer 'that overwhelmed my dear friend Michael Duff'.‡[48]

Cecil did not survive long into the new decade. On 14 January 1980 he celebrated his seventy-sixth birthday with a luncheon party given by Mary Pembroke. 'I had quite a nice day with a large lunch given for me,' Cecil wrote to Michael Wishart. 'By the time I had finished it I was very ready for bed.'[49] On the evening of 17 January, Billy Henderson, his old friend from Wavell days and for many years a neighbour at Tisbury, came over to read to Cecil as was his regular habit. Cecil seemed depressed at dinner; that night he had difficulty with his breathing. Grant summoned Dr Brown, who recalled Cecil's last words: 'Funny sending for you – doctor – in the middle of the night!'[50] A few minutes later with Grant and the doctor in attendance, Cecil slipped peacefully away.

---

* Eileen's handwriting.
† Professor (Sir) Anthony Blunt, unmasked on 15 November 1979.
‡ Sir Michael died on 3 March 1980.

Curiously, a week before Cecil's death, the decision was taken that Timothy, the white cat, should be put to sleep the next time the vet called. Cecil went up to bed and Eileen telephoned. There was no urgency, but as it happened the vet called that very afternoon. Cecil wrote the last entry in a diary which spanned fifty-eight years about the passing of his much loved cat:

Timmy had only a moment of indecision then the knife had found its position and the delay was not postponed. The life of Timmy was quickly at an end. Timothy who had been seventeen years my friend was no longer.

Then Eileen and I had a troubled time sitting in the firelight thinking about Timmy's years. Suddenly tears could not be separated. The man had gone away leaving me with the loss.

Timmy had been the great friend of Smallpeice and of me. He had his own ways, which could not be altered. He liked the sunny side of the street.

Now all was over and Timmy was alone, parted from us, while we were very much alone parted from him. I took a long time in coming to grips with ordinary life. I felt very lonely as I spent my time winging through the past seventeen years. I was still alive but Timmy had gone through to oblivion. He was perhaps lucky? Who knows?[51]

41

No Fear of Oblivion

*He wished to make the camera do the work of a painter
or designer so that in portraits the sitter became subor-
dinate to the general composition. This perhaps touches
the core of the matter. He was a man of many talents,
and photography, the medium in which he did his most
creative work, the medium through which he had most
influence, was the one he wished to put behind him. In
his last working years it could almost be said to have
palled on him.*

The Countess of Avon,
Daily Telegraph, 19 January 1980

Cecil's death was announced on the national television news with a clip
from the black and white scene in the *My Fair Lady* film. The *Evening
Standard* devoted the front page to the headline: 'CECIL BEATON DIES'. There
were lengthy obituaries in the daily papers, in London, New York and Paris.
In the summer of 1935 Cecil had woken up crying after 'a very quick but
sad dream'. In a depressed mood, the thirty-one year old had written:

> I was almost at the end of my life and overcome by its futility and waste.
> My life was over and I was old and all that remained were a lot of scraps,
> letters, bills, counterfoils, some of my typewritten articles and quite a lot
> of loose dollar bills in a cupboard.[1]

But Cecil need not have feared. When death came thirty-five years later,
there was no fear of him being consigned to oblivion.

On 23 January 1980 a simple country funeral was held at All Saints
Church, Broadchalke, echoing the wintry day of his mother's funeral eighteen years before. The village was alive with press and television cameras,
police and 'no waiting' signs. After the simple service, Cecil was laid to rest
in Wiltshire soil, to remain for ever in the county he loved. The service was
attended by his family and by friends of all ages and all worlds: Dudley
Scholte, a Heath Mount contemporary; Jack Gold from Harrow; Lord David

Cecil, met at Oxford in 1922; Lady Diana Cooper, first spotted in the Times Bookshop fifty-seven years before; Rosemary Olivier (Edith's niece); Clarissa Avon, wartime friend and neighbour; Hal Burton, collaborator on plays; Felix Harbord, adorner of Reddish and Pelham Place; June Hutchinson, to whom he had proposed; Beatrix Miller, editor of London *Vogue*; Roy Strong, who staged his exhibition; the neighbours – the Trees, Pembrokes, and Heads; Richard Buckle; and his publisher, Lord Weidenfeld. Seated with the family were Eileen Hose, his faithful secretary; Grant, his manservant; Mrs Stokes, his daily; Jack Smallpeice, his gardener, with his wife; and other villagers and friends who had come to pay their respects. Those that could not attend sent wreaths – Anita Loos, Irving and Ellin Berlin, Irene Worth – but nothing came from Garbo. One of the most appropriate tributes was Diana Cooper's gold victor's crown with bayleaves: 'To Darling Cecil with much love'.

The days that followed at Reddish House were sad ones. As winter turned to spring, a creation of thirty-two years was slowly dismantled, bequests were collected or delivered. At first the house was run as though Cecil had gone to New York but, gradually, this atmosphere dissolved. Perhaps the worst day occurred in May when men came like locusts to remove the books, leaving sad, deserted shelves. In the peace of the empty house, Cecil's presence lingered for another ten days and then disappeared in a flash as Christie's and their men moved in. Meanwhile, memorial services were held simultaneously in London and New York.

The Reddish House sale in June 1980 was not the first to have taken place on that lawn. In June 1947 Cecil had put up a marquee and sold those items of furniture from Ashcombe which were unsuitable to his new abode. Two hundred people had attended – villagers with dog-carts, on bicycles, in invalid chairs and on crutches. The 1980 sale was a considerably grander affair, with television coverage and bidders arriving from far corners of the globe. The house itself was sold to Ursula, Countess of Chichester, a neighbour, and then the possessions of a lifetime came under the hammer, lot by lot. Although it had a sad aura, it was in part a festive occasion and the successful buyers carried their trophies home with pride. At the end of the second day Mrs Brown, the doctor's wife, said: 'How I wish I could now go and have tea with Cecil and tell him about it. He'd be so interested and he'd want to know every detail.'[2] Despite the undoubted truth of that remark, it did not seem entirely inappropriate that the day ended in a torrent of rain.

Inevitably the last years of a man's life, his death and the dispersal of his work and possessions bring a story to a sad end. However, in Cecil's case this is less true than normal, for since his death his reputation and stature have grown considerably. Since 1980 there has been an important exhibition of his war photographs at the Imperial War Museum (which was extended by popular demand). There has been a major sale of his stage designs, portraits, drawings and landscapes at Christie's, an event which filled three salerooms in an evening of that almost hysterical excitement which anything connected with Cecil now evokes. There was a BBC television documentary with home-movies, interviews and newsfilm. The next day two teenage girls on an aeroplane were overheard musing on Cecil's 'amazing life'. A further major exhibition is to be held in 1986 at the Barbican Art Gallery in London, and in New York.

Cecil is unlikely to be forgotten due in part to the considerable amount of work he left behind him. There are many thousands of negatives at Sotheby's in London. These cover the spectrum of twentieth-century life, ranging from the Sitwells to punk rock, wide areas of travel, still life, film, theatre, ballet and opera. To visit that archive is a continually rewarding exercise. The diversity of Cecil's endeavours is such that one can almost certainly find everything sought.

It is of no use going in search of a portrait of Audrey Hepburn. The decision must first be made: formal or informal, black and white or colour, in film costume or in high fashion, on the set, standing, seated, on a bicycle, with or without Rex Harrison, hair up or down, in her *own* costume or one of a hundred extras, 1954, 1963 or 1964, or perhaps another date. Similarly the file on Marilyn Monroe, one afternoon's labour, is as large as the average portfolio of the casual amateur.

In assessing the quality of the work there are several aspects with which to contend. Besides the quantity of work and the comprehensive collection of fascinating sitters, there is the theatrical strain which is very strong and there is what Truman Capote has described as 'visual intelligence'.[3] Capote pointed out that:

> ... it is as a photographer that Beaton attains cultural importance – not only because of the individual excellence of his own work, but because of its influence on the work of the finest photographers of the last two generations: whether or not they admit it, or are even conscious of it, there is almost no first-rate contemporary photographer of any nationality who is not to some degree indebted to Cecil Beaton.[4]

Capote continued:

> For all his quiet tread he is one of the most on the spot people alive; his visual intelligence is genius – the camera will never be invented that could capture or encompass all that he actually sees.[5]

Cecil himself declared: 'To me the most important thing is to be master of the camera, and to see the face from a fresh and enthusiastic point of view.'[6] Irving Penn thought Cecil would be remembered primarily for the historical interest of the people he photographed, something which grows annually more important. He said: 'There will never be another Cecil Beaton. Some of his pictures were jokes, caricatures, very funny – except to the sitter.'[7]

Colin Ford, director of the National Museum of Photography, has declared: 'For half a century the credit *Cecil Beaton* photograph has been a stamp of style, artistry, wit, imagination and an unsurpassed sense of design.'[8] Cecil also raised the status of photographer from 'a nonentity who crawled under a black velvet cloth and pressed a button'[9] to a man with a lucrative and fashionable career. And Ainsley Ellis, writing in *The British Journal of Photography*, opined:

> Wholly professional in his attitude to travelling, designing, lecturing and writing, he nevertheless brought to photography always the enthusiasm and freshness of the true amateur. He was a man who attempted everything for the pleasure to be found in learning to do something wonderfully well. It was a rare accomplishment that became a dramatic achievement.[10]

Not all his judges are so kind. There are those who put Cecil on the fringe of photographic achievement. Susan Sontag dismissed Cecil for placing subjects like the Sitwells and Cocteau in 'fanciful, luxurious decors'. She thought this turned them into 'over explicit, unconvincing effigies'.[11] Other photographers sometimes became irritable discussing his work. He was not a photographer's photographer. Another critic, Jed Perl, described Cecil's pictures as: 'A nostalgia that draws us in. A nostalgia full of nuances, shades of meaning.' He continued:

> A taste for the distinctive, the haunting, the beautiful; and a desire to capture it through photography. This is much of what unites, at least superficially, the divergent products of Beaton's camera. Although he was fond of the exotic, he disliked the bizarre or grotesque. He was very English in his rejection of extreme, shocking statements. He was very English in his indifference to the idea of art as a great, soaring adventure – I doubt if Beaton cared whether art expressed some essential 'truth'. When Beaton saw beauty in the whiteness of an oriental flour factory, he showed its beauty without searching, as Henri Cartier-Bresson might have, for a parable of the human condition.

Mr Perl concluded by saying:

> Beaton called the book he wrote with Gail Buckland *The Magic Image*. He believed in magic, as he believed in beauty, richness and pattern. How about saying that a look through his photographs is like a magic carpet ride?[12]

As we have seen, Cecil hated to be described as a photographer. Beginning this book I believed I was writing about a photographer. Ending it I find that it is a book of the theatre. Cecil had many careers – photographer, traveller, lecturer, designer, arbiter of taste and fashion, caricaturist, writer, diarist, (failed) playwright, host, wit, social historian – but none appealed as much as the theatre. It is an extraordinary life-long addiction that catches a child whose heart beats the faster for the rise of a curtain on a stage-set and the entrance of the first of the cast. Cecil was just such an addict and a frustrated one. Like Enid Bagnold and others, the fact that he was not an actor or playwright caused him to seek other means of self-expression. It is a maxim that if you ask a successful man: 'What would you *really* like to have been?', his eyes will light up for a moment and a secret alternative career will invariably be mentioned. For one reason or another a stage career had proved impossible to follow, and the same drive had found its outlet successfully elsewhere. Cecil would have loved to write, direct and act in his own play. It is perhaps for this reason that Eileen Hose has said: 'He was unfulfilled at the end of his life. He was always trying to find some new way of expressing himself.'[13]

One of the results of this self-expression was the considerable lift that Cecil gave to the profession of stage designers. Like Oliver Messel he was a gentleman-designer, and any production on which he worked bore his unmistakable style.

As a diarist he will become increasingly important. James Pope-Hennessy described Cecil's (unpublished) diary as 'the chronicle of our age'.[14] Talking to James Lees-Milne, he referred to Cecil's and Eddy Sackville-West's diaries and declared: 'We could not be hoisted to posterity on two spikier spikes.'[15] Cecil had an uncanny knack of being in the right place at the right time. Thus his diary is never parochial. It is a frank document about himself and his contemporaries. Unlike most diaries it is seldom a parade of names and facts. It is soul-searching, vividly written, and considerably more interesting than that of his old sparring partner, Noël Coward.

It is sad that Cecil's career as a photographer and exponent of glamour eclipsed his talents as a natural caricaturist. He adored caricatures from an early age and in them he found a balance to his work. Having spent a tiring morning creating a beautiful series of portrait photographs of a society lady, he might well return home, consign his private opinions to his diary and draw an extraordinarily wicked caricature. It was his way of letting off steam and obtaining some innocent fun. Unfortunately few caricatures remain amongst Cecil's surviving work. There are some people who view those that do as works of hatred, but as Cecil himself declared to David Bailey: 'Oh yes I can hate. I can hate unreasonably. ... A lot of the time I feel I'm only doing it for a gag, that I really don't hate this person.... But I take a line about certain people and stick to it.'[16]

During the course of writing this book I was often asked: 'Do you like Cecil Beaton?' Until now I have shirked the question, replying that it is not the role of the biographer to like or dislike his subject. It is obviously important that the biographer should support his subject (and to some extent *vice versa*) as they travel together through the story of a life. Had I met Cecil as a direct contemporary in, say, 1925, I feel I would not have liked him. He would have been too flamboyant, I would have been too reserved. This might have disconcerted him and he might have felt the need to deliver a withering remark in my direction. But when I met him in old age I liked him very much. I found a man who, although already infirm and nearer to death than either of us realized, seemed to me to understand life. He had laid aside the need to succeed socially – a battle won a clear half century ago – and he was now sympathetic, aware, sensitive and perceptive. Here was a man who by exploring and nurturing every talent he possessed (and even a few he did not) had acquired an insight (and not only a visual one) into the fundamental issues that have preoccupied great artists through many ages. Although he suffered from a strong streak of vanity, he was essentially a modest man, who at once cast aside any fulfilled achievement to set off in quest of a new challenge. He never felt that any reward came easily to him, and I am sorry that he was more often sad in his life than happy. He gave the world a considerable degree of delight in many different ways. I wish I could resurrect him and assure him of the esteem in which his name is now held. I wish I could tell him the prices his work now commands. With his inherent modesty he would have stared back in astonished disbelief.

Bibliography

It would not be practicable to list all the books consulted in the preparation of this biography. Here, however, is a list of the particularly useful books, the ones from which extracts are quoted and a few of the rarer ones.

A CHRONOLOGICAL LIST OF CECIL BEATON'S BOOKS

The Book of Beauty (Duckworth, London, 1930)

Cecil Beaton's Scrapbook (Batsford, London, 1937)

Cecil Beaton's New York (Batsford, London, 1938); *Portrait of New York* (Batsford, London, 1948)

My Royal Past (Batsford, London, 1939; republished by Weidenfeld & Nicolson, London, 1960)

History Under Fire, with James Pope-Hennessy (Batsford, London, 1941)

Time Exposure, with Peter Quennell (Batsford, London, 1941)

Air of Glory (HMSO, London, 1941)

Winged Squadrons (Hutchinson, London, 1942)

Near East (Batsford, London, 1943)

British Photographers (Collins, London, 1944)

Far East (Batsford, London, 1945)

Cecil Beaton's Indian Album (Batsford, London, 1945-6)

Cecil Beaton's Chinese Album (Batsford, London, 1945-6)

India (Thacker & Co., Bombay, 1945)

The Masque (Designs for the Theatre by Rex Whistler) (The Curtain Press Ltd, London, 1947)

Ashcombe (Batsford, London, 1949)

Photobiography (Odhams, London, 1951; also published in America by Doubleday, New York, 1951)

Ballet (Wingate, London, 1951)

Persona Grata, with Kenneth Tynan (Wingate, London, 1953)

The Glass of Fashion (Weidenfeld & Nicolson, London, 1954; also published in America by Doubleday, New York, 1954; in France as *Cinquante Ans d'Elégances et d'Art de Vivre*, Amiot-Dumont, Paris, 1954; and in Japan by Kern Associates, Tokyo, 1954)

It Gives me Great Pleasure (Weidenfeld & Nicolson, London, 1955; also published in America as *I Take Great Pleasure*, John Day, New York, 1956)

The Face of the World (Weidenfeld & Nicolson, London, 1957)

Japanese (Weidenfeld & Nicolson, London, 1959)

Cecil Beaton's Diaries: 1922-1939 The Wandering Years (Weidenfeld & Nicolson, London, 1961; also published in America by Little Brown, Boston, 1961)

Quail in Aspic (Weidenfeld & Nicolson, London, 1962; also published in America by Bobbs Merrill, New York, 1963)

Images (Weidenfeld & Nicolson, London, 1963; also published in America by Bobbs Merrill, New York, 1963)

Royal Portraits (Weidenfeld & Nicolson, London, 1963; also published in America by Bobbs Merrill, New York, 1963)

Cecil Beaton's 'Fair Lady' (Weidenfeld & Nicolson, London, 1964)

Cecil Beaton's Diaries: 1939-1944 The Years Between (Weidenfeld & Nicolson, London, 1965)

Beaton Portraits (HMSO, London, 1968)

The Best of Beaton (Weidenfeld & Nicolson, London, 1968)

Fashion: An Anthology by Cecil Beaton (HMSO, London, 1971)

My Bolivian Aunt (Weidenfeld & Nicolson, London, 1971)

Cecil Beaton's Diaries: 1944-1948 The Happy Years (Weidenfeld & Nicolson, London, 1972; also published in America as *Memoirs of the 40s*, McGraw-Hill, New York, 1972; and in France as *Les Années Heureuses*, Coedition Albin Michel–Opera Mundi, Paris, 1972)

Cecil Beaton's Diaries: 1948-1955 The Strenuous Years (Weidenfeld & Nicolson, London, 1973)

The Magic Image, with Gail Buckland (Weidenfeld & Nicolson, London, 1975)

Cecil Beaton's Diaries: 1955-1963 The Restless Years (Weidenfeld & Nicolson, London, 1976)

Cecil Beaton's Diaries: 1963-1974 The Parting

Years (Weidenfeld & Nicolson, London, 1978)
Self Portrait with Friends, Richard Buckle (ed.) (Weidenfeld & Nicolson, London, 1979; also published in America by Times Books, New York, 1979)

CONTRIBUTIONS

The Age of Extravagance, Mary E. Edes and Dudley Frasier (Weidenfeld & Nicolson, London, 1955)
Three Weeks, Elinor Glyn (Duckworth, London, 1974)
The Rise and Fall of the Matinée Idol, Anthony Curtis (ed.) (Weidenfeld & Nicolson, London, 1974)

ILLUSTRATIONS

Wings on her Shoulders, Katherine Bentley Beauman (Hutchinson, London, 1943)
Face to Face with China, Harold Rattenbury (Harrap, London, 1945)
The School for Scandal, Richard Brinsley Sheridan (The Folio Society, London, 1949)
Before the Sunset Fades, The Marchioness of Bath (Longleat Estate Company, 1951)
The Importance of Being Earnest, Oscar Wilde (The Folio Society, London, 1960)
First Garden, C.Z. Guest (Putnam, New York, 1976)

BOOK COVERS

The President's Hat, Robert Herring (Longmans, London, 1926)
All at Sea, Osbert and Sacheverell Sitwell (Duckworth, London, 1927)
Mrs Lesley and Myself, Hugh Smith (Duckworth, London, 1927)
The Spirit of Paris, Paul Cohen Portheim (Batsford, London, 1937)
West Indian Summer, James Pope-Hennessy (Batsford, London, 1943)
A Star Danced, Gertrude Lawrence (Doubleday, New York, 1945)
Wars I Have Seen, Gertrude Stein (Batsford, London, 1945)
The Blessing, Nancy Mitford (Hamish Hamilton, London, 1951)
The Roman Spring of Mrs Stone, Tennessee Williams (John Lehmann, London, 1950)
The Loved and Envied, Enid Bagnold (Heinemann, London, 1951); Doubleday, New York, 1951)
Quadrille, Noël Coward (Heinemann, London, 1952)
Madame de Pompadour, Nancy Mitford (Hamish Hamilton, London, 1954)
Voltaire in Love, Nancy Mitford (Hamish Hamilton, London, 1957)
Don't Tell Alfred, Nancy Mitford (Hamish Hamilton, London, 1960)

CATALOGUES

Photographic Images and other Material from the Beaton Studio (Sotheby Parke Bernet & Co., London, 21 November 1977)
Photographic Images and other Material from the Beaton Studio (Sotheby Parke Bernet & Co., London, 26 October 1979)
Reddish House, Broadchalke, Wiltshire (Christie, Manson & Woods, London, 9–10 June 1980)
1904–1980 Cecil Beaton Memorial Exhibition (Parkin Gallery, London, 1983)
Cecil Beaton (Christie, Manson & Woods, London, 7 June 1984)

SELECTED BIBLIOGRAPHY

Acosta, Mercedes de, *Here Lies the Heart* (André Deutsch, London, 1960)
Acton, Harold, *Memoirs of an Aesthete* (Methuen, London, 1948)
Acton, Harold, *Nancy Mitford* (Hamish Hamilton, London, 1975)
Alsop, Susan Mary, *To Marietta From Paris 1945–1960* (Doubleday, New York, 1975)
Amory, Mark (ed.), *The Letters of Evelyn Waugh* (Weidenfeld & Nicolson, London, 1983)
Bagnold, Enid, *The Loved and Envied* (Heinemann, London, 1951)
Bagnold, Enid, *Two Plays* (*Lottie Dundas* and *Poor Judas*) (Heinemann, London, 1951)
Bagnold, Enid, *Autobiography* (Heinemann, London, 1969)
Bainbridge, John, *Garbo* (Frederick Muller, London, 1955)
Balfour, Patrick, *Society Racket* (John Long, London, 1933)
Berners, Lord, *The Girls of Radcliff Hall* (privately printed)
Bing, Sir Rudolf, *A Knight at the Opera* (Putnams, New York, 1981)
Birkenhead, Earl of, *Walter Monckton* (Weidenfeld & Nicolson, London, 1969)
Black, Kitty, *Upper Circle* (Methuen, London, 1984)
Bolitho, Hector, *A Batsford Century* (Batsford, London, 1943)
Bourdet, Denise, *Edouard Bourdet et ses amis* (La Jeune Parque, Paris, 1945)
Bradford, Sarah, *Princess Grace* (Weidenfeld & Nicolson, London, 1984)
Brinnin, John Malcolm (ed.), *Sextet* (Dell Publications, New York, 1981)

Brown, Frederick, *An Impersonation of Angels* (Longmans, London, 1969)

Burnett, Hugh (ed.), *Face to Face* (Jonathan Cape, London, 1964)

Capote, Truman, *The Dogs Bark* (Random House, New York, 1951)

Casey, Maie, *Tides and Eddies* (Michael Joseph, London, 1966)

Clark, Kenneth, *The Other Half* (John Murray, London, 1977)

Coats, Peter, *Of Generals and Gardens* (Weidenfeld & Nicolson, London, 1972)

Connolly, Cyril, *Enemies of Promise* (Routledge & Kegan Paul, London, 1949)

Coxhead, Elizabeth, *Constance Spry* (William Luscombe, London, 1975)

Culver, Roland, *Not Quite a Gentleman* (William Kimber, London, 1979)

Danziger, James, *Beaton* (Secker & Warburg, London, 1980)

Daubeny, Peter, *Stage by Stage* (John Murray, London, 1952)

Davie, Michael (ed.), *The Diaries of Evelyn Waugh* (Weidenfeld & Nicolson, London, 1976)

Dillon, Millicent, *A Little Original Sin* (Holt, Rinehart & Winston, New York, 1981)

Edwards, Anne, *Vivien Leigh* (Simon & Schuster, New York, 1977)

Evans, Trefor E. (ed.), *The Killearn Diaries* (Sidgwick & Jackson, London, 1972)

Feti, Frank, and Moline, Karen, *Streisand through the Lens* (Delilah Books, New York, 1982)

Fielding, Daphne, *Mercury Presides* (Eyre & Spottiswoode, London, 1954)

Fonteyn, Margot, *Autobiography* (W.H. Allen, London, 1975)

Forbes, Brian, *Ned's Girl* (Elm Tree Books, London, 1977)

Garland, Madge, *The Changing Face of Beauty* (Weidenfeld & Nicolson, London, 1957)

Garner, Philippe, *The Great Photographers: Cecil Beaton* (Collins, London, 1983)

Gill, Brendan, and Zerbe, Jerome, *Happy Times* (Harcourt Brace Jovanovich, New York, 1973)

Glenconner, Pamela, *The Sayings of the Children* (Blackwell, London, 1918)

Glendinning, Victoria, *Edith Sitwell* (Weidenfeld & Nicolson, London, 1981)•

Gordon, Ruth, *Myself Among Others* (Atheneum, New York, 1971)

Gordon, Ruth, *An Open Book* (Doubleday, New York, 1980)

Green, Michael, *Children of the Sun* (Constable, London, 1977)

Halliwell, Leslie, *The Filmgoers Companion* (Macgibbon & Kee, London, 1965)

Hammerton, Sir J.A. (ed.), *The Concise Universal Biography*, Volumes 1 & 2 (The Amalgamated Press Limited, London, 1932)

Harper, Allanah, *All Trivial Fond Records* (The Grey Walls Press, London, 1950)

Harrison, Rex, *Rex* (Macmillan, London, 1974)

Herbert, David, *Second Son* (Peter Owen, London, 1972)

Herbert, John (ed.), *Christie's Revue of the Season 1980* (Studio Vista, London, 1980)

Higham, Charles, *Kate* (W.W. Norton, New York, 1975)

Hill, Paul, and Cooper, Thomas, *Dialogue with Photography* (Farrar, Straus & Giroux, New York, 1979)

Holloway, Stanley, *Wiv a Little Bit o'Luck* (Leslie Frewen, London, 1967)

Holroyd, Michael, *Augustus John:* Volume 1 *The Years of Innocence*, Volume 2 *The Years of Experience* (Heinemann, London, 1974)

Howell, Georgina, *In Vogue* (Allen Lane, London, 1975)

Hutton, Edward, *Highways and Byways in Wiltshire* (Macmillan, London, 1924)

Israel, Lee, *Miss Tallulah Bankhead* (Putnams, New York, 1972)

Koegler, Horst, *The Concise Oxford Dictionary of Ballet* (Oxford University Press, London, 1977)

Lambert, Gavin, *On Cukor* (Putnams, New York, 1972)

Laver, James, *The Year's Work in the Theatre* (Longmans, London, 1949)

Lees-Milne, James, *Ancestral Voices* (Chatto & Windus, London, 1977)

Lerner, Alan Jay, *The Street Where I Live* (W.W. Norton, New York, 1978)

Lerner, Alan Jay, *My Fair Lady* (Coward McCann, New York, 1956)

Lesley, Cole, *Remembered Laughter* (Knopf, New York, 1976)

Loos, Anita, *A Girl Like I* (Viking Press, New York, 1966)

Loos, Anita, *Kiss Hollywood Goodbye* (W.H. Allen, London, 1974)

Lynn, Olga, *Oggie* (Weidenfeld & Nicolson, London, 1955)

Margetson, Stella, *The Long Party* (Saxon House, London, 1974)

du Maurier, Angela, *It's Only the Sister* (Peter Davies, London, 1951)

Moon, Penderel (ed.), *The Viceroy's Journal* (Oxford University Press, London, 1973)

Morgan, Ted, *Somerset Maugham* (Jonathan Cape, London, 1980)

Morley, Sheridan, *A Talent to Amuse* (Heinemann, London, 1969)

Morley, Sheridan, *Gladys Cooper* (Heinemann, London, 1979)

Mosley, Leonard, *Castlerosse* (Arthur Barker, London, 1956)

Mosley, Nicholas, *Rules of the Game* (Secker & Warburg, London, 1982)

Myers, John Bernard, *Tracking the Marvellous* (Random House, New York, 1983)

Nesbitt, Cathleen, *A Little Love and Good Company* (Faber & Faber, London, 1975)

Newman, Arnold, *The Great British* (Weidenfeld & Nicolson, London, 1979)

Nichols, Beverley, *The Sweet and Twenties* (Weidenfeld & Nicolson, London, 1958)

Nichols, Beverley, *A Case of Human Bondage* (Secker & Warburg, London, 1966)

Nicolson, Nigel, and Trautman, Joanne (eds), *The Letters of Virginia Woolf*, Volume Three (Harcourt Brace Jovanovich, New York, 1977)

Norman, Philip, *The Stones* (Elm Tree Books, London, 1984)

O'Higgins, Patrick, *Madame* (Viking, London, 1971)

Olivier, Edith, *Without Knowing Mr Walkley* (Faber & Faber, London, 1938)

Orwell, Sonia (ed.), *The Collected Essays, Journalism and Letters of George Orwell* (Secker & Warburg, London, 1968)

Paley, William S., *As It Happened* (Doubleday, New York, 1979)

Payn, Graham, and Morley, Sheridan (eds), *The Noël Coward Diaries* (Weidenfeld & Nicolson, London, 1982)

Pearson, John, *Façades* (Macmillan, London, 1978)

Perona, John, *El Morocco Family Album* (privately printed, 1937)

Pinkham, Roger, *Oliver Messel* (Victoria and Albert Museum, London, 1983)

Quennell, Peter (ed.), *A Lonely Business* (Weidenfeld & Nicolson, London, 1980)

Quennell, Peter, *Customs and Characters* (Weidenfeld & Nicolson, London, 1980)

Rhodes James, Robert (ed.), *Chips, the Diaries of Sir Henry Channon* (Weidenfeld & Nicolson, London, 1967)

Roberts, Brian, *Randolph* (Hamish Hamilton, London, 1984)

Rose, Francis, *Saying Life* (Cassell, London, 1961)

Russell, Peter, *Butler Royal* (Hutchinson, London, 1982)

Russell Noble, Joan (ed.), *Recollections of Virginia Woolf* (Peter Owen, London, 1972)

Sands, Frederick, and Broman, Sven, *The Divine Garbo* (Grosset & Dunlap, New York, 1979)

Seebohm, Caroline, *The Man who was Vogue* (Weidenfeld & Nicolson, London, 1982)

Selznick, Irene Mayer, *A Private View* (Knopf, New York, 1983)

Shaughnessy, Alfred, *Both Ends of the Candle* (Peter Owen, London, 1978)

Smith, Lady Eleanor, *Life's a Circus* (Longmans, Green & Co., London, 1939)

Smith, Jane S., *Elsie de Wolfe* (Atheneum, New York, 1982)

Sontag, Susan, *On Photography* (Farrar, Straus & Giroux, New York, 1973)

Spencer, Charles, *Cecil Beaton, Stage and Film Designs* (Academy Editions, London, 1975)

Steegmuller, Francis, *Cocteau* (Little, Brown, Boston, 1970)

Stein, Jean, and Plimpton, George, *Edie* (Knopf, New York, 1982)

Steward, Samuel M., *Dear Sammy* (Houghton Mifflin, Boston, 1977)

Sykes, Christopher, *Evelyn Waugh* (Collins, London, 1975)

Thomson, George Malcolm, *Lord Castlerosse* (Weidenfeld & Nicolson, London, 1973)

Townsend, Group Captain Peter, *Earth My Friend* (Hodder & Stoughton, London, 1959)

Tyler, Parker, *The Divine Comedy of Pavel Tchelitchew* (Fleet, New York, 1967)

Vickers, Hugo (ed.), *Cocktails and Laughter* (Hamish Hamilton, London, 1983)

Vreeland, Diana, *Allure* (Doubleday, New York, 1980)

Waugh, Evelyn, *A Little Learning* (Chapman & Hall, London, 1964)

Westminster, Loelia Duchess of, *Grace and Favour* (Weidenfeld & Nicolson, London, 1961)

Who Was Who, A Cumulated Index 1897–1980 (Adam & Charles Black, London, 1981)

Wishart, Michael, *High Diver* (Blond & Briggs, London, 1977)

Woolman Chase, Edna, and Chase, Ilka, *Always in Vogue* (Gollancz, London, 1954)

Young, Kenneth (ed.), *The Diaries of Sir Robert Bruce Lockhart, 1915–1938* (Macmillan, London, 1973) and *1939–1965* (Macmillan, London, 1980)

Yoxall, H.W., *A Fashion of Life* (Taplinger, New York, 1967)

Ziegler, Philip, *Diana Cooper* (Hamish Hamilton, London, 1981)

Source References

Cecil Beaton's papers can be divided into the following categories:

DIARIES: One hundred and forty-five volumes of manuscript diaries from 1922 to 1980, together with miscellaneous diary notes on loose bits of paper (property of the literary executors, Miss Eileen Hose and Viscount Norwich).

LETTERS: The letters of his family and friends filed alphabetically. These range in date from 1904 to 1980 and include some thirty-seven from Greta Garbo. There are a long series of letters from the Countess of Avon, Enid Bagnold, Mrs Ernest Beaton, Truman Capote, Edna Woolman Chase, Lady Diana Cooper, Lady Juliet Duff, Mrs Ian Fleming, Lincoln Kirstein, James Pope-Hennessy, Eileen Hose, Madame Lilia Ralli, Dame Edith Sitwell, Lady Smiley and Diana Vreeland (property of the literary executors).

OFFICE PAPERS: The surviving office files relating to projects such as films, plays, *Vogue*, exhibitions, books, etc. (property of the literary executors).

PRESS CUTTINGS: Forty-nine volumes of press cuttings from birth to death, bequeathed to the Victoria and Albert Museum by Cecil Beaton and lodged there in 1985.

THE DIARIES

1. Cecil Beaton, *The Wandering Years*, p. 162
2. *Ibid.*, Introduction
3. James Pope-Hennessy to Cecil, 31 May 1959
4. Diary, 9 October 1923
5. *Ibid.*

INTRODUCTION

1. Diary, 1979
2. Eileen Hose to author, 30 January 1980
3. Diary, December 1964
4. Stephen Tennant to author, 1981
5. Oliver Smith to author, 30 June 1983
6. Alan Jay Lerner to author, 27 November 1984
7. Ina Claire to author, 21 June 1983
8. Julie Andrews to author, 14 December 1983
9. Audrey Hepburn to author, 22 March 1983
10. *Ibid.*
11. Julie Andrews to author, 14 December 1983
12. Lillian Gish to author, 16 November 1981
13. Dame Anna Neagle to author, 7 October 1981
14. Peter Quennell to author, 2 April 1980
15. Diana Vreeland to author, 22 June 1980
16. Lady Diana Cooper to author, 1980
17. *Harper's Bazaar*, October 1953
18. *Ibid.*
19. Diary, 13 February 1944
20. Michael Wishart to author, 22 July 1980
21. George Rylands to author, 16 December 1983
22. Truman Capote to author, 28 June 1983
23. Irene Selznick to author, 26 May 1981
24. David Bailey to author, 15 November 1981
25. Cecil Beaton, *Photobiography* p. 69
26. Private information, 1 April 1985
27. Patrick Leigh Fermor to author, 16 April 1984
28. Lady Caroline Lowell to author, 16 April 1985
29. Mrs Alfred Bloomingdale to author, 8 December 1982
30. Enid Bagnold to author, 11 January 1981
31. David Herbert to author, 2 June 1980
32. Ina Claire to author, 21 June 1983
33. Coral Browne to author, 24 February 1985
34. Kin to author, 8 July 1983
35. Cathleen Nesbitt to author, 30 November 1981

36. Oliver Smith to author, 30 June 1983
37. Irving Penn to author, 7 December 1982
38. *Palm Beach Post*, 16 January 1970
39. Enid Bagnold to Cecil, 9 February 1955
40. *Mirror-News*, Los Angeles, 23 September 1957
41. Cecil to Greta Garbo, 2 September 1948
42. Diary, 3 January 1948
43. *Ibid.*, 12 September 1938

I: THE BLACKSMITH AND THE CHEMIST

1. Alice Lowthian memoir (sent to Cecil by Alice Lowthian Rollande, 27 January 1966)
2. Cecil Beaton, *My Bolivian Aunt*, p. 9
3. Alice Lowthian memoir
4. Cecil Beaton, *My Bolivian Aunt*, p. 23
5. Diary, 7 March 1928
6. Cecil Beaton, *My Bolivian Aunt*, p. 2
7. Diary, 16 August 1923
8. *Ibid.*, 31 August 1923
9. *Ibid.*, 11 January 1923
10. *Ibid.*, 25 September 1965
11. Cecil Beaton, *My Bolivian Aunt*, p. 18
12. *Ibid.*
13. Diary, undated fragment (1955, cut from vol. 5 of diary)
14. *Ibid.*
15. *Ibid.*
16. *Ibid.*, 28 September 1923
17. Local newspaper, press cutting in Ernest Beaton's album
18. Cecil Beaton, *My Bolivian Aunt*, pp. 20–21
19. *Timber and Plywood*, 25 March 1933
20. Cecil Beaton, *The Glass of Fashion*, p. 12
21. Diary, 3 February 1923
22. Cecil Beaton, *The Glass of Fashion*, p. 33
23. *Ibid.*
24. Sir John Gielgud to author, 13 November 1982
25. Private conversation
26. Cecil Beaton, *Photobiography*, p. 13
27. Cecil Beaton, *My Bolivian Aunt*, p. 51
28. Diary, several places
29. Cecil Beaton, *The Glass of Fashion*, p. 16
30. *Ibid.*

2: A HARSHER REALITY

1. Diary, 20 May 1924
2. *Ibid.*, 26 October 1926
3. Evelyn Waugh, *A Little Learning* (Chapman & Hall, London, 1964), p. 80
4. *Ibid.*, p. 81

5. Cecil Beaton, *The Wandering Years*, p. 173
6. *Ibid.*
7. Lawyer's report on *The Wandering Years*, 10 May 1961
8. Evelyn Waugh, *A Little Learning*, p. 90
9. Hugh Burnett (ed.), *Face to Face* (Jonathan Cape, London, 1964), p. 39
10. Typed diary, 29 October 1950
11. *Ibid.*
12. Hugh Burnett (ed.), *Face to Face*, p. 38
13. Sonia Orwell (ed.), *The Collected Essays, Journalism & Letters of George Orwell* (Secker & Warburg, London, 1968), Vol. I, p. 362
14. *Ibid.*, Vol. IV, p. 346
15. Diary, July 1968
16. *Ibid.*
17. *Ibid.*
18. *Ibid.*, 8 April 1923
19. *Ibid.*, 29 November 1926
20. Cyril Connolly, *Enemies of Promise* (Routledge and Kegan Paul, London, 1949), p. 164
21. Cecil Beaton, *It Gives me Great Pleasure*, p. 65
22. *Ibid.*
23. Cyril Connolly, *Enemies of Promise*, p. 165
24. Diary, July 1968
25. *Ibid.*
26. *Ibid.*

3: ADOLESCENT EMOTIONS

1. Cecil's lecture
2. *Ibid.*
3. *The Harrovian*, summer term 1919
4. Cecil's lecture
5. Colonel T.H.H. Grayson to author, 7 May 1983
6. *The Harrovian*, 22 June 1918
7. Diary, 23 April 1923
8. *Ibid.*, (undated) 1921
9. *Ibid.*, 27 February 1925
10. Notes on Childhood Reminiscences written on Cunard *White Star* 'Samaria' (undated)
11. Jack Gold to author, 15 May 1983
12. Diary, 27 February 1924
13. *Ibid.*, 25 January 1926
14. *Ibid.*, early 1920s
15. *Ibid.*
16. C.T. Bennett to Cecil, 20 November 1963
17. Baba Beaton, unpublished essay on 'Ninnie'
18. Major E.W. Freeborn to B.W.F. Armitage, 21 July 1922 (St John's College Library, Cambridge)
19. *The Harrovian*, 2 February 1980

4: CAMBRIDGE AND THE PURSUIT OF PUB-
LICITY

1. Cecil's lecture
2. George Rylands to author, 16 December
1983
3. Diary, 4 October 1922
4. *Ibid.*, 28 February 1925
5. *Ibid.*, 22 October 1922
6. *Ibid.*
7. *Ibid.*
8. *Ibid.*, 26 November 1922
9. *Ibid.*, 22 August 1923
10. *Ibid.*, 22 October 1923
11. John Hill to author, autumn 1983
12. Diary, 3 November 1922
13. *Ibid.*, 5 November 1922
14. *Ibid.*, 6 November 1922
15. *Ibid.*
16. Stewart Perowne to author, 13 September 1980
17. Diary, 6 November 1922
18. *Ibid.*, 7 November 1922
19. *Ibid.*
20. *Ibid.*, 13 November 1922
21. *Ibid.*, 16 November 1922
22. *Ibid.*, 28 November 1922
23. *The Times*, 30 November 1922
24. Diary, 5 December 1922
25. Stewart Perowne to author, 27 October
1983
26. Dennis Arundell to author, 20 October
1980
27. George Rylands to author, 16 December 1983
28. Diary, 21 December 1922
29. *Ibid.*, 12 December 1922
30. *Ibid.*, 26 January 1923
31. *Ibid.*, 16 February 1923
32. *Ibid.*, 9 February 1923
33. *Ibid.*, 23 February 1923
34. *Ibid.*
35. *Ibid.*, 2 March 1923
36. W. Bullivant to Cecil, 17 November
1922
37. Diary, 27 January 1923
38. *Ibid.*
39. *Ibid.*
40. *Ibid.*
41. *Ibid.*, 16 January 1923
42. *Ibid.*
43. Vera Birch to author, 20 October
1982
44. Diary, undated *c.* July 1966
45. *Ibid.*, 26 January 1927
46. *Ibid.*, 4 February 1925
47. *Ibid.*, 3 May 1923
48. W.G. Butler to author, 14 September
1982
49. *Ibid.*

50. *Ibid.*
51. Diary 16 May 1923
52. *Ibid.*, 1 June 1923
53. *Ibid.*, 2 June 1923
54. *Ibid.*, 14 June 1923
55. *Ibid.*
56. *Ibid.*, 19 December 1922
57. *Ibid.*, 9 January 1923
58. *Ibid.*
59. *Ibid.*, 13 December 1922
60. *Ibid.*, 16 June 1923
61. *Ibid.*, 18 June 1923
62. *Ibid.*
63. *Ibid.*, 19 June 1923
64. *Ibid.*
65. *Ibid.*
66. *Ibid.*
67. *Ibid.*, 20 June 1923
68. *Ibid.*, 27 July 1923
69. *Ibid.*
70. *Ibid.*
71. *Ibid.*, 28 July 1923
72. *Ibid.*
73. *Ibid.*, 16 August 1923
74. *Ibid.*, 8 October 1923
75. *Ibid.*, 9 October 1923
76. *Ibid.*
77. *Ibid.*
78. *Ibid.*, 11 October 1923
79. *Ibid.*
80. Diana Vreeland, *Allure* (Doubleday,
New York, 1980), p. 116
81. Diary, December 1966
82 *Ibid.*, 15 November 1923
83. *Ibid.*, 28 November 1923
84. *Ibid.*, 21 November 1923
85. *Ibid.*, 8 December 1923
86. *Ibid.*, 28 November 1923
87. Sir Steven Runciman to author, 7 November 1982
88. Diary, 3 December 1923
89. *Ibid.*, 8 December 1923
90. *Ibid.*, 9 December 1923
91. *Ibid.*
92. *Ibid.*, 16 February 1924
93. *Ibid.*, 5 February 1924
94. *Ibid.*, 6 February 1924
95. *Ibid.*, 23 February 1924
96. Stewart Perowne to author, 13 September 1980
97. Diary, 7 February 1924
98. *Ibid.*, 7 March 1924
99. *The Eagle*, 7 March 1924, pp. 308–12
100. Diary, 12 April 1924
101. *Ibid.*, 21 April 1924
102. *Ibid.*, 13 May 1924
103. *Ibid.*, 15 May 1924
104. *Ibid.*, 24 May 1924
105. *Ibid.*, 1 June 1924
106. *Ibid.*, 5 June 1924

107. *Spectator*, 14 June 1924
108. *The Cherwell*, 21 June 1924
109. *Ibid.*
110. Diary, 23 June 1924
111. *Ibid.*, 7 December 1924
112. *Ibid.*, 13 October 1924
113. *Ibid.*, 24 October 1924
114. *Ibid.*, 13 April 1925
115. *Ibid.*, 4 May 1925
116. *Ibid.*, 16 May 1925
117. *Ibid.*, 4 June 1925
118. *Ibid.*, 2 June 1925
119. *Ibid.*, 5 June 1925
120. *Ibid.*, 8 June 1925
121. *Ibid.*, 10 June 1925
122. *Ibid.*
123. *Ibid.*, 16 June 1925
124. *Ibid.*

5: ANYTHING FOR THE UPRISE

1. Diary, 15 June 1925
2. Sir Brian Batsford to author, 27 April 1983
3. Diary, 22 September 1923
4. *Ibid.*, 18 November 1922
5. *Ibid.*, 25 April, 1925
6. *Ibid.*, 21 July 1923
7. *Ibid.*, 30 July 1924
8. *Ibid.*, 14 December 1924
9. *Ibid.*, 11 September 1923
10. *Ibid.*, 23 September 1923
11. *Ibid.*, 25 September 1924
12. *Ibid.*, 4 September 1923
13. *Ibid.*, 1 October 1924
14. *Ibid.*
15. Joan Russell Noble (ed.) *Recollections of Virginia Woolf* (Peter Owen, London, 1972), pp. 90–91
16. *Ibid.*, p. 172
17. *Ibid.*, pp. 90–91
18. Diary, 17 April 1925
19. *Ibid.*, 24 June 1925
20. *Ibid.*, 11 July 1925
21. *Ibid.*, 14 July 1925
22. *Ibid.*, 19 October 1925
23. *Ibid.*, several entries
24. *Ibid.*, 4 July 1924
25. *Ibid.*, 28 June 1925
26. Lady Diana Cooper to author, 1984
27. Diary, 1 July 1924
28. *Ibid.*, 10 July 1924
29. *Ibid.*, 3 November 1925
30. *Ibid.*, 30 June 1925
31. *Ibid.*
32. *Ibid.*, 22 July 1925
33. Paul Tanqueray to author, 18 October 1982
34. Diary, 22 July 1925

35. Paul Tanqueray to author, 18 October 1982
36. Diary, 29 July 1925
37. *Ibid.*
38. *Ibid.*, 24 December 1923
39. *Ibid.*, 13 April 1925
40. *Ibid.*, 23 August 1925
41. *Ibid.*, 24 August 1925
42. *Ibid.*, 7 September 1925
43. *Ibid.*, 20 October 1925
44. *Ibid.*, 29 August 1925
45. Vera Birch to author, 20 October 1982
46. Diary, 11 September 1925
47. *Ibid.*, 15 October 1925
48. *Ibid.*, 2 September 1925
49. *Ibid.*
50. *Ibid.*, 5 September 1925
51. *Ibid.*, 29 October 1925
52. *Ibid.*, 30 October 1925
53. *Ibid.*
54. *Ibid.*
55. *Ibid.*, 1 November 1925
56. *Ibid.*
57. *Ibid.*, 2 November 1925
58. *Ibid.*
59. *Ibid.*, 4 November 1925
60. *Ibid.*, 10 November 1925
61. *Ibid.*
62. *Ibid.*
63. *Ibid.*, 15 November 1925
64. *Ibid.*, 16 November 1925
65. *Ibid.*, 18 November 1925
66. *Ibid.*, 19 November 1925

6: THE OFFICE

1. Diary, 20 November 1925
2. *Ibid.*
3. *Ibid.*
4. *Ibid.*
5. *Ibid.*
6. *Ibid.*
7. *Ibid.*
8. *Ibid.*
9. *Ibid.*
10. *Ibid.*
11. *Ibid.*, 21 November 1925
12. *Ibid.*, 23 November 1925
13. *Ibid.*, 2 December 1925
14. *Ibid.*
15. *Ibid.*, 3 December 1925
16. *Ibid.*
17. *Ibid.*, 5 December 1925
18. *Ibid.*, 8 December 1925
19. *Ibid.*, 20 December 1925
20. *Ibid.*
21. *Ibid.*
22. *Ibid.*
23. *Ibid.*
24. *Ibid.*

25. *Ibid.*, 12 December 1925
26. *Ibid.*, 13 December 1925
27. *Ibid.*, 5 June 1926
28. *Ibid.*, 28 December 1925
29. *Ibid.*, 4 January 1926
30. *Ibid.*
31. *Ibid.*, 5 January 1926
32. *Ibid.*
33. *Ibid.*
34. *Ibid.*, 17 January 1926
35. *Ibid.*, 21 February 1926
36. *Ibid.*
37. *Ibid.*
38. *Ibid.*, 21 January 1926
39. *Eve*, 22 December 1926
40. Diary, 11 March 1926
41. *Ibid.*, 1 March 1926
42. *Ibid.*
43. *Ibid.*, 14 March 1926
44. *Ibid.*
45. *Ibid.*, 16 March 1926
46. *Ibid.*, 26 March 1926
47. *Ibid.*, 10 April 1926
48. *Ibid.*, 11 April 1926
49. *Ibid.*, 12 April 1926
50. *Ibid.*
51. *Ibid.*, 13 April 1926
52. *Ibid.*, 16 April 1926
53. *Ibid.*
54. *Ibid.*, 18 April 1926
55. *Ibid.*, 19 April 1926
56. *Ibid.*, 3 May 1926
57. *Ibid.*, 27 April 1926
58. *Ibid.*
59. *Ibid.*
60. *Ibid.*, 16 May 1926
61. *Ibid.*, 17 May 1926
62. *Ibid.*, 29 June 1926
63. *Ibid.*
64. *Ibid.*
65. *Ibid.*, 22 June 1926
66. Edward Le Bas to Cecil, summer 1926
67. Cecil to Edward Le Bas, 30 July 1926
68. Diary, 13 August 1926
69. *Ibid.*, 19 August 1926
70. *Ibid.*, 20 August 1926
71. *Ibid.*
72. *Ibid.*, 23 August 1926
73. *Ibid.*, 24 August 1926
74. *Ibid.*
75. *Ibid.*
76. *Ibid.*, 25 August 1926
77. *Ibid.*
78. *Ibid.*
79. *Ibid.*, 26 August 1926
80. *Ibid.*
81. *Ibid.*
82. *Ibid.*
83. *Ibid.*, 27 August 1926
84. *Ibid.*

85. *Ibid.*, 30 August 1926
86. *Ibid.*
87. *Ibid.*, 31 August 1926
88. *Ibid.*
89. *Ibid.*
90. *Ibid.*
91. *Ibid.*
92. Serge Lifar to author, 19 August 1983
93. Diary, 1 September 1926

7: THE BREAKTHROUGH

1. Cecil to Jack Gold, August 1926
2. Diary, 6 September 1926
3. *Ibid.*, 18 September 1926
4. *Ibid.*, 5 October 1926
5. Cecil Beaton, *Photobiography*, p. 55
6. Diary, 8 October 1926
7. *Ibid.*
8. *Ibid.*
9. *Ibid.*, 20 July 1923
10. *Ibid.*
11. Angela du Maurier, *It's Only the Sister* (Peter Davies, London, 1951), pp. 83–4
12. Diary, 21 October 1926
13. *Ibid.*, 10 November 1926
14. *Ibid.*, 15 (18) November 1926
15. *Ibid.*, 22 November 1926
16. *Ibid.*
17. *Ibid.*
18. *Ibid.*, 23 November 1926
19. *Ibid.*, 24 November 1926
20. *Ibid.*, 25 November 1926
21. *Ibid.*
22. *Ibid.*, 1 December 1926
23. *Ibid.*
24. *Ibid.*
25. *Ibid.*, 6 December 1926
26. *Ibid.*, 18 November 1926
27. *Ibid.*, 13 December 1926
28. *Ibid.*, 7 December 1926
29. *Ibid.*
30. *Ibid.*, 11 December 1926
31. *Ibid.*, 9 December 1926
32. *Ibid.*, 15 December 1926
33. *Ibid.*, 18 December 1926
34. *Ibid.*, 19 December 1926
35. *Ibid.*, 21 December 1926
36. *Ibid.*
37. *Ibid.*
38. *Ibid.*
39. Cynthia Asquith, *Remember and be Glad* (James Barrie, London, 1952), p. 192
40. Pamela Glenconner, *The Sayings of the Children* (Blackwell, Oxford, 1918), p. 91
41. Cecil Beaton, *The Wandering Years*, p. 153
42. *Ibid.*
43. Edith Olivier, *Without Knowing Mr*

Walkley (Faber and Faber, London, 1938), p. 256

44. W.B. Henderson to author, 26 March 1980
45. Stephen Tennant to Eileen Hose, July 1981
46. Diary, 21 December 1926
47. *Ibid.*, 22 December 1926
48. *Ibid.*
49. *Ibid.*
50. *Ibid.*
51. *Ibid.*, 31 December 1926
52. *Ibid.*, 3 January 1927
53. *Ibid.*
54. *Ibid.*, 4 January 1927
55. *Ibid.*, 5 January 1927
56. *Ibid.*, 6 January 1927
57. *Ibid.*, 8 January 1922
58. Edith Sitwell to Cecil, Thursday, 6 January 1927
59. *Ibid.*, Monday, 10 January 1927
60. Diary, 9 January 1927
61. *Ibid.*, 10 January 1927
62. Cecil to Nancy and Baba Beaton, 14 January 1927
63. *Ibid.*
64. *Ibid.*
65. *Ibid.*, 12 January 1927
66. *Ibid.*
67. *Ibid.*, 15 January 1927
68. *Ibid.*
69. *Ibid.*
70. *Ibid.*
71. *Ibid.*
72. *Ibid.*
73. *Ibid.*, 26 January 1927
74. *Ibid.*, 16 January 1927
75. *Ibid.*
76. *Ibid.*, 14 January 1927
77. Stephen Tennant to Eileen Hose, July 1981

8: CECIL MASKED AND UNMASKED

1. Stephen Tennant to Cecil, undated (1926)
2. Diary, 20 November 1928
3. *Ibid.*
4. Cecil Beaton, *The Wandering Years*, p. 164
5. *Ibid.*
6. Stephen Tennant to author, autumn 1980
7. Cecil Beaton, *Ashcombe*, p. 1
8. Charles Castle, *Noël* (W.H. Allen, London, 1972), p. 156
9. *Westminster Gazette*, 7 May 1927
10. Press cutting, 18 July 1927
11. Stephen Tennant to author, 1 March 1981

12. Nancy Mitford to Cecil, 15 April 1966
13. Stephen Tennant to author, 1982
14. Beverley Nichols, *The Sweet and Twenties* (Weidenfeld & Nicolson, London, 1958), p. 210
15. David Herbert, *Second Son* (Peter Owen, London, 1972), p. 44
16. Cecil Beaton, *The Wandering Years*, p. 171
17. *Ibid.*
18. David Herbert to author, 12 September 1984
19. Edith Sitwell to Cecil, undated but summer 1927
20. *Ibid.*
21. Stephen Tennant to Cecil, 30 August 1927
22. *Ibid.*, July 1927
23. *Vogue*, July 1927
24. Edna Woolman Chase, *Always in Vogue* (Victor Gollancz, London, 1954), p. 186
25. Paula Gellibrand to author, 27 January 1981
26. Osbert Sitwell, Introduction to Cooling Galleries Catalogue, 1927
27. *Ibid.*
28. Virginia Woolf to Cecil, 5 October 1927
29. Nigel Nicolson and Joanne Trautman (eds), *The Letters of Virginia Woolf* (Harcourt Brace Jovanovich, New York, 1977), Vol. III, p. 428
30. *Sunday News*, 27 November 1927
31. *Ibid.*
32. *British Journal of Photography*, 2 December 1927
33. *Ibid.*
34. *Sunday Express*, 28 November 1927
35. *Sunday Pictorial*, 27 November 1927
36. Edith Olivier to Cecil, 24 November 1927
37. Kyrle Leng to Cecil, 1 December 1927
38. *Vogue*, December 1927
39. *Pearsons Magazine*, March 1928
40. The *Daily News* quote in *The Englishman*, Calcutta, 27 February 1928
41. *Ibid.*
42. *Ibid.*
43. *Evening News*, 24 February 1928
44. *Ibid.*
45. Nicholas Mosley, *Rules of the Game* (Secker & Warburg, London, 1982), p. 114
46. Diary, 11 May 1928
47. Lady Minto to Lady Ellesmere, 13 July 1927 (Duke of Sutherland's collection)
48. *Evening News*, 11 July 1928
49. Cecil to Lady Ellesmere, 10 July 1928 (Duke of Sutherland's collection)
50. *Daily Express*, 11 July 1928
51. *Ibid.*, 13 July 1928
52. Lord Durham to Lady Ellesmere, 12

July 1928 (Duke of Sutherland's collection)
53. Duke of Northumberland to Lady Ellesmere, 12 July 1928 (Duke of Sutherland's collection)
54. Duchess of Roxburghe to Lady Ellesmere, 12 July 1928 (Duke of Sutherland's collection)
55. Lord Lambourne to Lady Ellesmere, 14 July 1928 (Duke of Sutherland's collection)
56. *Daily Express*, 4 July 1928
57. *Morning Post*, 12 July 1928
58. *Sunday Express*, 15 July 1928
59. Lady Mosley to author, 5 February 1981
60. Diary, 1 August 1928
61. *Ibid.*
62. 'Mary Hamilton to the Kirk Must Go'
63. *Tatler*, December 1928
64. Diary, 19 December 1928

9: THE AMERICANS

1. Diary, 3 November 1928
2. *Ibid.*
3. Beverley Nichols to Cecil, undated but late summer 1928
4. Diary, 9 November 1928
5. *Ibid.*, 11 November 1928
6. *Ibid.*
7. *Ibid.*, 13 November 1928
8. *Ibid.*, 14 November 1928
9. *Ibid.*, 21 November 1928 ·
10. Edna Woolman Chase, *Always in Vogue*, p. 186
11. Diary, 23 November 1928
12. *Ibid.*, 15 December 1928
13. *Ibid.*, 14 December 1928
14. *Ibid.*
15. *Ibid.*, 15 December 1928
16. *Ibid.*, 9 December 1928
17. *Ibid.*, 21 November 1928
18. *Ibid.*
19. *Ibid.*, 9 December 1928
20. Mrs Beaton to Cecil, 14 January 1929
21. Diary, 9 November 1928
22. *Ibid.*, 23 November 1928
23. *Ibid.*, 16 December 1928
24. Mercedes de Acosta, *Here Lies the Heart* (André Deutsch, London, 1960), p. 132
25. Diary, 9 December 1928
26. *Ibid.*, 4 December 1928
27. *Ibid.*
28. *Ibid.*, 19 November 1928
29. *Ibid.*
30. *Ibid.*, 4 December 1928
31. *Ibid.*, 12 November 1928
32. *Ibid.*
33. *Ibid.*
34. *Ibid.*
35. Lady Ashton to author, 8 March 1980
36. Diary, 17 December 1928
37. *Sunday Dispatch*, 23 December 1928
38. *New York Times*, 25 January 1929
39. *Ibid.*
40. *New York Atlanta Georgia Journal*, 23 January 1929
41. *New York City Journal*, 12 January 1929
42. *Ibid.*
43. *Palm Beach Florida News*, 11 February 1929
44. *Ibid.*, 12 February 1929
45. *Ibid.*, 14 February 1929
46. Cecil Beaton, *Photobiography*, pp. 54–5
47. *Vogue*, 8 June 1929
48. Cecil Beaton, *Photobiography*, p. 56
49. Stephen Tennant to Cecil, 16 April 1929
50. Mrs Beaton to Cecil, 4 March 1929
51. Diary, December 1929 (Introduction)
52. Reggie Beaton to Cecil, 24 February 1929
53. Diary, March 1928
54. *Amateur Photographer and Cinematographer*, 10 July 1929
55. Lady Diana Cooper to Cecil, undated but summer 1929
56. Lady Diana Cooper to author, 21 March 1980
57. Lady Diana Cooper to Cecil, undated *c.* 1930

10: THE FUNNIEST PLACE IN THE WORLD

1. *Evening Telegraph*, 13 November 1929
2. Diary, December 1929 (Introduction)
3. *Ibid.*
4. *Ibid.*
5. *Vogue*, April 1929
6. Cecil Beaton, *The Wandering Years*, p. 185
7. Cecil Beaton, *Cecil Beaton's New York*, pp. 233–4
8. Anita Loos, *Kiss Hollywood Goodbye* (W.H. Allen, London, 1974), p. 94
9. Diary, August 1937
10. *Ibid.*, 10 January 1924
11. *Ibid.*
12. *Ibid.*, 30 August 1924
13. *Vogue*, May 1929
14. Diary, December 1929 (Introduction)
15. *Ibid.*
16. *Ibid.*
17. *Ibid.*
18. *Ibid.*
19. *Ibid.*
20. *Ibid.*
21. *Ibid.*
22. *Ibid.*
23. *Ibid.*

24. *Ibid.*, 18 December 1929
25. *Ibid.*
26. *Ibid.*, 19 December 1929
27. *Ibid.*, 18 December 1929
28. Anita Loos to author, 11 June 1981
29. Diary, 20 December 1929
30. *Ibid.*, 23 December 1929
31. Cecil Beaton, *Photobiography*, p. 62
32. Diary, 24 December 1929
33. *Ibid.*
34. *Ibid.*, 26 December 1929
35. *Ibid.*, 22 December 1929
36. *Ibid.*, 24 December 1929
37. *Ibid.*
38. *Ibid.*, 26 December 1929
39. *Ibid.*, 27 December 1929
40. *Ibid.*, 29 December 1929
41. *Ibid.*, 30 December 1929
42. *Ibid.*, 31 December 1929
43. *Ibid.*
44. *Ibid.*
45. Osbert Sitwell, Introduction to Cooling Galleries Catalogue, 1930
46. Patrick Balfour, *Society Racket* (John Long Ltd, London, 1933), pp. 182-3
47. Diary, 1 January 1930
48. *Ibid.*, 3 January 1930
49. *Ibid.*
50. *Ibid.*
51. *Ibid.*
52. *Ibid.*, 6 January 1930
53. *Ibid.*
54. *Ibid.*
55. *Ibid.*
56. *Ibid.*
57. *Ibid.*
58. *Ibid.*, 7 January 1930
59. *Ibid.*
60. *Ibid.*
61. *Ibid.*, 8 January 1930
62. *Ibid.*
63. *Ibid.*, 25 January 1930
64. *Ibid.*, 19 January 1930
65. Lord Weidenfeld to author, 14 August 1983
66. Diary, 18 January 1930
67. *Ibid.*, 25 January 1930
68. *Ibid.*, 23 January 1930
69. *Ibid.*
70. *Ibid.*, 25 January 1930
71. *Ibid.*, 26 January 1930
72. *Ibid.*, 28 January 1930
73. *Ibid.*, 29 January 1930
74. *Ibid.*
75. *Ibid.*, 1 February 1930
76. *Ibid.*
77. *Ibid.*
78. *Ibid.*, 8 February 1930
79. *Ibid.*
80. *Ibid.*, 9 February 1930
81. *Ibid.*, 6 March 1930
82. *Ibid.*, 4 March 1930
83. *Ibid.*, 3 February 1930
84. *Ibid.*, 23 February 1930
85. *Ibid.*, 22 February 1930
86. *Ibid.*, 21 February 1930
87. *Ibid.*, 3 March 1930
88. *Ibid.*, 13 March 1930
89. *Ibid.*, 5 February 1930
90. *Ibid.*
91. *Ibid.*, 6 February 1930
92. *Ibid.*, 13 March 1930
93. *Ibid.*, 20 March 1930
94. Anita Loos to Cecil, 15 March 1930

11: CECIL IN ARCADIA

1. Cecil Beaton, *Ashcombe*, p. 3
2. *Ibid.*, pp. 4-5
3. *Ibid.*
4. Edith Olivier to Cecil, 11 April 1930
5. *Ibid.*, 18 April 1930
6. R.W. Borley to Cecil, 23 April 1930
7. Edith Olivier to Cecil, 30 April 1930
8. *Ibid.*
9. Cecil Beaton, *Ashcombe*, p. 13
10. *Sunday Dispatch*, 11 May 1930
11. *World's Press News*, 5 June 1930
12. *Sunday Chronicle*, 22 June 1930
13. *Ibid.*, 29 June 1930
14. *Ibid.*, 22 June 1930
15. *Ibid.*, 29 June 1930
16. *Ibid.*, 6 July 1930
17. Stephen Tennant to Cecil, 1930
18. Diary, 15 May 1930
19. *Ibid.*
20. Edith Olivier to Cecil, 3 October 1930
21. *Ibid.*
22. *Ibid.*, 12 November 1930
23. *New Statesman*, 6 December 1930
24. *Daily Mail*, 27 November 1930
25. Cecil Beaton, *The Wandering Years*, p. 224
26. Lady Colefax to Cecil, undated but November 1930
27. *The Nation and the Athenaeum*, 29 November 1930
28. *Ibid.*
29. *Ibid.*, 13 December 1930
30. *Ibid.*, 20 December 1930
31. *Ibid.*, 3 January 1931
32. Diary, October 1931

12: I LOVE YOU, MR WATSON

1. Alan Pryce-Jones, *ADAM* International Revue, Nos 385-90, p. 91
2. Sir Stephen Spender, unpublished diary, 5 May 1956
3. *Ibid.*

4. Alan Pryce-Jones, *ADAM* International Revue, Nos 385–90, p. 91
5. Michael Wishart, *ADAM* International Revue, Nos 385–90, p. 98
6. Diary, 6 May 1956
7. *Ibid.*
8. *Ibid.*, 1930 (undated)
9. *Ibid.*, 6 May 1956
10. *Ibid.*
11. *Ibid.*, October 1931 (resumé)
12. *Ibid.*, 6 May 1956
13. *Ibid.*
14. *Ibid.*, 19 October 1931
15. *Ibid.*, 6 May 1956
16. *Ibid.*, October 1931 (resumé)
17. *Ibid.*, February 1931
18. Cecil to Patrick Balfour, 16 February 1931
19. Diary, 2 February 1931
20. *Ibid.*, 6 May 1956
21. *Ibid.*, October 1931
22. Press cutting, 1931
23. Diary, March 1931
24. *Ibid.*
25. Edna Woolman Chase to Cecil, 26 March 1931
26. Diary, October 1931
27. *Ibid.*
28. *Ibid.*
29. *Ibid.*, August 1931
30. *Ibid.*, 6 May 1956
31. *Ibid.*, August 1931

13: ROSES AND TUBEROSES AND CHALK WHITE FLOWERS

1. Diary, October 1931
2. *Ibid.*, March 1932
3. *Ibid.*
4. Cecil Beaton, *Photobiography*, p. 58
5. *Ibid.*
6. Diary, March 1932
7. Cecil Beaton, *The Wandering Years*, p. 256
8. *Ibid.*
9. *Ibid.*
10. *Ibid.*, pp. 257–60
11. Diary, March 1932
12. Cecil Beaton, *The Wandering Years*, p. 260
13. *Ibid.*, p. 259
14. *Ibid.*, p. 260
15. Mercedes de Acosta to Cecil, winter 1933
16. Anita Loos to Cecil, 29 September 1932
17. *Ibid.*
18. *Sketch*, 25 July 1934
19. Diary, undated but summer 1932
20. *Ibid.*, 28 June 1932
21. *Ibid.*, July 1932

22. Lady Diana Cooper to author
23. Diary, September 1932
24. *Ibid.*
25. Peter Watson to Cecil, 17 September 1932
26. Diary, undated but September 1934
27. *Ibid.*, September 1932
28. Private information
29. Lord Berners, *The Girls of Radcliff Hall* (privately printed), p. 27
30. Daphne Fielding to author, 24 November 1981
31. Peter Quennell to author, 21 October 1981
32. Diary, November 1969
33. Private information
34. Diana Vreeland to author, 10 February 1984
35. Diary, marked 26 February 1933 but 26 January 1933
36. Press cutting, 12 July 1933
37. *Vogue*, 1 May 1933
38. Elizabeth Coxhead, *Constance Spry* (William Luscombe, London, 1975), p. 103
39. Diary, 30 January 1933
40. *Ibid.*
41. *Ibid.*, April 1933
42. Cecil Beaton, *Cecil Beaton's Scrapbook*, p. 69
43. *World's Press News*, 26 October 1933
44. Diary, April 1933
45. *Ibid.*
46. *Ibid.*, 3 March 1933
48. *Ibid.*
49. *Ibid.*
50. *Ibid.*, April 1933
51. *Ibid.*, May 1933
52. *Ibid.*, undated but May 1933
53. *Ibid.*
54. *Ibid.*, 23 May 1933
55. *Ibid.*, May 1933
56. Lady Castlerosse to Cecil, 16 May 1933
57. Diary, May 1933
58. *Ibid.*, 26 May 1933
59. *Ibid.*, May 1933
60. *Ibid.*
61. *Ibid.*
62. Cecil to Peter Watson, May 1933
63. Diary, 10 July 1933
64. Peter Watson to Cecil, May 1933
65. Diary, 10 July 1933
66. *Ibid.*, 2 September 1933
67. *Ibid.*, summer 1933
68. *Ibid.*, 16 October 1933
69. *Ibid.*, October 1933
70. *Daily Telegraph*, 21 October 1933
71. Diary, October 1933
72. Edith Sitwell to Cecil, undated but October 1933

73. Mercedes de Acosta to Cecil, undated but winter 1934
74. Alice Collard to Mrs Beaton, 7 November 1933
75. Diary, October 1933
76. *Ibid.*

14: THE GIRLS OF RADCLIFF HALL

1. Michael Duff, *The Power of a Parasol* (A Marlowe Publication, privately printed), p. 94
2. Lord Berners to Cecil, 4 October 1933
3. *Ibid.*
4. *Ibid.*, 15 October 1933
5. Mrs Beaton to Cecil, 14 November 1933
6. Diary, August 1936
7. *Ibid.*, 11 December 1933
8. Cecil Beaton, *Photobiography*, p. 66
9. Diary, December 1933
10. *Ibid.*, 6 January 1934
11. *Ibid.*
12. *Ibid.*
13. *Ibid.*, 1 May 1934
14. *Ibid.*, July 1934
15. *Ibid.*, summer 1934
16. *Ibid.*
17. *The Times*, 3 August 1957
18. Parker Tyler, *The Divine Comedy of Pavlev Tchelitchew* (Fleet Publication Corporation, New York, 1967), p. 352
19. Victoria Glendinning, *Edith Sitwell* (Weidenfeld & Nicolson, London, 1981), p. 180: Edith Sitwell to Allen Tanner, August 1933
20. Cecil Beaton, *The Wandering Years*, p. 226
21. Diary, summer 1934
22. *Ibid.*
23. *Ibid.*
24. *Ibid.*
25. *Ibid.*
26. *Sunday Times*, 30 September 1934
27. Diary, summer 1934
28. *Ibid.*, September 1934
29. *Ibid.*
30. Dr Leahy's cards, 5 October 1934
31. Diary, 6 May 1956
32. *Ibid.*, 16 December 1934
33. *Tatler*, 14 November 1934
34. Diary, December 1934
35. *Ibid.*
36. Mrs Beaton to Cecil, 7 April 1935

15: MALICE IN WONDERLAND

1. Diary, February 1935
2. *Ibid.*
3. *Ibid.*
4. *Ibid.*
5. *Ibid.*, undated but 1935

6. *Ibid.*, February 1935
7. *Ibid.*
8. Lady Dufferin to author, 4 March 1985
9. Diary, May 1935
10. Marlene Dietrich to Cecil, undated but 1935
11. Diary, May 1935
12. *Ibid.*
13. *Ibid.*
14. *Ibid.*
15. *Ibid.*, June 1935
16. *Ibid.*
17. *Ibid.*
18. *Ibid.*
19. *Ibid.*
20. *Ibid.*
21. *Ibid.*
22. *Ibid.*
23. *Ibid.*
24. *Ibid.*
25. *Ibid.*
26. *Ibid.*
27. *Vogue*, 4 September 1935, pp. 45, 89
28. *Ibid.*, p. 89
29. Caroline Seebohm, *The Man who was Vogue* (Weidenfeld & Nicolson, London, 1982), p. 185
30. *Ibid.*, p. 220
31. Diary, November/December 1935
32. *Ibid.*
33. *Ibid.*
34. Margot Fonteyn, *Autobiography* (W.H. Allen, London, 1975), pp. 60–62
35. *Observer*, 23 October 1966
36. *Sunday Times*, 16 February 1936
37. *New Statesman and Nation*, 15 February 1936
38. Peter Watson to Cecil, March 1936
39. Constant Lambert to Cecil, 19 February 1936
40. Diary, May 1936
41. *Ibid.*, April 1936
42. *Ibid.*, June 1936
43. *Ibid.*
44. *Ibid.*
45. Valentina Schlee to author, 11 February 1984
46. Diary, June 1936
47. *Ibid.*
48. *Ibid.*
49. *Pittsburgh Press*, 27 July 1936
50. Boris Kochno to Cecil, August 1936
51. Diary, August 1936
52. *Evening News*, 12 August 1936
53. *Manchester Guardian*, 13 August 1936
54. *New Statesman and Nation*, 15 August 1936
55. Diary, undated
56. *Ibid.*, August 1936
57. *Ibid.*

58. *Ibid.*
59. *Ibid.*
60. *Ibid.*
61. *Ibid.*
62. Mrs Beaton to Cecil, 2 September 1936
63. Diary, November 1936
64. *Ibid.*
65. *New Statesman and Nation*, 14 November 1936

16: THE MEANS TO AN ACHIEVEMENT

1. Diary, (*c.* 20) November 1936
2. *Ibid.*
3. *Ibid.*
4. *Ibid.*
5. *Vogue*, 21 August 1935, p. 27
6. *Ibid.*
7. Diary, (*c.* 20) November 1936
8. *Ibid.*
9. *Ibid.*
10. *Ibid.*
11. *Ibid.*, January 1937
12. Duchess of Windsor to Cecil, 3 January 1937
13. *Ibid.*
14. Peter Watson to Cecil, January 1937
15. Diary, March 1937
16. Lady Oxford to Cecil, 8 May 1937
17. Diary, May 1937
18. Duchess of Gloucester to Cecil, 1935
19. Diary, spring 1937
20. *Ibid.*
21. *Ibid.*
22. *Ibid.*
23. *Ibid.*
24. *Ibid.*
25. *Ibid.*
26. Duchess of Windsor to Cecil, May 1937
27. Diary, 12 May 1937
28. *Ibid.*
29. *Ibid.*
30. *Ibid.*
31. *Ibid.*, June 1937
32. *Ibid.*
33. *Ibid.*
34. *Ibid.*
35. *Ibid.*
36. *Ibid.*
37. Edna Woolman Chase to Cecil, 4 June 1937
38. Cecil to Edna Woolman Chase, 4 June 1937
39. Diary, June 1937

17: ALL THE DAMNED KIKES IN TOWN

1. Diary, July 1937
2. *Ibid.*
3. *Ibid.*

4. *Ibid.*, August 1937
5. *Ibid.*, April 1937
6. *Ibid.*, August 1937
7. Lilia Ralli to Cecil, undated
8. Diary, 29 May 1936
9. James Lees-Milne, *Prophesying Peace* (Chatto and Windus, London, 1977), p. 41
10. Hector Bolitho, *A Batsford Century* (Batsford, London, 1943), p. 84
11. Sir Brian Batsford to author, 27 April 1983
12. Diary, summer 1937
13. Peter Watson to Cecil, September 1932
14. Diary, September 1937
15. Stephen Tennant to Cecil, 23 September 1937
16. *New Statesman and Nation*, 23 October 1937
17. Raymond Mortimer to Cecil, 3 December 1937
18. Diary, September 1937
19. *Ibid.*
20. *Ibid.*
21. *Ibid.*, November 1937
22. Cecil Beaton, *Photobiography*, p. 72
23. *Ibid.*
24. *Ibid.*, p. 73
25. Cecil to Edna Woolman Chase, 8 January 1937
26. *Ibid.*
27. *Ibid.*
28. Dr Agha, quoted by Cecil to Edna Woolman Chase, 12 January 1937
29. Cecil to Edna Woolman Chase, 8 January 1937
30. *Ibid.*
31. Diary, 22 November 1937
32. *Ibid.*
33. Lee Israel, *Miss Tallulah Bankhead* (Putnams, New York, 1972), pp. 179–80
34. Diary, November 1937
35. *Ibid.*, 7 January 1938
36. *Ibid.*
37. *Ibid.*
38. *Ibid.*
39. *Ibid.*
40. *New York Daily Mirror*, 24 January 1938
41. *Ibid.*
42. *Ibid.*
43. Diary, January 1938
44. *Ibid.*
45. *Time*, 7 February 1938
46. Diary, January 1938
47. *Ibid.*
48. Lady Rosse to author, 1 August 1983
49. Condé Nast to Cecil, 24 January 1938
50. Diary, January 1938
51. *Ibid.*
52. *Ibid.*

53. Gertrude Lawrence to Cecil, 30 January 1938

54. Lilia Ralli to Cecil, undated but February 1938

55. Diary, January 1938

56. *Ibid.*

57. *Ibid.*

58. Caroline Seebohm, *The Man who was Vogue*, p. 214

59. Edna Woolman Chase to Cecil, 26 January 1938

60. Diary, January 1938

61. *Ibid.*

62. Eleanor Lambert to author, 11 February 1984

63. *New Masses*, 2 February 1938

64. Diary, April 1938

65. Condé Nast to Cecil, April 1938

66. Cecil to Condé Nast, 5 May 1938

67. Cecil Beaton, *Cecil Beaton's New York*, p. 250

68. Cecil Beaton, *My Royal Past*, by Baroness von Bülop, p. 141

69. Cecil Beaton, *Cecil Beaton's New York*, p. 65

70. Irene Selznick to author, 26 May 1981

18: REST AND RECUPERATION

1. Cecil to Rudolf Kommer, 1 February 1939

2. Edna Woolman Chase to Cecil, 13 December 1938

3. Rudolf Kommer to Cecil, 9 January 1939

4. *Ibid.*, 14 February 1939

5. *Ibid.*

6. *Ibid.*, 22 February 1939

7. *New York Daily Mirror*, 6 March 1939

8. Frank Crowninshield to Walter Winchell, 27 April 1939

9. Cecil to Eleanor Lambert, 24 March 1939

10. Lady Ashton to author, 8 March 1980

11. Diary, April 1938

12. *Ibid.*, September 1938

13. *Ibid.*, August 1938

14. David Herbert, *Second Son*, p. 61

15. Diary, August 1938

16. *Ibid.*

17. *Ibid.*

18. *Ibid.*

19. David Herbert, *Second Son*, p. 81

20. Diary, September 1938

21. Michael Wishart, *High Diver* (Blond & Briggs, London, 1977), p. 92

22. Lady Lindsay to author, January 1984

23. Diary, September 1938

24. *Ibid.*

25. *Ibid.*

26. Grand Hotel writing paper

27. Diary, September 1938

28. *Ibid.*

29. *Ibid.*, April 1938

30. *Ibid.*

31. *Ibid.*

32. *Ibid.*, September 1938

33. Francis Rose, *Saying Life* (Cassell, London, 1961), p. 359

34. *Ibid.*

35. *Ibid.*

36. *Ibid.*, p. 327

37. Diary, (c. 22) September 1938

38. *Ibid.*, September 1938

39. *Ibid.*

40. *Ibid.*

41. John Sutro to author, 18 September 1981

42. Diary, September 1938

43. *Ibid.*

44. *Ibid.*, (c. 21) September 1938

45. *Ibid.*, (c. 22) September 1938

46. *Ibid.*

47. *Ibid.*

48. *Ibid.*, September 1938

49. *Ibid.*

50. *Ibid.*, September/October 1938

51. *Ibid.*, November 1938

52. *Ibid.*

53. *Ibid.*

54. *Ibid.*

55. *Ibid.*

56. *Ibid.*

57. *Ibid.*

58. *Ibid.*, early 1939

59. Cecil to Rudolf Kommer, 24 March 1939

60. Diary, March 1939

61. *Ibid.*

62. *Ibid.*, 17 April 1939

63. *Ibid.*

64. *Ibid.*, May 1939

65. *Ibid.*

66. *Ibid.*

67. *Ibid.*, 7 June 1939

68. *Ibid.*

69. *Ibid.*, June 1939

70. *Ibid.*

71. *Ibid.*

72. *Ibid.*

73. *Ibid.*

74. *Ibid.*, July 1939

75. *Ibid.*

76. *Ibid.*

77. Eleanor Lambert to Cecil, 23 August 1939

78. Diary, July 1939

79. *Ibid.*

80. *Ibid.*

81. *Ibid.*

82. *Ibid.*

83. *Ibid.*
84. Princess Olga to author, 28 March 1984
85. Diary, July 1939
86. *Ibid.*, 26 April 1923
87. *Ibid.*, December 1923
88. *Ibid.*, July 1939
89. *Ibid.*
90. *Ibid.*
91. *Ibid.*
92. *Ibid.*
93. *Ibid.*
94. *Ibid.*
95. *Ibid.*
96. *Ibid.*
97. *Ibid.*, August 1939
98. *Ibid.*
99. *Ibid.*
100. *Ibid.*
101. Samuel M. Steward, *Dear Sammy* (Houghton Mifflin, Boston, 1977), p. 79
102. Francis Rose, *Saying Life*, p. 385
103. *Ibid.*
104. Diary, September 1939
105. *Ibid.*, September/October 1938
106. *Britannia and Eve*, February 1940
107. *Spectator*, 21 October 1960
108. Diary, late November 1938
109. *Ibid.*, early 1920s
110. *Ibid.*, summer 1934
111. *Ibid.*, 1938
112. *Ibid.*, August/September 1937
113. *Ibid.*, 1937
114. Peter Watson to Cecil, 12 December 1939

19: WINGED SQUADRONS

1. Diary, 2 September 1939
2. *Ibid.*, August 1938
3. *Ibid.*, September 1939
4. *Ibid.*
5. *Ibid.*
6. *Ibid.*
7. Harold Acton, *Memoirs of an Aesthete* (Methuen, London, 1948), p. 88
8. Diary, September 1939
9. *Daily Sketch*, 1940
10. Charles Henri Ford to Cecil, 22 March 1940
11. Diary, 5 December 1939
12. *Ibid.*, December 1939–February 1940
13. *Ibid.*, 27 February 1940
14. *Ibid.*
15. *Ibid.*
16. *Daily Express*, 6 January 1940
17. Augustus John to Cecil, 4 January 1940
18. Enid Bagnold, *Autobiography* (Heinemann, London, 1969), p. 212
19. *Ibid.*
20. Diary, spring 1940
21. Robert Rhodes Jones (ed.), *Chips: The Diaries of Sir Henry Channon* (Weidenfeld & Nicolson, London, 1967), p. 262
22. Diary, March 1940
23. *Ibid.*
24. *Ibid.*
25. *Ibid.*
26. *Ibid.*
27. *Ibid.*
28. Kenneth Clark, *The Other Half* (John Murray, London, 1977), p. 15
29. Kenneth Clark to Cecil, 29 April 1940
30. Diary, spring 1940
31. *Ibid.*, 22 May 1940
32. *Ibid.*, May 1940
33. *Ibid.*, 2 July 1940
34. *Ibid.*
35. *Ibid.*
36. *Ibid.*
37. *Ibid.*, 8 August 1940
38. *Ibid.*, August 1940
39. *Ibid.*, September 1940
40. *Ibid.*, October 1940
41. *Vogue*, February 1941
42. Michael Redgrave to Cecil, 11 March 1941
43. Film script 'The Young Mr Pitt'
44. *Time and Tide*, 3 May 1941
45. Diary, 12 May 1941
46. Frances Day to Cecil, 29 May 1941
47. Diary, September 1940
48. *Ibid.*
49. *Ibid.*
50. *Ibid.*, 10 November 1940
51. *Ibid.*
52. *Ibid.*
53. *Ibid.*
54. *Ibid.*
55. *Ibid.*, November 1940
56. *Ibid.*
57. *Ibid.*, c. September 1940
58. *Ibid.*, 30 August 1940
59. *Ibid.*
60. *Ibid.*, September 1940
61. *Ibid.*, end of September 1940
62. Cecil to Enid Bagnold, summer 1940
63. Diary, December 1940
64. James Pope-Hennessy to Cecil, 14 December 1940
65. *Ibid.*, 21 December 1940
66. Peter Quennell (ed.), *A Lonely Business* (Weidenfeld & Nicolson, London, 1980), p. 36
67. *Spectator*, 11 July 1941
68. James Pope-Hennessy to Cecil, 2 December 1940
69. Cecil to Clarissa Churchill, 10 September 1941
70. Diary, 12 October 1940

71. *Women's Illustrated*, June 1941
72. Dr Agha to Mrs Chase, 6 January 1942
73. Diary, October 1940
74. *Ibid.*
75. *Ibid.*, February 1941
76. Cecil Beaton, *Winged Squadrons*, p. 6
77. Diary, February 1941
78. Cecil to Francis Rose, May 1941
79. Edna Chase to Cecil, 4 June 1941
80. Cecil Beaton, *Winged Squadrons*, p. 36
81. *New Statesman and Nation*, 6 June 1942
82. Diary, May 1941
83. Gail Buckland, *Cecil Beaton War Photographs, 1939–45* (Imperial War Museum/Jane's, London, 1981), p. 7
84. Cecil Beaton, *Time Exposure*, p. vii
85. Press cutting (unidentified), 1941
86. *Spectator*, 7 August 1941
87. *Horizon*, September 1941, Vol. IV, No. 21, pp. 213–14
88. *Ibid.*
89. *New Statesman and Nation*, 6 September 1941
90. Osbert Sitwell to Cecil, 4 September 1941
91. *Ibid.*
92. Cecil to Osbert Sitwell, September 1941 (draft letter)
93. Osbert Sitwell to Cecil, Sunday, September 1941
94. Siegfried Sassoon to Cecil, 20 September 1941
95. Lord Berners to Cecil, undated but September 1941
96. Lily Elsie to Cecil, 23 July 1941
97. Diary, 3 August 1941
98. Cecil to Lady Diana Cooper, 1 June 1941
99. Diary, September 1941
100. Coral Browne to author, 24 February 1985
101. Mrs Reginald Beaton to Mrs Ernest Beaton, 1941
102. Diary, December 1941
103. *Ibid.*, 14 January 1942
104. *Ibid.*
105. *Ibid.*, January 1942
106. *Ibid.*, February 1942

20: NEAR EAST

1. Cecil Beaton, *Near East*, p. 3
2. *Ibid.*, p. 4
3. *Ibid.*, p. 10
4. *Ibid.*, p. 12
5. *Ibid.*
6. *Ibid.*, p. 19
7. *Ibid.*, p. 26
8. Frank Scarlett to author, 22 December 1980
9. Cecil to Derek Adkins. 22 April 1942
10. Diary, April 1942
11. Cecil Beaton, *Near East*, p. 38
12. Diary, 29 April 1942
13. *Ibid.*, 3 May 1942
14. *Ibid.*, 30 April 1942
15. *Ibid.*, 1 May 1942
16. *Ibid.*, 3 May 1942
17. *Ibid.*
18. *Ibid.*, May 1942
19. *Ibid.*
20. *Ibid.*
21. *Ibid.*
22. *Ibid.*
23. *Ibid.*
24. *Ibid.*
25. *Ibid.*
26. Cecil to Lady Juliet Duff, 17 May 1942
27. Diary, May 1942
28. *Ibid.*, 19 May 1942
29. *Sunday Times Magazine*, 17 September 1967
30. Earl of Birkenhead, *Walter Monckton* (Weidenfeld & Nicolson, London, 1969), p. 201
31. Cecil to Lady Juliet Duff, 3 June 1942
32. 28 May 1942
33. *Ibid.*, 20 May 1942
34. *Ibid.*, 27 May 1942
35. *Ibid.*
36. *Ibid.*, 20 May 1942
37. *Ibid.*, 29 May 1942
38. Cecil to Lady Juliet Duff, 3 June 1942
39. *Ibid.*
40. Rudolf Kommer to Cecil, 1 September 1942
41. Diary, 31 May 1942
42. Cecil to Clarissa Churchill, 7 June 1942
43. Diary, 7 June 1942
44. *Ibid.*, 9 June 1942
45. *Ibid.*
46. *Ibid.*
47. *Ibid.*, 13 June 1942
48. *Ibid.*
49. Stewart Perowne to author, 4 February 1981
50. Diary, 13 June 1942
51. *Ibid.*
52. Stewart Perowne to author, 4 February 1981
53. Diary, 13 June 1942
54. *Ibid.*, 16 June 1942
55. *Ibid.*
56. *Ibid.*, 17 June 1942
57. *Ibid.*
58. *Ibid.*, 18 June 1942
59. Cecil Beaton, *Near East*, p. 119
60. Diary, 22 June 1942
61. *Ibid.*, 23 June 1942

62. Princess Aly Khan to author, 30 October 1980
63. Diary, 28 June 1942
64. Maie Casey, *Tides and Eddies* (Michael Joseph, London, 1966), p. 109
65. Diary, June 1942
66. *Ibid.*, 1 July 1942
67. *Ibid.*, 2 July 1942
68. *Ibid.*, 6 July 1942
69. *Ibid.*, 11 July 1942
70. *Ibid.*, 10 July 1942
71. *Ibid.*, 13 July 1942
72. *Vogue*, November 1942
73. Diary, 15 July 1942
74. *Ibid.*, July 1942
75. *New Statesman and Nation*, 17 July 1943
76. Diary, 8 August 1942
77. James Lees-Milne, *Ancestral Voices* (Chatto & Windus, London, 1975), pp. 159–60
78. Diary, 1943
79. *Ibid.*
80. *Ibid.*, 23 October 1942
81. *Ibid.*
82. *Ibid.*
83. *Ibid.*
84. Noël Coward to Cecil, 21 October 1942
85. Cecil Beaton, *The Years Between*, p. 231
86. Cecil to Enid Bagnold, March 1943
87. *Ibid.*
88. John Burrell to Cecil, 28 February 1943
89. Brian Forbes, *Ned's Girl* (Elm Tree Books, London, 1977), p. 205
90. Enid Bagnold to Cecil, 8 November 1943
91. *Ibid.*
92. Diary, June 1944
93. Maud Nelson to Cecil, 8 May 1944
94. Edna Woolman Chase to Cecil, 29 January 1943
95. Audrey Withers to Cecil, 30 April 1943
96. *Ibid.*, 22 July 1943
97. Edna Woolman Chase to Cecil, 6 October 1943
98. *Tatler*, 7 June 1944
99. *New Statesman*, 24 June 1944
100. James Lees-Milne, *Ancestral Voices*, pp. 159–60
101. *Ibid.*, p. 183
102. Diary, 1943
103. Hugh Francis to Cecil, 14 January 1944
104. Diary, December 1943
105. *Ibid.*
106. *Ibid.*
107. *Ibid.*, 16 July 1944
108. Lord Balfour of Inchrye to Cecil, 19 October 1965

21: FAR EAST

1. Peter Coats, *Of Generals and Gardens* (Weidenfeld & Nicolson, London, 1976), p. 218
2. Trefor E. Evans (ed.), *The Killearn Diaries* (Sidgwick & Jackson, London, 1972), p. 272
3. Diary, 21 December 1943
4. *Ibid.*
5. Cecil to Mrs Beaton, 21 December 1943
6. Peter Coats, *Of Generals and Gardens*, p. 218
7. Penderel Moon (ed.), *The Viceroy's Journal* (Oxford University Press, Oxford, 1973), p. 49
8. Diary, 15 July 1944
9. *Ibid.*, 1 January 1944
10. *Ibid.*, 19 March 1944
11. *Ibid.*, 28 December 1943
12. *Ibid.*, 2 January 1944
13. *Ibid.*
14. *Ibid.*
15. *Ibid.*
16. *Ibid.*, 5 January 1944
17. Cecil to Clarissa Churchill, 26 January 1944
18. Cecil to Lady Diana Cooper, 27 January 1944
19. Diary, 15 January 1944
20. *Ibid.*, 14 January 1944
21. *Ibid.*, 19 January 1944
22. *Ibid.*, 21 January 1944
23. Maie Casey, *Tides and Eddies*, pp. 141–2
24. Diary, 9 February 1944
25. *Ibid.*, 11 February 1944
26. *Ibid.*, 28 January 1944
27. *Ibid.*, 3 February 1944
28. *Ibid.*, 16 February 1944
29. *Ibid.*
30. *Ibid.*, 17 February 1944
31. *Ibid.*, 23 February 1944
32. *Ibid.*, 24 February 1944
33. *Ibid.*
34. Cecil to Clarissa Churchill, March 1944
35. Diary, 1 March 1944
36. *Ibid.*, 5 March 1944
37. *Ibid.*
38. *Ibid.*, 13 March 1944
39. Cecil to Clarissa Churchill, 20 March 1944
40. *Ibid.*, 25 March 1944
41. Diary, 29 March 1944
42. *Ibid.*, 30 March 1944
43. *Ibid.*
44. Hugh Francis to Cecil, 3 April 1944
45. *Ibid.*
46. Diary, 8 April 1944
47. *Ibid.*
48. *Ibid.*
49. *Ibid.*

50. *Ibid.*, 9 April 1944
51. Lady Seymour, unpublished diary, 10 April 1944
52. *Ibid.*, 11 April 1944
53. Cecil to Lady Diana Cooper, 30 May 1944
54. Diary, 15 April 1944
55. Åke Hartman to Cecil, 31 October 1965
56. Philip Smith to author, 2 September 1984
58. Diary, 16 April 1944
59. Leo Handley-Derry to author, 10 October 1984
60. Diary, 23 April 1944
61. *Ibid.*
62. *Ibid.*, 24 April 1944
63. *Ibid.*
64. *Ibid.*
65. *Ibid.*, 25 April 1944
66. Cecil to Lady Diana Cooper, 26 April 1944
67. Cecil to Clarissa Churchill, 27 April 1944
68. Diary, 29 April 1944
69. Cecil to Enid Bagnold, 23 May 1944
70. Diary, 17 May 1944
71. *Ibid.*
72. Cecil to Clarissa Churchill, 24 May 1944
73. Erik Watts to Cecil, 27 May 1944, quoting telegram from Hugh Francis
74. *Ibid.*
75. Diary, 29 May 1944
76. *Ibid.*, 31 May 1944
77. *Ibid.*, 5 June 1944
78. *Ibid.*, 6 June 1944
79. Cecil to Lady Diana Cooper, 30 May 1944
80. Diary, 3 June 1944
81. *Ibid.*
82. *Ibid.*, 5 June 1944
83. *Ibid.*, 20 June 1944
84. *Ibid.*
85. Cecil to Lady Juliet Duff, 18 June 1944
86. Diary, 21 June 1944
87. *Ibid.*, May 1945
88. *Ibid.*, 1 July 1944
89. *Ibid.*, 2 July 1944
90. *Ibid.*, 3 July 1944
91. *Ibid.*
92. *Ibid.*
93. *Ibid.*
94. *Ibid.*, 18 July 1944
95. Cecil to Clarissa Churchill, 10 July 1944
96. Diary, 24 July 1944
97. *Ibid.*
98. *Ibid.*, 5 August 1944
99. *Ibid.*, 11 August 1944
100. *Ibid.*, 8 September 1944
101. *Ibid.*, 21 September 1944
102. *Ibid.*, 5 September 1944
103. Alexander Liberman to Cecil, 27 October 1944
104. Diary, 23 September 1944
105. *Ibid.*, 11 November 1944
106. *Ibid.*, 4 May 1945
107. *Daily Mail*, 16 March 1946
108. *Sunday Times*, 25 November 1945
109. Edith Olivier to Cecil, 21 November 1945
110. Diary, 7 February 1962
111. Gail Buckland, *Cecil Beaton War Photographs 1939–45*, pp. 32–3

22: THE PASSING OF A HOUSE

1. Diary, July 1945
2. *Ibid.*
3. John Sutro to Cecil, 22 August 1945
4. Peter Watson to Cecil, September 1945
5. Edith Olivier to Cecil, 1 September 1945
6. Lord Wavell to Cecil, 29 March 1950
7. *Sunday Times*, 26 February 1950
8. Sir John Gielgud to author, 13 November 1982
9. *Oxford Magazine*, 2 June 1945
10. *Time & Tide*, 1 September 1945
11. Cecil to Lady Diana Cooper, September 1945
12. *Ibid.*
13. Diary, October 1942
14. Lady Diana Cooper to author, 6 May 1980
15. Diary, January 1947
16. *Ibid.*
17. *Ibid.*
18. Cecil Beaton, *The Happy Years*, p. 75
19. Quoted in letter Cecil to Garbo, 9 March 1947
20. Diary, March 1946
21. *Ibid.*
22. *Ibid.*
23. *Ibid.*
24. Cecil Beaton, *The Happy Years*, p. 92
25. *Ibid.*, p. 93
26. *Ibid.*
27. Mrs Beaton to Cecil, 26 April 1946
28. Maud Nelson to Cecil, 26 April 1946
29. *Ibid.*
30. *Ibid.*
31. Diary, January 1947
32. Cecil to Enid Bagnold, June 1947
33. Clarissa Churchill to Cecil, October 1946
34. Mrs Beaton to Cecil, 7 September 1946
35. Diary, September 1946
36. *Ibid.*, 7 October 1946
37. *Ibid.*, December 1946

38. *Ibid.*
39. *Ibid.*, January 1947
40. Cecil to Lady Diana Cooper, 17 September 1946
41. John Gielgud to Cecil, 25 August 1946
42. Oliver Smith to author, 30 June 1983
43. Waldemar Hansen to author, 12 December 1982
44. Lincoln Kirstein to Cecil, 18 December 1946
45. *New York Post*, 24 October 1946
46. Cecil to Clarissa Churchill, 1 September 1946
47. *Ibid.*
48. *Ibid.*
49. Clarissa Churchill to Cecil, 9 September 1946
50. James Pope-Hennessy to Cecil, 12 August 1946
51. Diary, September 1946
52. *Ibid.*, January 1947
53. Sir Anton Dolin to author, 4 July 1982
54. Clarissa Churchill to Cecil (undated)
55. Cecil to Clarissa Churchill, 14 November 1946
56. Diary, January 1947
57. *Ibid.*
58. Maud Nelson to Cecil, 16 November 1946
59. Diary, January 1947
60. *Ibid.*
61. *Ibid.*
62. *Ibid.*
63. *Ibid.*, May 1947
64. *Ibid.*
65. *Ibid.*
66. *Ibid.*
67. *Ibid.*
68. *Ibid.*
69. *Ibid.*, 11 May 1955
70. *Ibid.*, May 1947
71. Christine Norden and Michael Thornton, unpublished autobiography of Christine Norden
72. Stephen Tennent to Cecil, 5 June 1947
73. *Ibid.*, 24 May 1947
74. Margaret Case to Cecil, undated but 1947
75. Alice B. Toklas to Cecil, 25 August 1946
76. Diary, October 1947
77. *Ibid.*
78. Cecil to Lady Diana Cooper, 12 February 1948
79. *Ibid.*
80. Diary, 24 February 1947
81. *Ibid.*
82. Edward Hutton, *Highways and Byways in Wiltshire* (Macmillan, London, 1924), p. 206
83. *Ibid.*
84. Cecil to Garbo, 24 June 1947

23: MY GREATEST TRIUMPH

1. *Associated Press*, 15 October 1932
2. Diary, 6 February 1948
3. *Ibid.*, 15 April 1963
4. *New York Times*, 6 October 1964
5. Valentina Schlee to author, 17 August 1983
6. *Ibid.*
7. Cecil Beaton, *Photobiography*, p. 178
8. Cecil to Garbo, 9 March 1947
9. *Ibid.*
10. *Ibid.*, 15 May 1947
11. *Ibid.*
12. *Ibid.*, 2 August 1947
13. *Ibid.*, 7 August 1947
14. *Ibid.*, 12 August 1947
15. *Press Association*, 25 August 1947
16. Cecil to Garbo, 27 August 1947
17. *Ibid.*, 15 September 1947
18. *Ibid.*, 29 September 1947
19. *Ibid.*
20. *Ibid.*
21. *Ibid.*
22. *Ibid.*, 1 September 1947
23. Diary, June 1946
24. Geoffrey Toone to Cecil, Wednesday night (1946)
25. Diary, March 1944
26. *Ibid.*, 23 October 1947
27. *Ibid.*, 23 (28) October 1947
28. *Ibid.*
29. *Ibid.*
30. *Ibid.*
31. *Ibid.*, 3 November 1947
32. *Ibid.*
33. *Ibid.*
34. *Ibid.*, 4 November 1947
35. *Ibid.*, November 1947
36. *Ibid.*
37. *Ibid.*
38. *Ibid.*
39. *Ibid.*
40. *Ibid.*
41. *Ibid.*, (c. 19) November 1947
42. *Ibid.*, 24 November 1947
43. *Ibid.*, 26 November 1947
44. *Ibid.*, 1 December 1947
45. *Ibid.*
46. *Ibid.*
47. *Ibid.*
48. *Ibid.*, 3 December 1947
49. *Ibid.*, 4 December 1947
50. *Ibid.*
51. *Ibid.*, 8 December 1947
52. *Ibid.*
53. *Ibid.*, 11 December 1947

54. *Ibid.*
55. *Ibid.*, 12 December 1947
56. *Ibid.*
57. Cecil to Simon Fleet, 12 December 1947.
58. *Ibid.*
59. Diary, 20 December 1947
60. *Ibid.*
61. *Ibid.*
62. Cecil to Clarissa Churchill, 23 December 1947
63. Diary, 23 December 1947
64. *Ibid.*, 24 December 1947
65. *Ibid.*
66. *Ibid.*, 25 December 1947
67. *Ibid.*
68. *Ibid.*
69. *Ibid.*, 26 December 1947
70. *Ibid.*, 29 December 1947
71. *Ibid.*
72. *Ibid.*, 31 December 1947
73. *Ibid.*
74. *Ibid.*
75. *Ibid.*, 3 January 1948
76. *Ibid.*
77. *Ibid.*
78. *Ibid.*
79. *Ibid.*
80. *Ibid.*
81. *Ibid.*, 4 January 1948
82. *Ibid.*
83. Cecil to Lady Juliet Duff, January 1948
84. Lady Diana Cooper to Cecil, 30 January 1948
85. Cecil to Lady Diana Cooper, 12 January 1948
86. Diary, 4 January 1948
87. *Ibid.*, 6 January 1948
88. *Ibid.*, 13 January 1948
89. *Ibid.*
90. *Ibid.*, 6 March 1948
91. *Ibid.*, 14 January 1948
92. Cecil to Clarissa Churchill, 21 January 1948
93. Diary, January 1948
94. *Ibid.*
95. *Ibid.*
96. *Ibid.*
97. *Ibid.*
98. *Ibid.*
99. *Ibid.*, 13 February 1948
100. Cecil to Clarissa Churchill, 18 February 1948
101. Diary, (*c.* 15) February 1948
102. *Ibid.*
103. *Ibid.*
104. *Ibid.*, 21 February 1948
105. *Ibid.*, 23 February 1948
106. *Ibid.*
107. Cecil to Garbo, 28 February 1948

108. Garbo to Cecil, 28 February 1948
109. Diary, 3 March 1948
110. *Ibid.*
111. *Ibid.*, 4 March 1948
112. *Ibid.*
113. *Ibid.*
114. *Ibid.*
115. *Ibid.*
116. *Ibid.*
117. *Ibid.*
118. *Ibid.*
119. *Ibid.*
120. *Ibid.*, 8 March 1948
121. *Ibid.*, 9 March 1948
122. *Ibid.*, 12 March 1948
123. *Ibid.*
124. *Ibid.*, 13 March 1948
125. *Ibid.*, 14 March 1948
126. *Ibid.*
127. *Ibid.*
128. *Ibid.*
129. *Ibid.*, 15 March 1948
130. *Ibid.*
131. *Ibid.*

24: THE RETURN OF THE PRODIGAL

1. Ruth Gordon, *Myself Among Others* (Atheneum, New York, 1971), p. 77
2. Cecil to Garbo, 21 March 1948
3. *Ibid.*, 4 April 1948
4. *Ibid.*, April/May 1948
5. *Ibid.*, 17 May 1948
6. David Herbert, *Second Son*, p. 158
7. Cecil to Garbo, 17 May 1948
8. *Ibid.*
9. *Ibid.*, June 1948
10. Samuel M. Steward, *Dear Sammy*, p. 166: Alice B. Toklas to Samuel M. Steward, 22 July 1948
11. Cecil to Garbo, 21 February 1949
12. *Ibid.*, 16 July 1950
13. Oliver Smith to author, 30 June 1983
14. *Ibid.*
15. Cecil to Garbo, May/June 1948
16. *Ibid.*, 24 August 1948
17. Clarissa Churchill to Cecil, 29 September 1948
18. James Laver, *The Year's Work in the Theatre* (Longman's, London, 1949), p. 36
19. Hugh Beaumont to Cecil, 20 January 1949
20. Martin Battersby to Cecil, 9 December 1947
21. *Ibid.*, 20 January 1948
22. Maud Nelson to Cecil, 20 January 1948
23. Cecil to Garbo, 5 December 1948
24. James Laver, *The Year's Work in the Theatre*, p. 19

25. Dennis Arundell, quoted in letter from Simon Fleet to Cecil, 25 January 1949
26. Oliviers to Cecil, 21 January 1949
27. Cecil to Garbo, 6 March 1949
28. Cecil Beaton, *The Strenuous Years*, pp. 8–21
29. Cecil to Garbo, 16 May 1949
30. *Ibid.*, 24 April 1950
31. *Ibid.*, 11 November 1950
32. Cecil to Eileen Hose, 11 March 1956
33. Cecil to Garbo, 29 March 1949
34. Diary, 18 June 1949
35. Cecil to Garbo, 27 June 1949
36. *Ibid.*, 10 July 1949
37. Diary, autumn 1949
38. *Ibid.*, 27 June 1949
39. Cecil to Garbo, 27 June 1949
40. Diary, 5 August 1949
41. Cecil to Garbo, 22 August 1949
42. Diary, August 1949
43. *Ibid.*
44. *Ibid.*
45. Oliver Smith to author, 30 June 1983
46. John Malcolm Brinnin (ed.), *Sextet* (Dell Publications, New York, 1982), p. 45
47. Diary, 28 September 1949
48. *Ibid.*
49. *Ibid.*, winter 1948/49
50. *Ibid.*, November 1948
51. *Ibid.*, December 1948
52. *Ibid.*, early 1949
53. Cecil to Garbo, 27 June 1949
54. Diary, 2 October 1949
55. *Ibid.*
56. *Ibid.*
57. *Ibid.*
58. *Ibid.*, autumn 1949
59. *Ibid.*
60. Cecil to Lady Juliet Duff, 11 January 1950
61. Diary, 9 January 1950
62. *Daily Mirror*, 4 December 1950
63. John Bernard Myers, *Tracking the Marvellous* (Randon House, New York, 1983), p. 85
64. Cecil to Garbo, July 1950
65. *Ibid.*
66. John Piper to Cecil, 21 July 1950
67. Lincoln Kirstein to Cecil, 8 April 1967
68. *New York Times*, 8 April 1967
69. Roy Strong, *Homage to Beaton* (Parkin Gallery Catalogue, 1976)
70. *Daily Mail*, 30 November 1950
71. Cecil's telegram, 15 August 1950
72. Cecil to Garbo, 19 September 1950
73. *Ibid.*, 8 August 1950
74. Truman Capote to Cecil, 27 June 1950
75. Secretary's note, 14 September 1950
76. Irving Penn to author, 7 December 1982
77. Irving Penn to Cecil, 30 October 1950
78. *Ibid.*
79. Irving Penn to author, 7 December 1982
80. *Ibid.*
81. *Ibid.*
82. Cecil to Garbo, 20 June 1949
83. *Ibid.*, undated but late 1950
84. Diary, December 1950
85. *Ibid.*
86. Lincoln Kirstein to Cecil, 7 December 1951
87. Diary, early 1951
88. Ann Fleming to Lady Diana Cooper, 10 February 1951
89. *Observer*, 16 September 1951
90. Sir Osbert Sitwell to Cecil, 4 July 1951
91. Lady Diana Cooper to Cecil, 29 July 1951

25: MAN PROPOSES, GOD DISPOSES

1. Diary, 11 November 1928
2. Garson Kanin to Cecil, 6 May 1948
3. Cecil to Garbo, 20 September 1948
4. Enid Bagnold to Cecil, 5 October 1948
5. Cecil to Mrs Beaton, 8 November 1948
6. Diary, 11 February 1949
7. *Ibid.*
8. Cecil to Garbo, 2 May 1949
9. Diary, 24 June 1951
10. *Ibid.*
11. *Ibid.*, 14 July 1951
12. *Ibid.*, 28 July 1951
13. *Ibid.*
14. Cecil to Arnold Weissberger, 14 September 1951
15. Diary, 28 July 1951
16. *Ibid.*
17. Duff Cooper to Cecil, 17 July 1951
18. *Evening Standard*, 18 July 1951
19. Cecil to Garbo, 22 July 1951
20. Cecil to Hal Burton, 28 December 1951
21. Hal Burton to author, 19 July 1982
22. Diary, early 1952
23. *Ibid.*, June 1952
24. Peter Quennell (ed.), *A Lonely Business*, p. 78: James Pope-Hennessy to Nolwen de Janzé, 2 December 1951
25. Daphne Fielding to author, 24 November 1981
26. Augustus John to Cecil, 1951/2
27. Private information
28. Lady Hartwell to author, 14 May 1980
29. *Ibid.*
30. Cecil to Lady Diana Cooper, November 1951
31. Lady Diana Cooper to author
32. Susan Mary Alsop, *To Marietta from*

Paris 1945–1960 (Doubleday, New York, 1975), p. 190
33. Diary, early 1952
34. Cecil to Lady Diana Cooper, 4 April 1952
35. Diary, June 1952
36. Cecil to Hal Burton, 28 December 1951
37. Diary, January 1952
38. *Ibid.*
39. Cecil to Clarissa Churchill, 29 March 1952
40. Cecil Beaton, *Cecil Beaton's Scrapbook*, p. 55
41. Diary, April 1952
42. Cecil to Hal Burton, 10 February 1952
43. *Ibid.*, 3 March 1952
44. Cecil to Maud Nelson, 14 March 1941
45. John Malcolm Brinnin, *Sextet*, p. 59
46. Virgil Thomson, *Virgil Thomson* (Knopf, New York, 1966), pp. 396–7
47. Cecil to Maud Nelson, 17 March 1952
48. Sheridan Morley, *A Talent to Amuse* (Heinemann, London, 1969), p. 272
49. Diary, 1952
50. *Ibid.*
51. *Ibid.*
52. Graham Payn and Sheridan Morley (eds), *The Noël Coward Diaries* (Weidenfeld & Nicolson, London, 1982), p. 193: Noël's diary, 7 May 1952
53. Cecil to Enid Bagnold, 7 January 1956
54. Stephen Tennant to Eileen Hose, July 1981
55. Peter Daubeny, *Stage by Stage* (John Murray, London, 1952), pp. 96–7
56. Cecil to Garbo, 4 September 1952
57. Diary, June 1952
58. Cecil to Clarissa Churchill, summer 1952
59. James Pope-Hennessy to Cecil, June 1952
60. Diary, 4 November 1952
61. *Ibid.*
62. *Ibid.*
63. *Ibid.*, 14 November 1952
64. Truman Capote to Cecil, 8 November 1952
65. Diary, 19 December 1952
66. *Ibid.*
67. *Ibid.*, December 1952

26: TUNNELLING TOWARDS SOMETHING NEW

1. John Bernard Myers, *Tracking the Marvellous*, p. 63
2. *Ibid.*, p. 63
3. Diary, 1952/3
4. *Ibid.*

5. Truman Capote to Cecil, 21 January 1953
6. *Ibid.*
7. Diary, 22 January 1954
8. *Ibid.*
9. Princess Grace to author, 23 September 1981
10. *Ibid.*
11. Grace Kelly to Cecil, 23 July 1954
12. Diary, 14 January 1954
13. *Ibid.*, 1954
14. *Ibid.*, January 1954
15. Enid Bagnold to Cecil, 11 January 1956
16. Diary, June 1953
17. Cecil to Hal Burton, undated but 1953
18. *Ibid.*, 1953
19. Diary, 31 May 1953
20. *Ibid.*
21. *Ibid.*
22. *Ibid.*, 2 June 1953
23. *Ibid.*
24. *Ibid.*
25. *Ibid.*
26. *Ibid.*
27. *Ibid.*, June 1953
28. *Ibid.*
29. *Ibid.*, summer 1953
30. *Ibid.*, August 1953
31. *Ibid.*
32. Sir Max Beerbohm to Cecil, October 1953
33. Cecil Beaton, *Face of the World*, p. 175
34. Diary, November 1953
35. *Ibid.*, October 1953
36. *Ibid.*, 9 October 1953
37. *Ibid.*, November 1953
38. *Ibid.*
39. *Ibid.*, 14 January 1954
40. Cecil to Lady Diana Cooper, 9 March 1954
41. *Ibid.*, 3 May 1950
42. Diary, October 1953
43. Waldemar Hansen to author, 12 December 1982
44. Mark Amory (ed.), *Letters to Evelyn Waugh* (Weidenfeld & Nicolson, London, 1983), p. 424
45. *Ibid.*
46. Cecil's lecture
47. Diary, June 1954
48. Waldemar Hansen to author, 12 December 1982
49. *Ibid.*
50. *Ibid.*
51. *Ibid.*
52. *Sunday Times*, 4 July 1954
53. *New York Herald Tribune*, c. January 1954

54. Waldemar Hansen to author, 12 December 1982

55. Mark Amory, *The Letters of Evelyn Waugh*, p.425: Evelyn Waugh to Nancy Mitford, 18 June 1954

56. *Ibid.*, pp.426–7: Evelyn Waugh to Lady Mary Lygon, 28 June 1954

57. Diary, April 1954

58. *Ibid.*, summer 1954

59. Sir John Gielgud to Cecil, 6 November 1954

60. Sir Anthony Quayle to Cecil, 10 December 1954

61. Cathleen Nesbitt, *A Little Love and Good Company* (Faber & Faber, London, 1975), p.213

62. *Ibid.*

63. Diary, January 1954

64. *Ibid.*

65. *Ibid.*, December 1954

66. *Ibid.*, 5 December 1954

67. *Ibid.*

68. *Ibid.*

69. *Ibid.*

70. Cecil to Garbo, 11 January 1955 (draft letter)

71. Edna Woolman Chase to Cecil, 1 May 1953

72. Audrey Withers to Cecil, 10 February 1955

73. Harry Yoxall, *A Fashion of Life* (Taplinger, New York, 1967), p.105

74. Edna Woolman Chase to Cecil, 3 May 1955

75. Edna Woolman Chase's inscription in Cecil's copy, 1954

76. Cecil to Lady Diana Cooper, 22 February 1955

77. Queen Helen of Romania to Cecil, 10 May 1955

78. Mary McCarthy to Cecil, 20 July 1955

79. Bernard Berenson to Cecil, 3 July 1955

80. Audrey Withers to Eileen Hose, 16 August 1955

81. Dame Rose Macaulay to Cecil, undated

82. Nancy Mitford to Cecil, undated

83. Diary, July 1955

84. Cecil to Eileen Hose, November 1955

85. Diary, November 1955

86. *Ibid.*

87. *Ibid.*

88. *Ibid.*

27: MAGPIES AGAINST A WHITE DROP

1. Cecil Beaton, *Cecil Beaton's Fair Lady*, p. 5

2. *Ibid.*

3. Enid Bagnold to Cecil, 8 May 1943

4. *Ibid.*, 11 January 1956

5. *Ibid.*, 13 January 1952

6. Cecil to Lady Juliet Duff, 7 February 1952

7. Cecil to Lady Diana Cooper, 21 November 1954

8. Enid Bagnold to Cecil, 26 December 1953

9. Enid Bagnold, *Autobiography*, p.228

10. Irene Selznick, quoted in a letter from Cecil to Eileen Hose, 1955

11. Enid Bagnold to Cecil, 20 October 1955

12. *Ibid.*, 25 November 1954

13. Cecil to Lady Diana Cooper, undated but 1954

14. Enid Bagnold to Cecil, 20 May 1955

15. *Ibid.*

16. *Ibid.*, Friday night

17. Diary, 14 August 1955

18. Irene Selznick to author, 26 May 1981

19. Cecil to Lady Diana Cooper, (*c.*) 15 September 1955

20. Cecil to Lady Diana Cooper, 22 September 1955

21. Enid Bagnold to Cecil, 23 May 1956

22. Cecil to Eileen Hose, October 1955

23. Truman Capote to Cecil, 12 November 1955

24. Cecil to Eileen Hose, 11 January 1956

25. *Ibid.*

26. *Ibid.*

27. Irene Selznick to author, 26 May 1981

28. *Ibid.*, 14 November 1981

29. Cecil to Enid Bagnold, quoted in letter from Cecil to Eileen Hose, 1956

30. Cecil to Enid Bagnold, January/February 1956

31. Enid Bagnold to Cecil, 10 February 1956

32. *Ibid.*

33. *Ibid.*

34. Sir John Gielgud to author, 13 November 1982

35. *Spectator*, April 1956

36. Enid Bagnold to Cecil, 23 May 1956

37. *Ibid.*

38. Cecil to Enid Bagnold, 30 May 1956

39. *Ibid.*

40. *Ibid.*

41. Enid Bagnold to Cecil, 31 May 1956

42. Irene Mayer Selznick, *A Private View* (Knopf, New York, 1983), p. 353

43. Enid Bagnold, *Autobiography*, p. 232

44. Cecil Beaton, *Cecil Beaton's Fair Lady*, pp. 5–6

45. Alan Jay Lerner, *The Street Where I Live* (W.W. Norton, New York, 1978), p. 30

46. *Ibid.*

47. *Ibid.*, p. 48

48. Herman Levin to author, 5 December 1982

49. Oliver Smith to author, 30 June 1983

50. Julie Andrews to author, 14 December 1983
51. File article by Cecil on *My Fair Lady*
52. Cathleen Nesbitt, *A Little Love and Good Company*, p. 253
-53. Cecil to Eileen Hose, 10 October 1955
54. Cecil to Mrs Beaton, 14 October 1955
55. Julie Andrews to author, 14 December 1983
56. *Ibid.*
57. *Ibid.*
58. Cecil to Eileen Hose, 15 January 1956
59. Diary, April 1956
60. *Ibid.*
61. *Ibid.*
62. Jim Benton to Eileen Hose, 30 January 1956
63. Julie Andrews to author, 14 December 1983
64. Jim Benton to Eileen Hose, 30 January 1956
65. Alan Jay Lerner, *The Street Where I Live*, p. 105
66. Julie Andrews to author, 14 December 1983
67. *Ibid.*
68. Cecil to Eileen Hose, February 1956
69. Diary, April 1956
70. Cecil Beaton, *The Face of the World*, p. 184
71. Cecil to Eileen Hose, Wednesday morning (February 1956)
72. *Ibid.*
73. Waldemar Hansen to author, 12 December 1982
74. *Ibid.*
75. *Ibid.*
76. Cecil to Eileen Hose, 16 March 1956
77. *Ibid.*
78. Fan letter to Cecil, quoted by Jim Benton to Eileen Hose, 30 March 1956
79. Truman Capote to Cecil, 21 June 1956
80. Cecil to Eileen Hose, Friday evening (March 1956)
81. *Ibid.*, 1956
82. Diary, April 1956
83. *Ibid.*, summer 1958

28: THE CREST OF A WAVE

1. Diary, 6 May 1956
2. *Ibid.*
3. *Ibid.*
4. *Ibid.*
5. *Ibid.*
6. *Ibid.*
7. Cecil to Garbo, 4/5 May 1956
8. *Ibid.*
9. Diary, 6 May 1956

10. Truman Capote to author, 28 June 1983
11. Michael Wishart, *High Diver*, p. 60
12. Diary, 6 May 1956
13. *Ibid.*
14. Cecil to Waldemar Hansen, 4/5 May 1956
15. Truman Capote to Cecil, 15 May 1956
16. Diary, September 1956
17. *Ibid.*
18. Cecil to Eileen Hose, September 1956
19. Diary, October 1956
20. *Ibid.*
21. *Ibid.*
22. *Ibid.*
23. *Ibid.*, 17 October 1956
24. *Ibid.*, 18 October 1956
25. *Ibid.*
26. *Ibid.*, October 1956
27. *Ibid.*, 29 November 1956
28. Cecil to Louise Dahl-Wolfe, 25 November 1958
29. Cecil to Eileen Hose, 17 December 1956
30. Cecil to Mrs Beaton, 16 December 1956
31. Jim Benton to Eileen Hose, 8 February 1957
32. Cecil to Sir Anthony Eden, 23 December 1956
33. Cecil to Mrs Beaton, December 1956
34. Mrs Beaton to Cecil, undated
35. Ann Fleming to Cecil, 15 January 1957
36. Clarissa Eden to Cecil, 16 March 1957
37. Diary, December 1956
38. *Ibid.*, 1 January 1957
39. Truman Capote to author, 28 June 1983
40. Diary, 6 January 1957
41. *Ibid.*
42. *Ibid.*, January 1951
43. *Ibid.*
44. *Ibid.*
45. Group Captain Peter Townsend, *Earth My Friend* (Hodder & Stoughton, London, 1959), p. 87
46. Diary, January 1957
47. *Ibid.*
48. Cecil to Eileen Hose, 22 January 1957
49. Patrick O'Higgins, *Madame* (Viking, London, 1971), p. 239
50. *Ibid.*, p. 240
51. *Ibid.*, p. 241
52. Diary, January 1957
53. *Ibid.*
54. *Ibid.*
55. Cecil to Eileen Hose, October 1957
56. *Ibid.*
57. Truman Capote to Cecil, undated but 1957
58. Diary, 2 June 1963
59. *Ibid.*, 29 January 1957

60. *Ibid.*
61. *Ibid.*, 8 February 1957
62. *Ibid.*, February 1957
63. *Ibid.*
64. Cecil to Eileen Hose, 12 February 1957
65. Diary, February 1957
66. Cecil to Eileen Hose, February 1957
67. Stephen Tennant to author, 1981
68. Patrick O'Higgins, *Madame*, p. 242
69. *Ibid.*
70. T.S. Eliot to Cecil, 31 July 1956
71. *Daily Express*, 7 November 1957
72. Cecil to Eileen Hose, *c.* 17 February 1957
73. Alan Jay Lerner, *The Street Where I Live*, p. 158
74. Diary, summer 1957
75. *Sunday Times*, 8 February 1959
76. Diary, 11 August 1957
77. *Ibid.*
78. *Ibid.*
79. *Ibid.*
80. *Ibid.*
81. *Ibid.*
82. *Ibid.*
83. *Ibid.*
84. *Ibid.*
85. Cecil to Mrs Beaton, 18 September 1957
86. Cecil to Eileen Hose, 28 September 1957
87. Diary, 14 October 1957
88. *Ibid.*
89. Beverley Nichols to Cecil, May 1959
90. Mike Todd to Cecil, 6 March 1958
91. Diana Vreeland to Cecil, 31 May 1958
92. *New Republic*, 9 June 1958
93. *Sunday Times*, 8 February 1959
94. Cecil to Arnold Weissberger, 9 April 1959

29: NOSES TO THE GRIND

1. *News Chronicle*, 29 May 1958
2. Diary, 29 May 1958
3. *Ibid.*
4. Clarissa Eden to Cecil, 4 June 1958
5. Diary, 29 May 1958
6. *Ibid.*
7. *Ibid.*
8. *Ibid.*
9. *Ibid.*
10. *Ibid.*
11. *Ibid.*
12. Cecil to Eileen Hose, 16 January 1959
13. Diary, summer 1958
14. *Ibid.*
15. *Ibid.*
16. *Ibid.*
17. *Ibid.*
18. Waldemar Hansen to Cecil, 10 October 1958
19. Diary, summer 1958
20. *Ibid.*
21. Truman Capote to Cecil, 4 September 1958
22. Diary September 1958
23. Cecil to Eileen Hose, 17 January 1959
24. Eileen Hose to Cecil, 21 January 1959
25. Diary, January 1959
26. *Time*, 16 March 1959
27. *New York Times*, 5 February 1959
28. Jack Minster to Cecil, 28 April 1959
29. Diary, 23 August 1959
30. Sir Donald Wolfit to Cecil, 9 May 1959
31. Diary, 23 August 1959
32. *Ibid.*
33. Mona Washbourne to author, 27 September 1984
34. Ann Firbank to author, 3 June 1982
35. Diary, 23 August 1959
36. *Ibid.*, 21 September 1959
37. *Ibid.*
38. *Ibid.*
39. Jack Minster to Cecil, 22 September 1959
40. Cecil to Sir Donald Wolfit, September 1959
41. Cecil's statement, September 1959
42. Jim Benton to Eileen Hose, 5 October 1959
43. Cecil to Eileen Hose, October 1959
44. Diary, 23 September 1959
45. *Ibid.*
46. Cecil to Eileen Hose, October 1959
47. Diana Vreeland to Cecil, 26 October 1959
48. *New York Daily News*, 8 December 1959
49. Cecil to Eileen Hose, October 1959
50. Eileen Hose to Jim Benton, 4 January 1960
51. *Ibid.*
52. Diary, 8 September 1970
53. *Ibid.*, 10 September 1960
54. *Ibid.*, September 1960
55. *New York Herald Tribune*, 18 October 1960
56. *Time*, 31 October 1960
57. Diary, 26 October 1960
58. *Ibid.*
59. *Ibid.*, September 1960
60. *Ibid.*
61. *Ibid.*, January 1961
62. *Ibid.*
63. *Ibid.*
64. *Ibid.*
65. *Ibid.*
66. *Ibid.*, spring 1961
67. Contemporary magazine cutting

68. Graham Payn and Sheridan Morley (eds), *The Noël Coward Diaries*, p. 465: 28 February 1961
69. *New Yorker*, 4 March 1961
70. Rudolf Bing to Cecil, 23 October 1962
71. Cecil to Rudolf Bing, 21 March 1961
72. Cecil to Ed Wittstein, 26 July 1961
73. Herman E. Krawitz to Cecil, 22 August 1961
74. Cecil to Eileen Hose, September 1966
75. *New York Times*, 24 September 1966
76. Waldemar Hansen to author, 12 December 1982

30: JUNE

1. Alastair Forbes to author
2. Mrs Beaton to Cecil, undated but May 1958
3. Diary, May 1958
4. *Ibid.*, autumn 1958
5. *Ibid.*
6. *Ibid.*
7. *Ibid.*
8. *Ibid.*
9. *Ibid.*
10. *Ibid.*
11. Lady Hutchinson to author, 30 January 1985
12. Diary, autumn 1958
13. *Ibid.*, spring 1959
14. *Ibid.*, 31 January 1959
15. *Ibid.*
16. *Ibid.*, spring 1959
17. *Ibid.*, summer 1959
18. Cecil to Lady Diana Cooper, June 1959
19. Diary, 12 January 1960
20. *Ibid.*
21. *Ibid.*
22. *Ibid.*
23. *Ibid.*
24. *Ibid.*
25. *Ibid.*
26. *Ibid.*
27. *Ibid.*
28. *Ibid.*
29. *Ibid.*
30. *Ibid.*
31. *Ibid.*
32. *Ibid.*
33. *Ibid.*
34. *Ibid.*
35. Lady Hutchinson to author, 30 January 1985
36. June Osborn to Cecil, 25 December 1959
37. *Ibid.*
38. Truman Capote to Cecil, 21 January 1960
39. Diary, January 1960

40. *Ibid.*, 13 August 1960
41. Truman Capote to Cecil, summer 1960
42. Diary, 13 August 1960
43. *Ibid.*
44. June Osborn to Cecil, September 1960
45. Truman Capote to Cecil, 26 September 1960
46. *Ibid.*, September 1960
47. Diary, autumn 1960
48. June Osborn to Cecil, (undated) 1966

31: ROYAL PHOTOGRAPHER

1. Cecil to Eileen Hose, October 1957
2. *Ibid.*
3. Diary, February 1958
4. *Ibid.*
5. *Ibid.*
6. *Ibid.*
7. *Ibid.*, spring 1960
8. *Ibid.*
9. *Ibid.*
10. John Sutro to author, 18 September 1981
11. Diary, spring 1960
12. *Ibid.*
13. *Ibid.*
14. *Ibid.*
15. *Ibid.*, May 1960
16. *Ibid.*
17. *Ibid.*
18. *Ibid.*, March 1960
19. *Ibid.*
20. *Ibid.*
21. *Ibid.*
22. *Ibid.*
23. *Ibid.*
24. *Ibid.*
25. *Ibid.*
26. *Ibid.*
27. *Ibid.*
28. *Ibid.*
29. Unidentified press cutting, April 1960
30. Diary, 28 May 1960
31. *Ibid.*
32. *Ibid.*, December 1960
33. *Ibid.*, 1 April 1961
34. *Ibid.*, spring 1961
35. *Ibid.*
36. *Ibid.*
37. *Ibid.*, 11 June 1961
38. *Ibid.*
39. *Ibid.*
40. Peter Russell, *Butler Royal* (Hutchinson, London, 1982), p. 180
41. Diary, spring 1961
42. *Ibid.*
43. *Ibid.*
44. *Ibid.*

45. Sir Roy Strong to author, 23 January 1985
46. Queen Mother to Cecil, 27 October 1963

32: THE SEVERING OF LINKS

1. Truman Capote to Cecil (*c.* 1959)
2. Diary, August 1961
3. *Sunday Express*, 23 July 1961
4. *Spectator*, 21 July 1961
5. *Observer*, 16 July 1961
6. Diary, August 1961
7. *Ibid.*
8. *Sunday Times*, 16 July 1961
9. Diary, August 1961
10. *Ibid.*, June 1961
11. Mary, Countess of Pembroke, to author, 29 May 1980
12. Sacheverell Sitwell to Cecil, 24 July 1961
13. Diary, August 1961
14. *Ibid.*, August/September 1961
15. *Ibid.*, October 1961
16. *Ibid.*
17. *Ibid.*, January 1962
18. *Ibid.*, 16 November 1957
19. *Ibid.*, February 1960
20. *Ibid.*
21. *Ibid.*
22. *Ibid.*
23. *Ibid.*
24. *Ibid.*, Christmas 1961
25. *Ibid.*
26. *Ibid.*, Januuary 1962
27. *Ibid.*, 23 January 1962
28. Hugh Burnett (ed.), *Face to Face*, p. 4
29. *Ibid.*, p. 39
30. *Ibid.*, p. 40
31. *New Statesman*, 23 February 1962
32. *Queen*, 6 March 1962
33. Alastair Forbes to Cecil, 18 February 1962
34. Raymond Mortimer to Cecil, 23 February 1962
35. Laura Canfield to Cecil, 18 February 1962
36. Diary, 23 February 1962
37. *Ibid.*
38. *Ibid.*
39. *Ibid.*
40. Ava, Lady Waverley, to Cecil, 1 March 1962
41. Lily Elsie to Cecil, 8 June 1962
42. Diary, December 1962
43. Mrs Stacey Ramsey to author, 10 July 1980
44. Diary, May 1962
45. *Ibid.*
46. *Ibid.*

47. *Ibid.*
48. *Ibid.*
49. *Ibid.*
50. *Ibid.*
51. Cléo de Mérode to Cecil, 8 May 1962
52. Diary, May 1962
53. *Ibid.*, 24 May 1962
54. *Ibid.*, June 1962
55. *Ibid.*
56. *Ibid.*, spring 1961
57. *Ibid.*, August 1961
58. *Ibid.*, summer 1961
59. *Ibid.*, June 1962
60. *Ibid.*
61. *Ibid.*
62. *Ibid.*
63. *Ibid.*
64. *Ibid.*, January 1960
65. *Ibid.*
66. *Ibid.*
67. *Ibid.*
68. *Ibid.*
69. *Ibid.*
70. *Ibid.*
71. *Ibid.*
72. Anne Cockerell to author, 31 October 1984
73. Diary, summer 1962
74. *Ibid.*
75. *Ibid.*
76. *Ibid.*, 10 August 1962
77. *Ibid.*
78. *Ibid.*
79. *Ibid.*, 11 August 1962
80. *Ibid.*
81. *Ibid.*, 25 August 1962
82. *Ibid.*
83. Clara Svendsen to Cecil, 26 September 1962
84. Dame Edith Sitwell to Cecil, 16 August 1962
85. *Ibid.*, 17 November 1962
86. *Ibid.*, 19 November 1962
87. Diary, 29 November 1962
88. *Ibid.*
89. *Ibid.*
90. *Ibid.*
91. *Ibid.*
92. *Ibid.*
93. *Ibid.*
94. *Ibid.*
95. *Ibid.*
96. *Ibid.*
97. Queen Mother to Cecil, 30 November 1962
98. Dame Edith Sitwell to Cecil, 30 November 1962
99. Diary, December 1962
100. *Ibid.*
101. *Ibid.*

102. *Ibid.*
103. *Ibid.*, January 1963
104. Cecil to Eileen Hose, 15 March 1963
105. *Dance & Dancers*, April 1963
106. Diary, 20 January 1963
107. *Ibid.*
108. *Ibid.*

33: CECIL GOES TO HOLLYWOOD

1. Diary, 4 October 1963
2. Cecil to Eileen Hose, 19 February 1963
3. Diary, 2 March 1963
4. *Ibid.*, 17 May 1963
5. *Ibid.*, 15 May 1963
6. *Ibid.*, 2 April 1963
7. Lesley Blanch to author, 18 September 1981
8. Cecil to Diana Vreeland, 6 March 1963
9. Diary, 22 May 1963
10. *Ibid.*, 2 May 1963
11. *Ibid.*, 11 July 1963
12. *Ibid.*, 22 August 1963
13. *Ibid.*, 16 March 1963
14. *Ibid.*, 10 June 1963
15. *Ibid.*
16. *Ibid.*, 5 August 1963
17. Stanley Holloway, *Wiv a Little Bit o' Luck* (Leslie Frewen, London, 1967), p. 314
18. Diary, 18 June 1963
19. *Ibid.*, 20 March 1963
20. *Ibid.*, 10 October 1963
21. *Ibid.*, 29 March 1963
22. *Ibid.*, 25 April 1963
23. *Ibid.*, 22 May 1963
24. *Ibid.*, 12 March 1963
25. *Ibid.*, 26 March 1963
26. *Ibid.*, 26 April 1963
27. *Ibid.*, 13 March 1963
28. Lesley Blanch to author, 18 September 1981
29. *Ibid.*
30. Diary, 11 May 1963
31. *Ibid.*, 13 May 1963
32. *Ibid.*, 18 May 1963
33. *Ibid.*, July 1953 (*sic*)
34. *Ibid.*, 13 June 1963
35. Audrey Hepburn to author, 22 March 1983
36. Diary, 29 May 1963
37. *Ibid.*
38. *Ibid.*, 5 June 1963
39. *Ibid.*
40. Audrey Hepburn to Cecil, June 1963
41. Cecil to Eileen Hose, 9 June 1963
42. Diary, 17 June 1963
43. *Ibid.*, 28 April 1963
44. *Ibid.*, 17 June 1963
45. Cecil to Eileen Hose, 19 June 1963
46. Diary, 19 June 1963

47. *Ibid.*
48. *Ibid.*, 21 June 1963
49. *Ibid.*, 3 July 1963
50. *Ibid.*, 17 July 1963
51. *Ibid.*
52. *Ibid.*
53. Cecil to Eileen Hose, 20 July 1963
54. Diary, 30 July 1963
55. *Ibid.*
56. *Ibid.*, 4 August 1963
57. *Ibid.*, 23 August 1963
58. *Ibid.*, 28 May 1963
59. Cecil to Eileen Hose, June 1963
60. Cecil to Hal Burton, 4 August 1963
61. Diary, 9 August 1963
62. *Ibid.*
63. *Ibid.*
64. *New York Times*, 14 August 1963
65. Cecil to Eileen Hose, 14 August 1963
66. Diary, 4 September 1963
67. Cecil to Eileen Hose, 27 August 1963
68. Diary, 20 October 1963
69. Gerda Robison to Cecil, 10 October 1963
70. Edie Goetz to Cecil, 11 October 1963
71. Diary, 14 October 1963
72. *Ibid.*
73. *Ibid.*
74. *Ibid.*, 20 October 1963
75. *Ibid.*
76. *Ibid.*, 17 October 1963
77. *Ibid.*, 13 November 1963
78. Cecil to George Cukor, quoted in Cecil's diary, 19 November 1963
79. *Ibid.*
80. *Ibid.*, 22 November 1963
81. *Ibid.*
82. *Ibid.*, 28 November 1963
83. William S. Paley, *As It Happened* (Doubleday, New York, 1979), p. 336
84. *Los Angeles Times*, 10 January 1964
85. Diary, 25 October 1964
86. Gavin Lambert, *On Cukor* (G.P. Putnams, New York, 1972), p. 241
87. *Film '73* shown on BBC1, 29 May 1973
88. Alastair Forbes statement, 26 June 1973
89. Irene Selznick to author, 26 May 1981
90. Cecil to Eileen Hose, Friday October 1964
91. Alan Jay Lerner, *The Street Where I Live*, p. 187
92. Diary, June 1964
93. *Guardian*, 23 October 1964
94. *Ibid.*
95. Audrey Hepburn to Cecil, 20 April 1965

34: KIN

1. Diary, 23 March 1963
2. *Ibid.*, 24 March 1963
3. Kin to author, 26 February 1985
4. Diary, 24 February 1965 (*sic*)
5. *Ibid.*, 24 March 1963
6. *Ibid.*, 2 April 1963
7. *Ibid.*, 4 May 1963
8. *Ibid.*, 19 April 1963
9. *Ibid.*, 22 April 1963
10. Christopher Isherwood to Cecil, 25 April 1963
11. Kin to author, 22 June 1983
12. Diary, 4 May 1963
13. *Ibid.*, 12 May 1963
14. *Ibid.*, 25 May 1963
15. Cecil to Eileen Hose, 18 June 1963
16. Diary, 4 May 1963
17. *Ibid.*, 15 June 1963
18. *Ibid.*, 17 June 1963
19. *Ibid.*, 5 July 1963
20. *Ibid.*, 7 July 1963
21. Kin to author, 26 February 1985
22. Diary, 22 September 1963
23. *Ibid.*, 4 August 1963
24. *Ibid.*, 6 September 1963
25. *Ibid.*, 7 September 1963
26. *Ibid.*, 21 September 1963
27. Stephen Tennant to author, 8 May 1981
28. Diary, 22 September 1963
29. Kin to author, 26 February 1985
30. *Ibid.*
31. *Ibid.*
32. *Ibid.*, 22 June 1983
33. Diary, 20 October 1963
34. *Ibid.*
35. *Ibid.*, 10 November 1963
36. *Ibid.*, 16 November 1963
37. *Ibid.*, 20 November 1963
38. *Ibid.*, 9 December 1963
39. *Ibid.*, 11 December 1963
40. *Ibid.*, 16 December 1963
41. *Ibid.*, 26 January 1964
42. *Ibid.*, 17 February 1964
43. Eileen Hose to Cecil, 13 November 1963
44. Diary, *c.* January 1964
45. Prince Felix Youssoupoff to Cecil, 22 February 1964
46. Diary, April 1965
47. Diana Vreeland to Cecil, 7 January 1964
48. *Ibid.*, 6 January 1964
49. Diary, 9 January 1964
50. *Evening Standard*, 14 January 1964
51. Diary, 1 March 1964
52. *Ibid.*
53. *Ibid.*, 30 March 1964
54. *Ibid.*, 19 April 1963
55. Cecil to Eileen Hose, 2 May 1964
56. Diary, May 1964
57. *Ibid.*
58. *Ibid.*
59. *Ibid.*, 22 May 1964
60. *Ibid.*
61. *Ibid.*
62. *Ibid.*, May/June 1964
63. *Ibid.*, June 1964
64. *Ibid.*
65. *Ibid.*
66. Kin to author, 22 June 1983
67. *Ibid.*, 26 February 1985
68. Ina Claire to author, 21 June 1983
69. Lady Diana Cooper to author, undated
70. Eileen Hose to author, undated
71. Kin to author, 26 February 1985
72. Diary, June 1964
73. *Ibid.*
74. *Ibid.*
75. *Ibid.*
76. *Ibid.*, July 1964
77. *Ibid.*, 14 July 1964
78. *Ibid.*, July 1964
79. *Ibid.*, 24 July 1964
80. *Ibid.*, 11 August 1964
81. *Ibid.*, 19 August 1964
82. *Ibid.*, 20 August 1964
83. *Ibid.*, 2 September 1964
84. *Ibid.*
85. *Ibid.*, 3 September 1964
86. *Ibid.*, 16 October 1964
87. *Ibid.*, October 1964
88. *Evening Standard*, 6 October 1964
89. Dame Rebecca West to Cecil, 29 October 1962
90. *Chicago Sun-Times Family Magazine*, 24 September 1963
91. Diary, 6 December 1964
92. *Burlington Magazine*, January 1965
93. L.E. Hallett to Cecil, 19 January 1965
94. Audrey Hepburn to Cecil, January 1965
95. Diary, 23 January 1965
96. Jack Warner to Cecil, 20 January 1965
97. Hal Burton to Cecil, 27 February 1965
98. Diary, 23 January 1965
99. *Ibid.*
100. *Ibid.*, 20 January 1965
101. *Ibid.*
102. *Ibid.*
103. *Ibid.*
104. *Ibid.*, January 1965
105. *Ibid.*
106. *Ibid.*, 30 January 1965
107. *Ibid.*, February 1965
108. *Ibid.*, 14 February 1965
109. *Ibid.*, April 1965

110. Graham Sutherland to Cecil, 24 June 1965
111. Diary, summer 1965
112. *Ibid.*, June 1965
113. *Ibid.*
114. Kin to author, 25 February 1985
115. Diary, June 1965
116. Kin to author, 25 February 1985
117. *Ibid.*
118. *Ibid.*
119. *Ibid.*
120. Truman Capote to author, 28 June 1983
121. Diary, July 1965

35: RIP-VAN-WITH-IT

1. Diana Vreeland to Cecil, 28 December 1964
2. *Ibid.*
3. *Ibid.*, 4 May 1965
4. *Ibid.*
5. Diary, 5 October 1963
6. *Ibid.*
7. Cecil Day-Lewis to Cecil, 21 August 1965
8. Sir Harold Acton to Cecil, 3 April 1966
9. Noël Coward to Cecil, December 1965
10. *Sunday Times*, 18 July 1965
11. *Financial Times*, 29 July 1965
12. *New York Herald Tribune*, 29 October 1965
13. Diary, summer 1965
14. *New York Times*, 6 October 1964
15. Diana Vreeland to author, 15 November 1981
16. *Ibid.*
17. Valentina Schlee to author, 12 August 1983
18. Diary, August 1965
19. *Ibid.*
20. *Ibid.*, July 1965
21. *Ibid.*, August 1965
22. *Ibid.*
23. *Ibid.*
24. Cecil to Eileen Hose, 12 August 1965
25. Diary, summer 1965
26. *Ibid.*
27. Stephen Tennant to Cecil, undated but 1960
28. *Ibid.*, 29 June 1960
29. *Ibid.*, 8 July 1960
30. Diary, summer 1961
31. *Ibid.*
32. *Ibid.*
33. *Ibid.*
34. John Perry to Cecil, 25 January 1979
35. Diary, October 1965
36. Princess Grace to author, 23 September 1981

37. Diary, 25 September 1965
38. Truman Capote to Cecil, 19 April 1965
39. Diary, November 1965
40. Marianne Moore to Cecil, 18 December 1965
41. *New York Herald Tribune*, 29 October 1965
42. Diary, November 1965
43. *Ibid.*, 27 November 1965
44. *Ibid.*, 27 January 1966
45. *Ibid.*, January 1966
46. *Burlington Magazine*, March 1966
47. Diary, 29 January 1966
48. *Ibid.*
49. Desmond Corcoran to author, 24 September 1983
50. Cecil to Eileen Hose, 4 February 1966
51. Laura, Duchess of Marlborough, to author, November 1979
52. Diary, February 1966
53. *Ibid.*
54. *Ibid.*, 4 April 1966
55. *Ibid.*, January 1966
56. Cecil to Michael Wishart, 12 April 1966
57. Mary Quant to Cecil, April 1966
58. *Professional News*, 1968
59. *Sunday Times*, 13 March 1966
60. Coral Browne to author, 24 February 1985
61. Diary, 2 July 1966
62. Coral Browne to author, 24 February 1985
63. Hugh Beaumont to Cecil, 24 August 1966
64. Cecil to Stewart Perowne, undated (1966)
65. Diary, February 1967
66. *Ibid.*, July 1966
67. Aubrey Ensor to Cecil, October 1966
68. Diary, 30 October 1966
69. *Ibid.*
70. *Beaton by Bailey* film, 1971
71. Diary, 27 September 1966
72. *Ibid.*, 29 September 1966
73. *Ibid.*
74. *Ibid.*, 20 November 1966
75. *Ibid.*
76. Cecil to Eileen Hose, 28 November 1966
77. Diary, 24 December 1966
78. Cecil to Clarissa Avon, 26 December 1966

36: GROWING OLD, STAYING YOUNG

1. *Observer*, 16 January 1966
2. *Ibid.*
3. Cecil to Eileen Hose, 20 February 1967
4. *Ibid.*, 11 March 1967

6. Philip Norman, *The Stones* (Elm Tree Books, London, 1984), p. 183
7. Diary, March 1967
8. *Ibid.*
9. *Ibid.*
10. *Ibid.*
11. *Ibid.*
12. *Ibid.*
13. *Ibid.*
14. *Beaton by Bailey* film, 1971
15. Diary, March 1967
16. Diana Vreeland to Cecil, 8 May 1967
17. Diary, summer 1967
18. *Weekend Telegraph*, 17 November 1967
19. Diary, June 1967
20. *Ibid.*
21. Christopher Gibbs to author, 26 January 1985
22. *Ibid.*
23. Diary, 3 June 1967
24. *Ibid.*
25. Cecil to Eileen Hose, June 1967
26. Diary, June 1967
27. Cecil to Eileen Hose, June 1967
28. Diary, June 1967
29. *Ibid.*
30. *Ibid.*
31. *Ibid.*, July 1967
32. *Ibid.*.
33. *Ibid.*, 25 August 1967
34. *Ibid.*, July 1967
35. *Ibid.*
36. *Ibid.*, September 1967
37. *Ibid.*, 13 September 1967
38. Cecil to Diana Vreeland, 17 September 1967
39. Diary, September 1967
40. Cecil to Diana Vreeland, 12 September 1967
41. *The Times*, 6 October 1967
42. Diary, 21 September 1967
43. Christopher Isherwood to Cecil, 17 October 1967
44. Diary, 18 November 1967
45. *Ibid.*, November 1967
46. *Ibid.*
47. *Ibid.*, April 1968
48. *Ibid.*
49. *Ibid.*
50. Princess Marina to Cecil, 7 April 1968
51. Diana Vreeland to Cecil, March 1968
52. Anita Loos to Cecil, 27 March 1968
53. Diary, April 1968
54. *Ibid.*
55. *Ibid.*, November 1967
56. *Ibid.*, 5 January 1968
57. *Ibid.*
58. Eileen Hose to Cecil, January 1968
59. Cecil to Eileen Hose, 9 January 1968

60. Diary, January 1968
61. *Ibid.*
62. *Ibid.*
63. Truman Capote to Cecil, undated
64. Diary, 27 January 1968
65. Cecil to Eileen Hose, 31 January 1968
66. Diary, 8 February 1968
67. *Ibid.*
68. *Ibid.*, February 1968
69. *Ibid.*, 19 February 1968
70. *Ibid.*, April 1968
71. *Ibid.*, 10 April 1968
72. Sir Roy Strong, unpublished diary, 10 April 1968
73. Eileen Hose to Cecil, April 1968
74. Diary, April 1968
75. *Ibid.*
76. *Ibid.*
77. *Ibid.*, June 1968
78. *Ibid.*, 14 May 1968
79. *Ibid.*, 6 June 1968
80. Madame Yevonde to Cecil, 7 August 1968
81. Diary, August 1968
82. *Ibid.*
83. *Ibid.*
84. *Ibid.*
85. *Ibid.*
86. *Ibid.*
87. Princess Alexandra to Cecil, September 1968

37: FORTY YEARS ON

1. Diary, 12 August 1967
2. Lord Kenyon to Cecil, 26 September 1968
3. Diary, August 1968
4. Roy Strong to Cecil, July 1968
5. *Ibid.*
6. Earl Russell to Cecil, 16 August 1968
7. Sir Martin Charteris to Cecil, 11 September 1968
8. *Ibid.*
9. Diary, 18 October 1968
10. *Ibid.*
11. *Ibid.*
12. *Ibid.*
13. *Ibid.*, September 1968
14. *Ibid.*
15. *Ibid.*
16. *Ibid.*
17. *Ibid.*
18. *Ibid.*, 27 October 1968
19. *Ibid.*, 4 November 1968
20. *Ibid.*, 30 October 1968
21. Lady Bonham Carter to author, 17 December 1979
22. Diary, 30 October 1968
23. *Ibid.*, 4 November 1968

24. *Ibid.*
25. *Ibid.*
26. *Tatler*, January 1969
27. *British Journal of Photography*, 22 November 1968
28. *Apollo*, November 1968
29. *Burlington Magazine*, December 1968
30. Prince of Wales to Cecil, 13 December 1968
31. Cecil to Clarissa Avon, January 1969
32. Philip Norman, *The Stones*, p. 248
33. *Daily Express*, 5 November 1968
34. Diary, December 1968
35. *Ibid.*
36. Frank Teti and Karen Moline, *Streisand Through the Lens* (Delilah Books, New York, 1982), p. 58
37. Diary, 20 December 1968
38. Cecil to Arnold Weissberger, 11 April 1968
39. Howard W. Koch to Arnold Weissberger, 5 February 1969
40. Diary, January 1969
41. *Ibid.*, 13 January 1969
42. *Ibid.*, February 1969
43. *Ibid.*, 3 February 1969
44. *Ibid.*, July 1969
45. Earl of Pembroke to Cecil, 30 March 1969
46. Enid Bagnold to Cecil, 21 February 1968
47. Diary, 26 December 1969
48. Cecil to Enid Bagnold, 27 December 1969
49. Enid Bagnold to Cecil, 31 December 1969
50. Enid Bagnold to author, 1980
51. Sir John Gielgud to Cecil, 4 November 1968
52. *Ibid.*
53. Cecil to Sir John Gielgud, 4 November 1968
54. Diary, 1 April 1969
55. *Ibid.*, 3 April 1969
56. *Ibid.*, 4 April 1969
57. *Ibid.*
58. *Ibid.*, 6 April 1969
59. *Ibid.*, 7 April 1969
60. Diana Vreeland to Cecil, 31 March 1969
61. Cecil to Diana Vreeland, 6 October 1969
62. Howard W. Koch to Cecil, 17 April 1969
63. Cecil to Arnold Weissberger, 9 April 1969
64. Diary, spring/summer 1971
65. *Daily News*, 1 May 1969
66. Diary, April 1969
67. *New York Times*, 11 May 1969

68. Diary, April 1969
69. *Ibid.*
70. *Ibid.*, May 1969
71. *Ibid.*
72. Cecil to Diana Vreeland, 19 October 1970
73. Diary, July 1969
74. *Ibid.*, 14 August 1969
75. *Ibid.*
76. *Ibid.*, 22 August 1969
77. *Ibid.*, August 1969

38: LITTLE BLACK DRESSES

1. Cecil to Arnold Weissberger, 6 May 1966
2. *Ibid.*, 21 August 1969
3. Diary, 3 February 1967
4. Cecil to Diana Vreeland, 30 June 1969
5. *Ibid.*
6. Cecil Beaton, *Cecil Beaton's Scrapbook*, pp. 31–3
7. Ben Rosenberg to Arnold Weissberger, 22 July 1969
8. Theatrical Costume Designer's Contract, August 1969
9. Diary, 21 September 1969
10. *Ibid.*
11. *Ibid.*, 25 September 1969
12. *Ibid.*, 2 November 1969
13. *Ibid.*, 14 November 1969
14. *Ibid.*, 22 November 1969
15. Anita Loos to Cecil, 28 November 1969
16. *New York Times*, 25 November 1969
17. Diary, 25 November 1969
18. *New York Times*, 19 December 1969
19. Joan Crawford to Cecil, 23 April 1970
20. Milton Goldman to Cecil, 12 January 1971
21. Diary, December 1969
22. *Ibid.*, 25 September 1969
23. *Ibid.*, 20 November 1969
24. *Ibid.*, January 1970
25. *Ibid.*, 27 January 1970
26. *Ibid.*
27. *Ibid.*, 29 January 1970
28. Cecil to Clarissa Avon, 15 February 1970
29. Diary, 19 February 1970
30. *Ibid.*, April/May 1970
31. *Daily Telegraph*, 19 January 1980
32. Enid Bagnold to Cecil, 30 April 1970
33. Diary, April/May 1970
34. Cecil to Diana Vreeland, 10 June 1970
35. Diary, June 1970
36. *Ibid.*, 19 June 1970
37. Sir Roy Strong, unpublished diary, 11 July 1970
38. Cecil to Diana Vreeland, 19 August 1970

39. Cecil to Eileen Hose, August 1970
40. Diary, August 1970
41. Cathleen Nesbitt to author, 20 November 1981
42. Diary, September 1970
43. *Ibid.*, October 1970
44. *Ibid.*
45. *Ibid.*
46. Sir Roy Strong, unpublished diary, 22 October 1970
47. Diary, 30 December 1970
48. *Ibid.*
49. *Ibid.*, 19 January 1971
50. Cecil to Clarissa Avon, 6 February 1971
51. Diary, 23 February 1971
52. Chiquita Astor to author, July 1984
53. Diary, 29 March 1971
54. *Ibid.*, July 1971
55. Cecil to Diana Vreeland, 27 October 1971
56. David Bailey to author, 15 November 1981
57. Cecil to Alexander Liberman, 15 April 1971
58. Diary, 30 May 1971
59. Cecil to Alexander Liberman, 12 May 1970
60. Diary, June 1971
61. Margaret Case to Cecil, 22 August 1971
62. *Ibid.*
63. Diary, 14 September 1971
64. *Ibid.*, April 1970
65. *Guardian*, 27 October 1971
66. Cecil Beaton, *Fashion* (Victoria & Albert Museum catalogue, HMSO, London, 1971), p. 5
67. Diary, June 1971
68. Cecil to Bob Lavine, 18 August 1971
69. Diary, April 1970
70. Sir Roy Strong to author, 23 January 1985
71. Cecil to Diana Vreeland, October 1971
72. *Ibid.*

39: GARBO REVIEWED

1. Peter Quennell to author, 15 April 1985
2. Peter Quennell to Cecil, 11 August 1967
3. *Ibid.*
4. Diary, December 1967
5. *Ibid.*, September 1968
6. *Ibid.*, 21 November 1971
7. *Ibid.*
8. *Ibid.*
9. R.A. Armstrong to Cecil, 17 November 1971
10. Diary, 11 December 1971
11. *Ibid.*
12. Cable Grace Mirabella/Alexander Liberman to Cecil, 14 December 1971
13. Diary, December 1971
14. Cecil to Horst, 19 October 1971
15. *Ibid.*, 30 December 1971
16. Enid Bagnold to Cecil, 1 January 1972
17. Lady Clark to Cecil, 1 January 1972
18. Nancy Mitford to Cecil, 3 January 1972
19. Lady Hartwell to Cecil, 1 January 1972
20. Sir John Gielgud to Cecil, 1 January 1972
21. Hal Burton to Cecil, 1 January 1972
22. Dame Sybil Thorndike to Cecil, 2 January 1972
23. Cathleen Nesbitt to Cecil, 9 January 1972
24. Sir John Betjeman to Cecil, 2 January 1972
25. Clarissa Avon to Cecil, 4 January 1972
26. Sir Martin Charteris to Cecil, 23 January 1972
27. James Lees-Milne to Cecil, 5 January 1972
28. Mrs Graham Sutherland to Cecil, 5 January 1972
29. Cecil to Diana Vreeland, 8 January 1972
30. Diary, 30 February 1972
31. *Ibid.*
32. *Ibid.*
33. Cecil to Eileen Hose, 13 March 1972
34. Diary, March 1972
35. Cecil to Eileen Hose, 19 March 1972
36. Diary, March 1972
37. *Ibid.*, 19 May 1972
38. *Ibid.*, 21 May 1972
39. *Ibid.*
40. Irene Worth to author, 6 May 1983
41. Isabel Jeans to Cecil, 3 April 1972
42. Geoffrey Toone to author, 5 March 1985
43. Diary, 5 June 1972
44. *Ibid.*
45. *Ibid.*
46. Lesley Blanch to Cecil, 31 March 1972
47. *Spectator*, 27 May 1972
48. *Sunday Times*, 28 May 1972
49. *Listener*, 1 June 1972
50. *Harper's & Queen*, April 1972
51. *Chicago Tribune*, 8 April 1983
52. Diary, 13 April 1973
53. Cyril Connolly to Cecil, 2 June 1972
54. Cecil's note on the above letter
55. Diary, April 1973
56. *Ibid.*, August 1972
57. *Ibid.*
58. Cole Lesley, *Remembered Laughter* (Alfred A. Knopf, 1971), p. 461
59. Diary, September 1972

60. Enid Bagnold to Cecil, 25 March 1973
61. Diary, June 1973
62. Cecil to Patrick O'Higgins, 20 June 1973
63. Charles James to Cecil, 29 July 1973
64. *Ibid.*, 30 July 1973
65. *Ibid.*
66. Diary, August 1973
67. Cecil Beaton and Gail Buckland, *The Magic Image*, p. 8
68. *New York Times*, 7 December 1975
69. Diary, August 1973
70. *Observer*, 23 September 1973
71. Diary, September 1973
72. Cecil to Eileen Hose, undated (1973)
73. Eileen Hose to Cecil, undated (1973)
74. Eileen Hose to author, 22 April 1985
75. *Ibid.*
76. Diary, 13 December 1973
77. *Ibid.*, November 1973
78. *Ibid.*
79. *Ibid.*
80. *Ibid.*, 28 January 1974
81. *Ibid.*, February 1974
82. *Ibid.*
83. *Ibid.*, March 1974
84. *Ibid.*
85. *Ibid.*
86. W.D. Pack of Linklaters & Paines to Cecil, 16 April 1974
87. Diary, April 1974
88. *Ibid.*
89. Stephen Tennant to Cecil, 28 May 1974
90. Diary, June 1974
91. Lord Weidenfeld to author, 3 June 1982
92. Clarissa Avon to author, 12 July 1982
93. Lady Anne Tree to author, 22 October 1982
94. Mrs John Sutro to author, 18 September 1981
95. Stephen Tennant to author, 1980
96. Hal Burton to Cecil, 13 May 1974
97. Diary, 17 May 1974
98. *Ibid.*, June 1974

40: THE STROKE

1. Cecil to author, 15 January 1980
2. Constance de Hamel to author, 13 February 1981
3. Eileen Hose to Jane Lady Abdy, 26 July 1974
4. Lady Clark to Cecil, 1975
5. Dr Christopher Brown to author, 14 July 1984
6. Kin to Cecil, 28 August 1974
7. Jane Abdy, unpublished diary, 14 September 1974
8. Eileen Hose to Patrick O'Higgins, late 1975
9. Irving Penn to Cecil, 29 June 1975
10. *Ibid.*, May 1976
11. *Western Daily News*, 7 March 1978
12. Cecil to Alastair Forbes, 1975
13. Cecil to Paul Tanqueray, 1975
14. Cecil to Patrick O'Higgins, 1975
15. Eileen Hose to author, 7 April 1980
16. Sir Roy Strong, unpublished diary, 23 October 1975
17. Allan Davis to author, 23 November 1984
18. Bob Lavine to Diana Vreeland, 5 June 1977
19. *Ibid.*
20. Diana Vreeland to author, 21 June 1980
21. Eileen Hose to Patrick O'Higgins, 3 March 1978
22. Oliver Messel to Cecil, 28 May 1978
23. Diary, July 1978
24. *Ibid.*
25. *Ibid.*, September 1978
26. *Ibid.*
27. Cecil to Patrick O'Higgins, September 1978
28. Stephen Tennant to Cecil, 1974
29. *Ibid.*, undated but 1978
30. Diary, summer 1978
31. Alfred Shaughnessy, *Both Ends of the Candle* (Peter Owen, London, 1978), p. 51
32. Press file note (*Time* magazine), 14 September 1978
33. Diary, late 1978
34. Cecil to Horst, undated but 1979
35. Cecil to Diana Vreeland, January 1979
36. Meredith Etherington-Smith to author, 10 March 1985
37. Cecil to Patrick O'Higgins, February 1979
38. *Ibid.*, November 1979
39. Alastair Forbes to author, 1982
40. Diary, August 1979
41. W. Grant to author, March 1980
42. Cecil to Jane Abdy, 25 September 1979
43. Cecil to Patrick O'Higgins, October 1979
44. *Ibid.*, November 1979
45. *Ibid.*
46. *Ibid.*
47. *Ibid.*
48. Diary, December 1979
49. Cecil to Michael Wishart, 16 January 1980
50. Dr Christopher Brown to author, 14 July 1984
51. Diary, 9 January 1980

41: NO FEAR OF OBLIVION

1. Diary, August 1935
2. Mrs Christopher Brown to author, 10 June 1980
3. Cecil Beaton, *The Best of Beaton*, p. 11
4. *Ibid.*
5. *Ibid.*
6. *The British Journal of Photography*, 15 February 1980
7. Irving Penn to author, 7 December 1982
8. *Art at Auction 1977–78* (Sotheby Parke Bernet, London, 1978)
9. Cecil Beaton, *Cecil Beaton's Scrapbook*, p. 88
10. *The British Journal of Photography*, 15 February 1980
11. Susan Sontag, *On Photography* (Farrar, Strauss & Giroux, New York, 1977), p. 53
12. Essay by Jed Perl, 'Beaton: Takes: Notes'
13. Eileen Hose to author, 1981
14. James Lees-Milne, *Ancestral Voices*, p. 217
15. *Ibid.*
16. *Beaton by Bailey* film, 1971

Index

Abbey, Eleanor, 237
Abbott, George (b. 1886), 422 & n
Adbullah I of Jordan, HM King (1881–1951), 264
Abdy, Lady Diana (1907–67), 166 n, 168, 178, 226, 374
Abdy, Jane Lady, 574, 576, 581
Abdy, Bt, Sir Robert (1896–1976), 166 n, 168, 178, 226, 374, 430
Aberconway, Christabel Lady (1890–1970), 142, 153
Acton, Sir Harold (b. 1904), 45, 70, 236, 497
Adkins, Derek, 248–9, 257–8, 260, 560
Adrian (1903–59), 153
Adrian, Max (1903–73), 307
Agate, James (1877–1947), 176, 207
Agha, Dr Mehemed, 127, 135, 180, 186, 205, 208, 242, 248, 267, 271
Agnelli, Giovanni (b. 1921), 413, 417
Akins, Zoe (1886–1958), 334
Alba, Duke of (1878–1953), 197
Albania, HM King Zog of (1895–1961), 248
Albaret, Celeste (1891–1984), 503
Albery, Sir Bronson (1881–1971), 423
Alcock, Gordon, 48
Aldrich, Richard (b. 1902), 352
Alexander, Lady (d. 1946), 38, 54, 55, 82–3, 101, 230, 300, 568
Alexander, Sir George (1858–1918), 54 & n, 300
Alexandra, HM Queen (1844–1925), 52, 62, 84, 183, 340, 553
Alexandra, Hon. Mrs Angus Ogilvy, HRH Princess (b. 1936), 368, 462, 485, 561; letter to C, 523
Alington, (Lord) Napier (1896–1940), 240
Alison, Barley, 443
Allen, Adrianne (Mrs Raymond Massey) (b. 1907), 153
Allen, Gene, 462, 471, 475
Allen, Trevor, 230
Alphand, Hervé (b. 1907), 465
Alsop, Susan Mary, 355
Aly Khan, HH Princess Joan (b. 1908), 265–6, 581
Ames, Preston, 412

Amies, Hardy (b. 1909), 414
André, Gwili (1908–59), 158
Andrew, HRH The Prince (b. 1960), 432, 437–9, 485
Andrew, Mr R., 201, 208
Andrews, Eamonn (b. 1922), 457 & n
Andrews, Julie (b. 1935), XXV–XXVI, 387, 390–91, 392 & n, 413, 542
Andrews, Robert ('Bobbie') (1895–1981), 31, 39
Anglesey, (Marjorie) Marchioness of (1883–1946), 198
Anne, Mrs Mark Phillips, HRH The Princess (b. 1950), 346–7, 380, 435, 436, 438, 551, 569
Annenberg, Walter (b. 1908), 546
Annigoni, Pietro (b. 1910), 435–6, 525
Anouilh, Jean (b. 1907), 345
Aoyama, Yoshio, 423
Aramayo, Eduardo, 4
Arden, Elizabeth (d. 1966), 135
Argyll, HRH The Princess Louise, Duchess of (1848–1939), 164
Argyll, Margaret Duchess of (b. 1912), 107, 163, 178
Arias, Dr Roberto (b. 1918), 413
Armitage, B.W.F., 25–6, 28–9, 33, 35, 45–6
Armstrong-Jones, see Rosse and Snowdon
Arno, Peter (1906–68), 423
Arundell, Dennis (b. 1898), XXIII, 28, 30–33, 41, 339
Ascough, Bessie, 10
Ashcombe, 137–9, 148–50, 154–5, 159, 160, 165, 168–70, 174–5, 178–9, 184–5, 199, 201, 203, 220–21, 224, 227, 236, 248, 297–9, 389, 400, 487, 544, 585
Ashcroft, Dame Peggy (b. 1907), 7, 434
Ashley, (Sylvia) Lady (1904–77), 308
Ashley, Cooper, see Head
Ashley-Cooper, Lady Lettice (b. 1911), 458–9
Ashraf, HIH Princess (b. 1919), 263
Ashton, see Garland
Ashton, Sir Frederick (b. 1904), 84, 186–7, 230, 271, 304, 307, 345, 349, 356, 445, 453–4, 458, 461, 480, 527, 559, 581

Askowith, Bathsheba, 195 & n, 205, 206
Asquith, *see* Oxford
Asquith, Lady Cynthia (1887–1960), 85
Astaire, Adèle (1896–1981), 60 n, 118, 123–5, 133–4, 151, 153 & n, 154 n, 400
Astaire, Fred (b. 1899), 118, 123, 124, 153, 241
Astley, Major the Hon. Simon (1919–46), 275
Astor, Hon. Mrs Ana Inez (Chiquita), 451, 549, 566
Astor, Helen, *see* Hull, Mrs Lytle
Astor, Hon. Sir John (Jakie) (b. 1918), 451, 504, 520
Astor, Mary (b. 1906), 130
Astor, Hon. Michael (1916–80), 428
Astor, Vincent (1891–1959), 190
Astor, Mrs Vincent (Brooke), 534
Astor, (Nancy) Viscountess (1879–1964), 239
Athlone, HRH Princess Alice, Countess of (1883–1981), 514
Atkinson, Brooks (1895–1984), 282, 417
Aubrey, John (1626–97), 311, 513
Auchincloss, Louis (b. 1917), 534
Auchinleck, FM Sir Claud (1884–1981), 276
Auchinleck, Lady, 276 & n
Auden, W.H. (1907–73), 337
Auric, Georges (1899–1983), 217, 301
Auric, Mme Georges (Nora), 217, 301
Avon, the Countess of (Clarissa) (b. 1920), 247–8, 262, 277, 279, 280–81, 286, 291, 293 n, 304–7, 322, 331, 337–8, 354, 356; marries, 358; 399, 401, 413, 445, 454, 486–7, 505, 508–9, 544, 561, 565, 571, 575–6, 584–5
Avon, 1st Earl of (1897–1977), 239–40, 358, 399, 401, 445, 501, 571
Aylmer, Sir Felix (1889–1979), 415
Azaid, Sidi, 367

Baba, *see* Beaton
Bacall, Lauren (b. 1924), 542
Bachardy, Don, 465, 468, 501
Bache, Jules, 132
Bacon, Francis (b. 1909), 337, 397, 428, 446–7, 504, 536
Baddeley, Angela (1900–70), 352 & n
Bagnold, Enid (Lady Jones) (1889–1981), XXVIII, 238–9, 239 n, 247, 252, 269–70, 286–7, 301, 304, 344 & n, 351, 365, 401, 544, 560, 567, 588; and *The Chalk Garden*, 381–6; reconciled with C, 531–2
Bailey, David (b. 1938), XXVII, 436, 510, 527, 546, 547, 549–52, 556, 582, 588

Bailey, James (d. 1981), 237
Baillieu, Joanna (b. 1946), 520
Balanchine, George (1904–83), 182, 349, 520
Balenciaga, Cristobal (1895–1972), 373, 448, 453, 497
Balfour of Inchrye, (Harold) 1st Lord (b. 1897), 272–3
Balfour, Mrs Neil (Serena) (b. 1944), 451
Balfour, Patrick, *see* Kinross
Balston, Thomas (1883–1967), 141
Balthus, 513
Bankhead, Tallulah (1902–68), 51, 55, 70, 82, 96, 100, 102–3, 140, 205–6
Banks-Smith, Nancy, 551
Bannerman, Margaret (b. 1896), 39
Barber, Samuel (1910–81), 407
Bardot, Brigitte (b. 1934), 507
Baring, Hon. Maurice (1874–1945), 32, 239
Barlassina, Monsignor, 264
Barnes, Clive (b. 1927), 345, 541–2
Baron (1907–56), 367–8
Baronova, Irina (b. 1919), 190
Barrymore, Ethel (1882–1942), 158 n, 167 n
Barrymore, Lionel (1878–1954), 158 n
Bath, Marquess of (b. 1905), 354, 515
Batsford, B.T. Ltd, 203, 228, 250, 267, 307
Batsford, Sir Brian (Brian Cook) (b. 1910), 51, 203–4, 216
Battersby, Martin (1913–82), 338, 352
Baxter, Jane (b. 1909), 369
Baylis, Lilian (1874–1937), 187
Bea, *see* Gausbeck, Beatrice
Beardsley, Aubrey (1874–98), 345
Beaton, Barbara (Baba) (Mrs Alec Hambro) (C's sister) (1912–73), 7, 8, 12, 24, 52–3, 56–7, 62, 65, 69, 71–2, 79, 82, 87–9, 96, 101, 103, 107, 112, 116, 119–20, 140–41, 149, 154–5, 163, 165, 168, 173, 179, 191, 211, 269, 354, 359, 414, 447, 449, 463, 490, 552; birth, 7; engaged, 163; married, 178 & n; death, 566–7
Beaton, Brice (C's great-uncle), 5, 7
Beaton, Cecil (C's uncle) (1872–1949), 6, 7, 112
Beaton, Sir Cecil (1904–80): diaries of, XVII–XVIII; friends discuss, XXIII–XXIX

PART ONE – THE FORMATIVE YEARS
ancestors, 1–8; birth, 6; early influences, 9–11; home life, 12–13, 36–9, 46; education, 13–26; Heath Mount, 13–16; Evelyn Waugh tortures, 13–14; learns facts of life, 15; Harrow, 20–26; sex at Harrow,

22–4; Cambridge, 27–48; meets tutor, 28–9; and Kyrle Leng, 29–30; Bullivant's advice, 33–4, 39–40; acts in *The Rose and the Ring*, 30–32, *Volpone*, 32–4, *The Gyp's Princess*, 42, college revue, 44, *Henry IV*, 44–6, *Footlights*, 46–8; on homosexuality, 41; sex at Cambridge, 40–41, 42–3; painting, 20–21, 41; photography, 24–5, 41; early interest in publicity, 36–9; 43–4

PART TWO – THE STRUGGLING YEARS
home life, 51–71, 77–90, 91–2; photography, 52–3, 55–7, 69, 78–82; influence on sisters, 52–3, 65–6, 71, 87; publicity, 53, 65–6, 88; office life, 62–3, 68–71; worries over career, 55–8, 68, 71, 78; family rows, 55, 59; interest in stars, 51–2; wild parties, 59–60, 63–4, 89–90; at *Façade*, 69–70; play writing, 77–8; social climbing, 53–5, 65–6, 67, 80, 82–4; meets Stephen Tennant, 85–7; breakthrough, 85; at Wilsford, 90–92

PART THREE – THE WILD YEARS
at Cap Ferrat, 95–6; costume parties, 96–7; his voice, 97–8; Wilton ducking, 98–9; photos Sitwells, 99; and *Vogue*, 99–100, 111–12, 119, 135–6; Cooling Galleries exhibition (1927), 100–101; Virginia Woolf row, 101, 141–2; as arbiter of beauty, 102, 117–18; lives expensively, 102–3; Ellesmere Ball row, 103–6; insulted at theatre, 106–7; and Lady Mary Beaton row, 107–8; on photography, 102; in NY (1928–9), 109–19; meets Steichen, 111; impresses Crowninshield, 112; Kommer's advice, 112; social life, 110–14; Beverley Nichols rebukes, 114; BN alarms, 115–16; and Charles James, 116; exhibitions, 117, 118; Ziegfeld row, 117–18; home life, 119–21; and Lady Diana Cooper, 121; in NY (1929), 122; affair with Marjorie Oelrichs, 123, 132–3; and with Adèle Astaire, 123–4, 133–4; in Hollywood (1929–30), 124–8, 130–31; photos stars, 126–8, 130–31; at Hearst ranch, 128–9; quest for Garbo, 130–31; in Palm Beach, 131; in NY, 131–6; and black boxer, 134–5; finds Ashcombe, 137–9; and Frankau row, 139–40; English social life, 140–41; and *Book of Beauty*, 141–3

PART FOUR – THE LOVELORN YEARS
in Vienna, 148–9; in Venice, 149; meets Peter Watson, 148; glance of sympathy, 149; obsessed by PW, 148–57, 160–63, 165–75, 177–8; works on book and Ashcombe, 149–50; travels to NY with PW, 151; further American travels, 151–3; and pillow fights, 152; in Hollywood (1931), 152–3; photos stars, 153; in NY, 153–4; *Vogue* pay rise, 154; reunited with PW, 154; sleepless nights, 155; summer travels with PW, (1931) 155–6, (1932) 160–61; takes cut in *Vogue* salary, 157; tableaux vivants in Chicago, 157–8; photos stars in Hollywood, 158; meets Garbo (1932), 158–60; high jinks at Ashcombe, 160; affair with Doris Castlerosse, 161–3, 165; and Nancy's wedding, 163–4; 1st royal sitters, 164; in USA (1933), 164–5; baroque fashion photography of, 164–5; family life, 165; sightseeing with Odom, 166–7; writes farewell letter to PW, 167; with PW at Ashcombe, 168; and death of Reggie, 168–70; as character in *Girls of Radcliff Hall*, 171–2; forces PW to give car to, 172; visits Morocco with Hoyningen-Huene, 173; adopts Rolleiflex, 173; in NY (1934), 173–4; depression and extravagance of, 175; in Spain with Tchelitchew, 175–6; early Cochran work, 176–7; visits mind healer, 177; PW situation relaxes, 178; and Baba's wedding, 178; and broken life of father, 178–9; Paris life of (1935), 180–81, 184; in company of Bérard, 180–81, 184; Cocteau takes seriously, 181; pounces on Lady Dufferin, 181–2; and NY social whirl, 182–3; and Silver Jubilee, 183; in Rome with Lord Berners, 183; and Ashcombe life, 184–5; and filming *Sailor's Return*, 185; and *Vogue* problems, 185–6; ballet work, 186–8, 190–91; visits Russia, 186–7; spring travels (1936), 188; *Queen Mary* maiden voyage, 188; in NY in summer, 188–9; with Cocteau at automat, 189; summoned from Kammer, 191; and father's death, 191–2; photos Mrs Simpson, 193–4, 197–9; meets Edward VIII, 194–5; NY exhibition (1937), 195; advised by clairvoyant, 195; *Vogue* Coronation photos, 196; and Duchess of Gloucester, 196, 215; and Duchess of Kent, 196–7; at Candé with Mrs Simpson, 197–8, 198–9; Coronation (1937), 198; Windsor wedding, 199;

PART FOUR – THE LOVELORN YEARS – *cont.*

Windsor photos drama, 199–200; Ashcombe *fête champêtre*, 201–2; travels with Lilia Ralli, 202; publishes *Scrapbook*, 202–4; last NY season (1937–8), 204–13; disenchanted with *Vogue*, 205; designs for Tallulah Bankhead, 205–6; deteriorating health of, 204, 206; and Tchelitchew's influence, 297; Kike drama, 207–13; offensive drawing, 209; sacked from *Vogue* (1938), 210; Kommer rescues, 214–15; lengthy cruise, 215–16; in Venice, 216–17; in Tamaris, 217–20; makes friends with Francis Rose, 217–18, 222; painted by Bérard, 218–20; returns to London, 220; and New York book, 220–21; in Paris (1938), 221–2; with David Herbert in Tangiers, 222–3; and Francis Rose's East End misadventure, 223–4; career prospects revive, 224; photos Prince and Princess Paul, 224–5; photos Queen Elizabeth (1939), 225–7; and Merle Oberon costumes, 224, 226; with Gertrude Stein at Ain, 227–8; gets lost, 227–8; and outbreak of war, 228; and *My Royal Past*, 228–31

PART FIVE – THE WAR YEARS

wartime experiences, 235–92; war affects life of, 235; ARP work, 235–6; visits Queen Elizabeth, 236–7; Queen's photos released, 237; and *Heil Cinderella*, 237–9; photos war leaders, 239–40; visits USA, 241; works for Min. of Information in GB, 241–2, 246–50, 253–4; bandaged child photo, 242; in favour with *Vogue* again, 242; film work, 242–4; photos of Churchill, 244–6; and hysteria of Mrs Churchill, 245–6; photos London bomb damage, 246–7; escorted to police station, 246–7; collaborates with James Pope-Hennessy, 247; make friends with Clarissa Churchill, 247–8; visits WRNS, 248; and RAF work, 248–9; publishes *Time Exposure*, 250–52; and Osbert Sitwell row, 251–2; and Lord Berners' joke, 252; affair with Coral Browne, 252–3; visits Scotland, 253; muses on past, 254; earns respect of Noël Coward, 254; in Near East, 256–66; sails to Freetown, 255; in Canal Zone, 256; in desert, 257–60; memorable war photos, 258–60; grim hospital visit, 259; and SAS, 260; in Alexandria with Lilia, 260; in Cairo, 260–62, 266; photos captured General, 262; in Teheran, 262–3; in Iraq, 263–4; in Jerusalem, 264; in Jordan, 264–6; sick with panic, 265; with Mrs Casey, 266; in Lagos, 266–7; Near East work reviewed, 267–8; and royal photography, 268–9; photos Mrs Roosevelt, 268; and theatre and film work, 269–70; and *Vogue* problems, 270–71; and aeroplane accident, 272–3, 274; in Far East, 274–93; in India, 274–82, 289–91; pours glass into tweed overcoat, 274; at Viceroy's House, Delhi, 274–6; photos Mountbatten on double bed, 276; photos Lord Wavell, 276; and ADC life, 275, 278, 280, 281, 290, 291; visits Calcutta, 276–7, 278, 281–2; in jungle, 277–8; suffers dengue fever, 278; in Delhi, 278, 281; visits NW Frontier, 279, visits Bombay, 279–81; sees leopard hunt, 281; in Jaipur, 281; ill, 281–2; regrets quality of photos, 282; goes over the Hump, 282; in China, 282–9; in Chungking, 282–3, 287–9; on trip to Pihu, 283–7; in Chinese bath, 283; smokes opium, 283; with Secret Service, 283–4; and Chinese generals, 284–5; describes trip, 286; avoids truck accident, 286–7; discomforts of trip, 287; photos Chinese celebrities, 288; work criticized, 288, 289; 2nd Indian visit, 289–91; bumps into Noël Coward, 289–90; questioned by Viceroy, 290–91; homewards, 291–3; flies to USA, 291; bored by photography, 291; in Paris (1944), 292; change in character as war ends, 292–3; Far East war work reviewed, 293

PART SIX – THE GARBO YEARS

loses Ashcombe, 297–9; theatre work, 299–300, 306–7; ambition to write play, 300–301; in Paris with la Bande, 301; goes on stage in California, 301–2, 305, 306; on stage in NY, 306; meets Garbo again (1946), 302; judges GG's looks, 302; and her vertebrae, 302; proposes, 303; passport photo drama, 303, 304; writes bombshell letters, 303; telephones GG, 304; Emerald Cunard intrigues, 305–6; Korda work, 307–10; and Vivien Leigh's hands, 309; period of change, 310; finds Reddish House, 310–11, 314; writes to GG, 314–16; and GG's London visit, 315–16; Maud lights candles for, 316; love affair with GG, 312, 317–33; romantic complications, 316–17; massages GG's back, 317; GG draws curtains, 317; walks with GG, 318; and his curious role, 318; and Mona's advice, 319; new campaign begins, 319; GG stares at in theatre, 319–20; GG admits to room, 321; proposes again, 321; goes away for weekend, 322; GG's bath with, 322; seeks to make delights more binding, 322; and Christmas Day (1947), 323; New Year's Eve, 324; and Mr Winston scandal, 325; GG rebukes, 325–6; GG accuses of writing, 326; shocked by GG's accusation, 326; NY meetings continue, 327–9; in California with GG, 329–32; departs in tears, 332; writes to GG, 334–5; English life of, 335; friendship with Duchess of Kent, 336, 340; and with Truman Capote, 337; Lucian Freud paints, 337; further theatre and ballet work, 338–9, 344, 345–6, 349, 356–8; and Olivier row, 339; photos Prince Charles (1948), 339–40; and royal photography, 340; stays with Somerset Maugham, 340–41; PW stays with, 341; in Tangiers (1949), 341–2; further brushes with GG, 342; and with Schlee, 342–3; in Paris with GG and Schlee, 343–4; row with Maud Nelson, 346; photos Princess Anne (1950), 346–7; in Taormina, 347; encounters leg in deep sea, 347; Irving Penn photos, 347–8; GG complications, 348; and *Gainsborough Girls* play (1951), 350–53; and GG's two-month stay in England, 354–5; GG devastates in NY, 355–6; and Clarissa's marriage, 358; GG very difficult with, 359

PART SEVEN – THE VICTORIOUS YEARS
John Myers warns, 363–4; lecture tours of, 364–5; Princess Grace on, 364; considers life, 365; sacks Maud Nelson, 365–6; engages Eileen Hose, 366–7; and the Coronation, 367–8; and the Christie trial, 368–9; in Portofino, Rapallo and Venice, 369–70; at Slade, 370–71; and Broadchalke life, 371; as fastidious dresser, 371–2; working with Waldemar Hansen, 372–4, 393–4, 415–16; and Adonis in Capri, 374; theatre work, 374–5; row with GG (1954), 375–7; row with *Vogue*, 377–8; portrait photos of, 378–9; photos Queen, 379–80; and *The Chalk Garden*, 381–6; seething rage over London production, 384–5; remonstrates with Enid Bagnold, 385–6; and *My Fair Lady*, 386–95; work-

ing with Oliver Smith, 387; Julie Andrews on, 387, 390, 392; photos Marilyn Monroe, 393; and Joan Crawford, 393–4; and death of Peter Watson, 396–7; and fashion Oscar, 398; with GG in Paris (1956), 398; smuggles GG into London, 398; in London with GG, 399–400; and Sagittarius Gallery exhibition, 400; receives CBE (1957), 401; Japan trip with Truman Capote (1957), 401–6; more photos, 407; *Gigi* work, 408–12; Café Royal Party (1958), 413–15; and *Landscape with Figures* endeavour, 415–16, 418–20; financial problems of, 417; theatre and opera work, 407, 415, 417–18, 421–5; romance with June Osborn, 426–34; proposes to June, 431, 433; romance concludes, 434; as royal photographer, 435–42; and Princess Margaret's photos, 435–6; rivalry with Lord Snowdon, 436; horror at Princess Margaret's engagement, 436–7; photos Prince Andrew (1960), 437–9; Prince Philip's antipathy to, 438; decorates Covent Garden gala, 439; stays at Vaynol with Duchess of Kent, 439–40; dines with Queen Mother, 440, 453–4; photos Duke of Kent, 440; and Kent wedding, 441; and Gloucesters, 441; Roy Strong on, as royal photographer, 441–2; Queen Mother's appraisal of in letter to, 442; publishes 1st volume of diaries, 443–4; ambition of, 444; cold streak in, 444–5; attends Barbara Hutton's ball, 445; meets and kisses Nureyev, 445–6; painted by Francis Bacon, 446–7; and by Augustus John, 446–7; death of mother, 447–9; and *Face to Face* interview, 448; in Nigeria (1962), 449; and Francis Rose in hard times, 449; and Comédie Française work, 450; photo portraits, 450–51; stately home life, 451–2; close examination of Windsor dinner-party, 452–3; photos beautiful fledglings, 453; bad health, 453; and Broadchalke garden, 454; envy and jealousy of, 454, 456; considers own lot, 456; photos dying Isak Dinesen, 456–7; and Edith Sitwell encounters, 457–8; entertains Queen Mother to lunch, 457–8; on Kenya safari (1962), 458–9; ballet work and Nureyev, 459–60; and *My Fair Lady* film (1963), 461–74; works with Cukor, 461; designs sets and costumes, 462–5; selects extras, 464–5; daily routine, 465; weekend life,

PART SEVEN – THE VICTORIOUS YEARS – *cont.*
465; Hollywood vulgarity, 465–6; and Audrey Hepburn, 467–8; hostility to Cukor, 468; rage with Cukor, 469; shooting of film commences, 470; further row with Cukor, 472; attempt at reconciliation, 473–4; results of film, 474–6; sues BBC over Cukor, 475; wins two Oscars, 476; attitude to sex, 477; meets Kin in bar, 477–8; weekends with Kin, 478–80; Kin on Cecil, 481–2; London life, 482–3; photographs Plisetskaya, 483–4; sixtieth birthday, 484; in St Moritz, 484; in Morocco, 485; photos Princess Marina, 485; falls in lake at Vaynol, 485; photos Prince Edward (1964), 485; arrival of Kin in London, 485; integration of Kin, 486–7; panic *re* Kin, 487; travels with Kin, 487–9; Syrie Maugham memorial, 489; Redfern exhibition, 489–90; lunch with Queen Mother (1964), 490; Hon. FRPS, 490; on Kin's image, 490–91; with Kin at Broadchalke, 490–91; in France, 491; flies off the handle, 492; Kin announces wish to leave, 492–3; Kin concludes on relationship with, 493; Kin departs, 493–4

PART EIGHT – THE SWINGING YEARS
in changing times, 497; publishes war diaries, 497–8; Greek cruise with GG, 498, 499–500; and death of Schlee, 498–9; loneliness of, 500; visits to Stephen Tennant, 501–2; and death of Juliet Duff, 502; in Monaco, 502; concerned at Truman's success, 502–3, 508; photos in Paris, 503; suffers shingles, 503–4; Lefevre Gallery exhibition (1966), 504; Caribbean rest, 505; involved with young swingers, 505–6; theatre work, 506–7; becomes FIIP, 507; in NY and New Mexico, 508; and Simon Fleet's funeral, 508–9; and the Rolling Stones, 510–12; photos Mick Jagger, 511–12; technical hazards for, 512; takes psychedelic photos, 512; absorbed into Swinging Sixties, 513; puffs dope, 513; in Venice, 513; meets Greek Royal Family, 514; photos Twiggy, 514; in Stockholm, 514–15; tours Poland and Czechoslovakia, 515; suffers headaches, 515; and Francis Rose dramas, 516, 549; in NY, 516; and *Don't Count the Candles* row, 516–18; photos Margot Fonteyn in NY, 518; in Palm Beach, 519; Australian tour (1968), 519–20; takes Jackie Kennedy to *Don Quixote*, 520; Queen Mother lunches with, 520–21; flies off the handle, 521; Wright Hepburn Gallery exhibition, 521; takes mescalin tablets in NY, 522; and death of Princess Marina (1968), 523; National Portrait Gallery exhibition (1968), 524–8; '600 Faces by Beaton', 534–6; photos Queen, 525; and Prince Charles, 526–7; Prince Charles writes to, 528; on set of *Performance*, 528–9; works on *On a Clear Day*, 529, 532–4; and Barbra Streisand, 529, 533–4; sartorial elegance of 530; takes cure, 530–31; reconciliation with Enid Bagnold, 531–2; and with John Gielgud, 532; Hockney draws, 536; summer life (1969), 536–7; and *Coco*, 538–42; antipathy to Katharine Hepburn, 539–42; row with Alan Jay Lerner, 540; on *Oh Calcutta!*, 542; Palm Beach exhibition (1970), 543; with Kin (1970), 543; in South America, 544; prostate operation of, 544–6; photos Queen Mother, 545; at Windsor ball, 545; Cathleen Nesbitt becomes friend, 546; and *Beaton by Bailey* film, 546, 547, 549–52; at Mouton, 546; in Rio de Janeiro, 548; *Vogue* problems, 550; and suicide of Margaret Case, 550; delighted by Raymond Mortimer review, 551; V&A fashion exhibition, 551–3

PART NINE – THE DECLINING YEARS
vexed over Garbo revelations, 557–9; offered knighthood, 559; row with Horst, 559; becomes Knight Bachelor (1972), 560; letters of congratulation, 560–61; invested by Queen, 561–2; in Egypt, 562–3; in Cyprus, 563; savaged by Cecile de Rothschild, 563; *Plays and Players* articles, 563; and Duke of Windsor's funeral, 564; and publication of *The Happy Years*, 564–5; GG's reaction to, 565–6; summer holidays of, 566; death of Baba, 566–7; and Patrick O'Higgins' article, 567; and Charles James accusations, 567–8; encounter with Valentina Schlee, 568; and his garden, 569; at Princess Anne's party (1973), 569; admiration for Edward Heath, 569–70; and murder of James Pope-Hennessy (1974), 570; in Mexico (1974), 570; knocked down by Robert Heber-Percy, 570–71; Kodak exhibition row, 571; sadness at end of an era, 571; isolation from friends, 571–2; intense

loneliness of, 572; latest verdict on play, 572; last active summer of, 572–3; suffers stroke, 573; effects of stroke, 574; gradual recuperation, 574–9; GG visits (1975), 577; sells photographic studio, 578; visits NY, 578; visits Stephen Tennant, 579; resumes photography, 580; *Vogue* work in Paris, 580–81; seventy-sixth birthday, 582; death, 582–3; funeral, 584–5; Reddish House sale, 585; conclusion, 585–9

BOOKS

Air of Glory, 249; *Ashcombe*, 298–9; *Ballet*, 349; *British Photographers*, 271; *The Best of Beaton*, 522, 525, 568; *The Book of Beauty*, 120, 122, 126, 141–3, 149, 159, 177, 211; *Cecil Beaton's Chinese Album*, 293 n; *Cecil Beaton's Diaries: 1944–1948 The Happy Years*, 500, 521, 557–9, 564–5, 567–8, 570; *Cecil Beaton's Diaries: 1963–1974 The Parting Years*, 557, 579; *Cecil Beaton's Diaries: 1955–1963 The Restless Years*, 451, 530; *Cecil Beaton's Diaries: 1948–1955 The Strenuous Years*, 339, 368, 369, 521, 568; *Cecil Beaton's Diaries: 1922–1939 The Wandering Years*, 98, 123, 159–60, 226 n, 227 n, 443–4; *Cecil Beaton's Diaries: 1939–1944 The Years Between*, 269 n, 497, 498, 557; *Cecil Beaton's 'Fair Lady'*, 468, 485; *Cecil Beaton's Indian Album*, 293 n; *Cecil Beaton's New York*, 123, 203, 213, 214, 372; *Cecil Beaton's Scrapbook*, 160, 202–4, 251, 356, 376, 407, 539; *The Face of the World*, 393, 395, 407, 409; *Far East*, 292–3; *The Glass of Fashion*, 372, 373–4, 378, 574; *History Under Fire*, 247–8, 250; *Images*, 485; *India*, 293 n; *It Gives me Great Pleasure*, 365; *Japanese*, 416; *The Masque*, 310; *The Magic Image*, 568, 576–7; *My Bolivian Aunt*, 344, 551; *My Royal Past*, 213, 228–31, 254, 376, 453; *Near East*, 267–8; *Persona Grata*, 369; *Photobiography*, 135 n, 226 n, 227 n, 349; *Quail in Aspic*, 435 & n, 485; *Royal Portraits*, 442, 485; *Self Portrait with Friends*, 199 n, 226 n, 577; *Time Exposure*, 250–52; *Winged Squadrons*, 249–50

PRODUCTIONS

Adriana Lecouvreur, 425; *All the Vogue* (1925), 47; *Anna Karenina* (1948), 307–8; *Antony and Cleopatra*, 205–6; *Apparitions*, (1936) 187, 188, (1949) 339, 407, 459;

Aren't We All (1953), 369, 569; *Black Vanities* (1941), 243–4; *Camille* (1946), 306–7; *Casse-Noisette* (1951), 349; *The Chalk Garden* (1955), 357, 381–6, 388, 531–2; *Charley's Aunt* (1947), 310; *Coco* (1969), 529, 537, 538–42; *Crisis in Heaven* (1944), 270, 278; *Cry of the Peacock* (1950), 345; *Cyrano de Bergerac*, 301; *Dandy Dick* (1945), 300; *Dangerous Moonlight* (1941), 243; *Devoirs de Vacances* (1949), 344; *The Doctor's Dilemma* (1959), 253, 415; *A Family and a Fortune* (1966), 507; *First Class Passengers Only* (1927), 102; *Follow the Sun* including *The First Shoot* (1935), 186, 187; *The Gainsborough Girls*, 300–301, 335, (1951) 350–3, 355, 395, 415–16, renamed *Landscape with Figures* 418–21, 531, 566, 572; *Gigi* (1958), 242, 408–12, 415, 450; *The Grass Harp* (1952), 356–7; *The Gyp's Princess* (1923), 32–3, 34; *Heartbreak House* (1943), 9, 269–70; *Heil Cinderella* (1940), 237–9, 381; *Henry IV* (1924), 448 n–5; *Les Illuminations* (1950), 345, 394; *Kipps* (1941), 242–3; *Lady Windermere's Fan* (1945), 299–300, 301, 305–6, 316, 335, 338, 400, 407, 408, 448, (1966) 506; *Landscape with Figures*, see *The Gainsborough Girls*; *The Little Glass Clock* (1956), 391, 393; *Look After Lulu* (1959), 417, 429; *Major Barbara* (1941), 243; *Marguerite and Armand* (1963), 459–60, 500; *My Fair Lady*, 9, 65, 139, 242, (1956) 385, 386–94, (1958) 395, 396, 398, 407, 408, 412, 417, 422, 425, 426, 444, 449, (1964) 461–74, 474–5, 476, 477, 489, 489–90, 491, 529, 578; *On Approval* (1944), 270, 278; *On A Clear Day You Can See Forever* (1970), 529, 530, 531, 532–3, 534; *Our Betters* (1946), 307; *Our Lady's Tumbler* (1951), 349; *Les Patineurs* (1946), 307; *Le Pavillon* (1936), 190–91; *Picnic at Tintagel* (1952), 356; *Portrait of a Lady* (1954), 375; *Quadrille* (1952), 357–8, 407, (1954) 358; *The Return of the Prodigal* (1948), 338; *Romeo and Juliet*, 174; *The Rose and the Ring* (1922), 30, 32, 548; *The School for Scandal* (1949), 338–9; *The Second Mrs Tanqueray* (1950), 345–6, 448, 524; *Les Sirenes* (1946), 304, 307; *Streamline* (1934), 176; *Swan Lake* (1951), 349; *Tenderloin* (1959), 422; *La Traviata* (1966), 425, 487, 489; *The Truth About Women* (1958), 407; *Turandot* (1961),

PRODUCTIONS – *cont.*

423–5; *The Two Gentlemen of Verona*, 421; *Volpone* (1923), 32–3, 34; *The Young Mr Pitt* (1942), 243

Beaton, Ernest (C's father) (1867–1936): background, 5–6, 7–8; 10, 11, 12, 25, 36, 37, 38, 44, 52, 53, 56, 58, 59, 61–5, 67–9, 71–2, 77, 107–9, 113, 119–20, 165; death of Reggie, 169, 172, 178–9; death, 191–2; mentioned, 254, 298, 372, 531

Beaton, Etty (C's mother) (1872–1962): background, 3–10, 12, 36, 37–9, 46, 52, 54, 55, 59, 61, 64, 71, 88, 91, 97, 113, 119; death of Reggie, 169; 179; and Mr B's death, 191–2; 203, 206, 211, 220, 236, 253, 260, 267, 275, 303, 304, 305, 310–11, 346, 352, 354; heart attack and eightieth birthday, 359; 390, 401; drinking, 426–7; 433, 437, 458; death, 447–9; mentioned, 488, 531, 549, 559, 562, 584

Beaton, Frank (1914–41), 253

Beaton, John (1804–72), 6

Beaton, Lady Mary (d. *c.* 1599), 5, 87, 107

Beaton, Nancy (Lady Smiley) (C's sister) (b. 1909), 7, 8, 12, 24, 38, 52–3, 56–7, 60, 62, 65, 67, 71–2, 78–9, 81–2, 87–9, 101, 103–7, 112, 116, 119–20, 141, 149, 154–5, 168, 178, 191, 211, 269, 354, 359, 449, 552, 562, 571; birth, 7; married, 163–4, 163 *n*

Beaton, Reginald (C's brother) (1905–33), 7–10, 12–13, 15–16, 24, 37, 44, 46, 53, 56, 62–3, 67, 78, 120, 549; birth, 7; death, 168–70, 173

Beaton, Mrs Reginald (Aunt Lilias) (1878–1959), 37, 253

Beaton, Theodore, 119

Beaton, Walter Hardy (1841–1904), 6

Beaton, Wilfred (C's uncle) (1874–1940), 6, 7, 112

Beaton, William, 6

Beatrice, HRH The Princess (1857–1944), 65–6, 196

Beatty, (Diana) Countess (b. 1941), 452

Beauchamp, Antony (1918–57), 277–8

Beauchamp, Irene (Bubbles) (1899–1951), 37 & *n*

Beaufort, *see* Somerset

Beaufort, 10th Duke of (1900–84), 489

Beaufort, Mary Duchess of (b. 1897), 489

Beauman, Katharine Bentley, 250 *n*

Beaumont, Etienne de, 224, 341

Beaumont, Hugh (Binkie) (1908–73), 269, 299–300, 338, 351, 352, 357, 369, 384, 385 & *n*, 386, 401, 414–15, 502, 506, 561; death, 567

Beaverbrook, 1st Lord (1879–1964), 162

Beck, Maurice (1886–1960), 52, 53, 83

Becker, Baronne René de, 377

Bedaux, Mr and Mrs Charles, 197

Bedford, Sybille (b. 1911), 58

Beerbohm, Sir Max (1872–1956), 53, 203, 369

Beistigui, Don Carlos de (1895–1970), 354, 445, 462

Beit, Bt, Sir Alfred (b. 1903), 162 & *n*

Bekinson, John, 311

Bell, Clive (1881–1964), 33, 67

Belline, Ira (d. 1971), 341, 512

Benavides, Carmen, 549

Bender, Marylin, 541

Benito, Eduardo, 172

Bennett, Mr, 35

Bennett, Arnold (1867–1931), 68

Bennett, C.T. (1902–79), 23–4, 40, 43, 254, 579

Benson, Rev. Niale (1911–80), 577

Benthall, Michael (1919–74), 351, 540

Benton, Jim, 391–2, 394–5, 401, 420, 422

Berar, HH The Princess of (b. 1913), 280, 320

Berard, Christian (Bébé) (1902–49), 167, 173, 174, 180, 184, 186, 188, 202; at Tamaris, 217–20; 221–2, 224, 230, 239, 301, 314, 328, 335–6; death, 336–7; 345, 369, 397, 445, 447, 450

Bercutt, Max, 469, 471–2

Berenson, Bernard (1865–1959), 379

Berenson, Marisa (b. 1948), 559

Berger, Helmut (b. 1944), 568

Bergerac, Jacques (b. 1927), 410

Berlin, Irving (b. 1888), 122, 125–6, 130, 585

Berlin, Mrs Irving (Ellin) (b. 1903), 122, 125, 585

Bernays, Mr, 301

Berners, 14th Lord (1883–1950), 74–6, 141–2, 155, 168, 171–2, 174, 183, 225, 228, 230, 239, 248, 252, 304, 310

Berry, Lady Pamela (Lady Hartwell) (1914–82), 355, 358, 560

Betjeman, Sir John (1906–84), 185, 203, 454, 547, 561

Bevin, Rt Hon. Ernest (1881–1951), 240

Bibesco, Princess Marthe (1888–1973), 503

Bing, Sir Rudolf (b. 1902), 423–5, 505

Birch, Frank (1889–1956), 28, 32–4, 42–5

Birch, Hon. Mrs (Vera) (1899–1983), 34 & *n*, 57

Birkenhead, 1st Earl of (1872–1930), 36, 81

Birkenhead, 2nd Earl of (1907–75), 443–4

Birkin, Jane (b. 1946), 559, 580

Birley, Lady (Rhoda) (d. 1980), 433–4

Birrell, Francis (1889–1935), 33

Bishop, Adrian (d. 1942), 34 & *n*, 264

Bishron, 290

Bismarck, Prince Eddie von (d. 1971), 374

Bismarck, Princess (Mona Harrison Williams) (d. 1983), 111, 113 & *n*, 161, 168, 181, 182, 188–9, 201–2, 212, 221, 241, 303, 319, 323–4, 374, 452–3, 551

Black, George (b. 1911), 243

Blackwood, Caroline (Lady Caroline Lowell) (b. 1931), xxvii–xxviii, 370–71

Blanch, Lesley (Mrs Romain Gary) (b. 1907), 242–3, 462–3, 564

Blandford, (Tina) Marchioness of (d. 1975), 451

Blass, Bill, 578

Blixen, *see* Dinesen

Bloomingdale, Mr Alfred (Betsy), xxviii, 465

Blow, Detmar (1867–1939), 85, 310

Blundell, Sir Robert (1901–67), 29–30

Blunt, Professor Anthony (1907–83), 490, 582 & *n*

Bogarde, Dirk (b. 1920), 415

Bohan, Marc, 450

Boldini, Giovanni (1845–1931), 450, 490

Bolitho, Hector (1897–1974), 268

Bonham Carter, Lady (Charlotte) (b. 1893), 527

Booth Luce, Clare, *see* Luce

Borenius, Professor Tancred (1885–1948), xxvii

Borges, Jorge Luis (b. 1899), 564

Borley, Hugh, 297, 299

Borley, R.W., 138, 297–8

Bouquet, Carol, 579

Bourdet, Edouard (d. 1945), 217

Bourdet, Mme Edouard (Denise), 217, 219, 301, 372 *n*, 450

Bousquet, Marie-Louise (1874–1967), 301, 398, 448

Bowen, Elizabeth (1899–1973), 271

Bowles, Mrs Paul (Jane) (1917–73), 337, 341

Bowles, Paul (b. 1911), 337

Box, Muriel (b. 1905), 407

Box, Sydney (1907–83), 407

Boxer, Lady Arabella (b. 1934), 502

Boxer, Mark (b. 1931), 407, 502

Bracken, 1st Viscount (Brendan) (1901–58), 253, 289

Bradshaw, Jon, 515

Braham, Mrs Frank, 54, 57, 59, 65, 66

Brando, Marlon (b. 1924), 405

Brandolini, Count Brando, 413, 416–17, 473, 488, 500

Brandolini, Countess (Christina), 413, 416–17, 473, 486, 488, 500

Brandt, Herr Willy (b. 1913), 530

Bray, W/Cdr Charles, 256–7

Bream, Julian (b. 1933), 527

Brennan, Hank, xxvii

Brennan, Mrs, 58, 65, 67

Brett, Jeremy (b. 1935), 470, 473

Bridgeman, Hon. Sir Maurice (1904–80), 59, 60 *n*

Brinnin, John Malcolm, 356

Brisson, Frederick (1915–84), 529, 539–42

Britten, Benjamin (Lord) (1913–76), 270, 337, 345, 525

Broadbent, Peggy (Lady Harris) (d. 1978), 29 & *n*

Broadchalke (Reddish House), 310–11, 314–15, 335, 337, 341, 350, 397, 415–17, 445, 487, 491, 500–503, 506, 514, 521, 529, 549, 550, 569, 571, 572–3, 574–5, 577–83, 584–5

Brodie, Paddy, 89 & *n*, 107

Broglie, Princesse Jeanne-Marie de, 498, 500

Brokaw, *see* Booth Luce

Brook, Clive (1887–1974), 270

Brook, Peter (b. 1925), 357, 506, 508

Brooke, Rupert (1887–1915), xxix, 25, 87, 307

Brougham, Hon. Eleanor (1883–1966), 89, 90

Brown, Charlotte (Mrs Coudert Nast), 103–4

Brown, Dr Christopher (d. 1985), 560, 582

Brown, Mrs Christopher, 585

Brown, Dudley, 15, 46

Brown, Mrs Dudley, 110

Brown, Ivor (1891–1974), 338–9

Browne, Coral (b. 1913) xxviii, 252–3, 506

Browne, Irene (1891–1965), 110

Bruce, Christopher (b. 1945), 525

Bruce, Mrs David (Evangeline), 527

Bryant, Sir Arthur (1899–1985), 299, 371

Buccleuch, (Mary) Duchess of (b. 1900), 196, 414

Buckland, Gail (b. 1948), 293, 568, 576, 587

Buckle, Richard (b. 1916), xvii, 349, 502, 508, 524, 526–7, 531, 575, 585

Buckmaster, Joan (Mrs Robert Morley), 163

Bullivant, Billie, 25, 31, 33–4, 39–40, 43, 46 & *n*

Burke, Billie (1885—), 117
Burnier, Raymond, 278, 281
Burns, Pamela (d. 1944), XVII, 261
Burrell, John (1910–72), 269, 388
Burton, Hal (b. 1908), 270, 350, 353–5, 357, 366–7, 382, 399–400, 416, 429 n, 447, 470, 490, 560, 569, 572, 585
Butler of Saffron Walden, Lord (1900–80), 27
Butler, W.G., 35
Byam Shaw, Glen (b. 1904), 415

Cabrol, Baronne de, 465
Cada, Aunt, *see* Chattock
Callas, Maria (1923–77), 400
Calthrop, Gladys (1897–1980), 290, 527
Calvert, Phyllis (b. 1915), 243
Cameron, Julia Margaret, 141 & n
Cameron, Roderick (Rory) (1914–85), 519
Camoys, the Dowager Lady (b. 1913), 169
Campbell, Mrs Patrick (1865–1940), 206
Campbell, Mrs Turia, 225
Canfield, Laura, *see* Marlborough
Capel, Captain Arthur (Boy) (d. 1920), 427, 552
Capote, Truman (1924–84), XXVII; meets C, 337; in Tangiers, 341–2; in Taormina, 347; and *The Grass Harp*, 356–7; advises C on GG, 359; on C's lectures, 364; in Portofino, 369; mother's suicide, 374; on *The Chalk Garden*, 384; on *My Fair Lady*, 394; on Peter's death, 398; Japan trip, 401–7; and *Sayonara*, 401–2, 404–5; C stays with (1958), 416; on *Saratoga*, 421; on June, 429, 430, 432 & n, 433; on C's diaries, 443; Isak Dinesen on, 456; at royal lunch, 457–8; in Hollywood, 473; on Kin, 482, 493; success with *In Cold Blood*, 502–3, 508, 519; black and white ball, 508; friendship with C blighted, 516–17; in Bailey film, 549; C criticizes, 557; opinion of C, 586; mentioned, 147, 148, 312, 330, 346, 386, 397, 454, 466, 479, 522, 568
Carcano, Miguel (1889–1978), 549
Carisbrooke, the Marchioness of (1890–1956), 196
Carmencita, *see* Benavides, Carmen
Carmona, General (President of Portugal 1928–51) (1869–1951), 267
Carnarvon Countess of, *see* Losch
Carnarvon, 6th Earl of (b. 1898), 183 n
Carnegie, Lady Maud (1893–1945), 103, 240
Carnes, Simon, *see* Fleet
Caron, Leslie (b. 1931), 344, 409–11, 415

Carter, Howard (1873–1939), 562
Cartier-Bresson, Henri (b. 1908), 525–6, 587
Carton de Wiart, Lt-Gen. Sir Adrian (1880–1963), 288 & n
Cartwright, Mrs, 397
Casa Maury, *see* Dudley-Ward *and* Gellibrand
Casa Maury, (Bobby) Marquis de (d. 1968), 52, 112, 114, 172
Case, Margaret (1891–1971), 112, 135, 208, 211, 241, 242, 302, 310, 324, 325, 327, 421, 473; suicide, 550
Casey, Donn (2nd Lord) (b. 1931), 278
Casey, Lady (Maie) (d. 1983), 261 & n, 266, 277–8, 282, 290, 293 n, 519–20
Casey, 1st Lord (1890–1976), 261 & n, 277, 278 & n, 282, 519
Casler, Dick, 425
Castle, Mrs Vernon (Irene) (1893–1969), 18, 38–9, 141–2, 522 n
Castlerosse, Viscount (1891–1943), 105–6, 162, 163 & n, 217, 243
Castlerosse, Viscountess (Doris) (1901–42), 161–3, 165–8, 170–1, 173–4, 180, 182, 195, 202, 204, 216–17, 217 n, 243
Cavanagh, John (b. 1914), 552
Cavendish, Lady Elizabeth (b. 1926), 414
Cavendish, Lord Charles (1905–44), 19, 59, 60 & n, 63–4, 153 n, 154 n
Cavendish-Bentinck, Lord Morven (1900–50), 29
Cecil, Hugh, 38–9, 52, 55
Cecil, Lord David (1902–86), 29, 96, 98, 235, 311, 355, 546, 549, 584–5
Cerezeira, Cardinal Gonsalves, 267
Cerf, Bennett (1898–1971), 214
Chagall, Marc (1877–1985), XXI, 341
Chamberlain, Rt Hon. Neville (1869–1940), 220, 235
Champion de Crespigny, A/V/M H.V. (1897–1969), 263
Chanel, 'Coco' (1883–1971), 480, 491, 507, 529, 537, 540, 541; death, 542; 552, 553
Channon, Sir Henry (Chips) (1897–1958), 57, 161, 165, 168, 194, 239, 275, 299, 401 n
Chaplin, Sir Charles (1889–1977), 166
Chapman, John, 421, 425
Chapman-Walker, Mark, 261
Charisse, Cyd (b. 1923), 410, 465
Charles, Lallie, 10, 522
Charles, Prince, *see* Wales
Charteris of Amisfield, Lady (Gay) (b. 1919), 561, 571

Charteris of Amisfield, Lord (Martin) (b. 1913), 379, 525, 561, 571

Chase, Edna Woolman (1877–1957), 99–100, 110–12, 117, 154, 172, 185, 200, 205, 210–11, 214, 249, 253, 270–71, 291, 363, 378, 534

Chattock, Claud (d. 1915), 4, 5 n

Chattock, Mrs Richard (Aunt Cada) (1879–1970), 3–5, 37, 79, 339, 531 & n, 559, 576

Chattock, Richard (1865–1936), 5 n

Chattock, Tecia (Mrs Frank Fearnley-Whittingstall) (b. 1907), 5 n, 168, 178

Chattock, Tess (Mrs John Ellert) (b. 1910), 178

Cheke, Sir Marcus (1905–60), 267

Chen, Miss, 289

Chennault, Gen. C.L., 283

Chetwode, Hon. Roger (1906–40), 98

Chevalier, Maurice (1887–1972), 408, 410–12, 450

Chiang Chung-kuo, 284

Chiang Kai-shek, Generalissimo (1887–1975), 284, 289

Chiang Kai-shek, Madame, 289

Childs, Mrs, 77–8

Cholmondeley, Lady Caroline (b. 1952), 564

Cholmondeley, Lady George (d. 1925), 103

Cholmondeley, Sybil, Marchioness of (b. 1894), 198, 488, 551

Christie, John (1899–1953), 368–9

Churchill, Clarissa, *see* Avon

Churchill, Diana (Mrs Duncan Sandys) (1904–63), 157, 244

Churchill, Marguerite (b. 1910), 130

Churchill, Mary (Lady Soames) (b. 1922), 240

Churchill, Mrs Randolph (Pamela) (Mrs Averill Harriman) (b. 1920), 240, 414

Churchill, Hon. Randolph (1911–68), 160, 161, 224, 246, 254, 266, 367, 522, 535 n

Churchill, Sarah (Lady Audley) (1914–82), 186

Churchill, Mrs Winston (Clementine) (Baroness Spencer-Churchill) (1885–1977), 157, 244–6, 379

Churchill, Rt Hon. Sir Winston (1874–1965), 157 & n, 162, 186, 193, 217 n, 244–6, 292, 379, 491

Cilento, Diane (b. 1933), 407

Claire, Ina (1892–1985), xxv, xxviii, 18 & n, 115, 118, 120, 128, 151, 406, 567

Clark, Ossie, 547, 551

Clark, Mrs Ossie (Celia), 547

Clark, Lady (Jane) (1902–76), 251, 260, 574–5

Clark, Lord (Kenneth) (1903–83), 240, 241, 245, 247, 271, 542, 574–5

Cleghorn, Louann, 318, 324

Clerk, Rt Hon. Sir George (1874–1951), 180

Clowes, David, 278

Coats, Major Peter (b. 1910), 274–6, 291, 368

Cochran, (C.B.) Sir Charles (1872–1951), 66, 68, 176, 186, 188, 241

Cocteau, Jean (1889–1963), 53, 59, 167, 174, 180–81, 184, 186, 189–90, 214–15, 217–18, 221, 301, 328, 336, 374, 450, 587

Cohen, Al, 128

Cohen-Portheim, Paul, 68

Colefax, Lady Sibyl (d. 1950), 101, 142, 150, 160, 168, 220, 221, 291, 310

Coleman, Robert, 345

Colette (1873–1954), 408

Collard, Alice (Ninnie), 24–5, 74, 79, 89, 100, 169, 264

Collier, Constance (1878–1955), 39, 308, 330, 353, 378

Collins, Joan (b. 1933), 466

Colville, Charles, 560

Colville, Hon. Lady (Lady Clydesmuir) (1890–1970), 280

Colville, Lady Cynthia (1884–1968), 320 n

Colville, Col Hon. Sir John (1st Lord Clydesmuir) (1894–1954), 280 & n

Colville, Mary (Hon. Mrs Dalrymple-Hamilton) (1922–81), 280

Colville, Cdr Sir Richard (1907–75), 379

Compton, Fay (1894–1978), 30

Compton-Burnett, Dame Ivy (1892–1969), 507

Coningham, A/V/M Sir Arthur (1895–1948), 258–9

Connaught, HRH Princess Arthur of (1891–1959), 55, 96

Connolly, Cyril (1903–74), 16–18, 28, 62, 148, 203, 251, 267, 271, 398, 423, 443–4, 504, 506, 512, 549, 551 n, 564–5

Cook, Brian, *see* Batsford

Cooke, Alistair (b. 1908), 475

Cooper, Hon. Artemis (b. 1953), 566

Cooper, Lady Diana (b. 1892), xxi, xxiii, xxvi, 52, 54, 55, 73–6, 117–18, 121, 139, 161, 165, 168, 177, 241, 252, 270, 274, 277, 286, 288, 292, 300, 301, 305, 308, 325, 343, 344 & n, 349, 354–5, 370,

Cooper, Lady Diana – *cont.*
378, 382–3, 384, 398, 427, 428, 430,
432–4, 445, 449, 463, 484, 486, 489,
500, 506, 520, 527, 544, 547, 548, 552,
565–8, 578, 581–2, 585
Cooper, Douglas (1911–84), 491
Cooper, Rt Hon. Duff (1st Viscount Norwich)
(1890–1954), 161, 168, 252, 292, 343–
4, 353, 355, 374, 482
Cooper, Gary (1901–61), 127–8, 152, 153,
411
Cooper, Dame Gladys (1888–1971), 47, 51, 59,
82, 97, 383, 463, 465, 471; death, 559
Cooper, Jackie (b. 1921), 158
Cooper, Michael (d. 1972), 512 n
Corbett, Frank, 47–8
Corbett, Leonora (1907–60), 345
Corcoran, Desmond, 504
Corelli, Franco (b. 1924), 423–4
Cornwallis, Lady, 264
Cornwallis, Sir Kinahan (Ambassador to
Baghdad 1941–5) (1883–1959), 264
Corrigan, Mrs Laura (d. 1948), 77, 161, 201,
310
Courtneidge, Dame Cicely (1893–1980),
561–2
Coward, Sir Noël (1899–1973), 39, 51, 85,
91, 96, 113–14, 115, 119, 120, 161,
221, 254, 269, 289–90, 308, 357–8,
393, 417, 424, 429, 454, 479, 489,
497–8, 527, 550, 566; death, 567; 570
Craig, Edward Gordon (1872–1966), 451
Cranborne, *see* Salisbury
Cranborne, Viscountess (Mollie) (*now* Mar-
chioness of Salisbury), 414
Crawford, Joan (1904–77), 130, 158 n, 393–
4, 542
Craxton, John, 397
Crevel, René (d. 1935), 184
Crocker, Henry, 306
Crowninshield, Frank (1872–1947), 110,
112, 207
Crüwell, Gen. Ludwig (1892–1958), 262 & n
Cukor, George (1899–1983), 207, 312, 330,
382, 411, 444, 461, 463–4, 468–75,
489, 540
Culver, Roland (1900–84), 270
Cunard, Lady (Emerald) (1872–1948), 141,
161, 177, 194, 241, 271, 289, 305–6;
death, 335
Cunard, Nancy (1896–1965), 89
Cunningham, Sir George (1888–1963), 279
Curtiss, Mina (b. 1896), 535
Curzon, Lady Georgiana (b. 1910), 107

Curzon of Kedleston, Marchioness (d. 1958),
57, 77
Curzon, Mary (Countess Howe) (1887–1962),
47, 142
Cushing, Mrs, 464

Dahl, Roald (b. 1916), 575
Dahl-Wolfe, Louise (b. 1896), 291, 400
Daladier, Edouard (1884–1970), 240
Dali, Salvador (b. 1904), 195, 201, 239, 323,
374
d'Annunzio, Gabriele (1864–1938), 550
Dare, Zena (1887–1975), 66, 448, 510, 552
Darlington, W.A. (1890–1979), 33
Darrieux, Danielle (b. 1917), 542
Daubeny, Sir Peter (1921–75), 358
Davies, Marion (1898–1961), 128–30, 151
Davis, Allan (b. 1913), 415, 578
Davis, Charles, 140
Davis, George, 323, 337
Davison, Jimmy, 530, 543
Dawkins, Lady Bertha (1886–1943), 320 n
Day, Frances (b. 1908), 243–4
Day-Lewis, Cecil (1904–72), 250, 497
de Acosta, Mercedes (d. 1968), 80, 114, 134,
159, 169, 312, 314, 321, 323, 348, 416,
499, 505, 558 & n
Dean, Basil (1888–1978), 40
Dean Paul, Brenda (1907–59), 80
de Basil, Colonel (1888–1951), 190 & n, 191
de Bear, Archibald (1889—), 105
de Gaulle, Gen. Charles (1890–1970), 292,
439
de Grey, Lady, 365
de la Fressange, Ines, 580
Delavigne, Doris, *see* Castlerosse
Dell, Claudia (b. 1910), 117
del Renzio, Tony, 396
del Rio, Dolores (1905–83), 126, 130, 158
de Meyer, Baron Gayne (1869–1946), 75,
112
Dempster, Nigel (b. 1941), 106, 515
Denistoun, Miss, 223
d'Erlanger, Baba, *see* Faucigny-Lucinge
d'Erlanger, Baroness (Catherine), 73–5, 331
d'Erlanger, Leo (1898–1978), 520
d'Erlanger, Myrtle, 110
d'Erlanger, Mrs Robin, 74
Deslys, Gaby, 10, 11, 373, 463
Desmond, Florence (b. 1905), 176
de Valois, Dame Ninette (b. 1898), 187, 460
Devonshire, (Debo) Duchess of (b. 1920), 413,
451–2

Devonshire, Evelyn Duchess of (1870–1960), 198

Devonshire, (Mary) Dowager Duchess of (b. 1897), 367, 437

Devonshire, 11th Duke of (b. 1920), 451

Dewey, Mrs Alvin, 508

de Wolfe, Elsie, *see* Mendl

Diaghilev, Serge (1872–1929), 75–6, 158 n, 180–81, 190 n, 500

Dickinson, Emily (1830–86), 95

Dickson, Dorothy (b. 1898), 270, 307

Dietrich, Marlene (b. 1902), 151, 158, 182, 576

Dilé, Madame, 537

Dillon, Major Arthur (18th Viscount) (1875–1934), 22

Dillon, Mrs Arthur (Viscountess) (1874–1966), 32

Dinesen, Isak (1885–1962), 456–7

Dior, Christian (1905–57), 202 n, 372 n

Dobell, 504

Dobson, Frank (1888–1963), 140

Dolin, Sir Anton (1904–83), 158 n, 306–7

Domville, Valerie (1914–48), 103

Donat, Robert (1905–58), 243, 270

Dorman–Smith, Rt Hon. Sir Reginald (1899–1977), 272

Dotrice, Roy (b. 1923), 512–13

Doubleday, Mrs Nelson, 118

Doubrovska, Felia (1896–1981), xxiv & n

Douglas, Tom, 55, 84

Dowell, Anthony (b. 1943), 535

Down, Lesley-Anne (b. 1954), 580

Downey, Thomas, 230

Drawbell, J.W. (1899–1979), 240

Driberg, Tom (Lord Bradwell) (1905–76), 106, 211

Drogheda, Kathleen, Countess of (d. 1966), 90

Drummond-Hay, Lady Margaret (b. 1907), 237

Duchin, Eddy, 195

Duchin, Peter (b. 1937), 195 n

Dudley, (Eric) Earl of (1894–1969), 414

Dudley-Ward, Freda (Marquise de Casa Maury) (1894–1983), 36, 71, 98, 172

Dudley-Ward, Penelope (Lady Reed) (1914–82), 243, 305

Duff, Lady Juliet (1881–1965), 161, 165, 170, 178, 216, 222, 226, 235, 237, 238–9, 260, 261, 262, 289, 340, 344, 365, 397, 400, 414, 444; death, 502, 508

Duff, Bt, Sir Michael (1907–80), 165, 171–2, 173–4, 182, 201, 230, 315, 320 n, 327, 355, 439, 464, 574, 582 & n

Dufferin and Ava (Sheridan) 5th Marquess of (b. 1938), 505

Dufferin and Ava, Maureen, Marchioness of (b. 1907), 82, 98, 181–2, 439

Duke, Doris (b. 1912), 161, 406

du Maurier, Angela, 66, 79, 88

du Maurier, Dame Daphne (b. 1907), 79, 88

du Maurier, Sir Gerald (1873–1934), 79

Duncan, Isadora (1877–1927), 451, 531

Duncan, Ronald (1914–81), 349

Dunn, Lady (*now* Beaverbrook), 368

Dunn, Lady Mary (b. 1912), 60 n, 566

Dunn, Sir James (1874–1956), 368

Dunn, Bt, Sir Philip (1905–76), 59, 60 & n

Dunne, Eileen, 242

Dunphy, Jack, 416

Durham, 3rd Earl of (1855–1928), 105

Duse, Eleanora (1859–1924), 195 n

Duvivier, Julien (1896–1967), 308

Dylan, Bob (b. 1941), 497

Earp, T.W. (1892–1958), 141

Eccles, (David) 1st Viscount (b. 1905), 267

Eden, *see* Avon

Eden, Eleanor, 243

Edge, David, 445

Edinburgh, HRH Prince Philip, Duke of (b. 1921), 103, 217, 359, 367, 368, 435, 437–8, 454, 530, 546

Edward VIII, HM King, *see* Windsor, Duke of

Edward, HRH The Prince (b. 1964), 485

Egerton, Lady Anne (d. 1964), 103

Egerton, Lady Jane (*now* Scrope), 103

Eggar, Samantha (b. 1940), 419 n

Egypt, HM King Farouk of (1920–65), 256, 263 n, 264

Ekland, Britt (b. 1942), 506

Eliot, T.S. (1888–1965), 46, 95, 407

Elizabeth II, HM Queen (b. 1926), 268–9, 320 n, 340, 359, 367, 368, 369, 379–80, 395, 435, 437–9, 441, 454, 462, 485, 518, 525, 534–5, 552, 559, 562, 563, 569, 574

Elizabeth The Queen Mother, HM Queen (b. 1900), 60, 193, 196, 198; photographed by C (1939), 225–7, 227 n; 230, 231, 236–7, 244, 268–9, 310, 314, 339; photographed by C (1950), 346; 349; as Queen Mother, 367, 368, 369, 437, 440, 453–4, 459, 488, 490, 527, 536, 544, 545 & n, 551 & n, 561, 567; letters to C, 442, 458; lunches with C, 457–8, 520–21

Ellesmere, Violet, Countess of (1880–1977), 103–6, 110, 139

Elliott, Maxine (1871–1940), 160, 168, 215

Ellis, Ainsley, 528, 587

Elsie, Lily (d. 1962), 9–11, 120–21, 252, 272, 278; death 449; 463

Elsom, Isobel (1893–1980), 13, 54, 463–4, 464 n

Elton, A/V/M. John (b. 1905), 256

Elvey, Maurice (1887–1967), 307

Emerson, John (1872–1956), 122, 124–6, 128–9, 131, 133

Engelhard, Mrs Charles (Jane), 466

Englebrecht, 34, 103

Ensor, Aubrey, 15, 463, 507, 561

Epstein, Sir Jacob (1880–1959), 90, 435

Erickson, Carl, 112

Errazuriz, Madame, 373

Erté (b. 1893), 553

Ervine, St John (1888–1971), 32

Escande, Maurice, 450

Etherington-Smith, Meredith, 580–81

Euston, Hugh Earl of (Duke of Grafton) (b. 1919), 275

Evans, Dame Edith (1888–1976), 9, 269–70

Evans, Laurence, 353

Evans, 1st Lord (1903–63), 439

Everly, Mr, 323

Faber, Anne (*now* Cockerell), 453 & n

Fairbanks, Jr, Douglas (b. 1907), 204, 368

Fairfax, James, 520

Faithfull, Marianne (b. 1947), 510, 513

Faucigny-Lucinge, Prince Jean-Louis de, 548

Faucigny-Lucinge, Princesse Jean-Louis de (Baba), 58, 73

Fearnley-Whittingstall, Tecia, *see* Chattock

Fearnley-Whittingstall, Frank (1894–1945), 168

Feder, Abe, 388

Fell-Clark, Gordon (1903–45), 23, 25

Fellowes, Hon. Mrs Reginald (Daisy) (d. 1962), 120, 160, 161, 166, 167, 215–16, 413, 414, 443

Ferguson, Lady, 45

Fergusson, Sir Bernard (*later* Lord Ballantrae) (1911–80), 284

Fermor, *see* Leigh Fermor

Fermoy, Ruth Lady (b. 1908), 490

Ferrer, José (b. 1912), 301

Ferrer, Mel (b. 1917), 415, 474, 484

Feversham, 3rd Earl of (Sim) (1906–63), 98 & n

Février, Jacques, 397

Field, Audrey (1902–68), 180

Fielding, Hon. Mrs Daphne (*formerly* Marchioness of Bath) (b. 1904), 162, 165

Fielding, Fenella (b. 1934), 563

Finn, Christine, 419 n

Firbank, Ann, 419

Firbank, Ronald (1886–1926), 5, 220

Fish, Michael, 551

FitzGerald, Captain Hon. and Mrs Evelyn, 97

Flanagan, Bud (1896–1968), 243

Fleet, Simon (1913–66), 237–8, 322, 414, 500, 502, 508–9

Fleitman, Mrs, 110

Fleming, Caspar (1952–75), 358

Fleming, Ian (1906–64), 236

Fleming, Mrs Ian (Ann) (*formerly* Viscountess Rothermere) (1913–81), 236, 344, 349, 358, 401, 428, 492, 571

Flemyng, Robert (b. 1912), 375

Fletcher, Cyril, 279

Fletcher, Sir Walter (1892–1956), 287–8

Flick Hoffman, Mrs Eleanor, 217

Fontanne, Lynn (1887–1983), 118–19, 299, 313, 337, 357–9, 406

Fonteyn, Dame Margot (b. 1919), 187, 188, 413, 445, 459, 518, 521, 561

Forbes, Alastair (b. 1918), 448, 475, 548, 577, 581

Ford, Charles Henri, 175–6, 183, 206, 218, 237

Ford, Ruth (b. 1920), 175, 205, 206, 534, 552

Forsythe, Robert, 212

Foss, George, 163

Fouts, Denham (d. 1948), 178, 201, 397, 478, 479

Fowler, Norman, 396 & n, 398

Fox, Edward (b. 1937), 564

Fox, James (b. 1939), 528

Francis, Hugh, 240, 241, 267, 282, 288

Francis, Kay (1899–1968), 130, 262

Francis, Noel, 117

Frankau, Capt. Gilbert (1884–1952), 139–40

Fraser, John, 78

Fraser, Robert (d. 1986), 510–12, 512 n, 513

Freeborn, Major E.W. (1874–1945), 21–2, 25–6

Freeborn, Mrs E.W., 21

Freed, Arthur (1894–1973), 409, 475

Freedom, Mr, 552

Freeman, Rt Hon. John (b. 1915), 14, 447–8

Freud, Lucian (b. 1922), 337, 370, 397, 398, 413, 428

Frost, David (b. 1939), 447

Fry, Charles (d. 1958), 58, 84, 89, 203, 204, 267

Fry, Jeremy, 436

Fry, Roger (1866–1934), 33, 53

Furness, Thelma Viscountess (1904–70), 193
Furtwängler, Wilhelm (1886–1954), 210

Gabor, Eva (b. 1921), 393, 407, 410
Gabor, Zsa Zsa (b. 1919), 393
Gaffran, Charlotte, 571
Gage, Sir Berkeley (b. 1904), 403
Gage, 6th Viscount (1895–1982), 57
Gainsbourg, Serge, 559
Gandarillas, Baron Tony de (d. 1970), 184, 230, 445
Garbo, Greta (b. 1905), xxviii–ix; Cecil's quest to photo, 122, 128, 130–31; in *Book of Beauty*, 141; meets C (1932), 158–9; and *Scrapbook*, 203, 204, 356, 376–7; 2nd meeting with C (1946), 302; C proposes, 303; 1946 romance, 302–4; passport drama, 304–5; silence, 306; affair with C, 312–32; background, 312–14; C writes to, 314–16; in London, 315; C contacts, 316–17; the love affair – in NY, 317–29; in California, 329–32; C writes to, 334–5, 337–9, 341, 350–52, 358; meets C in Paris, 342–4; meets C in NY, 344–5, 348; becomes American citizen, 348; C discusses marriage, 349; in Bermuda, 352; contemplates visit to C, 353; stays with C at Broadchalke, 354–5; in Paris with C, 355; cools relationship, 355–6, 359; uneasy times with C, 375–6; major row with C, 376–7; reconciliation with C, 391; C meets in Paris 398; in London with C, 398–400; C considers impossible, 427; *re* June, 429 & *n*; on Greek cruise (1965), 498, 499–500; and Schlee's death, 498–9; C publishes diaries about, 557–9, 563, 564–6, 568; visits C (1975), 577–8; refuses to see C, 578; mentioned, 98 *n*, 125, 134, 139, 151, 350 & *n*, 364, 397, 407, 410, 416, 436, 444, 460, 462, 465 *n*, 466, 473, 481, 505, 523, 531, 539, 542, 552, 570, 585
Garland, Madge (*later* Lady Ashton), 53, 67, 70, 79, 80, 83, 84, 89, 116, 210, 215, 528
Garland, Patrick (b. 1935), 531
Garson, Greer (b. 1908), 306
Gathorne-Hardy, Hon. Edward (1901–78), 89–90
Gathorne-Hardy, Hon. Robert (1902–73), 29, 101 *n*
Gausbeck, Beatrice, 549
Gellibrand, Paula (Marquise de Casa Maury, *now* Mrs Long), 51–2, 90, 100, 101, 112, 114, 155, 572

Geoghegan, minor, 15
George, Prince, *see* Kent, Duke of
George V, HM King (1865–1936), 103, 183, 188
George VI, HM King (1895–1952), 198, 224, 226, 230, 237, 268–9, 292, 320 *n*, 339, 357, 442
Gibbs, Christopher (b. 1938), 502, 513, 528
Gibson, Miss, 75
Gide, André (1869–1951), 59
Gielgud, Sir John (b. 1904), 47, & *n*, 84, 270, 299–300, 305, 338, 351, 369, 374, 385 & *n*, 401, 532, 560
Gilbert, John (1895–1936), 120, 125, 128
Giles, Frank (b. 1919), 523
Giraudoux, Jean (1882–1944), 217
Gish, Lillian (b. 1896), xxvi, 115, 126, 134, 151
Givenchy, Baron Hubert de, 453, 471
Gladstone, Lady (Rosamund Hambro) (b. 1939), 178 *n*
Gladwyn, *see* Noble
Glanville, Professor Hugh, 575
Glenconner, Pamela Lady, *see* Grey
Glendevon, Lady (Liza) (b. 1915), 113
Glenville, Peter (b. 1913), 219, 351, 415, 517
Gloucester, HRH Princess Alice, Duchess of (b. 1901): letter to C, 196; 198, 215, 250, 441, 453 *n*
Gloucester, HRH The Duke of (1900–74), 368, 441
Gloucester, HRH Prince William of (1941–72), 320 *n*, 441
Glubb, Lt-Gen. Sir John (b. 1897), 264–5
Glyn, Elinor (1864–1943), 22
Glyn, Gertrude, 10
Goddard, Paulette (b. 1911), 281, 307–8, 309
Goebbels, Joseph, 215, 292
Goetz, William (1903–69), 404
Goetz, Mrs William (Edie), 404, 465, 470
Gold, Jack (b. 1904), 22, 29, 59–60, 77–8, 584
Goldman, Milton, 542
Goldschmidt-Rothschild, Baron Eric (b. 1894), 358
Goldsmid, Baroness, 54
Goldsmith, Isabel (b. 1954), 580
Goldsmith, Sir James (b. 1933), 581
Goldwyn, Mrs Sam, 207
Goodman, Francis, 484
Goodman, Lord (b. 1913), 525
Gopal, Ram (b. 1920), 281
Gordon, John (1890–1974), 340

Gordon, Ruth (1896–1985), 321–2, 330, 334 & *n*, 350, 351–2

Gordon-Moore, Peggy, 65, 82, 88

Gottfried, Dr, 444, 462

Gould, Len, 354, 355

Goulding, Edmund (1891–1959), 158 & *n*, 159

Goulding, Mrs Edmund (Marjorie Moss), 158 & *n*, 159

Gounod, 450

Grace, Princess, *see* Monaco

Grafton, *see* Euston

Grant, Duncan (1885–1978), 44, 515

Grant, William, 578, 580–82, 585

Graves, Charles (1884–1971), 139 & *n*

Gray, Dulcie (b. 1919), 299

Gray, Edith (1887–1965), 118

Gray, Sally (b. 1915), 243

Grayson, Col Tristram (1902–84), 21, 23

Greece, *see* Edinburgh *and* Spain

Greece, HRH Prince Andrew of (1882–1944), 103

Greece, HRH Princess Andrew of (1885–1969), 103

Greece, HM Queen Anne Marie of (b. 1946), 513

Greece, Princess Aspasia of (1896–1972), 103, 217

Greece, HRH Princess Cecilie of, *see* Hesse

Greece, HM King Constantine of (b. 1940), 513

Greece, HM Queen Frederica of (1917–81), 513

Greece, HM King George II of (1890–1947), 107

Greece, HRH Princess Irene of (b. 1942), 513

Greece, Princess Peter of (b. 1904), 264

Green, Ada, 341

Green, Ferida, 341

Green, Jessie, 223, 341

Green, Mitzi (1920–69), 128 & *n*

Green, Samuel Adams, 505, 536, 543–4, 546, 568, 570, 577, 578

Gregory, Maundy (d. 1941), 147

Grenfell, Granville, 14

Grenfell, Joyce (1910–79), 278, 385

Grès, Madame, 551

Grey of Falloden, 1st Viscount (1862–1933), 85, 105 *n*

Grey of Falloden, Viscountess (Pamela) (1800–1929), 85–6, 90–91, 95–6, 501

Griffith-Jones, Mark, 47

Grimes, Tammy (b. 1934), 552

Grimsdale, Maj.-Gen. Gordon, 282, 283–6

Gross, John (b. 1935), 448

Groult, Nicole, 67

Grove, Sir Gerald, 170

Grundy, Sydney, 372

Guedalla, Philip (1889–1944), 36, 48

Guest, Mrs Winston (Cee Zee), 577

Guinness, *see* Dufferin *and* Mosley

Guinness, Sir Alec (b. 1914), 504, 561

Guinness, Mrs Benjamin (d. 1931), 82–3, 84, 97

Guinness, Loel (b. 1906), 341, 543

Guinness, Mrs Loel (Gloria) (1913–80), 543, 577 *n*

Guinness, Meraud (b. 1904), 85–7

Guinness, Mrs Richard (Beatrice) (d. 1942), 82

Guinness, Tanis (Mrs Edward Phillips), 84, 85–7

Gunning, Anne (Lady Nutting), 410

Gunther, John (1901–70), 376 & *n*, 499

Gunther, Mrs John (Jane), 376 & *n*

Gunzburg, Baron Nicolas de, 154, 325

Gurton, Ray, 506, 515, 518, 531, 545, 558–9

Guthrie, Sir Tyrone (1900–71), 351

Gutierrez-Pons, Madame, 53, 54

Haddon, Dayle, 580

Hahn, Reynaldo (1875–1947), 450

Hale, Binnie (1899–1984), 55

Halifax, (Dorothy) Countess of (1885–1976), 248

Halifax, 1st Earl of (1881–1959), 98, 240

Hall, David (Buck), 472

Hall, Sir Peter (b. 1930), 411, 415, 421–2

Hall, Stanley, 506

Halle, Kay, 207

Hambleden, (Patricia) Dowager Viscountess of (b. 1904), 98

Hambro, *see* Beaton

Hambro, Alec (1910–43), 163, 173, 178 & *n*

Hambro, Capt. Angus (1883–1957), 178

Hambro, Eric, 260

Hammerstein, Mrs Oscar, 534

Handl, Irene (b. 1902), 532

Handley-Derry, Major Leo, 283, 285, 287

Hankin, St John (1869–1909), 388

Hansen, Waldemar, 305, 371, 372–3, 391, 393–4, 395, 398, 406, 415–16, 425, 443, 479

Harbord, Felix (d. 1981), 256, 532, 567, 585

Harding, Gilbert (1907–60), 447–8

Harding, Laura, 383

Hardy, Laurence, 352

Harewood, 7th Earl of (b. 1923), 551

Harlech, Lady (d. 1967), 512, 513
Harper, Allanah (b. 1904), 36, 58–9, 67, 69–70, 80–81, 83, 84
Harper, Kenneth, 505
Harris, Julie (b. 1925), 407, 415
Harris, Karen (d. 1964), 178
Harris, Lady, 230
Harrison, Major, 298
Harrison, Rex (b. 1908), 243, 299, 387, 389 & n, 391, 392 & n, 394, 395, 414, 464, 468, 470, 471, 473, 515
Harrison Williams, *see* Bismarck
Harrison Williams, Mr, 111, 181, 323
Harrod, Henry (b. 1939), 490
Hart, Derek, 516, 517
Hart, Moss (1904–61), 391, 393, 394, 395
Hartman, Ake (d. 1977), 283 & n, 284
Hartnell, Sir Norman (1901–79), 27, 34, 35–6, 46, 196, 226, 527, 552
Hartwell, *see* Berry
Harty, Russell, 577
Harvey, Laurence (1929–73), 407
Harvey, Sir Oliver and Lady, 355
Haslam, Nicholas (b. 1939), 530, 543
Hauser, Gayelord (d. 1984), 312–13, 359
Haw-Haw, Lord (William Joyce) (1904–46), 265
Hay, Sir Philip (b. 1900), 441
Hayes, Helen (b. 1900), 164
Hayward, Leland (1902–71), 415, 534
Head, 1st Viscount (1906–83), 449, 585
Head, Viscountess (b. 1907), 82, 449, 585
Hearst, William Randolph (1863–1951), 129–30, 154, 159
Heath, Rt Hon. Edward (b. 1916), 433–4, 545, 569–70
Heber-Percy, Robert (b. 1911), 168, 171–2, 566, 570–71
Heber-Percy, Victoria (*now* Zinovieff), 439
Heinz, Mrs H. J., 565
Helena Victoria, HH Princess (1870–1948), 320 n
Helpmann, Sir Robert (b. 1909), 187, 519
Henderson, William (Billy), 275, 278, 281, 291, 582
Henley, Hon. Mrs Sylvia (1882–1980), 552
Henry, Victor, 512
Hepburn, Audrey (b. 1929), xxv, 408, 461, 463, 467–74, 476, 484–5, 489, 490, 529, 551, 559, 568
Hepburn, Katharine (b. 1909), 203, 313, 330, 353, 383, 529, 534, 537, 538–42, 550
Hepworth, Dame Barbara (1903–75), 454
Herbage, Mr, 32
Herbert, *see* Pembroke
Herbert, Hon. David (b. 1908), xxviii, 98, 147, 165, 170, 171, 173–4, 182, 191, 192, 202, 213, 215–16, 221, 222–3, 230, 236, 238, 310, 315, 335, 341–2, 366 n, 445, 485, 512, 547, 567, 571, 577
Herlie, Eileen (b. 1919), 346
Herring, Robert (1903–75), 70, 79, 89
Hesketh, Christian Lady (b. 1929), 520
Hesse, HSH Grand Duke of (1906–37), 196
Hesse, HSH Grand Duchess of (Princess Cecilie) (1911–37), 103, 196
Hewlett, Maurice (1861–1923), 311 & n
Hiatt, Joe, 470
Hicks, Sir Seymour (1871–1949), 66 & n
Hill, Derek (b. 1916), 204, 537, 571
Hill, John, 30, 78
Hiller, Dame Wendy (b. 1912), 243, 299
Hine, W. Egerton (d. 1926), 21, 370
Hinks, Roger (1903–63), 31
Hirschfeld, 567
Hitchcock, Sir Alfred (1899–1980), 327 & n
Hitler, Adolf (1899–1945), 208, 211, 216, 218, 220, 222, 227, 237, 245, 292
Hoare, Gerald, 55
Hobson, Anthony and Tanya, 512
Hockney, David (b. 1937), 491, 504, 505, 527, 534, 536, 544, 547
Hodgkin, Eliot (b. 1905), 22
Hogg, Teddy (E.S.) (b. 1901), 29
Hokinson, Helen E., 364
Holden, Inez, 80, 83
Holloway, Stanley (1890–1982), 461, 464, 470, 475, 559
Hope-Wallace, Philip (1911–79), 300
Hopkin, Mary (b. 1950), 525
Hopper, Hedda (1890–1966), 474
Hordern, Sir Michael (b. 1911), 512
Horner, David (1901–84), 183 & n
Horner, Miss, 104
Horst, Horst P. (b. 1906), 167, 185, 202, 543, 559–60, 580
Horstmann, Lalli and Freddy, 186
Horton, Robert (1903–24), 22
Hose, Eileen (b. 1919), xviii, xxi, xxii, xxiii, 366–7, 371, 379, 388, 389, 391, 394, 397, 398–9, 400–401, 404, 408, 415; on C's finances, 417, 483; 422, 430, 435, 437, 440, 448, 449, 456, 457, 459, 460, 461, 468, 470, 471, 486, 487, 492, 505, 507, 508, 516, 518, 519, 521, 524, 538, 546, 549, 558, 559, 560, 568, 569, 571, 574–80, 583, 585, 588

Houseman, John (b. 1902), 206
Howard, Brian (1905–58), 58, 84–5, 86, 89 & *n*, 90, 99, 220, 271
Howard, Leslie (1893–1943), 220
Howard, Ronald, 352
Howard, Sydney (1885–1946), 115, 300
Howe, *see* Curzon
Hoyningen-Huene, Baron George (1900–68), 167, 173, 180, 202, 221, 501
Hudson, Bt, Sir Austin (1897–1956), 29 *n*
Hugo, Jean (1895–1984), 397
Hull (Helen Astor), Mrs Lytle, 218, 418
Humphries, Barry (b. 1934), 520
Hunt, Martita (1900–69), 308
Hurst, Brian Desmond (b. 1900), 243
Hutchinson, *see* Osborn
Hutchinson of Lullington, Lord (Jeremy) (b. 1915), 434 & *n*
Hutchinson, Mary St John, 567
Hutton, Barbara (1913–79), 445
Hutton, Edward, 311
Huxley, Aldous (1894–1963), 501
Hyderabad, HIH The Nizam of (1886–1967), 280
Hyde White, Wilfrid (b. 1903), 470, 471, 472, 473, 506
Hynchcliffe, Mr, 14
Hyson, Dorothy (Lady Quayle) (b. 1918), 299

Ipi, Fakir, 279
Iraq, HM King Faisal II (1935–58), 263–4
Iraq, Regent of (Abd al Ilah) (1914–58), 263–4
Ironside, FM Lord (1880–1959), 239–40
Irwin, John, XXVI, 290
Isaac, H.F. (Fred), 559
Isherwood, Christopher (1904–86), 178, 337, 411, 465, 477, 478–80, 501, 516
Ismail, Sir Miras (1883–1959), 281
Italy, HRH Princess Maria Pia of (b. 1934), 378, 417
Italy, HM Queen Marie-Jose of (b. 1906), 378
Italy, HM King Umberto of (1904–83), 74, 378

Jagger, Bianca (b. 1943), 568, 578, 580
Jagger, Mick (b. 1943), 510–12, 512 *n*, 513, 528–9, 578
Jaipur, HIH The Maharanee of, 281
Jaipur, HIH The Maharajah of (1911–70), 281

James, Charles (1906–78), 22, 116, 118, 134, 149, 218, 372, 395, 552, 567–8; death, 579
James, Edward (1907–84), 183 *n*, 552
James, Henry (1843–1916), 375
James, Adm. Sir William (1881–1973), 248
Janis, Elsie (1889–1956), 127, 131
Janze, Countesse Phyllis de (1894–1943), 373
Jeans, Isabel (1891–1985), 269, 299, 300, 305, 410, 411, 463, 506, 512, 563
Jeffress, Arthur (1904–61), 22 & *n*
Jenkinson, Anthony, 60
Jessie, Aunt, *see* Suarez
Jimmy, 134–5
John, Augustus (1878–1961), 70, 250, 354–5, 447
John, Admiral of the Fleet Sir Caspar (1903–84), 250
John, Elizabeth (Poppet) (b. 1912), 238
Johnson, Amy (1903–41), 140
Johnson, Lynda Bird (b. 1944), 515
Johnson, Mrs Lyndon B. (b. 1912), 543
Johnson, President Lyndon B. (1908–73), 542
Johnston, (Natasha) Lady (1914–84), 520
Johnston, Sir Charles (b. 1912), 520
Johnstone, Johnnie, 383
Jones, *see* Bagnold
Jones, Brian (1942–69), 510–12, 512 *n*, 513
Jones, Jennifer (Mrs David O. Selznick) (b. 1919), 375, 382
Jones, Sir Roderick (1877–1962), XXVIII, 270
Jordan, HM King Husain of (b. 1935), 264
Joseph, Dorothy (d. 1983), 141 & *n*, 195, 200, 240
Jourdan, Louis (b. 1919), 409, 410, 411–12
June, *see* Osborn
Jungman, Teresa ('Baby') (Mrs Cuthbertson), 70, 81, 82, 84, 88, 90–91
Jungman, Zita (Mrs Arthur James), 58, 67, 70, 74–5, 81, 82, 84, 88, 90–91

Kahn, Otto (1867–1934), 109
Kahn, Mrs Otto, 135
Kanin, Garson (b. 1912), 321–2, 330, 334, 350, 351–2
Kargere, Jocelyn, 580
Karinska, Madame (d. 1983), 187 & *n*, 188, 190, 201, 309, 349, 389, 393, 408, 450
Katsina, Usman Nagogo, 10th Emir of, 449
Kauffman, Stanley, 412
Kaufman, Al, 127
Kawabata, Yasunari (1899–1972), 404
Kaye, Danny (b. 1913), 543

Keaton, Buster (1895–1966), 130
Keel, Howard (b. 1919), 421 & *n*
Kelly, Sir Gerald (1879–1972), 269
Kelly, Grace, *see* Monaco
Kemsley, 1st Viscount (1883–1968), 306
Kemble-Cooper, Lily, 463
Kendall, Kay (Mrs Rex Harrison) (1927–59), 414
Kennedy, Caroline (b. 1957), 491
Kennedy, John (b. 1960), 491
Kennedy, President John F. (1917–63)́, 441, 456, 474, 577 *n*
Kennedy, Mrs John F. (Jackie Onassis) (b. 1929), 451, 462, 474, 491, 520, 522
Kennedy, Ludovic (b. 1919), 268
Kennedy, Senator Robert (1925–68), 522, 535 *n*
Kennedy, Mrs Rose (b. 1890), 548
Kent, HRH The Duchess of (Katharine) (b. 1933), 440–41, 552–3
Kent, HRH The Duke of (Edward) (b. 1935), 368, 435, 440–41
Kent, HRH The Duke of (George) (1902–42), 164, 196–7, 202, 216, 239, 250, 268, 407, 440
Kent, HRH Princess Marina, Duchess of (1906–68),, 193, 196–8, 202 & *n*, 216, 225, 230, 236, 239, 268, 320 *n*, 335–6, 339, 340, 346, 368, 407, 413, 437, 439–40, 441, 485, 512, 521, 526, 527; death, 523; letter to C, 517
Kent, HRH Prince Michael of (b. 1942), 268, 320 *n*, 368
Kent, HRH Princess Michael of (b. 1945), 582
Kenyon, Lord (b. 1917), 524
Kerr, Deborah (b. 1921), 243, 270, 272
Kerr, Walter, 417, 422
Kerridge, Mary (Mrs John Counsell) (b. 1914), 308
Keynes, 1st Lord (Maynard) (1883–1946), 42, 44
Khill, Marcel (k. 1940), 189
Kin (b. 1934), XXVIII, 466 & *n*, 477–94, 498, 500, 503, 507, 516, 520, 522–3, 529, 531, 536, 543–4, 557, 566, 576
Kinross, (Patrick) Lord (1904–76), 129, 151, 262, 414, 452
Kirkpatrick, Nigel, 18
Kirstein, Lincoln (b. 1907), 97, 305, 345, 349, 535
Klee, Paul (1879–1940), 345
Klossowski de Rola, Prince Stanislas, 513
'Knickerbocker, Suzy', 512, 534–5
Knoblock, Edward (1874–1945), 115

Knollys, Eardley, 29
Koch, Howard W. (b. 1916), 530, 533–4
Kochno, Boris (b. 1904), 180, 190, 314, 344, 450
Kommer, Dr Rudolf (Kaetchen) (d. 1943), 112 & *n*, 210–11, 212, 214, 217 *n*, 222, 262
Korda, Sir Alexander (1893–1956), 224, 307–10, 316, 327, 328, 330, 338, 462
Korda, Vincent (1897–1979), 307
Kramer, Hilton, 535, 568
Krawitz, Herman, 425
Kung, Dr, 288
Kyrssa, 505

Lacretelle, Jacques de (b. 1888), 217, 341
Lafaille, Comtesse de, 341–2
Lamb, Mrs Michael (Alexandra Hambro) (b. 1935), 178 *n*
Lambe, Charles, 31
Lambert, Constant (1905–51), 80, 188, 518
Lambert, Eleanor, 195 & *n*, 212, 215, 224, 241, 291–2, 421, 552
Lambert, Gavin (b. 1924), 475
Lambert, J. W. (b. 1917), 498
Lambourne, Lord (1847–1928), 105
Lambton, Lady, 413, 414, 488
Lambton, Lady Lucinda (b. 1943), 462, 482, 490, 522
Lambton, Lord (b. 1922), 106, 581
Lampson, Sir Miles (Lord Killearn) (1880–1946), 262, 274
Lampson, Lady (Jacqueline, Lady Killearn), 262, 274
Lancaster, Sir Osbert (b. 1908), 178, 230, 251, 300, 515, 568
Landsberg, Bertie, 73
Langley-Moore, Doris, 253
Langtry, Lillie (1852–1929), 141
Lascelles, Sir Alan (1887–1981), 65
Lasker, Mary, 425, 534, 542
Laski, Marghanita (b. 1915), 230
Latta, Lady, 37 & *n*, 63
Laughton, Charles (1899–1962), 415
Laurençin, Marie (1885–1956), 67, 101, 120
Laver, James (1899–1975), 338
Lavery, Hazel (d. 1935), 25, 51, 110
Lavine, Robert, 552, 578
Lawford, Valentine (Nicholas), 543
Lawrence, Gertrude (1898–1952), 118, 135, 162, 211, 317, 352; death 357; 528
Laycock, Maj.-Gen. Sir Robert (1907–68), 98
Lazar, Irving Paul (Swifty), 461, 470, 472
Lazenby, George (b. 1939), 533

Leahy, Dr, 177
Le Bas, Edward (Boy) (1904–66), 21–2, 24, 30–31, 35, 40–41, 43–5, 57, 61, 67, 71, 72 & n, 78
Le Bas, Gwen (k. 1944), 12, 290
Le Bas, Molly, 12, 72 n
Le Bas, Mr and Mrs, 37, 54, 56, 59, 61
Ledebur, Graf Friedrich von, 498–500
Lee of Ashbridge, Baroness (b. 1904), 528
Lees-Milne, James (b. 1908), 268, 271, 561, 588
Lehár, Franz (1870–1948), 10
Leigh, Vivien (1913–67), 207 n, 253, 301, 308–9, 338–9, 351, 401, 418, 506
Leigh Fermor, Patrick (b. 1915), xxvII, 163, 414
Leighton, Margaret (b. 1922), 299
Lelong, Lucien (1889–1958), 99, 167 n
Leng, Kyrle (d. 1958), 29–31, 33, 40, 78, 81, 95, 101 & n, 172 n
Lenin (1870–1924), 186
Lerner, Alan Jay (b. 1918), xxI, xxIV–v, 66, 386, 392, 408, 411–12, 422, 461–2, 468, 475, 529–30, 534, 538–41
Leslie, Anita (1914–85), 106
Levin, Herman (b. 1907), 386, 387, 388–9, 392, 578
Lewis, Robert, 356
Liberman, Alexander (b. 1912), 271, 292, 303, 503, 517, 533, 537
Lichfield, 5th Earl of (b. 1939), 436, 515, 533, 547, 553
Lichter, Mort, 471, 472
Liehm, A.J., 516
Lifar, Serge (b. 1905), 76, 160, 500, 568
Lilias, Aunt, *see* Beaton, Mrs Reginald
Lillie, Beatrice (Lady Peel) (b. 1894), 51, 270
Li Mo-an, General, 284–5
Li Mo-an, Madame, 284–5
Lindbergh, Charles (1902–74), 109
Linklater, Major Eric (1899–1974), 270, 278, 564
Linlithgow, (Doreen) Marchioness of (1886–1965), 275
Linn, Mrs Howard, 158
Lippincott, Joseph, 214
Little Bo Bitch, 581
Livesey, Roger (1906–76), 418
Lloyd Thomas, Penelope, 307
Lockyer, Chief Inspector Frank, 577
Loewe, Fritz (b. 1901), 66, 386, 408
Logan, Joshua (b. 1908), 342, 401–2, 404, 405, 534
Logan, Mrs Joshua (Nedda), 342, 401–2, 404, 405, 534

Lohr, Marie (1890–1975), 369
Long, Ray, 135
Longman, Robert, 70
Lonsdale, 5th Earl of (1857–1944), 102
Lonsdale, Frederick (1881–1954), 211, 270, 369
Loos, Anita (1888–1981), 118, 120, 121, 122–6, 128–36, 139, 148, 149, 153, 241, 251–2, 321–2, 351, 372, 443, 517–18, 540–41, 579, 585
Lopokova, Lydia (Lady Keynes) (1892–1981), 33, 353
Losch, Tilly (Countess of Carnarvon) (1903–75), 100, 120, 134, 157, 165, 176, 183 & n, 184, 230, 341
Loubet, President Emile (1838–1929), 439
Lovat Fraser, Claud (1890–1921), 45 & n
Love, Bessie (b. 1898), 128
Lowe, Edmund (1892–1971), 130
Lowell, *see* Blackwood
Lowndes, Elizabeth Belloc (Countess of Iddesleigh), 104
Lowry, McNeil, 535
Lowthian, Alice, 3–4
Lubitsch, Ernst (1892–1947), 127 & n
Lucas, Topsy (d. 1966), 33, 34, 35, 46, 64
Luce, Hon. Clare Boothe (b. 1903), 206, 211, 214, 262
Luce, Henry (1898–1967), 211
Lunt, Alfred (1893–1977), 118–19, 337, 357–8, 406, 425, 485
Lycett Green, Rupert (b. 1938), 503
Lygon, Lady Mary (1910–82), 373–4
Lynn, Olga (1882–1961), 82, 160, 238, 240, 306 & n, 464, 480

Macaulay, Dame Rose (1881–1958), 379
MacCarthy, Sir Desmond (1877–1952), 293
McCarthy, Lillah (Lady Keeble) (1875–1960), 463
McCarthy, Mary (b. 1912), 378
McCowen, Alec (b. 1925), 525
McCullers, Carson (b. 1917–67), 337
Macdonald, Mrs, 186–7
MacGregor, Helen, 53, 69, 83, 95
McIlhenny, Henry, 537
McKenna, Siobhan (b. 1923), 384
Mackenzie, Sir Compton (1883–1972), 22
McLaren, Christabel, *see* Aberconway
Maclean, Hon. Lady (Veronica) (b. 1920), 488
Macmillan, Rt Hon. Harold (1st Earl of Stockton) (b. 1894), 399, 570
McMullin, Johnnie (1889–1944), 166 & n, 211, 215

Macpherson, Aimée Semple, 128
Mainbocher, 180
Mann, Cathleen (Marchioness of Queens-berry) (1897–1959), 176
Manning, Olivia (1915–80), 260
Marais, Jean (b. 1913), 189, 221
Marbury, Elisabeth (d. 1933), 110, 111, 114, 151 & n
Margadale, the Lady (1908–80), xxi
Margaret, Countess of Snowdon, HRH The Princess (b. 1930), 268–9, 340, 349, 355, 369, 403, 407, 432, 435–7, 440, 454, 459, 460, 486, 490–91, 518, 561
Mariano, Nicky (1887–1968), 366
Marie Louise, HH Princess (1872–1956), 320 n, 340
Marina, HRH Princess, see Kent, Duchess of
Markévitch, Igor (1912–83), 397
Markova, Dame Alicia (b. 1910), 306
Marlborough, Gladys Duchess of (1881–1977), xxi, 99–100
Marlborough, Laura Duchess of (b. 1915), 448, 505, 570
Marlborough, (Mary) Duchess of (1900–61), 196
Marlborough, 9th Duke of (1871–1934), 52
Marlborough, 10th Duke of (1897–1972), 451
Marre, Albert, 383
Marriott, Lady (Momo) (d. 1960), 261, 413
Marriott, Maj.-Gen. Sir John (1895–1978), 261, 413
Marshall, Norman (1901–80), 352
Marshall, Tom, 43
Mary, HM Queen (1867–1953), 101, 104, 183, 197, 198, 230, 320 n, 552, 553
Mary, (Princess Royal) HRH Princess (1897–1965), 96, 107, 380, 407, 553
Marx Brothers, The, 158
Mason, James (1909–84), 343
Massari, Fritzi (1882–1969), 465, 530
Massenet, Jules (1842–1912), 450
Matthews, A.E. (1869–1960), 300
Matthews, Sir Stanley (b. 1915), 401 & n
Maugham, Liza, see Glendevon
Maugham, Syrie (1879–1955), 102–3, 110, 112, 160, 218, 489, 557 n
Maugham, 2nd Viscount (Robin) (1916–81), 519
Maugham, W. Somerset (1874–1965), 110, 115, 221, 340–41, 351, 489
Mauriac, François (1885–1970), 217
Maxwell, Elsa (d. 1963), 160, 305, 322, 327, 413, 424, 453, 519

Mayer, Louis B. (1885–1957), xxvii, 204
Mehta, Jamna Das, 275
Mendelssohn, Eleanora von, 191
Mendelssohn, Francesco von, 165
Mendl, Lady (Elsie de Wolfe) (1865–1950), 110, 111, 116–17, 155, 161, 166, 194, 215, 218, 306, 310, 330, 337, 418
Mendl, Sir Charles (1871–1958), 330
Mennin, Peter, 535
Menotti, Gian-Carlo (b. 1911), 407
Merchant, Vivien (Mrs Harold Pinter) (1929–82), 512
Mérode, Cléo de (1881–1966), 450–51
Merryman, Mrs Bessie (1864–1964), 194
Messel, Oliver (1904–78), xxvii, 82, 84–5, 97, 98, 109, 115, 129, 148–50, 152, 154–5, 160–61, 171, 194, 219, 225, 278, 300, 301, 349, 354, 399, 414, 436, 440, 484, 504, 505, 579, 588
Metcalfe, Lady Alexandra (b. 1904), 564
Michelham, (Bertha) Lady (d. 1961), 427
Milbanke, Sheila Lady (1898–1969), 100
Milbanke, Bt, Sir Ralph (Toby) (1907–49), 106 & n, 107
Milford Haven, (Nada) Marchioness of (1896–1963), 70
Millar, Gertie (Countess of Dudley) (1879–1952), 10, 11
Miller, Gilbert (1884–1969), 131, 322, 413, 487
Miller, Mrs Gilbert (Kitty) (1900–79), 124, 131–3, 322, 325, 413, 566, 582
Miller, Lee (Lady Penrose) (d. 1977), 398
Mills, Sir John (b. 1908), 243
Mills, Juliet (b. 1941), 506
Milnes-Gaskell, Lady Constance (1885–1964), 320 n
Minnelli, Vincente (b. 1913), 408, 409, 410, 533
Minster, Jack (d. 1966), 418–20
Minto, The Countess of (d. 1940), 104
Mishima, Yukio (1925–70), 404
Mitchell, Julian (b. 1935), 507
Mitchell-Innes, Norma (b. 1896), 65
Mitford, Hon. Jessica (b. 1917), 452
Mitford, Hon. Nancy (1904–73), 86, 97, 256 n, 271, 371, 373, 374 n, 379, 524, 546, 551, 560, death, 567
Mitford, Hon. Unity (1914–48), 247
Mizner, Addison, 128, 131, 133
Mizner, Wilson, 128
Mlinaric, David, 515
Mo, 520
Moffat, Ivan (b. 1918), 238

Moffo, Anna (b. 1932), 425
Mohamed Ali, Prince (1875–1955), 256
Molyneux, Capt. Edward (1891–1974), 34
Monaco, HSH Princess Caroline of (b. 1957), 580
Monaco, HSH Princess Grace of (1928–82), 364, 415, 502, 522 n, 559
Monaco, HSH Princess Stephanie of (b. 1965), 502
Monckton of Brenchley, 1st Viscount (Walter) (1891–1965), 256, 261
Monroe, Marilyn (1926–62), 393, 394, 527
Monsell, Hon. Joan (Mrs Leigh Fermor), 163
Montagu, Judy (Mrs Milton Gendel) (1923–72), 240
Montagu-Douglas-Scott, Lady Alice, see Gloucester, Duchess of
Montagu-Douglas-Scott, Charmian (Mrs Stirling) (b. 1942), 439, 453 & n
Montgomery of Alamein, FM Viscount (1887–1976), 266
Moore, Grace (1901–47), 135
Moore, Henry (b. 1898), 374, 527
Moore, Kieron (b. 1925), 328
Moore, Marianne (1887–1972), 503
Moran, 1st Lord (1882–1977), 557
Morand, Paul (1889–1975), 217
Morley, Robert (b. 1908), 163, 254, 299, 415
Morosini, Countess, 216, 369–70
Morrell, Lady Ottoline (1873–1938), 52, 117
Morocco, HM King Hassan of (b. 1929), 485
Mortimer, Raymond (1895–1980), 67, 89, 204, 221, 250, 271, 443, 448, 458–9, 548, 551 & n, 560, 562
Morton, Digby (1906–83), 372
Mosley, Lady Cynthia (1898–1933), 103, 166
Mosley, Hon. Lady (Diana) (b. 1910), 106, 220
Mosley, Bt, Sir Oswald (1896–1980), 103, 220
Moss, Marjorie, see Goulding
Mountbatten of Burma, Countess (1901–60), 248, 276, 320 n, 553
Mountbatten of Burma, A.F. 1st Earl (1900–79), 180, 276, 290, 553, 561
Munroe, Mrs, 111
Munster, Frosca, 217
Murdoch, Mrs, 368
Murray, Mae (1889–1965), 453
Murphy, Charles, 348
Mussolini, Benito (1883–1945), 292
Myers, John, 237
Myers, John Bernard, 345, 363–4, 372

Myers, Richard, 352–3
Myers, Mrs Richard, 353

Nabokov, Nicolas (b. 1903), 182, 191, 195, 520
Nancy, see Beaton
Nast, see Brown
Nast, Condé (1873–1942), 53, 110, 111, 118–19, 126–7, 136, 151, 154, 157, 175, 186, 200, 208, 210–13, 215, 241, 242
Nast, Natica (Mrs Gerald F. Warburg) (b. 1905), 111–12
Neagle, Dame Anna (b. 1904), XXVI
Neal, Patricia (Mrs Roald Dahl) (b. 1926), 575
Nelson, Maud (d. 1969), 101, 240–41, 253, 270, 274, 303, 305, 306 n, 307, 310–11, 316, 338, 344, 346, 350, 352, 353, 354, 365–6, 366 n
Nesbitt, Cathleen (1888–1982), XXVIII, 51, 87, 307, 375, 388, 420, 465, 546–8, 561
Nesbitt, Robert, 13
Netherlands, HM Queen (now Princess) Juliana of the (b. 1909), 564
Nevelson, Louise, 579
Neville, John, 374
Neville-Willing, Major Donald, 281
Newall, A/C/M Sir Cyril (Lord) (1886–1963), 240
Niarchos, Charlotte Ford, 534
Niarchos, Mrs Stavros (Eugenie) (d. 1970), 414, 439, 445, 552
Niarchos, Stavros (b. 1909), 416, 445
Nichols, Beverley (1898–1983), 97–8, 109–10, 114, 115–16, 129, 139, 141, 412, 489, 519, 557, 564
Nicolson, Hon. Sir Harold (1886–1968), 247, 515
Nillson, Birgit (b. 1918), 423–4
Ninnie, see Collard
Noailles, Vicomte Charles de (1891–1981), 217
Noailles, Vicomtesse Marie-Laure de (1902–70), 215, 397, 445, 450
Noble, Cynthia (Lady Gladwyn), 84
Norden, Christine (b. 1924), 309
Norman, Barry (b. 1933), 475
Norrie, Lt-Gen. Lord (1893–1977), 259–60
Northumberland, Helen Duchess of (1887–1965), 196
Northumberland, 8th Duke of (1880–1930), 105
Norway, HM Queen Maud of (1869–1938), 230

Norwich, 2nd Viscount (b. 1929), 121, 309
Novak, Kim (b. 1933), 195 n
Novello, Ivor (1893–1951), 31, 39, 82, 270, 299, 310, 315
Novello, Marie, 80
Nunburnholme, Marjorie Lady (1880–1968), 196
Nureyev, Rudolf (b. 1938), 445–6, 459–60, 521, 531
Nuri-es-Said, General (1888–1958), 264

Oakie, Jack (b. 1903), 130
Oberon, Merle (1911–79), 224, 226, 465
Obolensky, *see* von Hofmannsthal
Obolensky, Prince Serge (1890–1978), 318, 344, 505
O'Brien, Edna (b. 1936), 547, 564
O'Brien, Margery, 169
Odom, William, 166 & n, 168, 210, 216–17
Oelrichs, *see* Strange
Oelrichs, Marjorie (Mrs Eddy Duchin) (d. 1937), 123–5, 132–3, 151, 153, 165, 167 & n, 188, 195; death 195 n; 202
Ogden, Graham, 31
Ogdon, John (b. 1937), 451
Ogilvy, James (b. 1964), 485
Ogilvy-Dalgleish, W/Cdr James (1888–1969), 107
O'Higgins, Patrick (d. 1980), 404, 407, 566–7, 576–9, 581
O'Keefe, Georgia (b. 1887), 508
Oldcorn, Elizabeth (1835–98), 3–4
Olga, HRH Princess, *see* Yugoslavia, Princess Paul of
Olivier, Edith (1872–1948), 86, 96, 98, 101, 137–9, 141, 154–5, 170, 203, 220, 235, 236, 237, 293, 298, 310; death 335; 585
Olivier, Lord (Laurence) (b. 1907), 96, 309, 338–9, 401, 418, 454, 521
Onassis, Aristotle (1906–75), 417
O'Neill, Lady (Ann), *see* Fleming
Ormsby-Gore, Hon. Jane (Mrs Rainey) (b. 1942), 513
Orwell, George (1903–50), 16–17, 19
Osborn, Christopher, 431, 432
Osborn, Franz, 427
Osborn, June (Lady Hutchinson of Lullington) (b. 1920), 190 n, 426–34, 444, 458, 493, 527, 585
Osborne, John (b. 1929), 448, 454, 502
Otis-Skinner, Cornelia (1901–79), 305
O'Toole, Sheamus, 449
Oxford & Asquith (Margot) Countess of (1864–1945), 103, 196, 202, 254

Page, Anita, 130
Pagès, Jean, 172
Paget, (Bridget) Lady Victor (1892–1975), 247
Paget, Lady Caroline (*later* Duff) (1913–76), 185, 191, 216, 439 & n
Paget, Lady Elizabeth (*later* von Hofmann-sthal) (1916–80), 191, 202 n, 216, 224
Paget, Lady Muriel (1876–1938), 103–4
Painter, George (b. 1914), 506
Pakenham, Lady Violet (*now* Powell) (b. 1912), 163
Palewski, Gaston (1901–84), 256 & n
Paley, Princess Natasha (Mrs Jack Wilson) (1905–81), 164, 167 & n, 182, 318–19, 323, 374
Paley, William S. (b. 1901), 304, 321, 389 n, 394, 461, 474, 508, 534
Paley, Mrs William S. (Barbara Cushing) (Babe) (d. 1976), 394, 508, 534, 550
Pallenberg, Anita, 510–11, 528–9
Palmer, Lilli (b. 1914), 307, 415
Pansa, Janie, 347
Panzo, Mario, 207
Papp, Joeseph (b. 1921), 579
Parker, Dorothy (1893–1967), 313
Parkinson, Norman (b. 1913), 380, 548, 569
Parr, Tom, 505, 531
Parsons, Alan, 140
Parsons, Lady Bridget (1907–72), 230
Parsons, Hon. Desmond (1910–37), 201
Parsons, Schuyler, 109, 110, 111
Partridge, Mrs Frances (b. 1900), 43
Pascal, Gabriel (1894–1954), 243, 301, 386–7
Pasha, Russell, *see* Russell Sir Thomas
Patriarch in Jerusalem, Greek, 264
Paul, Prince and Princess, *see* Yugoslavia
Pavitt, Burnet, 13, 14
Pavlova, Anna (1881–1931), 21, 483
Payne, Barbara, 301
Pears, Sir Peter (b. 1910), 337
Peel, Rex, 278
Peirse, A/C/M Sir Richard (1892–1970), 276 n
Pelly, Claire (*later* Countess of Pembroke, *now* Mrs Tertius Murray-Threipland) (b. 1943), 505, 548, 582, 585
Pemberton, Reece, 386
Pembroke, Countess of, *see* Pelly
Pembroke, Dowager Countess of (Bea) (1883–1973), 98, 183, 236, 237, 238, 355
Pembroke, 15th Earl of (1880–1960), 183, 235

Pembroke, (Sidney) 16th Earl of (1906–69), 98, 227 n, 436, 514, 531
Pembroke, 17th Earl of (b. 1939), 98, 505, 513, 531, 547, 581, 582, 585
Pembroke, Mary Countess of, 445
Penn, Irving (b. 1917), xxvii, 347–8, 576–7, 578, 586
Penrose, Alec (1896–1950), 32 & n, 33
Penrose, Sir Roland (1900–84), 32 n, 398
Percy, Eileen, 130
Perl, Jed, 587
Perowne, Stewart (b. 1901), xxiii, 32–3, 263–4
Perry, Mrs Elfie, 299, 389
Perry, John (b. 1906), 274, 502
Persia, HIM Shah of (Muhammed Reza .Pahlavi) (1919–80), 263, 264
Persia, HIM Shahbanou of (Fawzieh) (b. 1921), 263
Peto, Gladys (1890–1977), 574
Philip, Prince, see Edinburgh, Duke of
Phipps, Diana, 546, 568
Picasso, Pablo (1881–1973), 53, 59, 228, 239, 365, 479, 491, 504
Picasso, Paloma (b. 1949), 580
Pickford, Mary (1893–1979), 153, 330
Pierrefeu, 223
Pile, Gen. Sir Frederick (1884–1976), 366
Pinchot, Rosamond (1904–38), 118, 207, 211
Pinter, Harold (b. 1930), 502
Piper, John (b. 1903), 142–3, 247, 345
Pirandello, Luigi (1867–1936), 44
Pitman, Robert, 557
Pitt-Rivers, Michael (b. 1917), 444–5
Platt-Lynes, George (1907–55), 331
Playfair, Sir Nigel (1874–1934), 65
Plisetskaya, Maya (b. 1925), 483–4
Plomley, Roy (1914–85), 27
Plunket, 7th Lord (Patrick) (1923–75), 379, 438
Plunket-Greene, David (1904–41), 104 & n
Poiret (1879–1944), 553
Polignac, Marie-Blanche de, 184
Pons, Helene, 389, 390, 391
Ponsonby, Elizabeth (1900–40), 84, 298
Ponsonby, Loelia, see Westminster
Poole, Sally (HH Begum Aga Khan), 414
Pope-Hennessy, James (1916–74), xvii, 247–8, 271, 274, 306, 353, 354, 358, 444, 537, 588; murder, 570
Pope-Hennessy, Sir John (b. 1913), 487, 489, 551
Porel, Jacques, 503

Porter, Alan, 323
Porter, Cole (1893–1964), 204, 216, 305, 322, 411
Porter, Linda Cole, 322
Porter, Eric (b. 1928), 374
Porter, Katharine Anne (1890–1980), 331
Porter, Thea (b. 1927), 552
Portland, (Ivy) Duchess of (1887–1982), 198
Powell, Anthony (b. 1905), 163
Powell, Dilys (b. 1901), 412
Powell, William (1892–1984), 127 & n
Previn, André (b. 1929), 470
Priddle, Mary, 6
Prince, Harold S. (Hal) (b. 1928), 422
Pritchett, Sir Victor (V. S.) (b. 1900), 251, 268
Procul Harum, 516
Procktor, Patrick (b. 1936), 508, 521, 527, 531, 544, 581
Proust, Marcel (1871–1922), 53, 450, 500, 503, 506
Pryce-Jones, Alan (b. 1908), 147–8
Pussy, see Milnes-Gaskell, Lady Constance, 320 n

Quant, Mary (b. 1934), 104 n, 506, 552
Quartermaine, Leon (1876–1967), 39
Quayle, Sir Anthony (b. 1913), 351, 374–5, 415, 506
Quennell, Peter (b. 1905), 250, 293, 435, 443, 498, 557, 570
Quick, Diana, 581

Radclyffe, Christine, 183
Radiguet, Raymond (1903–23), 189 & n
Radziminski, Wayne, 577
Radziwill, Princess Stanislas (Lee) 521–2, 527
Radziwill, Princess Stanislas (Grace) (now Grace, Countess of Dudley), 368, 414
Rainey, Michael, 513
Rains, Claude (1889–1967), 301
Ralli, Madame Jean (Lilia) (d. 1977), 184, 202 & n, 211, 216, 224–5, 257, 260, 340, 343, 414, 428, 568
Ramsay, Adm. Hon. Sir Alexander (1881–1972), 517
Ramsay, Lady Patricia (1886–1974), 517 & n
Ramsden, John (d. 1948), 59, 60 & n
Ramsey of Canterbury, Rt Rev. Lord (Michael) (Archbishop of Canterbury) (b. 1904), 27
Rattigan, Sir Terence (1911–77), 299
Raven, Simon (b. 1927), 444, 445
Ravensdale, Baroness (Irene) (1896–1966), 103

Raybould, Robin, 576
Reading, Stella, Dowager Marchioness of (1894–1971), 245
Reddish House, *see* Broadchalke
Redgrave, Sir Michael (1908–85), 243
Redgrave, Vanessa (b. 1937), 531
Reed, Sir Carol (1906–1976), 242–3
Reinhardt, Django, 527
Reith, 1st Lord (1889–1971), 240
Réjane, Madame (1857–1920), 503
Renshaw, Micky, 563
Rhodes, Zandra (b. 1940), 581
Ribblesdale, Ava Lady (d. 1958), 190 & *n*
Ribblesdale, 4th Lord (1854–1925), 427
Richard, Keith (b. 1943), 510–11, 512 *n*, 529
Richardson, Maurice (1907–78), 568
Richardson, Sir Ralph (1902–83), 351, 581
Richey, Paul, 267–8
Ritchie, Gen. Sir Neil (1897–1983), 259
Roberts, Keith, 490, 504, 528
Roberts, Leslie, 276
Robertson, Miss, 69, 71
Robertson, Sir Dennis (1890–1963), 30 & *n*, 31
Robinson, Edward G. (1893–1973), 262
Robinson, John (b. 1908), 415
Robson, Cecil, 345
Rogers, Ginger (b. 1911), 410
Rogers, Herman (1895–1957), 197
Rolfe, Frederick (Baron Corvo) (1891–1944), 73
Romania, HM Queen Helen of (1896–1982), 378
Rommel, FM Erwin (1891–1944), 262, 265
Roosevelt, Mrs Franklin, D. (Eleanor) (1884–1962), 268
Roosevelt, President Franklin D. (1882–1945), 245, 268, 291
Rose, Bt, Sir Francis (1909–79), 217–18, 222, 223–4, 227–8, 230, 236, 249, 271, 311, 443, 449, 504, 516, 531, 548; death, 582
Rose, Frederica Lady (Mrs Sproul-Bolton), 271
Rose, Susan, 431
Rosen, Mrs Walter, 117
Rosenauer, Michael, 139, 148
Rosse, Anne Countess of, 97, 210, 436, 518
Rosse, 6th Earl of (1906–79), 201, 210, 436
Rothenstein, Sir William (1872–1945), 80
Rothermere, *see* Fleming
Rothermere, 2nd Viscount (Esmond) (1898–1978), 236, 414, 521, 553
Rothschild, Baroness Bina Goldsmid, 465 & *n*

Rothschild, Baronne Cecile de (b. 1913), 398–400, 498–9, 563
Rothschild, Baronne Eugene de (Kitty) (1885–1952), 180
Rothschild, Baronne Elie de (Liliane), 515
Rothschild, Lord (Victor) (b. 1910), 429
Rothschild, Madame Olympia de, 580
Rothschild, Baron Philippe de (b. 1902), 413, 456, 488, 546, 548
Rothschild, Baronne Philippe de (Pauline Potter) (1908–76), 413, 456 & *n*, 486, 488, 546
Rowe, Sister, 438–9
Rowse, Prof. A. L. (b. 1903), 451
Roxburghe, The Duchess of (d. 1937), 103, 105
Royal, Princess, *see* Mary, Princess
Rubinstein, Helena (1871–1965), 206, 404, 407
Ruby, Jack, 474
Ruffer, Mrs (d. 1925), 57
Ruffer, Nada, 155
Runciman, Hon, Sir Steven (b. 1903), 30, 32, 34, 35, 41–2, 79, 90, 454
Russell, 3rd Earl (Bertrand) (1872–1970), 525
Russell, Mrs Henry, 114
Russell, John (b. 1906), 504
Russell, Sir Thomas (1879–1954), 262, 263
Russia, HH Prince George of (1903–38), 104
Russia, HH Grand Duchess Marie of (1890–1958), 189
Rutherford, Sir Thomas (1886–1957), 276
Ryan, Mrs Allan (Janet Rhinelander Stewart), 153, 534
Ryan, Mrs John Barry (Nin), 181–2, 413–14, 519–20
Rydon, John, 355
Rylands, George (b. 1902), XXVII, 27–8, 30–32, 41, 43–4, 46, 79, 175
Ryskamp, Charles (b. 1928), 535

St Laurent, Yves (b. 1936), 414, 450, 497
Sackville-West, Edward (5th Lord Sackville) (1901–65), 29, 251, 371, 588
Sackville-West, Hon. Vita (1892–1962), 101
Sainsbury, Sir Robert (b. 1906), 446 & *n*
Saint-Subber, Arnold, 356
Salisbury, Elizabeth, Marchioness of (1897–1982), 567, 582
Salisbury, 5th Marquess of (1893–1972), 241, 367, 567
Salisbury, The Marchioness of (d. 1955), 270
Sandford, 'Laddie', 132

Sandford, Mrs 'Laddie' (Jane), 132

Sandys, Diana, *see* Churchill, Diana

San Faustino, Princess Jane di, 161

Sanson, Mrs, 318

Sargeant, Winthrop, 424

Sassoon, Siegfried (1886–1967), 96, 251–2

Sassoon, 3rd Bt, Sir Victor (1881–1961), 280

Sauget, Henri (b. 1901), 397, 418

Scarlett, Frank (1900–81), 256–7

Schenck, Joseph (1878–1961), 124 & n

Schiaparelli, Madame Elsa (d. 1975), 186, 552, 553

Schiff, Mrs, 114

Schlee, Georges (d. 1964): background, 313–14; in London with GG, 315–16; in NY with GG, 320, 321, 322, 327, 328; ill, 321, 325; at C's party, 323; in Paris with GG, 342–3; in Bermuda with GG, 352; C prises GG from, 354; brings GG to heel, 356; GG speaks of, 359; rings GG, 376, death, 498–9; mentioned, 302, 304, 348, 353, 375, 377

Schlee, Mrs Georges (Valentina): background, 313–14; and Schlee's death, 498–9; antipathy to Garbo, 499; gives C a dress, 552–3; meets C in Venice, 568; mentioned, 189, 304, 327, 375

Schmiegelow, Mr, 68–9, 71

Schofield, A. F. (1884–1969), 34 & n

Scholte, Dudley (b. 1905), 13, 15, 531, 584

Scofield, Paul (b. 1922), 563

Scott, Maj.-Gen. Bruce, 279

Scott-Elliot, Walter (1895–1977), 29 n

Scriabin, Alexander (1872–1915), 445

Seale, Douglas, 418

Segovia, Andres (b. 1893), 135

Sekers, Sir Nicholas (1910–72), 504

Sellers, Peter (1925–80), 506

Selznick, David O. (1902–65), 207, 212, 473

Selznick, Mrs Irene (b. 1910), XXVII, 207, 212–13, 313, 357, and *The Chalk Garden*, 381–6; 404, 469, 475, 534

Sentener, David P., 117

Sert, Misia (1872–1950), 135

Seton, Marie (1910–85), 107 & n

Settle, Alison (1891–1980), 65, 70, 72–6, 99, 170

Seyler, Athene (b. 1889), 33, 299, 300

Seymour, Sir Horace (1885–1978), 282 & n, 287, 289

Seymour, Lady (Violet), 282 & n, 283, 287–8, 289

Shaughnessy, Alfred (b. 1916), 580

Shaw, George Bernard (1856–1950), 9, 269–70, 301, 386–7, 394

Shaw, Irwin (1913–84), 461

Shaw, Philip, 48

Shaw, Sebastian (b. 1905), 458

Shearer, Norma (1900–83), 131, 151

Sheean, Vincent (1899–1975), 337

Sheppard, Sir John (1881–1968), 34 & n

Sherek, Henry (1900–67), 352

Sherry, Gordon, 47–8

Shrimpton, Jean, 485, 505, 549, 552

Sickert, Walter (1860–1942), 248, 490

Sim, Alastair (1900–76), 415

Simon, 1st Viscount (John) (1873–1954), 239

Simpson, Wallis, *see* Windsor, Duchess of

Simpson-Smith, Col, 259

Sinatra, Frank (b. 1915), 485

Sisson, Cada, *see* Chattock

Sisson, Ella (1861–1902), 3, 5

Sisson, Esther, *see* Beaton, Mrs Ernest

Sisson, Jessie, *see* Suarez

Sisson, Joseph (1830–1907), 3–5

Sitwell, Dame Edith (1887–1964), 58, 69–70, 83, 88, 89, 95, 99, 101, 106, 139, 167, 169, 175–6, 230, 251–2, 349, 364, 439, 457–8, 508, 552, 578, 586–7

Sitwell, Lady (Georgia) (1905–80), XXVII, 70, 80, 168, 414, 548

Sitwell, Bt, Sir Osbert (1892–1969), 86–7, 95, 99, 100–102, 106, 110, 117, 129, 140, 141, 183, 186, 251–2, 349, 586–7

Sitwell, Bt, Sir Sacheverell (b. 1897), XXVII, 80, 95, 99, 102, 106, 168, 364, 423, 445, 548, 586–7

Sitwell, Lady Ida (1869–1937), 166

Sitwell, Reresby (b. 1927), 166

Skinner, Mr, 69, 71

Small, Susan, 552

Smallpeice, Jack, 569, 583, 585

Smallpeice, Mrs Jack, 569, 585

Smiley, *see* Beaton

Smiley, Bt, Sir Hugh (b. 1905), 163 & n

Smiley, John (b. 1934), 163 n

Smith, Arnold, 266

Smith, Hon. William (3rd Viscount Hambleden) (1903–48), 29

Smith, Dodie (b. 1896), 220

Smith, Lady Eleanor (1902–45), 36, 58, 67, 80, 81, 139

Smith, Oliver (b. 1918), XXIV, XXVIII, 305, 337, 341, 387, 392, 541

Smith, Lady Pamela, *see* Berry

Smith, Philip, 284

Smith, Stanley, 282
Smithson, Florence, 10, 11
Smuts, FM Rt Hon. Jan (1870–1950), 257, 272
Snell, Olive, 112
Snow, Carmel (d. 1961), 111–12, 130, 136, 321, 395
Snowdon, 1st Earl of (b. 1930), 414, 435–7, 440, 454, 489, 490, 516–18, 533, 550
Solov, Zachary (b. 1923), 379
Somerset, David (11th Duke of Beaufort) (b. 1928), 414
Sontag, Susan, 587
Soong, T. V., 288
Soper, Mr, 199–200
Southby, Vera, 283 n
Spaak, Paul-Henri (1899–1972), xxi
Spain, Nancy (1918–66), 407
Spain, HM Queen Sofia of (b. 1938), 513
Spain, HM Queen Victoria Eugenie of (1887–1969), 500–501
Spears, Gen. Sir Edward (1886–1974), 265
Spender, Lady (Natasha), 548
Spender, Sir Stephen (b. 1909), 148, 398, 548
Spiegel, Sam (1901–86), 530
Sprott, Sebastian (1897–1971), 33
Sproul-Bolton, Mrs, *see* Rose
Spry, Constance (1886–1960), 163
Squire, Sir John (J.C.) (1884–1958), 70, 311
Squire, Ronald (1886–1958), 369
Stanley of Alderley (Audrey) Lady (b. 1910), 253
Stark, Dame Freya (b. 1893), 264
Stebbing, 14
Steichen, Edward (1879–1973), 111, 112
Stein, Gertrude (1874–1946), 215, 218, 221, 224, 227–8, 310, 364, 445, 536, 550
Steward, Samuel M., 228, 336
Stewart, Janet Rhinelander, *see* Ryan
Stewart of Fulham, Lord (Michael) (b. 1906), 530
Stewart, Peter, 248
Stiebel, Victor, 187
Stirling, Lt-Col. David (b. 1915), 260
Stockton, *see* Macmillan
Stockwood, Rt Rev. Mervyn (b. 1913), 581
Stokowski, Leopold (1882–1977), 312, 424, 563
Stone, Rev. William, 6
Stourton, Hon. Jeanne, *see* Camoys
Strachan, D. W., 21
Strachey, Lytton (1880–1932), 42, 45, 64, 97
Strange, Michael (1890–1950), 167 n

Stravinsky, Igor (1882–1971), 512
Street, A. G. (1892–1966), 96
Streisand, Barbra (b. 1942), 466 & n, 529, 533–4, 537
Strickling, Howard, 131, 410
Strong, Sir Roy (b. 1935), 345–6, 441–2, 513, 520–21, 524–5, 527–8, 536, 545, 547, 552, 578, 585
Stroughill, Louise (1848–99), 6
Suarez, Jessie (Cecil's aunt) (1863–1950), 3–5, 8–10, 36–7, 53, 59, 215–16, 236, 267, 310, 339; death, 344, 373 n, 389, 543, 549, 559
Suarez, Don Pedro, 4, 5, 9, 10, 37, 544
Suarez, Romulo, 4
Sudley, Viscount (1903–58), 29, 172
Suffield-Jones, 55
Sullivan, Ed, 345
Sun Yat-sen, Madame (1892–1981), 282
Sutherland, The Duchess of (1891–1943), 196
Sutherland, Graham (1903–80), 22, 239, 341, 398, 440, 445, 454, 491
Sutherland, Mrs Graham (Kathy), 445, 491, 561
Sutro, John (1904–85), 185, 201, 217, 219, 220, 230, 236, 237, 241, 246, 254, 297–8, 436, 440
Sutro, Mrs John (Gillian), 297, 571
Svendsen, Clara, 457
Swanson, Gloria (1899–1983), 128
Sweeny, Charles, 163, 178
Sykes, Christopher (b. 1907), 263
Sykes, Bt, Sir Richard (1905–78), 59–60 & n, 64, 82, 161

Tagg, Alan (b. 1928), 382, 416, 437, 482, 483, 487, 550, 560
Talbot, Mrs, 433, 447, 448
Tandy, Ted, 5
Tangiers, 222–3, 341–2, 445, 529
Tanqueray, Paul (b. 1905), 55–7, 577
Taras, John, 344
Tashman, Lilyan (1899–1934), 130, 151, 153, 174
Taylor, Elizabeth (b. 1932), 410, 520, 559
Taylor, Mary, 164 & n, 188, 205
Tchelitchew, Pavel (Pavlik) (1898–1957), 167, 173, 175–6, 182–3, 186, 188, 189, 207, 212, 218, 230, 239, 326, 349, 397, 454
Tedder, MRAF Lord (1890–1967), 256
Temple, Shirley (b. 1928), 292, 454

Tennant, Lady Anne (*now* Lady Glenconner), 515

Tennant, Lady Emma (b. 1943), 512

Tennant, Hon. Stephen (b. 1906): on Cecil, XXIII–XXIV, 86, 91–2, 204, 251, 309, 310, 358, 407, 572; meets C, 85; background, 85–6; at Wilsford, 88–9, 90–92, 99, 170, 236, 501–2, 512; letters *re* NY, 109, 119; rebukes C, 140; rejects C, 579; mentioned, 86–7, 95–7, 103, 104–5, 105 *n*, 107, 176, 183, 220, 230, 454, 527 *n*, 550, 571

Terriss, Ellaline (Lady Hicks) (1871–1971), 66 & *n*

Terry, Dame Ellen (1848–1928), 451

Terry, Emilio, 397

Terry-Lewis, Mabel (1872–1957), 300

Thomas, Benjamin C. (1902–75), 42 & *n*, 43

Thomas, Robin, 171

Thomson, Virgil (b. 1896), 356–7

Thorndike, Dame Sybil (1882–1976), 39, 55, 239 *n*, 338, 561

Todd, Ann (b. 1909), 239 *n*, 374

Todd, Dorothy, 53, 70, 80 & *n*, 89

Todd, Mike (1907–58), 412

Toklas, Alice B. (1877–1967), 218, 224, 227–8, 310, 336, 445, 536

Tomlin, Stephen (1901–37), 137

Toone, Geoffrey, 316, 329, 563

Toscanini, Arturo (1867–1959), 202

Toussaint, Madame Jeanne, 408

Townsend, Group Capt. Peter (b. 1914), 403–4, 437

Traboulsi, Madame Samir, 581

Traill, Sir Alan (b. 1935), 14 *n*

Traill, George, 14

Train, Susan, 484 & *n*

Tree, Lady Anne (b. 1927), 414, 430, 440, 445, 454, 480, 530, 551, 566, 571, 575–6, 585

Tree, Sir Herbert Beerbohm (1853–1917), 8

Tree, Iris (1897–1968), 58, 498, 509

Tree, Michael (b. 1921), 414, 430, 440, 445, 482, 484, 550, 585

Tree, Penelope (b. 1949), 527, 546, 547, 566

Tree, Ronald (1897–1976), 505

Tree, Viola (1884–1939), 140

Trefusis, Violet (1894–1972), 372 *n*

Trilling, Steve, 469, 472

Turner, E. S., 564

Turner, Dame Eva (b. 1892), 531

Turner, W. J. (1889–1946), 271

Twiggy (b. 1946), 514, 518, 551

Tyler, Parker, 207

Tynan, Kenneth (1927–80), XXVI, 353, 369, 504, 542

Ulanova (b. 1910), 399

Umberto, *see* Italy

Unwin, Miradia, 43, 57, 72 *n*

Ure, Mary (1933–75), 415

Uribura, Clara, 97

Utaemon, 404

Valentina, *see* Schlee

Valentino, Madame Rudolph, 39

Vallance, Mr, 21

Vallee, Rudy (b. 1901), 166

Vanbrugh, Violet (1867–1942), 79

Vanderbilt, Mrs Grace (1871–1953), 110, 211

Van der Kemp, Gerald, 450, 465

Van Someren, Mrs Ernest (Ivy), 73 & *n*

Van Vechten, Carl (1880–1964), 114

Van Voren, Monique, 409

Verdura, Fulco, Duke of (1899–1978), 383

Verushka, 525

Vian, A. F. Sir Philip (1894–1968), 257

Viertel, Salka (1889–1978), 331

Vincent, Sybil, 83

Vivian, Charles, 102

Vivier, Roger, 507

Volpi, Contesse Lili, 216, 445, 560

von Hofmannsthal, *see* Paget

von Hofmannsthal, Alice (1902–56), 190, 191, 202 *n*, 224, 373

von Hofmannsthal, Raimund (1906–74), 202 *n*, 211, 216, 224

von Thyssen, Fiona, 445

Vreeland, Diana, XXVI, 41, 162, 201, 204, 323, 364, 373, 412, 421, 463, 466, 483, 497, 499, 508, 512, 515, 517, 522, 523–4, 537, 545, 549–50, 553, 561, 565, 568, 578–81

Vreeland, T. Reed (d. 1966), 201, 499

Vulliamy, 32–3

Vyvyan, Lady, 77

Wales, Prince of, *see* Windsor, Duke of

Wales, HRH The Prince of (b. 1948), 339–40, 347, 371, 435, 436, 438, 526–7; letter to C, 528

Walpole, Lady (d. 1926), 54, 107

Walton, Tony, 413

Walton, Sir William (1902–83), 70, 80, 186, 344, 578

Ware, Valentine, *see* Whitaker

Warhol, Andy (b. 1926), 497, 513, 535 & *n*, 540, 568

Waring, Lady Clementine (1879–1964), 53
Warner, David (b. 1941), 491, 504
Warner, Jack L. (1892–1978), 465–6, 467, 469, 472, 474, 490, 542
Warrender, Harry (1903–53), 46 & *n*, 47 *n*, 48
Washbourne, Mona (b. 1903), 418–19, 464, 473
Watson, Bertie, 531
Watson, Bt, Sir George (1861–1930), 147, 148
Watson, Victor William (Peter) (1908–56): background, 147–8; meets C, 148; with Oliver Messel, 148–50; obsesses C, 149–56, 157, 160–63, 165–70, 171–5, 177–8; on C's work, 188, 203, 230–31; at Kammer, 202; in Venice, 216; meets C again, 223; at Reddish, 341; meets Garbo, 354; death, 396–8; mentioned, 180, 195, 201, 206, 221–2, 236, 254, 272, 304, 320, 331, 399, 431, 436, 444, 479, 481, 482, 488, 531, 566, 570
Waugh, Auberon (b. 1939), 564
Waugh, Evelyn (1903–66), 13–14, 27, 89 *n*, 98 *n*, 107, 139–40, 371, 373–4, 374 *n*, 407, 443, 448, 454, 499, 551 *n*, 565 & *n*
Wavell, Eugenie, Countess (b. 1887), 275, 281–2, 291, 368
Wavell, FM Earl (1883–1950), 275, 276, 281–2, 290–91, 293 *n*, 299
Waverley, Ava Lady (1896–1974), 401, 449, 464
Weatherill, Bernard, 276 & *n*
Webb, Allan (1906–82), 563
Webb, Clifton (1893–1966), 110, 330, 411
Webb, Nella, 348
Weidenfeld, Lord (George) (b. 1919), 132, 485, 546, 559, 571, 585
Weiller, Commandant Paul-Louis (b. 1893), 340
Weissberger, Arnold (1906–81), 301, 391, 394, 530, 534, 539–40, 542
Weissmuller, Johnny (1904–84), 158
Welldon, Julia, 206
Welles, Orson (1915–85), 206, 211
Wellesley, Lord Gerald (7th Duke of Wellington) (1885–1972), 261 & *n*, 367, 561 & *n*
Wellman, Mrs, 111
Wells, H. G. (1866–1946), 48, 242
West, Mae (1892–1980), 115, 123, 543
West, Dame Rebecca (1892–1983), 53, 489
Westcott, Glenway, 207, 548

Westminster, Loelia, Duchess of (*formerly* Ponsonby, *now* Lady Lindsay of Dowhill) (b. 1902), 74–5, 196, 206, 217, 236, 240, 319 *n*, 327, 413, 512
Westmorland, Diana Countess of (1893–1983), 427
Weymouth, Viscountess, *see* Fielding, Daphne
Wharton, 9th Lord (1908–69), 280
Wheeler, Monroe, 351, 422, 548
Wheeler, Mrs Post, 38
Whigham, Margaret, *see* Argyll, Duchess of
Whish, Mary Diana, 72–3
Whish, Mrs, 65, 67, 72–5, 77, 81, 82, 88
Whistler, Rex (1905–44), 86, 96, 97, 119, 137–9, 149, 169–70, 176, 191, 216, 218, 228, 230, 237, 271; death, 291; mentioned, 310
Whitaker, Valentine (1904–30), 43 & *n*
White, Bill, 133
White, Dr Denham, 281
White, Patrick (b. 1912), 520, 525
Whitney, John Hay (1904–82), 212, 440
Whitney, Mrs John Hay (Betsey), 440
Whitney, Liz, 241
Wiasemsksy, Prince, 308
Wiborg, Mary Hoyt (1887–1964), 135
Wildbaum, Mrs, 341
Wilde, Dorothy (d. 1941), 90–91
Wilde, Oscar (1854–1900), 33, 90, 305
Wilding, Dorothy, 47, 199
Wilding, Michael (1912–79), 308
Wilkes, Mr and Mrs Vaughan, 16–17, 19
Williams, Billy, *see* Herring, Robert
Williams, Emlyn (b. 1905), 299
Williams, Peter, 459–60
Williams, Rowland, 311
Williams, Tennessee (1912–83), 322, 435
Williamson, Frank, 3
Wilson, Sir Angus (b. 1913), 448
Wilson, Cecil, 346
Wilson of Rievaulx, Lord (Harold) (b. 1916), 518, 530, 559
Wilson of Libya, FM Lord (Henry) (1881–1964), 261, 265
Wilson, John C. (Jack) (1899–1961), 167 *n*, 171, 182, 318 *n*
Wilson, Mrs Jack, *see* Paley, Natasha
Winchell, Walter (1897–1972), 207–8, 214–15
Windsor, Duchess of (b. 1896), 193–5, 197–200, 205, 215, 221, 236, 322, 324, 340, 441–2, 452–3, 521, 546, 552, 559
Windsor, HRH The Duke of (1894–1972), XVII, 36, 65, 71, 180, 193–5, 198–9,

Windsor, H R H The Duke of – *cont.*
205, 215, 230, 322, 323, 324, 340, 348,
441–2, 452–3, 462, 546; death, 564
Winn, Godfrey (1908–71), 44 *n*, 46, 139,
190
Winston, Norman (1899–1977), 325 & *n*,
326
Winston, Mrs Norman (Rosita), 325 & *n*, 326
Winston, Samuel, 395, 567
Winwood, Estelle (1883–1984), 305
Wishart, Michael (b. 1928), xxvii, 148, 397,
482, 505–6, 513, 582
Withers, Audrey, 271, 378, 379, 549
Withers, Googie (b. 1917), 270
Wittstein, Ed, 425
Wolfe, Dr, 204
Wolfe, Humbert (1886–1940), 45, 206
Wolfenden, Lord (1906–85), 41
Wolfit, Sir Donald (1902–68), 418–20
Wood, Christopher, (d. 1930), 310–11
Wood, Rt Hon. Sir Kingsley (1881–1943),
240
Woodward, Edward (b. 1930), 564
Woolf, Virginia (1882–1941), 53, 95, 101,
134, 142
Woollcott, Alexander (1887–1943), 313
Worsley, Katharine, *see* Kent, Duchess of
Worsley, T. C. (b. 1907), 531

Worth, Irene (b. 1916), 512, 520, 537, 547,
563, 564, 573, 585
Wray, Fay (b. 1907), 130, 153
Wrightsman, Mr & Mrs Charles, 445, 507,
513–14, 516, 522, 546
Wu, Kuo Cheng (1904–84), 288
Wu, Mrs K. C., 288
Wylie, Jim, 222
Wyndham, Lady (1861–1931), 54, 84
Wynyard, Diana (1906–64), 299

Yevonde, Mme, 522
York, Duchess of, *see* Elizabeth, the Queen
Mother
Young, Loretta (b. 1913), 153
Youssoupoff, Prince Felix (1887–1967), 483
Yoxall, Harry (1896–1984), 242, 378
Yugoslavia, HRH Prince Alexander of
(b. 1924), 378, 417
Yugoslavia, HRH Prince Paul of (1893–1976),
211, 224–5, 417, 485
Yugoslavia, HRH Princess Paul of (b. 1903),
224–5, 336, 417, 485, 527

Zetterling, Mai (b. 1925), 407
Ziegfeld, Florenz (1869–1932), 117–18
Zinkeisen, Doris, 176